EMPLOYMENT LAW IN SCOTLAND

EMPLOYMENT LAW IN SCOTLAND

by

Victor Craig
Solicitor,
Senior Lecturer in Law
Heriot-Watt University

Kenneth Miller
Senior Lecturer in Law
University of Strathclyde

T&T CLARK
EDINBURGH

T&T CLARK
59 GEORGE STREET
EDINBURGH EH2 2LQ
SCOTLAND

First Published 1991

British Library Cataloguing in Publication Data

A catalogue record for this book is
available from the British Library

ISBN 0 567 29187 1

Typeset by Trinity Typesetting, Edinburgh
Printed and bound in Great Britain by Billing & Sons Ltd, Worcester

CONTENTS

PREFACE

It is the purpose of this book to provide a detailed and accurate statement of the law of employment as it applies in Scotland. We believe that a book aimed specifically at Scots employment law is long overdue. This may seem strange given that a great deal of employment law is statute-based so that much of it is common throughout Great Britain. Yet differences in the law do exist. This is particularly the case in those areas of employment law where common law rules still operate. Thus, for example, the Scottish rules concerning the formation of the contract of employment differ from those operative in England and Wales. It is also the case that in the area of industrial conflict law the Scottish common law delicts are not nearly as well developed as their English counterparts. This fact has important implications for the ways in which the statutory immunities are applied by the Scottish courts.

Moreover, even in those areas where statute law applies it is not unusual for the Employment Appeal Tribunal in Scotland or the Court of Session to interpret these statutory provisions differently from their English colleagues. Thus there has been disagreement in the past over the correct interpretation to be placed on the Transfer of Undertakings (Protection of Employment) Regulations 1981, on the extent of a reasonable procedure where redundancy dismissals are being challenged as unfair and the purpose of the protective award where there has been a failure to consult a recognised trade union over redundancies. At time of writing, disagreement continues as to the correct meaning of 'wages' under the Wages Act 1986. It is also true that there are important differences in the procedure which are applied to employment law disputes in Scotland. This is most obvious in cases before the Scottish civil courts but Scotland also has its own separate rules of procedure for industrial tribunals and has modified the procedural rules applying to the Employment Appeal Tribunal.

Thus it is a major aim of this book to explain the law in Scotland and to emphasise the differences which exist in employment law between the two legal systems. The book also seeks to locate employment law within the legal system of Scotland. Equally, in areas where Scots employment law is underdeveloped (such as in the area of trade disputes law) the book discusses what we regard as being the major English decisions and speculates as to the likelihood of these decisions being followed and applied in Scotland.

As has already been stated, our aim in writing this book is to describe the current state of employment law in Scotland in a clear and concise way. If we have succeeded in achieving this aim, we are sure that our book will fill the need for an up-to-date student textbook which highlights the Scottish position. However, we believe that the book will also serve the requirements of the labour law practitioner, the personnel specialist and the trade union official. It has certainly been one of our objectives to write a book which will benefit all the various groups of people who may wish to ascertain and to comprehend the current state of Scots employment law.

Originally, Brian Napier was to have been involved in this venture. However, when he became Professor of Information Technology Law at Queen Mary and Westfield College he had to withdraw because of pressure of other work. We thank Brian for the help and encouragement which he has given to the authors over the years. We would also like to express our particular gratitude to him for allowing us to use his draft as the basis for Chapter One. We also gratefully acknowledge the significant assistance which we received from Professor Joe Thomson. Joe read drafts of many of the chapters and made numerous insightful and helpful suggestions for improvement. It is fair to say that most of these have found their way into this book.

We would also like to thank our colleagues at Heriot-Watt University and at the University of Strathclyde for their support and encouragement, T & T Clark for making sure that the book actually got published (there was certainly a time when the authors thought it would not), and Barbara Syme and Joyce Spencer for their word processing skills. Finally, our thanks go to our wives and families for their patience and understanding.

Any errors or omissions remain those of the authors and we have sought to state the law as at 1 July 1991.

Vic Craig & Kenny Miller
Edinburgh and Glasgow
15 July 1991

TABLE OF CASES

TABLE OF STATUTES

1

European Communities

STATUTORY INSTRUMENTS

ABBREVIATIONS

Statutes

TUA 1871	Trade Union Act 1871
CPPA 1875	Conspiracy and Protection of Property Act 1875
TDA 1906	Trade Disputes Act 1906
TUA 1913	Trade Union Act 1913
EqPA 1970	Equal Pay Act 1970
IRA 1971	Industrial Relations Act 1971
TULRA 1974	Trade Union and Labour Relations Act 1974
EPA 1975	Employment Protection Act 1975
SDA 1975	Sex Discrimination Act 1975
TUL(A)A 1976	Trade Union and Labour Relations (Amendment) Act 1976
RRA 1976	Race Relations Act 1976
EPCA 1978	Employment Protection (Consolidation) Act 1978
EA 1980	Employment Act 1980
EA 1982	Employment Act 1982
TUA 1984	Trade Union Act 1984
WA 1986	Wages Act 1986
SDA 1986	Sex Discrimination Act 1986
EA 1988	Employment Act 1988
EA 1989	Employment Act 1989
EA 1990	Employment Act 1990

Institutions

ACAS	Advisory, Conciliation and Arbitration Service
CA	Court of Appeal
CAC	Central Arbitration Committee
CBI	Confederation of British Industry
CIR	Commission on Industrial Relations
CO	Certification Officer
CRE	Commission for Racial Equality
CROTUM	Commissioner for the Rights of Trade Union Members
DE	Department of Employment
EAT	Employment Appeal Tribunal
ECJ	European Court of Justice
EEC	European Economic Community
EOC	Equal Opportunities Commission
HC	High Court of Justice
HL	House of Lords
IH	Inner House of the Court of Session
IT	Industrial Tribunal
JIC	Joint Industrial Council
OH	Outer House of the Court of Session
TUC	Trades Union Congress
STUC	Scottish Trades Union Congress
WC	Wages Council

Law Reports and Journals

AC	Appeal Cases
All ER	All England Reports
BJIR	British Journal of Industrial Relations
Ch	Chancery Cases
CLJ	Cambridge Law Journal
GWD	Green's Weekly Digest
ICR	Industrial Cases Reports
ILJ	Industrial Law Journal
IRLR	Industrial Relations Law Reports
IRRR	Industrial Relations Review and Report
ITR	Industrial Tribunals Reports
JC	Justiciary Cases
JR	Juridical Review
KIR	Knight's Industrial Reports
LQR	Law Quarterly Review
MLR	Modern Law Review
QB	Queen's Bench Reports
SC	Session Cases
SLT	Scots Law Times
WLR	Weekly Law Reports

Other Abbreviations

GOQ	Genuine Occupational Qualification
LOST	Lay Off or Short Time
UMA	Union Membership Agreement or Arrangement

Chapter One

DEVELOPMENT OF MODERN LABOUR LAW

1.1 The early law of master and servant

Before the last century, the relationship of master and servant was, in Scotland as in England, primarily a matter of status rather than consensual agreement. This did not mean that service entailed a servile or even quasi-servile role, though this was the case in a few exceptional occupations such as collier or salter,[1] where workers were *adscriptae glebae* and were conveyed along with the lands on which they worked. The category of servants which Erskine[2] describes as "necessary" (and contrasts with "voluntary") were also required by law to take work when it was offered to them. Stair, however, distinguishes between the position of the bondsman and that of the hired labourer, and observes[3] "Servants with us, which now retain that name, are judged free persons, and have but hired their labour and work to their masters for a time, which is a kind of contract betwixt them." The state of slavery itself was described as incompatible with the law of Scotland in *Knight v. Wedderburn*.[4] But while it is true that a degree of freedom was seen as existing from Stair's time both with regard to the decision to enter into employment and the terms and conditions that applied when this was done, content of the employment relationship itself was largely determined in advance of it being entered into. It was shaped not only by the custom and practice of the particular trade, but also by legislation which fixed, through rules of criminal law, wage rates and penalised unauthorised absences on the part of employees. It was only in the nineteenth century, when it became accepted practice to explain reciprocal obligations through the medium of consensual agreement and a philosophy of individualism[5] that the contract of employment began to take on the central role which it still has today. "[T]he Victorian era witnessed a radical change in this as in many other matters. The contract of service is the result of a purely voluntary consent on both sides. It may contain such terms as the parties thereto agree upon. The obligations which it imposes are strictly mutual."[6] Despite the optimism inherent in Maine's famous remark; this particular movement from a kind of status to contract was not necessarily associated with social reform or improvements in legal protections for the weaker party to the relationship. In *Bartonshill Coal Co. v. Reid*,[7]

---

[1] For an account of the special features of certain early employment relationships in Scotland, see J. R. Philip, "Early Labour in Scotland" (1934) 46 J.R. 121. Erskine *Principles*, I, VII, 60. See, generally, O. Kahn-Freund, "Blackstone's Neglected Child: the Contract of Employment" (1977) 93 L.Q.R. 508.

[2] *Principles* I, VII, 61.

[3] *Institutions* I.3.15.

[4] (1778) M. 14545

[5] P. S. Atiyah, *The Rise and Fall of Freedom of Contract* 1979, pp. 226-237.

[6] Umpherston, *The Law of Master and Servant* (1904) p. v.

[7] (1858) 3 Macqueen 266.

1

for example, the House of Lords imposed on the Scottish courts the doctrine of common employment, by which a servant was deemed to have agreed, as an implied term of his contract of employment, that he would not sue his master to recover damages for injuries caused by the negligence of a fellow-servant. Prior to that decision the Scottish courts had had no truck with the doctrine, "a principle as distasteful as it was alien to Scottish jurisprudence";[8] after it, the Scottish courts were, obliged to operate this fictional agreement within the contract as a means of limiting delictual liability.[9]

1.2 The spread of contract

Apart from being influenced by the general enthusiasm for contract as a basis for the ordering of society, the rise of the contract of employment as a legal device was also attributable to its usefulness to the parliamentary draftsmen of the late nineteenth and early twentieth centuries who had the task of defining the scope of legislation. This was important as statute law in the area of employment was introduced on a large scale to complement the older common law rules.[10] For example, the early provision made for industrial injury under the Workmen's Compensation Act 1906 applied generally only to those who were employed under a contract of service or apprenticeship,[11] and similarly the National Insurance Act 1911, which first made general provision for unemployment and sickness insurance and so can be described as one of the precursors of the welfare state, applied only to persons in this category. The increase in legislation dealing with welfare and employment thus contributed to the success of the contract of employment (or service) as a technical legal advice. The result was the unification of working relationships so that, in legal theory, the great majority of working people, whatever the content of the jobs they did, came to be seen as working under the same legal framework. It was this tendency (which was further developed in the course of the present century) which led Kahn-Freund to make his famous judgment that the contract of employment is the "cornerstone" of British labour law.[12] But it is worth remembering that this unity was not always a feature of the law. One may point by way of contrast to Bell's treatment of the employment relationship and note the distinctions he draws between the rules applied to the hiring of domestic servants, managers, ordinary labour and skilled labour. For each of these categories there are a separate set of legal rules to be applied.[13] In modern times the contract of employment continues to play a central role in defining employment rights, but the growth of statutory measures has meant that, as a fundamental institution of employment law, it is parallelled in importance by the technical concept of continuity of employment.[14]

---

[8]   *Radcliffe v. Ribble Motor Services Ltd* [1939] A.C. 215, 235 *per* Lord MacMillan; *Dixon v. Rankin* (1852) 14 D. 420.

[9]   See Fraser, *Master and Servant* (2nd edn., 1872) pp. 198-229; A. C. Gibb, *Law From Over the Border*, 1950, pp. 99-100.

[10] Fraser, *Master and Servant* p. 243.

[11] S. 13. Some of the early decisions made under this legislation are still of practical importance. See, *e.g.* the reliance placed on *Simmons v. Health Laundry Co.* [1910] 1 KB 543, CA by Sir John Donaldson MR in *O'Kelly v. Trusthouse Forte plc* [1982] IRLR 369, CA.

[12] *The System of Industrial Relations in Great Britain*, A. D. Flanders and H. A. Clegg (eds.), 1954, p. 45.

[13] *Principles* s. 190.

[14] See para. 3.2.

1.3 Collective labour relations

The growth of industrial employment in the nineteenth century led directly to the formation of trade unions, which sought to regulate relations between employers and employed by means of collective bargaining. In the course of the century both the nature and functions of trade unionism radically altered. Originally the descendants of organisations which had brought together skilled workmen in selected professions, the unions by the end of the century had extended to cover also large sections of the unskilled workforce, and in so doing had become a powerful political force. It has been remarked that, despite periods of oppression and difficulty, trade unions had, by the end of the Victorian period, become an integrated part of the economic and political life of society.[15] But this acceptance of trade unions by society at large was perhaps less evident in Scotland than elsewhere in the United Kingdom, where an industrial system founded on cheap labour in manufacturing industries bred a class consciousness and class hostility that was to prove long-lasting and divisive.[16] In any event, the gradual assimilation of unions within British society was a movement not reflected in the attitudes of the common law. Throughout the century, the judges (at first with the active assistance of Parliament, later in opposition to the prevailing tendency of legislation) developed and extended forms of liabilities, both civil and criminal, which restricted the activities of unions in general, and in the organisation of strikes and picketing in particular. The legislative milestones in this period of development were the reform of the Combination Acts in 1824, and the statutes of 1871 and 1875[17] which granted immunities from judge-made liabilities. But of equal importance to these direct reforms were the acts which in 1832, 1867 and 1884 extended the Parliamentary franchise. The liberalising measures of the 1870s were directly attributable to the new political power wielded by the working class, manifested in the Trades Union Congress, which first met in 1868. The reforming measures of 1871 and 1875 introduced immunities in respect of conspiracy (criminal and civil), and allowed the unions some freedom of action in the organisation of their affairs, internal and external. But as late as 1901 the House of Lords was able to deliver a crippling blow to union activity in the *Taff Vale* decision,[18] by holding that unions could be sued for damages in respect of wrongs committed by its officials. This decision required legislative reversal, which came in the shape of the great "settlement" of the Trade Disputes Act 1906. This statute set, for more than 60 years, the framework within which unions enjoyed a freedom — always relative, and varying according to the attitudes taken by the judiciary at different times — sufficient to allow them to operate without perpetual legal opposition; in common with the legal systems of Western Europe, organised labour in Britain may be said to have passed through an environment first of legal repression, then toleration, followed by recognition.[19] The hostility which the movement met from the judiciary during its formative period contributed, however, to a distrust on the part of unions of legislation which had to be applied by the courts[20] and to the tradition of "abstentionism" (*i.e.* the exclusion of the law from relations

---

[15] H. Phelps-Brown, *The Origins of Trade Union Power* (1983), Ch. I.

[16] T. C. Smout, *A Century of the Scottish People, 1830-1950* (1986), p. 4.

[17] Trade Union Act 1871; Conspiracy and Protection of Property Act 1875.

[18] [1901] AC 426. See Chapter Eleven.

[19] A. Jacobs in *The Making of Labour Law in Europe* (Bob Hepple (ed.)), 1986, pp. 194 ff.

[20] *Kahn-Freund's Labour and the Law* (3rd edn., P. Davies and M. R. Freedland (eds.), 1986), p. 53.

between employers and unions) which characterised British labour law until the 1970s.

1.4 Acceptance of the legitimacy and desirability of trade unions within the general social fabric was, however, a feature of successive governments, Conservative and Labour, throughout most of the present century. This acceptance was marked by several features: the acceptance of international standards demonstrating a commitment to freedom of association,[21] the acceptance of collective bargaining, conducted through representative unions, by government, in its capacity as employer, and by a commitment to collective bargaining as the preferred method for settling disputes over terms and conditions of employment in different industries. In the years since 1970, however, collective labour law has undergone a series of transformations. The Royal Commission on Trades Unions and Employers Associations (the Donovan Commission), which reported in 1968, recommended major changes in collective bargaining, but argued for the preservation of the voluntarist traditions. However, the Conservative government of 1971 tried, through the Industrial Relations Act 1971, to effect a reform of industrial relations posited on a new framework of legal controls on trades unions. And the 1980s have seen an even more profound attack on unionism, by a government which sees unions as responsible for many of the inadequacies of the labour market, and has accordingly drastically reduced the statutory immunities which allowed trade unions to operate free of legal intervention. In the last decade the principle of legal support for collective bargaining has been progressively and seriously eroded,[22] and it is no longer possible to identify positive governmental support for this activity.

1.5 Contract and statute

We have seen that in the nineteenth century the contract of employment achieved its pivotal position in explaining the relationship between employer and employee. Important through the contract of employment is, however, it must be considered alongside the various statutes which also regulate employment terms and conditions. Statutory intervention designed to protect the interests of employees has a long history. The Truck Acts 1831-1897 for over 150 years stood to protect the full payment of wages without unauthorised deductions to persons engaged in manual labour until their repeal in 1986.[23] In the field of health and safety at work too, statutory regulation dates back to the nineteenth century. Yet these early legislative incursions into the content of the employment relationship are often viewed as the exception rather than the rule in a system which we have said was characterised by legal "abstentionism".[24] In the last 25 years, however, there are indications that a new approach towards legislation has become established. Whereas in the period 1950 to 1959 there were five general Acts of Parliament regulating employment, the total increased to 16 in 1960 to 1969 and 30 in the period 1970 to 1979.[25] The reasons for this

---

[21] *E.g.* International Labour Organisation, Conventions No. 87, 98.

[22] See Chapters Nine and Eleven. See also R. Lewis, "The Role of the Law in Employment Relations" in R. Lewis (ed.) *Labour Law in Britain*, 1986, pp. 7-8.

[23] Wages Act 1986. See para 3.19.

[24] See, *e.g.*, R. Lewis, "The Historical Development of Labour Law" (1976), *British Journal of Industrial Relations*, Vol. XIV, No. 1, 1, 7.

[25] B. Hepple, "Individual Labour Law" in *Industrial Relations in Britain* (G. S. Bain (ed.)), 1983.

proliferation of statute law are diverse. In part it can be explained by the entry of the United Kingdom into the European Economic Community, which brought with it the continuing obligation to amend and reform our law to comply with the requirements of the Treaty of Rome and the Directives made under it. In part it is to be attributed to the politicisation of employment law which took place in the 1970s following the enactment of the Industrial Relations Act 1971. It has also happened (as in the case of the Health and Safety at Work Act 1974) that statutory reform of out-dated legislation has occurred at a time when other events were taking place. Thus employment legislation has been used by governments in recent years as a means of promoting particular economic policies. A good example is the Redundancy Payments Act 1965 which, by offering financial compensation to individuals whose jobs disappeared, was intended to encourage the adoption of new technology and a corresponding rise in productive efficiency.[26] But state intervention in the fixing of terms and conditions of employment may proceed from less obvious sources. The consensus among politicians of the 1960s that there was a need to reform the voluntarist system of collective bargaining in order to control inflation, led directly to the imposition of prices and incomes policies which interfered with the operation of free collective bargaining in the setting of rates of pay. Furthermore, when a different and more combative strategy of controlling the power of trades unions was tried by a Conservative government in 1971 with the passing of the Industrial Relations Act, concessions in the shape of the introduction of statutory protection for individuals against unfair dismissal were made by the government, arguably in order to make the total package of reforms more acceptable to the union movement. The use of labour law reform as an inducement to obtain political co-operation from interest groups within society is not the prerogative of any one political party. Many rights for individuals were introduced in the Employment Protection Act 1975, legislation which the Labour government of the day hoped would be instrumental in securing the support of the trade union movement for its policies as part of its incomes policy, which went by the name of a "social contract".[27] All these provide reasons for the large-scale reform of individual employment law through statute which took place between 1963 and 1979.

1.6 The reduction of employment law

In the period since 1979, the main characteristic of individual employment law has been the limitation or removal of many of the rights which statute granted in the previous decade to employed persons. Although this change is perhaps most widely appreciated in relation to the law of industrial conflict where legislation has very substantially reduced the range of circumstances in which industrial action may be organised free from civil liability,[28] this movement towards the restriction of rights is also to be found in individual employment law. Thus, for example, the period of continuous employment generally required before an employee may claim unfair dismissal, which stood at six months in

---

[26] P. Lewis, *Twenty Years of Statutory Redundancy Payments in Great Britain,* Universities of Leeds and Nottingham, Occasional Papers in *Industrial Relations* No. 8, 1985.

[27] See H. Phelps-Brown, *The Origins of Trade Union Power*, 1983, Ch. XI; P. Davies and M. R. Freedland, "Labour Law and the Public Interest — Collective Bargaining and Economic Policy" in Wedderburn and Murphy (eds.), *Labour Law and the Community: Perspectives for the 1980s*, 1983.

[28] See Chapter Eleven.

1978, is now two years.[29] Another example is the powers of wages councils; following the repeal of the Wages Council Act 1979[30] the power of these bodies to impose terms and conditions of employment in sectors of industry where trade unionism is weak have been very much reduced, and abolished altogether in the case of workers under twenty-one.[31] The motivation behind such changes is the desire to promote an industrial policy which places its emphasis on removing or easing impediments to taking on workers or taking up work. Deregulation, that is to say the removal of institutional restrictions which hamper the efficient working of the labour market, emerged as a key theme in the government's plans for the British economy of the 1980s — an objective which stretches beyond labour law to cover the provision of industrial training and the operation of the social security system, but there is no denying its considerable impact on employment legislation.[32]

As part of its programme of radical change, the United Kingdom has also withdrawn from a number of international standards which would otherwise have limited the government's plans to reduce the range of statutory controls on employment,[33] and has indicated its strong opposition to proposed legislation on the part of the European Community in relation to the communication of information to employees (the "Vredling" proposals), protection for part-time and temporary workers, and parental leave.

INTERACTION WITH INDUSTRIAL RELATIONS

1.7 General characteristics

The British system of industrial relations is traditionally characterised by a combination of features: (1) a high level of union membership, (2) extensive reliance on free collective bargaining as the principal method of settling terms and conditions of employment, (3) the non-intervention, or "abstention" of the law in the day-to-day management of industrial affairs. The continuation of these characteristics in any description of the system is now, however, open to question in the light of the changes which in recent years have altered the shape of British industrial relations.

1.8 Union membership and the closed shop

Trade union membership reached a peak of 13.2 million in 1979, but fell to 10.5 million by 1987; in the period 1979 to 1987, it dropped by 12 per cent. During the same period the number of persons eligible for membership increased slightly from 24.3 million to 24.7 million. Union membership has fallen each year since 1979. Increasing unemployment may be expected to lead to a fall in

---

[29] EPCA s. 64 (1) (a).

[30] Wages Act 1986.

[31] See para. 3.12. And see the Employment Act 1989, s. 13 (relaxing the duty to give written particulars of disciplinary procedures), s. 15 (increasing the period of continuous employment for receiving written reasons for dismissal) and the subordinate legislation on pre-hearing reviews of industrial tribunal complaints to be made under s. 20 of that Act.

[32] *Employment. The Challenge for the Nation*, Cmnd. 9474, p. 11. See also the discussion document "Burdens on Business", Department of Trade and Industry, 1985. For an assessment of attempts to introduce flexibility into the labour market, see G. Standing *Unemployment and Labour Market Flexibility: the United Kingdom*, 1986, ch. 7.

[33] *E.g.* ILO Convention No. 94 on Labour Clauses (Public Contracts); ILO Convention No. 41 on Night Work for Women; ILO Convention No. 95 on Protection of Wages.

union numbers, but the effects of economic depression on the unions has been exacerbated by structural changes in the economy. Many of the jobs which have gone have been in the manufacturing sector, where traditionally unions were strongly represented. Unions have proved more successful in retaining high membership levels in the public sector than they have in the private. Present indications are that new employment growth, where it occurs, is increasingly to be found in the area of self-employment and part-time work, areas where unions find recruitment difficult. Many unions have taken steps to try to increase membership by seeking to recruit from sections of the working population — especially women and ethnic minorities — where previously they have had relatively little impact.[34] It is uncertain whether such new strategies will be successful in bringing the period of declining membership to an end.

With this decline in membership there has also been a dramatic decline of the importance of the "closed shop",[35] under which the holding of union membership is accepted by both union and employer as a prerequisite for continued employment. The institution of the closed shop raises in sharp focus the conflict between individual and collective values in industrial relations, and its entrenched status in Britain has long been a thorn in the flesh for Conservative governments.

The decline in the closed shop during the 1980s was undoubtedly hastened by the new legal rules which progressively increased the legal obstacles surrounding its implementation.[36] Since 1979 the government has expressed its opposition to the practice on both moral and economic grounds.[37] The weakening of the institution has had the consequence of inhibiting the power of unions to conduct industrial action, for the controlling discipline which the closed shop gives to a union over its members is an important part of the union's industrial strength. In 1986 the official figures for working days lost due to industrial disputes were at their lowest for over twenty years and while those figures had doubled by 1989 the number of stoppages begun has continued to fall and the number of workers involved has not significantly increased.[38]

Despite the setbacks which the trade union movement has received both from government policy and the effects of the economic recession, it is still true that nearly one half of the workforce is organised within Britain, a figure notably higher than that found in other countries of Western Europe or North America, and higher than the membership figures for Britain for the 1950s and 1960s.[39]

1.9 Collective bargaining[40]

Collective bargaining was first extensively developed within British industry in the nineteenth century, and has continued since then to occupy a central role in the regulation of terms and conditions of employment in both public and private sectors. In the 1970s (following the reforms set in train as a consequence of the

---

[34] M. Stevens and A. Waking "Union density and workforce composition", *Employment Gazette*, August 1990.

[35] See M. Stevens, N. Millward and D. Smart "Trade Union Membership and the Closed Shop in 1989", *Employment Gazette*, November 1989.

[36] As to the present position see paras 5.57, 6.2.

[37] "The Government's view of the closed shop is clear: it is opposed to the principles underlying it. That people should be required to join a union as a condition of getting or holding a job runs contrary to the general traditions of personal liberty in this country." *Trade Union Immunities* Cmnd. 8128, 1981, p. 66.

[38] Labour Market Data *Employment Gazette*, 1989.

[39] See note 34 above.

[40] See Chapter Nine.

recommendations made by the Donovan Commission) there were various formal attempts made to reform the structure of collective bargaining. Assistance by the state for the improvement and extension of collective bargaining was forthcoming, first through the short-lived Commission on Industrial Relations (CIR), latterly through the Advisory Conciliation and Arbitration Service (ACAS). By statute[41] ACAS is charged with the general duty to promote the improvement of industrial relations, and in particular to encourage the extension of collective bargaining and the development and reform of collective bargaining machinery. Since 1980 ACAS has operated on a voluntary basis, that is to say its intervention is always subject to the co-operation of the parties involved, but in the period 1976-1980 it had a central responsibility for the scheme which envisaged the extension of trade union recognition to organisations by statutory means. That part of its jurisdiction was removed with the repeal of the relevant legislation by the Employment Act 1980. In recent years the structure and content of collective bargaining has undergone considerable change, so that now greater emphasis is placed on factory-level agreements and less on industry-wide national bargaining. The moves towards decentralisation of bargaining are particularly prevalent in the private sector, although the government has indicated it would like to see similar movement in public sector collective bargaining too.[42]

One relatively recent innovation in bargaining is the "single-union agreement", where recognition is given by management to a single union for all or most of the workers employed in an undertaking, irrespective of different job functions amongst the workforce. These arrangements are most frequently found in connection with the establishment of new manufacturing operations, and are particularly associated with job flexibility, acceptance of arbitration as a means of settling disputes and, most controversially, undertakings on the union side not to have recourse to strikes. These agreements have been and are a cause of great controversy within the union movement, and have highlighted the differences between traditional left-wing unions with a continuing commitment to socialist values, and the new "business" unions (such as the E.E.P.T.U.) which have prospered in the 1980s and are primarily concerned with achieving the best possible terms of employment for their members, with far fewer political scruples about how this is done.

1.10 The role of statute law

The judgment that, apart from regulatory legislation such as the Truck and Factories Acts and certain other particular measures, statute had little concern with fixing terms and conditions of employment, was most accurately applied to the British system of industrial relations in the 1950s. As already mentioned, the years since 1963 have seen a general growth in the significance of statute based rights. Although these rights will usually take precedence over the rules of the common law if there is conflict between them, it would be wrong to deduce from this evolution that the doctrines of the common law — particularly those concerned with the implication and interpretation of contractual terms — have become less important.[43] The contract of employment remains of central impor-

---

[41] Employment Protection Act 1975, s. 1.

[42] See *e.g.* B. C. Roberts, "Recent trends in collective bargaining in the United Kingdom" *International Labour Review*, vol. 123, May-June 1984, p. 287. Advisory Conciliation and Arbitration Service, *Collective Bargaining in Britain: its Extent and Level* Discussion Paper No. 2, February 1983.

[43] The significance of the implied term can be seen especially in the context of constructive dismissal; see para. 5.18.

tance in judging the availability and the implementation of statutory rights.[44]

The main statutory provisions dealing with employment protection in individual employment law are given below.[45]

(1) Employment Protection (Consolidation) Act 1978. This contains measures relating to the provision of written particulars to persons entering employment (ss. 1-7); itemised pay statements (ss. 8-10); guarantee payments which provide a degree of income maintenance to employees temporarily deprived of work (ss. 12-18); rights to time-off work (ss. 27-30); minimum periods of notice of termination (ss. 49-52); written statement of reasons for dismissal (s. 53); right not to be unfairly dismissed (Part V); redundancy payments (Part VI); protection of wages and other rights in the event of insolvency (ss. 121-127).

(2) Equal Pay Act 1970: claims based on like work (s. 1 (2) (a); work rated as equivalent (s. 1 (2) (b)); equal value (s. 1 (2)) (c)).

(3) Sex Discrimination Acts 1975, 1986: claims based on direct discrimination (s. 1 (2) (a)); indirect discrimination (s. 1 (1) (b)).

(4) Race Relations Act 1976: claims based on direct discrimination (s. 1 (1) (a)); indirect discrimination (s. 1 (1) (b)).

(5) Transfer of Undertakings (Protection of Employment) Regulations 1981:[46] transfer of contracts of employment of employees in businesses sold or transferred.

(6) Wages Act 1986: protection of wages against unauthorised deductions (Part 1).

(7) Employment Act 1990: protection against refusal of employment on grounds related to union membership (s. 1).

PARTICULAR LEGAL DEVELOPMENTS

1.11 The new statute-based regime of employment protection rights that has grown up has made extensive use of a new semi-obligatory source of standards, in the form of codes of practice. It has also, more particularly, provided the basis for extensive consideration of the role of European Community standards within the national legal system of the United Kingdom.

1.12 Codes of practice

The Advisory Conciliation and Arbitration Service (ACAS) is empowered[47] to issue "Codes of practice containing such practical guidance as the Service thinks fit for the purpose of promoting the improvement of industrial relations." A power in identical terms is given to the Secretary of State for Employment.[48] The Equal Opportunities Commission (EOC),[49] the Commission for Racial Equality (CRE),[50] and the Health and Safety Commission[51] also may issue codes of

---

[44] See para. 2.1.
[45] As amended by subsequent legislation.
[46] S.I. 1981 No. 1794.
[47] Employment Protection Act 1975, s. 6 (1).
[48] Employment Act 1980, s. 3 (1).
[49] Sex Discrimination Act 1986, s. 3 (1). See para. 7.21.
[50] Race Relations Act 1976, s. 47 (1). See para 7.28.
[51] Health and Safety at Work Act 1974, s. 16.

practice. These powers have been exercised by these bodies on a number of occasions.[52]

1.13 Other codes

The Manpower Services Commission issued in 1984 a Code of Good Practice on the employment of disabled people. This stands as a purely voluntary document giving guidance as to employment policies and does not have the statutory status of the codes mentioned in para. 1.21.

1.14 Function

Codes of practice have a general educational function in providing information to the general public about conduct which is thought by the issuing bodies to be useful in promoting their objectives. In addition, however, the codes have a specific function with regard to the adjudication of employment rights and related matters. Statute provides with regard to codes issued by ACAS that "A failure on the part of any person to observe any provision of a code of practice shall not of itself render him liable to any proceedings, but in proceedings before an industrial tribunal or the Central Arbitration Committee (CAC) any code of practice issued under this section shall be admissible in evidence."[53] A similar rule applies to codes issued by the Secretary of State, with the difference that codes issued by him may also be taken into account in proceedings before a court (as well as before an industrial tribunal or the CAC).[54] Codes issued by the EOC and the CRE may be taken into account only in proceedings before industrial tribunals.[55] The effect and interpretation of individual codes of practice is further considered below, under the appropriate subject headings.

1.15 The law of the European Community

To an unusual extent, employment law has provided a setting for consideration of the extent to which the legislative provisions of the EC are enforceable by individuals within the United Kingdom. The problems that have arisen concern in the main the effect of Directives within domestic law. The position with regard to the effect of provisions of the Treaty of Rome itself and the Regulations has proved less problematical.[56]

---

[52] *E.g.* ACAS has issued codes in respect of disciplinary practices and procedure (1977), disclosure of information to trade unions for collective bargaining purposes (1977), and time off for trade union duties and activities (1978). A new general code on industrial relations failed to find approval from the Secretary of State for Employment in 1987, and in its place ACAS has issued a booklet giving general guidance on discipline at work, but lacking the status of a statutory code of practice. The Secretary of State has issued codes on picketing (1980), closed shop agreements and arrangements (1983) and on trade union ballots on industrial action (1990). The Equal Opportunities Commission and the Commission for Racial Equality have issued codes in respect of the elimination of discrimination in employment, the current versions of which were published in 1985 and 1983 respectively. The Health and Safety Commission has issued a code in respect of safety representatives (1978).

[53] Employment Protection Act 1975, s. 6 (11).

[54] Employment Act 1980, s. 3 (B).

[55] Sex Discrimination Act 1975, s. 56A (10); Race Relations Act 1976, s. 47 (10).

[56] The decision of the European Court of Justice in *Defrenne v. SABENA S.A.* [1976] ICR 547 is to the effect that Article 119 of the Treaty of Rome might be relied upon by individuals in their national legal systems, to the extent their complaint was of discrimination in pay. See para. 7.11. As to Directives see *Duke v. GEC Reliance* [1988] IRLR 118, HL and *Foster v. British Gas plc, The Times* April 19, 1991, HL.

1.16 Equal pay and sex discrimination

The influence of Community standards is not restricted to the area of sex discrimination, but it is in relation to these issues that the fullest discussion of reach of Community law has taken place. The detailed rules regarding equal pay and sex discrimination are considered below,[57] but here it may be mentioned that, at least in some situations, it is possible for individuals to reply on community standards to achieve better rights than are available to them under the law of Scotland (or England). This has occurred on two notable occasions. In *McCarthys Ltd. v. Smith*[58] the European Court of Justice ruled that a woman could, on a proper interpretation of a claim for equal pay under Article 119 of the EEC Treaty, make comparison with a man who had been recently but was not presently employed on like work by her employer. This right to make comparison with a male predecessor was not permitted under the terms of the Equal Pay Act 1970[59] but this consideration did not stand in the way of the European Court of Justice's interpretation of the superior norm expressed in Article 119. So too, in *Marshall v. Southampton and South-West Hampshire Area Health Authority (Teaching)*[60] an individual was held entitled to rely directly on a provision of Community law which was contrary to the content of the Sex Discrimination Act 1975.[61] In *Marshall*, however, the crucial feature was the fact that the community provision was contained in a Directive and not in the Treaty itself.[62] The case establishes that the provisions of a directive, if unconditional and sufficiently precise, may be relied upon by an individual against the state, where the state has not properly implemented the directive in its domestic law. Domestic law cannot therefore validly detract from the standards guaranteed by Community law, though it does not follow from this that in all circumstances it is open to an individual to rely on the content of the relevant Community measure before his or her own courts of law.[63] Usually it will be a matter for the European Court of Justice to determine whether Community law displaces domestic law, but the House of Lords has shown that in appropriate cases — for example where domestic law has been passed to give effect to Community law — it is not necessary for recourse to be made to the European Court.[64]

Binding authority for the direct applicability of directive dealing with sex discrimination is restricted to the situation where attempts are being made to enforce them against the state. There is a rule, however, that in construing domestic legislation enacted after the relevant community standard has been adopted, the courts should do their best to make their interpretation consistent

---

[57] See Chapter Seven.
[58] [1980] ICR 672.
[59] S. 1 (2). See the decision of the Court of Appeal [1979] ICR 672.
[60] [1986] IRLR 140, ECJ.
[61] S. 6 (4), which allowed discrimination on the ground of sex if this arises from a provision concerned with retirement.
[62] Directive 76/207, Article 5 (1).
[63] See for example the sequel to the decision of the ECJ in *Marshall* to the effect that Art. 6 of Dir. 76/207 did not override the limit as to compensation contained in the Sex Discrimination Act 1975, s. 65 (2) (*Marshall v. Southampton and South West Hampshire Area Health Authority (Teaching) (No. 2)* [1990] IRLR 481.
[64] *Pickstone v. Freemans plc* [1988] IRLR 357, HL; *Litster v. Forth Dry Dock & Engineering Co Ltd* [1989] IRLR 161, HL.

with what the Community measure states, at least when the British state is enacted subsequent to the Community measure.[65]

It may be of course that a United Kingdom statute makes available more extensive rights than are to be found in the corresponding Community standards.[66] In this case there is no reason why more favourable domestic provisions should not be relied upon by suitably qualified individuals.

1.17 Collective redundancies

Apart from sex discrimination, there are two other important areas where the rules of Scots and English employment law have been directly influenced by Directives of the EC. The procedure for the handling of collective redundancies and the giving of advance warning to trade unions representing individual workers affected are regulated by the Employment Protection Act 1975,[67] which is the British response to a Council Directive of 1975.[68] Unlike the position with regard to the parent directives in sex discrimination law, there has been no attempt so far in the reported cases to argue either that the Directive is directly enforceable, or that the provisions in British law fall short of what is required by European law. But there are differences between the two sets of standards; notably in relation to the situations in which the duty to consult arises. Under the British scheme, the duty to consult arises only when the employer intends to impose redundancies, as defined by the Employment Protection (Consolidation) Act 1978, s. 81 (2); the Directive itself refers to "dismissals effected by an employer for one or more reasons not related to the individual worker concerned".[69] Not all dismissals falling within this latter definition are encompassed by the technical notion of redundancy in British law.[70]

1.18 Transfer of undertakings

The Transfer of Undertakings (Protection of Employment) Regulations 1981[71] seek to implement Council Directive 77/187[72] and the House of Lords has resorted to the Directive for the purpose of interpreting the domestic regulations.[73]

---

[65] *Garland v. British Railway Engineering Ltd* [1982] IRLR 257, HL; *Von Colson and Kamann v. Land Nordrhein-Westfahlen* [1984] ECR 1891, ECJ. European Communities Act 1972, s. 2 (1); *cf. Duke v. GEC Reliance* [1988] IRLR 118, HL. And see *Marleasing SA v. La Commercial Internacional de Alimentacion SA* (Case 106/89, unreported, ECJ).

[66] *Jenkins v. Kingsgate (Clothing Productions) Ltd* [1981] ICR 715.

[67] Ss. 99-107.

[68] Directive 75/129, on the approximation of the Laws of the Member States Relating to Collective Redundancies. See too para. 9.25.

[69] *Ibid.* Article 1.

[70] There are other differences too; Article 2 of the Directive requires consultation to be carried out "with a view to reaching agreement", but this is no part of the British regulations. See further P. O'Higgins, "International Standards and British Labour Law" in R. Lewis, *Labour Law in Britain*, 1986.

[71] S.I. 1981 No. 1794.

[72] On the Approximation of the Laws of the Member States Relating to the Safeguarding of Employees Rights in the Event of Transfers of Undertakings, Businesses or Parts of Businesses.

[73] *Litster v. Forth Dry Dock and Engineering Co Ltd* [1989] IRLR 161, HL; and see *Delabole Slate Ltd v. Berriman* [1985] IRLR 305, CA, 308, *per* Browne-Wilkinson LJ and *Secretary of State for Employment v. Anchor Hotel (Kippford) Ltd* [1985] IRLR 452, 453 *per* Waite J.

Chapter Two

THE CONTRACT OF EMPLOYMENT
AND ITS CONSTITUTION

2.1 The contract of employment

The contract of employment (or contract of service) has to be distinguished from the contract for services[1] and is of central importance to modern employment law. Perhaps strangely, this is so not because the rights of employees and employers are determined directly by the terms of the contract in contract law actions but for four distinct but related reasons.

(1) Many strategically significant employment rights and duties are created by statutes which are, in the main, applicable only where the work relationship takes the form of a contract of employment. The best example of such a statute is the Employment Protection (Consolidation) Act 1978.[2] Although other statutes are of wider application it is clear that they also — and most frequently — apply to the contract of employment.[3] Thus the contract of employment is the main medium through which access to modern substantive employment rights is achieved.

(2) Furthermore once access to the various statutory codes has been achieved it quickly becomes apparent that although the rights are intrinsically statutory their application and adjudication involve an appreciation of contract law issues. Two examples suffice to illustrate the close connection between statute rights and contract law. In the law of unfair dismissal[4] whether an employee has been "constructively dismissed"[5] depends essentially on whether the conduct of the employer which causes the employee to leave is either a repudiation or an anticipatory breach of the contract of employment and not merely conduct on the part of the employer which may be characterised as unreasonable.[6] Whether the statutory definition of redundancy[7] is satisfied depends to a large extent on whether the needs of a business for employees to carry out "work of a particular kind" in "the place where the employee was employed" have reduced.[8] Both issues of "work of a particular kind" and "the place where the employee was

---

[1] See paras. 1.2, 2.2.
[2] S. 153 defines an employee as "an individual who has entered into or works under a contract of employment".
[3] See for example the Equal Pay Act 1970 s. 6(1), the Sex Discrimination Act 1975 s. 82(1) and the Wages Act 1986 s. 8(1).
[4] See Chapter Five.
[5] See Chapter Five para. 5.17.
[6] *Western Excavating (ECC) Ltd v. Sharp* [1978] IRLR 27 (CA).
[7] EPCA, s. 81 (2) and see Chapter Six.
[8] *Ibid.*

employed" are to be determined by reference to the terms of the contract of employment and not merely by a test of actuality.[9]

(3) Because the contract of employment is a specific type of contract in the absence of express provisions being agreed by the parties the law implies into the contract various term. As will be seen later in this chapter the contract of employment can often be validly constituted orally or by implication with little more than a bare agreement to do certain work for wages.[10] However once it is clear that the contract is one of employment the relationship between the employer and employee is regulated not just by the express term but by a complex range of additional terms implied by law into each contract of employment.[11] Two examples suffice. There is implied into the contract of employment an obligation that the employer will not act in such a way as is likely to damage the trust and confidence on which the employment contract is based.[12] Also implied into the contract is an obligation that the employee will execute his duties with reasonable care.[13] However if the contract is not one of employment such terms are not implied automatically.

(4) When a contract of employment is created the employer becomes vicariously liable for the negligence of his employee while acting in the scope of his employment[14] whereas if the contract is for services generally [15] the employer or person who agrees with the contractor that the work should be done will have no liability for the negligence of the contractor or his employees in carrying out the contract.[16]

2.2 Identifying the contract of employment

Being able to identify the contract of employment or contract of service, and to distinguish it from other working relationships — particularly the contract under which the independent contractor provides services to another, the contract for services — is therefore not merely of academic interest. It has important legal and practical consequences. The modern distinction between the contract of employment and the contract for services reflects the distinction in Roman law between *locatio conductio operis* and *locatio conductio operarum*[17] and modern law makes no distinction between contracts of employment for ordinary as distinguished from skilled work or labour.[18] Although previously courts attached much significance to the control — either actual or potential — exercis-

---

[9] *Nelson v. BBC* [1977] ICR 649, [1977] IRLR 148, CA; *United Kingdom Atomic Energy Authority v. Claydon* [1974] IRLR 6, [1974] ICR 128, NIRC.

[10] In Scots law express agreement regarding wages is not essential since it is presumed that services are performed in return for wages (*Thomson v. Thomson's Trs.* (1889) 16 R 333).

[11] But note express terms may have the effect of creating a relationship other than a contract of employment. See paras. 2.2, 2.3.

[12] *Courtaulds Northern Textiles Ltd v. Andrew* [1979] IRLR 84, EAT; *Woods v. W M Car Services (Peterborough) Ltd* [1981] ICR 666, EAT.

[13] *Clydesdale Bank Ltd v. Beatson* (1882) 10 R 88. And post para 3.28.

[14] On vicarious liability in the course of employment see Gloag and Henderson, *Introduction to the Law of Scotland* (9th edn.) para 34.31.

[15] The exceptions would be where the contractor is subject to the control of the employer and where the contractor contracts with the Crown (Crown Proceedings Act 1947, ss. 2 & 38 (2)).

[16] *Stephen v. Thurso Police Commissioners* (1876) 3 R 535; and see *Marshall v. William Sharp and Sons* 1991 SLT 114, (IH).

[17] *Cf.* Lord Fraser, *Master and Servant* (3rd edn.) ch. 1.

[18] *Cassidy v. Minister of Health* [1951] 2 KB 343 whereas the distinction is emphasised by Bell (*Principles*, ss. 146-152).

able by one party (the employer) over the other (the employee)[19] it soon became apparent that control, although continuing to be a relevant criterion was too restrictive to be regarded as the absolute one[20] and the test which now finds judicial favour includes control only as one of many and varied factors.[21] The test now generally[22] applied to differentiate the contract of employment from the contract for services is one which, by examining a range of factors, seeks to determine the substance or economic reality of the relationship.[23] It is frequently referred to as the "multiple and variable test" because it permits consideration of a multiplicity of factors with different factors possibly receiving greater or less weight according to the circumstances of the employment. There is no exclusive list of relevant factors but many of the factors which will call for consideration are listed in *Market Investigations Ltd v. Ministry of Social Security*.[24] In particular circumstances other factors would include whether the work is performed as part of a business or merely ancillary to it[25] and, especially where the work is performed on a casual basis or as an outworker, the respective extents to which the employer is required to provide work and the employee is required to perform work when it is available for provided.[26]

2.3 Whether or not a contract of employment exists is a question of law;[27] however, answering that question involves an appreciation and evaluation of questions of fact and degree.[28] Since the existence of relevant factors may be a matter of inference for the tribunal of fact it may be difficult to challenge the

---

[19] See for example *Performing Right Society Ltd v. Mitchell and Booker (Palais de Danse) Ltd* [1924] 1 KB 762, CA; *Stagecraft Ltd v. Minister of National Insurance* [1952] SC 288; *Cassidy v. Minister of Health* [1951] 2 KB.

[20] *AEU v. Ministry of Pensions* [1963] 1 All ER 864 in which Megaw J. stated ". . . the question of the control of an employee is an important element in deciding whether the contract is one of service, but it is a test or criteria which is far from being an absolute one. The nature of the control which is required to bring the employment within the scope of a contract of service varies almost infinitely with the general nature of the duties involved."

[21] In *Argent v. Minister of Social Security* [1968] 3 All ER 208 Roskill J. neatly summarises the change in emphasis from control, through integration into a business, to "what in modern parlance is called economic reality."

[22] In cases of secondment of employees or employment *pro hae vice* the authority to control the work objective and method is still of critical importance. See para. 2.41.

[23] *E.g. Global Plant Ltd v. Secretary of State for Health and Social Security* [1972] 1 QB 139.

[24] [1968] 3 All ER 732. "The most that can be said is that control will no doubt have to be considered, although it can no longer be regarded as the sole determining factor; and factors which maybe of importance are such matters as whether he who performs the services provides his own tools and equipment, whether he hires his own helpers, what degree of financial risk he takes, what degree of responsibility for investment and management he has and whether and how far he has the opportunity of profiting from sound management in the performance of the task" *per* Cooke J.

[25] *Stevenson Jordan and Harrison Ltd v. McDonald and Evans* [1952] TLR 101, CA; *Whittaker v. Minister of Pensions and National Insurance* [1967] 1 QB 156.

[26] *O'Kelly v. Trusthouse Forte plc* [1983] IRLR 369, CA; *Nethermere (St Neots) Ltd v. Taverna and Gardiner* [1984] IRLR 240, CA. And contrast *Hellyer Brothers Ltd v. McLeod* [1987] ICR 526, CA with *Boyd Line Ltd v. Pitts* [1986] ICR 244, EAT.

[27] *Davies v. Presbyterian Church of Wales* [1986] ICR 280, HL.

[28] *O'Kelly v. Trusthouse Forte plc* [1983] IRLR 369, CA; *Sidey v. Phillips (Inpsector of Taxes)* (1987) 131 SJ 76, *The Times* December 12, 1986; *Lee v. Chung* [1990] IRLR 237, PC.

decision of a tribunal of first instance unless it can be shown that no reasonable tribunal acting judicially could have arrived at that decision. Thus in *Nethermere (St Neots) Ltd v. Taverna and Gardiner*[29] the existence of "the irreducible minimum of obligation on each side"[30] (to provide work and to do it when provided) was entirely a matter of inference; although the evidence before the industrial tribunal was "tenuous"[31] there was sufficient to allow the tribunal to find that the relationship between Nethermere Ltd and the homeworkers could be described as an "umbrella" or "global" contract thus satisfying the need to have an irreducible minimum of mutual obligation.[32] The scope entrusted to tribunals of fact is illustrated by contrasting *Hellyer Brothers Ltd v. McLeod*[33] with *Boyd Line Ltd v. Pitts*.[34] Both cases involved the redundancy of trawlermen and in each case the question arose as to whether during the periods between various voyages undertaken by McLeod and Pitts there was sufficient mutuality of obligation for these periods to be covered by a contract of employment. In the latter case the Employment Appeal Tribunal held there was evidence on which the industrial tribunal *could*[35] find there was a "global" or "umbrella" contract whereas in the former the findings of the majority of the industrial tribunal precluded the Employment Appeal Tribunal and the Court of Appeal arriving at a similar conclusion.[36] What type of contract the parties intend to create is also a relevant factor.[37] However, because the contract of employment is a legal concept there are several limitations on the freedom of the parties purporting to create a contract of employment. Thus a contract of employment under which the parties agree not to make deductions for income tax and national insurance contributions is likely to be illegal and void.[38] Where A and B enter a contract by which one of them is to work exclusively for C the contract is one *sui generis*[39] and although an express declaration that the contract is to be one of employment will not *per se* ensure the contract is of the same type as the label or description given to it by the parties [40] the court will recognise the clearly stated genuine intentions of the parties provided the other terms of the

---

[29] [1984] IRLR 240, CA.

[30] *Ibid., per* Stephenson L.J.

[31] *Ibid.*

[32] L.J. Stephenson could "not see why well founded expectations of continuing homework should not be hardened or refined into enforceable contracts by regular giving and taking of work for periods of a year or more . . ."

[33] [1987] ICR 526, CA.

[34] [1986] ICR 244, EAT.

[35] EAT's emphasis.

[36] In *Hellyer* the industrial tribunal's findings, reported in the decision of the EAT ([1986] ICR 122), included "(3) Any trawlerman was free to work for an owner other than the one for whom he had just sailed, if he wished. . . . (6) Owners had the right, if they wished, not to re-engage any trawlermen after completion of a particular voyage, and that right continued for as long as the shipowner might wish."

[37] *Massey v. Crown Life Insurance Co.* [1978] IRLR 31, CA.

[38] *Tomlinson v. Dick Evans "U" Drive Ltd* [1978] IRLR 77, EAT, *Jennings v. Westwood Engineering Ltd* [1975] IRLR 245, Ind. Trib.

[39] *Construction Industry Training Board v. Labour Force Ltd* [1970] 9 KIR 269.

[40] *Ferguson v. Dawson & Partners Ltd* [1976] IRLR 346, CA; *Young & Woods Ltd v. West* [1980] IRLR 201, CA.

contract are not inconsistent with that type of contract especially where the other factors are not conclusive of the matter.[41]

2.4 Special cases

Some employment types and situations deserve special mention.

(a) Pro hac vice. The normal rule is that because the contract of employment is based on the notion of *delectus personae*[42] the right under the contract cannot be assigned without the parties' consent.[43] Thus an employer cannot unilaterally transfer an employee to another employer without the employee's consent.[44] However this rule does not prevent an employer from instructing his employee to work for another.[45] Where this occurs although there is no change in the responsibilities of employer or employee under the contract of employment there arises the question of who is vicariously liable for the negligence of the employee when he is performing his contract of employment for the purposes of the other person; is he still the employee of his employer or has he become the employee *pro hac vice* of the other person?[46] If the employee (A) of X has become the employee of Y *pro hac vice* the latter is liable to third parties injured as a result of his negligence. However the onus of proving that A has become the *pro hac vice* employee of Y rests on X, the original employer,[47] and, although all the facts and circumstances have to be taken into account, which of the two employers has the authority to direct not merely the use made of the plant etc. but also the manner in which it is operated is often the critical factor.[48] In *Mersey Docks &*

---

[41] *Massey v. Crown Life Insurance Co.* [1978] IRLR 31, CA; *B.S.M. v. Secretary of State for Social Services* [1978] ICR 894. *Cf. Global Plant Ltd v. Secretary of State for Health and Social Security* [1971] 3 WLR 269; *Narich Pty. Ltd v. Commissioner of Pay-roll Tax* [1984] ICR 286, QBD.

[42] A contract is said to involve *delectus personae* when the personal and other individual characteristics of the contracting parties are material considerations in determining whether and on what terms to enter the contract. For a full description of *delectus personae* see Gloag on *Contract* (2nd edn. 1929), pp. 416-421.

[43] An exception is to be found in the Transfer of Undertaking (Protection) of Employment Regulations 1981, reg. 7. Note particularly reg. 5 (5) that an employee shall not have the right to rescind a contract of employment "by reason only that . . . the identity of his employer changes . . . unless the change is significant and to his detriment." Also in redundancy law an employee's refusal to accept an offer of employment from his employer's successor may result in a loss of a redundancy. And see paras 5.69, 6.7.

[44] *Nokes v. Doncaster Amalgamated Collieries Ltd* [1940] AC 1014, HL. Also it would be a material breach for an employer to tell his employee who enquires about payment of his wages to look to another employer for whom work has been performed.

[45] Frequently but not necessarily this will involve operating a vehicle or plant or equipment owned by the employee's employer for the purposes of another — typically a person who has entered into a contract of hire with the employee's employer; the contract of hire will often include the services of an operative — an employee of the owner of the vehicle, etc.

[46] Such a question only arises in cases of liability to a third party injured as a result of the employee's negligence (*County Plant Hire Ltd. v. Jackson & Lane Brothers Ltd* [1970] VIII KIR 989, *per* Denning MR). And see *Savory v. Holland & Hannen & Cubitts* [1964] 1 WLR 1158 at 1165.

[47] *Malley v. L.M.S. Railway Co.* 1944 SC 129; *Mersey Docks and Harbour Board v. Coggins & Giffith* [1947] AC 1, HL.

[48] *Mersey Docks and Harbour Board v. Coggins & Griffith Ltd* [1947] AC 1, HL; *McGregor v. J. S. Duthie Ltd* 1966 SLT 133, IH; *Kerr v. Hailes (Plant) Ltd* 1974 SLT (Notes) 31, OH. While in practice the location of the authority to exercise detailed control over the method of the work is the most influential factor, as indicated by the approach of L.J. Clk. Cooper in *Malley v. L.M.S. Railway Co.* 1944 SC 129, the matter is more complex.

Harbour Board v. Coggins & Griffith Ltd[49] the board hired out to Coggins & Griffith Ltd, a firm of stevedores, a crane with a driver. On whether the driver had become their employee, *pro hac vice* Lord McMillan stated *"Prima facie* he (the driver) was the Board's employee. But it is always open to an employer to show that he has for a particular purpose temporarily transferred the services of one of his general servants to another so as to constitute him *pro hac vice* the servant of that other party. The burden is on the general employer to establish such transference has been effected. The stevedores were entitled to tell him what parcels to pick up, where to go etc., that is to say they could direct him as to what they wanted him to do; but they had no authority to tell him how to handle his crane in doing the work." However in *McGregor v. J. S. Duthie Ltd*[50] the general employer was able to show that his employee was acting *pro hac vice* the employee of another (J. S. Duthie Ltd) whose lorry their employee was driving at the time two passengers were injured as a result of his negligence.[51] Who has the right to exercise control of the manner of the work is what is important and not who had *de facto* control[52] and a provision in a commercial contract for the liability of the contracting parties *inter se* will not affect the question of whether an employee has become *pro hac vice* the employee of another.[53]

(b) Apprentices. The essential differences between a contract of employment and a contract of apprenticeship are that the latter requires writing of some sort[54] for its proper constitution[55] and must involve an obligation to instruct the apprentice on the master's or employer's part.[56] Also, unlike the contract of employment[57] there is probably no right to terminate the apprenticeship contract by paying wages in lieu of notice because the apprentice is entitled to be so instructed in his trade or profession that his wages or salary on completion will reflect his completed training and instruction.[58] Although it has been doubted

---

[49] [1947] AC 1, HL.

[50] 1966 SLT 133, IH. Transfer *pro hac vice* also occurred in *Gibb v. United Steel Companies* [1957] 1 WLR 668.

[51] The negligent driver was in the general employment of a partnership which had entered a commercial contract with J. S. Duthie Ltd for sawing timber but it was agreed that he would drive one of Duthie's lorries when required and his general employers would be reimbursed his wages — "There is no doubt that from the time he left Kingairloch until he reached Fort William he (the driver) was engaged on Duthie's business and acting in accordance with instructions they had a right to give. I do not think the partnership (the general employers) would have had any right to instruct (the driver) . . . when he was driving their lorry, it was Duthie and Duthie alone who had the right to control the work he did" (*McGregor v. J. S. Duthie Ltd* 1966 SLT 133, *per* L. J.-C. Grant).

[52] This is emphasised by the fact that the presence of one of the partners in the lorry at the time of the accident was regarded by L. J.-C. Grant as irrelevant — he was "a mere hitchhiker". And see *McAllister v. Oban Transport and Trading Co Ltd* 1971 SLT (Notes) 51.

[53] *Arthur White v. Tarmac Civil Engineering* [1967] 1 WLR 1508; *Kerr v. Hailes (Plant) Ltd* 1974 SLT (Notes) 31.

[54] Either probative writing or informal writing followed by *rei interventus*.

[55] *Murray v. M'Gilchrist* (1863) 4 Irv. 461. However whether the contract be of apprenticeship or employment it seems contracting without a curator's consent may not render the contract void — *McFeetridge v. Stewart and Lloyds* 1913 SC 773; *Faulds v. BSC* 1977 SLT (Notes) 18. See W. McBryde, 1979 SLT (News) p. 29.

[56] *Gardner v. Smith* 1775 M. 593; *Royce v. Greig* 1902 2 SLT 298. Equally a perverse or determined refusal to learn would be a breach on the part of the apprentice (*Butler v. Dillon* [1952] 87 Irish Law Times Reports, 95).

[57] See para. 4.2.

[58] *Lyle v. Service* (1863) 2 MacQ. 115; *Dunk v. George Waller & Son Ltd* [1970] 2 QB 163, CA.

whether Scots law would follow English law that the obligations in the apprenticeship contract are so independent that misconduct by the apprentice does not justify his dismissal,[59] there is no doubt that in the context of statutory unfair dismissal law[60] apprentices are required to be treated more leniently than mature, qualified employees.[61]

(c) Directors. Because a limited company has a legal personality distinct from its shareholders and officers[62] it is quite logical for a director also to have a contract of employment (or "service agreement" as it is often called) with the company.[63] Where a service agreement is entered into between a company and a director a copy of such agreement or a written memorandum of its terms must be kept at the registered office or the principal place of business of the company[64] and service agreements for five years or more require approval by shareholders.[65] As previously stated, whether a contract of employment exists is a question of law involving a detailed evaluation of matters of fact[66] and such a process is particularly important in determining the true status of a company director. Equally, the size of a director's shareholding is not conclusive;[67] what matters is what functions the director actually carried out and the extent to which he was subject to the control of the company.[68] Each case will depend on its own facts and evidence is required to establish that a director is employed by a company.[69] While it is not possible to lay down firm rules the following issues will often be influential: (1) Is the director required to devote his whole time to the affairs of the company and is he employed on terms that his employment may be determined by notice? (2) Is he subject to control by the company? (3) Does he draw a weekly wage or salary? (4) Is there a written service agreement or a board minute or memorandum?[70]

(d) Public employment. Although the employment of many employees who work for public or governmental agencies is regulated by the terms of their

---

[59] See the comments of on *Waterman v. Fryer* [1922] 1 KB 499 in Gloag on *Contract* (2nd edn.), p. 593; and see the English decisions of *Maloney v. St Helens Industrial Co-operative Society* [1933] 1KB 293, CA to the effect that illness will not justify dismissal of apprentice and *Newell v. Gillingham Corporation* [1941] 1 KB 552.

[60] See Chapter Five.

[61] See, for example, *Stamton v. Wolfenden Cranes Ltd* [1972] IRLR 82.

[62] *Lee v. Lee's Air Farming Ltd* [1961] AC 12.

[63] For an interesting discussion of the possible "duality" of a director's tenure see R. R. Pennington, *Company Law* (6th edn.) p. 550.

[64] Companies Act 1985, s. 318. However the failure to preserve such a copy or to reduce the agreement to writing (unless it is for a period of more than a year) will not prevent the conclusion that the relationship between director and company is one of employment (*Folami v. Nigerline (UK)* [1978] ICR 277, EAT).

[65] Companies Act 1985, s. 319 (1). But note the exception regarding successive contracts where the second contract is entered into in the 6 months before the expiry of the first contract (s. 319 (2)).

[66] See para. 2.2.

[67] *Road Transport Industry Training Board v. Readers Garage* [1969] VI KIR 137.

[68] "The issue would depend on exactly what Mr Reader did. If for instance his main work was that of director, and he only occasionally stepped into the shoes of a workman that might be one thing; but if, on the other hand, he kept regular hours at the petrol pumps and only worked for a short period on the administrative side . . . there might be a different conclusion." *Ibid* per Lord Parker of Waddington CJ, at p. 141.

[69] *McMillan v. Guest* [1942] AC 562; *Trussed Steel Concrete Co v. Green* [1946] Ch. 115; *Robinson v. Sorby Ltd* [1967] 2 ITR 148; *Eaton v. Robert Eaton Ltd* [1988] IRLR 83, EAT.

[70] *Parsons (A J) Ltd v. Parson* [1979] IRLR 117, CA; *Eaton v. Robert Eaton Ltd* [1988] IRLR 83, EAT.

contracts of employment as supplemented by statutory provisions contained in legislation, principally the Employment Protection (Consolidation) Act 1978, some in public employment (especially those who occupy senior positions or hold particular offices) have their relationships regulated not only by their contracts of employment — supplemented in the way mentioned — but by certain rules of public law. A distinction must be made between public employees whose employment merely has a "statutory flavour" and those whose employment is truly regulated by public law or statute. The former are in no different position than employees who work in the private sector of industry and commerce;[71] the latter however derive additional protection *via* the medium of public law particularly the remedy of judicial review[72] which allows the grant of reduction, declarator and interdict.[73] These orders are significant in that they can achieve for the public employee something neither the law of contract nor employment protection legislation can generally[74] achieve for the private sector employee — they may declare a purported dismissal "invalid" thus depriving it of legal effect. Where such a declaration of invalidity occurs no question of reinstatement arises because there has never been a lawful dismissal.[75]

Certain groups of public employees require special mention. Holders of public offices (*munera publica*) derive their tenure and its incidents from the fact of their office-holding as protected by the common law.[75a] Consideration of the relationship between the Crown and the civil servant[76] involves two apparently conflicting schools of thought. The first, exemplified by *Riordan v. War Office*[77] is to the effect that as the Crown cannot effectively fetter its future executive action by contract[78] the relationship between the Crown and the civil servant, being terminable at the pleasure of the Crown, cannot sensibly be described as contractual; this has led to the wife of a civil servant being unable to arrest her husband's salary,[79] although the right to dismiss at pleasure can be lawfully restricted by legislation.[80] The second school of thought is typified by

---

[71] See for example *University Council of the Vidyodaya University of Ceylon v. Silva* [1965] 1 WLR 77, PC; *Tehrani v. Argyll & Clyde Health Board (No 2)* 1989 SLT 118, IH. Cf. *R. v. University of Hull, The Times,* April 2, 1991.

[72] For a survey of the flexible remedy of judicial review see J. St Clair and N. F. Davidson, *Judicial Review in Scotland.*

[73] See *Vine v. National Dock Labour Board* [1957] AC 488, HL; *Malloch v. Aberdeen Corporation* 1973 SC 227. Cf. *Tehrani v. Argyll & Clyde Glasgow Health Board 1 (No 2)* 1989 SLT 118, IH.

[74] It is true that, exceptionally, the effect of a dismissal potentially unfair by virtue of sec. 58 of EPCA can be postponed (EPCA, s. 77 (as amended by EA 1982, s. 8)) and that the English courts are more prepared to grant injunctions to restrain a dismissal in breach of contract where the relationship between employer and employee has not broken down; see para 3.35.

[75] Thus in *Malloch v. Aberdeen Corporation* 1973 SC 227, the effect of the order was to reduce Malloch's purported dismissal to a legal nullity with the result that he continued to be entitled to his salary.

[75a] *Hastie v. McMurtie* (1889) 16R. 715; *Rothesay Magistrates v. Carse* (1903) 5F 383; *McKay and Esslemont v. L. A.* 1937 SC 860.

[76] The Civil Service has been described as "A body of officials in the service of the Crown, who discharge duties belonging to the exercise of the Queen's executive powers, but not being members of Her Majesty's naval, military or air forces, and not being the holders of political offices" (Mustoe, *The Law and Organisation of the British Civil Service,* p. 26).

[77] [1961] 1 WLR 210.

[78] *Rederiaktiebolaget Amphitrite v. R.* [1921] 3 KB 500.

[79] *Mulvenna v. The Admiralty* 1952 SC 165, disapproved in *Kodeeswaraan v. Att. Gen. of Ceylon* [1970] 2 WLR 456.

[80] *Gould v. Stuart* 1896 AC 575; *Reilly v. R.* [1934] AC 176.

Kodeeswaran v. Att. Gen. of Ceylon[81] in which Lord Diplock reviewed the law and concluded that prior to *Mulvenna v. The Admiralty*[82] the arrears of salary of a civil servant were recoverable in England; the right to determine a contract at will being not inconsistent with the existence of a contract until so terminated. This school of thought recognises the need and the right of the Crown to terminate at pleasure the employment of the civil servant while preventing the abuse of such a power to dictate changes in contractual terms unilaterally.[83] More recently, although it has been recognised that there is nothing unconstitutional about civil servants being employed under contracts of employment, whether or not the relationship is to be regarded as contractual has been resolved by considering whether there was evidence that the parties intended that such a relationship should be created.[84] On appointment a police constable affirms that he will "faithfully discharge the duties of the office of constable"[85]; a police constable does not have a contract of employment[86] and this has not been altered by the statutory provision[87] which makes the chief constable liable in reparation in respect of any wrongful act or omission on the part of a constable under his general direction "as a master is . . . liable in respect of a wrongful act or omission on the part of a servant in the course of [his] employment."[88] While a police authority may enter into contracts of employment with officers (not being constables) for the assistance of constables,[89] a police cadet is not employed under a contract of employment and is therefore unable to claim unfair dismissal[90] and in England it has been held that a special constable is not employed under a contract because there was no intention to enter into a contractual relationship.[91] However although a police constable's legal status deprives him of the protection afforded to those who have contracts of employment[92] the

---

[81]   [1970] 2 WLR 456, PC. And see *Cameron v. Lord Advocate* 1952 SC 165.
[82]   1926 SC 842.
[83]   *Kodeeswaran v. Att. Gen. of Ceylon* [1970] 1 WLR 456, PC. And see *Att. Gen. for Guyana v. Nobrega* [1969] 3 All ER 1604, P.C.
[84]   *Regina v. Civil Service Appeal Board, ex parte Bruce* [1988] ICR 649, QBD. On the evidence it was clear the Crown did not intend to create a contract of employment. One important practical effect of *ex parte Bruce* is Employment Act 1988, s. 30 which, for their purposes of the law of industrial conflict deems the relationship between the Crown and the civil servant to be contractual. And note EPCA, s. 138 which has a similar effect for individual employment protection law.
[85]   The Police (Scotland) Regulations 1976, reg. 10.
[86]   *Young v. Magistrates and Town Council of Glasgow* (1891) 18 R 825; *Girdwood v. Standing Joint Committee of Midlothian* (1894) 22 R 11; *Yates v. Lancashire C.C.* [1975] ITR 20, IT. And see *Ridge v. Baldwin* [1964] AC 40, HL.
[87]   Police (Scotland) Act 1967, s. 39. And see s. 8 (2) regarding police cadets.
[88]   *Robertson v. Bell* 1969 SLT 119. S. 39 is a procedural device and does not alter the substance of the officer's relationship with the chief constable.
[89]   Police (Scotland) Act 1967, s. 9. And see *R. v. Derbyshire County Council, ex parte Noble* [1990] IRLR 332, CA (refusal of judicial review because police surgeon was appointed under ordinary contract for services).
[90]   *Wiltshire Police Authority v. Wynn* [1980] ICR 649. CA.
[91]   *Sheikh v. Anderton, The Times* July 18, 1988, EAT. But see *post* para. 2.9.
[92]   The most significant exclusion is EPCA, s. 146 (2). And see *Yates v. Lancashire C.C.* [1975] ITR 20. Other legislation (*e.g.* Sex Discrimination Act 1975, s. 17) treats holding the office of constable as employment. Cf. *Sheikh v. Anderton, The Times* July 18, 1988, EAT (special constable could not bring a complaint under the Race Relations act 1976 because he did not have a contract).

official or public law element involved will permit application for judicial review.[93]

2.5 The constitution of the contract of employment

Although the usual rules about the constitution and proof of contracts generally apply equally to the contract of employment, the coincidence of different factors distinguishes it from other contracts. First the terms of the contract of employment are very often not the subject of direct negotiation between the parties (they are invariably imposed by the more powerful of the two as individuals — the employer) or are the result, at least in part, of negotiations between a trade union and an employer or an association of employers. Secondly, even if the terms on which the employment contract is initially agreed can be clearly ascertained — although this is likely to involve an expedition through letters of appointment, statutory statements of particulars of employment, works' rulebooks, notices on display on the office wall and collective agreements both local and national — by the time any issue or dispute arises it is likely that the original agreement will have been the subject of variation or modification, often the subject of some remote negotiations, or just not observed or applied. Few, if any, contracts entered into by the ordinary person, without professional representation or advice, can rival the contract of employment for its informality and fluidity and it is these factors together which sometimes suggest that the contract of employment is not an ideal subject for the application of the usual rules of contract. However, few provisions special to the contract of employment have been developed and this, no doubt, is why statute has enacted modest provisions to ensure minimum formalities will accompany many, but not all, employment relationships.[94]

2.6 Thus the constitution of a valid contract of employment or apprenticeship requires that the parties have adequate capacity and that the contract is not illegal. In Scots law pupils (boys under 14 years and girls under 12 years) have no contractual capacity[95] — their contracts are void, not merely voidable.[96] A pupil who wishes to enter a contract must do so through his tutor. On the other hand, minors (boys between 14 and 18 and girls between 12 and 18[97]) may have either full or limited contractual capacity depending on whether he/she has a curator and the type of contract involved. A minor who has no curator, who is forisfamiliated[98] or whose curator is absent or abroad, has full contractual

---

[93] *R. v. Chief Constable of South Wales, ex parte Thornhill* [1987] IRLR 313, CA; *R. v. Chief Constable of Thames Valley Police, ex parte Stevenson, The Times* April 22, 1987, QB. However in a discplinary matter an investigating officer does not owe a common law duty of care towards the officers under investigation and neither legislation nor regulations create a private law right of action for breach of statutory duty thus excluding any claim for damages (*Calveley v. Chief Constable of Merseyside Police, The Times*, July 9, 1988, CA.).

[94] See *e.g.* EPCA, ss. 1-7 requiring the issue of written particulars of terms of employment.

[95] Bell, *Principles*, s. 2067. For a detailed discussion see W. W. McBryde, *The Law of Contract in Scotland*, Chapter 8.

[96] And see the interesting survey of discriminatory legislation in the Consultative Document published by the Department of Employment "Restrictions on Employment of Young People the Removal of Sex Discrimination in Legislation" (1987).

[97] Age of Majority (Scotland) Act 1969.

[98] Forisfamiliation describes the process by which a minor makes his/her own way in life independently of his family or curator; whether or not forisfamiliation has occurred is largely a question of fact.

capacity but his contracts are voidable on the grounds of *laesio enormis*[99] until the expiry of the *quadriennium utile*[100] — the period of four years beginning from the day the minor reaches majority (18).[101] However, where a minor has a curator a contract entered into without the curator's consent is generally void[102]; exceptions are said to exist in respect of contract of employment and apprenticeship[103] but there is no clear line of authority to this effect[104] and any exceptions which may exist will not extend to collateral or subsidiary agreements related to employment.[105] Unless contracts of employment and apprenticeship are the subject of exceptions they are null and void when entered into by minors without the consent of their curator so that they can be reduced even after the expiry of the *quadriennium utile* and without proof of *laesio enormis*.[106]

2.7 Assuming adequate contractual capacity, contracts of all types including those of employment and apprenticeship are enforceable only insofar as they are not illegal nor offend against public policy.[107] Of particular significance are the provisions of the Children and Young Persons (Scotland) Act 1937[108] to the effect that, subject to local authority bye-laws, no child shall be employed so long as he is under the age of 13 years.[109] More generally a contract of em-

---

[99] Literally "of great disadvantage". To decide what constitutes *laesio enormis* one should contrast a contract which was proper and reasonable at the time with one that was "immoderately disproportionate to what might have been got" (*Robertson v. S. Henderson & Sons Ltd* (1905) 13 SLT 180).

[100] Bell, *Commentaries*, I., 129 SC 534. *M'Feetridge v. Stewarts and Lloyds Ltd* 1913 SC 773, HL; *O'Donnell v. Brownieside Coal Co Ltd* 1934 SC 534. Cf. *Faulds v. BSC* 1977 SLT (Notes) 18, OH.

[101] Lord Fraser, *Parent and Child* (3rd edn.) p. 200.

[102] Fraser, *Master and Servant* (3rd edn.) p. 9, citing Erskine 1, 7, 33.

[103] *Stevenson v. Adair* (1872) 10 M 919; *M'Feetridge v. Stewarts and Lloyds Ltd* 1913 SC 773.

[104] Thus in *Stevenson v. Adair* (1872) 10 M 919 Lord Ardmillan seems to have been more concerned to ensure the law kept up with contemporary conditions and in *M'Feetridge* (ante) the minor was regarded as forisfamiliated. And note that the Scottish Law Commission has expressed the view that the law in this area is "bedevilled with uncertainty" (*Report on the Legal Capacity and Responsibility of Unions and Pupils* (1987) para. 2.17) thereby echoing the opinion of Lord Fraser, *Master and Servant* (1882) (3rd edn.) p. 13.

[105] Such agreements would include agreements comprising settlements of claims against an employer under legislation or claims for personal injury — *O'Donnell v. Brownieside Coal Co Ltd* 1934 SC 534; *Faulds v. B.S.C.* 1977 SLT (Notes) 18.

[106] An interesting issue might arise where a minor, without his curator's consent, enters into a contract of training or sponsorship which includes a term that fees will be repaid in the event of premature termination of employment after a period of training or education; see *Strathclyde Regional Council v. Neill* 1983 SLT (Sh. Ct.) 89.

[107] See W. W. McBryde, *The Law of Contract in Scotland*, pp. 628-632. Examples of statutory illegality include an alien failing to obtain the permission of the Secretary of State before changing his employment (*Rastegarnia v. Richmond Designs*, unreported, COIT 764/38), a barmaid under 18 years of age being employed contrary to licensing laws (*Lay v. Hamilton*, unreported, COIT 1394/211).

[108] S. 28 as amended by Children and Young Persons Act 1963, ss. 34, 64 and the Children Act 1972, s. 1. Note the Employment of Children Act 1973 has not yet been brought into force.

[109] On other restrictions or employment of minors see Chapter Three, paras. 3.26 *et seq.*

ployment for an illegal or immoral purpose will not be enforced[110] and cannot establish a period of continuous employment for the purpose of asserting a statutory right.[111] However it seems that if only part of the contract is tainted with illegality then it does not necessarily follow that the entire contract is unenforceable[112]; and where a contract is illegal only in is method of performance a party who is ignorant of the illegality will be able to enforce the contract.[113] Most contracts which purport to reduce or exclude statutory employment rights, although not strictly illegal, are declared to be void[114] and such statutory avoidance of a contract is in addition to rules of common law which also render it void.[115]

2.8 Formalities

Generally the contract of employment can be created without the need for any formal writing. Thus it can be constituted orally, by implication,[116] or by a written contract, or indeed by a mixture of these methods. However, a contract of employment for a period of more than one year and a contract of apprenticeship[117] require to be constituted by probative writing[118] and cannot be proved by parole.[118a] Improbative writings followed by *rei*

---

[110] In *Coral Leisure Group Ltd v. Barnett* [1981] ICR 502, EAT, while it was affirmed that a contract for immoral purposes was illegal and could not form the basis of a claim for unfair dismissal that had to be distinguished from a contract whose terms and purpose were not illegal although immoral acts (procuration of prostitutes) were committed in the course of his employment. And see *R. v. Salford Area Health Authority, ex parte Janaway, The Times*, December 2, 1988 HL, s. 4 of Abortion Act 1967 that "no person shall be under any duty . . . by contract . . . to participate in any treatment . . . to which he has a conscientious objection."

[111] *Tomlinson v. Dick Evans "U" Drive* [1978] ICR 639, EAT; *Hyland v. J. H. Barker (North West) Ltd* [1985] ICR 861 EAT. Both cases involved illegal tax-free payments to the employee and although in *Hyland* the tax-free allowance did not render the entire contract unenforceable, because it occurred during the period of continuous employment necessary to qualify for unfair dismissal protection — a period ending with the date of dismissal — no unfair dismissal right accrued. But see *Wilkinson v. Lugg* [1990] ICR 599, EAT.

[112] W. W. McBryde, *The Law of Contract in Scotland*, paras. 26-29. Cf. *Napier v. National Business Agency* [1951] 1 All ER 264, CA.

[113] *Newland v. Simons & Willer (Hairdressers) Ltd* [1981] IRLR 359, EAT.

[114] See, for example, EPCA, s. 140, SDA, 1975 s. 77 and Wages Act 1986, s. 6 (3).

[115] *Hennessy v. Craigmyle & Co* [1986] ICR 461 in which the Court of Appeal held that a contract settling an unfair dismissal complaint even although arrived under the auspices of a Conciliation Officer could nevertheless be avoided on a successful plea of duress (force and fear).

[116] A good example can be seen in *Taylor v. Furness, Withy and Co Ltd* [1969] VI KIR 488 in which the existence of the contract was implied from the issue of a letter welcoming T. as an employee of the company and an identity card.

[117] *Grant v. Ramage & Ferguson* (1897) 25 R 35.

[118] Bell, *Principles*, secs. 173, 190; *Nisbet v. Percy* 1951 SC 350. For an explanation of the origin of this rule see Fraser, *Master and Servant* (3rd edn.) p. 28. Cf. *Walker v. Greenock & District Hospital Board* 1951 SLT 329. Similarly where employment for more than one year is contained in a contract dealing with other matters writing is required (*Cook v. Grubb* 1963 SC 1).

[118a] But see the interesting observations in the Scottish Law Commission's Consultative Memorandum No. 66 (1985) paras. 2.17-2.19.

interventus[119] will perfect the agreement for the whole of the period agreed upon.[120] The improbative writing must be the writ of at least one of the parties.[121] Also, although there is no strict rule, contracts which have special or unusual terms may require written evidence of their terms.[122] In addition to these common law rules some statutes require certain formalities to be observed when employment contracts are entered.[123] Although in the ordinary case the contract can be created without writing, the current practice — no doubt stimulated by provisions originally contained in the Contract of Employment Act 1963[124] — is to set out the elements of the contract in writing, either in a single comprehensive document or, more usually in respect of employees in large workforces, in a series of documents, for example collective agreements, which frequently are tied into the contract of employment by adoption or incorporation.[125] When the contract is created orally or by implication difficulties arise in proving the terms of the contract.[126]

2.9 Contractual intention

The contract of employment is no exception to the rule that the purpose of the parties must be to oblige each other by seriously consenting to their respective obligations; it has been suggested that this state of mind falls short of the doctrine of English law that agreements are not binding as a contract if they are made without the intention of creating legal relations.[127] Nevertheless, although a serious agreement defective in form (for example an unwritten contract of employment for more than a year) is not a legally enforceable contract, in the context of business or commerce it is difficult to show that an agreement was

---

[119] According to Bell (*Principles*, secs. 26) "*Rei interventus* is inferred from any proceedings not unimportant on the part of the obligee, known to and permitted by the obligor to take place on the faith of the contract as if it were perfect; provided they are unequivocally referable to the agreement, and productive of alteration of circumstances, loss or inconvenience, though not unretrievable." And see *Tojeiro v. McKettrick-Agnew & Co Ltd* 1967 SLT (Notes) 11, OH, in which the failure to aver facts unequivocally referable to a contract for more than a year was fatal and *Heneaghan v. Aero Technologies Ltd* 1990 GWD 13-692 in which it was held there was no agreement on which rei *interventus* could operate in spite of the existence of a draft. And see para. 2.10.

[120] *Campbell v. Baird* (1827) 5 S 335.

[121] In *Nisbet v. Percy* 1951 SC 350 the statement that the position was for 3 years in the trade union rule book was held not to be improbative writing of either party and in *Gow v. McEwan* 1901 8 SLT 484, an unsigned handwritten memorandum showing a name, starting date and a scale of wages was too vague to found *rei interventus* because the deficiencies were of substance, not merely of form. And see *Heneaghan v. Aero Technologies Ltd* 1990 GWD 13-692.

[122] *Davies v. City of Glasgow Friendly Society* 1935 SC 224. "I have grave doubt whether a contract of service with such exceptional conditions (that the employee should receive increments related to sales volume generated by him) can competently be established by parole evidence . . ." *per* Lord Murray, *obiter*.

[123] Thus the Merchant Shipping Act 1974, s. 1, provides ". . . an agreement in writing shall be made between each person employed as a seaman on a ship registered in the UK and the persons employing him and shall be signed by both him and by or on behalf of them." And see para 2.43 regarding service contracts of directors.

[124] Ss. 4, 5. The equivalent current provisions are now in EPCA, ss. 1-7; see para. 2.10.

[125] See paras 2.14, 2.15.

[126] See M. R. Freedland, *The Contract of Employment*, p. 19. However some terms will be implied into such informal or incompleted contracts by law.

[127] See W. W. McBryde, *The Law of Contract in Scotland*, pp. 51-54.

not intended to create legal relations.[128] Thus where an employer enters an agreement — frequently in some form of writing and signed or at least acknowledged by the parties — in which he undertakes to make payment (and perform other obligations) and the worker agrees to obey his directions[129] it is improbable that it would be held that there is no contract because of the absence of a serious consent or purpose. However difficulties can arise where parties to a contract of employment, which, as already observed, is subject to periodic, informal and remote modifications,[130] alter their standards of performance. Are such modifications accompanied by the "serious consent" necessary to vary the original contract or are they merely some forms of non-binding extra-contractual agreements, arrangements or tolerance? The problem arises particularly where the contract of employment is in practice relaxed or departed from (and is intensified by the rule that the conclusion of a collective agreement does not automatically alter terms of the individual contract in the industry or undertaking concerned[131]) and a distinction is to be made between proper cases of consensual variation of the contract[132] and those cases in which an element of flexibility is introduced without any change in the legal obligations contained in the contract. Thus the English courts have held that a relaxation of the contract was to be attributed to a gesture of co-operation by the employee[133] or the assumption of obligations by the employer *ex gratia*[134] and in Scotland it has been held that the employer's representative lacked the authority to make the contract the employee argued existed.[134a]

---

[128] *Edwards v. Skyways Ltd* [1964] 1 All ER 494; and note the opinion of Lord President Clyde in *R. & J. Dempster v. Motherwell Bridge and Engineering Co* 1964 SC 308 at 328 that "the essence of commerce is making bargains, and unenforceable arrangements are the exception and not the rule."

[129] It is not being suggested that these are the essentials of a contract of employment merely that there is usually some agreement about these matters.

[130] See *ante* para. 2.1.

[131] See para. 2.14.

[132] See, for example, *Armstrong, Whitworth, Rolls Ltd v. Mustard* [1971] ITR 79, in which the term regarding the normal working week incorporated from a collective agreement was consensually varied by Mustard's working 60 hours a week for a period of 7 years when the collective agreement provided for 40 hours a week only. The inference was that the parties must have intended to alter the contract.

[133] See *Turiff Construction v. Bryant* [1967] II KIR 659, DC, and *Saxton v. NCB* [1970] ITR 196, DC; in *Bryant* local site negotiations which altered the working hours were regarded a "co-operation not contract" while in *Saxton* Lord Parker C.J. stated "Here was a man who was being called upon to co-operate to help his employers to run down this colliery, and one would think that in those circumstances it was difficult to say that he was working as he did otherwise than without prejudice . . . I do not think, in these circumstances, one can possibly say that there has been a consensual variation of the terms of his contract of employment."

[134] *Loman v. Merseyside Transport Services Ltd* [1968] 3 ITR 108, DC. And see K. W. Wedderburn *The Legal Force of Plant Bargains*, 1969, 32 MLR 99.

[134a] *Hoogerbeets v. British Coal* 1991 GWD 2-113, (OH). Contrast with *Hawker Siddeley Power Engineering Ltd v. Rump* [1979] IRLR 425, EAT that oral undertaking by employer's representative was unaffected by employee signing contradictory contract.

2.10 The statutory written statement of particulars

It is also necessary to distinguish the contract of employment from the written statement of particulars of terms of employment which employers are required to give all qualifying employees[135] not later than thirteen weeks after[136] employment begins.[137] In *Robertson & Jackson v. British Gas Corporation*[138] the Court of Appeal reiterated the Employment Appeal Tribunal in *System Floors (UK) Ltd v. Daniel*[139] that "the status of the written statement is this. It provides very strong *prima facie* evidence of what were the terms of the contract between the parties but it does not constitute a written contract between the parties. Nor are the statements of the terms conclusive."[140] Unlike a contract it is essentially a unilateral statement given to the employee by the employer showing what he (the employer) believes the terms of employment to be,[141] and no doubt it is designed to compensate for the position at common law whereby no written contract is generally required and to eliminate disputes between employer and employees.[142] However, it is clear that the employer's written statement when construed as an offer of employment on the stated terms can be converted into a contract by acceptance by the employee. Thus in *Gascol Conversions v. Mercer*[143] the employee, by signing a statement in the following terms "I confirm receipt of a new Contract of Employment . . . which sets out, as required by [the Act] the terms and conditions of my employment", had converted a unilateral statement into a binding bilateral written contract which excluded extraneous evidence. If the written statement can be expressly accepted as the contract presumably it can also become such by acquiescence[144]; and it would seem that a written statement showing the period of employment to be for a fixed period of more than one year[145] could, say, in the event of the employee not completing the necessary formality of probative acceptance, be

---

[135] Qualifying employees are those whose contracts normally involve employment for 16 hours or more per week or exceptionally those whose contracts normally involve employment for between 8 and 16 hours per week and have been employed for 5 years or more (EPCA, s. 146 (4)). Also employees who have written contracts which already contain the statutory particulars are excluded as are certain other employees — see EPCA, ss. 5, 5A, 141, 145, 146 (5)-(7) and 149.

[136] Given that an employed earner, who leaves his employment without just cause may be disqualified from receiving unemployment benefit for up to 26 weeks (Social Security Act 1986, s. 20) it could have been expected that he be entitled to receive confirmation of his terms before the end of 13 weeks.

[137] EPCA, s. 1. A fresh statement need not be given where a second period of employment begins within 6 months of a previous one and the terms of employment have not changed (EPCA, s. 2 (4)) as substituted by EA 1989, s. 13 (2).

[138] [1983] ICR 351.

[139] [1982] ICR 54.

[140] And see *Turiff Construction v. Bryant* [1962] II KIR 659 and *Greater Glasgow Health Board v. Pate* 1983 SLT 90, IH, in which a job title was not to be regarded as conclusive of Pate's contractual duties.

[141] And see J. T. Cameron, *The Contract of Employment Act 1963*, 1963 SLT (News) 203.

[142] See *Cole v. Midland Display Ltd* [1973] IRLR 62, NIRC.

[143] [1974] IRLR 155, CA.

[144] *Davies v. City of Glasgow Friendly Society* 1935 SC 224. But see *Evenden v. Guildford City Association Football Club Ltd* [1975] ICR 367, CA, and *Jones v. Associated Tunnelling Co Ltd* [1981] IRLR 477.

[145] EPCA, s. 2 (2).

the basis for *rei interventus*.[146] The written statement must identify the parties,[147] specify the date when the employment began and the date on which the employee's period of continuous employment began (taking into account any employment with a previous employer which counts towards that period).[148] The written statement must contain "particulars"[149] of the following terms of employment which were applicable not more than one week before the statement is given[150] — (1) remuneration, including method and intervals of payment, (2) hours of work and particularly normal working hours, (3) entitlement to holidays, holiday pay (including accrued holiday pay on termination), sick leave/pay and pensions, (4) notice of termination[151] and the title of job the employee is employed to do.[152] A job title is to be distinguished from the more detailed job description. Only the former is required to be given although many employers choose to make the responsibilities of employees clear by issuing detailed job descriptions. Where a job title is incorporated into the contract of employment tribunals are likely to construe it in a way which includes ancillary duties.[153] In addition to these particulars normally[154] the statement must specify or refer to any disciplinary rules applicable to the employee as well as indicating initial and subsequent procedures for redressing disciplinary and other grievances except those relating to health and safety at work; it must also indicate whether, in relation to pensions, a contracting-out certificate is in force.[155] However this basic obligation to give a statement to each employee is subject to the important qualification that, for the purpose of informing an employee of the particulars of his terms of employment, an employer may merely refer the employee to "some document" (frequently a collective agreement or works/staff handbook) which the employee has reasonable opportunities of reading in the course of his employment or which is made accessible to him in some other way.[156] Where, as inevitably is the case, changes occur in an employee's terms of employment, the employer is required, not more than one month after the change, to "inform the employee of the nature of the change by a written state-

---

[146] Even an unsigned document, provided it contains all the essentials of a contract, can be the basis for a plea of *rei interventus* — *Bell v. Goodall* (1883) 10 R 905 *per* Inglis at p. 908; *Wares v. Duff-Dunbar's Trs* 1920 SC 5. *Cf. Gow v. McEwan* (1901) 8 SLT 484.

[147] This can be critical in the case where there are several companies all with similar names embraced by a large conglomerate.

[148] EPCA, s. 1 (2) as amended by EA 1982, Sch 2. Whether or not employment is "continuous employment" depends on compliance with a set of statutory rules in EPCA, Sch. 13; accordingly where qualification for a statutory right is concerned what matters is compliance with the rules and not what is contained in the written statement. See paras 3.2-3.6.

[149] It has been indicated by the NIRC in *Owens v. Multilux Ltd* [1974] IRLR 113 that stating a salary of "£2,500 p.a. net of deductions" would be sufficiently detailed even although it left unclear whether payment was net or gross of income tax.

[150] EPCA, s. 1 (3). If no particulars are to be entered under s. 1 (3) (a)-(g) or under s. 1 (2) that shall be stated (s 2 (1)).

[151] If the contract is for a fixed period its date of expiry must be stated (EPCA, s. 2 (2)).

[152] EPCA, s. 1 (3).

[153] *Churcher v. Weyside Engineering (1926) Ltd* [1976] IRLR 402, IT; *Glitz v. Watford Electric Co* [1979] IRLR 89, EAT; and *Greater Glasgow Health Board v. Pate* 1983 SLT 90, IH.

[154] An exception exists in respect of employers whose workforce is less than 20 employees. See EPCA, s. 2A added by EA 1989, s. 13 (3), (4), (5).

[155] EPCA, s. 1 (4), (5).

[156] EPCA, s. 2 (3).

ment."[157] The information can be conveyed by giving the employee an amended written statement or by referring him to some accessible document setting out the nature of the change.[158] However the employee's basic entitlement to have an up-to-date written statement is further diluted by the employer's option of indicating to the employee, either when an initial statement is given or when changes occur, that future changes will be entered up in the document or recorded in some other way.[159] Provided changes are entered into the document or recorded within one month no further statements need be issued.[160] Thus where an employer exercises this option of referring to, and entering changes in, a document the onus is on the employee to consult the document on a regular basis to ascertain whether any changes in his terms of employment have occurred.

2.11 Where an employer fails to comply with his obligations to give a statement or notify or enter up changes in terms of employment, an employee may refer the matter to an industrial tribunal[161] which may determine the particulars which ought to have been included or confirm, amend or substitute particulars.[162] However, the industrial tribunal is unable to determine the meaning ot a term or indicate what might be reasonable notice for termination of the contract[163]; and it has been stated that the industrial tribunal has "no power to make award of wages or . . . payment . . . and the circumstances surrounding the applicant's dismissal do not concern [it]." The tribunal treats "the application as one for the determination of the conditions of the employee's . . . employment, leaving the applicant to make such use of [the] determination as he thinks fit."[164] Thus because of the somewhat inconclusive nature of the tribunal procedure when considered in isolation, applications for a determination of particulars are more usefully combined with applications relating to unfair dismissal, redundancy payments and unlawful deductions from wages, and, although there is no penalty that an industrial tribunal can impose for an employer's failure to comply with his obligation to give a written statement,[165] the real advantage for the employer is the knowledge that his workforce are in no doubt as to the terms of their employment along with the corresponding industrial relations benefits.

2.12 The terms of the contract — express and implied

The terms of the contract of employment, like those of many other nominate or innominate contracts, can be express or implied. An express term will often be

---

[157] *Ibid.* s. 4 (1). And by s. 4 (4) even changes of name and changes in the identity of the employer which have no effect on continuity of employment are included.

[158] *Ibid.* s. 4 (1), (2).

[159] *Ibid.* s. 4 (3).

[160] *Ibid.*

[161] *Ibid.* s. 11. In some cases an employer can also apply to an industrial tribunal (s. 11 (2), (30)). No reference may be entertained more than 3 months after employment has ceased. (s. 11 (9)).

[162] *Ibid.* s. 11 (1), (2) (a), (3). The procedures by which a reference may be made seem unnecessarily complicated especially in view of the limited effect of the tribunal's determination; see *Mears v. Safecar Security Ltd* [1982] 3 WLR 366, CA.

[163] *Owens v. Multilux Ltd* [1974] IRLR 113, NIRC; *Cuthbertson v. A.M.L. Distributors* [1975] IRLR 228, IT; and see *Simmons v. Garner Motors Ltd* [1972] ITR 246.

[164] *McKay v. W. B. Henderson Ltd* [1967] ITR 98, IT; and see *Eagland v. British Telecommunications* [1990] IRLR 328, EAT.

[165] Strictly an employer can refuse to issue any statements leaving industrial tribunals to do the work instead.

written in what may be described as primary contractual documents like letters of appointment and acceptance or in formal contracts themselves but equally can be found in secondary sources like collective agreements or works notices or handbooks. However, an express term does not have to be written; in an oral contract of employment it is perfectly possible for the parties to be express about particular issues or terms — an express term merely describes the situation in which the contracting parties (or one of them) having considered a matter relevant to their dealings, consciously and deliberately give(s) expression to their agreement by specific writings or words.[166] Where terms are express and questions of interpretation[167] and construction arise for the performance of the contract,[168] the normal rules of construction will apply, although the Employment Appeal Tribunal has been reluctant to apply the *contra proferentem* rule[169] or the extrinsic evidence rule[170] in relation to the contract of employment.[171] However, although there may be a dispute about the meaning of express terms, they have the advantage that generally[171a] they cannot be contradicted by implied terms.[172] On the other hand, the express words used by the contracting parties may be too vague in meaning to be enforced[173] and where they have the effect of conferring a discretion on one party it is legitimate for a court or tribunal to imply a term requiring the discretion to be exercised reasonably.[173a]

---

[166] Express terms may be found in advertisements (*Tayside Regional Co v. McIntosh* [1982] IRLR 272; *Deeley v. British Rail Engineering* [1980] IRLR 147, CA), notices (*Petrie v. McFisheries* [1940] 1 KB 258), works rules (*Murray v. Robert & Rome Ltd* 1968 SLT (Notes) 90) collective agreements etc. (*N.C.B. v. Galley* [1958] 1 WLR 16).

[167] See for example, *Associated British Ports v. TGWU* [1989] IRLR 399, HL; *Burroughs Machines Ltd v. Timmoney* 1977 SC 393, IH.

[168] On the construction and interpretation of contracts see W. W. McBryde, *The Law of Contract in Scotland*, Ch. 19.

[169] The effect of this rule is that ambiguous terms of contract are to be construed against the party pleading or founding on them.

[170] The effect of this is that normally (there are various exceptions) once a contract has been reduced to writing it is incompetent to contradict its terms by parole evidence. But see the cases referred to in the Scottish Law Commission's Consultative Memorandum No. 66 (1985), paras. 2.17-2.19.

[171] *Tayside Regional Council v. McIntosh* [1982] IRLR 272 — reducing the contract to writing did not exclude evidence of the obligation to possess a driving licence which was stated in the newspaper advertisement in response to which the job was obtained but to which no reference occurred in the written contract. And see *Pederson v. Camden London Borough Council* [1981] ICR 674, CA. *Cf. Gascol Conversions v. Mercer* [1974] IRLR 155, CA. And see Bell, *Principles*, s. 136. *Pollock v. McAndrew* (1828) 7 S 189.

[171a] In *Johnstone v. Bloomsbury Health Authority* [1991] ICR 269 the Court of Appeal accepted that an express term regarding hours of work could be overridden by the employer's implied duty to take reasonable care for the employee's safety.

[172] *Cummings v. Charles Connell & Co (Shipbuilders) Ltd* 1968 SC 305, *M'Whirter v. Longmuir* 1948 SC 577.

[173] In *Cook v. Grubb* 1963 SC 1, OH, the phrase "permanent employment" was too vague to be enforced and in *Jacques v. Lloyd D. George & Partners Ltd* [1968] 2 All ER 187, the words "should you be instrumental in introducing a person willing to sign a document capable of becoming a contract to purchase" were similarly treated. *Cf. Lawrie v. Brown & Co Ltd* 1908 SC 705 ("regular employment"); *NCB v. Galley* [1958] 1 WLR 16, CA ("to work such days or part days in each week as may be reasonably required by the management").

[173a] *British Broadcasting Corporation v. Beckett* [1983] IRLR 43, EAT; *United Bank v. Akhtar* [1989] IRLR 507, EAT.

2.13 Implied terms

Broadly, implied terms can fall into two categories — (1) those terms which may be implied into the contract having regard to the facts and circumstances of the particular contract and (2) those terms which are implied by law (common law or statute). In the first category, although terms may also be implied by the custom of a trade and form a course of dealing, perhaps the most significant method of implying a term is a positive desire on the part of courts and tribunals to give a contract business efficacy.[174] In relation to the contract of employment the following are examples of terms being implied from the circumstances — *Sagar v. Ridehalgh & Son Ltd*[175] (implied term regarding deductions from wages for poor performance), *Bristol Garage (Brighton) Ltd v. Lowen*[176] (implied term limiting employee's liability to make good financial loss), *Murco Petroleum Ltd v. Forge*[177] (implied term entitling employee to wage increase), *Bliss v. South East Thames Regional Health Authority*[178] (no implied term that employer could require Bliss to submit to psychiatric examination), *Sim v. Rotherham Metropolitan B.C.*[179] (implied term that schoolteacher will comply with administrative arrangements (covering for absent colleagues for running school) and *Sybron Corporation v. Rochem Ltd*[180] (implied term that employee had duty to disclose misconduct of fellow employee). Many terms are implied into the contract of employment from collective agreements which are treated separately.[181] Because the contract of employment is a nominate or specific contract the second category comprises certain terms implied as part of the general law. Thus common law implies into the contract of employment various terms: for example, that the employee will carry out his duties with reasonable care[182] and will serve his employer with good faith and fidelity[183] and that an employer will not conduct himself in a manner likely to seriously damage the relationship of trust and confidence on which the employment relationship is based.[184] The substance of these and other implied terms is discussed later.[185] The significance of these legally implied terms is that in the absence of express terms dealing with the matter they are incorporated automatically into every contract of employment. Thus although the parties to a contract of employment may only express terms dealing with, say, wages and hours of work, their complete contractual relationship is to be judged not only according to these express terms but according to such terms as supplemented by such addi-

---

[174] Perhaps the best known *dictum* on the business efficacy method of implying a term is that of Bowen L.J. in *The Moorcock* (1889) 14 PD 64, CA. And see *M'Whirter v. Longmuir* 1948 SC 577, at p. 589. *Cf. Gallagher v. Post Office* [1970] 3 All ER 713, NIRC. Another similar method of implying a term is to refer to what an "officious bystander" would have agreed (*Shirlaw v. Southern Counties (1926) Ltd* [1939] 2KB 206, CA).

[175] [1931] 1 Ch 310, CA.

[176] [1979] IRLR 86, EAT.

[177] [1987] ICR 282 EAT.

[178] [1987] ICR 200, CA.

[179] [1983] ICR 801, CA.

[180] [1983] ICR 801, CA.

[181] See para. 2.14.

[182] *Lister v. Romford Ice and Cold Storage Co Ltd* [1957] AC 555, HL.

[183] *Graham v. R. S. Paton Ltd* 1917 SC 203; *Hivac Ltd v. Park Royal Scientific Instruments Ltd* [1946] Ch 169, CA.

[184] *Courtaulds Northern Textiles Ltd v. Andrew* [1979] IRLR 84, EAT; *Woods v. W M Car Services (Peterborough) Ltd* [1981] ICR 666, EAT.

[185] See Chapter Three.

tional terms that the law implies. Accordingly, a positive response to the following question brings into play a whole range of contractual rights and duties — "Will you work as my employee for 38 hours each week at £3.50 per hour?" Occasionally statute implies terms into the contract of employment. However, although this is relatively unusual — most modern employment rights are statutory and do not depend on actual or fictional contractual provisions[186] — the following statutorily implied contractual terms may be noted. (1) By the Equal Pay Act 1970[187] the terms of a contract of employment[188] shall be deemed to include an "equality clause" whereby men and women doing particular work[189] are entitled to equal pay. Because the clause is essentially contractual, claims based on it may be raised in either the ordinary courts or in industrial tribunals. (2) Quite oddly the final steps to enforce an employer's obligation to disclose information to a trade union for collective bargaining are achieved by implying into individual contracts of employment the terms of an award of the Central Arbitration Committee.[190] (3) By the Wages Act 1986[191] an employee who receives less than the statutory minimum remuneration specified in a Wages Council Order is entitled under his contract[192] to be paid the difference between the rate he receives and the statutory minimum.

2.14 Collective agreements

Collective agreements[193] lead a "Jekyll and Hyde" existence in employment law, for although an argument can be made for collective agreements to be legally enforceable in Scots law,[194] current practice is reflected by the statutory provision[195] that collective agreements will generally not be treated as legally enforceable contracts.[196] However this provision relates only to the status of the

---

[186] Also most statutes expressly prohibit contractual interference with or exclusion of their respective statutory rights. See, for example, EPCA, s. 140, SDA 1975 s. 77 (as applied by SDA 1986 s. 6).

[187] EqPA 1970, s. 1 (1).

[188] The Equal Pay Act also applies to contracts of apprenticeship and contracts to personally execute work (EqPA, s. 1 (6) (a)).

[189] For detailed coverage of equal pay see Chapter Seven.

[190] EPA, s. 21 (6), (7). *Cf.* EPA, Part IV — Procedure for Handling Redundancies. And see Chapter Nine.

[191] S. 16 (1).

[192] By Wages Act, s. 8 (2) contracts of employment, apprenticeship and for personal performance of work are included.

[193] The Trade Union and Labour Relations Act 1974, s. 30 (1) defines a collective agreement as any agreement or arrangement made by or on behalf of one or more trade unions and one or more employers or employer's associations relating to the matters referred to in s. 29 (1) of that Act as amended by Employment Act 1982, s. 18. And see Chapter Eleven.

[194] See J. Casey, "Collective Agreements: Some Scottish Footnotes" 1973 JR 22 and R. L. C. Hunter "Collective Agreement Fair Wages Clause and the Employment Relationship in Scots Law" 1975 JR 47.

[195] Trade Union and Labour Relations Act 1974, s. 18 provides that any collective agreement "shall be conclusively presumed not to have been intended by the parties to be a legally enforceable contract unless the agreement — (a) is in writing and (b) contains a provision which (however expressed) states that the parties intended that the agreement shall be a legally enforceable contract" but that where conditions (a) and (b) are satisfied the agreement is conclusively presumed to have been intended to be a legally enforceable contract. And see *NCB v. NUM* [1986] ICR 439 in which a statement in a collective agreement that the parties were to "be bound by this agreement" did not satisfy condition (b) above.

[196] According to W. W. McBryde, *The Law of Contract in Scotland*, Scots law does not require that contracts be preceded by this degree of *animus* or intention. See para 2.9 (*ante*).

collective agreement between the trade union(s) and the employer(s) and does not prevent the terms of a collective agreement — itself not an enforceable contract — being productive of legally binding rights and duties when incorporated expressly or by implication into a contract of employment.[197] When such incorporation occurs the legal quality of the collectively agreed terms derives not from the collective agreement but from the individual contract of employment of which it has become a part. A collective agreement (or part of it)[198] may be incorporated into a contract of employment either expressly or by implication[199] and this is so whether or not the employee is a member of the relevant trade union or the employer is represented at the collective negotiations.[200] And the Court of Appeal has rejected as quite untenable the proposition that where a closed shop agreement was in force rules of the trade union were implied into the contract of employment of every employee covered by the closed shop agreement.[201] Express incorporation occurs where in the contract of employment there is a clear reference to a specific collective agreement[202] or where there is a more general reference to "such national and county (collective) agreements as are in force."[203] The words of reference may be specific resulting in the incorporation of only particular provisions of a collective agreement[204] or they may be couched in more general terms in which case all appropriate provisions in the collective agreement will become part of the individual's contract of employment.[205] Where such general reference occurs an employee will not be able to resist the incorporation of a collective term of which he does not approve.[206]

In the absence of express incorporation a collectively agreed term may nevertheless become part of the individual employee's contract of employment by implication. However it is wrong to assume that collectively agreed terms (or,

---

[197] See in this respect the important decision of the Court of Appeal in *Marley v. Forward Trust Group Ltd* [1986] IRLR 369 overturning the Employment Appeal Tribunal [1986] IRLR 43, that a term in a collective agreement stated to be binding in honour only was not binding even if incorporated into the contract of employment.

[198] Some terms of collective agreements are not regarded as suitable for or capable of incorporation into the contract of employment; see post.

[199] It is necessary to note that the process of incorporation is not restricted to collective agreements; contracting parties are generally free to agree that their terms of contract are to be found in or determined by an extraneous document or source, but by far the most common document to be incorporated is the collective agreement.

[200] *Cf.* Patents Act 1977, s. 40.

[201] *Associated Newspapers Ltd v. Wade* [1979] IRLR 201.

[202] The following is an example of express incorporation — "The terms of your employment are subject to the Agreement on Wages and Conditions of Employment dated 1973 made between the Hawick Knitwear Manufacturers' Association and the GMBATU . . .".

[203] *NCB v. Galley* [1958] 1 WLR 16.

[204] See, for example, *Pearson v. William Jones Ltd* [1967] 1 WLR 1140 where the collective agreement was referred to only for overtime working.

[205] An individual's contract of employment may require him to work under, for example, "the terms of the national agreement" or "such terms as may be negotiated from time to time with the recognised trade unions".

[206] *NCB v. Galley* [1958] 1 WLR 16, CA; *Callison v. Ford Motor Co Ltd* [1969] ITR 74. In *Galley* the employee's situation was exacerbated by his union agreeing to a term of which *Galley* (and others) did not approve but also by the loose wording of the term incorporated — "to work such days or part days . . . as may be reasonably required by management". And see *Lombard Tricity Finance Ltd v. Paton, The Times* October 31, 1988, CA, to effect that although it was unusual a contract could provide for its terms to be varied unilaterally by one party in his absolute discretion to the detriment of the other party.

for that matter, terms set out in some other document to which no express reference is made in the contract of employment itself) will automatically become incorporated into contracts of employment[207] because whether or not the collectively agreed term is to be implied into the contract will depend on whether the implication satisfies one or more methods which, by the principles of contract law, permit such an implication. In essence therefore, whether a collective agreement (or part of it), can, in the absence of an express reference, be implied into the contract of employment, depends on whether implication of the term(s) is justified in the particular circumstances[208] or to give the contract "business efficacy" and, where there have been previous employments, a course of dealing.[209] Thus merely because an employer observes the terms of a collective agreement does not *per se* mean it is incorporated into contract of employment because "the application of the collective agreement . . . was equally consistent with the view that [the employers] did so as policy, not necessarily because they were bound to do";[210] although membership of an employer's association may require the introduction of collective agreements into contracts of employment entered into by associated employers.[210a]

However the potential for express or implied incorporation of collective agreements is subject to the term being suitable or appropriate for incorporation into an individual's contract of employment and a special statutory provision regarding what may be briefly described as a "no-strike clause". Collective agreements, particularly industry-wide or national agreements, frequently cover a wide range of matters of interest to the parties — trade unions and employers. Many of these matters are primarily concerned with negotiating machinery and institutions and long term strategy — essentially collective issues relevant to the industry or parties. Equally however the agreements will include more mundane issues like pay rates, sick leave entitlement, redundancy compensation packages, job mobility/transfer schemes etc. — issues which readily translate into terms of individual contracts of employment. The significance of this distinction is reflected by a judicial reluctance to incorporate "collective" provisions into individual contracts of employment.[211] Thus a provision in a collective agreement which involved interviewing potentially redundant employees prior to the preparation of a list showing which employees preferred retraining to redundancy was regarded as a long term plan regarding the policy of redundancy

---

[207] Thus in *Singh v. BSC* [1974] IRLR 131 the conclusion of a new collective agreement with the recognised trade unions *per se* had no effect on Singh's contract of employment. And see *Rodwell v. Thomas* [1944] 1 KB 596.

[208] An example of circumstantial incorporation is seen in *Joel v. Cammell Laird* [1969] ITR 206 in which the industrial tribunal specified satisfaction of the following three conditions before implied incorporation could take place: (1) specific knowledge of the collective term by the party alleged to be bound, (2) conduct on the part of that person which indicated he accepted the collective agreement and (3) clarity of the mechanics of incorporation. And see *Maclea v. Essex Line Ltd* [1933] 45 Lloyd's Rep. 254, KBD, in which the terms and conditions of the National Maritime Board were implied into the contract between Maclea and the Essex Line Ltd; however from the judgment of Lord Acton it is obvious that the Board conditions could have been implied on the basis of custom of the trade or a previous course of dealing.

[209] This is recognised by EPCA, s. 2 (4) in relation to giving a written statement of particulars.

[210] *Young v. Canadian Northern Railway Co* [1931] AC 1129, PC, *per* Lord Russell of Killowen. And see *Hamilton v. Futura Floors Ltd* [1990] IRLR 478, OH.

[210a] *Hamilton v. Futura Floors Ltd* [1990] IRLR 478, OH.

[211] *Burroughs Machines v. Timmoney* 1977 SC 393.

implementation rather than the rights of individual employees.[212] Similarly part of the collective agreement arrived at in 1946 between the National Coal Board and the National Union of Mineworkers which created a National Reference Tribunal (a tribunal to deal with disputes) were intended to resolve disputes between employer and trade union and were not intended to be enforceable between the board and its individual employees.[213] On the other hand, a collective provision dealing with transferring employees from one type of work to another has been held to be incorporated into the contract of employment,[214] as have terms which provided that employees who accepted significantly different alternative employment would have six months to assess the suitability of the new job without prejudice to enhanced redundancy benefits.[215] However, it is respectfully suggested that care needs to be taken when deciding whether a collectively agreed term — especially one that is referred to expressly — is suitable or appropriate for incorporation into a contract of employment. Provided a collectively agreed term is neither too vague nor too indefinite to be enforced,[215] the fact that the parties to the collective agreement did not envisage that a term of that agreement would be incorporated into an individual's contract of employment is of limited importance in the face of evidence that the contracting parties (the employer and the employee) themselves intended that it be so incorporated.[217] However this suggestion is subject to the statutory provision[218] that no term of a collective agreement which prohibits or restricts (or has the effect of prohibiting or restricting) the right[219] of workers[220] to engage in a strike or other industrial action shall not either expressly or by implication form part of the contract between the worker and his employer unless the collective agreement satisfies certain conditions which cannot be overridden by the collective agreement or the contract of employment.[221] Arguably a collective agreement would restrict the right to take industrial action if, say, as part of a dispute procedure it is provided that there will be no resort to industrial action until the procedure has been exhausted but given that the circumstances which led to the enactment of sec. 18 (4) are unlikely to be repeated,[222] that it applies only to incorporation of terms from collective agreements and that the industrial action

---

[212] *British Leyland v. McQuilken* [1978] IRLR 245, EAT.

[213] *NCB v. NUM* [1986] ICR 736, Ch D.

[214] *Joel v. Cammell Laird (Ship Repairers) Ltd* [1969] ITR 206.

[215] *Marley v. Forward Trust Ltd* [1986] ICR 891, CA.

[216] On the question of contracts being void from uncertainty see W. W. McBryde, *The Law of Contract in Scotland*, para. 4-18 *et seq.*

[217] And see *Marley v. Forward Trust Ltd* [1986] ICR 891, CA.

[218] TULRA, s. 18 (4)

[219] It is very debatable whether British workers have a "right" to engage in industrial action; most workers who take industrial action — whether or not supported by a majority in a ballot — will break their contracts of employment and if dismissed may not have a right to claim unfair dismissal. See Chapters Three and Five.

[220] Strictly s. 18 (4) is not limited to those who have contracts of employment (TULRA, s. 30 (1)).

[221] These conditions are (i) the collective agreement is in writing, (ii) it expressly provides the "no-strike" clause may be incorporated into a contract of employment, (iii) it is reasonably accessible to, and available for consultation by, the worker during his working hours and (iv) the trade union(s) which is (are) parties to the collective agreement are independent trade unions. (TULRA s. 18 (4)).

[222] It is generally believed s. 18 (4) was enacted to prevent the recurrence of the concession made in *Rookes v. Barnard* [1964] AC 1129 that a "no strike" clause in a collective agreement was incorporated into individual contracts of employment. See Chapter Eleven.

itself is likely to be a breach of contract the provision of sec. 18 (4) should not be overemphasised because it is by no means certain such "no strike" clauses would have been regarded as appropriate for inclusion in individual contracts.[223]

2.15 The effect of incorporation

Once the collective term is incorporated into the contract of employment it becomes, like any other term of the contract, removable or alterable only with the consent of the parties. Accordingly, the fact that the employer terminates the collective agreement or leaves the employer's organisation which concluded the agreement, will have no effect on the term as incorporated into the contract of employment.[224] Thus where an employee's contract of employment was subject to the condition that "wages and conditions of service shall be in accordance with national or local agreements for the time being in force", by which employees became entitled to a guaranteed weekly payment, the employee's right to such a payment was unaffected by the employer's decision to terminate the relevant collective agreement.[225]

2.16 Custom and agency

Terms of the contract of employment may also originate in custom and through an intermediary or agent. Where a custom or trade practice is well-known and well-settled in a trade or industry, is not contrary to a rule of law and is reasonable in the circumstances, it will, in the absence of a contrary term, become a term of the contract without proof of its express communication to the contracting party when the contract is entered into.[226] Thus, where no express term regarding remuneration was made, the customary wage rate for the locality was implied into the contract[227] and where merchant seamen were engaged "simply by being told to join a ship without anything more, it is always assumed on both sides that the engagement is upon the terms and conditions of the National Maritime Board".[228] Also while acceptance of employment on terms known to include the provisions of rule books, notices etc. will result in those terms being implied into the contract,[229] a policy adopted by management unilaterally cannot become a term of employees' contracts on the grounds that it is an established practice unless it is at least shown that the policy has been drawn to

---

[223] On the other hand trade unions can now include "no strike" clauses in collective agreements in the knowledge that they need not be translated into contractual duties at the level of the individual. Where they are incorporated it could be argued that provided, say, the dispute procedure was exhausted first the industrial action would not be a breach of contract.

[224] *Burroughs Machines Ltd v. Timmoney* [1977] IRLR 404, IH; *Robertson v. Jackson v. British Gas Corporation* [1983] ICR 351, CA. And see *Hamilton v. Futura Floors Ltd* [1990] IRLR 478, OH.

[225] *Gibbons v. Associated British Ports* [1985] IRLR 276. The position is summarised neatly by Kerr LJ in *Robertson & Jackson v. British Gas Corporation* [1983] IRLR 302 thus "The terms of an individual contract are in part to be found in the agreed collective agreements as they exist from time to time, and if these cease to exist as collective agreements, then the term as expressly varied between the individual and the employer will remain as they were by reference to the last agreed collective agreement incorporated into the individual contracts."

[226] *Hogarth v. Leith Cotton & Seed Co Ltd* 1909 SC 955.

[227] *Stuart v. McLeod* 1901 9 SLT 192.

[228] *Maclea v. Essex Line* [1933] 45 Lloyd's Reps. 254.

[229] See D. M. Walker, *The Law of Contracts and Related Obligations in Scotland* (2nd edn.), p. 390 and the cases referred to.

the attention of the employees or has been followed without exception for a substantial period.[230] Although there is no insurmountable legal impediment to a trade union becoming the duly authorised agent of those members it represents in collective bargaining,[231] the present position would seem to be that generally trade union members neither expressly nor impliedly confer any authority on the trade union or its negotiators so as to ensure that the collective agreement when made — or at least those parts of it which create legal obligations — will form a set of legal rights and duties between on the one hand the member and those employers represented at the collective negotiations and on the other hand the union (agent) and its members (principals). Of course, while many trade unions are authorised at the commencement of collective negotiations to achieve a particular target, such authorisation seldom emanates from individual members but almost universally from a representative conference or committee. Furthermore the result of the now customary membership ballots indicates that proof of the negotiators' authority to act as agent for all members would be elusive. The current legal position — although there are *dicta* to the contrary[232] — is that in the absence of special circumstances[233] a trade union negotiating a collective agreement does not act as the duly authorised agent of its members so that they are bound as principals.[234] Until there is a radical change in the attitudes of unions, their members or the legislature, the impact of collective agreements on employment terms of employer and employee — whether members of the trade union or employers' organisations — will continue to depend on incorporation into the contract of employment.

---

[230] *Duke v. Reliance Systems Ltd* [1982] ICR 449, EAT.

[231] Because of the number of principals likely to be involved it would be a case of acting on behalf of principals whose identities were undisclosed; new members could be dealt with by the application of the rules of ratification although a question might arise about whether the principal was in existence at the time of the collective negotiations. On Agency see Gloag and Henderson's *Introduction to the Law of Scotland* (9th edn), Ch 23.

[232] See the observations of Denning MR in *Chappell v. Times Newspapers Ltd* [1975] IRLR 91.

[233] See, for example, *Edwards v. Skyways Ltd* [1964] 1 WLR 349; *Sutherland v. Montrose Fishing Co Ltd* (1921) 37 Sh. Ct. Rep. 239.

[234] *Holland v. London Society of Compositors* [1924] 40 TLR 440; *Rodwell v. Thomas* [1944] 1 KB 596; *Burton Group v. Smith* [1977] IRLR 351; EAT; *Gray Dunn & Co v. Edwards* [1980] IRLR 23, EAT.

Chapter Three

RIGHTS AND DUTIES ARISING DURING THE CONTRACT OF EMPLOYMENT

3.1 Introduction

Once the contract of employment has been created different types of legal rights and duties come into play. The relationship between employer and employee is sufficiently close to bring into operation the "neighbour" principle of the law of reparation so that an employer must take reasonable care to ensure the safety of his employees. Obviously contractual rights and duties will also come into play. Rights and duties which arise from the law of reparation and the law of contract have their origins in the common law. Especially since the 1960s, however, many employment law rights and duties have been created by statute, for example, (1) redundancy payments,[1] (2) unfair dismissal[2] and (3) sexual and racial discrimination.[3] However statutory employment rights can be distinguished from those which are based on the common law in at least two ways. First nearly all statutory employment rights are enforced through the medium of the industrial tribunals[4] whereas rights in the employment field which originate in the law of delict or contract are enforced through the ordinary courts.[4a] Secondly the majority[5] of statutory employment rights are conferred only on those employees who have accumulated the relevant period of continuous employment.[6] Accordingly whether or not an employee possesses a period of continuous employment is often of critical importance and must be considered as a prelude to the operation of the statutory rules relating to the substance of the statutory right claimed. At the end of this section[7] there is a table showing the periods of continuous employment required for entitlement to the various statutory rights which operate in employment and which are enforced through the industrial tribunals.

---

[1] See Chapter Six.
[2] See Chapter Five.
[3] See Chapter Seven.
[4] Chapter Eight
[4a] At the time of writing an order extending the jurisdiction of industrial tribunals to deal with certain contract law disputes has not yet been made under EPCA, s. 131.
[5] The main exceptions are rights relating to sexual and racial discrimination and the part of unfair dismissal law dealing with union membership and contained in EPCA, s. 58 as amended by EA 1988, s. 11. And see the Employment Act 1990, s. 1.
[6] Usually it has to be continuous employment with the employer against whom the claim is being made but there are special rules permitting employment with other employers to be considered. See para. 3.5.
[7] See para. 3.46.

CONTINUOUS EMPLOYMENT

3.2 General

Whether employment is continuous depends on a set of statutory rules[8] contained in the Employment Protection (Consolidation) Act 1978[9] but irrespective of these rules no period of employment can be counted if it took place under an illegal contract of employment.[10] Although the length of a period of continuous employment is calculated in calendar months or years the basic unit is the week.[11] Thus to determine whether or not an employee has, say, two years' continuous employment it is necessary to apply the statutory rules to each of the weeks in that two year period. Normally[12] a week which cannot be taken into account also interrupts any period of continuous employment already accumulated as does the receipt of a redundancy payment[12a] and the employee will have to recommence the qualifying process. Except for redundancy payments (for which employment below 18 years of age is ignored[13]) an employee's period of continuous employment begins with the day on which he starts work[14] and ends with the day by reference to which the period has to be ascertained[15] and, unless the contrary is proved, employment with one employer[16] is presumed to have been continuous.[17]

3.3 Which weeks count towards continuous employment?

The following weeks are to be taken into account to determine a period of continuous employment.

(a)   A week in which the employee is employed for 16 hours or more.[18]

(b)   A week during which there is a contract[19] which normally involves employment for 16 hours or more[20] although weeks in which the contractual hours are reduced to between 8 and 16 per week can, subject to a maximum of

---

[8]   The rules are mandatory and cannot be altered by agreement (*Secretary of State for Employment v. Globe Elastic Thread Co. Ltd.* [1979] ICR 706, H L; *Hanson v. Fashion Industries Ltd* [1980] IRLR 393, EAT).

[9]   S. 151 and sch. 13 (as amended by EA 1982, s. 20, sch. 2).

[10]   *Hyland v. J. H. Barker (North West) Ltd* [1985] ICR 861, EAT. Cf. *Wilkinson v. Lugg* [1990] ICR 599, EAT.

[11]   EPCA, s. 151 (1), (2).

[12]   The exception is a week during which the employee takes part in a strike or is locked out. (EPCA, s. 151, Sch. 13 para. 15.)

[12a]   EPCA, Sch. 13 para. 12.

[13]   EPCA. Sch. 13 para. 15.

[14]   As to "starts work" see *Salvation Army General Council v. Dewsbury* [1984] IRLR 222, EAT.

[15]   EPCA, s. 151 (3). A week is deemed to end on a Saturday (*ibid.*, Sch. 13 para. 24 (1)).

[16]   *Secretary of State for Employment v. Cohen and Beaupress Ltd.* [1986] IRLR 169, EAT. And see *Tipper v. Roofdec Ltd* [1989] IRLR 419, EAT to effect that where there are successive periods of employment with one employer the reason for the termination of the earlier one is of no significance.

[17]   EPCA, Sch. 13 para. 1 (3).

[18]   EPCA, Sch. 13, para. 3. Note this is a test of actuality and the fact that the contractual hours are less than 16 will probably not prevent the week from counting if the actual hours are 16 or more.

[19]   Crown employees are deemed to have contracts (EPCA, Sch. 13, para. 19).

[20]   Sch. 13, para. 4. As *Weston v. Vega Space Systems Engineering Ltd* [1989] IRLR 429, EAT, illustrates for para. 4 the important question is the number of hours the contract normally involves and not the number actually worked.

26, count.[21] While it is not permissible to aggregate the hours under concurrent contracts,[22] where a contract of employment requires preparatory work to be done but makes no specific provision for it, the time spent on such work is to be added to such working hours as may be expressed in the contract.[23]

(c)   A week in which the contract involves employment between 8 and 16 hours per week and the employee has in other respects been continuously employed for 5 years.[24]

(d)   A week in which the employee is, for part of or the whole of the week, incapable of working because of illness, pregnancy or confinement,[25] or is absent on account of a temporary cessation of work, or an arrangement or custom whereby continuity of employment is to be preserved.[26] What constitutes a "temporary cessation of work" has produced much litigation which has resulted in support for the following propositions — (i) a temporary cessation of work can occur between two (or more) fixed term contracts[27], (ii) the provision relates to temporary cessation of paid work[28], (iii) the amount of work has to cease and no longer be available for the employer to give to the employee.[29] Whether a temporary cessation of work has occurred is a question of fact and degree including the whole history of the employment and although it is possible to compare periods when work continues with periods when it has ceased such a "mathematical" approach is not appropriate where the pattern of work and cessation of work is irregular.[30] In *Sillars v. Charrington Fuels Ltd*[31] although the lay members of the EAT approved of the broad approach set out in *Fitzgerald* and *Flack* because the "mathematical" approach might result in unfairness, the industrial tribunal had been correct to apply the "mathematical" approach in the circumstances.

(e)   A week of absence because of pregnancy where a woman has exercised her statutory right to return to work.[32]

---

[21] Sch. 13 para. 5. In relation to "on-call" hours it is necessary to distinguish between a duty to be available for work and actual work itself (*Suffolk County Council v. Secretary of State for the Environment and Alcock* [1984] ICR 882, HL). And see the special provision for employees who are required to live on the premises in Sch. 13 para. 24 (2).

[22] Thus a school teacher who had several different but concurrent part-time contracts with the same employer could not attain the 16 hours required by adding together the hours under the various contracts (*Lewis v. Surrey County Council* [1987] IRLR 509, HL).

[23] *Society of Licensed Victuallers v. Chamberlain* [1989] IRLR 421, EAT. *Cf. Girls' Public Day School Trust v. Khanna* [1987] ICR 339, EAT.

[24] EPCA, Sch. 13 para. 6. In *Letheby & Christopher Ltd v. Bond* [1988] ICR 480, EAT it was held that para. 6 only applied to contracts to last for more than a week. And see *Harber v. North London Polytechnic* [1990] IRLR 199, CA.

[25] Sch. 13 para. 9 (1). The maximum permitted absence for illness and pregnancy under this provision is 26 weeks.

[26] *Ibid.* In *Letheby & Christopher Ltd v. Bond* [1988] ICR 480, EAT it was held para. 9 (1) (c) required the tribunal to determine whether the parties regarded the employment as continuing and that the use of separate contracts (for each spell of work) suggested they did not regard it as continuing.

[27] *Ford v. Warwickshire County Council* [1983] IRLR 126, HL; cf. *Moncrieff v. Tayside Regional Council* 1983 SLT 378, IH.

[28] *University of Aston in Birmingham v. Malik* [1984] ICR 492, EAT.

[29] *Byrne v. Birmingham District Council* [1987] IRLR 191, CA. (Allocating work to employees in a pool of workers does not mean there is a temporary cessation of work in respect of those employees to whom work is periodically not offered.)

[30] *Fitzgerald v. Hall Russell & Co Ltd* [1970] SC (HL) 1; *Flack v. Kodak Ltd* [1986] ICR 775, CA.

[31] [1988] IRLR 180, EAT; affirmed [1989] IRLR 152, CA.

[32] EPCA, Sch. 13, para. 10.

(f)   A week which is covered by the statutory provision[33] which postpones the effective date of termination[34] or is between dismissal for redundancy and a renewal or re-engagement.[35]

3.4 Strikes and lock-outs

However, even if a week falls into one of the paragraphs (a)-(e) above it will not count if, during that week the employee takes part in a strike or is locked out.[36] "Strike" is defined to mean "the cessation of work by a body of persons employed acting in combination, or a concerted refusal or a refusal under a common understanding of any number of persons employed to continue to work for an employer in consequence of a dispute, done as a means of compelling their employer or any person or body of persons employed, to accept or not to accept terms or conditions of or affecting employment"[37] and "lock-out" means "the closing of a place of employment or the suspension of work, or the refusal by an employer to continue to employ any number of persons employed by him in consequence of a dispute, done with a view to compelling those persons, or to aid another employer in compelling persons employed by him, to accept terms or conditions of or affecting employment".[38] It must be emphasised that these definitions are provided for dealing with questions of continuity of employment although they may be of assistance when the meaning of "strike" or "lock-out" arises in relation to other questions (for example where an employer claims an employee has been dismissed during a strike or lock-out.)[39] However the rule that weeks on strike or when locked out do not count is tempered by the further provisions that (i) in calculating the *length* of a period of continuous employment the beginning of that period is postponed only by the days of strike or lock-out[40] and (ii) continuity of employment is not fractured by a strike or lock-out.[41] The latter provision is of great significance because without it employees would be extremely vulnerable and greatly inhibited from taking strike action.[42]

3.5 Different employers

Normally the rules of continuous employment permit consideration of employment with a particular employer; each time an employee changes his employer he has to start afresh to accumulate continuous employment.[43] However in the following situations it is permitted to have regard to employment with more than one employer —

(a)   where a trade, business or undertaking is transferred a period of employment with the transferor counts as a period of employment with the transferee (the new owner) in respect of any employee who is employed by the transferor

---

[33] EPCA, ss. 55 (5), (b), 90 (3).
[34] See para. 5.27.
[35] EPCA, Sch. 13 para. 11.
[36] *Ibid.* Sch. 13 para. 15 (1), (4)
[37] *Ibid.* Sch. 13 para. 24 (1).
[38] *Ibid.*
[39] See Chapter Eight.
[40] *Ibid.* s. 151 (5), (6) (b).
[41] *Ibid.* Sch. 13 para 15 (2), (4).
[42] *Cf.* Employment Act 1990 s. 7 regarding employees who take part in unofficial action.
[43] *Ibid.* s. 151, Sch. 13 para. 17 (1). And see *Secretary of State for Employment v. Cohen and Beaupress Ltd* [1987] IRLR 169, EAT.

at the time of the transfer.[44] Whether a business has been transferred is a mixed question of fact and law and it is important to distinguish between the transfer of a business as a going concern and the mere transfer of the assets of the business.[45] Thus in *Melon v. Hector Powe Ltd*[46] where a factory which made suits was transferred there was no transfer of a business because the new owners made suits not merely for their own retail outlets but for sale to any retail outlets which wished to sell them. As Lord Fraser of Tullybelton remarked in *Melon v. Hector Powe Ltd* "individual employees may continue to do the same work in the same environment and they may not appreciate that they are working in a different business".[47] The above provisions apply to the transfer of any trade, business or undertaking whether private or public and this latter category includes the functions of ministers and government departments.[48] Where the undertaking is in the nature of a commercial venture the provisions of the Transfer of Undertakings (Protection of Employment) Regulations 1981[49] also have to be considered. The main effect of these regulations is that after the transfer, contracts of employees in the undertaking at the time of the transfer and those who but for their unfair dismissal would have been employed at that time[50] continue to have effect as if they were made between such employees and the transferee, and all the rights and liabilities of the transferor under or in connection with the contract of employment attach to the transferee.[51] Thus in a situation to which these regulations apply an employee whose contracts of employment subsists at the time of the transfer[52] can, after the transfer, exercise any rights against the transferee on the basis of his employment with both transferor and transferee in so far as the other rules regarding continuity are met;

(b)   where by Act of Parliament one body corporate is substituted for another in a contract of employment, employment with both bodies counts towards continuous employment;[53]

(c)   where after the death of an employer employment is continued by trustees or representatives of the deceased employer, employment before and after the employer's death counts towards continuous employment;[54]

---

[44]   EPCA, Sch. 13 para. 17 (2).

[45]   *Bailey's Exrs v. Co-operative Wholesale Society Ltd* 1976 SLT 92. And see *Rastill v. Automatic Refreshment Services Ltd* [1978] ICR 289, EAT; *Mannin Management Services v. Ward* IDS Brief 393, CA.

[46]   [1980] IRLR 477, HL. Cf. *Gibson v. Motortune* [1990] ICR 740, EAT.

[47]   *Ibid.* If employees have cause to doubt that the business has been transferred they should consider making claims against the transferor before the relevant time limits expire.

[48]   EPCA, Sch. 13 para. 19 (5).

[49]   SI 1981 No. 1794.

[50]   *Litster v. Forth Dry Dock and Engineering Co Ltd* [1989] ICR 341, HL.

[51]   Transfer of Undertakings (Protection of Employment) Regulations 1981, reg. 3.

[52]   In *Brook Lane Finance Ltd v. Bradley* [1988] IRLR 283 the EAT expressed the view that para. 17 (2) of Sch. 13 to EPCA and the Transfer of Undertakings etc. Regulations should receive the same meaning so that in accordance with *Secretary of State for Employment v. Spence* [1986] IRLR 248, CA a transfer of a business is to be regarded as taking place at a particular time not over an extended period. More recently another EAT has declined to follow *Brook Lane Finance Ltd* because it was given before the decision in *Litster v. Forth Dry Dock & Engineering Co Ltd* [1989] ICR 341, HL and chose to interpret para. 17 (2) to preserve continuity: *Macer v. Abafast Ltd* [1990] IRLR 137.

[53]   EPCA, Sch. 13 para. 17 (3).

[54]   *Ibid.* Sch. 13 para. 17 (4). And see the similar provision relating to the change in the composition of a partnership or trustees (para. 17(5)) and *Jeetle v. Elster* [1985] IRLR 227, EAT.

(d)   where an employee transfers to an employer who is an associated employer of the other employer employment with both employers counts towards continuous employment.[55]

3.6 Re-engagement

Where, following a complaint of unfair dismissal (or action taken by a conciliation officer[56]) an employee is re-instated or re-engaged the period between dismissal and re-employment counts towards continuous employment.[57] Continuity is also preserved where an employee is re-employed before the complaint of unfair dismissal is heard[58] or where no complaint at all is made and re-employment results from a settlement or arrangement.[59] Also where a liquidator re-engages employees whose contracts have been terminated by the winding up of the company for which the employees had worked the liquidator is regarded as continuing their employment "for and on behalf of the company".[60]

REMUNERATION

3.7 Introduction

The rights and duties of the employer and employee relating to remuneration are regulated both by contractual provisions and statutory rules. Thus whether wages are due during periods of sickness[61] and whether they can be withheld during industrial action are matters to be determined by the contract while entitlement to medical suspension pay, guarantee and redundancy payments are regulated by statute,[62] as are deductions from wages.[63] It has been observed that "remuneration" can connote a *quid pro quo* for services rendered including payment in kind[63a] or more specifically a monetary payment[63b] depending on the circumstances.[63c]

---

[55] *Ibid.* Sch. 13 para. 18. Employers are "associated " if "one is a company of which the other (directly or indirectly) has control, or if both are companies of which a third person (directly or indirectly) has control" (EPCA, s. 153 (4)). This definition is exhaustive and must embrace at least one limited company — *Merton London Borough Council v. Gardiner* [1980] IRLR 472, CA. "Control" means control by a majority of votes attaching to shares exercised in a general meeting and not *de facto* managerial control; however evidence might show that one person in practice controls the voting powers attaching to the shares of another so that he controls his own shares as well as those of the other person —*South West Launderettes Ltd v. Laidler* [1986] IRLR 305, EAT — or that one person holds shares as a nominee of another — *Payne v. Secretary of State for Employment* [1989] IRLR 352, CA. And note the alertness of the EAT when confronted with companies forming a partnership or joint venture: *Pinkney v. Sandpipe Drilling Ltd* [1990] IRLR 425. The company may be registered abroad: *Hancill v. Marcon Engineering Ltd* [1990] IRLR 51, EAT.

[56] See para. 5.9.

[57] Labour Relations (Continuity of Employment) Regulations 1976 (SI 1976 No. 660) whose effect is continued by EPCA, Sch. 15 para. 4.

[58] *Smith v. Carlisle City Council* (1983 unreported EAT).

[59] EPCA, Sch. 13 para. 9(1)(c); *Ingram v. Foxon* [1985] IRLR 5, EAT.

[60] *Smith v. Lord Advocate* 1978 SC 159.

[61] This must be distinguished from statutory sick pay which is paid by employers on behalf of the Department of Social Security; see para. 3.17.

[62] See EPCA, ss. 19, 12, 81; and see paras. 3.25, 3.16 and Chapter Six.

[63] See Wages Act 1986, s. 1; and see para. 3.21.

[63a] Eg. *R v. Postmaster General* [1876] 1 QBD 658.

[63b] Eg. *S & U Stores Ltd v. Wilkes* [1974] 3 All ER 401.

[63c] *Chapman v. Aberdeen Construction Group plc* 1990 GWD 18-1012.

3.8 The contractual terms

Wages. Contractual terms regarding the payment of wages or salary are usually express.[64] However in the absence of an express term there is a rebuttable presumption that services are given for payment.[65] While by a clear contractual term it is permissible to leave for future determination the precise amount of wages due[66] such a power of determination will not justify withholding all wages.[67] Where there is neither an express nor implied term regarding the amount of remuneration to be paid the parties can have resort to the equitable principle of *quantum meruit.*[68] Where performance ceases between two payment dates the question whether an employee has a right to accrued wages may arise. Where the contract is indivisible it seems that no right to wages for part performance will arise unless it is due to the employee's death or illness.[69] In contracts which may be terminated by notice whether wages accrue in respect of past performance and the rate of accrual may be implied from the terms of the contract and the practice of the contracting parties.[70] Although the Apportionment Act 1870 allocates on a *per diem* basis annuities including salaries[71] it is not settled whether the Act applies to payment made under a contract of employment[72] What may be of more practical significance is (1) failure to perform his duties under the contract will deprive him of the opportunity of compelling the employer to pay wages and will bring into play the principles of compensation where the employer has suffered damage[73] and (2) where wages are not paid an employee does not have a lien over his employer's moveables.[74]

[64] Although it is not a contract the written statement required to be issued under EPCA, s. 1 has to specify particulars of "the scale or rate of remuneration, or the method of calculating remuneration" and "the intervals at which remuneration is paid (that is whether it is weekly, or monthly or by some other period)."

[65] *Thomson v. Thomson's Trustees* (1889) 16 R 333. *Cf.* Lord Fraser, *Master and Servant* (3rd edn. 1881) p. 39 *et seq* where many of the cases discussed feature services by near relatives; also in some of the older cases the issue was whether wages were due in addition to board and/or accommodation.

[66] *Re Richmond Gate Property Co Ltd* [1964] 3 All ER 936.

[67] Lord Fraser, *Master and Servant,* p. 135. In *Richmond Gate* the board's power to determine the salary of the managing director was superseded by the company's liquidation.

[68] *McKenzie v. Baird's Trustees* 1907 SC 838; *Powell v. Braun* [1954] 1 All ER 484, CA. Cf. *McNaughton v. Brunton* (1882) 10 R 111.

[69] Bell, *Principles,* 179; Erskine, *Institutes* III, 3, 16. Cf. *Douglas v. Argyll* 1736 Mor 11102 and *Cutter v. Powell* (1795) 6 Term Rep. 320 in which entitlement to wages seems to have been conditioned on completion of the voyage.

[70] *McGill v. Park* (1829) 2 F 272; and see *Buchanan v. Strathclyde Regional Council* 1981, OH (unreported). Merely because there is a right to terminate by notice to expire on a date before the next payment of wages/salary is due will not necessarily mean that payments will have accrued for the period up to the expiry of the notice (*Diamond v. English Sewing Cotton Co Ltd* [1922] WN 237, CA).

[71] Apportionment Act 1870, ss. 2, 5.

[72] Contrast *McGill v. Park* (1889) 2 F 272 with *Inman v. Ackroyd and Best Ltd* [1901] 1 QB 613, CA. In *Sim v. Rotherham Metropolitan Borough Council* [1986] ICR 897 Scott, J was prepared to hold that the Apportionment Act 1870 applied to the salary of a school teacher. And see Mathews, "Salaries in the Apportionment Act 1870" [1982] 2 *Legal Studies* 302.

[73] Erskine, *Institutes* III, 3, 16; *Scottish North-Eastern Railway Co v. Napier* (1859) 21 D 700 OH; *Pegler v. Northern Agricultural Implement Co* (1877) 4 R 435. And see G. H. L. Fridman, *Modern Law of Employment* (1963) p. 484.

[74] Bell, *Principles* 1412; *Barnton Hotel Co Ltd v. Cook* (1899) 1 F 1190. According to W. M. Gloag, *The Law of Contract* (2nd edn.) p. 632 *Findlay v. Waddell* 1910 SC 670 indicates the distinction between an employee who is merely a custodier of his employer's moveables and others who obtain, for example, books and papers for a particular piece of

3.9 *Withholding wages.* In accordance with the rule of mutual contracts where either party to the contract of employment is in material breach he is unable to compel performance by the other party.[75] Thus a ship's engineer failed in an action for payment of salary when his employer pleaded he was relieved of his duty of paying salary because of the pursuer's continued misconduct and neglect of duty.[76] The same rule applies to an employee who takes industrial action which is in breach of contract[77]; he cannot enforce a contractual right to wages withheld by his employer in respect of the period during which the industrial action occurred.[78] And the employer faced with a breach by the employee is not required to rescind the contract before he is entitled to withhold wages (or other performance).[79] However it is doubtful whether an insignificant breach justifies the withholding of wages[80] although it would seem that, provided the breach does justify withholding remuneration, the amount withheld cannot be challenged.[81] However it is arguable that the conduct of the employer towards an employee in breach may indicate acceptance of partial performance and justify a finding that the employer has affirmed the contract.[82] Thus where a local government employee's breach of contract was confined to a refusal to deal with enquiries from councillors the employer's right to withhold wages was not defeated by permitting the employee to attend and perform his other duties because it had been made clear to the employee on his arrival each day for work that he was not required to work except in full compliance with his

work; the former has "custody only on which no right of retention can be founded" whereas the latter have "possession and a right to retain".

[75] *Turnbull v. McLean* (1874) 1 R 230; *Graham & Co v. United Turkey Red Co Ltd* 1922 SC 533.
[76] *Sharp v. Rettie* (1884) 11 R 745, IH; Lord President Inglis stated "The defence to the action is not a challenge of the amount said to be due . . . but an averment that the pursuer has committed a breach of contract and is therefore not entitled to sue on the contract . . . It is always competent when one party sues upon a contract . . . for the latter to say — You broke the contract and instead of my being in debt to you, you are in debt to me. This form of defence amounts in substance to an action in damages and is in fact an action for damages for real injury done by the pursuer to . . . the defender . . ."
[77] Industrial action does not always involve a breach of contract by the employee (*Powerpacking Casemakers v. Faust* [1983] ICR 292, CA) nor does a lock-out always involve a breach of contract by employer (*Express and Star Ltd v. Bunday* [1988] IRC 379, CA). And see para. 5.64.
[78] *Buchanan v. Strathclyde Regional Council*, 1981 (unreported); *Laurie v. British Steel Corporation* 1988 SLT 17, OH. See also *Miles v. Wakefield Metropolitan District Council* [1987] IRLR 19, HL; *Wiluszynski v. London Borough of Tower Hamlets* [1989] IRLR 259, CA. And see para. 3.41.
[79] *Laurie v. British Steel Corporation* 1988 SLT 17, OH; *Cresswell v. Board of Inland Revenue* [1984] IRLR 190.
[80] See W. M. Gloag, *Law of Contract* (2nd edn.) p. 623 ". . . a failure in the performance of a contract may not be so material as to justify the rescission of the contract, yet may be sufficiently material to entitle the other party to withhold counter-performance." Cf. *Sim v. Rotherham Metropolitan Borough Council* [1986] IRLR 391 in which it was held that a teacher's failure to cover for an absent colleague for one period of 35 minutes was sufficient "to impeach the plaintiff's title to his full contractual salary." Also in *Wiluszynski v. London Borough of Tower Hamlets* [1989] IRLR 259, CA, all the employee failed to do was to deal with enquiries from councillors of which there were only 2 or 3 *per* week.
[81] Ibid. This, together with the exceptional provision in EPCA, ss. 62, 62A, places an employee who takes industrial action in a vulnerable situation.
[82] *Royle v. Trafford Borough Council* [1984] IRLR 184; *McPherson v. London Borough of Barnet* [1988] IRLR 470.

contract and that any work he did would be voluntary and unpaid,[83] although giving the employee directions to work would have resulted in a finding of affirmation of part performance of the contract and could not have been accompanied by a withholding of all wages.[84] Also, to be entitled to his full contractual wages an employee must be prepared to work in accordance with his employer's lawful instructions.[85] Although the Wages Act 1986 regulates deductions from wages or salary it does not apply to any deduction from a worker's wages made on account of his having taken part in industrial action;[86] indeed it is arguable that since, by virtue of the worker's breach of contract, wages are not "payable"[87] the Wages Act has no application at all to instances of withholding of wages.[88]

3.10 *Suspension, lay-off and late payment.* Although statutory provision is now made to protect — in a very modest way — income of employees whose employer does not, for certain reasons, provide work,[89] employees whose remuneration is paid on a time basis (by the hour/day etc) are entitled to be paid at the appropriate rate for the contracted number of hours and paying less than the agreed rate, laying off or suspending the employee without pay will, in the absence of a clear contractual term entitling the employer so to act, be a material breach of contract entitling the employee to rescind and/or damages.[90] However where the contract gives an employer the right to lay off an employee without pay the employer will not be in breach merely by continuing to lay off for a long time.[91] Where the remuneration is related to the amount of work done, an employer is required to provide a steady supply of work while the contract exists[92] although an established custom may provide that in certain circumstances the obligation to pay wages may be suspended.[93] Where wages are not paid on time it is arguable that the employee is entitled to interest on the amount unpaid[94] but late payment will only be regarded as a material breach of contract if it indicates an intention no longer to be bound by the contract.[95]

---

[83] *Wiluszynsky v. London Borough of Tower Hamlets* [1989] IRLR 259, CA.

[84] *Ibid.*

[85] In *Cresswell v. Board of Inland Revenue* [1984] IRLR 190 it was held that withholding all remuneration was justified for the period during which the employee was not prepared to operate new technology even though he was prepared to do the same task manually. And see *McPherson v. London Borough of Barnet* [1988] IRLR 470.

[86] WA 1986, s. 1(5)(e).

[87] By the Wages Act 1986, s. 7(1) wages mean "any sums *payable* to the worker by his employer . . ."; and s. 8 (3) provides that "where the total amount of wages that are paid . . . is less than total amount of the wages that are *properly payable* . . . on that occasion the amount of the deficiency shall be treated as a deduction."

[88] *Bird v. British Celanese Ltd* [1945] KB 336.

[89] See EPCA, s. 12. And see para. 3.15.

[90] *D. & J. McKenzie Ltd v. Smith* 1976 SLT 216, OH; *Burroughs Machines Ltd v. Timmoney* 1978 SLT (Notes) 10.

[91] *Kenneth McRae & Co Ltd v. Dawson* [1984] IRLR 5, EAT.

[92] Bell, *Principles* s. 192; *Cowdenbeath Coal Co v. Drylie* (1886) 3 Sh. Ct. Rep. 3.

[93] *Devonald v. Rosser & Sons* [1906] 2 KB 728, CA.

[94] Lord Fraser, *Master and Servant* (3rd edn.) p. 138; F.A. Umpherston, *The Law of Master and Servant*, p. 61; *Mansfield v. Scott* (1831) 9. S. 780. *Cf. Wallace v. Geddes* (1821) 1 Sh. App. 42.

[95] *Hanlon v. Allied Breweries UK Ltd* [1975] IRLR 321, IT; *Adams v. Charles Zub and Associates Ltd* [1978] IRLR 551, EAT.

3.11 *Wages during illness of employee.* Although the income of an employee unable to work during periods because of incapacity for work is now protected by the introduction of statutory sick pay (SSP)[96] a question may still arise regarding an employee's contractual entitlement to receive wages during illness. In the absence of an express provision it has been held in England[97] that a doubt may be resolved by resorting to "the presumption that the wage is to be paid till the employment is ended".[98] However where a contractual term regarding sick pay[99] exists then, in the absence of an express provision, the employer's obligation to pay sick pay continues only for such a period as is reasonable.[100] The position in Scotland has not been the subject of recent judicial pronouncement but it is arguable that where the contract is for a fixed period the employer must continue to pay wages during short periods of illness[101] whereas in other contracts an employee's right to wages depends on a term being implied from the facts or circumstances because there is no Scots authority reflecting the English rule that where no term about sick pay can be implied there is a presumption that wages will be payable until the contract is determined.[102] Of course whether the contract be for a fixed period or terminable by notice the incapacity of the employee may be such as to frustrate the contract.[103]

3.12 Remuneration and statute

Although in most cases an entitlement to receive, and an obligation to pay, wages are settled by reference to the terms of the contract various statutory provisions seek to protect the income of employees in a variety of measures relating to: (1) guarantee payments, (2) medical suspension pay, (3) pay during notice, (4) itemised pay statements, (5) deductions from wages and (6) wages councils orders, and these are dealt with here. However, statute also enacts rights to redundancy payments,[104] maternity pay[105] and equal pay for men and women[106] and these are dealt with elsewhere as indicated.

Week's pay. The statutory concept of a week's pay is relevant to various issues in modern employment law like, for example, the computation of a redundancy payment and the basic award of unfair dismissal; statute determines the amount of these (and other) statutory payments by reference to the week's pay of the relevant employee. The rules for computing a week's pay are set out in Employment Protection (Consolidation) Act 1978, Sch. 14 and vary depend-

---

[96] Social Security and Housing Benefit Act 1982, s. 1; and see para. 3.17. Where a contractual right to wages does exist any SSP paid by the employer is set off against the contractual claim *pro tanto* and *vice versa* (*ibid.* s. 3(3)).

[97] *Mears v. Safecar Security Ltd* [1982] ICR 626, CA disapproving *Orman v. Saville Sportswear* [1960] 1 WLR 1055.

[98] *Mears v. Safecar Security Ltd* [1982] ICR 626 at 651 *per* Stephenson LJ.

[99] In *Howman & Sons v. Blyth* [1983] ICR 416 the EAT emphasised the distinction between sick pay and wages.

[100] *Howman & Sons v. Blyth* [1983] ICR 416.

[101] Stair, *Institutions*, I, 15, 2; Bell, *Principle*, s. 179. Cf. *White v. Baillie* (1794) Mor 10147.

[102] Lord Fraser, *Master and Servant* (3rd edn.) p. 141; V. Craig, "*Wages during Sickness in Scotland*" 1982 SLT (News) 252.

[103] See para. 4.6.

[104] See paras. Chapter Six.

[105] See para. 3.18.

[106] See Chapter Seven.

ing on whether the employee has, or has not, normal working hours.[107] Before summarising these rules it is necessary to note that although "week's pay" means the gross amount due to the employee by virtue of his contract[108] it does not include expenses[109], tips[110] or travelling or subsistence allowances[111]; overtime earnings are included in a week's pay only if the employer has a duty to provide it and the employee a duty to work it when provided.[112] However for the purposes of calculating some statutory payments, for example a redundancy payment and the basic award of compensation for unfair dismissal,[113] statute prescribes the maximum amount that may be taken into account.[114] Broadly, where the employee has normal working hours his week's pay is:

(a)   where pay does not vary according to the work done (i.e. time rates) the amount payable by the employer under the contract if the employee works throughout his normal working hours in a week;[115]

(b)   in other cases (i.e. piecework and work paid by commission) the average hourly rate calculated over the 12 week period before the calculation date[116] — in effect the total pay divided by the total hours over 12 weeks multiplied by the normal working hours;[117] or

(c)   where the normal working hours vary from week to week (e.g. shiftwork) the average week's pay over 12 weeks prior to calculation date.[118]

Where the employee has no normal working hours his week's pay is the average week's pay over the 12 weeks prior to the calculation date.[119]

3.13 *Wages councils.* Although there is no general minimum wage legislation in the United Kingdom the wage rates of workers in particular industries have been the subject of statutory control since 1909[120] through various instruments,

---

[107] Particulars of normal working hours should be contained in the written statement issued under EPCA, s. 1 (see para. 2.10) and generally exclude hours paid at overtime rates unless the minimum contractual hours include some hours paid at overtime rates in which case the normal working hours are the minimum contractual hours (EPCA Sch. 14, paras. 1, 2).

[108] *Secretary of State for Employment v. John Woodrow & Sons (Builders) Ltd* [1983] ICR 582, EAT; *Murphy Telecommunications (Systems) Ltd v. Henderson* [1973] ICR 581, NIRC. It may also include commission (*J. & S. Bickley Ltd v. Washer* [1977] ICR 425, EAT).

[109] *S & U Stoves Ltd v. Wilkes* [1974] ICR 645, NIRC.

[110] *Palmanor Ltd v. Cedron* [1978] ICR 1008, EAT.

[111] *A M Carmichael Ltd v. Laing* [1972] ITR 1, DC.

[112] *Tarmac Roadstone Holdings Ltd v. Peacock* [1973] ICR 273, CA. And see *A & B Marcusfield Ltd v. Melhuish* [1977] IRLR 484, EAT regarding bonus payments.

[113] *Cf.* the special award payable only where a dismissal is unfair under EPCA, s. 58 (union membership/activities). See paras. 5.57 *et seq.*

[114] EPCA, Sch. 14 para. 8. By the Employment Protection (Variation of Limits) Order 1991 the maximum is presently £198.00.

[115] EPCA, Sch. 14, para. 3(2).

[116] As to the meaning of "calculation date" see *ibid.* para. 7.

[117] See *British Coal plc v. Cheesborough* [1990] IRLR 148, HL.

[118] Sch. 14 paras. 3(3), 4; weeks in which no work is done and weeks in which no remuneration is payable are disregarded (para. 5). Whether remuneration is "payable" see *Secretary of State for Employment v. Crane* [1988] IRLR 238, EAT. And note the effect of *British Coal plc v. Cheesborough* [1990] IRLR 148, HL, that by para. 5(1) the average is to be arrived at by taking account of all hours (basic and overtime) and all remuneration with any overtime premium stripped out — workers who worked overtime may receive a smaller redundancy payment.

[119] *Ibid.* para. 6; again weeks in which no remuneration is paid are disregarded (*ibid.*). And see special provisions in para. 9 for employees employed for period so short that averaging is difficult.

[120] Trade Boards Act 1909, now repealed.

notably,[121] wages councils,[122] independent but official arbitration machinery[123] and the Fair Wages Resolutions of the House of Commons.[124] The main reasons for such official interventions into the area of wage rates were (1) to protect the income of workers in industries where worker organisation was poor or non-existent with the result that collective bargaining was ineffective, and (2) to ensure that competition for lucrative contracts awarded by central or local government did not result in payment of unfairly low wages. Since 1980 the trend has been to remove or limit such statutory or official attempts to maintain wages rates. Thus Sch. 11 to the Employment Protection Act 1975 has been repealed[125] and in 1982 the United Kingdom denounced I.L.O. Convention No. 94 and the House of Commons voted to revoke the Fair Wages Resolution. Most significantly however the Wages Act 1986, although leaving the wages council system intact,[126] repealed[127] the Wages Councils Act 1979,[128] reduced the powers of existing wages councils[129] and made new provisions for the abolition of, or variation of the scope of, wages councils.[130]

3.14 *Composition and powers of wages councils.* A wages council is a tripartite body with representatives of employers[131] and workers and usually three but not more than five independent persons.[132] It can, after consultation, be abolished or have the scope of its operation varied by statutory instrument although this shall not affect any rights or liabilities which have accrued prior to the statutory instrument having effect.[133] The procedure[134] which is required to precede the making of a wages order can be summarised thus — Stage 1: the wages council publishes notice of the wage rate it proposes to fix and receives written representations from affected persons; Stage 2: consideration by the wages council of any written representations received; Stage 3: the wages council makes an order in terms of the proposal or amended proposal; Stage 4: publication of the order followed by its coming into effect after an interval of not less than 28 days.[135] Wages councils cannot include in a wages order any provision to apply to workers under the age of 21[136] and in respect of time workers[137] an order must

---

[121] See also Agricultural Wages (Scotland) Act 1949, Road Haulage Wages Act 1938 repealed by EA 1980, s. 19(c).

[122] Wages Councils Acts 1948, 1979, also repealed.

[123] See Terms and Conditions of Employment Act 1959 repealed and superseded by EA 1975, s. 98, Sch. 11, now also repealed by EA 1980, s. 19.

[124] The Fair Wages Resolution of 1891 was superseded by a similar Resolution of 1946.

[125] EA 1980, s. 19 (c).

[126] About 2.7 million workers are still covered by 24 wages councils.

[127] S. 12, Sch. 5 Pt. II.

[128] Thus no new wages council can be established except by exercise by the Secretary of State of the power given by Wages Act 1986 s. 13(4) to bring workers previously under one wages council under another one.

[129] Ss. 12, 14-18.

[130] S. 13.

[131] Where appropriate small businesses must be represented (WA, Sch. 2 para. 2(3)).

[132] WA 1986, s. 12(4), Sch. 2. By the Agricultural Wages (Scotland) Act 1949 the Agricultural Wages Board always has five independent numbers.

[133] WA 1986, s. 13.

[134] WA Sch. 3.

[135] *Ibid.*

[136] WA 1986, s. 12(3).

[137] A time worker is a worker other than a piece worker whether his remuneration is determined by reference to the actual number of hours worked or not (s. 26(1)).

be limited to: (1) fixing a single minimum hourly rate for all the time worked in a week, (2) fixing a single minimum hourly rate of remuneration up to a total amount (the basic hours) and a single minimum hourly overtime rate for hours in excess of the basic hours, and (3) fixing (where applicable) a limit to deductions or payments in respect of the provision of living accommodation by his employer.[138] Thus a wages council can no longer include in an order provisions regarding differential rates, holidays or other terms of employment. However before making an order (except one relating only to limits for payments or deductions for living accommodation) a wages council must have regard to the effect of the proposed wage rate on the level of employment among the workers to whom it will apply.[139]

3.15 *Effect of wages order.* Once an order is made it applies to all workers employed in the industry or sector for which the wages council operates[140] and if the amount of remuneration paid[141] is less than that prescribed by the wages order the worker is to be taken to be entitled under his contract to be paid the difference and the worker's employer is guilty of an offence and is liable to a fine.[142] Without derogating from any other right to recover by civil proceedings a criminal court may order an employer to pay to the worker the difference between the actual remuneration and the statutory minimum remuneration for any week in which an offence was committed unless the week was part of a cycle and the aggregate remuneration was not less than the aggregate statutory remuneration.[143] Also a failure to pay the rate prescribed may be treated as an unlawful deduction under the Wages Act 1986.[143a]

3.16 *Guarantee payments.* A system of guaranteeing an employee's income when his employer is unable to employ him throughout a day was first introduced by the Employment Protection Act 1975[144] but the current provisions are now contained in Employment Protection (Consolidation) Act 1978.[145] However the provisions are modest and are dependent on the employee satisfying various conditions. Unless excluded,[146] an employee with one month's continuous employment[147] is entitled to a guarantee payment for a day throughout which he is

---

[138] S. 14(1). Special provision is made for piece workers in s. 15.

[139] S. 14(6).

[140] "Worker" is defined to mean those who work (or worked) under contract of service, apprenticeship (but only those over 21 will be covered) and contracts for personal performance of work or services and homeworkers who may employ up to 2 helpers; but there is excluded from this definition "an individual who is wholly employed other than for the purposes of the business of the person employing him" (s. 26(1), (2)).

[141] To determine what is the amount of remuneration paid regard must be had to s. 17 (computation of remuneration) and s. 18 (apportionment of remuneration).

[142] S. 16(1), (2).

[143] S. 16 (3), (5). Such an order to pay the difference can be made in respect of any week falling up to two years before the week in which the offence was committed.

[143a] See, for example, *Reid v. Camphill Engravers* [1990] IRLR 268, EAT.

[144] Ss. 22-28.

[145] Ss. 12-18 as amended by EA 1982, Schs. 2, 3.

[146] Exclusions cover share fishermen (EPCA, s. 144(2)) employees who ordinarily work outside Great Britain (EPCA, s. 141(2)) and employees who are employed under a contract for a fixed term of 3 months or less or for a specific task which is not expected to last for more than 3 months unless his continuous employment actually exceeds 3 months (EPCA, s. 12(2)).

[147] See paras. 3.2, *et seq.*

not provided with work.[148] However a payment is only due in respect of a day during any part of which the employee would normally be required to work in accordance with his contract of employment.[149] Thus no payment is due for holidays or rest days[150] or for days on which the employee has agreed not to work.[151] Also the reasons for the employer's failure to provide work must be because of a diminution in the requirements of the business for the kind of work the employee is employed to do or "any other occurrence affecting the normal running of the business".[152] However, the fact that the failure to provide work is due to a trade dispute will only disentitle the employee to a payment if the dispute results in a strike, lock-out or other industrial action involving an employee of the laying-off employer or an associated employer.[153] However, an employee will lose the right to a guarantee payment by unreasonably refusing to carry out suitable alternative work (which may be outside the terms of the existing contract of employment)[154] or by failing to comply with reasonable requirements to ensure the availability of his services.[155] Employers will also be excluded from receiving guarantee payments as such if the Secretary of State has made an order exempting the industry from the application of the general statutory rules.[156] However, guarantee payments are put into perspective by the provision[157] which limits the daily rate of a guarantee payment to £13.65[158] and the number of days in respect of which entitlement to a guarantee payment may arise to five in any period of three months[159] and that which permits setting off any liability to pay a statutory guarantee payment against any contractual right to receive remuneration for workless days.[160] In the event of an employer fail-

---

[148] EPCA, s. 12(1).

[149] *Mailway (Southern) Ltd v. Willsher* [1978] IRLR 322, EAT.

[150] In *North v. Pavleigh* [1979] IRLR 461, IT, the employers gave employees 2 days of "unpaid holidays" but as the contract contained no provision for such they were days on which the employees were normally required to work.

[151] *Clemens v. Peter Richards Ltd* [1977] IRLR 332; *Daley v. Strathclyde Regional Council* [1977] IRLR 441. Cf. *Robinson v. Claxton & Garland Ltd* [1977] IRLR 159, IT, in which it has held that a day on which an employee was suspended without pay was still a day he was normally required to work in accordance with his contract. And see s. 15(4)).

[152] EPCA, s. 12(3). This phrase is extremely wide and would cover an employer's inability to heat the workplace to the correct temperature (*Meadows v. Faithful Overalls Ltd* [1977] IRLR 461, IT), a machine breakdown, a failure of supplies or power etc.

[153] EPCA, s. 13(1) as amended EA 1980, Sch. 3. Cf. *Garvey v. Maybank (Oldham) Ltd* [1979] IRLR 408, IT, which illustrates the width of the exclusion prior to amendment. As to "associated employer" see para. 3.5, f. 55.

[154] See, for example, *Purdy v. Willowbrook International Ltd* [1977] IRLR 388, IT.

[155] EPCA, s. 13(2). In *Meadows v. Faithful Overalls Ltd* [1977] IRLR 330, an industrial tribunal held that an employee who declined her employer's offer of refreshments in the canteen and went home pending the arrival of heating oil failed to comply with reasonable requirements to ensure the availability of her services.

[156] EPCA, s. 18 permits an order to be made where a collective agreement or a wages order already guarantees remuneration and provides for disputes to be resolved by independent arbitration or adjudication or by an industrial tribunal.

[157] EPCA, s. 15, as amended by EA 1980, s. 14(4) and by subsequent ministerial orders.

[158] Employment Protection (Variation of Limits) Order 1991 (SI 1991 No 464). This figure is subject to an annual review (EPCA, s. 148(1)).

[159] EPCA, s. 15(1), (2).

[160] EPCA, s. 16. This also results in entitlement to contractual remuneration for 5 days in a period of 3 months preventing entitlement to a guarantee payment for additional workless days in the same 3 month period (*Cartwright v. G. Clancey Ltd* [1983] ICR 852, EAT).

ing to pay a guarantee payment the employee's remedy is by way of a complaint to an industrial tribunal which can order the payment to be made.[161]

3.17 *Medical suspension pay.* An employee who has been continuously employed[162] for one month, provided he is not incapable of work by reason of disease or bodily or mental disablement, is entitled to be paid remuneration by his employer during periods when he is suspended from work[163] on medical grounds in consequence of — (1) any requirement imposed by or under any provision of any legislation[164] or (2) any recommendation in any provision of a code of practice issued or approved under the Health and Safety at Work etc. Act 1974.[165] For each week in which suspension occurs an employee is entitled to a week's pay[166] for up to a maximum of twenty-six weeks[167] but any contractual remuneration paid for any period goes toward discharging an employer's liability to pay medical suspension pay and *vice versa.*[168] However, an employee who is employed under a fixed term contract of three months or less or under a contract for a specific task not expected to last more than three months (unless it does result in more than three months' continuous employment), who unreasonably declines his employer's offer of suitable alternative work (which need not fall within the work he has contracted to do) or who fails to comply with his employer's reasonable requirements to ensure the availability of his services, is not entitled to medical suspension pay.[169] In the event of an employer failing to pay medical suspension pay the employee's remedy is by presenting (within three months or further period as the tribunal considers reasonable) a complaint to an industrial tribunal which can order payment of the appropriate amount.[170] The purpose of these provisions is to protect the income of an employee who is capable of work but who is suspended from work on medical grounds, for example, the need to avoid the employee's (continued) exposure to a health hazard. The provisions do not themselves entitle an employer to suspend work or pay or both and any suspension to comply with a requirement or recommendation referred to in the Employment Protection (Consolidation) Act 1978, s. 19(1) for which the employer does not have a contractual right would in most instances support a claim of constructive dismissal and it has to be noted that such a constructive dismissal will found an unfair dismissal complaint after only four weeks' continuous employment.[171]

---

[161] EPCA, s. 17. A complaint must be presented within three months although the tribunal has a discretion to accept late complaints.

[162] See paras. 3.2, *et seq.*

[163] An employee is regarded as suspended from work only while he continues to be employed by his employer but is not provided with work or does not perform the work he normally performed (EPCA s.19(2)).

[164] Both primary and delegated legislation are included.

[165] EPCA, s. 19. The relevant provisions are set out in EPCA, Sch. 1, as amended by subsequent orders, *e.g.* SI 1980 No. 1581.

[166] "Week's pay" is defined in EPCA, Sch. 14; and see para. 3.11.

[167] EPCA, ss. 19, 21. If in any week remuneration is payable only in respect of part of a week the amount of a week's pay shall be reduced accordingly.

[168] EPCA, s. 21(3).

[169] EPCA, s. 20 as amended by EA 1982, Sch. 2.

[170] EPCA, s. 22.

[171] EPCA, s. 64(2). Of course the dismissal may be fair; alternatively the contract might have become frustrated (supervening illegality) in which case there would be no dismissal. And see para. 5.25. *Cf. Johnstone v. Bloomsbury Health Authority* [1991] IRLR 118, CA.

3.18 *Statutory sick pay.* Statutory Sick Pay (SSP) was introduced by the Social Security and Housing Benefits Act 1982[172] essentially to simplify the system of income maintenance for those who were unable to work for short periods because of sickness[173] and had been heralded by the introduction of "self-certification" for claiming the first week of Sickness Benefit.[174] The effect of the scheme is to require employers to pay for a maximum of 28 weeks[175] to incapacitated employees an amount equivalent to what would have been paid by way of state benefit.[176] Thus subject to the employee meeting certain qualifying conditions[177] an employer is liable to pay to the employee, for a day of incapacity for work in relation to his contract of service, a payment (to be known as "statutory sick pay") in respect of that day.[178] However certain employees are excluded — (1) those over pensionable age, (2) those with contracts for a specified period of not more than three months, (3) those who have not yet started work, (4) those who fall sick while there is a trade dispute,[179] (5) those who have received SSP for the maximum period of entitlement in respect of the employer (28 weeks) and (6) those who are pregnant in respect of any days after the beginning of the eleventh week before the expected week of confinement.[180] Entitlement to SSP is in addition to any contractual rights and cannot be limited or excluded by agreement.[181] The amount of SSP is subject to review by the Secretary of State[182] and currently there are two rates in operation.[183] Disputes about entitlement to SSP are dealt with by Adjudication Officers and Social Security Appeal Tribunals.[184]

3.19 *Statutory maternity pay.* The right to statutory pay complements the right not to be dismissed because of pregnancy,[185] the right to return to work after pregnancy[186] and the right to time-off for ante-natal care.[187] A statutory right to receive payment during maternity leave was first introduced in 1975[188] and until April 1987 the right to such a payment (which was granted only to employees

---

[172] Ss. 1-27. And see the Statutory Sick Pay (General) Regulations 1982 (SI. No. 894).

[173] See the White Paper "Income During initial Sickness" Cmnd. 7864 (1980).

[174] S.I. 1982 No. 699.

[175] Social Security and Housing Benefits Act 1982, s. 5(4).

[176] For a detailed coverage of SSP see D. Bonner *et al, Non-Means Tested Benefits: The Legislation* (1990 edn.) and Ogus & Barendt *The Law of Social Security* (3rd edn.), 229-230.

[177] Briefly, the day for which payment is made (1) must form part of a "period of incapacity for work" which itself means a period of at least 4 consecutive days, (2) must fall within a period of entitlement and (3) must be a day on which employee would normally be expected to work (a qualifying day) (Social Security and Housing Benefits Act 1982, ss. 2, 3, 4 as amended by Social Security Act 1985, s. 18; Social Security Act 1986, Sch. 10).

[178] *Ibid.* s. 1(1).

[179] Unless the employee proves he did not participate in nor have a direct interest in the trade dispute.

[180] *Ibid.* Sch. 1, paras. 1, 2, 7. Note also employees, to be eligible at all, must earn more than the minimum earnings on which national insurance contributions are paid.

[181] *Ibid.* s. 1(2)

[182] *Ibid.* s. 7 as amended by Social Security Act 1986, s. 67.

[183] For employees whose earnings exceed £185 p.w. — £52.50 and for those with lower earnings but above the minimum rate on which NI contributions become payable — £43.50.

[184] Social Security Act 1986, s. 52.

[185] See para. 5.55.

[186] See para. 5.55.

[187] See para. 3.26.

[188] Employment Protection Act 1975, s. 36.

who had at least two years' continuous employment) operated in addition to the right to receive state maternity allowance payable by the Department of Social Security.[189] However, this was a cumbersome and unnecessarily complicated procedure[190] and by Part V of the Social Security Act 1986 Statutory Maternity Pay (SMP) was introduced.[191] Provided a woman (1) is earning above the lower limit for National Insurance Contributions,[192] (2) gives, in a prescribed form, medical evidence of pregnancy and (3) gives her employer at least three weeks' notice of leaving work, she is entitled to receive SMP at the lower rate[193] if by the qualifying week[194] she has been employed by that employer for 26 weeks; where she has by the qualifying week been employed by the employer for 2 years she is paid at the higher rate — nine tenths of her week's pay[195] — for the first six weeks of the maximum period of entitlement of 18 weeks.[196] In effect the employer is being cast in the role of an agent for the Department of Social Security and in addition to being entitled to recover all payments made[197] he is entitled to deduct 7.5% to compensate for the extra National Insurance contributions that are due on the paid out on SMP.[198] To further emphasise the employer's role as social security agent, disputes regarding entitlement to SMP lie to an Adjudication officer with rights of appeal to a Social Security Appeal Tribunal.

3.20 *Pay during notice.* Where an employee has been given contractual notice he will have a contractual right to receive his remuneration for the period of notice. Alternatively where his contract is, in the absence of his repudiating his contract, terminated without notice, he is entitled to payment in lieu of notice.[199] Whether such a payment should be gross or net of deductions like income tax would seem to depend on whether the payment is viewed as damages for breach or merely a payment due under the contract. In England it has been held that where an employer has an obligation to pay wages in lieu it is truly a payment of damages and therefore to be net of deductions.[199a] In Scotland the employer has an implied right to end the contract without notice provided wages and other emoluments are paid for in lieu[199b]; arguably such a payment should be gross being the amount due under the contract. In addition however, to

---

[189] For detailed coverage of SMP see Ogus and Barendt, *The Law of Social Security* (3rd edn.) 229-232.

[190] Any state maternity allowance was deducted from maternity pay (EPCA, s. 35(1)) and the employer received a rebate from the Maternity Pay Fund (EPCA, s. 39(1)).

[191] And see Statutory Maternity Pay (General) Regulations 1986 (S.I. 1986 No. 1960).

[192] In 1991 £52.00 p.w.

[193] In 1991 the lower rate was £44.50 p.w.

[194] *I.e.* the fifteenth week before the expected week of confinement (*ibid.*).

[195] Social Security Act 1986, s. 48.

[196] This is reduced by every week the employee continues to work after the sixth week before her expected week of confinement (Social Security Act 1986, s. 47; Statutory Maternity Pay (General) Regulations 1986).

[197] This is done by adjusting the amount of his contribution to the National Insurance Fund.

[198] Statutory Maternity Pay (Compensation of Employers) Regulations. 1987 (S.I. 1987 No. 91).

[199] See paras. 4.2, *et seq*.

[199a] *Foster Wheeler Ltd v. Jackson* [1990] IRLR 412, EAT; *cf. Gothard v. Mirror Group Newspapers Ltd* [1988] IRLR 396, CA.

[199b] See Chapter Four, para. 4.2.

complement the statutory right to minimum periods of notice[200] legislative provision[201] exists to protect the wages of an employee during the period of notice required by statute[202] who gives or receives notice and, in the event of an employer failing to give the statutory notice, an employee's right to receive his remuneration during the period of that notice shall be taken into account in assessing liability for breach of contract.[203] The extent to which an employee's remuneration is protected during notice largely depends on whether or not the employee has "normal working hours".[204] Where an employee has normal working hours he is entitled to be paid during the period of notice at his normal hourly rate[205] if during the period in question (1) he is ready and willing to work but work is not provided, (2) he is incapable of work because of sickness or injury or (3) he is absent from work in accordance with the terms of his employment relating to holidays.[206] Where the employee does not have normal working hours the employer is required to pay not less than a week's pay for each week of notice and this obligation operates while the employee is incapable of work through sickness or injury or is on contractual holiday leave although at other times it is conditional on the employee's readiness and willingness to do enough work to earn a week's pay.[207] However where notice of termination is given by the employee liability to make payment is postponed until the notice expires[208] and no liability at all arises under these provisions[209] where the employee has requested and has been granted time off[210] or takes part in a strike during the notice period.[211]

3.21 *Itemised pay statements.* Every employee has the right to be given by his employer a written itemised pay statement containing particulars of (1) the gross wage or salary,[212] (2) variable or fixed deductions and the purposes for which

---

[200] EPCA, s. 49. Although the minimum periods of notice are prescribed by statute (EPCA, s. 49) the remedy is an action of damages for breach of contract and could now be pursued as an unlawful deduction under the Wages Act 1986 (*Westwood v. Secretary of State for Employment* [1985] ICR 209, HL). And see para. 4.3.

[201] EPCA, s. 50, Sch. 3. The provision does not extend to those employees who are entitled to receive notice of termination which is at least one week more than the minimum prescribed by EPCA, s. 49 (EPCA, s. 50(3)).

[202] EPCA, s. 49.

[203] EPCA, s. 51.

[204] EPCA, Sch. 3. Although "normal working hours" are defined by EPCA, Sch. 14, for calculating a "week's pay" that definition does not extend to Sch. 3 for which it would seem whether an employee has normal working hours would be a matter of fact for an industrial tribunal which would be able to take guidance from Sch. 14.

[205] The normal hourly rate is arrived at by dividing his week's pay by his normal working hours (EPCA, Sch. 3, para. 2).

[206] EPCA, Sch. 3 para. 2. Other payments (SSP, holiday pay etc.) go towards meeting the employer's liability (*ibid.*). And see Sch. 3 paras. 4 (sickness benefit and industrial injuries) and 7 (breach during notice period).

[207] EPCA, Sch. 3 para. 3. Again other payments go towards meeting the employer's liability. And see Sch. 3 paras. 7 (breach during notice) and 4 (sickness benefit).

[208] EPCA, Sch. 3 paras. 2(3), 3(4).

[209] Of course a liability might arise from any agreement.

[210] EPCA, Sch. 3 para. 5.

[211] EPCA, Sch. 3 paras. 6.

[212] But this excludes "tips" because they are not monies paid by the employer under the contract of employment (*Cofone v. Spaghetti House Ltd* [1980] ICR 155, EAT).

they are made,[213] (3) the net wage or salary and (4) where different parts of the net amount are paid in different ways, the amount and method of payment of each part payment.[214] Where a dispute arises as to what particulars ought to have been included in such an itemised statement or where an employer fails to give such a statement application may be made to an industrial tribunal[215] which can (1) confirm, amend or substitute particulars or (2) where an employer fails to give any statement or gives an incomplete statement, make a declaration to that effect and order payment of the aggregate of unnotified deductions made during the thirteen weeks prior to the reference.[216]

3.22 *Deductions from wages and methods of payment.* The law regarding deductions from wages and methods of payment was overhauled by the Wages Act 1986 which repealed the Truck Acts 1831-1940 and the Payment of Wages Act 1960 as well as other legislation dealing with deductions from wages in particular industries.[217] The Truck Acts had provided for the wages of manual workers to be paid only in cash[218] and had imposed strict conditions on deductions from the wages of such workers.[219] However by the 1980s it was debatable whether the tenets of the Truck Acts were in keeping with modern conditions[220] and the Wages Act 1986 removes the special protections conferred on manual workers. Now all workers[221] may be paid in whatever way the parties to the contract choose and most contracts now include an express term;[222] where there is no express term it may be arguable that there is an implied right to be paid in particular way. With regard to deductions,[223] although additional provision is made

---

[213] EPCA, s. 9 permits the omission of particulars of fixed deductions provided the statement contains an aggregate amount of fixed deductions and there has been given to the employee before the issue of the particular pay statement a written standing statement of fixed deduction which gives details of how the aggregate is comprised; standing statements have to be re-issued at intervals of not more than 12 months.

[214] EPCA, s. 8.

[215] Where the employment has ceased the reference must occur within 3 months of it ceasing (EPCA, s. 11(9)).

[216] EPCA, s. 11. The tribunal may make a penal award (*Scott v. Creager* [1979] IRLR 162, EAT). And note that where a deduction is unlawful because it contravenes the Wages Act 1986 the aggregate payments ordered may not exceed the amount of the deduction (WA 1986, s. 6(2)).

[217] Wages Act 1986, s. 32(2). The particular legislation and the extent to which it is repealed set out in Sch. 5, Pt. III.

[218] Although by the Payment of Wages Act 1960 workers could agree to be paid other than by cash they were free to revoke such agreements at any time.

[219] For an interesting survey of the truck system see G. W. Hilton, *The Truck System* (1960).

[220] Ironically in the years leading up to the repeal of the Truck Acts several cases suggested that a measure of protection was still required. See *Riley v. Frisby Ltd* [1982] IRLR 479, *Bristow v. City Petroleum Ltd* [1985] IRLR 459, *Sealand Petroleum Co Ltd v. Barratt* [1986] ICR 423. And see "Deductions from Pay and Repeal of the Truck Acts", Goriely, 1983 ILJ 236.

[221] "Worker" is defined to mean those who work under contracts of service and apprenticeship and other contracts under which an individual undertakes to perform personally any work or services for another party who is not a client or customer of a business carried on by the individual (WA 1986, s. 8(1), (2)).

[222] Where an express term is used it may be advisable to provide for a degree of flexibility.

[223] The same rules apply to payments made by workers (WA, s. 1(2)). WA 1986, s. 8(3) provides "where the total amount of any wages that are paid on any occasion by an employer to any worker . . . is less than the total amount of the wages that are properly payable . . . on that occasion (after deductions) then except in so far as the deficiency is

in respect of retail workers, the basic rules which now apply to all workers (retail and non-retail) provide that no deduction from wages[224] may be made unless (1) it is required or authorised by statute[225] or a relevant provision of the worker's contract, or (2) the worker has previously consented to it in writing.[226] A provision is a relevant position if: (1) it is in a written contract of which a copy has been given to the worker before the deduction is made, or (2) whether the contract is in writing or not and whether the term(s) is (are) express or implied the worker has received written notice of the existence of the term(s) and its (their) effect prior to the deduction being made.[227] The effect of these provisions is that, statutorily authorised deductions excepted, deductions from wages must be consented to by the worker and must be preceded by written notice of the term(s). A failure to comply with these requirements will render the deduction (or payment) unlawful unless covered by one of the following six exceptions relating to deductions (or payments): (1) for reimbursing overpayments of wages or expenses, (2) in consequence of disciplinary proceedings held by virtue of any statutory provisions, (3) the employer is required by statute to make a pay over to a public authority, (4) of sums (typically trade union dues under a check-off agreement[228]) for onward payment to a third person; it should be noted however that this exception is conditional on the worker having consented in writing and the third person (the trade union, in relation to a check-off agreement) notifying the employer of the amounts to be deducted, (5) where the worker has taken part in a strike or other industrial action and the deduction is made on that account[229] (6) for satisfying a court or tribunal order requiring payment to be made by the worker to the employer provided the worker has

attributable to an error of computation the amount of the deficiency shall be treated . . . as a deduction . . . from wages on that occasion". It follows that a total or part failure to pay the wages that are "properly payable" may be characterised as a deduction; and regarding pay in lieu of notice see *Kournavous v. Masterton & Sons* [1990] IRLR 119, EAT.

[224] In this context "wages" are to be given the meaning in WA, s. 7; although various payments are excluded (a loan or advance of wages, expenses in carrying out employment, retirement/compensation for loss of office, redundancy monies, and monies paid other than in his capacity as a worker) "wages" means any sums payable in connection with the worker's employment including emoluments referable to his employment payable under the contract or otherwise, payments under EPCA, ss. 69, 77, 122 (4)(a)-(d), SSP and SMP and have been held to include wages in lieu of notice (*Kournavous v. Masterton & Sons* [1990] IRLR 119, EAT; *cf. Delaney v. Staples* [1991] IRLR 112, CA).

[225] For example legislation regarding national insurance contributions, income tax; and see *Slater v. Grampian Regional Council* 1991 GWD 13-825 and Debtors (Scotland) Act 1987, s. 71 which brings the fee of an employer arrester within WA, s. 1(1)(a). S. 1(6) preserves statutory provisions regulating deductions from payments other than wages.

[226] WA, s. 1(1).

[227] WA, s. 1(3); by s. 1(4) where a contract is varied or consent is given to permit a deduction no retrospective effect is possible. However it is not necessary for a collective agreement which introduces the variation to be in writing but the effect of the new collectively agreed term must be notified in writing to the worker (*York City and District Travel Ltd v. Smith* [1990] ICR 344, EAT).

[228] A check-off agreement is an agreement or understanding between an employer and a trade union whereby the employer agrees (usually as part of a recognition agreement) to deduct union subscriptions from employees who are union members and pay the aggregate amount to the union.

[229] The need for such an exception is arguable because where a worker fails to perform his contract by taking industrial action it is doubtful whether wages are "payable". See WA, s. 7(1) and para. 3.8.

consented in writing.[230] Where a deduction (or payment) falls within one of the above exceptions whether it is lawful depends on the common law or other legislation dealing with deductions.[231] So, for example, where an overpayment has been made whether it can be recovered will depend on whether the payment falls within the *condictio indebiti*[232] and, on the assumption that it can be recovered, whether recovery can take place *via* deduction would turn on whether a contractual term to that effect can be supported by the evidence. On the other hand where a deduction (or payment) does not fall within one of the exceptions its legality is determined by reference to the Wages Act 1986, s. 1(1)-(4) unless the worker is in retail employment in respect of which special provisions are made.

3.23 *Retail workers.* It must be noted that these special provisions are in addition to the general rules about the legality of deductions (and payments) already discussed.[233] Where the worker is employed in retail employment[234] then, except in respect of the final instalment of wages,[235] the maximum deduction (or payment required to the employer by the worker) that may be made on account of one or more cash shortages[236] or stock deficiencies[237] must not exceed one-tenth of the gross wages payable on any occasion.[238] This provision is to protect retail workers who were required to accept a contractual term to the effect that they would suffer a deduction from wages to cover any cash or stock shortages occurring during their employment often whether or not due to their own fault. According to some contractual terms the entire amount of the shortage could be deducted from a single wage payment thereby upsetting the worker's budget and expenditure arrangements. Deductions (and payments) on account of a cash shortage or stock deficiency include those made on account of: (1) the worker's dishonesty or conduct, or (2) any other event in respect of which he (alone or with others) has contractual liability and this is so whether or not the amount reflects the exact shortage or deficiency[239] and special provision is made to avoid the employer pleading that what has occurred is not a deduction from the retail worker's wages but merely part of the method of calculating wages.[240] Also, even if all the other provisions are complied with no deduction (or first

---

[230] WA, s.1(5)(a)-(f).

[231] *E.g.* EPCA, ss. 8-11.

[232] A remedy for recovering money paid under the mistaken belief that it was due; see generally Gloag & Henderson's *Introduction to the Law of Scotland* (9th edn.) para. 14.4 *et seq.*

[233] Thus s. 2(1) provides "Where in accordance with section 1(1) the employer . . . makes a deduction . . .".

[234] By s. 2(2) this means employment (regular or casual) involving (1) carrying out by the worker of retail transactions (*viz.* the sale or supply of goods or services) directly with members of the public or with fellow workers or other individuals in their personal capacities or (2) collection by the worker of amounts payable in connection with retail transactions (*viz.* the sale or supply of goods or services) carried out by other persons directly with members of the public or with fellow workers or other individuals in their personal capacities.

[235] WA, s. 4(2); final instalment of wages mean (1) the wages payable in respet of the last period he is employed prior to termination of his contract excluding any wages referable to an earlier period (for example "lying time" or holiday pay) or (2) pay in lieu of notice if paid after amounts paid in (1) (WA, s. 4(1)).

[236] *Viz.* "a deficit arising in relation to amounts received in connection with retail transactions" (WA, s. 2(2)).

[237] *Viz.* "a stock deficiency arising in the course of retail transactions" (WA, s. 2(2)).

[238] WA, ss. 2(1), 3(4).

[239] WA, s. 4(6).

[240] WA, s. 2(4), (5).

deduction) from wages of a retail worker may be lawfully made later than 12 months after the date the shortage or deficiency was established.[241] On the assumption that the general rules[242] have been complied with the propriety of a retail worker's employer receiving payment for a cash shortage or stock deficiency depends on him satisfying the following conditions — (1) prior written notice to the worker of his total liability in respect of the particular shortage or deficiency, (2) issuing to the worker a written demand for payment on one of his pay days and (3) not demanding payment before the first pay day following a day the worker is notified of his total liability or later than the end of the period of 12 months beginning with the employer establishing the shortage or deficiency.[243]

3.24 *Remedy for unlawful deductions and payments.* The remedy of a worker in respect of unlawful deductions and payments is by way of a complaint to an industrial tribunal "and not otherwise".[244] Like other disputes concerning statutory employment rights a complaint of a contravention of the Wages Act may be conclusively settled by agreement arrived at under the auspices of a Conciliation Officer but any other agreement which purports to exclude or limit the operation of Part I of the Act is void.[245] The following may be the subject of a complaint to an industrial tribunal[246] — (1) deductions from the wages of a worker which are unlawful by virtue of s. 1(1) or s. 2(3),[247] (2) payments received from a worker which are unlawful by virtue of s. 1(2) or s. 3(1), (3) deduction from the wages of retail workers exceeding one-tenth of the gross wages payable and (4) payments received from a retail worker which exceed one tenth of the gross wages payable on the relevant day.[248] Where a tribunal

---

[241] WA, s. 2(3); and in respect of payments by a retail worker to his employer see WA, s. 3(3) which has similar effect and s. 4(4) that no legal proceedings to recover a cash shortage or stock deficiency may be commenced after the period of 12 months referred to in s. 3(3)(b) unless a demand for payment has been made before the expiry of that period.

[242] As contained in WA, s. 1(1), (2).

[243] WA, s. 3(1), (2), (3); s. 3(5) permits an employer to discount amounts for which a demand has been made but not paid in calculating the amount that can be lawfully demanded on subsequent pay days.

[244] WA, s. 6(1). In an unreported decision (*Rickard v. PB Glass Supplies Ltd*, 10/4/89) the Court of Appeal has held that a dispute over the amount of commission payable was a simple common law claim for wages and therefore a contractual claim which was competent in the county court. However Parker LJ also observed that there was no evidence of what wages were "properly payable" and this, presumably, prevented treating as a deduction under WA s. 8(3) the difference between the commission paid and that the worker believed to be due. More recently the EAT has held that for s.8(3) there is no distinction between an undisputed deduction and one which is in dispute because the employer denies liability to make a payment (*Kournavous v. Masterton and Sons Ltd* [1990] IRLR 119).

[245] WA, s.6(1), (3).

[246] A complaint must be presented within 3 months of the deduction or payment although the tribunal may extend this period if timeous presentation was not reasonably practicable (WA. s.5 (2)).

[247] A failure to pay wages in lieu of notice is to be regarded as an unlawful deduction (*Kournavous v. Masterton and Sons Ltd* [1990] IRLR 119, EAT *cf. Delaney v. Staples* [1991] IRLR 112, CA. Also any failure to pay the full wages "payable" *e.g.* by paying less than a Wages Council Order, would give rise to a complaint to a tribunal: *Reid v. Camphill Engravers*. [1990] IRLR 268, EAT.

[248] WA, s. 5(1). Note that by s. 3(4) and (6) the employer's demand for payment need be restricted to one-tenth of the gross wage only where the demand is made "on any pay day". Thus it seems no such restriction operates to demands made on other days. But where a court orders payment to recover a cash shortage or stock deficiency (provided the

upholds a complaint it shall issue a declaration to that effect and, depending on the nature of the employer's unlawful action, order payment or repayment of such amounts as have been deducted or paid in contravention of the Wages Act 1986[249] and although there is no scope for a punitive award of compensation, where a tribunal has ordered payment or repayment by an employer provision is made to prevent the employer recovering the amount of such payments of repayments by raising an action in the civil courts.[250]

3.25 *Wages and other payments in event of employer's insolvency.*[250a] Special statutory provisions exists to protect sums due to an employee in the event of his employer's insolvency; the provisions do two things — (1) treat as preferred debts certain payments due by the employer to the employee;[251] (2) require the Secretary of State for Employment to make payment out of the Redundancy Fund[252] certain payments due to an employee by an insolvent employer.[253]

(1)   A preferred debt is an unsecured debt which ranks before all other secured debts in bankruptcy or winding up.[254] Subject to a statutory maximum [255] the following are treated as preferred debts: (1) remuneration (including commission) payable in respect of the period of four months before the relevant date,[256] (2) accrued holiday pay,[257] (3) guarantee payment,[258] (4) medical suspension pay,[259] (5) pay during certain time-off,[260] (6) statutory sick pay[261] and (7)

employer has complied with the requirements of s. 1(1)(a) or (b)) it shall ensure payment is made at a rate not more than that set out in s. 3 (one-tenth of gross wage) unless payment is ordered after the worker has received his final instalment of wages (WA. s. 4(5)).

[249] WA, s. 5(4). And see s. 5(5) and (6) which require a tribunal to take account of (1) the employer complying with either s. 1(1)(a) or (b) but only with regard to some of the deductions or payments and (2) any monies already paid or repaid to the worker.

[250] WA, s. 5(7), (8). Clearly such civil proceedings would be possible where the employer had a contractual right to receive a payment but in respect of which he has not complied with the relevant provisions of the WA. However a contractual term entitling a payment to be received (without complying with the relevant provisions of the WA) would be void by s. 6(3).

[250a] And see Chapter Four, para. 4.9.

[251] Bankruptcy (Scotland) Act 1985, s. 51(1)(e), Sch. 3 paras. 5, 6.

[252] The Employment Act 1990 merges this with the National Insurance Fund.

[253] For purposes of EPCA ss. 122-126 an employer is insolvent if (a) sequestration is awarded, he executes a trust deed for creditors or enters a composition contract; (b) he has died and a judicial factor is required by Judicial Factors (Scotland) Act 1889, s. 11A to divide insolvent's estate among his creditors or (c) a winding up order is made or a resolution for a voluntary winding up is passed or a receiver is appointed (EPCA, s. 122(2) as amended by Bankruptcy (Scotland) Act 1985).

[254] As to priority among preferred debts see Bankruptcy (Scotland) Act 1985, s. 51(4).

[255] Bankruptcy (Scotland) Act 1985, Sch. 3. paras. 5, 6; Insolvency Act 1986, Sch. 6 paras. 9, 12.

[256] Bankruptcy (Scotland) Act 1985, Sch. 3 para. 5 (1); Insolvency Act 1986, Sch. 6 para. 9. "Relevant date" is defined to mean (a) date of sequestration or date of death (Bankruptcy (Scotland) Act 1985, Sch. 3 para. 7); (b) date of administration order (Insolvency Act 1986, s. 387 (3)(a)); (c) the date of appointment of provisional liquidator or the date of winding up order; (d) date of voluntary winding up resolution and (e) date of appointment of a receiver (s. 387(3)(b)(c)).

[257] Bankruptcy (Scotland) Act 1985, Sch. 3 para. 5; Insolvency Act 1986, Sch. 6, para. 10.

[258] *Ibid.* paras. 9(2), 13(2); and see para. 3.16.

[259] *Ibid.*; and see para. 3.17.

[260] *Ibid.*; and see para. 3.30.

[260] *Ibid.*; and see para. 3.30.

[261] *Ibid.*; and see para. 3.18.

pay due during a protective award.[262] Contributions (payable by employer or employee) to the National Insurance Fund and to certain occupational pensions schemes also rank as preferred debts.[263]

(2)   Although the above debts are preferred the employer's financial position may prevent any payments being made and it is to protect employees[264] against such an eventuality that the Secretary of State for Employment is required to make in respect of employees whose employment has been terminated[265] the following payments[266] out of the Redundancy Fund — (a) arrears of pay (including the payments specified in the Employment Protection (Consolidation) Act 1978, s. 122(4)[267] in respect of up to eight weeks,[268] (b) pay in respect of statutory notice,[269] (c) up to six weeks' holiday pay,[270] (d) basic award of unfair dismissal compensation[271] and (e) a reasonable sum payable as reimbursement of a fee or premium paid by an apprentice or articled clerk.[272] However the total amount payable in respect of any such debts where the amount is referable to a period of time is subject to a maximum weekly limit[273] and on making a payment the Secretary of State is subrogated to any rights the employee has directly against his employer.[274] To receive a payment from the Redundancy Fund a written application must be made to the Secretary of State for Employment who may require a written statement (from the person responsible for the insolvency procedures) of the amount which remains unpaid[275] with a right of complaint to an industrial tribunal in the event of the application being unsuccessful or met only in part.[276]

HOURS OF WORK AND TIME-OFF

3.26 Hours of work — general

Apart from statute providing that an employer must give certain employees written particulars of any terms or conditions of employment relating to hours of work,[277] generally, settling of terms of employment including hours of work is left to the contracting parties. However a contractual right to require an employee

---

[262] *Ibid.*; and see Chapter Nine paras. 9.24 *et seq.*

[263] Bankruptcy (Scotland) Act 1985, s. 55 (1)(e), (2); Insolvency Act 1986, s. 386.

[264] Certain employees are excluded. See EPCA, ss. 141 (2A), 144 (2), (4).

[265] EPCA, s. 122(1)(aa) as inserted by Insolvency Act 1985, s. 218(2).

[266] Note the extent to which a debt is preferred may not be the extent to which it can be claimed from the secretary of state. Compare EPCA, s. 122 (3) with Bankruptcy (Scotland) Act 1985, Sch. 3 paras. 5, 9.

[267] As amended by Insolvency Act 1985, s. 218.

[268] EPCA, s. 122 (3) as substituted by EA 1982, s. 21 (2).

[269] *Ibid.*

[270] *Ibid.* Holiday pay is defined by EPCA, s. 127(3).

[271] *Ibid.*

[272] *Ibid.* And see the provisions in s. 123 for payment by the Secretary of State of unpaid contributions to occupational pension schemes.

[273] EPCA, s. 122(5). Currently, by Employment Protection (Variation of Limits) Order 1991 the weekly limit is £198.00 making a maximum entitlement of arrears of wages of £1584.00 (8 x £198.00); and see *Morris v. Secretary of State for Employment* [1985] 492, EAT (weekly limit to be applied before deductions of income tax and national insurance).

[274] EPCA, s. 125(1).

[275] EPCA, s. 122(10), (11) as substituted by EA 1989 s. 18(2).

[276] EPCA, s. 124(1); the complaint must be submitted within 3 months of the Secretary of State's decision.

[277] EPCA, s. 1.

to work a specified number of hours per week may itself be subordinated to the employer's duty to take reasonable care for the safety of his employees.[278] Such restrictions as legislation imposes are selective and, frequently, subject to extension or modification by the appropriate authority where the circumstances justify a departure from the normal rules. Some restrictions on working hours are to protect the workforce[279] while others are primarily for the protection of the public[280] and breaches of the restrictions attract criminal penalties in some cases for the employee as well as the employer.[281] The extent and effect of such restrictions as do exist vary according to the nature of the work, where it is done and the age of the employees or a combination of these. Most of the statutory restrictions on the employment of females 18 years of age and over have been removed by the Sex Discrimination Act 1986 but note that any legislation for the protection of women (as regards (a) pregnancy or maternity or (b) other risks specifically affecting women) continues to have effect.[282] The statutory provisions affecting hours of work are varied and detailed but the following general rules may be stated.

3.27 *Adults — male and female.* There are presently[282a] very few restrictions on the working hours of adults.[283] The main exceptions are in relation to miners and certain drivers. Although this is subject to suspension or exception in respect of, *inter alia*, emergencies, national danger or economic disturbance due to the demand for coal, [284] no miner[285] may spend more than seven hours a day (including time going to and from his work station) below ground.[286]

The hours of work of drivers engaged in the carriage of passengers or goods by road are subject to different restrictions depending on whether the driving is regulated only by domestic legislation or domestic legislation as amended to accord with EC rules.[287] Whether the hours of work are regulated by EC rules depends on a variety of factors including the number of passengers a vehicle carries, its maximum weight when fully laden, the length of its regular route and whether the driver works only in Britain or in Britain as well as abroad.[288]

---

[278] See *Johnstone v. Bloomsbury Health Authority* [1991] IRLR 118, CA.

[279] See, for example, the Factories Act 1961, s. 86 (limits on the hours of work of young persons while employed in a factory) and the Coal Mines Regulation Act 1908, s. 1 (limits on the time spent underground by a miner).

[280] See, for example, the Transport Act 1968, Part VI (limits on hours of work of drivers of goods and certain public service vehicles).

[281] See Coal Mines Regulation Act 1908, s. 7 as amended by Mines and Quarries Act 1954, s. 187. And see *Anklagemyndigheden v. Hansen & Son, The Times*, August 14, 1990, ECJ.

[282] SDA 1975, s. 51 as substituted by EA 1989, s. 3(3). And note the legislation in EA 1989. Sch. 1 is expressly continued presumably because it is for the protection of women as regards pregnancy etc.

[283] Adults are those 18 years of age and over.

[282a] See the proposed EC Directive on Working Time (OJ 1990 C254/4).

[284] In mines of ironstone, shale or fireclay the limits are slightly longer: Coal Mines Regulation Act 1908, s. 1(1), (7).

[285] For others (deputy, pump-minder, fan-worker, etc.) the period is eight hours a day: Coal Mines Regulation Act 1908, s. 1(7) proviso (a), as amended.

[286] Coal Mines Regulation Act 1908, s. 1(1); the daily limit may be extended by up to 30 minutes at the mine manager's discretion (s. 3).

[287] Transport Act 1968, Part VI (as amended).

[288] See EC Council Regulation 3820/85 and the Community Road Transport Rules (Exemptions) Regulations 1978 S.I. 1978 No. 1158 as amended. For a specialist text reference may be made to Kitchin's *Road Transport Law* (25th edn., 1985).

Where the matter is regulated by domestic law a driver shall not drive[289] certain vehicles[290] on any working day[291] for more than 10 hours and, when he has been on duty[292] for 5½ hours without having had a break of at least 30 minutes, he must have such a break unless the expiry of the spell of 5½ hours coincides with the end of his working day[293] and the working day of a driver shall not exceed 11 hours although that limit may be increased to 12½ hours provided the driver has been off duty for a period(s) of not less than the period by which his working day exceeds 11 hours.[294] The driver's working week[295] must not require him to be on duty[296] for more than 60 hours and in each working week he must be off duty for a period of at least 24 hours.[297]

Where EC rules apply to the vehicle the hours of drivers are also restricted.[298] Thus for goods vehicles[299] the maximum spell of driving shall not exceed 4½ hours without a rest break of at least 45 minutes[300] and the driving period must not normally exceed 9 hours a day nor 90 in 2 consecutive weeks.[301] There must be a daily rest period of (normally) 11 consecutive hours during the 24 hours preceding the spell of driving or at work although these rules differ if the rest is taken at the crew's base or elsewhere and where a bunk is provided.[302] There must be a weekly rest period of 45 hours reducible in some circumstances to 24 hours.[303]

Persons who are employed on successive shift systems in a necessarily continuous process in the sheet glass industry have their shift period limited to 8 hours, and their weekly hours limited to not more than 42 hours with a compulsory interval of 16 hours between shifts.[304] The Baking Industry (Hours of Work) Act 1954 which regulated employment in night bakeries has been repealed.[305]

---

[289] Driving is defined to mean "being at the driving controls of the vehicle for the purpose of controlling its movement whether it is in motion or stationary with the engine running": Transport Act 1968, s. 103(3).

[290] The restrictions relate to driving of vehicles to which Part VI of the Transport Act 1968 relates; these are public service vehicles, vehicles constructed or adapted to carry more than 12 passengers, locomotives, motor tractors or articulated drawing units, or vehicles constructed or adpated to carry goods other than the effects of passengers: Transport Act 1968, s. 98 (2).

[291] Transport Act 1968, s. 103(1). And see *Carter v. Walton* [1985] RTR 378.

[292] Transport Act 1968, s. 103(4).

[293] *Ibid.* s. 96(2)(b).

[294] *ibid.* s. 96(3). The working day of the driver of an express or contract carriage (defined in s. 159(1)) may be extended to 14 hours: s. 96(3)(c)

[295] *Ibid.* s. 103(1).

[296] *Ibid.* s. 103(4).

[297] *Ibid.* s. 96(5), (6).

[298] A provision of domestic law which imposes strict liability on the employer of a driver who breaks EC rules is not unlawful: *Anklagemyndigheden v. Hansen & Son, The Times* August 14, 1990, ECJ.

[299] The permitted hours of work for drivers of passenger vehicles vary slightly.

[300] Council Regulation 3280/85. The requirement for a 45 minute break is modified where breaks are permitted during the 4½ hour spell and on vehicles over 20,000 kgs. the rest periods are longer (*ibid.*).

[301] *Ibid.* There is no weekly maximum but a weekly rest must be taken after not more than 6 days of driving.

[302] *Ibid.*

[303] *ibid.* As to the timing of the rest period see *Kelly v. Shulman, The Times* May 10, 1988.

[304] Hours of Employment (Conventions) Act 1936, s. 3.

[305] SDA 1986, s. 6.

3.28 *Women, young persons and children.* As noted previously the law regarding the employment of women has been radically altered by the Sex Discrimination Act 1986 and the Employment Act 1989. The former[306] removed the restrictions on the employment of women contained in (i) the Hours of Employment (Conventions) Act 1936, s. 1 (employment of women by night in industrial undertakings), (ii) the Mines and Quarries Act 1954 ss. 126, 126(1), 128, 131 (hours of work of women at a mine) and (iii) the Factories Act 1961 ss. 86, 88-102, 106-115 (hours of employment of women in factories), while the latter[307] (i) removed the restrictions on women being employed below ground in a working mine and from being employed on certain work in relation to mining and (ii) amended the Factories Act 1961, s. 20 (prohibition of cleaning of machinery by a woman) and the Offices, Shops and Railway Premises Act 1963, s. 17 (fencing of exposed machinery). The Employment Act 1989 also enacts two mutually dependent provisions — (i) any provision of an Act passed before the Sex Discrimination Act 1975[308] (or an instrument made thereunder) is of no effect if it requires an act which would be unlawful by virtue, *inter alia* of Part II of the Sex Discrimination Act 1975[309] but (ii) nothing in, *inter alia*, Part II of the Sex Discrimination Act 1975 shall render unlawful an act done to comply with a statutory provision concerning the protection of women as regards pregnancy, maternity or other risks specifically affecting women.[310] Although the special provisions for young persons employed as shop assistants have been repealed[311] certain general provisions relating to all shop assistants still remain. Thus shop assistants are entitled to have at least one half day off each week;[312] their meal times are regulated by statute[313] and seats have to be provided for female shop assistants.[314] The prohibition against opening a shop on a Sunday[315] does not apply to Scotland.[316] In keeping with the Government's desire to remove restrictions on recruitment and employment[317] many of the restrictions on the employment of young persons (those over compulsory school leaving age[318] but under 18 years of age) have been removed[319] while others have been amended so as generally not to apply to persons over school leaving age.[320]

[306] SDA 1986, ss. 7, 9.

[307] EA 1989, s. 9.

[308] Acts passed between the SDA 1975 and EA 1989 may be amended or repealed by order of the Secretary of State (EA 1989, s. 2).

[309] EA 1989, s. 1.

[310] SDA 1975, s. 51 as substituted by EA 1989, s. 3. And note the provisions in EA 1989, Sch. 1 which are, in effect, deemed to be for protection of women.

[311] See EA 1989, s. 10, Sch. 3.

[312] Shops Act 1950, s. 17(1).

[313] *Ibid.* s. 19, Third Schedule. As to the application of the rules regarding meal breaks see *Hutchison v. Cumming* 1926 JC 110.

[314] Shops Act 1950, s. 37.

[315] *Ibid.* s. 47.

[316] *Ibid.* s. 66.

[317] See "Building Businesses . . . not Barriers", Chapter Seven (Cmnd. 9794) and the Wages Act 1986, Part II.

[318] Education (Scotland) Act 1980, s. 135.

[319] See EA 1989, s. 10 and Sch. 3 which repeal many provisions including Employment of Women, Young Persons and Children Act 1920, s. 1 (3) (employment of young persons at night in industrial undertakings), Children and Young Persons (Scotland) Act 1937, s. 29 (power to make bye-laws for persons (not children) under 18), the Shops Act 1950, ss. 18, 20, 24-36, 68, 72 (holidays, meal times and hours of employment of young persons), the Mines and Quarries Act 1954, ss. 125-128, 130, 132 (hours of young persons) and the Factories Act 1961, ss. 86-94, 96-109, 112-11, 138, 140 (hours, holidays, occupation of young persons).

[320] See EA 1989, Sch. 3 parts II and III.

The employment of children is strictly regulated to prevent their exploitation, to ensure their safety and to avoid jeopardising their education. Thus a child[321] must not be employed in any factory or at any mine or quarry,[322] and generally the employment of a child under the age of thirteen is forbidden.[323] The hours of work and the type of employment of children over thirteen are also regulated by enactment[324] and local bye-laws.[325] No child may be employed during school hours on any school day or for more than two hours on any school day or Sunday.[326] However, these general restrictions are invariably supplemented by local legislation which may prohibit totally the employment of children in certain specified employments, require the employer of children to observe other conditions in relation to their employment or even raise the age below which children generally may not be employed.[327] Although legislation has been passed which will transfer to the Secretary of State the power to make regulations for the employment of children,[328] such legislation remains inoperative, the matter being still regulated by byelaws.

3.29 Time-off — General

Whether an employee is entitled to time-off work is generally to be settled by the contracting parties although there are several situations in which statutory rights to time-off work operate.[329] However before considering these statutory rights it is necessary to observe that an employee who takes unauthorised time-off will be in breach of this contract as will an employee who fails to return to work after a period of authorised time-off. However an agreement to the effect that an employee's failure to return to work timeously is to be treated as an automatic termination of the contract of employment may be void.[330]

---

[321] For the purpose of the education legislation "child" means a person who is not over school age (Education (Scotland) Act 1962, s. 145(12); Education (Scotland) Act 1980, s. 135(1)). For the purpose of any enactment relating to the prohibition or regulation of the employment of children, any person who is not over school age for the purpose of the Education (Scotland) Act 1980 is deemed to be a child within the meaning of that other enactment. (Education (Scotland) Act 1980, s. 125)).

[322] Education (Scotland) Act 1962, s. 136.

[323] Children and Young Persons (Scotland) Act 1937, s. 28(1)(a) (substituted by the Children Act 1972, s. 1(2). Education authority byelaws may, however, authorise such children to be employed by their parents or guardians in light agricultural or horticultural work and a child may take part in a performance under a licence (*ibid.*).

[324] See the Children and Young Persons (Scotland) Act 1937, Part III (ss. 28-38). See also the Shops Act 1950, s. 27.

[325] Byelaws may be made by education authorities under the Children and Young Persons (Scotland) Act 1937, s. 28(2). These are in addition to any restrictions contained in s. 28(1).

[326] *Ibid.*, s. 28(1)(b), (d), (e). Nor may he be employed before 7 am or after 7 pm on any day: s. 28(1)(c) (substituted by the Children and Young Persons Act 1963, s. 34). He must not be required to lift, carry or move anything so heavy as to be likely to injure him: Children and Young Persons (Scotland) Act 1937, s. 28(1)(f).

[327] *Ibid.*, s. 28(2)(b), (c). For example, the Lothian Region Byelaws provide that no child is to be employed until the education authority has issued an employment certificate to the effect that the proposed employment is not likely to be prejudicial to the child's well-being or to render him unfit to obtain the full benefit of education.

[328] See the Employment of Children Act 1973, s. 1(3), Sch. 1, Part I, para. 5, Part II. The Act received the royal assent on 23 May 1973, but no commencement order had been made under s. 3(4).

[329] And note at common law the right of certain workers to time-off for finding work at the end of a term (*Alexander v. Gardner* (1863) 1 Guthrie's Sh. Ct. Cases 369).

[330] Compare *Igbo v. Johnson Matthey Chemicals Ltd* [1986] IRLR 215, CA with *Logan Salton v. Durham C.C.* [1989] IRLR 99, EAT.

3.30 *Statutory time-off rights*. The rights to time-off for carrying out or participating in trade union duties or activities is dealt with elsewhere.[331] The following other time-off rights have been created:

(1)   An employer must permit employees who hold certain public offices or who are members of certain public bodies to take time off, without pay, to perform their public duties.[332] This provision embraces Justices of the Peace, members of a local authority,[333] a statutory tribunal, a Health Board, a school or college governing body and a river purification board.[334] The amount of time-off to be allowed is whatever is reasonable in the circumstances[335] and although membership of a local authority working party is not to be equated with membership of one of its committees or sub-commitees[336] it is a breach of an employee's right merely to re-time the classes of a lecturer whereby he does the same amount of work.[337]

(2)   An employee who is called for jury service commits an offence if he fails to attend unless he is disqualified, ineligible or excused.[338] Jurors are entitled to receive allowances at rates determined by the Secretary of State.[339]

(3)   An employee who has received notice of dismissal by reason of redundancy and who has sufficient continuous employment to receive a redundancy payment by the time the notice expires is entitled to reasonable time off with pay to look for new work or make arrangements for training for future employment.[340] Although no limit is imposed on the amount of time off to be allowed an employer may not be required to pay more than two fifths of a week's pay in respect of the notice period.[341]

(4)   Safety representatives are entitled to time off with pay for performing certain functions[342] and for undergoing reasonable training having regard to the code of practice approved by the Health and Safety Commission.[343] Payments made under the contract of employment and for time off for trade union duties go towards discharging any liability to make payment to safety representatives.[344]

(5)   A pregnant employee is entitled not to be unreasonably refused[345] time off for an ante-natal care appointment made on the advice of a doctor, midwife or health visitor.[346] For appointments other than the first the employee must if

---

[331] See Chapter Nine.

[332] EPCA, s. 29(1).

[333] And see *Ratcliffe v. Dorset C.C.* [1978] IRLR 191, IT; *R. v. Eden D.C. ex parte Moffat, The Times* November 24, 1988, CA.

[334] *Ibid.*, s. 29(5)(a)

[335] *Ibid.*, s. 29(4). And see Local Government and Housing Act 1989, s. 10 which limits local authorities who choose to pay employees who take time off for public duties.

[336] *R. v. Eden D.C. ex parte Moffat*, The Times November 24, 1988, CA.

[337] *Ratcliffe v. Dorset C.C.* 1978 IRLR 191, IT.

[338] Criminal Procedure (Scotland) Act 1975 s. 99(1) as amended by Law Reform (Miscellaneous Provisions) (Scotland) Act 1980, s. 2(3).

[339] Juries Act 1949 s. 24 as substituted by Law Reform (Miscellaneous Provisions) (Scotland) Act 1980 s. 28, Sch. 2.

[340] EPCA, s. 31; and see *Sutton v. Hawker Siddeley Aviation Ltd* [1978] ICR 1057, EAT.

[341] EPCA, s. 31(9). Contractual and statutory payments are set-off (*ibid.* s. 31(11)).

[342] The functions are set out in Safety Representatives and Safety Committees Regulations 1977, SI 1977 No 500, which also define "safety representatives" and contain provision regarding their appointment.

[343] Safety Representatives and Safety Committee Regulation 1977, reg. 4.

[344] *Ibid.*

[345] See *Gregory v. Tudsbury Ltd* [1982] IRLR 267, IT.

[346] EPCA, s. 31A as added by EA 1980 s. 13.

requested by her employer produce a certificate of pregnancy and an appointment card or similar document.[347] Where an employee is permitted to take time off she is entitled to be paid at the appropriate hourly rate which is to be determined according to statutory rules.[348]

The remedy of an employee who is denied any of these rights is to complain within three months to an industrial tribunal[349] which may make a declaratory order and an order requiring the employer to pay the employee the appropriate amount.[350]

SAFETY

3.31 The nature of the employer's duty

The law of delict imposes on employers a duty to promulgate and operate a reasonably safe system of work. However it is arguable that in some respects a similar duty may be implied into the contract of employment[351] in that an employee is entitled to terminate the contract on being required to do work — within the scope of the contract — if in the circumstances he would be exposed to undue personal risk or danger[352] and in the law of unfair dismissal industrial tribunals are used to accepting that a failure to take reasonable care for the safety of an employee may be a breach of the contract sufficiently material to found a constructive dismissal.[353] This is the result of the decision of the Court of Appeal in *Western Excavating (ECC) Ltd v. Sharp*[354] that for a constructive dismissal the employee must leave because the employer has broken the contract in a material way or has indicated he no longer intends to be bound by it.[355] However, while aspects of an employer's duty of devising and maintaining a reasonably safe system of work may thus be capable of expression as an implied term of the contract of employment it is well established that in its delictual form the duty is personal to the employer and cannot be discharged merely by delegating its performance to a third person, for example another employee.[356] In *McDermid v. Nash Dredging and Reclamation Co Ltd*[357] McDermid was

---

[347] *Ibid.*

[348] EPCA, s. 31A(4), (5) as added by EA 1980, s. 13.

[349] EPCA ss. 30(1), 31(7), 31A(6); Safety Representatives and Safety Committee Regulations 1977, reg. 11(2).

[350] EPCA ss. 30(2), 31(8), 31A(8); Safety Representatives and Safety Committee Regulations 1977, reg. 11(3), (4).

[351] *McKeating v. Frame* 1921 SC 382. In *Matthews v. Kuwait Bechtel Corpn* [1959] 2 QB 57 the Court of Appeal allowed an employee injured in the course of his employment to sue for damages on the footing that the employer was in breach of an implied contractual term to take care for the employee's safety. And see *Johnstone v. Bloomsbury Health Authority* [1991] IRLR 118, CA.

[352] See F. A. Umpherston, *The Law of Master and Servant* (1904) p. 48. *Cf. McKinnon v. Iberia Shipping Co Ltd* 1955 SC 20.

[353] See para. 5. 17.

[354] [1978] ICR 22.

[355] Instances of industrial tribunals holding that unsafe work practices have justified rescission by the employee are — *British Aircraft Corporation v. Austin* [1978] IRLR 332, EAT; *Keys v. Shoefayre Ltd* [1978] IRLR 476, IT; *Graham Oxley Tool Steel Ltd v. Firth* [1980] IRLR 135, EAT; *Dutton & Clark Ltd v. Daley* [1985] IRLR 363, EAT. *Cf. Jageo v. Smiths Industries* [1982] ICR 47, EAT.

[356] *Davie v. New Merton Board Mills Ltd* [1958] 1 QB 210 at 238 *per* Parker L.J. citing *Bain v. Fife Coal Co Ltd* 1935 SC 681. For a detailed text book on the delictual duty see D M Walker, *Delict*.

[357] [1987] ICR 917, HL.

required to work under a tugboat captain who was employed by a subsidiary company of McDermid's employer. He was injured when the tugboat captain failed to operate the system he had devised for McDermid's safety. In holding McDermid's employer personally liable Lord Brandon stated:

> "An employer owed his employee a duty to exercise reasonable care to ensure that the system of work provided for him was a safe one . . . The duty has been described as a personal or non-delegable one, which meant that if it was not performed, it was no defence for the employer to show that he had delegated its performance to a person, whether his servant or not, whom he had reasonably believed to be competent to perform it . . . I cannot accept that (the captain's) negligence had not been negligence in failing to operate the system that he had devised but rather casual negligence in the course of operating the system for which the employers, since (the captain) was not their servant, were not liable. (The captain's) negligence had not been casual but central. It had involved abandoning the safe system and operating in its place a manifestly unsafe system. In the result there had been a failure by the employers in operating a safe system of work."

It is also necessary to note that the common law duties relating to a reasonably safe system of work are distinct from and in addition to the many duties imposed by legislation on employers, occupiers of factories and others. Much protective legislation imposes duties which are enforced by criminal penalties. Thus the general duties of the Health and Safety at Work etc Act 1974 imposed on employers (and others) have no effect on civil law rights and duties[358] whereas certain provisions of other protective legislation may confer civil law rights on the intended beneficiaries of the legislation.[359]

3.32 The scope of the duty

While the duty is framed in general terms — to take care for the safety of employees — it does not extend to a general duty of care to take all reasonable steps to protect an employee's economic welfare while acting in the course of his employment by insuring an employee against special risks or advising of the existence of the risk so that the employee himself may effect appropriate insurance.[360] However, a health authority has been sued by a junior hospital doctor for failing to take reasonable care for his safety by requiring him to work "excessively long continuous periods without adequate provision for rest periods"[361] and it has been held that illness caused by exposure to fellow employees' cigarette smoke can be regarded as an industrial accident.[362] The duty

---

[358] Health and Safety at Work etc. Act 1974, s. 47(1).

[359] *Atkinson v. Newcastle Waterworks* (1877) 2 Ex D 411; *Grant v. NCB* 1956 SC (HL) 48. And see Gloag and Henderson's *Introduction to the Law of Scotland* (9th edn.) para. 34.3.

[360] *Reid v. Rush and Tompkins Group* [1989] IRLR 265, CA; and see *Rutherford v. Radio Rentals* 1990 GWD 28-1612. Note that by the Employers' Liability (Compulsory Insurance) Act 1969 an employer is required to maintain insurance against liability for bodily injury and disease sustained by his employees arising out of and in the course of their employment.

[361] See *Johnstone v. Bloomsbury Health Authority* [1991] IRLR 118, CA. And consider also the possibility of health care workers being exposed to injury by contact with patients infected with HIV unless reasonable precautions are taken. For a full account of exposure to HIV see Southam and Howard, *Aids and Employment Law* (1988).

[362] *The Times*, August 30, 1990.

to take reasonable care for an employee's safety may be conveniently studied by considering it in relation to the following headings —

(a) Safe system of work. Before requiring an employee to carry out work an employer must consider his operations and promulgate a reasonably safe system whereby his commercial objectives may be obtained[363] and where his employee has to work with employees of another employer or self-employed workers the system must embrace the co-ordination of the work.[364] Whether a safe system of work exists is a question of fact which will be influenced by the circumstances of each case, including the known disabilities of particular employees; it is determined by having regard to the standard of reasonable foresight[365] and may include guarding against risk of injury by criminals.[366] However to perform this aspect of his duty an employer need not employ specialist consultants[367] although in some circumstances obtaining sufficient information to appraise the risks an operation might involve could require specialist help.

(b) Competent staff. The personal duty to select competent staff or co-workers[368] is separate from his vicarious liability for a negligent employee acting in the course of his employment. Thus although an employee impliedly warrants his competence to do the job he accepts[369] in an issue with another employee it would seem an employer could not rely on such a warranty. Also, the duty to select competent staff extends to the dismissal of employees who behave in an unsafe way[370] and it has been held to be fair to dismiss an employee whose medical condition was such that a failure on his part could expose his fellow employees to toxic substances.[371]

(c) Plant, equipment and materials. An employer must provide such plant, equipment and materials as are necessary to ensure the employee's safety and to operate a system of maintenance and monitoring to detect failures.[372] However an employer who supplies defective plant, equipment or materials will only be liable for any resulting injury if he knew or ought to have known of the defect[373] and an employee's knowledge of the defect will not necessarily be imputed to the employer,[374] much depending on the responsibilities exercised by the employee. While at common law an employer is not liable for a latent defect which could not be revealed by reasonable inspection, by the Employers' Liability (Defective Equipment) Act 1969 where a defect in equipment, plant or

---

[363] *Sword v. Cameron* (1839) ID 493; *English v. Wilsons and Clyde Coal Co Ltd* 1937 SC (HL) 46.

[364] *McArdle v. Andmac Roofing* [1967] 1 WLR 356, CA; *McDermid v. Nash Dredging and Reclamation Co Ltd* [1987] ICR 917, HL.

[365] *Paris v. Stepney Borough Council* [1951] AC 367, HL.

[366] *Williams v. Grimshaw and Others* [1967] 3 KIR 610; *Houghton v. Hackney Borough Council* [1967] 3 KIR 615.

[367] *Charlton v. Forrest Printing Ink Co Ltd* [1980] IRLR 331, CA.

[368] *Bett v. Dalmeny Oil Co Ltd* (1905) 7 F 787. And see *Tossa Marine Co v. Alfred C. Toepfer Schiffartsgesellschaft GmbH* [1985] 2 Lloyd's Rep. 325 (Court of Appeal while agreeing that the warranty of seaworthiness also required the provision of adequate and competent crew, held it did not require that the employment conditions of the crew complied with the standards of the ITF).

[369] *Pinkerton v. Hollis Bros* 1989 SLT 165, OH.

[370] *Hudson v. Ridge Manufacturing Co Ltd* [1957] 2 QB 348, *per* Streatfield J.

[371] *Sing-Den v. Chloride Metals Ltd* [1976] IRLR 56, IT.

[372] *English v. Wilsons and Clyde Coal Co Ltd* 1937 SC (HL) 46.

[373] *Davie v. New Merton Board Mills* [1959]AC 604, HL.

[374] *Maclean v. Forestry Commission* 1970 SLT 265.

machinery (but not materials[375]) is attributable to the fault[376] of a third party the employer is liable for any resultant personal injury to an employee whether or not the defect could have been detected by the employer. Liability under the Act cannot be excluded by contract, and to the above liabilities in respect of plant, equipment and materials have been added recently enacted provisions relating to product liability.[376a]

(d) Safe place of work. The place of work together with access to and from it must be reasonably safe[377] but the standard of care may vary depending on, for example, whether the work is done outside or inside and whether special clothing is provided[378] and although the fact that the employee works on premises which are outwith his employer's control may affect the standard of care the employer will be expected to attain, it will not absolve him from all responsibility.[379] While it may not be practicable for the employer of a window cleaner to inspect every house where the employee will work the same would not apply to the employer of an employee sent to work at a fairground.[380] Some statutes expressly require employers to provide places for employees to leave clothing not worn during working hours[381] and particular provisions may be interpreted as conferring civil law rights.[382] However in the absence of such statutory provisions an employer's duty does not require that he protects the employee's property against theft[383] although where an employer provides places for storage and safe-keeping of employees property he may be regarded as a (gratuitous) depository[384] with an obligation to take reasonable care.[385]

PROVIDING WORK

3.33 The employer's contractual duties[385a]

Although it may seem purely academic, in certain situations there has arisen the question of whether an employee is entitled to have the opportunity of actually

---

[375] *Loch v. British Leyland (UK) Ltd* 1975 SLT (Notes) 67.

[376] "Fault" means negligence, breach of statutory duty or other act or omission which gives use to liability in damages in Scotland (Employers' Liability (Defective Equipment) Act 1969, s. 1(3)).

[376a] Consumer Protection Act 1987, Sch. 3.

[377] *Brydon v. Stuart* (1855) 2 Macq. 30, HL. *Cf. Ramsay v. George Wimpey & Co Ltd* 1951 SC 692.

[378] *Bradford v. Robinsons Rentals Ltd* [1967] 1 WLR 337.

[379] *McQuilter v. Goulandris Bros Ltd* 1951 SLT (Notes) 75.

[380] Compare *Wilson v. Tyneside Window Cleaning Co* [1978] 2 QB 110, CA with *McDowell v. FMC (Meat) Ltd* [1968] 3 KIR 595.

[381] See, for example, Factories Act 1961, s. 59 and Offices, Shops and Railway Premises Act 1963, s. 12. In *McCarthy v. Daily Mirror Newspapers Ltd* [1949] 1 All ER 801, CA, it was held that the forerunner of s. 59 required protection against risk of theft.

[382] Thus in *Barr v. Cruickshank & Co Ltd* 1959 SLT (Sh. Ct.) 9, the forerunner of s. 59 of Factories Act 1961 was held to confer a civil law action.

[383] *Deyong v. Shenburn* [1946] KB 227, CA; *Edwards v. West Herts Group Hospitals Management Committee* [1957] 1 WLR 415, CA.

[384] The deposit may be provided *prout de jure: Walter v. Scottish and Newcastle Breweries* 1970 SLT (Sh. Ct.) 21.

[385] Bell, *Principles*, ss. 212-218; *Copland v. Brogan* 1916 SC 277 in which it was held that the onus is on the depositary to explain the loss of an item deposited while in his custody or to show he had exercised reasonable care.

[385a] Regarding statutory duties see para. 3.16.

carrying out his work or whether his employer is merely required to pay him his wages and other contractual benefits while denying him the opportunity of working. However the question has a practical dimension. For example in *Langston v. Chrysler (UK) Ltd*[386] because a dispute had arisen between Langston and the Amalgamated Union of Engineering Workers, Chrysler (UK) Ltd suspended him with pay for several months while Langston maintained he had a right not just to contractual benefits but also to do his work. However in spite of *dicta* which seek to elevate the notion of "a right to work"[387] into a legal principle the courts have to date been much more cautious[388] although there is support for the following propositions. (1) While an employee who is paid on a piece-work basis is entitled to receive a constant supply of work until the contract is terminated[389] or to be paid wages as if he was given normal work.[390] (2) In other cases provided the employer pays the wages the employee would have earned under the contract he is not bound to provide work[391] unless from the nature and the circumstances of the employment a term to provide work may be implied.[392] Thus in contracts involving public appearances by the employee a term has been implied that the employer's obligation includes allowing the employee to make public appearances and thereby achieve the enhancement of his reputation which the contract envisaged.[393] Similarly where an employee would quickly lose his expertise or contacts if no opportunity to practise and maintain these were allowed a duty to secure such an opportunity by providing work could be implied.[394] (3) The fact that statute now provides, in a very modest way, for the protection of income during periods when no work is available[395] has not resulted in the general implication of a right to lay off when no work is available.[396] However, although an employer may breach the contract by denying an employee the opportunity of doing his work the employee's remedies would not extend to an order of specific implement.[397]

RESPECT

3.34 The employer's contractual duty

Even the older law while implying into the employment relationship obedience, submission and respect on the part of the employee recognised the employer's duty of "gentleness and moderation in his bearing towards his servant".[398] Thus habitual use of intemperate language or spiteful withholding of privileges or

---

[386] [1974] ICR 180.
[387] See, for example, the judgment of Lord Denning MR in *Langston* (*ibid.*).
[388] And see Kahn-Freund's comment that the "right to work" theory in its present inchoate form is unlikely to be of practical application: [1974] ILJ 186 at 197.
[389] Bell, *Principles*, s. 192; *Cowdenbeath Coal Co v. Drylie* (1886) 3 Sh. Ct. Rep. 3.
[390] *Devonald v. Rosser & Sons* [1906] 2 KB 728, CA.
[391] *Turner v. Sawdon & Co* [1901] 1 KB 653, CA.
[392] *Collier v. Sunday Referee Publishing Co Ltd* [1940] 2 KB 647.
[393] *Herbert Clayton and Jack Waller Ltd v. Oliver* [1930] AC 209, HL.
[394] *Breach v. Epsylon Industries Ltd* [1976] ICR 316, EAT. And see the *Bosworth v. Angus Jowett & Co Ltd* [1977] IRLR 374, (employee entitled to be provided with work until the end of his fixed term contract); and *Hemmings v. International Computers Ltd* [1976] IRLR 37, IT (circumstances in which a term to provide work were summarised).
[395] See para. 3.16.
[396] *Namyslo v. Secretary of State for Employment* [1979] IRLR 450, IT.
[397] See para. 3.57.
[398] Lord Fraser, *Master and Servant* (3rd edn.) p. 120.

benefits from one employee could allow him to rescind;[399] young employees and females particularly were entitled to proper treatment by their employer and an early attempt to protect female workers against sexual harassment is seen in the rule entitling a female employee to rescind her contract should her employer attempt her honour.[400] Modern law regards the relationship of employer and employee as one in which each owes the other a duty of "mutual respect"[401] and the content of such a duty will be largely influenced by the nature of the employment, the status of the employee[402] and contemporary values. Thus courts and tribunals have been prepared to imply into the modern contract of employment terms to the effect that (1) an employer will not, without proper cause, conduct himself in a manner likely seriously to damage the relationship of trust and confidence on which the employment relationship is based,[403] (2) a senior employee is entitled to his employer's support for his authority and status[404] and (3) an employer must not exercise a contractual disciplinary power harshly or unreasonably.[405] However, there is no implied term that an employer shall treat his employees reasonably[406] or that he may not carry out efficiency or work-study tests.[407] However, to these implied contractual terms there have to be added certain statutory rights which are also concerned with a failure to show proper respect towards employees. Thus an employer who sexually or racially harasses an employee will thereby subject the employee to a detriment.[408]

REFERENCES

3.35 The nature of the employer's duties

Unless it is the subject of an express term[409] an employer is not required to give a reference to an employee on completion of employment[410] and if he should give a reference it is protected by qualified privilege.[411] Recently however it has been held in England that an employer owes an employee a duty to take reasonable care to ensure that any reference which is given is accurate.[412] Also

[399] *Ibid.* pp. 120, 121.
[400] *Ibid.* p. 126; *McLean v. Miller* (1832) 5 Deas Rep. 270.
[401] *Wilson v. Racher* [1974] ICR 428, CA; *Palmanor Ltd v. Cedron* [1978] ICR 1008, EAT.
[402] Lord Fraser, *Master and Servant* (3rd edn.) p. 125.
[403] *Courtaulds Northern Textiles Ltd v. Andrew* [1979] IRLR 84, EAT; *Woods v. W M Car Services (Peterborough) Ltd* [1981] ICR 666, EAT. And see *Bliss v. South East Thames Regional Health Authority* [1985] IRLR 308 in which the Court of Appeal held that requiring an employee to undergo a psychiatric examination when there was nothing more than a breakdown of relationships between Bliss and other employees was a breach of the implied duty not to damage trust and confidence.
[404] *Associated Tyre Specialists (Eastern) Ltd v. Waterhouse* [1976] IRLR 386, EAT; *Wigan Borough Council v. Davies* [1979] ICR 411, EAT.
[405] *BBC v. Beckett* [1983] IRLR 43. EAT; *Cawley v. South Wales Electricity Board* [1985] IRLR 89, EAT.
[406] *Post Office v. Roberts* [1980] IRLR 347, EAT.
[407] *Davies v. Richard Johnson & Nephew Ltd* [1934] 51 TLR 115.
[408] *Strathclyde Regional Council v. Porcelli* [1986] ICR 504, IH; *De Souza v. Automobile Association* [1986] ICR 514, CA. And see Chapter Seven.
[409] *Grant v. Ramage & Ferguson Ltd* (1897) 25 R 35 *per* Lord Young at p. 39.
[410] Lord Fraser, *Master and Servant* (3rd edn.) p. 128.
[411] Bell, *Principles*, s. 188.
[412] *Lawton v. BOC Transhield* [1987] ICR 7. Although this decision might dissuade employers from giving references it has to be emphasised that for liability there has to be proof of negligence.

where an employee's record is kept by computer the Data Protection Act 1984 permits an employee (or ex-employee) to have access to the information as well as compensation for any inaccuracies.[413] However the Act does not apply to personal data which consist exclusively of an indication of an employer's intention as opposed to an expression of opinion.[414] Thus whether or not the Act entitles an employee to its remedies might turn on whether the employer's statement is regarded as an indication of intention or the expression of an opinion. It should also be noted that while the Rehabilitation of Offenders Act 1974[415] excuses the non-disclosure of a "spent" conviction it seems that if a spent conviction is disclosed, for example in a reference, the employer can plead *veritas*[416] in an action of defamation unless malice is proved.[417] Where an offer of employment is made "subject to satisfactory references" the question whether the references were satisfactory — was for the prospective employer to determine subjectively.[418]

COMPETENCE AND CAREFUL PERFORMANCE

3.36 Competence

Although there would seem to be a distinction between a competent employee performing his duties carelessly and an incompetent employee performing carefully[419] the distinction has not been developed. Indeed in England the employee's implied duty to perform his work with reasonable care is founded on a case in which the point at issue was whether an employee warranted his competence to perform the work he had undertaken[420] and more recently it has been held in Scotland that the employee's duty of careful performance subsumes capability or competence to perform carefully at his particular job.[421] While most employers today seek to satisfy themselves that employees have the necessary competence for the relevant work, for example by obtaining references and examining qualifications and in some cases requiring job applicants to undergo selection tests, it is implied that the employee has the ordinary skill and competence to perform the job.[422] Thus the employer would be entitled to rescind the

---

[413] Data Protection Act 1984, ss. 21-24.

[414] *Ibid.* s. 1 (3).

[415] S. 4(2), (3).

[416] To be defamatory a statement must be untrue and a plea of *veritas* is simply that the allegedly defamatory statement is true.

[417] Rehabilitation of Offenders Act 1974, s. 8(5); and see *Herbage v. Pressdram* [1984] 1 WLR 1160.

[418] *Wishart v. National Association of Citizens' Advice Bureaux Ltd, The Times* June 25, 1990, CA.

[419] Compare, for example, *Gunn v. Ramsay* 1801 Hume 384 in which it was held that an employer was not entitled to dismiss for incompetence a (careful) cook who had expressly qualified her cooking skills with *Clydesdale Bank v. Beatson* (1882) 10 R 88 in which an otherwise competent bank teller, through want of reasonable care, handed over the wrong denomination of bank notes was held liable for the employer's loss (£900).

[420] Although in *Lister v. Romford Ice and Cold Storage Co Ltd* [1957] AC 555 the House of Lords confirmed it was an implied term that an employee would perform the contract carefully, considerable reliance was placed on *Harmer v. Cornelius* [1858] 5 CBNS 236 which was concerned with the implication of a warranty of competence.

[421] *Pinkerton v. Hollis Bros* 1989 SLT 165, OH.

[422] Bell, *Commentaries* I, 489; Bell, *Principles* ss. 152-154, 178-189; *Gunn v. Ramsay* (1801) Hume 384. But note that in *Heddel v. Duncan*, 5 June 1810 FC it was held the employer could not expect of a 17 year old the prudence of a man where the employee had acted in good faith.

contract of a manager if it could be established that he lacked the competence necessary for performing the managerial tasks required by his contract.[423] However where the employer wishes to employ an expert or an employee with "superior skill" it is up to the employer to satisfy himself that the employee comes up to that higher standard.[424]

3.37 Reasonable care

It is equally clear that an employee must perform his duties with reasonable care.[425] Thus a bank teller who carelessly gave out £1,000 instead of £100 had to account to his employers for the difference.[426] In England it has been held in *Lister v. Romford Ice and Cold Storage Co Ltd*[427] that an employee who carries out his contractual duties negligently may be required to indemnify his employer against claims by a third party injured as a result of the employee's negligence. Following a claim by a fellow employee injured as a result of Lister's negligent driving, Lister's employer's insurers relying on their right of subrogation[428] insisted that Lister's employers sue him for breach of contract, namely, his failure to perform his duties with reasonable care. In partial mollification of this decision British insurance companies have, in a "gentleman's agreement", undertaken not to exercise subrogation rights against employees.[429] However where insurance contracts are not involved the ruling in *Lister*[430] highlights the vulnerability of an employee whose employer (or a liquidator) chooses to exercise his right of indemnity[431] and probably for this reason the English courts have attempted to curtail its impact.[432] Thus in *Harvey v. R. G. O'Dell Ltd*[433] the decision in *Lister* was distinguished on somewhat transparent grounds while in *Morris v. Ford Motor Co Ltd*[434] it was not regarded as just and equitable to force Ford Motor Co Ltd to allow their employee to be sued in their name and, in the industrial setting of the case, there was an implied term which excluded the

---

[423] *Pinkerton v. Hollis Bros* 1989 SLT 165, OH.

[424] Bell, *Principles* s. 153. *Gunn v. Ramsay* (1801) Hume 384; *McNally v. Welltrade* [1978] IRLR 497.

[425] Lord Fraser, *Master and Servant*, (3rd edn.) pp. 68, 69.

[426] *Clydesdale Bank v. Beatson* (1882) 1 Q R 88. And see *Janata Bank v. Ahmed* [1981] ICR 791, CA (bank employee allowed unsecured overdraft facilities without making adequate checks on the crediworthiness of the borrower).

[427] [1957] AC 555, HL.

[428] This is a right almost invariably found in contracts of insurance, indemnity and guarantee to the effect that, in the case of an insurance contract, the insurer is entitled to exercise any rights available to the insured to recover monies paid out under the insurance contract.

[429] There is the proviso that there is no wilful misconduct or collusion and the gentleman's agreement relates only to personal injury claims. See Glanville Williams, "Vicarious Liability and the Master's Indemnity" (1952) 20 MLR 220, 437; G. Gardiner "Reports of Committees', (1959) 22 MLR 652.

[430] By a majority of 3 to 2 their Lordships rejected the plea that if such a right of indemnity existed it was accompanied by the duty that the employer should maintain insurance to cover the employee's potential liability.

[431] See *Janata Bank v. Ahmed* [1981] ICR 791, CA.

[432] Arguably such an exercise should be undertaken by the legislature.

[433] [1958] 2 QB 78. And see *Vandyke v. Fender* [1970] 2 QB 292, CA, *per* Denning MR at p. 303.

[434] [1973] QB 792, CA.

exercise of subrogation rights against employees.[435] How the Scottish courts would react to circumstances similar to those in *Lister* or *Morris* is a matter of conjecture; while the underlying principles are similar[436] whether the attitudes demonstrated by *Morris* and *Harvey v. R. G. O'Dell*[437] would be reflected in Scotland must await further decision.

RESPECT AND OBEDIENCE

3.38 The attitude of the older law

The older law, perhaps because many employees worked in and around their employer's home, stressed the employee's duty of respectful behaviour towards his employer and family. Thus writing in 1882 Lord Fraser stated, "It is the duty of the servant at all times to conduct himself towards his master or mistress in a respectful manner; and there is no ground which the courts of law have been so uniform in holding a valid reason of dismissal as insolence on the part of the servant."[438] And while it was always accepted that the degree of respect required to be exhibited by the employee would depend much on the employer's station and the nature of the work the employee was employed to do, employees have been lawfully dismissed for disrespect in the form of laughing and sneering at their employer's instructions[439] and for demonstrating a "saucy and impertinent manner unbecoming the relative positions of the parties".[440]

3.39 The modern law

Modern employment law having been developed by statutory provisions which seek to redress the inequality often inherent in the contract of employment, for example by enacting laws protecting against unfair dismissal and discrimination, now implies into the contract of employment a duty of "mutual respect"[441] and an obligation not to do anything likely to undermine the trust and confidence on which the employment relationship is based.[442] Thus the extent to which an employee is contractually required to exhibit respect for his employer and other (senior) employees is to be determined having regard to these implied

---

[435] M was injured as a result of the negligence of an employee of Ford Motor Co Ltd; however by the commercial (cleaning) contract between Ford and M's employer (the cleaning contractors) the latter undertook to indemnify Ford against all claims by their own employees even if caused by the negligence of employees of Ford. M recovered damages from Ford which, on the basis of the indemnity, M's employers were required to meet, but the Court of Appeal refused to allow M's employers to subrogate themselves to the right of Ford and thereby recover the award of damages directly from the negligent employee.

[436] There is no Scottish equivalent to the English Civil Liability (Contribution) Act 1978 by which a vicariously liable employer can recover a contribution from the negligent employee. The employer and employee are not jointly and severally liable so s. 3(2) of the Law Reform (Miscellaneous Provisions) Act 1940 does not apply. But see D. M. Walker, *Delict*, (2nd edn.) pp. 125-126.

[437] [1958] 2 QB 78.

[438] *Master and Servant* (3rd edn.) p. 70.

[439] *Ibid.* p. 71.

[440] *Ibid.*

[441] *Wilson v. Racher* [1974] ICR 428, CA; and see para. 3.34.

[442] See para. 3.34. The implication of such a duty is often relied on by an employee to challenge the action of his employer (usually in the context of constructive dismissal).

obligations giving weight to the status of the employee involved[443] with the proviso that an isolated, occasional or provoked outburst of anger or disrespectful language will seldom entitle an employer to rescind the contract and dismiss without notice.[444] However, today the extent to which an employee's disrespect justifies termination of his employment more commonly occurs in the context of unfair dismissal law[445] which permits the fair dismissal of an employee where the reason for his dismissal relates to his conduct[446] or is for some other substantial reason.[447]

3.40 Obedience

The obligation of an employee to carry out his employer's instructions also straddles contract and unfair dismissal law and it is worth noting that although in an unfair dismissal complaint the essence of the matter is whether the employer acted fairly in dismissing the employee the extent of the employee's contractual duties will be relevant.[448] However it is trite law that an employee who deliberately refuses to carry out his employer's clearly communicated[449] and lawful instructions will be in material breach of his contract[450] and where an employer has issued rules or instructions whose purpose is to secure the efficient operation of his undertaking it will be a breach of the employee's implied duty if he sets about interpreting them in an unreasonable manner designed to defeat that purpose. Thus in *Secretary of State for Employment v. ASLEF (No 2)*[451] when members of the trade union ASLEF engaged in industrial action which took the form of a rigid adherence to the British Railways Board Rule Book, which contained 239 rules, they were held to breach the implied term of their contracts that they would "not, in obeying . . . lawful instructions, seek to obey them in a wholly unreasonable way which has the effect of disrupting the system, the efficient running of which (they are) employed to ensure."[452] Similarly, control of the work method is the prerogative of the employer subject to the proviso that any alteration of the work method must not fundamentally change the nature of the employee's job. Thus in *Cresswell v. Board of Inland Revenue*[453] employees who refused to use a computer to do their work which previously had been done manually using pen, paper and pocket calculator were acting in

---

[443] See Lord Fraser, *Master and Servant* (3rd edn.) p. 71.

[444] *Ibid.*; and see *Wilson v. Racher* [1974] ICR 428, CA. Cf. *Pepper v. Webb* [1969] 1 WLR 514, CA.

[445] See Chapter Five. In a contractual context any doubt as to whether the perceived lack of respect justifies termination can be avoided by either giving notice or wages in lieu of notice.

[446] EPCA, s. 57(2)(b). See *Whitlow v. Alkanet Construction* [1975] IRLR 321, IT (employee engaging in sexual activity with managing director's wife).

[447] EPCA, s. 57(1)(b). See *Boychuk v. H. J. Symons (Holdings) Ltd* [1977] IRLR 395, EAT (employer entitled to order the removal of lapel badges displaying the slogan "Lesbians Ignite" as potentially offensive to customers and fellow employees).

[448] *Wicks v. Charles A. Smethurst Ltd* [1973] IRLR 327.

[449] *Thomson v. Douglas* (1807) Hume 392.

[450] Lord Fraser, *Master and Servant* (3rd edn.) pp. 70-73; *Thomson v. Stewart* (1888) 15 R 806.

[451] [1972] 2 QB 455, CA.

[452] *Ibid. per* Roskill LJ. Alternatively by seeking to interpret the employer's instructions in an unreasonable way the employees could have been in breach of their implied duty of faithful service. See in particular the judgment of Buckley LJ.

[453] [1984] IRLR 190, Ch.

breach of contract by not observing their employer's instructions regarding how their tasks should be accomplished.[454]

3.41 Industrial action

In *Secretary of State for Employment v. ASLEF (No. 2)*[455] the industrial action can be described as a "work-to-rule". However most other forms of industrial action are likely to involve a breach of contract with the possible exception of a "work-to-contract" whereby employees deliberately restrict their performance to that which can be required by reference to the express terms of their contract. What must not be overlooked, however, is the ability of courts to supplement contracts by interpretation or implication of terms so that what employees regard as the limits of their contractual obligations are extended. A good example is seen in *Sim v. Rotherham Metropolitan Borough Council*[456] in which school-teachers refused to fill in for absent colleagues believing, in the absence of an express contractual term, they had no obligation to do so. It was held however that Sim, as a secondary schoolteacher had an implied obligation to stand in for absent colleagues on the basis that the contracts of professional employees could not normally be expected to detail the duties of the employee under the contract; the contractual obligations are largely defined by the nature of their professions and teachers have a professional obligation to co-operate in the running of the school in accordance with the timetable and other reasonable administrative arrangements. A strike is a breach of contract,[457] as is "blacking", whereby employees refuse to do particular duties usually as a result of a refusal to handle goods which, for example, have originated from an enterprise involved in a trade dispute[458] and, arguably, "go-slow".[459]

3.42 General limits

Industrial action by employees aside, it is clear that an employer's right to insist that employees carry out his instructions is subject to the following limitations:

(1)   Generally an employee is not required to carry out an instruction which would require him to do work outside the scope of his contract;[460] exceptionally in an emergency an employee is required to accommodate the urgent and necessary requirements of his employer's business.[461] In many cases the parameters of the scope of the contract will be contained in a job description which, either

---

[454] Note, however, the reservation of Walton J that the employer must provide any necessary training but that "it can hardly be considered that to ask an employee to acquire basic skills as to retrieving information from a computer or feeding such information into a computer is something in the slightest esoteric or . . . unusual".

[455] [1972] 2 QB 455, CA.

[456] [1986] ICR 897.

[457] *Simmons v. Hoover Ltd* [1977] ICR 61, EAT. And see paras. 2.14, 3.9.

[458] See, for example, *Hadmor Productions Ltd v. Hamilton* [1982] IRLR 102, HL.

[459] Kahn-Freund maintains in *Labour and the Law* (2nd edn.) p. 265 that a "go-slow" would be a breach of the implied obligation to work at a reasonable speed.

[460] *Moffat v. Boothby* (1894) 11 R 501; *London Borough of Redbridge v. Fishman* [1978] ICR 569, EAT.

[461] *Wilson v. Simpson* (1844) 6 D 1256; *Sim v. Rotherham Metropolitan Borough Council* [1986] ICR 897. And note the unreported decision of the NIRC (1972) in *Smith v. St Andrew's Scottish Ambulance Service* to the effect that it was fair to dismiss an employee who refused to pick up a seriously ill child because the journey could not have completed before the end of his contractual working hours.

expressly or by implication, will have been imported into the contract of employment. In such a case whether a particular function or task falls within the scope of the contract is a matter of interpretation but generally courts will be reluctant to extent an expressed range of specific duties or responsibilities. On the other hand where there is imported into the contract a brief job title or a general description of a particular post an extension to include related duties not previously performed will be relatively easy. Thus where an employee's job title was "clerk/typist" that was wide enough to include an obligation to do photocopying.[462] However it is important to note that in determining the scope of the contract it is necessary to take into account the circumstances surrounding the nomenclature of the job title. Thus in deciding whether an employee whose letter of appointment included the job title "assistant speech therapist" and who had always worked with school children could be required to work with geriatric patients and do a wide range of clerical and other duties, it was necessary to take account of (a) the fact that the employee's initial appointment was in the department of the director of education to whom the employee was responsible, (b) the subsequent actings of the employee and her employers and (c) the type of work the employee had actually done prior to the attempted change of duties.[463]

(2)   An employee is not required to carry out an instruction which would involve him committing an illegal act.[464] Thus an employee cannot be required to falsify a record that his employer requires him to keep.[465] However it has been held that it is not immoral to require employees to participate in broadcasts to a country which operates a policy of apartheid;[466] nor is a medical secretary who was required to type a letter arranging a patient's referral to a consultant to enable the formation of an opinion as to whether the patient's pregnancy should be terminated under the Abortion Act 1967 being required to "participate in any treatment" authorised by that Act.[467]

(3)   An employee is entitled to refuse to carry out an instruction which would expose him to an unreasonable risk which the employment did not contemplate. Thus the crew of a merchant vessel were entitled to refuse to sail the ship to Nagasaki in Japan even although that was within the articles the crew had signed because the ship's cargo (coal) had been declared contraband in the war between Russia and Japan; according to Lord Stormonth-Darling ". . . it had been held that in view of the proximity of belligerent ships, special risks, not covered by the crew's agreements did exist. It is therefore plain that the whole question turned . . . on whether the crew having signed an agreement to serve on an ordinary commercial voyage subject only to the perils of the sea, were justified in refusing to serve after the agreement had been broken by the shipowner requiring them to serve on a voyage, which although within the geo-

---

[462] *Glitz v. Watford Electric Co* [1979] IRLR 89, EAT; *Churcher v. Weyside Engineering (1926) Ltd* [1976] IRLR 402, IT.

[463] *Greater Glasgow Health Board v. Pate* [1983] SLT 90, IH; *Dunbar v. Baillie Bros* 1990 GWD 26-1487. Cf. *London Borough of Redbridge v. Fishman* [1978] ICR 569, EAT.

[464] Lord Fraser, *Master and Servant* (3rd edn.) p. 27.

[465] *Morrish v. Henlys (Folkstone) Ltd* [1973] ICR 482, NIRC.

[466] *British Broadcasting Corporation v. Hearn* [1977] ICR 685, CA. But consider the legislation preventing trade with certain foreign countries.

[467] *R v. Salford Area Health Authority, ex parte Janaway, The Times* December 2, 1988, HL.

graphical limits of the articles, was attended with risks not contemplated by these articles."[468]

FIDELITY

3.43 Introduction

While it does not involve *uberrima fides* (utmost good faith) and, generally, there is no duty on the employee to disclose his own misconduct or that of a fellow employee[469] there is no doubt that there is implied into the contract of employment an obligation of fidelity or loyalty on the employee's part. However as has been observed[470] this branch of the law of Scotland is "somewhat obscure and not fully developed". Perhaps because the limits of the implied obligation are unclear most employers seek to protect themselves against the risk of employees and ex-employees harming their businesses by requiring the employee to agree to an express contractual term — a restrictive covenant — by which such a risk may be eliminated or reduced. Such covenants are treated separately[471] and while, if properly drawn, they are generally more effective than relying on the implied term it is nevertheless necessary to consider the latter which will be of considerable significance where no express clause exists.[472]

3.44 The implied duty

Although the implied duty is couched in general terms of loyal service, litigation tends to relate to (1) restraints on an employee acting in competition with his employer, (2) protection of trade secrets and confidential information against misuse by employees, and (3) the rights of an employee to engage in spare-time work or to obtain earnings from secondary employment.[472a] However, before dealing with these issues it has been stated as a general principle that the loyal employee must, within the sphere of his employment, use all reasonable means to advance his employer's business and refrain from any activity which would injure that business[473] or in slightly different language that the employee has a duty to serve with good faith and fidelity[474] so that where a conflict arises he must place his employer's interests before his own[475] for example by informing his employer that one of his (major) clients is dissatisfied instead of saying nothing and accepting the client's offer of employment.[476] However it must be

---

[468] *Lang v. St Enoch Shipping Co Ltd* 1908 SC 103; and see *Burton v. Pinkerton* (1867) LR 2 Ex 340; *Ferrie v. Western District No 3 Council* [1973] IRLR 162, IT. Also contrast *Ottoman Bank v. Chakarian* [1930] AC 277, PC with *Bouzourou v. Ottoman Bank* [1930] AC 271, PC and *Walmsley v. Udec Refrigeration Ltd* [1972] IRLR 80, IT.

[469] *Sybron Corp v. Rochem Ltd* [1983] IRLR 253, CA.

[470] *Chill Foods (Scotland) Ltd v. Cool Foods Ltd* 1977 SLT 38 at p. 40, *per* Lord Maxwell.

[471] See para. 3.49.

[472] While there is no direct authority it seems that the implied term and the express covenant can co-exist and the former can be relied on in the event of the latter being unenforceable: *Roger Bullivant Ltd v. Ellis* [1987] IRLR 491, CA.

[472a] And see the political restrictions on certain local government employees: Local Government and Housing Act 1989, ss. 1-3.

[473] *Malloch v. Duffy* (1882) 19 SLR 697, OH; *Graham v. R. S. Paton* 1917 1 SLT 66, IH, *per* Lord McKenzie at 69.

[474] *Hivac Ltd v. Park Royal Scientific Instruments Ltd* [1946] Ch 169, CA; *Faccenda Chicken Ltd v. Fowler* [1986] ICR 297.

[475] *Boston Deep Sea Fishing & Ice Co Ltd v. Ansell* (1888) 39 Ch D 339, CA.

[476] *Sanders v. Parry* [1967] 1 WLR 753.

stressed that these are general principles whose effect and impact are largely influenced by the facts and circumstances of the employment[477]

3.45 *Competition.* The implied duty of fidelity does not prevent an employee from purchasing commodities in which his employer deals[478] nor from working as an unskilled employee for a competitor of his employer.[479] Although much will depend on the nature of the employment and the type of work in which the employee is engaged[480] it seems logical that the implied term should not enable the employer to prohibit all employment for a competitor in his spare time during the currency of the contract when such an objective cannot be obtained by an express term after the contract has ended and those decisions which relate the right to work for a competitor to the nature of the employment and the type of work[481] are to be preferred to those which suggest the implied term necessarily precludes any working for a competitor.[482]

3.46 *Confidential information.* Although it is not a crime for an employee dishonestly to exploit his employer's confidential information,[483] unless disclosure can be justified by considering the public interest[484] it is a breach of the employee's implied duty to reveal or misuse his employer's trade secrets or information imparted to him in confidence[485] and an employer to whom an employee (or ex-employee) owed a duty of confidence has a right to protect confidentiality against others (for example other employers) who had received the information with the knowledge that it has originally been communicated in confidence.[486] Clearly whether a duty of confidence exists in respect of information is a question of law[487] and although the limits of the duty will depend on the particular facts of the case it has been observed that "'confidential' does not merely mean secret . . . in this branch of the law the expression 'confidential' relates to information which is the subject of an obligation of confidence".[488] Thus the mere fact that the information has become known to a third party or

---

[477] *Faccenda Chicken Ltd v. Fowler* [1986] ICR 297, *per* Neill LJ at 309.

[478] *Graham v. R. S. Paton Ltd* 1917 1 SLT 66, IH in which Lord President Strathclyde seemed prepared to allow an employee to purchase commodities in which his employer dealt even if he knew this would prejudice the employer.

[479] *Nova Plastics Ltd v. Froggett* [1982] IRLR 146, EAT.

[480] See particularly the judgment of Lord Greene MR in *Hivac Ltd v. Park Royal Scientific Instruments Ltd* [1946] Ch 169, CA.

[481] *Hivac Ltd v. Park Royal Scientific Instruments Ltd, ibid.; Harris and Russell v. Slingsby* [1973] IRLR 221, NIRC; *United Sterling Corporation v. Felton and Mannion* [1974] IRLR 314, Ch; *Nova Plastics Ltd v. Froggett* [1982] IRLR 146, EAT.

[482] E.g. *Malloch v. Duffy* (1882) 19 SLR 697, OH.

[483] *Grant v. Allan* 1988 SLT 11.

[484] *Initial Services Ltd v. Putterill* [1958] 1 QB 396, CA; *Lion Laboratories Ltd v. Evans* [1985] QB 526, CA; *In Re A Company's Application* [1989] IRLR 477.

[485] Lord Fraser, *Master and Servant* (3rd edn.) p. 98; *Robb v. Green* [1895] 2 QB 315, CA in which Lord Esher MR stated ". . . it is impossible to suppose that an [employer] would have put an [employee] into a confidential position of this kind unless he thought that [he] would be bound to use good faith towards [the employer]; or that [the employee] would not know . . . the [employer] would rely on his observance of good faith in the confidential relation between them".

[486] *Lord Advocate v. Scotsman Publications Ltd* 1988 SLT 490, *per* L.J.-C. Ross at 503 where his Lordship also opines that the laws of Scotland and England are to the same effect.

[487] *General Nutritions Ltd v. Yates, The Times,* June 6, 1981.

[488] *Lord Advocate v. Scotsman Publications Ltd* 1988 SLT 490 *per* L. J.-C. Ross at 503.

has been published in some limited way will not *per se* mean that a court will not grant an interdict to prevent further disclosure of confidential information[489] although there must come a stage at which publication has become so widespread that the information can no longer be regarded as confidential.[490] In *Faccenda Chicken Ltd v. Fowler*[491] the Court of Appeal endorsed the rule that after the employment is terminated the implied duty in relation to confidential information — while still in existence — is considerably restricted to the obligation not to misuse or disclose information which is a secret process, design or method or information of a sufficiently high degree of confidentiality to amount to a trade secret unless the information has become part of the ex-employee's own skill or knowledge even though acquired during employment.[492] Where the employment is continuing then the employee must not misuse or disclose (1) information which is imparted to him in confidence, or (2) specific trade secrets even though he knows the information by heart.[493] The extent of the duty varies according to the nature of the contract but would be broken by an employee copying or memorising a list of his employer's customers for transmission to a third party or for use after his employment ended.[494]

3.47 *Confidential information after the contract ends.* The nature of the restriction regarding confidential information after termination of employment is well illustrated by *Faccenda Chicken Ltd v. Fowler* in which Fowler left his position as sales manager of Faccenda Chicken Ltd to set up business selling fresh chickens from refrigerated vans in the same area as that in which Faccenda Chicken Ltd operated a similar business. However Faccenda Chicken Ltd alleged that Fowler in his own enterprise was wrongly making use of their "sales information" comprising (1) the names and addresses of Faccenda's customers and their usual requirements, (2) the most convenient routes for the itinerant refrigerated vans as well as the customers' preferred delivery days and times and (3) the price structure used for respective customers which, they maintained, when taken as a whole constituted confidential information. Neill L. J. re-stated that while the ex-employee's obligation might cover secret processes of manufacture and other information of a high degree of confidentiality so as to amount to a trade secret it probably did not extend to information which was "confidential" only in that had it been disclosed while the contract of employment was subsisting it would have been a breach of the implied duty of fidelity[495] and in order to

---

[489] *Ibid.*; see also *Speed Seal Products Ltd v. Paddington* [1986] 1 All ER 91, CA.

[490] Compare for example *Lord Advocate v. Scotsman Publications Ltd* 1988 SLT 490 (*ante*) with *Att. Gen. v. Guardian Newspapers Ltd (No 2)* [1988] 2 WLR 805.

[491] [1986] ICR 297, CA.

[492] *E.g. United Sterling Corporation Ltd v. Felton and Mannion* [1974] IRLR 314.

[493] *Faccenda Chicken Ltd v. Fowler* [1986] ICR 297, CA; and see *Chill Foods (Scotland) Ltd v. Cool Foods Ltd* 1977 SLT 38, OH.

[494] *Ibid.* And see *Robb v. Green* [1895] 2 QB 315, CA; *Liverpool Victoria Friendly Society v. Houston* (1900) 3 F 42, IH.

[495] And see Cross J. in *Printers & Furnishers Ltd v. Holloway* [1965] RPC 239 at 253 — "In this connection. . . not all information which is given to a servant in confidence and which it would be a breach of his duty for him to disclose to another person during his employment is a trade secret which he can be prevented from using for his own advantage after the employment is over . . . It would have been a breach of duty [for Holloway] to divulge any of the [printing instructions handed to him to be used during his employment] to a stranger while he was employed, but many of these instructions are not really 'trade secrets' at all . . . but in so far as the instructions cannot be called 'trade secrets' and he carried them in his head, he is entitled to use them for his benefit or for the benefit of a future employer."

determine whether after employment the use or disclosure of information may be restricted he identified the following matters requiring consideration — (1) the nature of the employment, (2) the nature of the information, in particular can it be equated with a trade secret, (3) has the employer stressed to the employee the confidentiality of the information and (4) whether the (confidential) information can be easily isolated from that which the ex-employee is free to use and disclose. In the event the sales information was not regarded as having the degree of confidentiality to prevent its use or disclosure because the information was necessarily acquired by Fowler in his employment, was widely known at junior levels (van drivers and secretaries) and the confidential nature of the information had not been emphasised. The approach adopted in *Fowler* has been followed in Scotland in *Harben Pumps Ltd v. Lafferty*.[495a]

3.48 *Spare time working.* Where the contract of employment requires him to be at work the employee must apply himself exclusively to the performance of the contract at the relevant times.[496] Generally therefore employees are free to take on employment at other times subject to two provisos: (1) The other (subsidiary) work does not affect his efficient performance of the original (main) contract. So where a clerk of works engaged for a particular building project took on work for other building contractors and his main employers contended that by doing so he was in breach of his contract Lord Pearson who was unable to accept the contention stated, "of course if the accumulation of other work leads to the inefficient performance of the duties . . . the employer has a remedy . . . Here no suggestion is made that the pursuer's superintendence was in any sense inefficient. There is no stipulation in the contract as to giving whole time; and . . . I do not see my way to reach the conclusion that the remuneration stipulated is so high as to import an obligation to give his full time and take no other job."[497] However, consideration must be given to the possibility of skilled technical, research or senior employees revealing to a competitor, by spare time working, their main employer's technical or manufacturing data in which case a breach of the implied duty is at least arguable[498] whereas other classes of employee will require restrictions on their spare time activity to be the subject of an express clause.[499] (2) Any loss caused to the main employer as a result of subsidiary employment or activity in breach of the implied duty of fidelity is recoverable and secondary earnings or profits have to be accounted for.[500]

3.49 The express covenant

As indicated previously employers frequently seek to protect their interests against the activities of employees and ex-employees by inserting into the contract of employment[501] a clause or covenant which, for example, might restrict the em-

---

[495a] 1989 SLT 752.

[496] *Cameron & Co v. Gibb* (1967) 3 SLR 282.

[497] *Currie v. Glasgow Central Stores Ltd* 1905 12 SLT 651, OH.

[498] *Hivac Ltd v. Park Royal Scientific Instruments* [1946] Ch 169. CA.

[499] *Nova Plastics Ltd v. Froggatt* [1982] IRLR 146, EAT.

[500] *Boston Deep Sea Fishing and Ice Co v. Ansell* [1888] 39 Ch D 339, CA. And see *Reading v. Att. Gen.* 1951 AC 507, HL, in which a resourceful soldier by accompanying, in uniform, vehicles carrying illicit alcohol received about £20,000 when the vehicles, through his presence, avoided being examined by the police. He had no right to retain the money so earned.

[501] Typically, restrictive covenants are part of the contract of employment but equally may be contained in subsidiary or *ad hoc* agreements provided they are referable to the contract of employment: *Stenhouse Australia v. Phillips* [1974] AC 391, PC.

ployee's right to work in his spare time or, more commonly, to engage in new employment after termination of a previous contract.[502] Such restrictive covenants are to be construed fairly and it is the duty of a court to give effect to them as expressed and not to correct their errors and supply their omissions.[502a] Thus where a covenant prevented an employee/shareholder from "carrying on business in competition with the employer/company or any of its subsidiaries" without preventing him from becoming a director or employee of a competing business the Court, emphasising the distinction between an individual carrying on business and a company carrying on business, refused to interdict the employee/shareholder from becoming a director of a competing company;[503] and it has been queried whether a restrictive covenant is binding in a contract of employment which is the subject of the Transfer of Undertakings (Protection of Employment) Regulations 1981.[503a]

3.50 *Pacta illicita.* An employer's right to enforce restrictive covenants is subject to the following two overriding principles: (1) such covenants will be regarded by the courts as *pacta illicita* if the restriction is wider than necessary to protect the legitimate interests of the employer and (2) exclusion of competition *per se* is not a legitimate interest for protection because public policy demands that trade shall be free to everybody.[504] Thus while an employer is not permitted through such a covenant to secure for himself an advantage he would not otherwise be able to secure, he is entitled to prevent an ex-employee taking up particular employment if that is necessary to protect the employer's confidential information or trade connections.[505] In certain circumstances the provisions of the Restrictive Trade Practices Act 1976 may operate to invalidate an agreement.[505a]

3.51 *Reasonableness.* Having been satisfied that the employer has a legitimate interest to protect, it is then necessary to consider whether the particular covenant is reasonable as between the parties and in terms of the public interest.[506] This involves a consideration of the geographical area and the duration of the restraint as well as the duties of the ex-employee. Previous decisions are no more than examples of whether a restriction has been regarded as reasonable in the particular circumstances of the case. Thus a restrictive covenant in the contract of employment of a trainee manager employed by a company which manufactured jeans that for a period of two years after the end of his employment he would not perform any services for any person or business entity in competition with his employers has been held to be reasonable even though the restriction

---

[502] It is also helpful to insert an express clause that on termination the employee will deliver up all papers, property etc. of the employer which may be in his possession.

[502a] See para. 3.52.

[503] *WAC Ltd v. Whillock* [1990] IRLR 23, IH. Also note the (unanswered) question whether the rights of subsidiaries can be protected by means of a contract between the parent company and its employees/directors.

[503a] *Initial Services Ltd v. McCall* 1990, OH (unreported).

[504] *Scottish Farmers Dairy Co (Glasgow) Ltd v. M'Ghee* 1933 SC 148.

[505] See, for example, *A & D Bedrooms Ltd v. Michael* 1984 SLT 297; *Rentokil Ltd v. Hampton* 1982 SLT 422.

[505a] See *Donald Storrie Estate Agency Ltd v. Adams* 1989 SLT 305, OH.

[506] On this latter ground it would seem that individuals who are not parties to an agreement may challenge its validity as it affects them; see *Kores Manufacturing Co Ltd v. Kolok Manufacturing Co Ltd* [1959] Ch 108, CA; *Eastham v. Newcastle United FC Ltd* [1964] Ch 413.

was world-wide and it prevented him from working not merely in the jeans factories or departments of competitors but from being employed at all by a competitor during the short period of the restriction.[507] On the other hand a covenant that for a period of 18 months an employee would not work for any previous or present client of the pursuer's group of companies was held to be unreasonably wide because on the face of it it was world-wide and even if it were treated as applying only to the UK the restriction was too wide because the employee's areas of operation with his previous employer were both in Scotland.[508] While the facts of each case are obviously of great significance a contractual declaration of the reasonableness of a restrictive covenant is likely to be regarded as an illegitimate attempt to oust the jurisdiction of the court and therefore not conclusive and, generally, the reasonableness of a restriction has to be tested at the time the contract is made.[509] An example of a restriction being unreasonable in the public interest can be seen in *Bull v. Pitney-Bowes Ltd*[510] in which breach of the restraint resulted in a retired employee losing pension rights but the effect was to require a future employer to pay Bull an inflated salary to compensate for loss of his pension with the result that the costs of such a future employer would be artificially high and to that extent against the public interest.[511]

3.52 *Enforcement.* Where a covenant is valid[511a] the employer is entitled to prevent an ex-employee from contacting all customers who fall within its scope notwithstanding that some customers no longer wish to patronise the employer.[512] Similarly while an invalid covenant cannot be cured by limiting the extent to which it is to be enforced[513] a covenant which contains several restrictions of which one (or more) is invalid may nevertheless be enforced in its remainder if the invalid restriction(s) can be severed, provided the invalid restriction is capable of removal without adding to or altering what remains and the removal of the invalid parts does not change the character of the contract.[514] However it seems

---

[507] *Bluebell Apparel v. Dickinson* 1980 SLT 157.

[508] *Hinton and Higgs (UK) Ltd v. Murphy* 1989 SLT 450, OH; and see *Spencer v. Marchington* [1988] IRLR 393 in which the covenant which prohibited the ex-employee from being engaged in an employment agency or similar business within a radius of 25 miles of her former employer's place of business in Banbury was held to be too wide because the existing customers of the former employer were all, except one, within a 20 mile radius and, in practice, the restriction not only prevented the ex-employee from servicing customers inside the 25 mile radius but also for quite a distance outside because customers outside the area would look to Oxford or Northampton (within the 25 mile radius) and they would be prevented from going to an agency in which the ex-employee was concerned. And compare *Greer v. Sketchley Ltd* [1979] IRLR 445, CA, with *Littlewoods Organisation Ltd v. Harris* [1977] 1 WLR 1422.

[509] *Hinton and Higgs (UK) Ltd v. Murphy* 1989 SLT 450, OH.

[510] [1967] 1 WLR 273.

[511] Similarly it was pointed out in *Stenhouse Australia Ltd v. Phillips* [1974] AC 391, PC, that a restraint cannot be disguised by permitting an ex-employee to contact any of his former employer's customers provided the pays a premium for each customer solicited.

[511a] It is doubtful whether a restrictive covenant can survive a repudiation by the employer even if there is an express provision to that effect: *Briggs v. Oates* [1990] IRLR 472.

[512] *John Michael Design plc v. Cooke* [1987] ICR 445, CA.

[513] *Agma Chemical Co Ltd v. Hart* 1984 SLT 246, IH.

[514] *Sadler v. Imperial Life Assurance Co of Canada* [1988] IRLR 388; and see *T Lucas & Co Ltd v. Mitchell* [1974] Ch 129, CA; *Rentokil Ltd v. Hampton* 1982 SLT 422 where severance was suggested but rejected.

competent for the parties to agree that if part of a restriction is found to be unenforceable it will nevertheless be applied in its amended or reduced state. Thus where the employer and employee agreed that if "a restriction[515] would be valid if some part thereof were deleted or the period of application reduced, such restriction shall apply with such modifications as may be necessary to make them valid or effective" their agreement was applied by the court which distinguished it from a request that the court re-write the contract.[516]

PATENTS AND COPYRIGHT

3.53 Employee's inventions

As a result of the Patents Act 1977, notwithstanding any other rule of law, any invention[517] made by an employee, as between himself and his employer, is taken to belong to his employer if (a) the invention was made in the course of his normal duties or such other duties as were specifically assigned to him and an invention might reasonably be expected to result from carrying out those duties[518] or (b) the invention was made in the course of the employee's duties and at the time of making the invention, because of the nature of those duties and the responsibilities arising therefrom, the employee had a special obligation to further the interests of his employer's undertaking.[519] However any other invention belongs to the employee.[520] An example of neither condition (a) nor (b) being satisfied is seen in *Reiss Engineering Co Ltd v. Harris*[521] in which it was held that when Harris — who was employed as a sales manager in a company whose business involved the sale, but not the design or manufacture, of valves — invented a new kind of valve the invention belonged to him and not his employer, because he did not make the invention in the course of his normal or specially assigned duties and, unlike a managing director, Harris had no special duty to further his employer's interests. However even though an employer has the right to an invention as a result of either condition (a) or (b) being satisfied he will invalidate the patent if he falsely declares that he and not the employee is the inventor[522] and since the rights of employee and employer to an invention are regulated solely by s. 39 of the 1977 Act no recourse can or need be made to the employee's implied duty of fidelity to determine to whom an invention made by an employee belongs.[523]

---

[515] Which is found to be void.

[516] *Hinton and Higgs (UK) Ltd v. Murphy* 1989 SLT 450, OH. And see *WAC Ltd v. Whillock* [1990] IRLR 23, IH.

[517] An invention is patentable only if it is new, involves an inventive step, is capable of industrial application and the grant of a patent is not excluded by the Patents Act 1977, s. 1(2), (3) (Patents Act 1977, s.1(1)). Certain things are expressly excluded by Patents Act 1977 s.12); *e.g.* (1) scientific theories, schemes for playing a game or doing business and (2) literary, dramatic, musical and artistic works as well as computer programs but those in category (2) are the subject of copyright legislation.

[518] Patents Act 1977, s. 39(1)(a).

[519] *Ibid.* s. 39(1)(b).

[520] *Ibid.* s. 39(2).

[521] [1985] IRLR 232.

[522] Patents Act 1977, s. 13(2).

[523] *Reiss Engineering Ltd v. Harris* [1985] IRLR 232.

3.54 *Reduction of rights and compensation.* Any agreement[524] which purports to reduce an employee's rights to an invention is unenforceable,[525] and it is now provided[526] that where an invention belongs to an employee, nothing done by him in pursuing an application for a patent or performing or working the invention shall be taken to infringe any copyright or design right (in any model or document relating to the invention) to which, as between the employee and his employer, his employer is entitled. This is a useful provision because it attempts to ensure that an employee's rights in his own invention are not sterilized by the exercise of related design rights invested in his employer. Even where an invention of an employee belongs to his employer by virtue of s. 39 of the 1977 Act or where an employee has assigned his rights in an invention to his employer the employee-inventor may apply to the Comptroller-General of Patents, Designs and Trade Marks for an award of compensation under s. 40 of that Act.[527] The amount of the compensation should secure for the employee-inventor "a fair share of . . . the benefit" which the employer has derived or may derive.[528] However an employee's right to apply to the Comptroller-General for compensation is defeated if there is a relevant collective agreement which provides for compensation.[529]

3.55 *Copyright.* Although the law regarding copyright[530] has been substantially overhauled by the Copyright, Designs and Patents Act 1988[531] the law in respect of copyright in literary,[532] dramatic, musical or artistic works made by an employee in the course of his employment remains, in principle, as stated in the Copyright Act 1956 which the exception that the complicated provisions contained in s. 4 (2) of that Act are now removed.[533] Thus where an employee makes such a work in the course of his employment his employer is the first owner of any copyright in the work subject to any agreement[534] to the contrary.[535]

---

[524] Thus it would include contracts other than the contract of employment.

[525] Patents Act 1977, s. 42.

[526] Patents Act 1977, s. 39(3) introduced by the Copyright, Designs and Patents Act 1988, Sch. 5.

[527] However little use is made of this provision. See the Annual Reports of the Comptroller-General for 1986, 87, 88.

[528] Patents Act 1977, s. 41(1); relevant criteria for determining what is a fair share are set out in s. 41(4).

[529] "Collective agreement" has the meaning given by Trade Union and Labour Relations Act 1974, s. 30(1) and an agreement is "relevant" if it is in force at the time of the invention and is made between a trade union, of which the employee is a member, and his employer or an association of which the employer is a member (Patents Act 1977, s. 40(6)).

[530] The advantage of owning the copyright in material is the excusive right to copy the work, show it to the public, broadcast it and alter it (Copyright, Designs and Patents Act 1988, s. 16).

[531] Before any question of copyright can arise there must be a recording "in writing or otherwise" (Copyright, Designs and Patents Act 1988, s. 3(2)).

[532] Note "literary work" explicitly includes a table of compilation and a computer program (*ibid.*, s. 3(1)).

[533] The effect is that what matters now is whether there is a contract of employment or not; questions of whether the author was employed by the proprietor of a newspaper etc. no longer arise.

[534] By using the word "agreement" it would seem an employer's right to be first owner can be qualified not only by a contractual term but, for example a collective agreement or a set of employer's guidelines.

[535] Copyright, Patents and Designs Act 1988, s. 11(2); and see the similar provision in s. 215(3) in respect of a design right.

Accordingly, unless the work is made in the course of his employment an employee will be the first owner of any copyright in it[536] subject to any assignation of copyright prior to the work's creation.[537] It is worth noting that, unlike the Patents Act 1977, the Copyright, Patents and Designs Act 1988 makes no provision for compensating an employee the copyright in whose work is transferred to his employer, although there would seem no reason why matters like compensation could not be part of a modifying agreement.

BREACH OF CONTRACT

3.56 General

Breach of the contract of employment can take many forms, for example, non-payment of wages or requiring an employee to perform duties which are outwith the scope of the contract on the employer's part and disclosing trade secrets or failing to perform his contractual duties with reasonable care on the employee's part. Equally the breach might result in the contract being brought to an end, for example by wrongful dismissal or resignation. Wrongful dismissal means a dismissal in breach of the contract[538] and is to be contrasted with unfair dismissal which generally means a dismissal which does not conform with a statutory standard of fairness and reasonableness.[539] To determine whether or not a dismissal is unfair regard is had to the relevant statutory provisions, as supplemented by any relevant code of practice, and the contract of employment. To determine whether a dismissal is wrongful regard is had to the express and implied terms of the contract. Thus a wrongful dismissal occurs, for example, where an employee's contract is terminated without notice by the employer when the employee's conduct does not justify such an instant or summary dismissal. However, while it is a wrongful dismissal where, absent a breach by the employee, the employer gives insufficient notice, or where the employer prematurely terminates a contract for a fixed period or task, it is not wrongful to dismiss without notice provided wages in lieu are paid.[540]

3.57 Specific performance, interdict and wrongful termination

Because the law regards the contract of employment as one involving a personal relationship based on mutual trust and confidence the full range of contractual remedies is not available. Thus the common law rule that it is inconsistent with personal liberty that contracts which are merely for the performance of work[541] may not be specifically enforced[542] is now endorsed — as far as enforcement against the employee is concerned — by the statutory declaration that "No court

---

[536] *Ibid.* s. 11(1).

[537] *Ibid.* s. 91.

[538] Arguably it also encompasses a dismissal which occurs in breach of special statutory powers although strictly such dismissals are not merely wrongful but "invalid" and therefore of no legal effect; see *Malloch v. Aberdeen Corporation* 1974 SLT 253 and the terminology used therein.

[539] See Chapter Five.

[540] *Graham v. Thomson* (1822) 1 S 309; *Morrison v. Abernethy School Board* (1876) 3 R 945.

[541] Such contracts are termed *mera factae quae in meris faciendi finibus consistent* — contracts which consist of bare performance — as opposed to those which also involve transfer of property rights.

[542] *Stewart v. Stewart* (1832) 10 S 674; *De Francesco v. Barnum* (1890) 45 Ch D 430; *Skerret v. Oliver* (1896) 23 R 468; *Murray v. Dumbarton CC* 1935 SLT 239, OH.

shall by way of (a) an order for specific implement of a contract of employment or (b) an interdict restraining a breach . . . of such a contract compel an
employee to do any work or attend any place for the doing of any work."[543]
The result of the combination of these common law and statutory rules is that
where the breach involves, on the employee's part, a refusal to work (for example by a wrongful resignation) or, on the employer's part, a refusal to employ
(for example by a wrongful dismissal) generally the courts will not grant any
order whose effect would be to compel the continuation of employment[544] or
grant an order which prevents the appointment of a replacement;[545] nor is a
dismissed employee entitled to treat the contract as subsisting and claim wages.[546]

3.58 *Trust and confidence.* Recent decisions of the English courts demonstrate
that an injunction may[547] be granted to restrain or at least postpone a potentially
wrongful dismissal where there is sufficient confidence on the part of the employer in the employee's ability to do the job.[548] Thus in *Hughes v. London
Borough of Southwark*[549] an injunction was granted to restrain the transfer of
employees in breach of their employment contracts from hospital-based jobs to
work in the community because there was no question of their employers having
lost confidence in them; the proposed transfer was necessitated by the employer's
shortage of funds, whereas in *Ali v. London Borough of Southwark*[550] the employer's proposal to discipline Ali was not restrained by injunction because "it
was plain the employers had lost all confidence in (her) to carry out the duties
involved in the caring for others. Although they had not lost that confidence
irrevocably . . . they had lost it for the moment on reasonable grounds . . ."[551]
However, an order which would, in effect, decree specific performance of the
contract of employment has been granted even where it was impossible to
conclude that a workable situation would arise because there was no question
over the competence of the employee who was prepared to given an undertaking that he would work in accordance with his superior's instructions.[552] Similarly, English courts have been prepared to grant injunctions to restrain a dismissal which is wrongful in that it would be in breach of a procedure engrafted
on to a contract of employment.[553] Thus in *Irani v. Southampton and South*

---

[543] TULRA, s. 16. Also although an industrial tribunal may "order" the reinstatement of an
unfairly dismissed employee, breach of the order by the employer only permits the tribunal
to increase the compensation it would otherwise have been empowered to award — no
other penalty can be imposed on the employer (EPCA, ss. 68, 71).

[544] *Murray v. Dumbarton CC* 1935 SLT 239, OH. And see *Warren v. Mendy* [1989] IRLR
210, CA.

[545] *Page One Records Ltd v. Britton* [1968] 1 WLR 157; *Skerret v. Oliver* (1893) 23 R 468.

[546] *First Edinburgh Building Society v. Munro* (1884) 21 SLR 291.

[547] Interdict and injunction are discretionary remedies.

[548] *Hill v. CA Parsons & Co Ltd* 1972 Ch 305, CA; *Powell v. Brent London Borough Council*
[1987] IRLR 407, CA.

[549] [1987] IRLR 55.

[550] [1989] ICR 567.

[551] *Per* Millet J. at 582; and see *Chappell v. Times Newspapers Ltd* [1975] IRLR 90, CA.

[552] *Wadcock v. London Borough of Brent* [1990] IRLR 223.

[553] *R. v. BBC ex parte Lavelle* [1982] IRLR 404; A similar attitude was displayed in *Dietman
v. Brent London Borough Council* [1987] ICR 737 (affirmed [1988] ICR 842, CA) although ultimately Hodgson J would have refused the injunction because the dismissed
employee did not make her position clear at an early stage and thereby prevented the
employer from adopting the correct contractual procedure. And see *Wadcock v. London
Borough of Brent* [1990] IRLR 223.

West Hampshire Health Authority[554] the Health Authority was restrained by injunction from dismissing Irani without using the contractual procedures for resolving disputes between the employer and employees in circumstances in which there was no criticism of Irani's conduct or professional competence because damages would not have been an adequate remedy. However where the essential mutual trust and confidence has been lost the remedy for a wrongful dismissal is damages. Indeed where an employee is dismissed with wages and other contractual benefits paid in lieu of notice no action for damages will lie on the basis that the employer has an implied right to terminate the contract.[555]

3.59 Other breaches of the contract and interdict

Where the breach does not involve a wrongful termination of the contract with the result that the victim of the breach is not seeking to prolong a relationship which has broken down, interdict to restrain the breach of a particular term of the contract will more readily be granted. Accordingly it is common for an employee or ex-employee to be interdicted against working for a competitor in his spare time by virtue of his implied duty of fidelity or after the contract's termination by virtue of a restrictive covenant.[556] However, as a general rule interdict will not be granted to enforce a negative stipulation if it would have the effect of forcing the employee to work for the employer or to starve through being idle.[557] However, it may be possible to obviate the alternative of enforced idleness by offering to continue to pay the employee his full contractual benefits during the period for which the interdict is sought. Thus in *Evening Standard Ltd v. Henderson*,[558] in which Lawton L.J. suggested the law required fresh examination to reflect modern conditions,[559] Henderson was required by his contract to give a year's notice and not to work for any other company without his employer's permission but, having been offered a position with a competing newspaper, he gave his employers only two months' notice. Evening Standard Ltd were granted an injunction which restrained him from taking up his new employment until the expiry of his proper period of notice and the court's decision to grant the injunction was clearly influenced by Henderson's employers' willingness to provide him with all of his contractual benefits until the contract expired without (a) insisting that he performed his contractual obligations or (b) claiming damages for the period during which he did not work for them. More

---

[554] [1985] ICR 590; and see *Jones v. Lee and Guilding* [1980] IRLR 67, CA.

[555] *Graham v. Thomson* (1822) 1 S 309. However, it appears the employee does not have an equivalent right of termination (*Wallace v. Wishart* 1800 Hume 383). In England it seems that unless the contract expressly provides for termination by payment in lieu of notice, what the employee receives is treated as damages for breach of contract — see *Rex Stewart Jeffries Parker Ginsberg Ltd v. Parker* [1988] IRLR 483, CA, in which *Dixon v. Stenor* [1973] IRLR 28, NIRC, is distinguished, and *Delaney v. Staples* [1991] IRLR 112, CA.

[556] See para. 3.34.

[557] *Warner Brothers Pictures Inc v. Nelson* [1937] 1 KB 209.

[558] [1987] ICR 588, CA.

[559] At p. 594 Lawton L.J. stated "There is a great temptation for employees . . . to break their contracts and go to other employers, usually for higher salaries and when they do (assuming there is no question of confidential information), as the law stands at present, they can . . . say: 'You cannot obtain an injunction against me which will have the effect of forcing me either to come back and work out my notice or starve, and it is no good you talking . . . about damages because in the real world damages are impossible to quantify'. All the risk they are running in this kind of situation is that they will have to pay the costs of any legal proceedings . . . It is time that some court examined the matter fully."

recently in *Warren v. Mendy*[560] the Court of Appeal has re-affirmed the rule that enforcement of negative obligations will not be permitted if its effect will be to compel an employee to perform his positive obligation and has stated whether such compulsion exists is to be decided by having regard to the psychological, material and physical needs of the employee to maintain his skill and talent; the longer the period for which the injunction is sought, the more readily will compulsion be inferred; compulsion may be inferred where the injunction is sought, not against the employee, but a third party (another employer); and an employee's claim that he will be compelled to perform the contract's positive obligations should be examined sceptically, but once satisfied such compulsion exists, the court should refuse the employer's application for an injunction. Although it is competent for the Court of Session to make the equivalent of an "Anton Piller" order[560a] caution has been urged in the use of such orders in the context of employment.[560b]

3.60 Damages

Generally,[561] any breach of the contract will sound in damages; at the very least, nominal damages will be due.[562] An action for damages may be combined with the remedies of rescission where the breach is so serious as to amount to a repudiation of the contract,[563] interdict, lien and retention[564] or may be brought as a separate independent action. At common law it is an implied term of the contract of employment that the employer is entitled to dismiss without notice provided he pays wages and other contractual benefits due to the employee in lieu of notice.[565] Accordingly, in the ordinary case,[566] no action for damages will lie because no breach will have occurred.[567] Also while a contractual provision may restrict or exclude liability in respect of breach of contract such a provision may be rendered void by the Unfair Contract Terms Act 1977.[567a]

3.61 *Measure of damages.* Where damages are due the amount or measure of damages is determined according to the normal rules of ordinary and special

---

[560] [1989] IRLR 210, CA.

[560a] See MacPhail on *Evidence* (1987), 25.07.

[560b] *Lock International plc v. Beswick* [1990] IRLR 481.

[561] The main exception is in relation to late payment of money (Bell, *Principles*, s. 32); but see para. 3.10, n. 94.

[562] *Webster & Co v. Crammond Iron Co* (1875) 2 R 752; *Fife Coal Co Ltd v. McBain* 1935 SLT (Sh. Ct.) 6.

[563] See Chapter Four.

[564] See para. 3.8.

[565] See para. 3.59 and consider to what extent such an implied term is consistent with EPCA, s. 49(3) which on the one hand overrides contractual provisions for periods shorter than those set out in s. 49(1) and on the other hand expressly preserves an employee's right of "*accepting* a payment in lieu of notice." See the interesting arguments canvassed by M. R. Freedland, *The Contract of Employment* pp. 185-189. And see *Trotter v. Forth Ports Authority* 1991 GWD 17-1045 that s. 49(3) does not prevent waiving right to pay in lieu of notice as distinct from waiving right to notice itself.

[566] *Cf. Dunk v. George Waller & Son Ltd* [1970] 2 QB 163 (contract of apprenticeship), *Herbert Clayton and Jack Waller Ltd v. Oliver* [1930] AC 209, HL (contract involving an element of publicity that would enhance the employee's reputation).

[567] *Graham v. Thomson* (1822) 1 S 309.

[567a] See *Chapman v. Aberdeen Construction Group plc* 1990 GWD 18-1012; *Micklefield v. SAC Technology Ltd* [1990] IRLR 218.

damages.[568] The result of the application of those rules is that here the breach takes the form of a wrongful dismissal, damages will normally be the wages and other emoluments the employee would have received had the contract been performed in the least burdensome way by the employer.[569] Therefore, where a contract of employment can be terminated by giving notice, the employee's damages will not exceed what he could have earned during the period of notice to which he was contractually entitled.[570] Where the contract is for a fixed period with no provision for termination by notice before the expiry of the fixed term, damages will reflect the wages or salary and other parts of a remuneration package the employee would have received had the contract been allowed to run its full course, subject always to the employee's duty to mitigate his loss.[571] Damages will include all the parts of a remuneration package to which the employee was contractually entitled[572] and have been held to include the loss of (1) a subscription to a private health insurance scheme, (2) the free use of a car,[572a] (3) pension and insurance benefits, (4) rent-free accommodation and an entitlement to a share in profits.[573] However, damages will include neither the loss of a pay rise awarded after a wrongful dismissal because the dismissed employee would not have had a contractual right to it,[574] nor the expenses of submitting an unfair dismissal complaint,[575] on the ground that it could not be reasonably foreseen at the time of contracting. Similarly while a breach of contract — particularly a wrongful dismissal — may cause the innocent party to suffer injury to his feelings, the current view is that damages for breach of the contract of employment will not reflect such injury.[576] On the other hand damages

---

[568] For a concise statement of these rules see Gloag and Henderson's *Introduction to the Law of Scotland* (9th edn.) para. 13.28.

[569] *Baird v. Banff District Lunacy Board* 1914 SLT 284; *British Guiana Credit Corpn v. da Silva* [1965] 1 WLR 248, PC. *Cf. Rigby v. Ferodo Ltd* [1988] ICR 29, HL that limitation of damages to the notice period does not apply where the employee has not been dismissed and has chosen not to rescind in face of breach by the employer.

[570] And note the equivalent statutory provision in EPCA, s. 51 (in respect of employees covered by it) that damages for breach of contract will take into account the rights conferred by EPCA, s. 50.

[571] See, for example, *Yetton v. Eastwoods Froy Ltd* [1967] 1 WLR 104.

[572] However they will not include unpaid employee contributions to a pension scheme on the basis that being obliged to make the contributions they would not have formed part of his disposable income (*Dews v. NCB* [1987] IRLR, HL).

[572a] Regarding damages for loss of car see *Cull v. Oilfield Inspection Services Group plc* 1990 SLT 205, OH.

[573] *Baird v. Banff and District Lunacy Board* 1914 1 SLT 284; *Re Rubel Bronze and Metal Co and Vos* [1918] 1 KB 315; *Lindsay v. Queen's Hotel Co* [1919] 1 KB 212, DC; *Shove v. Downs Surgical plc* [1984] ICR 532.

[574] *Lavarack v. Woods of Colchester Ltd* [1967] 1 QB 278, CA. *Cf. Cull v. Oilfield Inspection Group plc* 1990 SLT 205, OH in which the pursuer failed to prove "a real likelihood" of salary increase.

[575] *Blyth v. Scottish Liberal Club* 1983 SLT 260, IH.

[576] *Addis v. Gramophone Co Ltd* [1909] AC 488, HL. In *Bliss v. SE Thames Regional Health Authority* [1988] ICR 700, CA, Dillon LJ disapproved of *Cox v. Philips Industries Ltd* [1976] ICR 138 and affirmed that standing the decision in *Addis* it was not possible for damages for breach of the contract of employment to include an award in respect of distress, vexation, frustration and consequent ill-health which were the result of the breach. See too *O'Laoire v. Jackel International Ltd* [1991] IRLR 170, CA. *Cf. Diesen v. Samson* 1971 SLT (Sh Ct) 49; *Heywood v. Wellers* [1976] QB 446. And note the contrary view expressed by Lord Fraser, *Master and Servant* (3rd edn.) p. 135.

will be awarded for the loss of statutory rights which are conditional on a period of continuous employment which was interrupted by a wrongful dismissal.[577]

Where the employee is in breach of contract whether a loss sustained by the employer will sound in damages depends on whether, taking account of the circumstances, it arose naturally from the breach or whether it could have been contemplated by the parties at the time of contracting.[578] Thus where an employee, without whose presence other employees are not permitted to work, refuses to work a shift the employer's loss will not be restricted to the cost of hiring a replacement but may extend to the loss of profit which the shift would have produced.[579] Where an employee receives the benefits of a training course at his employer's expense, to ensure he (the employer) derives some value from the employee's attendance at the course, he may require him to repay a proportion of the training or college fees in the event of his leaving his employment in breach of contract provided the obligation to repay is not regarded as a penalty.[580] Furthermore unless it is part of a clause of liquidated damage[581] the withholding of wages will not preclude recovery of additional losses by way of damages[582] although any wages or other contractual entitlements so withheld will be set off against the employer's loss arising from breach of the contract.[583]

3.62 Mitigation, taxation and receipt of benefits

The amount of damages recoverable however is also influenced by (1) the principle of mitigation of loss, (2) the incidence of taxation and (3) the receipt by the victim of the breach of benefits which arise as a consequence of the breach.

(a) Mitigation of loss. The victim of a breach of any contract is able to recover in damages only such losses which he could not reasonably avoid.[584] As has been remarked[585] it is inaccurate to talk of the victim of the breach having a "duty" to mitigate his loss; strictly, an employee who is dismissed in breach of his contract is entitled to remain idle and not seek other employment provided he recognises that by failing to take reasonable steps to obtain other employment he accepts that any award of damages he receives will be reduced accordingly.[586] What steps

---

[577] *Basnett v. J & A Jackson Ltd* [1976] ICR 63.

[578] *NCB v. Galley* [1958] 1 WLR 16, CA.

[579] *Ibid.*

[580] *Strathclyde Regional Council v. Neil* 1983 SLT (Sh Ct) 89; applied in *Electronic Data Systems Ltd v. Hubble* (*Financial Times* February 4, 1987) in which H's undertaking that if he left his employers within 2 year of completing a training course he would pay them £4,500 was enforced; it was not a penalty as it represented only a fraction of the real cost of the training programme.

[581] Contracting parties are free to stipulate that breach of a contract will require a specified amount to be paid by way of liquidated damages; such stipulations will be enforced provided they are not construed as penalties. On penalty clause and liquidated damages see generally Gloag and Henderson's *Introduction to Law of Scotland* (9th edn.) paras. 13.21-13.24.

[582] *Dingwall v. Burnett* 1912 SC 1097; *Gaumont-British Picture Corp Ltd v. Alexander* [1936] 2 All ER 1686.

[583] Lord Fraser, *Master and Servant* (3rd edn.) p. 113.

[584] *Ross v. McFarlane* (1894) 21 R 396; *Yetton v. Eastwoods Froy Ltd* [1967] 1 WLR 104. But note that conduct of the victim prior to the breach is irrelevant: *Prestwick Circuits Ltd v. McAndrew* [1990] IRLR 191, IH.

[585] W. W. McBryde, *The Law of Contract in Scotland*, paras. 20-28, 20-29.

[586] In fairness to L. J.-C. McDonald with whom McBryde disagrees (*ibid.*) a complete quotation leaves the reader in no doubt. Thus while his lordship did say an employee "was not entitled to sit idle and make no effort to find suitable employment" he adds in the next sentence "He must fairly and reasonably exert himself to earn his living, and can only come against the defender for the loss he sustains from his inability to secure a position as good as that which he (lost)".

are reasonable depends on the circumstances of each case[587] but generally an employer's damages will be reduced if he fails to seek a replacement employee just as the employee's damages will be reduced if he fails to seek other employment. Thus where an employee was wrongfully dismissed and a question arose whether he should have accepted alternative employment with the dismissing employers Crichton J opined "The test is this — Did the plaintiff act unreasonably in not taking up this lower-paid and lower-grade job? I have come to the conclusion that he did not. It was not incumbent upon him, having been a works manager, at the age of 59, to have to take a much humbler and less well-rewarded job especially with the defendants themselves and working with people who had been junior to him and would now be senior. I find he was not unreasonable."[588] However it is submitted that in the case of a contract for a fixed term, although during the period soon after the breach the dismissed employee will be able to reject employment on terms less favourable than those of the contract unlawfully terminated, eventually he may be reasonably expected to consider less well rewarded positions.[589] Similarly a dismissed employee might reasonably be expected to claim any statutory benefits to which he is entitled.[590]

(b) Incidence of taxation. Since the purpose of an award of damages is to compensate it is necessary to take into account, in the case where the employee is prevented from performing the contract, the income tax he would have had to pay on his earnings had the contract been allowed to run its course; if such taxation was not taken into account clearly a dismissed employee would on receipt of an award of damages be in a better position than if he had earned the money.[591] However although it is settled that taxation has to be taken into account, until recently the methods adopted have varied due principally to the provisions of the Income and Corporation Taxes Act 1988,[592] which requires that awards of compensation for loss of employment in excess of £30,000 be taxed. Thus where the award of damages exceeds that figure the court will require to take account of the income tax the employee would have paid if his contract had not been broken and the tax on the award of damages itself for which he will have to account to the Inland Revenue. The method adopted in Scotland is exemplified by *Stewart v. Glentaggart Ltd*[593] in which Lord Hunter, having arrived at a figure to compensate for the employee's loss, deducted therefrom an estimate of the income tax the employee would have had to pay had the contract not been unlawfully terminated, then observed that that figure would then have been subject to taxation as an award of damages so that after such taxation had been recovered by the Inland Revenue the victim of the breach would have been left with less than the figure required to compensate him for his loss and to avoid such a situation his lordship proceeded to add on to the sum left after deducting income tax such sum as the recipient would have to

---

[587] *Ross v. McFarlane* (1894) 21 R 396.

[588] *Basnett v. J. & A. Jackson* [1976] ICR 63.

[589] *Ibid.*; and see *Yetton v. Eastwoods Froy* [1967] 1 WLR 104.

[590] *Parsons v. BNM Laboratories Ltd* [1964] 1 QB 95 (Unemployment Benefit); *Basnett v. J. & A. Jackson Ltd* [1976] IRLR 154 (Supplementary Benefit).

[591] *British Transport Commission v. Gourley* [1956] AC 185, HL; *Spencer v. McMillan's Trs* 1958 SC 300; *Stewart v. Glentaggart Ltd* 1963 SLT 119.

[592] Ss. 148, 188.

[593] 1963 SLT 119. And see *Cull v. Oilfield Inspection Services Group plc* 1990 SLT 205, OH, in which it was held that the effect of ss. 148, 188 rendered the application of a multiplier (1.5) to Cull's salary inappropriate for calculating damages for breach of contract.

pay by way of tax on the award itself. For example, assume an employee's loss is £60,000.

Stage 1	
Loss of earnings	£60,000
Stage 2	
Deduct Income Tax, say	£20,000
	£40,000
Stage 3	
Since net award exceeds £30,000, Add estimate of tax on damages, say	£ 4,000
Total award	£44,000

Although this method involves a fair amount of estimate and prediction these are the hallmarks of many awards of compensation.[594]

(c) Benefits arising on the breach. Where the victim of a breach of the contract receives a payment or benefit in respect of the period to which the damages relate, the question arises should such payments or benefits be deducted in arriving at the net award of damages. Similar questions arise in delictual actions for personal injuries[595] and the principles applicable in those cases are generally[596] the same as those which require to be taken into account where the damages result from a breach of contract. Thus in *Redpath v. Belfast and County Down Rly*[597] Andrews CJ opined in a statement approved by Lord Reid in *Parry v. Cleaver:*[598] "Admittedly the present case differs from *British Westinghouse Electric and Manufacturing Co Ltd v. Underground Electric Railways of London Ltd*[599] . . . in one important respect, namely, that it was an action for breach of contract whilst in the present case we are concerned with the measure of damages in an action of tort; but I am unable to appreciate why any different principle should apply. The important consideration common to all cases, is that the circumstance relied upon in mitigation of damages arose independently of the cause of action, and was not naturally attributable to it. The defendants' wrongful act may in each case have been a *causa sine qua non* but in no true sense was it the *causa causans* of the circumstance relied on in mitigation of damages." The operation of the above principle can be seen in *Lavarack v. Woods of Colchester Ltd*[600] in which, as a result of Lavarack's wrongful dismissal he was released from a restrictive covenant in his contract of employment. This enabled him to take up employment with a company named Martindale in which he also acquired shares. He also acquired shares in another company (Ventilation) and the value of both holdings increased. Clearly while the salary he received by working for Martindale had to be taken into account

---

[594] A similar method has been adopted in England: *Shove v. Downs Surgical plc* [1984] ICR 532.

[595] See, for example, *Parry v. Cleaver* [1970] AC 1, HL; *Wilson v. NCB* 1981 SLT 67, HL; *Hodgson v. Trapp, The Times* November 14, 1988, HL. On the need to take account of mitigating benefits or payments see A. S. Burrows, *Remedies for Torts and Breach of Contract* (1987) pp. 106-115.

[596] *Cf.* Law Reform (Personal Injuries) Act 1948 s. 2; Administration of Justice Act 1982, s. 10.

[597] [1947] NI 167 at p. 187.

[598] [1970] AC 1 at p. 14.

[599] [1912] AC 673.

[600] [1967] 1 QB 278.

the Court of Appeal held that only the increased value of the shares in Martindale had to be deducted from the loss occasioned by the wrongful dismissal.[601] Where the victim of the breach receives incidental payments or benefits it is the net gain of which account must be taken. Thus in *Westwood v. Secretary of State for Employment*[602] W. was dismissed without notice or pay in lieu thereof when his contract entitled him to receive 12 weeks' notice of termination. He became entitled to unemployment benefit for one year, followed, on exhaustion, by supplementary benefit at a lower rate and the House of Lords held that there should be deducted from damages in respect of the 12 weeks for which he received neither notice nor pay in lieu his net gain, namely, not what W. actually received by way of unemployment benefit but the lesser sum he received by way of supplementary benefit after the premature exhaustion of his unemployment benefit. Similarly where an employer is freed from his obligation to pay wages because of a breach by the employee his loss is reduced *pro tanto*.[603] The following receipts[604] must be taken into account when calculating compensation — unpaid national insurance contributions,[605] unemployment benefit,[606] supplementary benefit,[607] family income supplement,[608] statutory sick pay[609] and attendance and mobility allowances.[610] There are conflicting decisions whether a statutory redundancy payment should be deducted from damages for a wrongful dismissal.[611] However, while emphasising the peculiar and exceptional circumstances of the case, the House of Lords has held that such a payment should be deducted from an award of damages in a delictual action[612] although Lord Scarman stated[613] that

---

[601] "I realise that L was only at liberty to invest in Ventilation because his employment was terminated. But nevertheless the benefit from that investment was not a direct result of his dismissal. It was an entirely collateral benefit . . . for which he need not account to his [former] employers . . . [but his shareholding in] Martindale stands on a different footing" *per* Lord Denning at p. 290-291.

[602] [1985] ICR 209, HL.

[603] Lord Fraser, *Master and Servant* (3rd ed.) p. 113.

[604] Where a benefit could have been received but was not (because the victim of the breach did not apply) logically it should still be taken into account.

[605] *Cooper v. Firth Brown Ltd* [1963] 1 WLR 418.

[606] *Parsons v. BNM Laboratories Ltd* [1964] 1 QB, CA; *Westwood v. Secretary of State for Employment* [1985] ICR 209, HL.

[607] *Westwood v. Secretary of State for Employment* [1985] ICR 209, HL.

[608] *Gaskell v. Preston* [1981] 3 All ER 427.

[609] *Palfrey v. Greater London Council* [1985] ICR 437.

[610] *Hodgson v. Trapp, The Times* November 14, 1988, HL, in which the purpose of the allowances was highlighted and Lord Bridge could find no general principle to support the opinion of Lord Reid in *Parry v. Cleaver* [1970] AC 1 that Parliament did not intend statutory benefits to be for the benefit of the wrongdoer.

[611] Contrast *Stocks v. Magna Merchants Ltd* [1973] 1 WLR 1505 in which a redundancy payment was deducted, with *Basnett v. J & A Jackson Ltd* [1976] ICR 63 in which it was not.

[612] *Wilson v. NCB* 1981 SLT 67, HL affirming the decision of the Court of Session (1981 SLT 67) in which Lord President Emslie opined "Once the intrinsic nature and purpose of redundancy payments are known (to compensate . . . for the loss of an established job . . . whether the recipient will or will not find new employment . . . even if the employee immediately secures another . . . better-paid job) . . . the question whether [a] redundancy payment . . . should . . . be disregarded must be resolved by application of the common law which treats the answer as one depending on justice, reasonableness and public policy . . . in this case I can discover no trace of public policy which could justify the pursuer's claim to receive damages for loss of earnings . . . and at the same time keep the redundancy payments as well . . . [but] I do not wish to be taken to be laying down any general rule."

[613] *Ibid.* p. 73.

in many cases it would not be reasonable or just to deduct a statutory redundancy payment from damages paid to compensate [an employee] for loss of future earnings. Certainly no deduction is made in respect of the basic award of compensation for unfair dismissal on the grounds that even if the termination had been lawful, protection against unfair dismissal would have been available[614] and this would seem to support the view that a statutory redundancy payment should not be deducted from damages.

PUBLIC LAW AND EMPLOYMENT

3.63 Judicial review

In Scotland the Court of Session and in England the High Court exercise similar jurisdictions to supervise the decision of inferior courts, tribunals and administrative bodies by way of judicial review. Thus Rule of Court 260B provides: "An application to the supervisory jurisdiction of the court which immediately before the coming into operation of this rule would have been made by way of summons or petition shall be made by way of an application for judicial review . . . and on such an application the court may make such order . . . as it thinks fit being an order which could be made in any action or petition and including an order for reduction, suspension, declarator, interdict, implement, restriction and payment."[615] One result of these administrative law jurisdictions is that decisions of tribunals or administrative bodies relating to employment matters may be subject to the supervision of the Court of Session. Examples of employees seeking to use this additional and special jurisdiction to redress the effect of decisions relating to employment can be seen in *Nahar v. Strathclyde Regional Council*[616] in which Nahar, a schoolteacher, sought a reduction of the decision of Strathclyde Regional Council to dismiss him on grounds of misconduct and *O'Neill v. Scottish Joint Negotiating Committee for Teaching Staff*[617] in which a schoolteacher sought reduction of a decision of the Committee for Teaching Staff in a question relating to entitlement to full salary during maternity leave.

3.64 *No alternative remedy.* A pre-condition of judicial review is that no alternative statutory remedy is available.[618] While doubt has been expressed on whether this prevents judicial review of a decision which could be the subject of an appeal to the Court of Session but only after passage through a hierarchy of statutory tribunals,[619] where an employee has elected to pursue his grievance by some alternative procedure — for example complaint to an industrial tribunal — any application for judicial review before the conclusion of the alternative procedure will be incompetent.[620]

---

[614] *Shove v. Downs Surgical plc* [1984] ICR 532. And see *O'Laoire v. Jackel International Ltd* [1991] IRLR 170, CA regarding the compensatory award.

[615] The English equivalent is rule 53 of the Rules of the Supreme Court. The wording of Rule 260B makes it clear that it is not the rule itself which describes the limits of judicial review but whether the application falls within the Court of Session's supervisory jurisdiction; and see the observations in *West v. Secretary of State for Scotland* 1991 GWD 16-952.

[616] 1986 SLT 570, OH.

[617] 1987 SLT 648, OH.

[618] Rule of Court 260 B(3); and see *British Railways Board v. Glasgow Corporation* 1976 SC 224.

[619] *Nahar v. Strathclyde Regional Council* 1986 SLT 570, *per* Lord Davidson 573-4.

[620] *Nahar v. Strathclyde Regional Council* 1986 SLT 570, OH.

3.65 *Public law element.* Perhaps the most significant restriction on judicial review is the need for a public law element to be involved and the preparedness of courts to hold that such an element is involved will determine the extent to which judicial review is available as an additional procedure in employment matters will be critical. The need for such a public law element was emphasised in *R. v. East Berkshire Health Authority, ex parte Walsh*[621] in which Walsh, a senior nursing officer, unsuccessfully sought judicial review of the health authority's decision to dismiss him because he was not trying to enforce a public right but his private contractual rights under his contract of employment. The following quotation from the judgment of Sir John Donaldson M.R. encapsulates the distinction between public and private law rights.

> "Parliament can underpin the position of public authority employers by directly restricting the freedom of the public authority to dismiss, thus giving the employee 'public law' rights and at least making him a potential candidate for administrative law remedies. Alternatively it can require the authority to contract with its employees on specified terms with a view to the employee acquiring 'private law' rights under the terms of the contract of employment. If the authority fails or refuses to thus create 'private law' rights for the employee, the employee will have 'public law' rights to compel compliance, the remedy being [an order] to require the authority so to contract or a declaration that the employee has those rights. If, however, the authority gives the employee the required contractual protection, a breach of that contract is not a matter of 'public law' and gives rise to no administrative law remedies."[622]

A similar approach has been adopted in Scotland in *Tehrani v. Argyll and Clyde Health Board*[623] in which an application for judicial review of the summary dismissal of a surgeon employed by the Argyll and Clyde Health Board was refused because the issue was essentially a matter of private law.[624] On similar grounds application for judicial review have been refused in the case of a university lecturer who was dissatisfied with how his employers had handled a grievance and a prison officer's complaint about his employer's refusal to pay him removal expenses even although the Crown was a party to the arrangement.[624a] However where judicial review does lie, the Court of Session has at its disposal a range of remedies not available in disputes regulated purely by private law.[625] Thus in *Malloch v. Aberdeen Corporation*[626] the effect of the court order was to reduce Malloch's purported dismissal to a legal nullity with the result that (a) he was required to be treated as never having been dismissed and therefore entitled to his salary and other benefits since his date of dismissal and (b) he was entitled to resume his position as a schoolteacher until his contract of employment was lawfully terminated. However even in the absence of

---

[621] [1984] ICR 743, CA.
[622] *Ibid.* p. 253.
[623] 1990 SLT 118, IH. Although in *Tehrani* the requirement of a public law element was conceded it has been accepted as binding on this point: *West v. Secretary of State for Scotland* 1991 GWD 16-952.
[624] *Cf. Vine v. National Dock Labour Board* [1957] AC 488; *Ridge v. Baldwin* [1964] AC 40; *Malloch v. Aberdeen Corporation* 1971 SC(HL) 85.
[624a] *Criper v. University of Edinburgh* 1991 SLT 129; *West v. Secretary of State for Scotland* 1991 GWD 16-952.
[625] The usual private law remedies are an action based on the contract of employment or a complaint of unfair dismissal.
[626] 1971 SC(HL) 85.

a public law element the Charter and Statutes of a university may restrict the grounds on which a dismissal may occur.[626a]

THE CONTRACT OF EMPLOYMENT AND THE CRIMINAL LAW

3.66 Since the Employers and Workmen Act 1875[627] removed the sanction of the criminal law for an employee's failure to perform his obligations under the contract the position is that, generally, a breach of the contract *simpliciter* by either the employer or the employee does not bring the criminal law into play. However special note should be made in respect of the following:

(a) Health and safety. As previously explained[628] it is an implied term of the contract of employment that the employer will take reasonable care for the safety of his employees. However in many cases the standard of care and provision required of employers is specified by statute, delegated legislation or a code of pracitce[629] which frequently are enforced through the criminal law. Perhaps of greatest significance is the Health and Safety at Work Act 1974 which combines general duties, cast in terms which are very similar to the employer's implied contractual obligation to take reasonable care, with criminal sanctions. Thus s. 2 of the 1974 Act provides: "it shall be the duty of every employer to ensure, so far as is reasonably practicable, the health, safety and welfare at work of all his employees".[630] The effect of such general provisions is that the same failing on the part of an employer can amount not just to breach of the contract but also to the breach of a prescribed statutory standard with the consequent criminal penalties.[631]

(b) The Conspiracy and Protection of Property Act 1875. This legislation is the nearest our law now comes to attaching criminal penalties for breach of the employment contract by providing that it is an offence for any person to wilfully and maliciously break a contract of service or hiring in the knowledge that the breach will probably endanger human life, cause serious bodily injury or expose valuable property to destruction or injury.[632] However the words "wilfully and maliciously"[633] clearly restrict the operation of the legislation and there is no record of any recent prosecutions.[634]

[626a] *R v. Visitor of University of Hull, The Times* April 2, 1991.

[627] Ss. 9, 14.

[628] See para. 3.31.

[629] See for example the Factories Act 1961, Control of Substances Hazardous to Health Regulations 1988, Code of Practice for Reducing the Exposure of Employed Persons to Noise.

[630] And see the other general duties imposed by ss. 2-9 mainly on employers. *Cf.* ss. 7 and 8 that (1) it shall be the duty of every employee to take reasonable care for the health and safety of himself and others at work and (2) no person shall intentionally or recklessly interfere with anything provided in the interests of health, safety or welfare in pursuance of any relevant statutory provision.

[631] And see, for example *Armour v. Skeen* 1977 SLT 71 and *Wotherspoon v. HMA* 1978 JC 74 demonstrating that criminal liability can attach to managers etc. as individuals.

[632] Conspiracy and Protection of Property Act 1875, s. 5. Note that s. 4 (as amended by Electricity Supply Act 1919, s. 31) which related only to workers in the gas, electricity and water industries, has been repealed (Industrial Relations Act 1971, s. 133).

[633] According to s. 15 of the 1875 Act "maliciously" shall be construed in accordance with the Malicious Damage Act 1856, s. 58.

[634] Although many provisions of the Conspiracy and Protection of Property Act 1875 have been repealed it is to be noted that among those not repealed is s. 6 which provides that it is an offence for an employer, in breach of a legal duty to do so, to wilfully or negligently fail to provide food, clothing, accommodation or medical aid with the result that the health of an employee or apprentice is likely to be seriously injured.

(c) *Malicious mischief.* At common law it is a crime wilfully and maliciously[635] to destroy or damage the property of another. Accordingly where an employee sets out deliberately to damage property of his employer — which would inevitably be a breach of an employee's implied duty of fidelity or good faith[636] — there is a considerable risk that the employee's conduct will justify a charge of malicious mischief. The risk of such a charge being sustained against an employee seems to have been increased since *H.M. Advocate v. Wilson*[637] in which it was held that physical damage to property is not essential to the crime. Thus an employee at a power station who wilfully and maliciously activated an emergency "stop" button with the result that generation of electricity was halted for several hours causing considerable financial loss to his employers committed the crime of malicious mischief. It is an interesting question whether an employee who, for example, deliberately inserted a virus into his employer's computing facility also commits the crime of malicious mischief. On the face of the decision in *H.M. Advocate v. Wilson*[638] those employees who wilfully and maliciously insert metaphorical as well as literal "spanners-in-the-works" would seem to commit the crime. On the other hand the statutory offence of vandalism[639] requires damage to or the destruction of property of another. However it is not a crime according to Scots law dishonestly to exploit the confidential information of another. Accordingly a charge that an employee had feloniously and without the authority of his employer made copies of a computer print-out with intent to sell them to his employer's competitors was held to be irrelevant although undoubtedly in breach of contract.[640]

(d) *Sit-ins.* Where employees take control of their employer's premises by a sit-in, work-in or some other form of unauthorised occupation[641] it is likely that such employees are in breach of their contracts of employment in at least two respects — (i) by disobeying their employer's lawful instructions with regard to access and egress to the workplace and (ii) acting in a manner wholly inconsistent with their implied duties of loyal service. However the occupation would probably support a charge of intimidation under the Conspiracy and Protection of Property Act 1875[642] on the view that those participating in the work-in or sit-in are, by depriving the employers of their use of the premises, preventing them from doing an act they had a legal right to do, namely to enter and leave the premises.[643] Although the Trespass (Scotland) Act 1865 has been used to prosecute "squatters" and travelling people[644] that Act has not been used to deal with workplace occupations.[645]

---

[635] It is probably sufficient if there is a deliberate disregard or indifference for the property rights of others (*Ward v. Robertson* 1938 JC 32).

[636] See para 3.43 *et seq.*

[637] 1984 SLT 117.

[638] *Ibid.*

[639] Criminal Justice (Scotland) Act 1980, s. 78.

[640] *Grant v. Allan* 1987 SLT 11.

[641] See Chapter Eleven.

[642] S. 7 provides "Every person who, with a view to compel any other person to abstain from doing or to do an act which such other person has a legal right to do or to abstain from doing, wrongfully and without legal authority . . . deprives him of or hinders him in the use of such property . . . shall, on conviction be liable to . . . a penalty . . .".

[643] *Galt v. Philp* 1984 SLT 28 in which it was also held that liability under Conspiracy and Protection of Property Act 1875, s. 7 was not affected by the civil law immunity contained in TULRA, s. 13.

[644] *Paterson v. Robertson* 1945 SLT 31.

[645] However those who took part in the occupation in *Galt v. Philp* 1984 SLT 28 were originally charged under the Trespass (Scotland) Act 1865.

Chapter Four

TERMINATION OF THE CONTRACT

The contract of employment may be terminated in a variety of ways: (1) by notice, (2) by rescission following repudiation, (3) by frustration, (4) by the dissolution of a partnership, the winding up of a limited company and sequestration and (5) by performance and passage of time and these are now considered in more detail.

NOTICE

4.1 The rules regarding the termination of the contract of employment are both common law and statutory in nature with some matters, for example the length of notice required for lawful termination of the contract, treated by both common law provisions and statutory provisions although the latter are conditional on the employee having the necessary period of continuous employment.[1] To determine whether proper notice of termination has been given it is therefore necessary to consider whether the statutory or common law rules apply and in this respect it is important to note that although any contractual provision which is shorter than that provided for by statute[2] will not have effect[3] it is possible that the length of notice required by common law will exceed the statutory standard. Accordingly as a matter of practice it is necessary to consider the following questions (1) Does a statutory provision apply? (2) What is the statutory notice entitlement? (3) Is there a more beneficial express contractual provision? (4) Where there is no such provision is there a more beneficial term to be implied from the circumstances or the common law?

4.2 The common law rules

Unless the appointment is *ad vitam aut culpam*[4] or the contract is for a determinate period,[5] where the contract makes no provision regarding the notice required for lawful termination[6] the contract of employment may be terminated by either party giving to the other reasonable notice of termination or, in the

---

[1] See paras. 3.2 *et seq.*
[2] EPCA, s. 49; and see para. 4.3.
[3] *Ibid.* s. 49(3).
[4] See *Mitchell v. School Board of Elgin* (1883) 10 R 982; *Hastie v. McMurtrie* (1883) 16 R 715.
[5] *Brennan v. Campbell's Trs.* (1898) 25 R 423. And see R. Hunter *Well and Wisely Fixed?* (1979) 24 JLSS 317 on the distinction between a contract for a determinate period and a "fixed term contract" under EPCA.
[6] Such a provision may be implied by custom (*Hamilton v. George Outram* (1885) 17 D 798).

case of termination by the employer, payment in lieu of notice.[7] The common law implies a condition that when an employer "dispenses with his (the employee's) services without cause . . . he (the employee) should be allowed the means of livelihood for a period within which he might reasonably be expected to find another situation".[8] Thus, it is not a breach of contract for an employer to dismiss without notice provided payment in lieu is made.[9] Since this is a payment due under the contract and not damages for breach, arguably it is to be made without deducting tax and national insurance contributions.[9a] What is reasonable notice depends on the facts and circumstances of each case.[10] Where the contract is for a term certain not exceeding one year, unless there is a custom or usage to the contrary,[11] reasonable notice (of termination) has to be given to prevent the renewal of the contract by tacit relocation for a similar period.[12] However this rule probably applies only to particular "classes of servants — agricultural, domestic and the like".[13] Where an employee is dismissed without notice the contract is ended when the dismissal is communicated.[14]

4.3 The statutory provisions

Statute[15] provides for minimum periods of notice for certain employees.[16] After one month's continuous employment[17] an employee is entitled to receive one week's notice until he has two years' continuous employment when he becomes entitled to one week's notice for every year of continuous employment up to a maximum entitlement of 12 weeks' notice.[18] An employee who has been continuously employed for one month is required to give one week's notice of

---

[7] *Forsyth v. Heathery Knowe Coal Co* (1880) 7 R 887; *Graham v. Thomson* (1882) 1 S 309.

[8] *Morrison v. Abernethy School Board* (1876) 3 R 945, *per* Lord Deas at p. 952. It seems that an employer wishing to terminate a contract by making a payment in lieu of notice is required to pay not merely *wages* in lieu of notice but an amount in respect of other contractual benefits lost too. Thus in *Morrison (ante)* Lord Deas said a payment or allowance in lieu of notice could "not . . . be . . . less than . . . a quarter's salary and emoluments (a dwellinghouse and a garden)".

[9] *Graham v. Thomson* (1822) 1 S 309; *Cooper v. Henderson* (1825) 3 S 619.

[9a] *CF.* the position in England where payment in lieu is a payment by way of damages: *Gothard v. Mirror Group Newspapers Ltd* [1988] IRLR 396, CA; *Foster Wheeler Ltd v. Jackson* [1990] IRLR 412, EAT.

[10] See *Forsyth v. Heathery Knowe Coal Co* (1880) 7 R 887; *Morrison v. Abernethy School Board* (1876) 3 R 945; *Wilson v. Anthony* 1958 SLT (Sh. Ct.) 651; *Currie v. Glasgow Central Stores* (1905) SLT 651; *Hill v. C. A. Parsons & Co Ltd* 1972 1 Ch 305, CA.

[11] *Morrison v. Allardyce* (1823) 2 S 434.

[12] Bell, *Principles,* s. 187; Lord Fraser, *Master & Servant* p. 58.

[13] *Lennox v. Allan and Sons* (1880) 8 R 38 *per* Lord J Clark Moncrieff; *Brennan v. Campbell's Trs.* (1898) 25 R 423. Cf. *Stevenson v. N B Railway Board* (1905) 7 F 1106; *Houston v. The Calico Printer's Association Ltd* (1903) 10 SLT 532. In England the presumption of yearly hiring has ceased (*Richardson v. Keofod* [1969] 3 All ER 1264).

[14] *Octavius Atkinson & Sons Ltd v. Morris* [1989] IRLR 158, CA.

[15] EPCA, s. 49 as amended by EA 1982, Sch. 2 para. 3. Note however that the rights conferred by ss. 49 & 50 are contractual and not independent statutory rights (*Westwood v. Secretary of State for Employment* [1985] ICR 209, HL).

[16] Employees are excluded if they have not been continuously employed for one month; others excluded are (a) those engaged in work outside Great Britain (EPCA, s. 141(1)), (b) those employed on specific task not expected to exceed 3 months and which does not exceed that time (EPCA, s. 49(4)(a)), (c) certain seamen (EPCA, s. 144), (d) dock-workers (EPCA, s. 145) and (e) those employed for or working less than 16 hours *per* week (EPCA, Sch. 13 paras. 3 and 4).

[17] See paras. 3.2 *et seq.*

[18] EPCA, s. 49(1).

termination but his obligation does not increase relative to his period of continuous employment. A term in a contract of employment for a shorter period of notice is void[19] and is superseded by the statutory provisions but either party may waive his rights[19a] under these provisions or accept payment in lieu of notice[20] and neither is prevented from terminating the contract without notice by virtue of the other party's repudiation.[21] However it is insufficient for one party merely to designate the conduct of the other as "gross misconduct" or repudiation; the facts have to support the existence of the repudiatory conduct before the statutory right to notice may be avoided.[22] Since only contractual terms for shorter periods of notice are invalidated, if common law reasonable notice exceeds the statutory provision the party is entitled to enforcement of the contract on the more beneficial term; if the contract of employment expressly incorporates the periods of notice specified by statute the contract will be enforced on that basis. Whether notice is given by the employer or employee the latter is ensured a minimum income during the period of notice.[23] However this protective measure disappears if the notice the employer must give to terminate the contract exceeds by at least one week the notice statute requires.[24]

4.4 Requirements of valid notice

While there is no rule that notice of termination must be in writing the contract may expressly require it and it is advisable that it should be so to avoid disputes. Verbal notice does not start to run until the day following the day on which it was given[25] and a notice which does not specify the date or contain material from which the date (of termination) is positively ascertainable has no effect on the contract and an employee who leaves on receipt of such an invalid notice will be deemed to have resigned.[26] Thus informing an employee that he will eventually be dismissed without specifying a date is not giving valid notice;[27] nor is an announcement that a factory is to close down by a specific date com-

---

[19] EPCA, s. 140(1)(a). Also an employer's failure to give the statutory notice shall be taken into account in computing damages for breach of contract (EPCA, s. 51).

[19a] It has been held that there is no difference between waiving a right to payment in lieu as opposed to a right to notice itself: *Trotter v. Forth Ports Authority* 1991 GWD 17-1045.

[20] And see *Secretary of State for Employment v. Staffordshire C.C.* [1989] IRLR 117, CA. And note the interesting discussion in M. R. Freedland, *The Contract of Employment* (1976) p. 186 whether an employee can insist on working out his notice instead of "accepting" wages in lieu. See also *Dedman v. British Building & Engineering Appliances Ltd* [1974] ICR 53 and *Cort & Son v. Chapman* [1981] ICR 816 regarding effect of EPCA, s. 55 (4) (effective date of termination) on dismissal with wages in lieu.

[21] EPCA, s. 49(5).

[22] *Lanton Leisure Ltd v. White and Gibson* [1987] IRLR 119, EAT.

[23] EPCA, s. 50 and Sch. 3. The rights conferred by ss. 49 and 50 are contractual and not independent statutory rights (*Westwood v. Secretary of State for Employment* [1985] ICR 209 HL, reversing [1983] ICR 820, CA).

[24] EPCA, s. 50(3).

[25] *West v. Kneels Ltd* [1986] IRLR 430, EAT.

[26] *Morton Sundour Fabrics Ltd v. Shaw* [1967] 2 ITR 84; *Hughes v. Gwynedd Area Health Authority* [1977] IRLR 436, EAT. However if his resignation followed a repudiation by the employer there will be a constructive dismissal for redundancy and unfair dismissal law. See Chapter Five.

[27] *Haseltine Lake & Co v. Dowler* [1981] ICR 222, EAT.

bined with an invitation to employees to seek alternative work,[28] or that the employer will depart from a particular term of the contract — for example the rate of wages — from a certain date.[29] On the other hand where an employee wrote "I am left with no option but to resign and instigate . . . proceedings against you. I look forward to hearing from you within seven days." a tribunal was entitled to read the letter as meaning that resignation would take effect, if there was no reply, within seven days.[29a] A valid notice once given cannot unilaterally be withdrawn before it expires;[30] it operates to terminate the contract. However an inadequate notice which is itself a repudiation of the contract needs to be accepted before it can affect the contract and it would seem therefore such a notice may be withdrawn at any time until it has been accepted by the other (innocent) party.[31]

REPUDIATION

4.5 The normal rule that the repudiation of a contract does not terminate it applies to the contract of employment,[32] and it has been stated[33] that those decisions[34] where the contract of employment was terminated by the repudiation and not by its acceptance (the "automatic termination" theory) were wrongly decided. Thus where an employee never accepted a wage reduction imposed by his employers but continued to work without notice being given or being dismissed his contract never came to an end and he was entitled to receive the wages to which he was contractually entitled.[35] Of course depending on the form or nature of the repudiatory breach the victim of the breach may have no practical alternative but to accept the repudiation and bring the contract to an

---

[28] *International Computers Ltd v. Kennedy* [1981] IRLR 28, EAT. Also an announcement of closure to trade union officials is not to be construed as notice of termination (*Doble v. Firestone Tyre & Rubber Co Ltd* [1981] IRLR 300, EAT). But see *Anderson v. Wishart* (1818) 1 Murr 429. Equally in view of the provision of the Transfer of Undertakings (Protection of Employment) Reguatlions 1981, it is unlikely that informing an employee that the business will be sold on a specific date will amount to a notice of termination.

[29] *Rigby v. Ferodo Ltd* [1987] 516, HL.

[29a] *Walmsley v. C & R Ferguson Ltd* 1989 SLT 258, IH.

[30] *Riordan v. The War Office* [1960] All ER 774, CA; *Harris and Russell Ltd v. Slingsby* [1973] ICR 545, NIRC.

[31] *Decro-Wall International S.A. v. Practitioners in Marketing Ltd* [1971] I WLR 361, CA, particularly Buckley L.J. at p. 235. "A repudiation and a notice of termination are clearly different things. A repudiation may be withdrawn at any time before acceptance: a notice of determination validly given cannot thereafter be withdrawn without agreement". And see *Norwest Holst Group Administration v. Harrison* [1985] ICR 668, CA.

[32] *London Transport Executive v. Clarke* [1981] ICR 355, CA; *Norris v. Southampton C.C.* [1982] ICR 177, EAT; *Boston Deep Sea Fishing and Ice Co Ltd v. Ansell* (1888) 39 Ch D 339. And see *Rasool v. Hepworth Pipework Co* (No. 1) [1980] IRLR 88, EAT and the instructive judgment of Megarry V.-C. in *Thomas Marshall (Exports) Ltd v. Guinle* [1978] IRLR 174. For an interesting discussion of and suggested solutions to the problems involved see McMullen, *A Synthesis of the Mode of Termination of Contracts of Employment* (1982) 41 CLJ 110.

[33] *London Transport Executive v. Clarke* [1981] ICR 355, *per* Dunn L.J. at p. 372.

[34] *Gannon v. J. C. Firth Ltd* [1976] IRLR 415, *Kallinos v. London Electricity Wire* [1980] IRLR 11, *Smith v. Avana Bakeries Ltd* [1979] IRLR 423.

[35] *Rigby v. Ferodo Ltd* [1987] IRLR 516 HL.

end.[36] The position is stated succinctly by Lord Oliver in *Rigby v. Ferodo Ltd*[37] "There was no reason in law or in logic why, leaving aside the extreme cases of outright dismissal or walk-out, a contract of employment should be on any different footing from any other contract regarding the principle that an unaccepted repudiation was a thing writ in water and of no value to anybody."

Whether a breach is material depends on the terms of the particular contract and although no general rule can be laid down[38] the nature of the breach itself and its impact on the contractual relations of the parties is of importance.[39] The effect of a breach and whether it indicates an intention not to be bound by the contract has to be assessed by reference to the standards of a reasonable person, the actual intentions of the party in breach being irrelevant.[40] Exceptionally the contract of employment may contain distinct severable obligations and a material failure in respect of one obligation may not result in the repudiation of the contract[41] but the cumulative effect of repeated non-material breaches may justify rescission.[42] Examples of material breach of the employment contract by the employer include the sale of business in which the employee works,[43] a failure to take reasonable steps to ensure an employee's safety,[44] oppressive use of a disciplinary power,[45] a failure to give support to a manager or supervisor[46] and

---

[36] Both Templeman and Dunn L.J.J. in *London Transport Executive v. Clarke (ante)* recognise that the rule may have to suffer some qualification. Thus Templeman L.J. at p. 368 states "If a worker walks out of his job and does not thereafter claim to be entitled to resume work, then he repudiates his contract and the employer accepts that repudiation by taking no action to affirm the contract. No question of unfair dismissal arises unless the worker claims he was constructively dismissed. If a worker walks out of his job or commits any other breach of contract, repudiatory or otherwise, but at any time he claims he is entitled to resume or continue his work, the his contract of employment is only determined if the employer expressly or impliedly asserts and accepts repudiation on the part of the workers", while at p. 373 Dunn L.J. admits there may be cases where the innocent party has no option but to accept the repudiation and terminate the contract. See also Salmon and Sachs L.J.J. in *Decro-Wall International S.A. v. Practitioners in Marketing Ltd* [1971] 1 WLR 361 and Lord McDonald in *Trust House Forte v. Murphy* [1977] IRLR 186; *Batchelor v. British Airways Board* [1987] IRLR 136, CA.

[37] [1987] IRLR 516, HL at p. 518.

[38] *Woods v. W. M. Car Services (Peterborough) Ltd* [1982] IRLR 413, CA.

[39] *Wade v. Waldon* 1909 SC 571, IH; *Millbrook Furnishing Industries Ltd v. McIntosh* [1981] IRLR 309, EAT.

[40] *Forslind v. Bechley-Crundall* 1922 SC (HL) 173; *BBC v. Beckett* [1983] IRLR 43, EAT; *Blyth v. Scottish Liberal Club* 1983 SLT 260, IH; *Millbrook Furnishing Industries Ltd v. McIntosh* [1981] IRLR 309, EAT.

[41] *Land v. West Yorkshire Metropolitan C.C.* [1981] IRLR 87, CA.

[42] See *Pepper v. Webb* [1969] 1 WLR 514; *Hanlon v. Allied Breweries* [1975] IRLR 321, IT; *Lewis v. Motorworld Garages Ltd* [1985] IRLR 465, CA. See also Lord Fraser, *Master and Servant* (3rd. edn.) p. 138; *Mansfield v. Scott* (1831) 9 S 780.

[43] *Ross v. McFarlane* (1894) 21 R 396; *Collier v. Sunday Referee Publishing Co* (1940) 2 KB 647. See also *Trevillion v. Hospital of St John and St Elizabeth* [1973] IRLR 176, NIRC. But note the provisions of the Transfer of Undertakings Regulations 1981 which transfer the contracts of employment of employees employed in the business at the time of the transfer. (Regulation 5).

[44] *Donovan v. Invicta Airways Ltd* [1970] 1 Lloyd's Rep. 486, CA; *British Aircraft Corporation v. Austin* [1978] IRLR 332, EAT.

[45] *BBC v. Beckett* [1983] IRLR 43, EAT; *Cawley v. South Wales Electricity Board* [1985] IRLR 89, EAT.

[46] *Associated Tyre Specialists (Eastern) Ltd v. Waterhouse* [1976] IRLR 386, EAT.

a failure to pay the agreed wages.[47] Unjustified summary dismissal is itself a repudiation of the contract which generally leaves the employee with no choice but to rescind.[48] Because of the remedy of unfair dismissal few modern cases turn on questions of contract law but the following are illustrations of material breach by the employee: refusal to carry out a lawful instruction,[49] breach of an obligation, express or implied, protecting trade secrets and confidential information,[50] and engaging in most forms of industrial action.[51]

The repudiation may take the form of an anticipatory breach entitling the victim of the breach to sue at once.[52] However a party who has committed an anticipatory breach is entitled to withdraw it before the innocent party has elected to accept[53] and it must be clear that a breach is inevitable.[54] Thus, the announcement of the imposition of new terms (to which employee did not agree) by a certain date justifies immediate termination by the employee.[55] However a genuine dispute regarding the terms of the contract is not an anticipatory breach.[56]

Certain conduct may be inconsistent with rescission although it is unlikely mere delay would indicate an affirmation of the contract.[57] While the circumstances of each case are important, going on strike, continued acceptance of

---

[47] *Industrial Rubber Products v. Gillon* [1977] IRLR 389 EAT; *Stokes v. Hampstead Wine Co* [1979] IRLR 298, EAT. However it is the materiality of the breach that is important and not whether it is an alteration in basic pay or an additional payment: *Gillies v. Richard Daniels & Co Ltd* [1979] IRLR 457, EAT.

[48] *Ross v. Pender* (1874) 1 R 352; *Murray v. Dumbarton C.C.* 1935 SLT 239. *Cf.* the special cases of *Hill v. (CA) Parsons & Co Ltd* [1972] 1 Ch 305; *R v. BBC, ex parte Lavelle* [1982] IRLR 404. But note the decision of Hodgson J. in *Dietman v. Brent London Borough Council* [1987] ICR 237 (affirmed [1988] ICR 842, CA) that even a repudiatory dismissal requires acceptance for the contract to be terminated - *sed quaere*.

[49] *Pepper v. Webb* [1969] 1 WLR 514. In emergencies an employee may be required to perform duties outwith normal contractual provisions: *Wilson v. Simson* (1844) 6 D 1256; *Millbrook Furnishing Industries Ltd v. McIntosh* [1981] IRLR 309, EAT. In certain circumstances refusal to obey may not be material (*Laws v. London Chronicle Ltd* [1959] 1 WLR 698).

[50] *Thomas Marshall (Exports) Ltd v. Guinle* [1978] IRLR 74; *Hivac Ltd v. Park Royal Scientific Instruments Ltd* [1946] Ch 169 (where only wartime regulations prevented instant dismissal).

[51] Not all forms of industrial action involve breach of the contract as in *Powerpacking Casemakers v. Faust* [1983] IRLR 117, EAT, where overtime could not be required under the contracts.

[52] *Hochester v. De La Tour* (1853) 2 E & B 678.

[53] *Norwest Holst Group Administration v. Harrison* [1985] ICR 668, CA. In fact in *Harrison* the Court of Appeal goes further and permits the withdrawal of the anticipatory breach any time before the innocent victim communicates his election to accept and rescind the contract.

[54] *Haseltine Lake Co v. Dowler* [1981] IRLR 25, EAT (an employee was told he had no future with the company but no date of dismissal was fixed and EAT held no anticipatory breach because nothing suggested he would be dismissed without proper notice). See also *Morton Sundour Fabrics Ltd v. Shaw* [1967] ITR 84 (announcement of likely redundancy) and *Maher v. Fram Gerrard Ltd* [1974] ICR 31 (intimation of transfer of employee against his will).

[55] *Wellworthy Ltd v. Ellis* (unreported) case no. 915/83, EAT; *Rigby v. Ferodo Ltd* [1987] IRLR 516, HL.

[56] *Financial Techniques Ltd v. Hughes* [1981] IRLR 32, CA.

[57] *Bashir v. Brillo Manufacturing Co* [1979] IRLR 295, EAT, distinguishing *Western Excavating (EEC) Ltd v. Sharp* [1979] IRLR 27, CA. See also *Ross v. Pender* (1874) 1 R 352. *Cf. Fraser v. Laing* (1878) 5 R 596.

wages and reporting for duty[58] have been held to be inconsistent with rescission. However, continuing to work after clear words showing acceptance (of the new or altered contractual terms) only under protest will not result in affirmation of the contract.[59] Conversely, a plea that a repudiatory dismissal had not been accepted so as to rescind the contract will not succeed where the victim of the breach (1) chose to fight the case on its merits (instead of pleading there was no termination at all), (2) presented a complaint to an industrial tribunal without stating it was merely to preserve rights, (3) failed to offer to continue working and (4) accepted a job with another employer.[60]

FRUSTRATION

4.6 Circumstances amounting to frustration [60a]

The death or inability to perform through illness of either party frustrates the contract.[61] Where illness is concerned the case must be judged according to its own circumstances[62] although the factors identified in *Marshall v. Harland and Wolf Ltd*[63] and *The Egg Stores (Stamford Hill) Ltd v. Leibovici*[64] will be relevant.[65] However in a case of frustration the contract is terminated by operation of law and the fact that the employer has issued a notice of dismissal does not prevent a plea of frustration and although the Employment Appeal Tribunal has cautioned against too easy an application of the doctrine of frustration[66] it is incorrect to hold that in the employment field frustration by illness is normally only relevant where the contract is for a long term which cannot be determined by notice.[67] Although inconsistent with Scots principles,[68] imprisonment of the employee may support a plea of frustration[69] because although the employee's

---

[58] *Grant v. Brown & Root Manpower Services* (unreported) case no. 167/84, EAT; *Hunt v. British Railways Board* [1979] IRLR 379. Cf. *Bliss v. South East Thames Regional Health Authority* [1985] IRLR 308, CA.

[59] *Marriott v. Oxford & District Co-operative Society Ltd* (No. 2) [1970] 1 QB 186, CA; *Burdett-Coutts & Ors v. Hertfordshire C.C.* [1984] IRLR 91; *Rigby v. Ferodo Ltd* [1987] IRLR 516, HL; *Bliss v. S.E. Thames Regional Health Authority* [1987] ICR 700, CA.

[60] *Dietman v. Brent London Borough Council* [1987] ICR 237, affirmed [1988] ICR 842, CA.

[60a] And see para. 5. 23.

[61] *Hoey v. McEwan and Auld* (1867) 5 M 814; *Poussard v. Spiers & Pond* [1876] 1 QBD 410; *Condor v. Barron Knights* [1966] 1 WLR 876; *Ranger v. Brown and Ors* [1978] ICR 603, EAT.

[62] *Westwood v. SMT Co* 1938 SN 8.

[63] [1972] 2 All ER 715.

[64] [1977] ICR 260.

[65] These factors include the terms of the contract, nature of the employment, its expected duration where no illness, the nature of the illness and prospects of recovery, period of past employment, was the person a "key" employee, the acquisition of statutory rights by replacement employee, payment of wages during absence, employer's actings (e.g. did he dismiss the employee) and whether a reasonable employer could be expected to wait any longer.

[66] *Williams v. Watson Luxury Coaches Ltd* [1990] IRLR 164, EAT.

[67] *Notcutt v. Universal Equipment Co Ltd* [1986] ICR 414, CA, disapproving *Harman v. Flexible Lamps Ltd* [1980] IRLR 418, EAT. And see *Hart v. A. R. Marshall & Sons (Bulwell) Ltd* [1977] IRLR 51, EAT.

[68] Lord Fraser, *Master and Servant*, p. 322 referring to Bell and Pothier. And see *McEwan v. Malcolm* (1867) 5 SLR 62.

[69] *E. C. Shepherd and Co Ltd v. Jerrom* [1986] IRLR 358, CA, disapproving *Hare v. Murphy Bros Ltd* [1974] ICR 603.

criminal conduct was deliberate it was the act of the judge in imposing the custodial sentence which affected the contract. Conscription or internment[70] and even a short period of legal disqualification from holding office can frustrate the contract.[71] Thus losing his HGV licence following a heart attack has frustrated the contract of an HGV driver.[71a] While parties may expressly provide that a particular event will not frustrate the contract[72] where frustration occurs the contract is valid until then and contractual claims relative to the period prior to frustration are competent.[73] Where the right to payment has not yet accrued at the time of frustration (e.g. holiday pay and pensions) an equitable remedy (on the principles of unjustified enrichment) would be available.[74]

DISSOLUTION OF PARTNERSHIP

4.7 Where the employer is a partnership possessing a legal personality distinct from the personalities of the partners[75] dissolution of the partnership may operate to terminate contracts of employment with the firm and where the dissolution is brought about by the death of a partner the contract will be frustrated[76] although the same might not result where the dissolution is deliberate.[77] However in a continuing partnership contracts of employment with the firm are not affected by death, resignation or assumption of a partner or partners.[78] In any event continuity of employment is preserved by statute[79] and where the reconstruction of the partnership takes the form of a transfer of a business from an old partnership to a new one the provisions of the Transfer of Undertakings (Protection of Employment) Regulations 1981 would apply so that the contracts of employment of employees employed in the firm at the time of the transfer of the business would be automatically transferred to the new firm.[80]

---

[70] *Marshall v. Glanville* (1917) 2 KB 87, *Unger v. Preston Corporation* (1942) 1 All ER 200. However enlistment would seem to be a repudiation.

[71] *Tarnesby v. Kensington & Chelsea & Westminster Area Health Authority* [1981] IRLR 369, HL. However in accordance with Scots principles is it not arguable that Tarnesby's professional misconduct leading to his suspension under the Medical Act 1956 was repudiation?

[71a] *Dunbar v. Baillie Bros.* 1990 GWD 26-1487.

[72] D. M. Walker, *The Law of Contracts and Voluntary Obligations in Scotland* (2nd edn.) para. 31.53. Whether the contract provides for there to be no frustration on the happening of a particular event will be a question of interpretation and in *F. C. Shepherd & Co Ltd v. Jerrom* [1986] IRLR 358, CA, it was held that imprisonment did frustrate the contract even where the contract included a suspensory power in respect of "wilful absence".

[73] Walker, *op. cit.*

[74] In England claims are dealt with under the Law Reform (Frustrated Contracts) Act 1943.

[75] Partnership Act 1890, s. 4(2).

[76] *Hoey v. McEwan & Auld* (1867) 5 M 814. Partnership Act 1890, s. 33(1) provides for dissolution by death of any partner in the absence of a term to contrary.

[77] See the judgment of Lord Deas in *Hoey v. M'Ewan & Auld* (1867) 5 M 814 and *Harkins v. Smith* (1841) SJ 381, decided on the employee's acceptance of the breach. And see the English decisions of *Phillips v. Alhambra Palace Co* [1901] 1 QB 59, DC; *Tunstall v. Condon* [1980] ICR 786, EAT.

[78] *Campbell v. Baird* (1827) 5 S 335. In *Berlitz School of Languages v. Duchene* (1903) 6 F 181 it was suggested that an alternative ground of decision was that the contract of employment contained an implied term to accept change in the composition of the partnership. Cf. *Garden Haig-Scott & Wallace v. Prudential Approved Society for Women* 1927 SLT 393, OH. Also see *Phillips v. Alhambra Palace Co* [1901] 1 QB 59.

[79] EPCA, Sch. 13 para. 17(2). And see *Allen & Son v. Coventry* [1979] IRLR 399, EAT.

[80] Transfer of Undertaking (Protection of Employment) Regulations 1981 (S.I. 1981 No. 1794), reg. 5.

SEQUESTRATION AND WINDING UP

4.8 The bankruptcy or insolvency of an employer is a breach of the contract and permits the employee to rescind the contract and claim damages.[81] The reasoning is that after the bankruptcy or insolvency the employee cannot expect to receive the stipulated wages.[82] A compulsory winding up order operates as a notice of termination of the contracts of employment then subsisting between the company and its employees[83] and where the employee continues his employment it will be under a new contract, express or inferred, entered by the liquidator, but for and on behalf of the company.[84] In such a case the liquidator is personally liable for the wages due under the new contracts.[85]

While a resolution for the voluntary winding up of a company may operate to terminate contracts of employment the effect of the voluntary winding up depends on the facts and circumstances of each case.[86] Thus where the voluntary winding up was coupled with a stated intention to cease business and insolvency there was a breach of contract by the company[87] but where the voluntary winding up was to facilitate a take-over it did not operate so as to repudiate the employee's contract.[88]

Where a receiver is appointed by the holder of a floating change or by the court on the application of the holder[89] the appointment itself will not affect subsisting contracts of employment with the company.[90] The position seems to be similar to that in England where a receiver appointed by debenture holders acts as the agent of the company and the appointment does not affect contracts of employment[91] unless the continuation of the particular employment contract is incompatible with the role of the receiver;[92] the receiver himself may expressly dismiss employees[93] or by his conduct, for example by selling the business, repudiate existing contracts of employment.[94] Where existing contracts of employment are continued or adopted by the receiver he is personally liable on such contracts subject to his statutory right of indemnity.[95] However with a

---

[81] Bell, *Principles*, s. 185; *Day v. Tait* (1900) 8 SLT 40, OH. As the employee's claim is for damages and not wages he ranks as an ordinary creditor.

[82] *Day v. Tait* (1900) 8 SLT 40, OH.

[83] *Day v. Tait* (1900) 8 SLT 40, OH. However, in view of the fact that inability to pay debts is not the sole ground on which a winding-up order may be made (see the Insolvency Act 1986, s. 122) where there is no insolvency the effect of the winding-up order may be different: see *Laing v. Gowans* (1902) 10 SLT 401, OH.

[84] *Smith v. Lord Advocate* 1979 SLT 233, IH.

[85] *Smith v. Lord Advocate* 1979 SLT 233 *per* Lord President Emslie at 241.

[86] *Reigate v. Union Manufacturing Co (Ramsbottom) Ltd* [1918] 1 KB 592, CA; *Ferguson v. Telford Grier and McKay & Co* [1967] ITR 387, IT; *Fox Brothers (Clothes) Ltd v. Bryant* [1979] ICR 64, EAT.

[87] *Reigate v. Union Manufacturing Co (Ramsbottom) Ltd* [1918] 1 KB 592, CA.

[88] *Midland Counties Bank Ltd v. Attwood* [1905] 1 Ch 355; *Ferguson v. Telford Grier and McKay & Co* [1967] ITR 387, IT.

[89] Insolvency Act 1986 s. 51 (1), (2).

[90] *Ibid.* s. 57(4).

[91] *Re Foster Clark Ltd's Indenture Trusts* [1966] 1 All ER 43; *Re Mack Trucks (Great Britain) Ltd* [1967] 1 WLR 780; *Nicoll v. Cutts* 1985 BCLC 322, CA.

[92] *Griffiths v. Secretary of State for Social Services* [1974] QB 468 where the functions of a manager were assumed by the receiver.

[93] Insolvency Act 1986, s. 55(2), Sch. 2 para. 11.

[94] *Re Foster Clark Ltd's Indenture Trusts* [1966] 1 All ER 43.

[95] Insolvency Act 1986, s. 57(3).

view to reducing the vulnerability of employees it is also provided that nothing the receiver does during the first fourteen days of his appointment is to be taken to amount to adoption of any contracts of employment.[96]

EMPLOYEE'S RIGHTS IN BANKRUPTCY AND INSOLVENCY

4.9 The rights of an employee in the event of his employer's bankruptcy or insolvency are protected in two ways. First certain payments due to the employee rank as preferential debts.[97] Secondly, where an insolvent[98] employer is liable to make certain payments to an employee whose employment has been terminated the employee may claim directly against the Secretary of State for Employment.[99] Payments falling into the first category of preferred debts include — (a) remuneration[100] of an employee in respect of the whole or any part of the period of four months prior to the relevant date[101] subject to a maximum prescribed by the Secretary of State,[102] (b) any accrued holiday pay of an employee whose employment has been terminated in respect of any period of employment prior to the relevant date,[103] (c) a guarantee payment,[104] (d) medical suspension pay,[105] (e) payments for time off for (i) trade union duties, (ii) looking for work in a redundancy situation and (iii) ante-natal care,[106] (f) statutory sick pay[107] and (g) remuneration due under a protective award.[108] The following payments fall into the second category and, subject to a statutory maximum,[109] may, in the event of the employer's assets being insufficient to meet even preferred debts, on

---

[96] *Ibid.* s. 57(5). However the statutory wording would not seem to extend to express acts of adoption.

[97] In receivership to have priority over the floating charge the debts must have been intimated, or otherwise have become known to the receiver, within 6 months of advertisement by him in the Edinburgh Gazette and a local newspaper (Insolvency Act 1986, s. 59(1), (2)).

[98] An employer is insolvent only if (a) there has been an award of sequestration, a trust deed or composition contract, (b) after death a judicial factor is required to divide his estate among his creditors or (c) there has been a winding up order or resolution, the appointment of a receiver or a voluntary arrangement (EPCA, s. 127(2)).

[99] EPCA, s. 122(1) as amended by the Insolvency Act 1985, s. 218.

[100] Remuneration includes wages or salary for time or piecework and commission (Bankruptcy (Scotland) Act 1985, Sch. 3, para. 9 (1)(a); Insolvency Act 1986, Sch. 6, paras. 9, 13) but not director's fees (*Re C. W. & A. C. Hughes Ltd* [1966] 1 WLR 1369).

[101] The relevant date is: (a) date of sequestration or death of insolvent debtor (Bankruptcy Act 1985, Sch. 3, para. 7); (b) date of (i) an administration order, (ii) appointment of provisional liquidator or (iii) winding up order (Insolvency Act 1986, s. 387 (3)(a), (b)); (c) date of winding up resolution (Insolvency Act 1986, s. 387(c)); and (d) date of appointment of receiver (Insolvency Act 1986, s. 387 (b)).

[102] Bankruptcy Act (Scotland) 1985, Sch. 3 paras. 5, 6; Insolvency Act 1986, Sch. 6 paras. 9, 12.

[103] Bankruptcy (Scotland) Act 1985, Sch. 3 paras. 5, 9; Insolvency Act 1986, Sch. 6 paras. 10, 13, 14. Note the definition of holiday pay in Bankruptcy (Scotland) Act 1985 Sch. 3 para. 9(3).

[104] Bankruptcy (Scotland) Act 1985 Sch. 3 para. 9; Insolvency Act 1986 Sch. 6 para. 13.

[105] *Ibid.*

[106] *Ibid.*

[107] *Ibid.* And see Bankruptcy (Scotland) Act 1985 Sch. 3 para. 9 (4) and Insolvency Act 1986 Sch. 6 para. 15 regarding contractual sick pay.

[108] *Ibid.* See Greene and Fletcher, *The Law and Practice of Receivership in Scotland*, para. 6.13.

[109] EPCA, s. 122(5).

application to the Secretary of State be met out of the National Insurance Fund[110] — (a) up to 8 weeks arrears of pay,[111] (b) pay during statutory notice or pay in lieu thereof, (c) up to 6 weeks' holiday pay[112] in respect of the 12 months prior to the date of insolvency, (d) a basic award of unfair dismissal compensation and (e) an apprenticeship premium.[113] The Secretary of State may also be required to pay into an occupational pension scheme[114] any unpaid contributions due by an insolvent employer either on his own accord or on behalf of an employee.[115] Employees[116] who apply to the Secretary of State but are partly or totally refused such a payment and those interested in an occupational pension scheme in respect of which the Secretary of State refuses — partly or totally — to make a payment may, within 3 months, complain to an industrial tribunal which may declare the amount of any payment the Secretary of State should make.[117] The correct approach is to apply the statutory maximum[118] and deduct therefrom, where appropriate, income tax and National Insurance deductions[119] and where the claim relates to a failure to give proper notice the employee must take reasonable steps to mitigate his loss.[120] Also where the Secretary of State makes a payment to an employee or to an occupational pension fund he becomes entitled to exercise any rights and remedies available to the employee and persons competent to act in respect of the pension scheme.[121]

TERMINATION BY PERFORMANCE AND PASSAGE OF TIME

4.10 Where the contract is to perform a particular and finite piece of work it is brought to an end or discharged when the work is completed.[122] Generally where the contract is for a fixed term it comes to an end when the term expires and strictly neither party is required to give notice of impending expiry.[123] Only in those classes of employment[124] where by well-established custom the contract is

---

[110] By EA 1990, s. 11 the Redundancy Fund is wound up and merged with the National Insurance Fund.

[111] These include (1) guarantee payments, (2) medical suspension pay, (3) time off payments and (4) payments under a protective award (EPCA, s. 122(4)).

[112] As defined in EPCA, s. 127(3).

[113] EPCA, s. 122 as amended by EA 1982 Sch. 3 paras. 3-5, Bankruptcy (Scotland) Act 1985, Sch. 7, Insolvency Act 1985 (s. 218) and 1986 (Sch. 14), and EA 1989 s. 18.

[114] As defined in EPCA, s. 127(3).

[115] EPCA, s. 123 as amended by EA 1989, s. 18(3).

[116] Various groups of employees are excluded. See EPCA, ss. 141(2A) (those who ordinarily work outside the territory of the European Communities); s. 144(2), (4), (5) (share fishermen and merchant seamen); s. 146(1) (police).

[117] EPCA, s. 124.

[118] EPCA, s. 122(5).

[119] *Morris v. Secretary of State for Employment* [1985] ICR 492, EAT; *Secretary of State for Employment v. Cooper* [1987] ICR 766, EAT. But note these decisions were on the basis that money paid in lieu of notice was a payment of damages.

[120] *Westwood v. Secretary of State for Employment* [1985] ICR 209, HL.

[121] EPCA, s. 125.

[122] Stair, *Institutions* I. 18, 3. See also *Ryan v. Shipboard Maintenance Ltd* [1980] ICR 88, EAT; *Wiltshire CC v. NATFHE* [1982] ICR 445, CA; *Brown v. Knowsley BC* [1986] IRLR 102. EAT.

[123] *Lennox v. Allan & Sons* (1880) 8 R 38; *Brennan v. Campbell's Trs.* (1898) 25 R 423. In *Robson v. Hawick School Board* (1900) 2 F 411 the very fact that the contract was for a fixed period was itself notice of dismissal.

[124] Viz. "agricultural, domestic etc." per L.J.-C. Moncrieff, *Lennox v. Allan & Sons* (1880) 8 R 38. Cf. *Campbell v. Fyfe* (1851) 13 D 1041; *Stevenson v. N B Railway Co* (1905) 7 F 1106.

renewed for a further similar period is notice of termination necessary to prevent tacit relocation.[125]

SPECIAL EMPLOYMENTS

4.11 In the case of the ordinary relationship of employer and employee there is no obligation at common law either to provide the dismissed employee with a statement of the reasons for his dismissal or to allow the employee the opportunity of a hearing before effecting a dismissal.[126] However the holder of a *munus publicum* is afforded special protection which will include observance of the principles of natural justice.[127] Equally where the employee enjoys a statutory status a failure to follow the proper procedure or to observe the rules of natural justice will render the dismissal null and invalid.[128] However, neither the fact that the employer is a public body nor that the employer's powers are based on statutes will *per se* restrict the employer's powers of termination by requiring observance of the rules of natural justice.[129] There has to be a public law element concerned before a public sector employee is entitled to have access to the administrative law remedy of judicial review.[130] Thus a consultant surgeon who was summarily dismissed with no right of appeal against dismissal to the Secretary of State could not seek judicial review of the decision to dismiss him even although the employing health board had to observe the rules of natural justice. The fact that these rules had to be observed was insufficient to elevate the surgeon's contract of employment into one within the domain of public administrative law.

Where a person holds a statutory status or public office the legal remedies for unlawful removal from office exceed the contractual and statutory remedies normally available with respect to the ordinary employer-employee relationship. Thus the reduction of an invalid or *ultra vires* dismissal may in practice operate as reinstatement at least until the correct legal process is carried through.[131]

STATUTORY STATEMENT OF REASONS FOR DISMISSAL

4.12 An employee[132] who, by the effective date of termination, has been continuously employed[133] for a period of not less than 2 years[134] is entitled, on his

---

[125] Bell, *Principles* s. 187; Lord Fraser, *Master and Servant* p. 58; W. M. Gloag, *The Law of Contract* (2nd edn.) p. 732.

[126] Fraser, *Master and Servant*, p. 120; *Vine v. NDLB* [1957] AC 488, HL; *Ridge v. Baldwin* [1964] AC 40, HL; *Vidyodaya University of Ceylon v. Silva* [1965] 1 WLR 77, PC.

[127] *Magistrates of Montrose v. Strachan* (1910) Mor 13118; *Rothesay Magistrates v. Carse* (1903) 5 F 383; *Ridge v. Baldwin* [1964] AC 40, HL.

[128] *Vine v. National Dock Labour Board* [1957] AC 488, HL; *Malloch v. Aberdeen Corporation* 1971 SLT 245, HL. Cf. *Barber v. Manchester Regional Hospital Board* [1958] 1 WLR 181.

[129] In *Malloch v. Aberdeen Corporation* 1971 SLT 245, HL, Lord Reid distinguished employees in higher grades or offices from others who are in the same position as employees in the private sector.

[130] *Tehrani v. Argyll and Clyde Health Board* 1990 SLT 119, IH.

[131] See, for example, *Malloch v. Aberdeen Corporation* 1971 SLT 245, HL; and see para. 3. 63 *et seq.*; where no valid dismissal arises entitlement to arrears of salary or pension contributions may arise.

[132] Certain employees are excluded from the right to receive a written statement of the reasons for dismissal: see EPCA, s. 138(3) members of the forces, s. 141(2) (employment outside Great Britain), s. 144(2) (share fishermen), s. 146(2) (dock workers) and s. 146(2) (police).

[133] See para. 3.2.

[134] EPCA, s. 53 (2) as amended by EA 1989, s. 15.

dismissal with or without notice or on the expiry of a fixed-term contract which is not renewed, to receive from his employer, within 14 days of requesting[134a] it, a written statement[135] giving particulars of the reasons for his dismissal.[136] Where an employer (1) unreasonably[137] refuses[138] to provide a written statement, or (2) provides a statement whose particulars the employee alleges are inadequate or untrue,[139] the employee may present a complaint to an industrial tribunal.[140] If the employee's complaint is upheld the tribunal (1) may make a declaration of what were the true reasons for dismissal,[141] and (2) must award the employee 2 weeks' pay.[142] No special technicalities are required of the employer, and he may refer the employee to another document, already given to the employee, which provides the particulars,[143] but to be adequate the statement must be such that the employee or anyone else who sees it can know from the statement why the employee was dismissed.[144]

[134a] S. 53 cannot be used to correct a statement which an employer has volunteered where no request has been made: *Catherine Haigh Harlequin Hair Design v. Seed* [1990 IRLR 175, EAT.

[135] The statement is admissible in evidence in any proceedings, EPCA, s. 53(3).

[136] *Ibid.* s. 53 (1). As to the purpose of the statutory entitlement, contrast *Horsley Smith and Sherry Ltd v. Dutton* [1977] ICR 594, [1977] IRLR 172, EAT, with *Charles Lang & Sons Ltd v. Aubrey* [1978] ICR 168, [1977] IRLR 354, EAT. In the former case Phillips J appreciated the social purpose of finding out the reason for a dismissal, whereas Lord McDonald viewed the provision as penal. In *Harvard Securities plc v. Younghusband* [1990] IRLR 17 the EAT observed the purpose of s. 53 is to tie down the employer to the reason on which he genuinely relied thus making clear to the employee the case he has to meet.

[137] Whether a refusal is unreasonable is a matter for the industrial tribunal. A tribunal has held that it is unreasonable for employers to refuse a statement just because the police asked them not to answer any correspondence in connection with the offence which led to the dismissal: *Daynecourt Insurance Brokers Ltd v. Iles* [1978] IRLR 335, EAT.

[138] There has to be a refusal: *Lowson v. Percy Main and District Social Club and Institute Ltd* [1979] ICR 568, [1979] IRLR 227, EAT. However, a prolonged failure to produce the statement may allow the tribunal to conclude that there has been a refusal: *Newland v. Simons and Willer (Hairdressers) Ltd* [1981] ICR 521, [1981] IRLR 359, EAT.

[139] But this does not permit a tribunal to examine the justification for the dismissal: *Harvard Securities plc v. Younghusband* [1990] IRLR 17, EAT.

[140] EPCA, s. 53(4). The time for presenting such a complaint is the same as that for making a complaint of unfair dismissals (s. 53(5)). Thus, unless the tribunal deems an earlier complaint not reasonably practicable the time limit will be 3 months beginning with the effective date of termination (s. 67(2), (4)).

[141] *Ibid.* s. 53(4)(a). This can have important implications for unfair dismissal; see Chapter Five.

[142] *Ibid.* s. 53(4)(b). There is no maximum for s. 53.

[143] *Merchant v. Earley Town Council* [1979] ICR 891, [1979] IRLR 311, EAT.

[144] *Horsley Smith and Sherry Ltd v. Dutton* [1979] ICR 594; [1977] IRLR 172, EAT. The import of the decision is that one single document or statement must contain the essential reasons for the dismissal, although it may refer to other documents for further details. And see *Harvard Securities plc v. Younghusband* [1990] IRLR 17, AT.

Chapter Five

UNFAIR DISMISSAL

INTRODUCTION

5.1 The law giving employees the right not to be unfairly dismissed was first introduced by the Industrial Relations Act 1971 and became effective on February 28, 1972. The present law on unfair dismissal is regulated by the Employment Protection (Consolidation) Act 1978 Part V. In particular, s. 54(1) declares that, subject to certain exceptions, every employee shall have the right not to be unfairly dismissed by his employer. The aim is to create a statutory regime whereby an employee has the right to complain to an industrial tribunal when his contract is terminated and the tribunal will assess the legitimacy of the dismissal on the basis of fairness and reasonableness. This arrangement complies with international standards[1] and fulfils the recommendation of the Donovan Commission in 1968 that statutory machinery should be created which would require the employer to prove that he had a valid reason connected with the capacity or conduct of the worker or based on the operational requirements of the undertaking for any dismissal.[2] The industrial tribunal was selected as the appropriate forum for such complaints because it was an agency which seemed to possess the virtues of relative accessibility, informality, speed and lack of expense[3] — vital requirements for this area of the law.

5.2 It should be noted that the law of unfair dismissal does nothing to remove an employee's common law right to seek damages for wrongful dismissal in the civil courts. Thus an employee may have two remedies in relation to dismissal — one involving a breach of contract claim in a civil court and the other a statute-based complaint before an industrial tribunal. In the former, the outcome will depend largely on the terms of the contract of employment; in the latter, the decision will turn on the tribunal's assessment of the reasonableness or otherwise of the conduct of the employer. In most cases, a complaint of unfair dismissal will be the preferable option since it should be a cheaper and much faster option and because it provides at least the possibility of re-employment. However, given the qualifying requirements for unfair dismissal and the practical limitations in terms of remedies, there might still be circumstances where a wrongful dismissal action is preferable[4] and, indeed, in some occasions it may be the only remedy.

5.3 Qualifying for the right, exclusions and time limits
The basic rule is that before an employee is eligible to complain of unfair dismissal he must, on the effective date of termination of the contract of em-

---

[1] See International Labour Organisation Recommendation No. 119.
[2] See the Report of the Royal Commission on Trade Unions and Employers' Associations Cmnd 3623 at para. 545.
[3] *Ibid.*, para. 572.
[4] See, for example *Dietman v. London Borough of Brent* [1987] IRLR 146, CA.

ployment, have been continuously employed[5] by his employer (or any associated employer[6]) for a minimum period of two years.[7] At one time the qualifying period was as low as 26 weeks.[8] The present qualifying period was introduced as part of the Conservative Government's policies aimed at encouraging the recruitment of new staff.[9] Clearly, it now provides a substantial period during which an employer can form a view as to an employee's suitability without the fear of unfair dismissal proceedings being raised against him should he decide to dismiss. However, there are certain special cases where an employee has a right to complain of unfair dismissal without serving any qualifying period. These apply where an employee is dismissed for an automatically unfair reason *viz* because of his wish to join or to take part in the activities of an independent trade union, or because of his refusal to become or remain a member of a trade union. In these two cases a person obtains unfair dismissal protection as soon as employment has commenced.[10] Moreover, where employees are dismissed because of their sex or race a complaint under the Sex Discrimination Act 1975 or Race Relations Act 1976 will be competent because neither of these Acts stipulates a minimum qualifying period.

5.4 There are a number of ways by which a person can be denied the right to complain of unfair dismissal even in circumstances where it appears that the two year qualifying period has been satisfied. First, the right not to be unfairly dismissed only applies to those persons who satisfy the statutory definition of employee.[11] Thus only people who are employed under a contract of employment or a contract of apprenticeship can bring a complaint. A self-employed person working under a contract for services is excluded. Equally, those employed on the basis of non-standard contractual arrangements such as police cadets[12] or ministers of religion[13] are excluded. Despite the uncertainty as to whether or not Crown servants are employed under contracts of employment they do qualify for unfair dismissal rights.[14] However, persons who are employed under contracts of employment can still be denied the right to complain if their contracts have an illegal objective such as a fraud on the Inland Revenue. If a contract is illegal it is considered as being void *ab initio* and, therefore, cannot exist as a

---

[5] A matter discussed in more detail in Chapter Three, paras. 3.2-3.6.

[6] Under EPCA, s. 153(4) any two employers are to be treated as associated if one is a company of which the other (either directly or indirectly) has control, or if both are companies of which a third person (directly or indirectly) has control.

[7] EPCA, s. 64 (1)(a).

[8] The qualifying period was increased on a number of occasions by the Conservative Government from the 26 week qualifying period which operated when the Conservatives came to power in 1979. The present two years qualifying period was set by the Unfair Dismissal (Variation of Qualifying Period) Order 1985, S.I. 1985 No. 782 where the period of continuous employment began on or after 1 June 1985.

[9] This issue has been a constant theme of the Government's industrial and economic policies. See, for example, *Lifting the Burden*, Cmnd 9571, 1985 and *Building Businesses Not Barriers*, Cmnd. 9794, 1986.

[10] EPCA, s. 64(3). And see s. 64(2) regarding dismissal for reasons stated in s. 19(1), Sch. 1 (health and safety).

[11] EPCA, s. 153(1). See also Chapter Two, paras. 2.2-2.3.

[12] *Wiltshire Police Authority v. Wynn* [1980] ICR 649, CA.

[13] *Methodist Conference President v. Parfitt* [1984] ICR 176, CA; *Davies v. Presbyterian Church of Wales* [1986] ICR 280, HL.

[14] There is an equivalent provision for House of Commons Staff in EPCA, s. 138 and s. 139.

means of creating any rights to unfair dismissal.[15] In this area much will depend upon the knowledge of the employee as to the existence of this illegality.[16] Given the consequences for the complainant the tribunals are reluctant to hold that a contract of employment is illegal for this purpose. Thus a contract which appears legal on its face but is performed in an illegal way has been accepted as lawful in unfair dismissal law.[17]

5.5 Exclusions

Also there is a number of exclusions which deny a person a right to complain. First, an employee who is above retirement age is excluded.[18] Thus there is no right of complaint if the employee has on or before the effective date of termination attained the following age

(1) If in the undertaking in which he was employed there was a normal retiring age for an employee holding the position which he held and the age was the same whether the employee holding that position was a man or a woman, that normal retiring age; and

(2) in any other case, the age of sixty-five.[19]

It is clear that if there is a non-discriminatory normal retiring age in the undertaking such an age will apply for the purposes of unfair dismissal law no matter whether this age is above or below normal pensionable age. If there is no such age in the undertaking the appropriate age will be 65 for both men and women.

5.6 Although the concept of a normal retiring age has caused disagreement amongst the judges of the Court of Appeal in the past,[20] it is now clear that there is a presumption that the normal retiring age will be the contractual retirement age applicable to all, or nearly all, the employees holding the position of the employee concerned.[21] However, this presumption can be displaced where there is evidence to show that the relevant employees had a reasonable expectation that a higher age of retirement would replace the contractual age.[22] In order to displace the presumption it is not necessary to establish an express abandonment; it is enough if there is evidence that it is regularly departed from in practice.[23] In deciding whether there is such a departure, the tribunal must examine the class of employees to which the dismissed employee belonged. Thus the normal retiring age would not be disturbed when there is an agreement with an individual employee to continue longer in employment since a normal retiring age involves

[15] *Tomlinson v. Dick Evans U Drive Ltd* [1978] ICR 639, EAT.
[16] *Tomlinson, ibid.*
[17] *Coral Leisure Group Ltd. v. Barnett* [1981] ICR 503, EAT.
[18] EPCA, s. 64(1)(b) (as amended by SDA 1986, s. 3(1)).
[19] This provision was substituted by SDA 1986, s. 3(1) in order to comply with the decision of the European Court of Justice in *Marshall v. Southampton and SW Hampshire Area Health Authority* [1986] ICR 335. For the position under the earlier law see *Nothman v. London Borough of Barnet* [1979] ICR 111, HL.
[20] *Cf. Post Office v. Wallser* [1981] IRLR 37 and *Howard v. Department for National Savings* [1981] ICR 208.
[21] *Per* Lord Fraser of Tullybelton in *Waite v. Government Communications Headquarters* [1983] ICR 653 at 662. See also *Highland and Islands Development Board v. MacGillivray* [1986] IRLR 210, IH.
[22] *Hughes v. Department of Health and Social Security* [1985] ICR 419, HL.
[23] *Whittle v. Manpower Services Commission* [1987] IRLR 441, EAT; *Secretary of State for Scotland v. Meikle* [1986] IRLR 208, EAT.

a comparison with other employees who hold the same position as the applicant.[24] If the contractual retiring age is not observed in practice and employees retire at a variety of different ages there can be no normal retiring age for that undertaking so that in such a case the age of retirement will be taken to be 65.[25]

5.7 Employees who under their contracts of employment ordinarily work outside Great Britain are excluded from unfair dismissal law.[26] In the past it was thought possible for an employee ordinarily to work both in Britain and abroad.[27] However, it is now clear as a result of the decision of the Court of Appeal in *Wilson v. Maynard Shipbuilding Consultants AB*[28] that an employee must either ordinarily work in or outside Great Britain; he cannot do both at once. As the statutory directions make clear, the starting point for discovering a person's place of work must be the contract of employment. This involves the tribunal looking at the relevant terms of the contract, express or implied, over the whole period of employment. The question cannot be answered simply by reference to what has actually happened during the period of employment before termination took place,[29] Frequently, however, the contractual terms will provide little, if any guidance as to the actual place of work. In such a case the correct approach is to examine all the facts in order to discover the employee's "base".[30] This base will usually be considered as the place where the employee ordinarily works even although the employee spends a considerable period of time in other places. Although all the facts should be considered in determining an employee's base, such facts as the place where the employee gets his orders; where the travels involved in his employment begin and end; where his private residence is or is expected to be; where, and in what currency, he is paid; and whether or not he pays British national insurance contributions[31] might be particularly significant.

5.8 Any agreement which limits an employee's statutory rights or denies him the opportunity of complaining to an industrial tribunal is void.[32] In the context of unfair dismissal law this would mean that any contractual term which denied an employee the right to complain to an industrial tribunal would be unenforceable.[33] Equally, any agreement by a dismissed employee to abandon a complaint of unfair dismissal would be ineffective even where the employer has made a severance payment to that employee consistent with his entitlement to compensation under unfair dismissal law.[34] However, there are some excep-

[24] *Age Concern (Scotland) Ltd v. Hines* [1983] IRLR 477, EAT.
[25] *Waite v. Government Communications Headquarters* [1983] ICR 653, HL.
[26] EPCA, s. 141(2). EPCA, s. 141(5) declares that a person employed to work on board a U.K. registered ship shall be regarded as ordinarily working in Great Britain unless his employment is wholly outside Great Britain or he is not ordinarily resident here.
[27] *Portec (UK) Ltd. v. Morgensen* [1976] ICR 396, EAT.
[28] [1978] ICR 376.
[29] *Wilson, ibid.*
[30] *Wilson, ibid.; Todd v. British Midland Airways Ltd* [1978] ICR 959, CA. But see the judgment of Donaldson L.J. in *Janata Bank v. Ahmed* [1981] ICR 791 who pointed out that the base test is only an aid to construction and reminded tribunals that they should adopt a "broad brush approach" when examining the contractual position.
[31] *Per* Megaw L.J. in *Wilson v. Maynard Shipbuilding Consultants AB* [1978] ICR 376.
[32] EPCA, s. 140(1).
[33] For the special position of the fixed term contract see para 5.10.
[34] *Council of Engineering Institutions v. Maddison* [1977] ICR 30 EAT.

tions to this general rule. In particular there can be no complaint to an industrial tribunal where the employee is covered by a "dismissal procedures agreement" for which a relevant order has been made by the Secretary of State after
joint application by all the parties to the agreement.[35] Such an agreement must
be in writing and must be made by or on behalf of one or more independent
trade unions and one or more employers or employers' associations.[36] Before
making the order the Secretary of State must be satisfied as to the following
(1)   the procedures are non-discriminatory;
(2)   the remedies provided by the agreement are on the whole as beneficial
as statutory unfair dismissal law;
(3)   there is a right to arbitration or adjudication by some independent body;
(4)   the provisions of the agreement can be determined with reasonable certainty as to whether or not a particular employee is covered by it.[37]

5.9 An employee will also be prevented from pursuing a complaint to an industrial tribunal where a conciliation officer of ACAS has taken action in relation
to that complaint by promoting a settlement.[38] In exercising this function a
conciliation officer is not obliged to follow any specific formula. An officer
would be held to have promoted a settlement where his involvement with the
parties was simply to ensure that they had truly reached an agreement.[39] A
settlement cannot be challenged because the conciliation officer did not explain
the applicant's rights to him — there must be some evidence of bad faith or
unfair methods;[40] or perhaps economic duress.[41] Although such settlements are
usually recorded on a form provided by ACAS which is signed by the parties,
it has been held that an oral agreement reached through the intermediary of an
ACAS conciliation officer was to exclude an unfair dismissal application.[42]
Despite the fact that the Employment Protection (Consolidation) Act 1978, s.
134(1), requires that a complaint be presented to a tribunal before a conciliation
officer can become involved, it has been accepted that an officer can act not
only where the employee has made a formal or express complaint but also
where a claim can be implied from the overt acts or attitudes of the employee.[43]

5.10 It has already been noted that an agreement is void if it excludes an employee's statutory rights. However, an exception is made for an employee who
is employed on a fixed term contract[44] of one year or more. Such an employee
can agree in writing before the contract's expiration to waive any rights as to
unfair dismissal but only insofar as the dismissal arises from the expiry and
non-renewal of the contract. Thus an employee working under a fixed term
contract only waives his unfair dismissal rights as far as the non-renewal of that
contract is concerned and this is so no matter what is the reason for the dismissal;
however his rights to complain of unfair dismissal in any other circumstance

---

[35]   EPCA, s. 140(2)(c).
[36]   EPCA, s. 153(1).
[37]   EPCA, s. 65. The only major exempt industry is the Electrical Contracting Industry.
[38]   EPCA, s. 140(2)(d), (e) and (g) and ss. 133 and 134.
[39]   *Moore v. Duport Furniture Products Ltd* [1982] IRLR 31, HL.
[40]   *Slack v. Greenham (Plant Hire) Ltd* [1983] ICR 617, EAT.
[41]   *Hennessy v. Craigmyle & Co Ltd* [1986] ICR 461 CA.
[42]   *Gilbert v. Kembridge Fibres Ltd* [1984] ICR 188 EAT.
[43]   *Moore v. Duport Furniture Products Ltd* [1982] IRLR 31, HL; and see EPCA, s. 134(3).
[44]   EPCA, s. 142(1).

remain unaffected by the agreement. A fixed term contract is a contract where the parties have agreed a definite termination date. However, in *Dixon v. British Broadcasting Corporation*[45] the Court of Appeal held that a contract is for a fixed term even although it provides for termination by notice on either side before the expiry of the term. On the other hand, a contract which is inherently temporary but which is indeterminate in time, such as a contract to work until a particular task is completed, is not a fixed term contract.[46]

5.11 A number of specific employments are excluded from the ambit of unfair dismissal law. Persons employed in the police service are excluded[47] as are members of the armed forces.[48] The unfair dismissal provisions also do not apply to employment as a master or as a member of the crew of a fishing vessel where the person is paid by means of a share in the profits or gross earnings of the vessel.[49] Although, as we have seen, civil servants enjoy the advantages of unfair dismissal law this protection can be lost if a certificate issued by a Minister of the Crown is in force excluding that person in order to safeguard national security.[50] At one time there were also exclusions for employed spouses[51] and registered dock workers.[52] Both of these groups of employees can now complain of unfair dismissal.

5.12 Time limits

An employee has three months from the effective date of termination[53] of his contract to complain to an industrial tribunal.[54] This period expires at midnight on the last day of the three months, even when this is a non-working day[55] and runs from the date of dismissal. This is not necessarily the date when the employee is informed that an appeal against dismissal has failed,[56] nor the date when he receives his P45.[57] A failure to present the complaint within this period will render the complaint time-barred. However, the tribunal has the power to extend this period when it is satisfied that it was not reasonably practicable for the complaint to be presented within the three months.[58] The issue of reasonable practicability is essentially a question of fact for the industrial tribunal.[59] It would seem that the correct question for the tribunal is to ask whether it was reasonably feasible for the complaint to be presented in time.[60] This is a test which the courts

---

[45] [1979] ICR 281.
[46] See, for example, *Wiltshire County Council v. NATFHE* [1980] ICR 455 CA.
[47] EPCA, s. 146(2) and (3).
[48] EPCA, s. 138(3).
[49] EPCA, s. 144(2).
[50] EPCA, s. 138(4). See also *Council for Civil Service Unions v. Minister for the Civil Service* [1985] ICR 14 HL. There is also a power to exclude non-civil servants on security grounds: EPCA, s. 138(5), sch. 9, para. 2.
[51] EPCA, s. 146(1) repealed by EA 1982, s. 21(2), sch. 3 para. 6.
[52] EPCA, s. 145 repealed by Dock Work Act 1989, s. 7(1) and sch. 1.
[53] See paras. 5.27 to 5.29.
[54] EPCA, s. 67(2). This period is extended to six months in the case of a selective re-engagement of employees involved in industrial action: EPCA, s. 67(3).
[55] *Swainston v. Hetton Victory Club Ltd* [1983] ICR 341 CA.
[56] *Savage v. J. Sainsbury Ltd* [1981] ICR 1 CA.
[57] *London Borough of Newham v. Ward* [1985] IRLR 509 CA.
[58] EPCA, s. 67(2).
[59] *Palmer v. Southend-on-Sea Borough Council* [1984] ICR 372 CA.
[60] *Palmer, ibid.*

and tribunals apply strictly. An applicant's ignorance of his rights would not normally be a ground for extending the three month period.[61] Equally, where the delay is the fault of the applicant or a mistake by his adviser[62] in not informing him fully of his rights, there will be no extension of the time limit.[63] A late application may be allowed where the mistake is reasonable so that there is a just cause and excuse for it.[64] Thus an employee who knew of the time limit but who thought that his complaint for unfair dismissal would be heard by the same tribunal which considered his complaint for unemployment benefit was held entitled to submit a late complaint because his mistake was genuine.[65]

5.13 There are two further problems concerning the three-month time limit. First, what is the position of an employee who awaits the outcome of a final internal appeal and then discovers that when this has failed a right to complain to an industrial tribunal has become time-barred? At one time there were conflicting decisions of the Employment Appeal Tribunal on this point.[66] However, the Court of Appeal has now made it clear that the mere fact that an employee has been pursuing an appeal through the employer's internal machinery does not mean that it was not reasonably practicable for the unfair dismissal application to be made in time.[67] Thus an employee in such a position would be well advised to submit an application anyway in order to protect his rights. The other problem concerns the case where material information comes to the employee's attention after the expiry of the three months. In *Machine Tool Industry Research Association v. Simpson*[68] the Court of Appeal considered that this would be a circumstance where a late application would be accepted so long as the information was crucial or important and was reasonably unknown to the applicant during the three months so that once it was acquired it gave the applicant a genuine belief that a claim should be brought. This decision has important implications, in particular, for the redundant employee who later discovers that someone has been hired to replace him.

MEANING OF DISMISSAL

5.14 It is crucial for unfair dismissal law that the termination of the employee's contract satisfies the statutory definition of dismissal. Usually, this is not a problem since it is obvious that the employee has been dismissed. However, where this is an issue the onus of proving statutory dismissal rests with the employee. Dismissal is defined to apply in the following four cases:

---

[61] *Dedman v. British Building and Engineering Appliances Ltd* [1974] ICR 53 CA.

[62] *Riley v. Tesco Stores Ltd* [1980] IRLR 103 CA. This case also makes it clear that an adviser who is a trade union official or CAB worker is to be treated in the same way as a solicitor.

[63] *Dedman v. British Building and Engineering Appliances Ltd* [1974] ICR 53; *Walls Meat Co Ltd v. Khan* [1979] ICR 52 CA; *Riley, ibid.*

[64] *Khan, ibid.; Riley, ibid.*

[65] *Khan, ibid.*

[66] *Crown Agents for Overseas Government and Administration v. Lawa* [1979] ICR 103, EAT (good reason for an extension); *Bodha v. Hampshire Area Health Authority* [1982] ICR 200 EAT (no extension).

[67] *Palmer v. Southend-on-Sea Borough Council* [1984] ICR 372.

[68] [1988] IRLR 212.

(a)   where the contract is terminated by the employer with or without notice;

(b)   where under a fixed term contract the term expires without being re-newed under the same contract;

(c)   where the employee terminates the contract with or without notice in circumstances entitling him to terminate without notice by reason of the employer's conduct;

(d)   where a woman is refused permission by her employer to return to work after maternity leave.[69]

5.15 Termination by the employer

There will be a dismissal where the employer's words are a clear instruction to the employee that his contract is being terminated with or without notice. However, if the words used are ambiguous, it is necessary to construe them in context. This would entail looking at such factors as the status of the employee and, if the language was verbal, the place and circumstances in which the words were used.[70] Only if the words remain ambiguous after looking at them in their context should the tribunal then consider how these words could reasonably be interpreted and decide whether they were so interpreted by the employee concerned.[71] Problems can sometimes arise when the employer uses unambiguous words of dismissal in the heat of the moment. Such language need not consti-tute dismissal so long as the words are withdrawn almost immediately.[72] It will be a question of degree as to whether or not a retraction can prevent dismissal. Where the employee uses unambiguous language consistent with resignation, the employer can accept that resignation. A tribunal is entitled to apply the natural meaning of the employee's language and accept the fact of the employer's understanding of it without the need to decide how the reasonable employer would have reacted.[73] The only exception to this rule would be where there is something in the context of the exchange or in the circumstances of the em-ployee himself that establishes, that despite appearances, there was no real res-ignation.[74] These special circumstances may include decisions taken in the heat of the moment, or involving an immature employee,[75] or where the employee is jostled into a decision by the employer.[76]

Another area of difficulty is the case where at first sight it may appear that the employee has resigned, but it can be shown that the resignation was forced upon the employee by the employer. It is clear that where the employer issues an ultimatum such as "resign or be sacked" this should be construed as dis-missal.[77] The same would also apply where the employee is pressurised into

---

[69]   EPCA, ss. 55(2), 56.

[70]   Problems can sometimes arise as to whether offensive language used by an employer is intended simply to be abusive or meant to terminate the contract. See, for example, *Futty v. D. & D. Brekkes Ltd* [1974] IRLR 130, IT.

[71]   *J. & J. Stern v. Simpson* [1983] IRLR 52, EAT.

[72]   *Martin v. Yeoman Aggregates Ltd* [1983] ICR 314, EAT.

[73]   *Sothern v. Franks, Charlesly & Co* [1981] IRLR 278, CA.

[74]   *Sovereign House Security Services Ltd v. Savage* [1989] IRLR 115, CA.

[75]   *Savage, ibid.*

[76]   *Barclay v. City of Glasgow District Council* [1983] IRLR 313, EAT. It was also held in this case that there may be occasions (*e.g.* where an employee is suffering from emotional stress) where the employer is required to take account of the employee's special circum-stances before deciding whether to treat the employee as having resigned.

[77]   *East Sussex County Council v. Walker* [1972] 7 ITR 280; *Sheffield v. Oxford Controls Ltd* [1979] IRLR 133, EAT.

resigning because of employer fraud.[78] The crucial test in such cases is to consider who really terminated the contract.[79] However, employer dismissal depends upon there being a causal link between the employer's threat and the employee's resignation. Thus it would not be dismissal for an employer to tell an employee that if he does not find a job elsewhere his employment will eventually be terminated.[80]

5.16 Non-renewal of contract

An employer's non-renewal of a fixed term contract is a dismissal. As already noted, a contract can be for a fixed term even although it contains a notice clause.[81] Problems can still arise with this type of contract. Thus, for example, it would not be a dismissal in law when the contract came to an end and was not renewed because the contract specified that it would last only as long as sufficient funds were provided by sponsors and no further funding was received. In this case the contract came to an end automatically on the happening or non-happening of a future event — there was no need for action by anybody.[82]

5.17 Constructive dismissal

The third type of dismissal is "constructive" dismissal. This arises where, although it is the employee who ends the contract by walking out or giving notice, the real reason for the termination is some prior conduct by the employer. Although there was some confusion in the past, it is now clear that for employee's resignation to constitute a dismissal in law, the act must be in response to a material breach of contract by the employer; it would not be sufficient if the employer had merely acted in an unreasonable manner towards the employee.[83] Thus the present test for constructive dismissal concentrates upon the terms of the contract of employment both express and implied.[84] In order to satisfy this test the employer's conduct must go to the root of the contract so as to indicate that he no longer intends to be bound by it. This intention is judged objectively so that there might still be a material breach even where the employer believes that he has acted in conformity with the contract.[85] Obvious examples of such a material breach would be a failure to pay wages;[86] a unilateral alteration in duties without contractual authority;[87] a suspension without pay where this is not au-

---

[78] *Caledonian Mining Co Ltd v. Bassett* [1987] ICR 425, EAT.

[79] *Martin v. MBS Fastenings (Glynwed) Distribution Ltd* [1983] ICR 511, CA.

[80] *Haseltine, Lake & Co v. Dowler* [1981] ICR 222, EAT.

[81] *BBC v. Dixon* [1979] ICR 281, CA.

[82] *Brown v. Knowsley Borough Council* [1986] IRLR 102, EAT.

[83] *Western Excavating ECC Ltd v. Sharp* [1978] ICR 221, CA applied in Scotland in *Greater Glasgow Health Board v. Pate* 1983 SLT 90.

[84] See, for example, *Woods v. W. M. Car Services (Peterborough) Ltd* [1982] ICR 693, CA.

[85] *Lewis v. Motorworld Garages Ltd* [1986] ICR 157, CA. See also *Blyth v. Scottish Liberal Club* 1982 SC 140.

[86] *Industrial Rubber Products v. Gillon* [1977] IRLR 389, EAT. However, it has been held that where the contract does not provide for regular pay increases, no such term can be implied so that a failure to increase wages would not necessarily be a material breach: *Murco Petroleum Ltd v. Forge* [1987] IRLR 50, EAT.

[87] Removal of an employee's important duties leaving him with duties of a humdrum nature is undoubtedly grounds for employee resignation: *Coleman v. S. & W. Baldwin* [1977] IRLR 342, EAT. Even a temporary change of duties could be a material breach: *McNeill v. Charles Crimin (Electrical Contractors) Ltd* [1984] IRLR 179, EAT. See also *Hogg v. Dover College* [1990] ICR 39, EAT.

thorised by the contract;[88] a demotion out of proportion to the offence[89] or a failure to follow the contractual disciplinary rules.[90] Usually a constructive dismissal will arise as a result of a single act of the employer. However, there might be occasions where the right to resign can arise after a series of incidents so that the employee is entitled to rely on their cumulative effect.[91]

5.18 To a large extent each constructive dismissal case will depend upon its own facts with the terms of the contract constituting a critical focus for analysis. Thus, for example, in a case where the employee argues that a change in his place of work constitutes a material breach the tribunal will be required to discover whether or not there is a clear and unambiguous mobility clause giving the employer the power to relocate work.[92] However, even where there is no express term in the contract stipulating the employee's place of work, a right to transfer that employee might be implied on the basis of business efficacy.[93] Usually a term will be implied permitting a change in place of work so long as it is within reasonable daily travelling distance of the employee's home.[94] However, insufficient notice of such a change is undoubtedly a material breach.[95] The implied terms of the contract are also important in the sense that an employee may have a ground for resignation where the employer is in breach of one of his implied contractual duties. In particular, a complaint alleging that the employer's conduct has destroyed or seriously damaged the relationship of mutual trust and confidence between the parties is a fruitful means of establishing constructive dismissal.[96] Examples of this type of material breach include employer use of offensive language towards an employee;[97] questioning an employee's competence when this is not a true opinion of his abilities;[98] and denying the employee protection from harassment by fellow employees.[99]

5.19 For a constructive dismissal complaint to succeed it is also necessary that the employee establishes a causal link between the employer's material breach and his decision to leave.[100] An employee who delays his decision to resign might be prevented from successfully arguing constructive dismissal on the basis that he has accepted a variation in the terms of his contract.[101] To avoid this the employee should leave as quickly as possible or, if there are circumstances

---

[88] *D. & J. McKenzie Ltd v. Smith* [1976] IRLR 345, IH.
[89] *BBC v. Becket* [1981] IRLR 515, EAT.
[90] *Post Office v. Strange* [1981] IRLR 515, EAT.
[91] *Lewis v. Motorworld Garages Ltd* [1985] IRLR 465, CA.
[92] *Rank Xerox v. Churchill* [1988] IRLR 280, EAT.
[93] *Courtaulds Northern Spinning Ltd v. Sibson* [1988] IRLR 305, CA.
[94] *Sibson, ibid; Jones v. Associated Tunnelling Co Ltd* [1981] IRLR 477, EAT.
[95] *Prestwick Circuits Ltd v. McAndrew* [1990] IRLR 191, IH.
[96] See, for example, the decision of the Court of Appeal in *Woods v. W. M. Car Services (Peterborough) Ltd* [1982] ICR 693.
[97] *Isle of Wight Tourist Board v. Coombes* [1976] IRLR 413, EAT.
[98] *Courtaulds Northern Textiles Ltd v. Andrew* [1979] IRLR 84, EAT.
[99] *Wigan Borough Council v. Davies* [1979] IRLR 127. An employer's failure to take seriously an employee's complaint of sexual harassment can be grounds for resignation: *Bracebridge Engineering Ltd v. Darby* [1990] IRLR 3, EAT.
[100] *Walker v. Josiah Wedgwood & Sons Ltd* [1978] ICR 744, EAT.
[101] *Western Excavating (ECC) Ltd v. Sharp* [1978] ICR 221, CA. However, this would not apply where the employer's breach is either a continuing breach or a breach which also involves a breach of statute: *Reid v. Camphill Engravers* [1990] IRLR 268, EAT.

preventing this, to indicate that he does not accept the employer's conduct and is continuing to work under protest.[102] Thus an employee who makes clear his objection to the employer's conduct, should not be taken to have affirmed the contract by continuing to work and draw pay for a limited period even where this is simply to enable him to find alternative work.[103] Once the employee has established constructive dismissal it is still open to the employer to show that the reason for the dismissal was fair,[104] although usually this would be difficult.

5.20 Save for the special case of the employee who is not allowed to return to her old job after confinement, which will be discussed shortly, a complaint of unfair dismissal lies only where termination takes one of these three forms. Thus it is not a relevant form of dismissal where the parties mutually agree to terminate the contract, unless there was some unlawful employer pressure which forced the employee to agree to the termination.[105] In the past the tribunals applied the concept of mutual termination narrowly. For example, it was still a relevant dismissal where the employer dismissed an employee who had volunteered to go or who had no objection to being dismissed.[106] However, this position must now be contrasted with the case where the employee applies for retirement and this is accepted by the employer. In such a case there will be mutual termination, notwithstanding that the retirement was at the employer's request and subject to the employer's approval.[107]

5.21 Automatic termination

However there is one important limitation on the concept of an agreed termination. For example, an employee, in return for being given extended leave, may agree that if he does-not return to work on a specific date his contract will have terminated automatically. The legitimacy of this approach was tested and approved by the Employment Appeal Tribunal in *British Leyland (UK) Ltd v. Ashraf*[108] where it was held that in the circumstances there was no dismissal in law. However, this decision has now been reversed by the Court of Appeal in *Igbo v. Johnson Matthey Chemicals Ltd*[109] where the court, concerned about the damaging consequences of this approach for employees,[110] argued that an agree-

---

[102] *W. E. Cox Toner (International) Ltd. v. Crook* [1981] ICR 823, EAT. An employee who performs acts which can only be construed as consistent with the continuation of the contract will lose his right to complain. On the other hand, if the employee is only continuing in order to allow the employer to remedy his breach a complaint of unfair dismissal may still succeded.

[103] *Marriott v. Oxford Cooperative Society (No. 2)* [1970] 1 QB 186.

[104] *Berriman v. Delabole Slate Ltd* [1985] ICR 546, CA; *Stephenson & Co. (Oxford) Ltd v. Austin* [1990] ICR 609, EAT. See also the decision of the Second Division in *Greater Glasgow Health Board v. Pate* 1983 SLT 90 but note the dissent of Lord Dunpark who argued that once it had been held that the complainant had been constructively dismissed there was no room for argument that her dismissal had been other than unfair.

[105] *Staffordshire County Council v. Donovan* [1981] IRLR 108, EAT. And see *Logan Salton v. Durham C.C.* [1989] IRLR 99, EAT.

[106] *Burton, Alton & Johnson Ltd. v. Peck* [1975] ICR 193.

[107] *Birch and Humber v. University of Liverpool* [1985] ICR 470, CA.

[108] [1978] ICR 979.

[109] [1986] ICR 505.

[110] The potential application of the *Ashraf* principle could have been very wide. For example, could it have been used to deal with the employee with a poor attendance record. The absurdities of this approach are discussed by Parker L.J. in *Igbo, ibid.* at 512.

ment of this kind was void[111] because it constituted an attempt to limit the operation of the Act.

5.22 Self-dismissal

One other potential problem area concerns the notion of self-dismissal and its recognition as a form of termination of a contract of employment. This involves arguing that where an employee has committed an act of gross misconduct, that act alone should be taken as terminating the contract without the need for any dismissal by the employer. The acceptance of this argument would also deny a tribunal jurisdiction on the basis that the ending of the contract in such circumstances did not involve a dismissal. The Employment Appeal Tribunal recognised its validity in *Gannon v. J. C. Firth Ltd*[112] where the employees, in the course of a dispute, walked out of the factory without informing the management and left the premises in a dangerous state. It was held that this conduct was repudiatory of the contract and that it also ended the contract so that the employees had not been dismissed and could not complain of unfair dismissal. However, this case has also been overruled by the Court of Appeal. In *London Transport Executive v. Clarke*[113] a majority of that court held that a repudiatory breach does not automatically terminate a contract of employment. Instead, it gives the innocent party the right to elect to terminate the contract or not. It is only once the innocent party has decided to accept the repudiation and terminate the contract that the relationship is ended. In the context of employee misconduct, this means that the employer must dismiss the employee in order to end the contract.[114] Hence, in such circumstances the employee will at least be able to complain to a tribunal, although it is likely that the employer will be able to satisfy the tribunal as to the fairness of this decision.

5.23 Frustration

One circumstance where an employee will be denied the opportunity of complaining to an industrial tribunal is where his contract is terminated by operation of law. It is a general rule applicable to all contracts that a contract will end automatically when there is some frustrating event which renders that contract impossible or illegal to perform or involves performance of a radically different kind from that originally envisaged by the parties. As discussed earlier this doctrine undoubtedly applies to contracts of employment[115] and has special significance in unfair dismissal law for sick employees or those serving prison sentences. Its application to the sick employee was reviewed by the National Industrial Relations Court in *Marshall v. Harland and Wolff Ltd*[116] where it was stated that in considering whether an employee's sickness could frustrate the contract the tribunals should take account of certain factors.[117]

---

[111] EPCA, s. 140.

[112] [1976] IRLR 415, followed in *Kallinos v. London Electric Wire* [1980] IRLR 11, EAT.

[113] [1981] ICR 355 (Templeman and Dunn L.JJ., Lord Denning M.R. dissenting). See also *Rasool v. Hepworth Pipe Co Ltd* [1980] ICR 495, EAT. And see Chapter Four para 4.5

[114] See Chapter Four para 4.5

[115] See generally W. W. McBryde *The Law of Contract in Scotland* at paras. 15-22 to 15-48.

[116] [1972] ICR 101.

[117] See Chapter Four para 4.6

5.24 The reference to contracts of longstanding led the Employment Appeal Tribunal to argue in *Egg Stores (Stamford Hill) Ltd v. Leibovici*[118] that frustration would not normally be relevant in the case of short term periodic contracts terminable at short notice. It was also argued that although there were a large number of issues which had to be considered before a contract would be treated a frustrated one critical consideration would be to discover whether the time had come when the employer could no longer be reasonably expected to keep the absent employee's post open for him. The Employment Appeal Tribunal also argued that much may turn on the reason for the employer's inaction (*e.g.* avoidance of his statutory obligations) should this moment arise and the employer do nothing.[119] Indeed, the Employment Appeal Tribunal has gone so far as to argue in *Harman v. Flexible Lamps Ltd*[120] that the doctrine of frustration should not apply at all to a contract of employment which could be terminated by notice and should be therefore restricted to long term contracts without notice provisions. This narrow view of the operation of the doctrine has been criticised by the Court of Appeal in *Notcutt v. Universal Equipment Co (London) Ltd.*[121] In this case it was argued that there was no reason in principle why a periodic contract of employment determinable by relatively short notice should not also be capable of being terminated by frustration. When considering this question it is not necessary to take account of the injustice to the parties of the rules of frustration. The *Notcutt* case undoubtedly ensures that it will be much easier for the employer to argue in the future that the contract of a sick employee has been frustrated.[122] Nonetheless, in *Williams v. Watson Luxury Coaches Ltd*[123] the Employment Appeal Tribunal counselled tribunals to guard against too easy an application of the doctrine of frustration and reiterated that the tribunal should always consider the factors discussed in *Marshall* and *Liebovici* in order to determine whether a contract of employment has genuinely been frustrated.

5.25 There is no doubt that the serving of a custodial sentence can also be a potentially frustrating event. However, just like the sick employee the circumstances of each case must be considered with due regard for such factors as the employee's position in the business and the expected period of his absence from work.[124] Although usually frustration can only apply where the frustrating event is not the fault of either party, an exception is made for the imprisoned employee. Thus although in some senses it is the employee's fault which creates the circumstances making performance impossible this would not bar the application of frustration so long as it is the employer who seeks to take advantage of the doctrine.[125]

---

[118] [1976] IRLR 376.
[119] *A. R. Marshall & Sons (Bulwell) Ltd* [1977] IRLR 15, EAT.
[120] [1980] IRLR 418.
[121] [1986] ICR 414.
[122] The *Notcutt* case was actually a claim for damages for contractual sick pay. However, the principles applicable here are the same as for unfair dismissal. In this case a contract which had run for 27 years and which could be terminated by twelve weeks notice was held to be frustrated by an eight months' absence.
[123] [1990] IRLR 164.
[124] *F. C. Shepherd & Co Ltd v. Jerrom* [1985] ICR 552, EAT.
[125] *F. C. Shepherd & Co Ltd v. Jerrom* [1986] ICR 802, CA.

5.26 Return to work after confinement

The final type of dismissal for unfair dismissal purposes applies in the case of the female employee seeking to return to work after confinement. When an employee is entitled to return to work and has exercised her right to do so, but is not permitted to return, she should be regarded as being continuously employed until the notified date of her return and treated as dismissed with effect from that day for the reason for which she was not permitted to return.[126]

5.27 Effective date of termination

One further important issue as regards dismissal is the establishment of the employee's effective date of termination (EDT). This is important because it fixes the date upon which the employee's period of continuous employment ends and it starts the three month period during which the employee must submit his complaint of unfair dismissal to the tribunal. Clearly the exact date of this event will vary depending upon the form of dismissal. EDT is defined as follows:

(a)   in the case of an employee whose contract is terminated by notice, whether given by the employer or employee, the EDT will be the date on which that notice expires;

(b)   in the case of an employee whose contract is terminated without notice, the EDT will be the date on which the termination takes effect; and

(c)   in the case of an employee employed under a fixed term contract, where that term expires without being renewed under the same contract, the EDT will be the date on which that term expires.[127]

5.28 It is clear that where dismissal is communicated to an employee in a letter, the contract of employment will not terminate until the employee has actually read the letter or had a reasonable opportunity of reading it. In such a case the EDT is the date when the employee either does read the letter or the date when he reasonably had the opportunity of knowing about it — it is not backdated to the date when the letter was written.[128] A dismissal will terminate the contract once it has been communicated to the employee even although the dismissal is in breach of contract.[129] In England a distinction has been made between a case where an employee is dismissed with notice but is given payment in lieu of working out that notice, and a case where no notice of dismissal is given but a payment is made in lieu of notice. In the former the EDT is the date when the notice expires; in the latter the EDT is the date of receipt of the payment.[130] Much will depend upon the tribunal's construction of the employer's letter in deciding which alternative applies in a given case.[131]

5.29 There are also special statutory rules applying in the case of constructive dismissal. Usually the EDT will be the date when the contract would have ended had the employee been given the statutory minimum notice.[132] This date

---

[126] EPCA, s. 56.

[127] EPCA, s. 55(4).

[128] *Brown v. Southall & Knight* [1980] ICR 617, EAT.

[129] *Stapp v. Shaftesbury Society* [1982] IRLR 326, CA; *Batchelor v. British Railways Board* [1987] IRLR 136, CA. But see Chapter Three para. 3.39 and Chapter Four para. 4.5.

[130] *Adams v. GKN Sankey Ltd* [1980] IRLR 416, EAT.

[131] *Chapman v. Letheby & Christopher Ltd* [1981] IRLR 440, EAT.

[132] See Chapter Four para. 4.3.

will be calculated as running from the date when the employee ended the contract, or gave notice of termination.[133] However, the position is different where the employee is under notice of termination from the employer and that employee gives counter notice to terminate the contract at an earlier date. In such a case the EDT will be the date when the counter notice expires. If the employee seeks to end the contract immediately in such circumstances it would seem that EDT is the date when that intention is communicated to the employer.

REASONS FOR DISMISSAL

5.30 In the normal unfair dismissal case it is for the employee to show on a balance of probabilities that he was dismissed. Thereafter, the burden of proof passes to the employer to show that the reason for the dismissal falls within one of the fair grounds of dismissal as recognised by statute. There are several issues which have to be considered at this point. First an employer is required to give on request a written statement of the reasons for dismissal.[134] Second, an employer is required to prove the reason or, if there is more than one, the principal reason for the dismissal[135] and that it fell within one of the recognised categories of fair dismissal.[136] These are

(1)   a reason related to the capability or qualifications of the employee for performing work of the kind which he was employed by the employer to do;

(2)   a reason related to the conduct of the employee;

(3)   the reason was the redundancy of the employee;

(4)   the reason was that the employee could not continue to work in the position which he held without contravention (either on his part or on that of his employer) of a statutory duty or restriction;[137] or

(5)   some other substantial reason of a kind such as to justify the dismissal of an employee holding the position which that employee held.[138]

Finally, it is for the tribunal to decide whether in the circumstances (including the size and administrative resources of the employer's undertaking) the employer acted reasonably or unreasonably in treating the reason as a sufficient reason for dismissing the employee; and that question is to be determined in accordance with equity and the substantial merits of the case.[139]

5.31 A reason for dismissal is a set of facts known to the employer or beliefs held by him which cause him to dismiss the employee.[140] An employer is not necessarily bound by the reason given to the employee at the time of the dismissal. Thus a wrong label applied by the employer at the time of dismissal need not be fatal to his case.[141] The critical issue is for the employer to lead some evidence before the tribunal which shows that the reason upon which he

---

[133] EPCA s, 55(6)(7).

[134] See Chapter Four para. 4.12.

[135] EPCA, s. 57(1)(a).

[136] See generally *UCATT v. Brain* [1981] ICR 542, CA.

[137] EPCA, s. 57(2)(a)-(d).

[138] EPCA, s. 57(1)(b)

[139] EPCA, s. 57(3) as amended by EA 1980, s. 6 to "neutralise" the onus of proof and to reduce the burden on employers.

[140] *Abernethy v. Mott, Hay & Anderson* [1974] ICR 323 CA.

[141] But see *Harvard Security Plc v. Younghusband* [1990] IRLR 17, EAT.

relied allowed him to form a belief as to the ground for dismissal. However, where the employer adduces one reason as the only reason for the dismissal and that reason proves to be unfounded, the tribunal would be entitled to find the dismissal unfair since the employer has failed to show a potentially valid reason for dismissal.[142] The more difficult case is where the employer puts forward a number of reasons for the dismissal. In such a case, the tribunal is directed to discover the principal reason for that dismissal. It has been held that this direction does not require the tribunal to dissect the employer's reasons in analytical detail.[143] However, an employer must be careful when a number of reasons are put forward and one of these reasons proves unfounded that that specific reason did not form an important part of the principal reason for dismissal. The other reasons must be the more important reasons for the dismissal and constitute the principal reason by themselves for the employer to prove that he had a relevant reason for dismissal.[144]

5.32 There is no doubt that generally the test for identifying the employer's reason for dismissal is subjective so that the tribunal should seek to discover what was in the employer's mind at the time of the dismissal. In this regard, it is a fundamental rule that an employer cannot rely on a reason for dismissal which he did not know about at the time of dismissal.[145] Thus, contrary to the position at common law, if an act of gross misconduct comes to the employer's attention after the date of dismissal that ground cannot be argued before the tribunal; although it may be used to reduce compensation. However, this basic rule is subject to one exception applicable in a case where there is a right to an internal appeal. Any information which comes to light in the course of that appeal can be considered by the tribunal so long as the new evidence relates to the original ground of dismissal.[146] A failure to grant a right to such an appeal may of itself render a dismissal unfair.[147] However, a tribunal, when ascertaining the reason for dismissal, must ignore any pressure on the employer by way of calling, organising, procuring or financing a strike or other industrial action, or by threatening to do so.[148]

5.33 Fair grounds

The next stage is for the employer to show that the reason for the dismissal can be accommodated within the fair grounds of dismissal noted above. Occasionally, it may be difficult to categorise exactly the ground of dismissal. There are certainly times when a dismissal on the ground of capability can overlap with a misconduct dismissal. It would seem that where the lack of capability is attributable to the employee's failure to exercise the skills he possesses as opposed to an inherent deficiency in his work, then, this would be a dismissal for mis-

---

[142] *Nelson v. BBC* [1977] ICR 649, CA.

[143] *Bates Farms & Dairy Ltd v. Scott* [1976] IRLR 214, EAT.

[144] *Smith v. City of Glasgow District Council* [1987] ICR 796, HL. See also *Carlin v. St Cuthberts Cooperative Society Ltd* [1974] IRLR 188, NIRC.

[145] *W. Devis & Sons Ltd v. Atkins* [1977] ICR 662, HL.

[146] *National Heart and Chest Hospitals v. Nambiar* [1981] ICR 441 approved by the House of Lords in *West Midlands Cooperative Society Ltd v. Tipton* [1986] ICR 192. Technically, of course, the employer is not changing the reason, he is merely adducing further evidence in support of it.

[147] *Tipton, ibid.*

[148] EPCA, s. 63.

conduct.[149] In such a case there would be a need for the employer to issue warnings so that the tribunal could assess the reasonableness or otherwise of his decision to dismiss. If an employer is seeking to argue that a dismissal is fair on the ground of redundancy, the onus is upon him to show on a balance of probabilities that it was genuinely for this reason. The usual presumption which applies in redundancy law, *viz.* that a dismissal is by reason of redundancy until the contrary is proved is not relevant in an unfair dismissal context. In the case of dismissal for breach of a statutory enactment it is necessary for the employer to show that the illegality actually exists. It is not enough for the employer simply to have a subjective belief that continued employment will break the law.[150] The final ground for dismissal — for some other substantial reason — is a deliberately wide category of dismissal which need not be construed *eiusdem generis* with the other reasons.[151] Thus the range of grounds for dismissal which fit this category is an open question so that this is one head where there are few limitations upon the exercise of managerial prerogative.[152]

THE ISSUE OF REASONABLENESS

5.34 Once the employer has proved that there is a fair reason for the dismissal, the tribunal must then consider whether in the circumstances he acted reasonably in treating it as a sufficient reason for dismissing the employee. In determining this question, there is no onus of proof upon either party, although the House of Lords has stated that the language of s. 57(3) requires the employer to show the reason for the dismissal so that the tribunal can consider whether the employer acted reasonably in treating that reason as a sufficient reason for dismissal.[153] In the end, legislation directs tribunals to reach their decisions on the basis of equity and the substantial merits of the case.[154] This is essentially a question of fact so that assuming that the correct test is applied the decision of the tribunal is really only challengeable on appeal where it can be shown that no reasonably instructed tribunal could have reached it.[155] There are a plethora of decisions bearing upon the issue of reasonableness. However, with a view to avoiding legalism and to encourage the parties to present their own cases tribunals have been advised to avoid a preoccupation with guideline authority and to frame their decisions in accordance with the statutory directions.[156] This means that previous decisions do not have the same status as precedents as they would have in other legal fields. Nevertheless, they are important as indicating the general approach of the tribunals to the question of reasonableness.

5.35 The statutory directions are also important in two specific senses. First, tribunals are instructed to take account of the size and administrative resources of the employer's undertaking.[157] This means that the reasonableness test is

---

[149] *Sutton & Gates (Luton) Ltd v. Boxall* [1979] ICR 67, EAT.

[150] *Bouchaala v. Trust House Forte Hotels Ltd* [1980] IRLR 382, EAT.

[151] *R. S. Components Ltd v. Irwin* [1973] IRLR 239, NIRC.

[152] See John Bowers and Andrew Clarke "Unfair Dismissal and Management Prerogative; A Study of 'Other Substantial Reason'" (1981) 10 ILJ 34.

[153] *Smith v. City of Glasgow District Council* [1987] ICR 796, HL.

[154] EPCA, s. 57(3).

[155] *Spook Erection Ltd v. Thackray* [1984] IRLR 116, IH.

[156] *Anandarajah v. Lord Chancellor's Department* [1984] IRLR 131, EAT. For recent developments on this issue see Chapter Eight, paras. 8.22-8.24.

[157] EPCA, s. 57(3).

variable and will not be applied so stringently in the case of a small employer as it would be for a large business. Second, tribunals are directed[158] to have regard to the ACAS Codes of Practice. In the context of unfair dismissal law, the ACAS Code on Disciplinary Practice and Procedures in Employment[159] provides valuable guidance to tribunals in cases of dismissal for misconduct. The Code can be used both as a point of comparison when considering the reasonableness of an employer's own disciplinary procedures and sets out model arrangements in cases where there are no internal disciplinary rules.

5.36 Substantive and procedural issues

The issue of reasonablness has both a substantive and a procedural element, although, in the end, the decision has to be made on the basis of all the circumstances of the case. In terms of the substance of the decision, the tribunal must be satisfied that it was reasonable in the circumstances. In this regard it is not for the tribunal to substitute its own decision because it disagrees with the employer's particular conclusion in the circumstances of the case. The correct approach is to consider whether the decision of the employer is within a band of reasonable responses. The nature of this test is best explained in the judgment of Lord Denning M.R. in *British Leyland UK Ltd v. Swift*[160] where he declared as follows:

> "The correct test is: was it reasonable for the employer to dismiss him? If no reasonable employer would have dismissed him, then the dismissal was unfair. But if a reasonable employer might reasonably have dismissed him, then the dismissal was fair. It must be remembered that in all these cases there is a band of reasonableness, within which one employer might reasonably take one view; another quite reasonably take a different view . . . if it was quite reasonable to dismiss him, then the dismissal must be upheld as fair; even though some other employers may not have dismissed him."

A tribunal should approach this issue in the following way,

(1)   the starting point must always be the statutory language;[161]
(2)   in applying this the tribunal must consider the reasonableness of the employer's conduct, not simply whether it considers the dismissal to be fair;
(3)   in judging reasonableness the tribunal must not substitute its decision as to what was the right course to adopt for that of the employer;
(4)   in many, though not all, cases there is a band of reasonable responses to the employee's conduct within which one employer might reasonably take one view, another quite reasonably take another;
(5)   the function of the industrial tribunal, as an industrial jury, is to determine whether in the particular circumstances of each case the decision to dismiss fell within the range of reasonable responses which a reasonable employer might have adopted.[162]

---

[158] EPA, s. 6(11).

[159] ACAS Code of Practice No. 1 effective from 20 June 1977. ACAS has tried to introduce a new and more extensive Code which was rejected by the Secretary of State. See (1987) D. of E. Gazette 150. However, there is now a useful ACAS handbook on Discipline and Dismissal.

[160] [1981] IRLR 91 applied in Scotland by the Inner House in *Gair v. Bevan Harris Ltd* 1983 SLT 487.

[161] EPCA, s. 57(3).

[162] See generally the decision of the EAT in *Iceland Frozen Foods Ltd v. Jones* [1983] ICR 17 particularly at pp. 24-25. Both *Swift* and *Jones* have been approved by the Second Division in *Scottish Midland Co-operative Society v. Cullion* [1991] IRLR 261.

Thus in the end it is the function of the tribunal, as an industrial jury, to determine whether in the particular circumstances of each case the employer's decision fell within the band of reasonable responses which a reasonable employer might have adopted. If the decision falls within that band the dismissal is fair; if the dismissal falls outside the band it is unfair.

5.37 A reasonable employer must not only have regard to the reason for the dismissal but also to the need for some sort of procedure relevant to the circumstances of the case. This is particularly important in misconduct cases where, as has already been noted, the ACAS Code of Practice must be a major focus of attention in order to establish the "procedural fairness" of the dismissal. Thus it might not be enough for an employer to have a fair substantive reason for dismissal he must also ensure that a fair procedure is adopted. This would entail such elements as a proper investigation,[163] issuing warnings, and in serious cases meriting dismissal a right to a hearing and an appeal against the decision to dismiss. The importance of procedural fairness as an element in an unfair dismissal case has varied over the years. At least initially procedural fairness was a critical factor which could render an otherwise fair dismissal unfair simply through a want of procedure.[164] Later, procedural fairness was relegated to being one of a number of factors which established the reasonableness of the employer's decision. This approach became encapsulated in the *British Labour Pump*[165] test which allowed an employer to succeed in an unfair dismissal claim even where there had been a failure to follow the correct procedure if he could prove on a balance of probabilities that if he had applied the correct procedure there would have been no difference and the employee would still have been dismissed.

5.38 The decision of the House of Lords in *Polkey v. A. E. Dayton Services Ltd*[166] breathes fresh life into the procedural aspects of an unfair dismissal case. In particular, it makes it clear that the *British Labour Pump* test is unsound because it is inconsistent with the decision of the House of Lords in the *Devis* case[167] that the reason for the employer's decision to dismiss must be judged in light of his knowledge at the date of dismissal and because it concentrates unnecessarily upon the question of injustice to the employee and ignores the statutory direction to judge the employer's actions on the basis of the reasonableness test. It is now the case, therefore, that the question whether a particular dismissal is unfair must be judged in the light of what the employer actually did and not what he might have done. This should mean that in most cases a failure to apply a proper procedure will lead to a finding that the dismissal was

---

[163] *British Home Stores Ltd v. Burchell* [1978] IRLR 379, EAT.
[164] See, for example, *Earl v. Slater & Wheeler (Airlyne) Ltd* [1972] IRLR
[165] *British Labour Pump Ltd v. Byrne* [1979] ICR 347, EAT. Approved by the EAT in Scotland in *Gray Dunn & Co Ltd v. Edwards* [1980] IRLR 23. See also the decision of the Court of Appeal in *W. & J. Wass Ltd. v. Binns* [1982] ICR 486.
[166] [1988] ICR 142.
[167] *Devis & Sons Ltd. v. Atkins* [1977] ICR 662.

unfair.[168] It is equally true that an employer who denies an employee a right to appeal against a decision to dismiss might also jeopardise his chances of proving that the dismissal was fair.[169] On the other hand, not every breach of an employee's contractual right of appeal renders a dismissal unfair. However, a dismissal is likely to be unfair, even where an employee has been granted an appeal, if the appellate procedure was defective because it could or should have found and demonstrated a flaw in the employer's disciplinary procedures and did not do so.[170]

5.39 It is clear that the tribunal must consider the reasonableness of the employer's decision in the circumstances of the case. One aspect of this is that the employer should take some account of the personal circumstances of the employee. Thus long-serving employees should obtain some recognition for that service when an employer is contemplating dismissal; although it is really the quality of that service which counts.[171] Length of service may be particularly important in redundancy cases and there can be no doubt that selection on the basis of last in first out is *prima facie* evidence of a reasonable choice by the employer. Another consideration, particularly in misconduct cases, is for the employer to act consistently so that employees in similar positions are treated in the same way and obtain the same sanctions for the same types of offence.[172] However, although the issue of consistency must be important so also must be the question of flexibility of approach. Thus although it would seem sensible to treat like cases alike the Employment Appeal Tribunal has counselled both tribunals and employers to avoid applying a tariff approach to industrial misconduct cases.[173] Everything turns on the circumstances of the particular case. In many ways it is difficult to separate the issue of reasonableness from the employer's chosen ground for dismissal, so the fair reasons for dismissal must be discussed in more detail.

---

[168] See, for example, the speech of Lord Bridge of Harwich in *Polkey v. A. E. Dayton Services ltd* [1988] ICR 142 at p. 163 who argued that the language of s. 57(3) ensured that in the case of incapacity an employer would not normally act reasonably unless he gives the employee fair warning and an opportunity to mend his ways and show that he can do the job; in the case of misconduct a reasonable employer would be expected to investigate the complaint fully and fairly and to hear the employee in his defence or in mitigation and in a redundancy case an employer would not normally act reasonably unless he warns and consults employees and adopts a fair basis of selection. For a recent application of *Polkey* in a misconduct case see the decisions of the EAT in *Spink v. Express Foods Group Ltd* [1990] IRLR 320 and *Louies v. Coventry Hood & Seating Co. Ltd.* [1990] IRLR 324.

[169] *West Midlands Cooperative Society Ltd v. Tipton* [1986] ICR 192 HL. This is most likely to be the case where the employee has a contractual right to an appeal and is still challenging the sufficiency of the employer's reasons.

[170] *Post Office v. Marney* [1990] IRLR 170, EAT.

[171] *AEI Cables Ltd v. McLay* 1980 SC 42, IH.

[172] *Post Office v. Fennell* [1981] IRLR 221, CA. It is no defence for an employer to argue that the manager who dealt with previous cases was not the one who considered the circumstances of the complainant's dismissal. Consistency must be consistency as between all employees of the employer. See *Cain v. Leeds Western Health Authority* [1990] IRLR 168, EAT.

[173] *Hadiioannou v. Coral Casinos Ltd* [1981] IRLR 352.

THE OPERATION OF THE FAIR REASONS

5.40 (a) Capability or qualifications

"Capability" is assessed by reference to skill, aptitude, health or any other physical or mental quality and "qualifications" as meaning any degree, diploma or other academic, technical or professional qualification relevant to the position which the employee held.[174] Clearly, dismissal for lack of capability is the more important reason. In some cases it may be difficult to establish that the employee is incompetent, and given that the qualifying period for a claim is now two years it must be assumed that many employees who are considered incompetent by their employers will be dismissed without qualifying for any unfair dismissal rights. However if an employee is being dismissed on the ground of incompetence it is usually the case that the employee cannot be dismissed for one single incompetent act; although there may be exceptions such as where the job involves such high standards that the employer cannot take the risk of repetition.[175]

5.41 To a large extent the requirement that the employee at least be given some warning that his job is at risk seeks to resolve the tension between the interest of the employer not to have his business affected adversely by an inefficient employee and the employee's right not to be treated unfairly. Ultimately, the tribunal must be satisfied that the employer honestly believed on reasonable grounds that the employee was incompetent and that there was a reasonable basis for that belief.[176] This test will require the employer to have conducted some sort of investigation into the employee's competence. There is also an obligation upon the employer to train the employee in the job and to ensure proper supervision. As far as the procedure for such dismissals is concerned, although the incompetent employee is not entitled to the same level of warnings as the employee who is guilty of misconduct, at the very least, he has the right to a fair warning from the employer.[177] This should inform the employee of the aspects of his work which he is not performing adequately and advise him of the likelihood of dismissal if there is no improvement in his work after having been given a reasonable opportunity to improve his performance.[178]

5.42 *Ill health dismissals.* The most difficult type of capability case is that applying to the sick employee. As has already been discussed, the contract of employment of a sick employee absent from work for a substantial period might well terminate automatically through the doctrine of frustration. However, it is the clear thrust of the decisions on this subject that it is much the better route for the employer to consider all the options, and, where appropriate, to take the decision to dismiss. In reaching such a decision the critical issue is to balance

---

[174] EPCA, s. 57(4).
[175] *Alidair Ltd v. Taylor* [1978] IRLR 82, CA.
[176] *Taylor, ibid.*
[177] See, for example, the speech of Lord Bridge of Harwick in *Polkey v. A. E. Dayton Services Ltd* [1988] ICR 142 at p. 163. It should be remembered that where an employee's incapacity is attributable to his failure to exercise the skills that he possesses this would be a dismissal for misconduct where a warnings approach would be required. See generally *Sutton and Gates (Luton) Ltd v. Boxall* [1979] ICR 67, EAT.
[178] *Winterhalter Gastronom Ltd v. Webb* [1973] ICR 245, NIRC.

the employer's need for the work to be done, against the need of the employee to be given time to recover from his illness.[179] In the end, the tribunal must ask itself whether the employer should be expected to wait any longer and, if so, how much longer before dismissing the sick employee.[180] Although warnings are clearly not applicable here,[181] it is important for the employer to consult with the employee and to discuss the matter with him so that the true medical position can be established.[182] Save in special circumstances, a failure to consult will show that the employer has acted unreasonably in the circumstances.[183]

5.43 In order to discover the true position it might also be important to discuss the employee's state of health with medical advisers and this may involve the employee undergoing an examination by a doctor nominated by the employer so long as there is contractual authority to this effect. But it has been stressed that the final decision to dismiss is not a medical one but one to be decided by the employer in the light of all the relevant facts.[184] Even where the employer forms the view that the sick employee is no longer capable of performing his work it does not necessarily follow that he should be dismissed. An employer should consider if there is other alternative work which the employee can do. The employer is certainly not obliged to create a special job for the sick employee.[185] However, an employer who does not consider this issue may be acting unreasonably; although it is certainly the case that he does not have to go out of his way to accommodate the sick employee.[186] Difficulties also arise in relation to the employee who is sick and absent from work on an intermittent basis. The Employment Appeal Tribunal has recently declared[187] that the correct approach in such a case is one based on sympathy, understanding and compassion and that a disciplinary approach is not appropriate. In the end there may come a time when the employee should be cautioned that his absences have reached the stage where it is impossible to continue with that employment.

5.44 (b) Misconduct

The sort of conduct which would justify dismissal has been described in *Thomson v. Alloa Motor Co Ltd*[188] as being actions of such a nature, whether done in the course of employment or outwith it, that reflect in some way upon the employer-employee relationship. In terms of conduct within employment usually one act of misconduct will not justify dismissal. Only acts of gross misconduct such as thefts or assaults would merit dismissal for a single act. In this field, therefore, much will depend upon the previous disciplinary record of the employee and the employer's own disciplinary rules or, failing these, the ACAS Code. Thus

---

[179] *Taylorplan Catering (Scotland) Ltd v. McInally* [1980] IRLR 53, EAT.

[180] *Spencer v. Paragon Wallpapers Ltd* [1976] IRLR 373, EAT.

[181] *Spencer, ibid.*

[182] *East Lindsay District Council v. Daubney* [1977] IRLR 81 EAT.

[183] *Leonard v. Fergus & Haynes Civil Engineering Ltd* [1979] IRLR 235, IH. In *A Links & Co Ltd v. Rose, The Scotsman* 19 June 1991 the First Division argued that the correct approach was for the tribunal to determine, as a matter of fact and judgments, what consultation, if any, was necessary or desirable in the circumstances, what consultation, if any, took place and whether or not that consultation process was adequate in the circumstances.

[184] *East Lindsey District Council v. Daubney* [1977] IRLR 81, EAT.

[185] *Merseyside & North Wales Electricity Board v. Taylor* [1975] IRLR 60.

[186] *Carricks (Caterers) Ltd v. Nolan* [1980] IRLR 259, EAT.

[187] *Lynock v. Cereal Packaging Ltd* [1988] IRLR 510, EAT.

[188] [1983] IRLR 403, EAT.

the issue of warnings for previous acts of misconduct is likely to be an important focus for discussion in most conduct dismissals. Save for cases of gross misconduct, the sanction applied to a particular act or omission will depend upon the gravity of the offence and the employee's previous record. An employee who commits a fairly minor act may find himself dismissed because of the cumulative effect of his previous warnings. Obviously, therefore, it is important for employers with their own disciplinary rules to specify clearly the various acts of misconduct which employees can commit and to set out the penalties which can apply to them. The ACAS Code certainly envisages that for first offenders who commit a minor offence the penalty should be a formal oral warning; in more serious cases the sanction should be a written warning and only in cases of gross misconduct should the employee be dismissed. It also recognises that the disciplinary rules will vary depending on the circumstances of the case. Thus it is open to employers when devising their disciplinary rules to categorise some relatively trivial act which might usually only merit a warning as an act of gross misconduct justifying dismissal for certain classes of employees because of the impact of this type of misconduct upon their businesses. In the end, of course, the employer cannot circumvent the statutory test of reasonableness and it will be for the tribunal to decide whether or not the employer's decision to dismiss for this type of misconduct is reasonable in the circumstances.[189]

5.45 *Proof in misconduct dismissals.* One important question which arises in misconduct dismissals concerns the level of proof that the employer requires. It is clear that the employer does not have to prove the employee's guilt; it is enough if he has a genuine belief in the employee's guilt.[190] The *Burchell* case laid down a threefold approach to this question. First, it is necessary for the employer to have a genuine belief in the employee's guilt; second, the employer must have reasonable grounds upon which to sustain that belief; and, third, there must have been as much investigation into the matter as was reasonable in all the circumstances of the case.[191] The test was developed originally to deal with dishonesty cases, but its application has now been approved in other cases of breach of discipline.[192] The level of investigation required by the *Burchell* test will vary depending upon the nature of the case. At the one extreme will be cases where the employee is virtually caught in the act and at the other end are cases where the issue is one of pure inference. As the scale moves towards a case based on inference so the amount of inquiry and investigation required of the employer will increase.[193] There is undoubtedly an obligation upon an employer to conduct a most stringent inquiry where his case depends entirely upon the uncorroborated evidence of an informant who refuses

---

[189] See the decision of the Inner House in *Ladbroke Racing Ltd v. Arnott* [1983] IRLR 154.

[190] *British Home Stores Ltd v. Burchell* [1978] IRLR 379, EAT approved by the Court of Appeal in *W. Weddell & Co Ltd v. Tepper* [1980] ICR 286.

[191] A tribunal must avoid substituting its own views when applying this test. See the decision of the Northern Ireland Court of Appeal in *Ulsterbus Ltd v. Henderson* [1989] IRLR 251.

[192] *Distillers Co (Bottling Services) Ltd v. Gardner* [1982] IRLR 47, EAT.

[193] *ILEA v. Gravett* [1988] IRLR 497, EAT. In *Scottish Midland Cooperative Society Ltd v. Cullion* [1991] IRLR 261 the Second Division argued that the correct approach was to discover whether the employer believed that the employee was guilty of misconduct and was entitled so to believe, having regard to the investigation carried out.

to be named.[194] Clearly, there is no requirement upon an employer to hold an investigation where the employee has already admitted the misconduct.[195] Equally, the full rigours of the *Burchell* test do not apply where the employer is convinced that one of two or three employees is responsible for an act of dishonesty but cannot identify the actual culprit. In such a case the employer would be entitled to dismiss all of the employees so long as three points are satisfied. First, the act must be one which if it had been committed by an identified individual would have justified dismissal; second, the tribunal must be satisfied that the act was committed by one or more of the group, all of whom can be shown to be individually capable of having committed the act complained of; and, third there must have been a proper investigation by the employer to identify the culprit.[196] These special rules are most likely to apply in dishonesty cases, although they may also operate in conduct cases generally and exceptionally in capability cases.[197]

5.46 The importance of procedural fairness in the wake of *Polkey v. A E Dayton Services Ltd*[198] has already been noted. In a misconduct case one would expect an employer to (1) investigate, (2) grant the employee a hearing and (3) permit an appeal where the employee is still challenging the grounds for dismissal. The right of the employee to be heard must be a critical step in a misconduct case. Its current importance can be guaged by *McLaren v. National Coal Board*[199] where it was held that an employee who had been dismissed for assault should have been given a hearing even although this would have been difficult to convene because of the miners' strike. In this case the court stressed that the standards of fairness are immutable. A useful case which spells out the various steps which an employer should follow for misconduct dismissals is *Whitbread & Co Plc v. Mills*[200] in which it was suggested the question of reasonableness could be approached by asking the following subsidiary questions:
(1)   Has the employer complied with the pre-dismissal procedures which a reasonable employer would have applied in the circumstances?
(2)   Where there is a contractual appeal process, has the employer carried it out in its essentials?
(3)   Where conduct is the main reason, has the employer proved that at the time of dismissal he had a reasonable suspicion amounting to a belief in the guilt of the employee and, if necessary, complied with the *Burchell* principles?
(4)   During the disciplinary hearing and the appeals process, has the employer dealt fairly with the employee?

---

[194] *Linfood Cash & Carry Ltd v. Thomson* [1989] IRLR 235, EAT. This case also contains a useful checklist of the steps which an employer should take when dealing with a misconduct complaint based upon the allegations of an informant. See Wood J. at pp. 237-238.
[195] *RSPB v. Croucher* [1984] IRLR 425, EAT.
[196] *Monie v. Coral Racing Co Ltd* [1980] IRLR 464 CA as developed by the EAT in *Whitbread & Co Plc v. Thomas* [1988] IRLR 43. See also *Parr v. Whitbread Plc* [1990] IRLR 39 where the EAT again reiterated the need for a tribunal to be satisfied that the employer acted reasonably in identifying the group and that as between members of this group the employer could not reasonably identify the individual perpetrator.
[197] *Thomas, ibid.*
[198] [1988] ICR 142, HL. Applied by the EAT in *Spink v. Express Fords Escort Ltd* [1990] IRLR 320 and *Louies v. Coventry Hood & Seating Co Ltd* [1990] IRLR 324.
[199] [1988] IRLR 215, CA.
[200] [1988] IRLR 501, EAT.

5.47 *Criminal offences.* The commission of a criminal offence, although a major act of misconduct, is merely one example of misconduct which may justify dismissal. Clearly, as far as criminal behaviour within employment is concerned, given that it is not necessary for an employer to prove guilt but merely to have a genuine belief as to the employee's misconduct which is based on reasonable grounds, an employer may be held to have dismissed fairly even although the employee is subsequently acquitted at his trial or the procurator fiscal decides not to proceed with the criminal charge.[201] In the end, the issue for the tribunal is to discover whether the employer's behaviour complied with the statutory test of fairness.[202] On the other hand, where the criminal offence relates to conduct outside employment an employer would be well advised to dismiss only after the employee has been convicted. Even then the employer must also be sure that the nature of the offence makes the employee unsuitable to continue in his job.[203] The important point is for the employer to make a connection between the offence and the duties which the employee performs at work. In one sense this is a very simple task since it might be argued that any conviction has a bearing on the employer/employee relationship. However, it is necessary for the employer to show either that his business will be affected by continued employment because of the impact upon customers or the effect upon fellow employees or that the commission of the offence has seriously damaged the relationship of trust and confidence between the parties.[204] The more senior the employee the easier it will be for the employer to establish this latter point.[205]

5.48 (c) Redundancy

Where the employer establishes that his principal reason for dismissing an employee was one of redundancy that dismissal will be considered fair and the employer's primary obligation will be to pay the relevant statutory redundancy payment. However, such dismissals can be challenged in two ways. First, a redundancy dismissal can be regarded as unfair if it can be shown that the circumstances constituting the redundancy applied equally to one or more other employees in the same undertaking who held similar positions and who were not dismissed, and either

(a)   the reason the applicant was selected was his union membership, non-membership or activities, or

(b)   he was selected for dismissal in contravention of a customary arrangement or agreed procedure and there were no special reasons justifying departure from that arrangement or agreement.[206]

---

[201] See, for example, the decision of the Inner House in *Carr v. Alexander Russell Ltd* [1976] ICR 39 where it was held that an employer could dismiss an employee before his trial where that employee had been caught red-handed by the police with the employer's property and later charged with theft. On the other hand the mere fact that an employee has been charged with theft would not of itself merit dismissal; in such a case an employer would be required to conduct some sort of investigation: *Scottish Special Housing Association v. Cooke* [1979] IRLR 264, EAT.

[202] *Harris (Ipswich) Ltd v. Harrison* [1978] IRLR 382, EAT.

[203] See, for example, ACAS Code para. 15(c). Cf. *Bradshaw v. Rugby Portland Cement Co Ltd* [1972] IRLR 46 and *Nottinghamshire County Council v. Bowly* [1978] IRLR 252, EAT.

[204] *Norfolk County Council v. Bernard* [1979] IRLR 220, EAT; *Moore v. C. and A. Modes Ltd* [1981] IRLR 71, EAT.

[205] *Richardson v. Bradford City Metropolitan Council* [1975] IRLR 296, EAT.

[206] EPCA, s. 59. As to the union membership etc see para. 5.57.

An agreed procedure can encompass both express agreed procedures and those existing by implication.[207] The question as to whether there are special reasons justifying a departure from the agreed procedure is essentially one for the tribunal as an industrial jury. An appeal against this type of decision will lie only when the tribunal has misdirected itself in law or has reached a decision which no properly instructed tribunal could have reached on the facts.[208] An employer who cannot rely on an agreed procedure may fall back upon a customary arrangement, but the normal practice of an employer to seek volunteers before declaring compulsory redundancies cannot be a customary arrangement because it is too vague.[209] At the very least the criteria applied in such an arrangement must be sufficiently certain so as to enable the tribunal to compare the position of the applicant with an employee who was not dismissed.

5.49 A dismissal for redundancy can also be unfair on the basis that the employer has handled the redundancy in such a way that he cannot be held to have acted reasonably in all the circumstances. In particular, a dismissal may be challenged on this basis either because there were no clearly adopted criteria to ascertain those selected for redundancy or that the criteria which were applied were inherently unreasonable. In England guidance has been provided in *Williams v. Compair Maxam Ltd*[210] where it was stated an employer should consider:
(1) the need to give as much warning as possible about impending redundancies;
(2) the need for consultation and discussion with trade unions so as criteria for selection can be agreed;
(3) even where union agreement cannot be obtained the employer should devise criteria which are objectively justifiable;
(4) those criteria should be applied fairly, taking account of any union representations;
(5) the need to consider whether those selected could be offered alternative employment.

5.50 In Scotland there has been some reluctance to accept the *Compair Maxam* principles. The Scottish approach has been to recognise that once the employer has shown that the dismissal is not in contravention of an agreed procedure or customary arrangement, in most cases it will be extremely difficult for the tribunal to hold that in dismissing the applicant the employer acted unreasonably.[211] Moreover, in Scotland it has been stated that the five principles were never intended to be considered in each and every redundancy case, nor that an employer had to comply with every one of the principles in order to avoid a finding of unfair dismissal.[212] Indeed, in Scotland it has been argued that the *Compair Maxam* principles only have relevance to large organisations where a significant number of redundancies are contemplated; they should not be applied to small employers, particularly if those employers do not recognise trade unions.[213] These comments

---

[207] *Henry v. Ellerman City Liners Ltd* [1984] IRLR 409, CA.
[208] See *Cross International v. Reid* [1985] IRLR 387, CA.
[209] *Rogers v. Vosper Thorneycroft (UK) Ltd* [1989] IRLR 82.
[210] [1982] ICR 156, EAT.
[211] See, for example, in *Atkinson v. George Lindsay & Co* [1980] IRLR 196 and *Buchanan v. Tilcon Ltd* [1983] IRLR 417, IH.
[212] *A. Simpson & Son (Motors) Ltd v. Reid* [1983] IRLR 401, EAT.
[213] *Meikle v. McPhail (Charleston Arms)* [1983] IRLR 351, EAT; *Gray v. Shetland Norse Preserving Co Ltd* [1985] IRLR 53, EAT.

are subject to two further points. First, since *Polkey v. A. E. Dayton Services Ltd*[214] in most cases the reasonable employer would be expected to consult with the employee concerned prior to dismissal. In fact, Lord Bridge even went so far as to argue that an employer would not be acting reasonably in most redundancy cases unless he consults with the employee or his representative, adopts a fair basis for selection and considers redeployment or staff! Second, although rarely referred to in Scottish cases, the Industrial Relations Code of Practice (1972) also provides guidance as to the procedural aspects of redundancy and also places particular emphasis upon the need for consultation.[215]

5.51 (d) Contravention of a statutory enactment

As has already been noted, for a dismissal to be accepted as fair under this head it is necessary for the employer to show that continued employment will contravene a statutory enactment and it has been held that this ground does not extend to encompass the idea of a genuine but erroneous belief on the part of the employer;[216] however such a belief may allow the employer to plead there was some other substantial reason for the dismissal.[217] A reasonable employer who does have an employee whose continued employment will break the law should consider whether that employee can be employed in any other capacity, or whether making some modifications in the employee's contractual duties will ensure that any further employment is lawful, for example, redeployment of a driver who has lost his driving licence.

5.52 (e) Some other substantial reason

This category has been used to justify a variety of different reasons for dismissal. Employers have successfully argued for its application in such disparate cases as dismissal of an employee because of a personality clash with other workers;[218] dismissal on the instructions of a major customer who had been upset by the employee's conduct;[219] and dismissal because of the employee's sexual preference.[220] In all of these cases the crucial factor for the employers was to establish that the continued employment of the employees concerned would have had an adverse effect upon their businesses. In the case of dismissal because of a personality difference, for example, the employer would be expected to show that the breakdown was irredeemable and that he had no other option but to dismiss. It is clear that this head of dismissal requires the tribunal to assess the reason for dismissal by reference to an employee — and not the actual employee who was dismissed — but an employee who holds the position which that employee held.[221] A dismissal for a substantial reason cannot be for a whimsical or capricious reason which no person of ordinary sense would entertain. On the other hand, if the employer can show that he had a fair reason in his mind at the time when he

---

[214] [1988] ICR 142, HL. This decision overruled the "no difference" rule in redundancy cases as devised by the EAT in *British United Shoe Machinery Co Ltd v. Clarke* [1978] ICR 70.

[215] See, in particular, paras. 45-46. It is likely that this Code will be repealed shortly under the powers granted to the Secretary of State by EA 1990, s. 12.

[216] *Bouchaala v. Trust House Forte Hotels Ltd* [1980] IRLR 382, EAT.

[217] *Bouchaala, ibid.*

[218] *Treganowan v. Robert Knee & Co Ltd* [1975] ICR 405.

[219] *Scott Packing & Warehousing Ltd v. Patterson* [1978] IRLR 166, EAT.

[220] *Saunders v. Scottish National Camps Association Ltd* [1981] IRLR 277, IH.

[221] *Dobie v. Burns International Security Services (UK) Ltd* [1984] ICR 812 CA.

decided on dismissal and that he genuinely believed it to be fair, this would bring the case within the category of some other substantial reason.[222]

5.53 *Business reorganisations.* The area of greatest controversy for some other substantial reason dismissals has been in relation to business reorganisations which fall short of redundancy. An employer may find that it is necessary to reorganise his business to make it more efficient or so as to react to a change in market conditions and this entails changing the employees' jobs or the duties that they perform. It has been accepted that an employer could be justified in dismissing an employee who refused to accept reasonable changes in his terms and conditions of employment on the basis of some other substantial reason.[223] Clearly as far as the common law is concerned an employer who unilaterally changes an employee's terms and conditions of employment is in danger of committing a material breach of contract. However, as far as unfair dismissal law is concerned an employer's decision to change terms may well lead to a fair dismissal even although a serious breach of contract has been committed in the process. Thus it has been held that a breach of contract by the employer, such as a change in the place of work, which justifies the employee resigning and claiming constructive dismissal, can nonetheless be a dismissal for some other substantial reason.[224] In the end the task for the tribunal is to consider whether in all the circumstances the employer has acted reasonably and the fact that the reorganisation entails a breach of the employees' contracts or disregards collectively agreed terms would not preclude a tribunal from holding that the dismissal was fair because of the other circumstances.

5.54 Although all the circumstances must be taken into account one important issue in these types of case will always be to consider whether the change in terms is necessary for the needs of the business. In one of the early cases it was stated that a dismissal of an employee who refused to accept new terms could only be for some other substantial reason on the basis that if the reorganisation were not done the whole business would be brought to a standstill.[225] This undoubtedly set too high a standard and in *Hollister v. National Farmers' Union*[226] the Court of Appeal argued that the correct approach was to discover whether there was some sound, good business reason for the reorganisation. This particular test views the issue from the employer's perspective and widens the scope of management discretion. In other cases, an attempt has been made to take some account of the interests of the employee.[227] The modern approach is that it is necessary for a tribunal when considering the issue of reasonableness

---

[222] See generally Lord McDonald in the EAT in *Harper v. National Coal Board* [1980] IRLR 260. See also the decision of the Court of Appeal in *Kent County Council v. Gilham (No 2)* [1985] IRLR 18 which referred to some other substantial reason being designed to deter employers dismissing for some trivial or unworthy reason.

[223] *R. S. Components Ltd v. Irwin* [1973] IRLR 239, NIRC.

[224] *Genower v. Ealing, Hammersmith & Hounslow Area Health Authority* [1980] IRLR 297, EAT.

[225] *Ellis v. Brighton Cooperative Society Ltd* [1976] IRLR 219 EAT.

[226] [1979] ICR 142.

[227] Thus in *Evan v. Elementa Holdings Ltd* [1982] ICR 323 the EAT argued that if it was reasonable for an employee to decline new contractual terms it would be unreasonable for an employer to dismiss for such a refusal but another EAT has criticised this approach as being inconsistent with *Hollister v. National Farmer's Union* [1979] ICR 142, CA: see *Chubb v. Fire Security Ltd v. Harper* [1983] IRLR 311, EAT.

to make a finding as to the advantages to the employer of the reorganisation, and to assess whether it was reasonable for him to rely on those advantages despite the disadvantages which the employee will suffer when the changes are implemented. However, it has been stressed that the question of weighing the advantages to the employer against the disadvantages to the employee is merely one factor which the tribunal has to take into account.[228] In the final analysis the tribunal must approach this issue as it must in all other reasonableness questions on the basis of the band of reasonable responses test.[229]

SPECIAL CASES

5.55 (a) Maternity

As we saw in chapter three pregnant employees have rights to maternity pay and a right to time-off work for ante-natal care. There is also an additional protection given to pregnant employees under unfair dismissal law. Thus an employee will be treated as unfairly dismissed if the reason or principal reason for her dismissal is that she is pregnant or is any other reason connected with her pregnancy.[230] It is not enough under this provision for an employee simply to be dismissed whilst pregnant. It must be shown that the employer knew or believed either that the woman was pregnant or that he was dismissing her for a reason connected with her pregnancy.[231] This right is subject to two exceptions. First she will not be held to have been unfairly dismissed if the employer can show that at the effective date of termination[232] she is or will have become, because of her pregnancy, incapable of adequately doing the work which she is employed to do.[233] Second, her dismissal will also be fair if, because of her pregnancy, she cannot or will not be able to continue after that date to do that work without contravention (either by her or by her employer) of a duty or restriction imposed by or under any enactment.[234] However, before an employer can dismiss on either of the above grounds he must first consider whether or not there is a suitable available vacancy. If there is, he must make the pregnant employee an offer of that job before or on the effective date of termination and must ensure that her new contractual terms and conditions are not substantially less favourable than the corresponding provisions of her previous contract.[235] If there is no suitable vacancy or the employee refuses the offer, then, the dismissal will be fair.

5.56 Pregnant employees have protection under these provisions when an employer is selecting employees for redundancy because in selecting for redundancy, the employer must ignore the inconvenience that may arise from a pregnant employee taking maternity leave.[236] If he does not do so and makes

---

[228] *Chubb, ibid.*

[229] *Richmond Precision Engineering Ltd v. Pearce* [1985] IRLR 179, EAT.

[230] EPCA s. 60 (1).

[231] *Del Monte Foods Ltd v. Mundon* [1980] IRLR 224, EAT. In accordance with the decision of the House of Lords in *Brown v. Stockton-on-Tees Borough Council* [1988] IRLR 263 the phrase "any other reason connected with her pregnancy" must be construed widely and includes a case where the employer's decision is based on the after-effects of the pregnancy. See *Clayton v. Vigers* [1990] IRLR 177, EAT.

[232] Discussed at paras 5.27-5.29 above.

[233] EPCA, s. 60(1)(a)

[234] EPCA, s. 60(1)(b)

[235] See generally EPCA, s. 60(2) and (3).

[236] *Brown v. Stockton-on-Tees Borough Council* [1988] IRLR 263, HL.

that absence the factor that determines the pregnant employee's dismissal, that dismissal will be deemed unfair. Although a dismissal because of pregnancy is automatically unfair an employee requires to fulfil the qualifying period for complaint although an employee who does not have sufficient service and is dismissed may have a claim under the Sex Discrimination Act 1975.[237]

Additionally, a woman who has exercised her statutory right to return to work and has complied with all the notice requirements[238] has the right to complain of unfair dismissal if the employer refuses to allow her to return. An employee who is entitled to return to work and has exercised her right to do so shall be treated as if she had been employed until her notified date of return, as having been continuously employed until that day and as having been dismissed on the day she should have returned to work for the reason that she was not permitted to return.[239] There are special rules[240] for employees employed by employers with less than six employees who are prevented from returning to work because it is not reasonably practicable.

5.57 (b) Union membership dismissals and rights of non-union members

A dismissal is automatically unfair if the reason for it (or, if more than one, the principal reason) was that the employee

(i)   was, or proposed to become, a member of an independent trade union;[241] or

(ii)   had taken part, or proposed to take part, in the activities of an independent trade union at an appropriate time; or

(iii)   was not a member of any trade union, or of a particular trade union, or one of a number of particular trade unions, or had refused or proposed to refuse to become or remain a union member.[242]

Employees dismissed on any of these grounds also enjoy an additional and unique benefit because there is no need for them to satisfy either the continuous employment requirements or be below the upper age limit in order to exercise these rights.[243]

5.58 The union membership and activities protections defined by heads (i) and (ii) are identical to the statutory protections against action short of dismissal.[244] All of these protections are discussed at some length later.[245] For present purposes it is enough simply to discuss a few issues raised by head (ii) First, it is clear that an employee's right to be protected from dismissal for union activities only applies in relation to activities exercised by him after the commencement of his employment with the dismissing employer.[246] It should be noted that this

---

[237] See *Hayes v. Malleable Working Men's Club and Institute* [1985] IRLR 367 EAT; *Webb v. Emo Air Cargo (UK) Ltd* [1990] IRLR 124, EAT. There may also be a claim under European law: see *Hertz v Aldi Marked K/S* [1991] IRLR 31, ECJ. See also Chapter Seven, para 7.14.

[238] EPCA, s. 47.

[239] EPCA, s. 56.

[240] EPCA, s. 56A.

[241] This phrase is defined by TULRA, s. 30(1). See Chapter Ten, para 10.15

[242] EPCA, s. 58(1).

[243] EPCA, s. 64(3).

[244] EPCA, s. 23.

[245] See Chapter Nine, paras 9.51 - 9.58

[246] *City of Birmingham District Council v. Beyer* [1977] IRLR 211, EAT.

position remains unchanged by the Employment Act 1990 since s. 1 of this Act only makes it unlawful to refuse a person employment because he is a union member.[247] Second, these activities must be exercised at an appropriate time. This is defined to be a time outside working hours or within working hours but with the consent of the employer,[248] but participation in industrial action is not taking part in trade union activities.[249] Dismissal whilst taking part in industrial action is subject to special rules discussed shortly.

5.59 *The Closed Shop.* Although previous legislation provided for the fair dismissal of employees who were not union members all such provisions have now been repealed;[250] dismissal of an employee because of his non-membership of any or a particular trade union is now automatically unfair.[251] This protects the employee from dismissal in all circumstances for not being a member of any union, or of a particular trade union, or of one of a number of particular trade unions, or for refusing or proposing to refuse to become or remain a member. Moreover, there is also an equivalent protection for action short of dismissal against the non-union member.[252] These protections are limited in the sense that they only apply once employment has commenced. However statute now regulates the pre-entry closed shop by making it unlawful to refuse a person employment because he is not a union member or because he is unwilling to accept a requirement to take steps to become a union member or to make payments to a third party (*e.g.* a charity) in the event of not being a union member.[253]

5.60 *Remedies for union membership dismissals.* There are also a number of other provisions which further enhance the rights relating to union membership, non-membership and activities. First, employees dismissed on these grounds have rights to a minimum basic award of £2,650[254] regardless of length of service and, in addition to their basic award and compensatory award, enjoy a right to a special award where they have sought reinstatement or re-engagement and they have not got their jobs back. If reinstatement or re-engagement were sought but not ordered by the tribunal the special award is 104 weeks' pay or £13,180 whichever is the greater up to a maximum of £26,290. Where the tribunal has made the relevant order but the employer has failed to comply with it the special award is 156 weeks' pay or £19,735 whichever is the greater, but, here, there is no maximum award.[255] The special award can be reduced in certain circumstances discussed later in this chapter. Union members and non-members also have a right to interim relief pending the hearing of their complaints of unfair dismissal.[256]

---

[247] Although in *Discount Tobacco & Confectionery Ltd v. Armitage* [1990] IRLR 15 the EAT held that "union membership" should be defined broadly to entail any incident of membership such as seeking the services of a union officer.

[248] EPCA, s. 58(2).

[249] *Drew v. St Edmundsbury Borough Council* [1980] ICR 513, EAT.

[250] EA, 1988, s. 11; and see original provisions of EPCA, s. 58(3). The then state of the law was discussed by the European Court of Human Rights in *Young, James and Webster v. United Kingdom* [1981] IRLR 408.

[251] EPCA, s. 58(1)(c).

[252] EPCA, s. 23.

[253] EA 1990, s. 1.

[254] EPCA, s. 73(4A). The Secretary of State can increase this sum by order. EPCA, s. 73(4B).

[255] See generally EPCA, s. 75A(1) and (2). These sums can also be increased by order of the Secretary of State. The figures stated here are those specified as operating from April 1, 1991.

[256] See para. 5.88.

5.61 There are two final points which have to be made in relation to the dismissal of the non-union member. First, unlike any other type of unfair dismissal complaint, it is possible for a third party to be sisted as a respondent to the proceedings in addition to the employer. Where either the employer or the complainant claims that the employer was induced to dismiss the complainant by pressure which a trade union or other person exercised on the employer by calling, organising, procuring or financing a strike or other industrial action, or by threatening to do so, and that the pressure was exercised because the complainant was not a union member the employer or the complainant may request the tribunal to direct that the person whom he claims exercised the pressure be sisted as a party to the proceedings.[257] If the employee succeeds in his complaint and an award of compensation is made that award can be made wholly or partly against the trade union or other person who has been sisted.[258] Secondly, the current law also protects the non-member who is dismissed because he refuses to pay a sum of money equivalent to the union dues to some other organisation such as a charity by providing that an employee who is dismissed because he failed to comply with a requirement that he make payments (either directly or by deduction from wages) to a third party if he refuses to become or ceases to remain a union member is to be treated as having been dismissed on the ground of non-union membership thus making his dismissal automatically unfair.[259] This provision fulfils the government's view that an employee should not be required to pay a financial price for his non-membership of a trade union.

5.62 (c) Industrial action dismissals

At common law, an employer is entitled to dismiss an employee who is taking part in industrial action because this is likely to constitute a material breach of contract. However, in unfair dismissal law special rules operate in cases of industrial action and lock-outs.[260] These rules deny an industrial tribunal jurisdiction to hear complaints of unfair dismissal when the employee was taking part in industrial action[261] or was locked out unless the employer has acted in a discriminatory or selective way either in terms of dismissal or as regards re-engagement of those who have been dismissed. There has been some disagreement as to the exact purpose of these special rules. On the one hand,[262] the rules were seen to be designed to protect the employer so that he could dismiss the entire labour force on strike and could take on another one without the stigma of any unfair dismissals. On the other hand, in more recent cases[263] it has been suggested that the purpose of this provision is to keep the law out of industrial disputes so that it can maintain an air of neutrality. This latter reason is more in keeping with the notion of collective laissez faire operative in other areas of

---

[257] EPCA, s. 76A(1). Under the original provisions which were added to EPCA by EA 1980 only the employer could sist. EA 1982, s. 7 extended this to cover the employee as well because the Government was concerned that employers were reluctant to exercise their sisting powers.

[258] EPCA, s. 76A(3).

[259] EPCA, s. 58(13), inserted by EA 1982 s. 3.

[260] EPCA, ss. 62 and 62A inserted by EA 1990 s.9

[261] As to the distinction between official and unofficial action see para 5. 68.

[262] *Heath v. J. F. Longman (Meat Salesmen) Ltd* [1973] ICR 407, NIRC.

[263] *Gallagher v. Wragg* [1977] ICR 175, EAT; *Faust v. Power Packing Casemakers Ltd* [1983] ICR 665, CA.

collective labour law. However the enactment of new rules applicable only where the industrial action is unofficial may require this purpose to be re-appraised.

5.63 *Official action.* The first question to be determined is whether at the date of dismissal either the employer was conducting a "lock-out" or the employee was taking part in "a strike or other industrial action." Although "lock-out" and "strike" are defined for determining whether there is continuity of employment[264] the general approach of the courts and tribunals has been to regard this lack of definition as deliberate and to ignore these definitions. Thus as far as lock-outs are concerned the Court of Appeal has held that the fact that this amounts to a breach of contract will be a material consideration although not conclusive. In the end, it is the task of the tribunal to decide the question on the facts and merits of each case using its industrial relations expertise.[265] This reluctance to regard the issue as a legal question is also true for strikes.[266] As far as other industrial action is concerned there has also been an unwillingness to lay down any hard and fast rules: although it would appear that there is no need for such action to be in breach of contract. The important issue is to discover whether the action was intended to have a disruptive effect upon the employer's business.[267]

5.64 In the case of dismissal for taking part in strikes or other industrial action the next question is to discuss the legal approach to the issue of employee participation. This question is important for two reasons. First, under the current provisions[268] it is necessary to discover whether or not the employee was taking part in the action on the date of his dismissal. Second, it is important to discover how other employees who were also taking part in the action were treated on that date. A tribunal will only have jurisdiction if there is discriminatory treatment as between the applicant and other employees who were taking part in the action at the date of his dismissal. This question is also one of fact since the meaning of taking part in a strike is just the kind of issue which the tribunal is best fitted to decide as an industrial jury.[269] The tribunal's finding should not be interfered with if there was evidence to supports its conclusion and the words were given a meaning of which they were reasonably capable.[270] This may mean that on the same primary facts two tribunals could reach diametrically opposite, but equally correct, conclusions as to whether employees took part in industrial action[271] — surely an unsatisfactory state of affairs. All that can be said with

---

[264] See Chapter Three.

[265] *Express & Star Ltd v. Bunday* [1988] ICR 379.

[266] See also *Bunday, ibid.*

[267] *Faust v. Power Packing Casemakers Ltd* [1983] ICR 665, CA.

[268] EPCA, s. 62 was amended by EA 1982, s. 9 to restrict the point of comparison to the date of the employee's dismissal. There was no such limitation under the original provisions of s. 62. This meant that an employer who allowed some strikers to return to work and then at some later date dismissed those who remained on strike could not rely on s. 62 to prevent a tribunal considering the fairness of those dismissals. See *Frank Jones (Tipton) Ltd v. Stock* [1978] ICR 347, HL. EA 1982, s. 9 reverses *Stock* and ensures that employees who do return to work on a date before the complainant's dismissal cannot be used as comparators.

[269] *Coates and Venables v. Modern Methods & Materials Ltd* [1982] ICR 763, CA.

[270] *Coates, ibid.*

[271] *Naylor v. Orton & Smith Ltd* [1983] IRLR 233, EAT.

any confidence is that an employer is entitled to judge the position on the basis of the employee's actions. Thus an employer would be justified in believing that an employee who failed to turn up for work during a strike was taking part in that action.[272] This would arise even although the reason for the employee's non-appearance was because of a fear that he would be subjected to abuse by pickets if he should try to get to work,[273] or because he had fallen ill during the strike.[274] Indeed, it would seem that an absent employee who is not taking part in the action has a duty to maintain contact with his employer in order to ensure that the employer understands that his absence was not as a result of the strike.[275] A sick employee whose absence from work pre-dated the strike and who continues to inform the employer of his medical condition should not be treated as taking part in it even although he sympathises with its objectives.[276]

5.65 Because of the need to treat relevant employeers equally it is necessary to consider which employees fall into this category. As far as lock-outs are concerned relevant employees are employees who were directly interested in the dispute in contemplation or furtherance of which the lock-out occurred.[277] It has been held that this issue involves a retrospective test.[278] This means that employees who have been able to return to work may still have a direct interest in the dispute and, therefore, be relevant employees so that the tribunal would have jurisdiction to consider the fairness of any subsequent dismissals. In the case of strikes or other industrial action, relevant employees are those employees at the establishment who were taking part in the action at the complainant's date of dismissal.[279] It has two results — (1) it means that the employee can only compare himself with other employees who were taking part in the action at the date of his dismissal[280] — employees who returned to work at an earlier date cannot be used as comparators; and (2) it enables employers to treat employees differently who are employed at different establishments.[281] Clearly, therefore, where an employer does dismiss all his employees who are taking part in industrial action at a particular establishment so that there is no selectivity, a tribunal lacks jurisdiction to consider the fairness of those dismissals.

5.66 *Re-engagement after dismissal.* What is the position if the employer should decide to re-engage some of these employees who were dismissed? A tribunal has jurisdiction to consider an unfair dismissal complaint if within three months

---

[272] *Coates and Venables v. Modern Methods & Materials Ltd* [1982] ICR 763 where by a majority the Court of Appeal held that an employer was not required to discover the reasons for an employee's failure to work before deciding to dismiss him for not taking part in industrial action. It has been stated that the question as to whether an employee is taking part in industrial action is one of objective fact. See *Bolton Broadways Ltd v. Edwards* [1987] IRLR 392, EAT approved in *Manifold Industries v. Sims* [1991] IRLR 242, EAT. *Cf McKenzie v. Crossville Motors Ltd* [1990] ICR 172, EAT.

[273] *Coates and Venables, ibid.*

[274] *Williams v. Mail & Echo Ltd* [1980] ICR 366, EAT.

[275] *McKenzie v. Crossville Motors Ltd* [1990] ICR 172, EAT.

[276] *Hindle Gears Ltd. v. McGinty* [1985] ICR 111, EAT.

[277] EPCA, s. 62(4)(b)(i).

[278] *H. Campey & Sons v. Bellwood* [1987] ICR 311, EAT.

[279] EPCA, s. 62(4)(b)(ii) (as amended by EA 1982 s. 9).

[280] In this context date of dismissal means time of dismissal. See *Hindle Gears Ltd v. McGinty* [1985] ICR 111, EAT.

[281] "Establishment" means that establishment of the employer at or from which the complainant works (EPCA, s. 62(4)(b)).

of the date of dismissal any employee in the same position as the complainant has been offered re-engagement and he has not[282] This means that an employer who does re-engage selectively during this period may have to face unfair dismissal complaints from those who have not been re-hired. However, if the employer can sit out the three month period without taking back staff, any subsequent re-engagements outwith this period will not permit staff not offered re-engagement to complain to an industrial tribunal.

Employees who are offered re-engagement can be taken back on terms different from the original contract so long as the nature of their work and the capacity and place where they work are the same.[283] Further, it is also legitimate for an employer to offer re-engagement to dismissed strikers at different times so long as he ensures that by the expiry of the three month period all the strikers have received offers of re-engagement.[284]

5.67 *Unofficial action.* The above rules do not apply where the employee has taken part in an unofficial strike or other unofficial industrial action. Where an employee at the time of his dismissal was taking part in unofficial industrial action he loses all right to complain of unfair dismissal.[285] A strike or other industrial action is unofficial in relation to the employee unless —

(a)   the employee is a member of a trade union and the action is authorised or endorsed by that union;[286] or

(b)   the employee is not a member of the union but there are amongst those taking part in the industrial action members of the union by which the action has been authorised or endorsed. Thus only action which the union has repudiated is capable of being classified as unofficial. The mere fact that industrial action has been called by a shop steward does not make it unofficial. It will only become so once the union has repudiated the authorisation in the manner specified in the Employment Act 1982 (as inserted by the Employment Act 1990).

A strike or other industrial action cannot be regarded as unofficial if none of those taking part in it are union members. However, in order to prevent union members from resigning *en masse* so as to avoid the action being treated as unofficial, an employee who was a member of the union when he began to take part in the action shall continue to be treated as a union member notwithstanding his resignation.[287] If a union decides to repudiate industrial action so that it must then be considered unofficial, the action cannot be treated as unofficial for unfair dismissal purposes until the end of the next working day after the day on which the repudiation takes place.[288] The effect of the above provisions is to enable an employer to dismiss selectively those of his employees who are taking part in unofficial industrial action without any of the employees so dismissed having recourse to an industrial tribunal. This state of affairs creates a major dilemma for a trade union. For if, on the one hand, it decides to endorse the industrial action it lays itself open to civil proceedings by the employer if

[282] EPCA, s. 62(2) (as amended by EA 1982, s. 9).
[283] *Williams v. National Theatre Board Ltd* [1982] IRLR 377, CA.
[284] *Highland Fabircators Ltd v. McLaughlin* [1985] ICR 183, EAT.
[285] EPCA, s. 62A(1), inserted by EA 1990 s.9
[286] The question of authorisation or endorsement is dealt with by EA 1982, s. 15(3)-(7) added by EA 1990, s 6(3)-(7) and is considered in Chapter Eleven, paras 11.50-11.51.
[287] EPCA, s. 62A(6).
[288] *ibid.*

the action should prove to be unlawful;[289] if, on the other hand, it repudiates the action the union takes the risk that some members (most probably the ringleaders of the action) will lose their jobs without any unfair dismissal rights.

5.68 (d) Dismissal on the transfer of an undertaking

Special rules regulate dismissals which take place because of the transfer of a commercial business.[290] As we have seen[291] statutory novation of contracts of employment occurs where a commercial business is transferred. Also unfair dismissal rights are conferred on employees who are dismissed either before or after such transfer,[292] so that where the transfer (or a reason connected with it) is the reason (or principal reason) for the dismissal, then, that employee is to be treated as having been unfairly dismissed. The effect of this provision which deems dismissals because of, or connected with, a business transfer to be automatically unfair is qualified significantly by the statutory declaration that where an economic, technical or organisational reason entailing changes in the workforce of either the transferee or transferor employer is the reason or principal reason for the dismissal that dismissal will be for a substantial reason and whether it is fair or not will depend upon the application of the reasonableness principle.[293]

5.69 It is clear that the economic, technical or organisational defence only applies when there are changes in the workforce and changes in the identity of the individuals who make up the workforce do not constitute changes in the workforce itself so long as the overall numbers and functions of the employees looked at as a whole remain unchanged. Therefore the Regulations would not operate where the employee resigned after the transfer because the transferees proposed to reduce his wages to that of their existing staff since the reason for the employer's decision was to produce standard rates of pay and was not intended to lead to a reduction in the number of employees.[294] On the other hand, there would be a change in the workforce when a transferee gives the employees who are kept on by him entirely different jobs to do since this entails changing the occupations of the workforce as a whole and amounts to much more than merely standardising their terms and conditions of employment.[295]

5.70 The statutory rules relating to dismissals and business transfers have been differently applied in the past. At one time in Scotland it was held that a dismissal that was for an economic, technical or organisational reason could not be for redundancy.[296] However Scottish tribunals are now at liberty to follow the English decision in *Gorictree Ltd v. Jenkinson*[297] that such dismissals do not entail

---

[289] The question of union repudiation is also discussed in Chapter Eleven.
[290] The Transfer of Undertakings (Protection of Employment) Regulations 1981, S.I. 1981 No. 1794.
[291] Chapter Three, para 3.5.
[292] S.I. 1981 No. 1794, reg. 8(1).
[293] *Ibid.*, reg. 8(2).
[294] *Berriman v. Delabole Slate Ltd* [1985] ICR 546, CA.
[295] *Crawford v. Swinton Insurance Brokers Ltd* [1990] IRLR 42, EAT.
[296] *Canning v. Niaz and McLaughlin* [1983] IRLR 431 EAT; *Meikle v. McPhail (Charleston Arms)* [1983] IRLR 351, EAT.
[297] [1985] ICR 51, EAT.

loss of redundancy rights.[298] Further, the most recent Scottish decision[299] on this issue has held that it would not be a dismissal for an economic, technical or organisational reason for the transferor to dismiss the workforce in order to comply with a condition of sale that the purchaser buy the business without staff. Hence such dismissals must now be automatically unfair. These arrangements are much less likely since the decision of the House of Lords in *Litster v. Forth Dry Dock and Engineering Co Ltd*[300] that employees dismissed by the transferor at some time before the moment of the transfer are nonetheless entitled to exercise their statutory rights in relation to such dismissals against the transferee provided the reason for their dismissal is the transfer of the business or a reason connected with it.

REMEDIES

5.71 Statute[301] creates a framework of remedies for employees whose complaints of unfair dismissal have been upheld by an industrial tribunal. The scheme of the legislation is to make re-employment — in the form of reinstatement or re-engagement — the primary remedy, although this has not been the case in practice,[302] with a right to compensation where an employee has not requested re-employment or it has not been ordered by the tribunal. Compensation is made up of two distinct elements — a basic award and a compensatory award. An employee who has sought re-employment and this has been ordered by the tribunal but has not been complied with by the employer also receives an additional award of compensation. Since 1982 an employee who has been dismissed for union membership, activities or non-membership also has a right to a special award.[303] A tribunal which finds a complaint to be well-founded must explain to the complainant the re-employment orders which can be made and ask him if he wishes to be reinstated or re-engaged. If re-employment is sought the tribunal must then consider whether or not to make the relevant order and must give both the complainant and the employer the opportunity to be heard before exercising its discretion.[304] In Scotland the practice is to hear the evidence pertaining to remedies with the evidence on the merits and not to create a separate stage of procedure after the decision in favour of the complainant has been announced.

5.72 (a) Reinstatement and re-engagement

An order of reinstatement entails the tribunal ordering the employer to treat the complainant in all respects as if he had not been dismissed[305] and taking an

---

[298] See generally *Anderson v. Dalkeith Engineering Ltd* [1985] ICR 66, EAT.

[299] See *Gateway Hotels Ltd v. Stewart* [1988] IRLR 287, EAT which follows the decision of the English EAT in *Wheeler v. Patel* [1987] ICR 631. But see also the decision in *Anderson, ibid.* and the judgment of Lord Dunpark in *Forth Dry Dock and Engineering Co Ltd v. Litster* [1988] IRLR 289 IH.

[300] [1989] IRLR 161.

[301] EPCA, ss. 67-79.

[302] In only 4.0% of successful cases in Scotland for the year 1 April 1990 to 31 March 1991 did the complainant obtain reinstatement or re-engagement. See Industrial Tribunals in Scotland Fact Sheet — May 1991.

[303] See para. 5.87.

[304] *Pirelli General Cable Works Ltd v. Murray* [1979] IRLR 190, EAT.

[305] EPCA, s. 69(2).

employee back on less favourable terms does not constitute reinstatement.[306] The order must specify —

(a)   the amount payable by the employer in respect of any benefit which the complainant might reasonably be expected to have had but for the dismissal, including arrears of pay;

(b)   any rights and privileges, including seniority and pension rights, which must be restored;

(c)   the date for compliance with the order.[307]

5.73 A tribunal is directed to make an order of re-engagement on such terms as it may decide.[308] This is an order that the complainant be engaged by the employer, or by a successor of the employer or by an associated employer, in employment comparable to that from which he was dismissed or other suitable employment.[309] The order must specify the terms on which re-engagement is to take place including —

(a)   the identity of the employer;

(b)   the nature of the employment;

(c)   the remuneration;

(d)   the amount payable by the employer in respect of any benefit which the complainant might reasonably be expected to have had but for the dismissal, including arrears of pay;

(e)   any rights and privileges, including seniority and pension rights, which must be restored;

(f)   the date for compliance with the order.[310]

5.74 There is a clear procedure which must be followed in re-employment cases. First, the tribunal must consider whether to order reinstatement and only if this is not ordered should it then consider re-engagement and on what terms.[311] In doing so it must take into account the following considerations —

(a)   the wishes of the complainant;

(b)   whether it is practicable for the employer to comply;

(c)   where the complainant caused or contributed to the dismissal, whether it would be just to make the order.[312]

Central to these provisions is the question of practicability. It is for the employer to show that re-employment is not practicable. It is worth noting that the employer can have two opportunities to show that it is not practicable to re-employ. First, when the tribunal is contemplating making the order; and, second, where the order has been made but not complied with and additional compensation becomes payable this can be avoided if the employer can satisfy the tribunal that it was not practicable to comply with the order.[313] Thus in Scotland a tribunal need not reach a final conclusion that re-employment is in fact practicable at the time when the order is made.[314]

---

[306] *Artisan Press v. Srawley* [1986] IRLR 126, EAT.

[307] EPCA, s. 69(2)(a)-(c).

[308] EPCA, s. 69(1).

[309] EPCA, s. 69(4).

[310] EPCA, s. 69(4)(a)-(f).

[311] EPCA, s. 69(6).

[312] EPCA, s. 69(6)(a)-(c).

[313] EPCA, s. 71(2)(b).

[314] *Timex Corporation v. Thomson* [1981] IRLR 522, EAT.

5.75 *Practicability.* One issue which might be important as regards the issue of practicability is the extent to which personal relationships may have deteriorated between employer and employee particularly in small firms so as to make re-employment impracticable. In *Enessy Co SA v. Minoprio*[315] it was declared that in the case of a small employer with few staff "where there must exist a close personal relationship, reinstatement can only be appropriate in exceptional circumstances and to enforce it upon a reluctant employer is not a course which an industrial tribunal should pursue unless persuaded by powerful evidence that it would succeed". It has been argued that these remarks were made in a case where the relationship was almost a domestic one and that tribunals should not shirk from their duty of inquiring into relationships, even in a small firm, to see whether the fears of continuing disharmony are exaggerated.[316] It is to be hoped that this latter view prevails since, as Smith and Wood point out, if the *Enessy* view were applied too widely it would resemble the old common law rules against enforcement of contracts of employment.[317] The only further statutory guidance on the question of practicability is that where the employer has engaged a permanent replacement for a dismissed employee, the tribunal shall not take that fact into account in determining whether it is practicable to comply with a re-employment order, unless the employer shows

(a) that it was not practicable to have the work done without engaging a permanent replacement; or

(b) that he engaged the replacement after the lapse of a reasonable period, without hearing from the complainant that he wished to be re-employed, and that when he engaged the replacement it was no longer reasonable for him to arrange for the work to be done except by a permanent replacement.[318]

5.76 As has already been noted, a complainant who does obtain an order of re-employment is also entitled to be paid an amount to cover loss of benefits such as arrears of pay for the period from the date of termination to the date of his re-employment. In calculating the sum to be awarded, the tribunal must take into account, so as to reduce the employer's liability, any sums which the complainant has received by way of wages in lieu of notice or ex gratia payments paid by the employer, remuneration for employment with another employer and such other benefits as the tribunal thinks appropriate in the circumstances.[319] There is no statutory upper limit on the amount which an employee can be awarded to compensate for arrears of pay when the tribunal decides to make an order of re-employment.

5.77 If the employer does reinstate or re-engage the complainant but does not comply fully with the terms of the order, the tribunal will make an award of compensation of such amount as it thinks fit having regard to the loss sustained by the employee in consequence of the employer's failure to comply fully with the order.[320] This award cannot exceed the maximum compensatory award.[321] It

---

[315] [1978] IRLR 489, EAT.
[316] "Re-Employment and the Industrial Tribunals" (1982) JLSS 216.
[317] *Industrial Law* (London, 4th edn.) at p. 336.
[318] EPCA, s. 70(1).
[319] EPCA, s. 70(2).
[320] EPCA, s. 71(1).
[321] EPCA, s. 75(1).

is much more likely that the above provision will be activated because the employer has failed completely to comply with the order. In such a case the employee becomes entitled to compensation and will certainly receive a basic award and a compensatory award. The tribunal also has the authority to make an additional award. However, as we have seen, this can be resisted by the employer if he can satisfy the tribunal that it was not practicable for him to comply with the order. The additional award will be between 26 and 52 weeks' pay in a case of race or sex discrimination and between 13 and 26 weeks' pay in any other case.[322] This award is not intended to be a precisely calculated substitute for financial loss but rather a genuine *solatium*. It is capable of being reduced because of a failure to mitigate loss but only if this question is treated as a general factor and not something producing a quantifiable reduction in the sum which would otherwise be awarded.[323]

5.78   Since all these awards including the additional award are subject to a statutory maximum, an employer's failure to comply with the re-employment order may have an unfortunate consequence for the complainant. For he may find himself receiving less by way of compensation for the employer's failure to comply with the order than he would have received for arrears of pay had the order been complied with! It was suggested[324] that the solution to this problem was for the tribunal to give the employee the option of receiving compensation for failure to obtain re-employment or to enforce the order for arrears of wages made as part of the original order of re-employment. However, the Court of Appeal in *O'Laoire v. Jackel International Ltd*[325] has made it clear that the employee does not have such an option because the statutory language is quite specific so that a complainant who has not been re-employed in pursuance of a tribunal order is only entitled to an award of compensation which is subject to a statutory maximum.

5.79 (b) Compensation

A complainant's compensation is made up of two elements — a basic award and a compensatory award. The basic award is dependent upon the complainant's length of service and age whereas the compensatory award is intended to compensate for loss consequent upon dismissal.

5.80 *(i) Basic award.* The basic award is calculated on the same basis as a redundancy payment. This means that the award is calculated by reference to the period, ending with the effective date of termination,[326] during which the employee has been continuously employed, by starting at the end of that period and reckoning backwards the number of years of employment and allowing —
(a)   one and a half weeks' pay for each year in which the employee was over the age of 41;
(b)   one week's pay for each year in which the employee was between 22 and 41; and
(c)   half a week's pay for each year of employment under 22.[327]

---

[322] EPCA, s. 71(3).
[323] See generally *Mabirizi v. National Hospital for Nervous Diseases* [1989] IRLR 133, EAT.
[324] *Cohoc (UK) Ltd v. Neal* [1989] IRLR 51, EAT.
[325] [1990] IRLR 70.
[326] See para. 5.27.
[327] EPCA, s. 73(3).

The maximum number of years which can be taken into account is twenty.[328] The amount of this award can be reduced in a number of circumstances. First, an employee who is aged over 64 has his basic award reduced by one twelfth for each whole month from the date of his last birthday (the specified anniversary) to his effective date of termination.[329] Thus an employee who is over 65 is ineligible to receive a basic award. The basic award is also reduced if the complainant has received a statutory redundancy payment,[330] or has received an ex gratia payment from his employer which is intended to satisfy his legal rights.[331] It is also possible for the basic award to be reduced on grounds of justice and equity if the complainant has unreasonably refused an offer of reinstatement.[332] Finally, there is also provision to reduce the basic award where the complainant has contributed to his dismissal.[333] This would apply where the tribunal considers it just and equitable to reduce the award because of the conduct of the complainant before his dismissal. As has already been noted, this is most likely to arise where the employee commits an act of misconduct which only comes to light after the employer has taken the decision to dismiss on other grounds or where there is procedural unfairness.[334] Finally, an employee who has been dismissed for an automatically unfair reason related to trade union membership, non-membership or activities has the right to minimum basic award before any reduction on any of the above grounds.[335]

5.81 *(ii) Compensatory award.* The compensatory award will be such amount as the tribunal considers just and equitable in all the circumstances having regard to the loss sustained by the complainant in consequence of the dismissal in so far as that loss is attributable to action taken by the employer.[336] The award is subject to a statutory maximum which is presently £10,000. Under this head of compensation the critical question is for the tribunal to ascertain the extent of the employee's loss. If there is no loss there can be no award. This might be the case, for example, where the tribunal holds that the employee has been unfairly dismissed but considers that he would have been dismissed in any event. Such a state of affairs might arise in a case where the dismissal is unfair simply because of a want of procedure or a failure to consult.[337] Equally, another occasion where the tribunal would be justified in holding that the complainant has suffered no loss is where more serious misconduct comes to the employer's attention after the date of dismissal.[338]

---

[328] EPCA, s. 73(4).
[329] EPCA, s. 73(5) and (6) as amended by SDA 1986, s. 3(2). Formerly the ages were 64 for a man and 59 for a woman.
[330] EPCA, s. 73(9).
[331] *Chelsea Football & Athletic Club v. Heath* [1981] ICR 323.
[332] EPCA, s. 73(7A).
[333] EPCA, s. 73(7B).
[334] *W. Devis & Sons Ltd v. Atkins* [1977] ICR 662, HL.
[335] EPCA, s. 73(4A) and see para. 5.60.
[336] EPCA, s. 74(1). For a discussion as to whether or not the compensatory award can be deducted from any award of damages for common law breach of contract see the decision of the Court of Appeal in *O'Laoire v. Jackel International Ltd* [1991] IRLR 170. See Chapter Three, para 3.62.
[337] *Polkey v. A. E. Dayton Services Ltd* [1988] ICR 142, HL; *Hough v. Leyland Daf Ltd* [1991] IRLR 194, EAT.
[338] *W. Devis & Sons Ltd v. Atkins* [1977] ICR 662, HL.

5.82 In particular, the award can compensate for

(a)   any expenses reasonably incurred by the complainant in consequence of the dismissal; and

(b)   loss of any benefit which he might reasonably be expected to have had but for the dismissal.[339]

However, where the complainant is being compensated for a loss of entitlement to a payment on redundancy, the compensatory award can only compensate him to the extent of the excess of this payment over his basic award.[340] A complainant has a duty to mitigate his loss and his compensatory award will be reduced if he has failed to do so.[341] Moreover, where an employee has received a payment on redundancy, whether statutory or otherwise, which exceeds the basic award, that excess must go to reduce the compensatory award.[342] The compensatory award can also be reduced on a just and equitable basis where the tribunal finds that the dismissal was to any extent caused or contributed to by the action of the complainant.[343] Finally, a tribunal is directed to ignore any pressure exercised on the employer through a real or threatened strike or other industrial action when calculating the award.[344]

5.83 *Calculating the compensatory award.* A number of principles have been developed for ascertaining those losses which are capable of being compensated by this award. The major aim of the compensatory award is to compensate the complainant fully for the pecuniary losses which flowed from his unfair dismissal. He is not entitled to any compensation for injury to feelings.[345] The method of calculating the compensatory award was first discussed in *Norton Tool Co Ltd v. Tewson*[346] — a decision under the unfair dismissal provisions of the Industrial Relations act 1971 but which is still relevant. This decision sets out the basic heads of compensation which the compensatory award is capable of covering. A tribunal which is assessing the compensatory award must consider each of these heads in turn and must calculate the amount to be awarded under each. The tribunal has a duty to raise the various categories of loss even where they are not raised by the complainant, although once a head of loss has been considered it is for the complainant actually to prove that he suffered a loss under it.[347]

5.84 *Heads of loss*

(1) *Immediate Loss of Wages.* This head compensates the complainant for his actual loss of earnings from the date of dismissal to the date of the hearing. This is done by calculating the complainant's net wage (i.e. his pay after deductions for tax and national insurance) and deducting from it any pay which he has received from other employment during the period from the date of the expiry of his notice until the hearing date.[348] If the complainant has obtained

---

[339] EPCA, s. 74(2).
[340] EPCA, s. 74(3).
[341] EPCA, s. 74(4).
[342] EPCA, s. 74(7). Cf. *Roadchef Ltd v. Hastings* [1988] IRLR 142, EAT.
[343] EPCA, s. 74(6)
[344] EPCA, s. 74(5).
[345] *Norton Tool Co Ltd v. Tewson* [1972] ICR 501, NIRC.
[346] [1972] ICR 501, NIRC.
[347] *Tidman v. Aveling Marshall Ltd* [1977] IRLR 218, EAT.
[348] See *Babcock FATA Ltd v. Addison* [1987] IRLR 173, CA.

other employment which he then loses before the date of the hearing, then, that dismissal should be ignored when ascertaining the extent of his loss.[349] It is now clear that a tribunal is also required to deduct any money which the complainant has received as wages in lieu of notice.[350] The value of other benefits to the complainant such as the loss of a company car or cheap loan facilities can be included as a relevant loss.[351] Equally, the tribunal can also take account of any expenses which the employee incurred as a result of his dismissal.[352] This could include any expenses associated with moving house.[353] although it does not include any legal expenses incurred in complaining to the tribunal.

(2) *Future loss.* If the complainant is still out of work at the date of the hearing, the tribunal must consider awarding an element to cover his future loss of wages. This award must involve a degree of speculation for the tribunal since it is required to assess the likely period of continued unemployment for the complainant. Equally, even where the complainant has obtained fresh employment there will still be a future loss of earnings if he is paid at a lower rate by his new employer. In such a case the tribunal also has the difficult task of establishing how long it will be before the complainant achieves parity with his previous earnings. In considering these issues the tribunal is likely to base its decision upon its collective knowledge of industrial relations in the area.[354] The quantification of the likely period of continued unemployment will be based upon the evidence[355] and the tribunal's consideration of the complainant's personal characteristics, for example, that he was elderly or in poor health.[356] This calculation can include a sum to take account of loss of earnings after the employee has reached normal retiring age.[357] The tribunal may also include any anticipated salary increases so long as there is a high probability that the complainant would have received them.[358] However, where there is evidence that the complainant might have lost his job in the future because of redundancy the tribunal will be justified in taking this factor into account and, therefore, reduce the period of future loss accordingly.[359] The number of weeks which constitute the complainant's period of future loss will be used as a multiplier when calculating the amount of compensation to be awarded under this head. Thus the tribunal will also calculate the complainant's actual loss per week and then multiply this figure by the number of weeks of future loss in order to arrive at the appropriate sum. Clearly, the complainant's actual loss per week will depend upon whether or not he has obtained fresh employment and the rate of pay if new employment has been obtained. When calculating the complainant's net losses the tribunal is entitled to take account of loss of fringe benefits and may also include any additional expenses incurred in the new job.

(3) *Loss of pension rights.* A complainant is entitled to compensation for loss of pension rights. The sum awarded under this head is likely to be substantial

---

[349] *Courtaulds Northern Spinning Ltd v. Moosa* [1984] IRLR 43, EAT.

[350] *Babcock FATA Ltd v. Addison* [1987] IRLR 173, CA disapproving *Finnie v. Top Hat Frozen Foods* [1985] IRLR 365, EAT.

[351] EPCA, s. 74(2)(b).

[352] EPCA, s. 72(2)(a).

[353] *Scottish Cooperative Wholesale Society v. Lloyd* [1973] IRLR 93, NIRC.

[354] *Bateman v. British Leyland (UK) Ltd* [1974] IRLR 104, NIRC.

[355] *Morganite Electrical Carbon Ltd v. Donne* [1987] IRLR 363, EAT.

[356] *Fougere v. Phoenix Motor Co Ltd* [1976] IRLR 259, EAT.

[357] *Barrel Plating & Phosphating Co Ltd v. Danks* [1976] IRLR 262, EAT.

[358] *York Trailer Co Ltd v. Sparkes* [1972] IRLR 348, NIRC.

[359] *Young's of Gosport Ltd v. Kendell* [1977] IRLR 433, EAT.

particularly where the complainant contributed to an occupational pension scheme and remains unemployed or cannot take advantage of his existing pension rights in his new job.[360] The types of loss which a tribunal should take into account under this head were discussed in *Copson v. Eversure Accessories Ltd*[361] where it was stressed that a tribunal should take a broad common sense approach. Two forms of loss were identified — (a) loss of the present pension position; and (b) loss of future pension (*i.e.* the opportunity to improve the position until the time of retiral). Usually the tribunal will base its assessment of loss upon the sum of the contributions already made. This approach is particularly useful in cases of relatively short service or when calculating future loss. However, where the complainant is dismissed shortly before his retirement age the better approach is to take an actuarial method and to assess the capital value of the pension and then discount it for accelerated payment. In 1980 the Government Actuary's Department (GAD) produced a paper which suggested ways of quantifying loss of pension rights.[362] A new set of guidelines entitled *Industrial Tribunals — Compensation for Loss of Pension Rights* was published by HMSO in 1990. These guidelines were prepared by three tribunal chairmen in consultation with GAD and are simpler to operate. The new guidelines contain a simplified actuarial method for calculating deferred pension rights based on age and assume that the employee would not have left his employment for any reason other than death or disability. Given the amount of uncertainty associated with calculating loss of pension rights, industrial tribunals are likely to rely on these guidelines although it should not be forgotten that they have no statutory force and that tribunals are encouraged to take a broad common sense view.

(4) *Loss arising from the manner of dismissal.* An employee has no right to any compensation for the distress caused by his dismissal. However, there may be rare occasions where an employee can claim compensation under this head when there is cogent evidence that the manner of the dismissal caused financial loss to him (*e.g.* by making it more difficult for him to find future employment.[363]

(5) *Loss of statutory protection.* An employee who is dismissed and who obtains other employment will lose all those employment protection rights which depend upon continuity of employment and particularly his rights in redundancy. In *Norton Tool*[364] it was recognised that an employee could receive a sum to compensate for this. However, since the introduction of the basic award which is calculated on the same basis as a redundancy payment it was thought that this head would be largely ignored or lead to a nominal award. Nonetheless in *Daley v. A. E. Dorset (Almar Dolls) Ltd*[365] it was accepted that loss of a service-related notice entitlement is a head of damage which can be reflected in the compensatory award and awarded a sum equivalent to half the employee's statutory notice entitlement. The Scottish position is that loss of the statutory right to long notice may in principle be a head of loss provided it can be quantified, but it is so remote as to be significant only in an exceptional case.[366]

---

[360] Since the Social Security Act 1986 it is now much easier to transfer occupational pensions.

[361] [1974] IRLR 247, NIRC.

[362] Discussed in (1980) 25 JLSS No 4 (Workshop).

[363] *Vaughan v. Weighpack Ltd* [1974] IRLR 105, NIRC.

[364] *Norton Tool Co Ltd v. Tewson* [1972] ICR. 501, NIRC.

[365] [1981] IRLR 385, EAT.

[366] *Gourley v. Kerr* 18 February 1982, EAT (unreported). Discussed in *Stair Memorial Encyclopaedia of the Laws of Scotland*, Vol. 9, *Employment*, at para. 281.

5.85 *Mitigation of loss and employee's contributory conduct.* As has already been noted the common law rules as regards mitigation of loss should apply in relation to the compensatory award.[367] The major issue as regards mitigation is to consider whether the employee has acted reasonably in the circumstances.[368] It is clear that this test does not require the employee to take any job that might be offered; although he should take employment that is reasonably and properly offered to him.[369] It is likely that an employee who fails to utilise the employer's grievance procedure after dismissal will not be taken to have failed to mitigate his loss.[370] Equally, an employee does not necessarily fail to mitigate his loss by setting up in business on his own account after dismissal rather than trying to get another job.[371] On the other hand, an employee is likely to find that a refusal by him to accept an offer of reinstatement from his employer amounts to a failure to mitigate so that he cannot claim for any loss.[372] The onus of proof as regards a failure to mitigate is likely to rest upon the employer.[373]

5.86 As has already been noted, the basic award can be reduced to any extent on a just and equitable basis because of the conduct of the complainant before his dismissal.[374] The compensatory award can also be reduced on a just and equitable basis where the tribunal finds that the dismissal was to any extent caused or contributed to by any action of the complainant.[375] In considering this question a tribunal is required to make three findings. First, that there was conduct on the part of the employee in connection with his dismissal which was culpable or blameworthy; second, that the matters to which the complaint relates were caused or contributed to, to some extent, by the culpable or blameworthy conduct; and, third, that it is just and equitable to reduce the assessment to a specified extent.[376] Culpable or blameworthy conduct includes not only breaches of contract and delicts but other conduct which is perverse or foolish or bloodyminded or simply unreasonable in the circumstances.[377] Tribunals have been advised to look at all the circumstances when conducting this exercise and to concentrate upon the realities rather than relying upon the technical reason for the dismissal.[378] This can entail the tribunal considering aspects of the complainant's conduct beyond those stated in the reasons for his dismissal.[379]

---

[367] EPCA, s. 74(4).

[368] *Bessenden Properties Ltd v. Corness* [1973] IRLR 365, NIRC.

[369] *Gallear v. J. F. Watson & Son Ltd* [1979] IRLR 306, EAT.

[370] *William Muir (Bond 9) Ltd. v. Lamb* [1985] IRLR 95, EAT doubting *Hoover Ltd v. Forde* [1980] ICR 239, EAT. It is now clear that as far as constructive dismissal cases are concerned there is no need to exercise grievance rights as far as mitigation is concerned; see *Seligman & Latz Ltd v. McHugh* [1979] IRLR 130, EAT.

[371] *Gardiner-Hill v. Roland Berger Technics Ltd* [1982] IRLR 498, EAT.

[372] *Sweetlove v. Redbridge and Waltham Forest Area Health Authority* [1979] IRLR 195, EAT.

[373] *Bessenden Properties Ltd v. Corness* [1974] IRLR 338, CA. Cf. *Scottish & Newcastle Breweries Plc v. Halliday* [1986] IRLR 291, EAT where the onus was placed on the employee.

[374] EPCA, s. 73(7B).

[375] EPCA, s. 74(6).

[376] *Nelson v. BBC (No 2)* [1979] IRLR 346, CA.

[377] *Nelson, ibid.*

[378] *Maris v. Rotherham County Borough Council* [1974] IRLR 147, NIRC.

[379] *Jamieson v. Aberdeen County Council* [1975] IRLR 348, EAT.

5.87 There is no doubt that a tribunal can reduce the compensatory award in a misconduct case where the dismissal has been held to be unfair because the employer failed to follow the correct procedure.[380] Equally, the compensatory award can be reduced because of other acts of misconduct which only came to light after the complainant's dismissal.[381] In both cases there is nothing to prevent the tribunal making a nil award. The question of contributory fault is more difficult to apply in a capability case. In *Kraft Foods Ltd v. Fox*[382] it was argued that contributory fault was best applied in misconduct cases or in capability cases where the employee is unwilling to increase his efforts; it had no place in cases of incapacity where the employee was doing his best but his best was not good enough because here the employee had no control over his actions. This proposition has been narrowed by the later case of *Moncur v. International Paint Co Ltd*[383] where it was stated that it could not be an absolute rule that an act or failing which is attributable to a defect of character or personality of the claimant, and which is not within his control to alter, can never be material when considering contributory fault. The *Moncur* view has been preferred by the EAT in Scotland.[384] The compensatory award is most likely to be reduced in a capability case where the employee is lazy, negligent or unwilling to improve.[385] However, the possibility cannot be ignored that the award might also be reduced in cases where the employee's lack of skill is genuinely beyond his control.

5.88 (c) Trade union dismissals

It has already been noted that employees dismissed for union membership or activities or non-membership reasons have a right to a minimum basic award and a right to a special award where they have sought reinstatement or re-engagement and they have not been re-employed. Both the basic award and the special award are subject to reductions on account of the complainant's age.[386] The special award can also be reduced on a just and equitable basis because of the employee's conduct before his dismissal or, where dismissal was with notice, his conduct before that notice was given.[387] A reduction can also be made to this award on a just and equitable basis where the tribunal finds that the employee has unreasonably prevented an order of reinstatement or re-engagement being complied with or has unreasonably refused an offer of reinstatement made by his employer otherwise than in compliance with such an order.[388]

5.89 *Interim relief.* Employees who have been dismissed on grounds of union membership, non-membership or activities also enjoy the right to interim relief. This may involve the employee being re-employed by the employer until his

---

[380] *W. Devis & Sons Ltd v. Atkins* [1977] ICR 662, HL; *Polkey v. A. E. Dayton Services Ltd* [1988] ICR 142, HL.

[381] *Devis, ibid.*

[382] [1977] IRLR 431, EAT.

[383] [1978] IRLR 223, EAT.

[384] See *Finnie v. Top Hat Frozen Foods* [1985] IRLR 365, EAT where it was held that the tribunal was entitled to take account of the employee's performance of his duties in assessing contributory fault.

[385] In such a case there is likely to be substantial reduction in the award; see *Sutton and Gates (Luton) Ltd v. Boxall* [1978] IRLR 486, EAT.

[386] EPCA, s. 73(5) (basic award); EPCA, s. 75A(2) (special award).

[387] EPCA, s. 75A(4).

[388] EPCA, s. 75A(5).

unfair dismissal complaint is resolved. However, it is more likely that the tribunal will continue the employee's rights to wages and other benefits until this time. An application for interim relief must be presented to the tribunal within seven days of the employee's effective date of termination.[389] Where the dismissal is alleged to be for trade union membership or activities the application must be accompanied by a certificate, signed by an authorised official of the employee's union, stating that at the date of dismissal the complainant was or had proposed to become a member of the union and that there appear to be reasonable grounds for supposing that the reason or the principal reason was one alleged in the complaint.[390] An interim relief application is determined as soon as practicable, although the employer is entitled to at least seven days notice of the application and the arrangements for the hearing.[391] The remedy will be awarded if it is likely that the tribunal which will later determine the complaint will find that the complainant was unfairly dismissed.[392] This has been interpreted as requiring the tribunal to consider whether the employee has a "pretty good" chance of succeeding — a higher standard than simply showing a reasonable prospect of success.[393]

5.90 If the tribunal upholds the application it must first ask the employer whether he is willing to reinstate or re-engage the complainant until the hearing and, if the employer is willing, it will make the appropriate order.[394] If the employer fails to attend the hearing or is unwilling to accept re-employment of the employee, the tribunal will make an order for the continuation of the employee's contract of employment.[395] This is an order continuing the employee's contract in force until the determination or settlement of his complaint but only for the purposes of pay or any other benefit derived from employment, seniority, pension rights and similar matters and as regards the computation of continuous employment.[396] The order must specify the amount which the employee is to receive at each normal pay period.[397] This will be the amount which he could reasonably have been expected to earn had he not been dismissed.[398] The employee can complain to the tribunal at any time (including at the hearing of his unfair dismissal complaint) that the employer has failed to comply with the relevant order. In the case of an order for reinstatement or re-engagement the tribunal has the power to order the continuation of the complainant's contract and may award such compensation as it considers just and equitable.[399] Where the employer has failed to comply with a continuation order the tribunal will determine the amount of pay owed and in any other case will award such compensation as it considers just and equitable.[400]

---

[389] EPCA, s. 77(2)(a).
[390] EPCA, s. 77(2)(b).
[391] EPCA, s. 77(3) and (3A).
[392] EPCA, s. 77(5).
[393] *Taplin v. C. Shippam Ltd* [1978] IRLR 450, EAT.
[394] EPCA, s. 77(5) and (7).
[395] EPCA, s. 77(9).
[396] EPCA, s. 78(1).
[397] EPCA, s. 78(2).
[398] EPCA, s. 78(6).
[399] EPCA, s. 79(2).
[400] EPCA, s. 79(3). Where this application is being dealt with at the same time as the unfair dismissal complaint, the tribunal must specify the amount of pay separately.

5.91 (d) Recoupment of benefits

A person who has been dismissed from employment may well be entitled to state benefits such as unemployment benefit or income support. The question is whether a tribunal should take such benefits into account when determining the amount of compensation to be paid to a complainant. This issue is now regulated by the Employment Protection (Recoupment of Unemployment Benefit and Supplementary Benefit) Regulations 1977[401] which permit the recovery of sums from the prescribed element in unfair dismissal compensation. This element is the amount which the employee has received to cover loss of wages for the period up until the conclusion of the hearing.[402] When the tribunal makes a monetary award to which the Regulations apply it must set out (a) the monetary award; (b) the amount of the prescribed element, if any (c); the dates of the period of the prescribed element and (d) the amount, if any, by which the monetary award exceeds the prescribed element.[403] The effect of the Regulations is to assess the employer for the whole of the monetary award but to postpone payment of the prescribed element until a recoupment notice has been served on the employer by the Department of Employment.[404] Initially, therefore, the employee only receives the excess of the monetary award over the prescribed element. The effect of the recoupment notice is to require the employer to pay back to the Department the amount of the benefits paid during the period of the prescribed element.[405] Once this has been done the employer will be required to pay the rest of the monetary award to the successful complainant.

---

[401] SI 1977 No. 674 as amended by SI 1980 No. 1608. These regulations only apply to an award by a tribunal; they do not apply to a negotiated settlement. This fact may be an incentive to the parties to agree to some sort of negotiated settlement.

[402] Reg. 3, and paras. 6-8 of Sched.

[403] Reg. 5(3).

[404] Reg. 8.

[405] Reg. 9(2).

Chapter Six

REDUNDANCY PAYMENTS

INTRODUCTION

6.1 When an employee becomes redundant various legal questions can arise. For example the selection for redundancy of part-time employees before full-time employees may raise issues of indirect sexual or marital status discrimination.[1] Alternatively the selection for redundancy may raise issues of the fairness of the dismissal and it is the case that a perfectly genuine dismissal for redundancy may, for want of proper procedure, become an unfair dismissal.[2] However this Chapter is concerned with the simple question of whether an employee is entitled to receive a redundancy payment which is a payment, calculated in accordance with strict statutory rules, an employee[3] with at least two years' continuous employment is entitled to receive from his employer[4] in the event of his dismissal on grounds of redundancy — in short, statutory compensation for loss of employment. The system of redundancy payments was first introduced by the Redundancy Payments Act 1965 and the current provisions are now contained in Part VI of the Employment Protection (Consolidation) Act 1978.[5] The issues involved in whether an employee is entitled to receive a redundancy payment are as follows:

(1) Has the employee been dismissed?

(2) Is the dismissal due to redundancy?

(3) Has the employee's right to receive a redundancy payment been defeated by his refusal of alternative employment?

(4) Has the business in which the redundant employee worked been transferred to another employer?

(5) Has the employee's right to redundancy payment been affected by his misconduct or a strike or lock-out?

(6) Is the employee covered by an exclusion or exemption?

(7) What rules are there for claiming and calculating a redundancy payment?

(8) What payments may be received from the Redundancy Fund?

---

[1]   See Chapter Seven, para. 7.15.

[2]   See Chapter Five, para. 5.49.

[3]   Defined to mean those employed under a contract of employment or apprenticehsip (EPCA, s. 153(1)); but note the special provisions made for others, *e.g.* office holders (ss. 115, 116, 117).

[4]   An employer's right to receive a rebate has been removed (WA, ss. 27-29; EA 1989, s. 17).

[5]   For a detailed analysis of purpose of redundancy payments and the law regarding redundancy, see respectively, *The Effect of the Redundancy Payments Scheme* (HMSO, 1971) and C. Grunfeld, *The Law of Redundancy* (3rd edn. 1989).

DISMISSAL

6.2 General

Generally[6] to become entitled to a redundancy payment an employee must have been dismissed. However redundancy law[7] like unfair dismissal law[8] provides that an employee is to be treated as dismissed by his employer only if his contract of employment is terminated in certain ways. As the statutory declaration of the situations which amount to dismissal is discussed in detail in the context of unfair dismissal law[9] it is sufficient here to set out the elements of the statutory declaration and consider any special rules which relate only to redundancy. Thus an employee is dismissed "if but only if[10]" (i) his contract is terminated by his employer with or without notice,[11] (ii) his fixed term contract expires without being renewed, or (iii) he terminates his contract with or without notice when his employer's conduct[12] entitles him (the employee) to terminate his contract without notice (*i.e.* rescind the contract) — commonly referred to as a constructive dismissal.

6.3 Special rules

(a) Employee leaving early. Although unfair dismissal and redundancy law both contain special rules which permit an employee who leaves by giving notice to terminate during a period of notice given by his employer to be regarded as dismissed[13] the rules which operate in relation to redundancy are more strict than those for unfair dismissal. The object of the rules is to ensure that an employee under notice is not forced to choose between an offer of employment available during the period of the employer's notice and his redundancy payment. However to preserve his right to a redundancy payment the employee's notice of earlier termination must be in writing[14] and it must be given during the "obligatory part" of the employer's notice.[15] The obligatory part of the employer's notice is the period of notice the employer is required by statute[16] to give. Thus if an employer's notice is longer than the period required by statute the employee must delay giving his notice of earlier termination until the obligatory part of the notice has commenced. Accordingly if an employer gives four weeks' notice to an employee who by statute is entitled to only two weeks' notice, the employee to preserve his entitlement to a redundancy payment must not give written notice before the last two of the four weeks.[17] How-

---

[6] The exceptions are where an employee has been put on short time or is laid off by his employer and where a dismissal is implied (see para. 6.3).

[7] EPCA, s. 83(2).

[8] EPCA, s. 55(2).

[9] See Chapter Five paras. 5.14-5.25.

[10] It is therefore an exclusive definition which cannot be circumvented by contract — see EPCA, s. 140.

[11] Cf. *Brown v. Knowsley Borough Council* [1986] IRLR 102, EAT.

[12] However a lock-out does not entitle termination without notice (EPCA, s. 92 (4)).

[13] The special rules are contained in EPCA, ss. 55(3) (unfair dismissal) and 85 (redundancy) respectively.

[14] EPCA, s. 85(1). Notice other than in writing results in loss of entitlement (*Brown v. Singer Manufacturing Co. Ltd.* [1967] ITR 213).

[15] EPCA, s. 85(1).

[16] EPCA, s. 49.

[17] Cf. *CPS Recruitment Ltd v. Bowen* [1982] IRLR 54 in which the EAT, perhaps to mollify the strictness of the rule, distinguished an employee's request for earlier termination (by the employer) from an employee's notice of earlier termination by himself.

ever even if an employee gives written notice at the correct time his right to a redundancy payment depends on his employer's reaction. If his employer does not object to the employee's earlier termination, other conditions being met, the employee will be entitled to receive a payment. However if the employer gives to the employee written notice requiring the employee to withdraw his notice but the employee persists in earlier termination whether the employee retains an entitlement to a redundancy payment is determined by an industrial tribunal.[18]

(b) Implied termination. The statutory concept[19] of "dismissal" already mentioned is extended[20] so that where, in accordance with a rule of law (a) any act on the part of or (b) any event (including his death) affecting an employer operates to terminate the contract of employment the act or event shall be treated as a termination by the employer. The result is that such implied or constructive terminations are deemed to be dismissals. Provision (b) above is to ensure that entitlement to a redundancy payment is not lost where the contract of employment is frustrated[21] by, for example, the death or long term illness or incapacity or an individual employer, a company's compulsory liquidation or the dissolution of a partnership.[22] However, obviously, there is no implied termination by an employer where it is the death illness or incapacity of the employee which results in the termination of the contract[23] and where an event affects both the employer and employee there is an implied termination by the employer only where its effect on the employer terminates the contract. Thus where statute transferred the policing functions at Heathrow Airport to the Metropolitan Police there was no implied termination of the employee's contract because it was brought about by his consenting to a transfer to the Metropolitan Police and not by the statutory transfer of functions.[24] On the other hand with regard to provision (a) above it is not clear what "acts on the part of an employer" (apart from those already declared to be a dismissal) operate to terminate the contract. It may have been intended to apply in a case where an employer, without expressly dismissing an employee, disposes of the business in which an employee is employed in the knowledge that the new owner will not offer him employment. However, strictly, because such an act would be a repudiation of the contract leaving the employee with no alternative but to rescind the contract there would be a dismissal within the statutory definition.[25] Additionally since the enactment of the Transfer of Undertakings (Protection of Employment) Regulations 1981[26] the sale of a commercial undertaking (or part of one) operates to transfer to the new owner contracts of employment subsisting at the time of the transfer of the undertaking.[27]

(c) Volunteers for redundancy. Because entitlement to a redundancy payment is conditional on a dismissal — as previously explained — occurring, it follows

[18] EPCA, s. 85(3), (4).
[19] EPCA, s. 83(1).
[20] EPCA, s. 93.
[21] See Chapter Four para. 4.6 and Chapter Five para. 5.68.
[22] See Chapter Four paras. 4.7, 4.8.
[23] Cf. *Thomas v. John Drake & Co Ltd* [1971] ITR 146, IT to effect that, the employer's intimation that he regarded the contract as frustrated was an act of the employer operating to terminate the contract.
[24] *British Airport Authority v. Fenerty* [1976] 361, DC.
[25] EPCA, s. 83(2)(c). However when EPCA, s. 93 was first enacted (see Redundancy Payment Act 1965, s. 22) the view may have been that certain repudiatory conduct itself terminated the contract.
[26] S.I. 1981 No. 1794.
[27] *Ibid.* Regulation 5. Also see para. 6.7.

that generally[28] a termination by agreement or by the employee leaving voluntarily will result in the loss of such entitlement. Because it is accepted as good industrial relations practice for employers to give advance warning of redundancies and, where possible, to reduce their workforce by inviting volunteers[29] it is sometimes difficult to know whether a dismissal has occurred. However the following principles have been established. After redundancies are announced without a date of dismissal being fixed or positively ascertainable an employee who terminates his employment is not treated as dismissed.[30] It is necessary to distinguish an employee who consents to the termination of his contract from one who consents or volunteers to be dismissed. In the former case there is no dismissal[31] whereas in the latter case there is a dismissal even if the employee went along with or encouraged it.[32] But to be a dismissal the eventual termination must be the act of the employer alone. Accordingly because an employer's acceptance of an employee's application for early retirement results in the contract being terminated not by the employer alone but by the employer and employee together it has been held there is no dismissal even although the employer had a discretion to accept or refuse the application.[33]

(d) Lay-off and short-time. An important exception to the rule that entitlement to a redundancy payment depends on the employee having been dismissed occurs where the employee has been laid-off or placed on short-time.[34] The purpose of the relevant provisions[35] is to prevent an employer avoiding liability for a redundancy payment by indefinite lay-off or short-time. Clearly, provided an employer had a contractual right to lay-off or impose short-time working he would be able to meet the reduction in requirements for employees to do work without ever having to dismiss an employee.[36] An employee is laid-off for any week in which he is not entitled to any remuneration[37] under his contract by reason of no work being provided by his employer[38] and an employee is on short-time in any week for which he receives less than half a week's pay because of a diminution of his work.[39]

---

[28]   EPCA, s. 83(2)(b) may be seen as an exception because it provides for a dismissal where termination takes the form of the expiry of a fixed term contract without the contract being renewed.

[29]   Code of Practice issued under the Industrial Relations Act 1971, paras. 45, 46.

[30]   *Morton Sundour Fabrics Ltd v. Shaw* [1976] ITR 84; *International Computers Ltd v. Kennedy* [1981] IRLR 28, EAT in which it was also held that an employer who indicated that those employees who leave at times convenient to the employer may be personally barred from subsequently pleading there was no dismissal.

[31]   This is of course not the case where the termination agreement has been induced by force and fear; see for example *Hennessy v. Craigmyle Laundry Ltd* [1986] ICR 461, CA.

[32]   *Burton, Allton and Johnson v. Peck* [1975] IRLR 81, EAT; *Morley v. C. T. Morley Ltd* [1985] ICR 499, EAT.

[33]   *Birch and Humber v. Liverpool University* [1985] IRLR 165, CA. The court was not prepared to separate the act of application from the act of acceptance and the contract was held to have been terminated by mutual consent.

[34]   EPCA, s. 81(1)(b).

[35]   EPCA, ss. 81(1)(b), 87, 88, 89.

[36]   Of course if he did not have such a contractual right by laying off or imposing short-time the employer would risk the employee rescinding the contract and claiming a constructive dismissal within EPCA, s. 83(2)(c). And see *D. & J. McKenzie Ltd v. Smith* 1976 SLT 216, OH.

[37]   See *Powell Duffryn Wagon Co Ltd v. House* [1974] ICR 123, NIRC.

[38]   EPCA, s. 87(1), which applies to piece-rate and time-rate workers. And see C. Grunfeld, *The Law of Redundancy* (2nd edn., 1980) p. 250.

[39]   EPCA, s. 87(2).

The effect of the provisions is that an employee who has been laid-off or on short-time (or a combination thereof) for at least 4 consecutive weeks or, in a period of 13 consecutive weeks, for 3 consecutive and 3 non-consecutive weeks is entitled to give his employer written notice[40] of his intention to claim a redundancy payment[41] and if this is accompanied by his giving the notice required to terminate his contract[42] the employee will become entitled to the appropriate redundancy payment unless (1) the employer gives to the employee "counter-notice" that he will contest his liability to make such a payment and (2) on the date of the employee's notice of intention to claim it was likely that within 4 weeks full employment lasting at least 13 weeks would be resumed.[43] While an offer of re-employment is not strictly a "counter-notice"[44] it has been held that the following was to be read as a week's notice of termination:

"As I have now been laid off for four consecutive weeks with no work I have been advised (by ACAS) that after such a time you must either re-employ me full-time for a minimum of 13 weeks or make me redundant. If you do not wish to do any of the above, then I am left with no option but to resign and instigate industrial tribunal proceedings against you. I look forward to hearing from you within 7 days."[45]

Where liability to make a redundancy payment is contested by an employer giving counter-notice the employee's entitlement to a payment is to be decided by an industrial tribunal.[46]

6.4 The relevant date

For various purposes[47] it is important to be able to ascertain the time of dismissal or as statute[48] describes it, the "relevant date".[49] The precise rules for determining the relevant date are complicated but they may be summarised thus.

(a) Termination with notice. The relevant date is the date the notice expires[50] unless the notice is given by the employer and it is shorter than that required by statute[51] in which case it is postponed until the date on which the statutory minimum notice would have expired if given on the date the actual (shorter) notice was given.[52] However although such a postponement applies "for the

---

[40] The time at which the various notices have to be given is strictly regulated by EPCA, ss. 88(1), (2), (3), (4), 89(5)(a)-(c); and see *Allinson v. Drew Simmons Engineering Ltd* [1985] ICR 488, EAT.

[41] EPCA, s. 88(1)(a), (b). However these provisions do not apply where the lay-off or short-time is attributable to a strike or a lock-out (EPCA, s. 89(3)).

[42] EPCA, s. 89(5) (a)-(c).

[43] *Ibid.* ss. 88(3), (4), 89(1).

[44] *Fabar Construction Ltd v. Race* [1979] ICR 529, EAT.

[45] *Walmsley v. C. & R. Ferguson Ltd* [1989] IRLR 112, IH.

[46] EPCA, s. 89(4).

[47] For (a) calculating continuous employment, (b) applying the time limits for making a claim and (c) applying the special rules regarding lay-off and short-time.

[48] EPCA, s. 90.

[49] In the law of unfair dismissal the equivalent concept is the "effective date of termination" as defined by EPCA, s. 55(4). And see Chapter Five, para. 5.27.

[50] EPCA, 90(1)(a). This also applies to notice of earlier termination given by the employee following notice by the employer (*Ibid.* s. 90(1)(e)).

[51] *Ibid.* s. 49(1).

[52] *Ibid.* s. 90(3).

purposes" specified[53] it has been held they are not words of limitation and merely mean that it is the same relevant date that is used to decide whether the employee has the two years' continuous employment required to qualify for a redundancy.[54] Accordingly previous decisions[55] on the meaning of section 90(3) the Employment Protection (consolidatior) Act 1978 will have to be reviewed.

(b) Termination without notice. The relevant date is the date of dismissal[56] unless the termination is by an employer who is not entitled — by reason of the employee's breach of contract — to terminate without giving notice in which case, it is postponed until the minimum statutory notice,[57] had it been given, would have expired.[58] Where termination is truly without notice (as opposed to with very short notice) the contract ends when the dismissal is communicated and does not continue until the employee had completed his journey home for which by his contract his employers were obliged to pay.[59] Furthermore although employees and employers may waive their respective rights to minimum statutory notice[60] where such a waiver takes place the relevant date is still postponed by statute[61] until the expiry of the notice required by section 49(1) because the fact that an employee has waived his right to notice or accepted a payment in lieu of notice under section 49(3) is relevant only to his rights in contract and not to his rights to a redundancy payment.[62] Where wages in lieu of notice are given the relevant date is the date of the dismissal but where the employee is merely excused from working out notice the relevant date is the date the notice expired.[63] Where termination occurs by the non-renewal of a fixed-term contract the relevant date is the date of the contract's expiry.[64]

(c) Special provisions. Special provisions determine the relevant date where there has been a trial period[65] and where the entitlement to a redundancy payment follows a period of lay-off or short-time.[66]

REDUNDANCY

6.5 The statutory definition of redundancy

Although the words "redundant" and "redundancy" are popularly used to denote "superfluous" or "outmoded" for the system of redundancy payments the concept of redundancy involves a two-part, technical legal definition.[67] Thus an

---

[53] *Ibid.* The specified purposes are for determining (1) a qualifying period, (2) a period of continuous employment and (3) a week's pay.

[54] *Secretary of State for Employment v. Staffordshire CC* [1989] IRLR 117, CA.

[55] *Slater v. John Swain & Co Ltd* [1981] ICR 554, EAT; *Smith v. Clark's College Ltd* [1969] ITR 78, IT.

[56] EPCA, s. 90(1)(b).

[57] *Ibid.* s. 49(1).

[58] *Ibid.* s. 90(3).

[59] *Octavius Atkinson and Sons v. Morris* [1989] IRLR 158, CA.

[60] *Ibid.*, s. 49(3).

[61] *Ibid.*, s. 90(3).

[62] *Secretary of State for Employment v. Staffordshire CC* [1989] IRLR 117, CA.

[63] Compare *Slater v. John Swain & Son Ltd* [1981] ICR 554, EAT, *Belling and Lee Ltd v. Burford* [1982] ICR 454, EAT with *Adams v. G K N Sankey Ltd* [1980] IRLR 416, EAT, *Chapman v. Letheby & Christopher Ltd* [1981] IRLR 440, EAT.

[64] EPCA, s. 90(1)(c).

[65] See para. 6.7.

[66] EPCA, s. 90(1)(d) (trial periods); *ibid.* s. 90(2) (lay-off and short-time).

[67] The Transfer of Undertakings (Protection of Employment) Regulations 1981 have not altered the definition (*Chapman v. CPS Computer Group plc,* [1987] IRLR 462, CA).

employee is redundant if his dismissal is attributable[68] wholly or mainly to the fact that

(a) his employer has ceased, or intends to cease, temporarily or permanently,[69] (generally or in the place the employee was employed) to carry on the business for the purposes of which the employee was employed,[70] or

(b) the requirements of that business for employees[71] to carry out work of a particular kind (generally or in the place the employee was employed) have ceased or diminished or are expected to cease or diminish temporarily or permanently.[72]

To satisfy either (a) or (b) it is permissible to have regard to the business(es) of an associated employer[73] and similarly the activities of local education authorities in respect of their schools may be treated as one business.[74] Although business is widely defined to include "a trade, profession or any other activity"[75] entitlement to a redundancy payment only occurs where the requirements of the business for the purposes of which the employee works has ceased or diminished. It is therefore necessary, occasionally, to be able to isolate the business for which the employee works from other business activities of the same employer. In *Babar Indian Restaurant v. Rawat*[76] two partners operated a restaurant, a frozen food shop and an off-sales shop. When the frozen food shop was closed down and an employee was transferred from there to the restaurant the dismissal of Rawat, a waiter in the restaurant, to accommodate the transfer of the employee from the frozen food was not due to redundancy in that the requirements of the restaurant business for whose purposes Rawat was employed had not ceased or diminished.[77] However had the three business (the restaurant, the off-sales and the frozen food shop) been carried on by associated employers[78] the three businesses could have been treated as one[79] and the dismissal of Rawat would have been by reason of redundancy.

---

[68] As to the meaning of "attributable" see *Fleming v. Wandsworth London Borough Council, The Times* December 23, 1985, CA.

[69] EPCA, s. 81(3). Thus closure of a business for a week has led to entitlement to a redundancy payment (*Whitworth v. Bilabbey Ltd* [1975] IRLR 206); *cf. Higgs and Hill Ltd v. Singh* [1977] ICR 193, EAT. And where there is a right to lay-off short term closures may be dealt with by that method. See para. 6.3(d).

[70] EPCA, s. 81(2)(a).

[71] Thus where one employee is replaced by another there is no redundancy because the requirements of the business for "employees" has not altered (*North Yorkshire CC v. Fay* [1985] IRLR 247, CA) and the opposite is the case where an employee is replaced by a self-employed person (*Gorictree Ltd v. Jenkinson* [1985] IRLR 3, EAT. And see *Willcox and Lane v. Hastings* [1987] IRLR 298, CA.

[72] EPCA, s. 81(2)(b), (3).

[73] As to the meaning of "associated employer" see Chapter Three para. 3.5(d).

[74] EPCA, s. 81(2), (2A).

[75] *Ibid.* s. 153(1). Cf. the Transfer of Undertakings (Protection of Employment) Regulations 1981 which relate only to undertakings in the nature of a commercial venture. And see para. 6.8.

[76] [1985] IRLR 57, EAT.

[77] In fact Rawat was unfairly dismissed because his employers did not prove the reason for his dismissal was redundancy.

[78] See Chapter Three para. 3.5(d).

[79] EPCA, s. 81(2). And see para. 6.7.

6.6 Place of work and work of a particular kind.

A key element in both parts of the definition of redundancy is "the place where the employee (is) employed"[80] and to determine an employee's place of employment it is necessary to consider where by his contract of employment[81] (taking account of any implied terms)[82] the employee may be required to work. Thus although an employer was entitled to transfer an employee to a different place of work it has been held this may be subject to the implied term that the transfer would be restricted to what was a reasonable distance and be preceded by reasonable notice[83] but where there is a clear express term permitting the transfer of an employee although there will be no scope for implying a qualification that it is limited by what is a daily travelling distance[84] it has been held[85] that where there is a clause allowing the employer to change an employee's place of work the employer must not apply the clause in such a way as to render it impossible for the employee to comply with his contractual obligation to move. The significance of an employee's place of work is that a contractual right to move an employee to a location where work is available from one where work is ceasing or diminishing will, in the event of the employee refusing to move, defeat his claim to a redundancy payment. Correspondingly in the event of unfair dismissal proceedings the employer will not be able to claim the reason for dismissal was redundancy.[86]

Another question in considering the statutory concept of redundancy is whether there has been a reduction in the needs of the business for employees to carry out "work of a particular kind".[87] This question is answered by examining the particular kind of work the employee is by his contract bound to do.[88] However as *Haden Ltd v. Cowen*[89] illustrates this requires careful examination of the particular contract of employment. Although Cowen, a divisional contracts surveyor, was by his contract "required to undertake, at the direction of the company, any and all duties which reasonably fall within the scope" of his capabilities he was dismissed by reason of redundancy when the requirements of the business for a divisional contracts surveyor ceased because the effect of these words did not give his employer (Haden Ltd) the right to transfer him from his job as divisional contracts surveyor to any job as a surveyor; it merely required him to perform any duties reasonably within the scope of his capabilities as divisional contracts surveyor.[90] Similarly although a job-title is to be construed

---

[80] *Ibid.* s. 81(2)(a), (b).

[81] *United Kingdom Atomic Energy Authority v. Claydon* [1974] ICR 128, NIRC; and see Chapter Two para. 2.13.

[82] *O'Brien v. Associated Fire Alarms Ltd* [1968] 1WLR 1916, CA; *Briggs v. Imperial Chemicals Industries Ltd* [1968] ITR 270, DC; in *Courtaulds Northern Spinning Ltd v. Sibson* [1988] IRLR 305, CA where there was no express term regarding the place of employment it was held that if the parties had directed their minds to the question of the mobility of the employee they would have agreed a power in the employer to direct the employee for any reason to work at any place within daily reach of his home.

[83] *Prestwick Circuits Ltd. v. McAndrew* [1990] IRLR 191, IH.

[84] *Rank Xerox Ltd v. Churchill* [1988] IRLR 280, EAT.

[85] *United Bank Ltd v. Akhtar* [1989] IRLR 507, EAT. Note also that the employer conceded that the operation of the mobility clause was limited by the employer's implied duties of cooperation and not to frustrate the employee's attempts to perform the contract.

[86] See Chapter Five para. 5.48.

[87] EPCA, s. 81(2)(b).

[88] *Nelson v. BBC* [1977] ICR 649, CA.

[89] [1982] IRLR 314, CA.

[90] CF. *Shook v. London Borough of Ealing* [1986] IRLR 46, EAT.

with flexibility[91] it is wrong to rely solely on a general job-title without taking account of the surrounding circumstances.[92] However where the kind of work the employee can be required to do is governed by an express term in the contract it is wrong to imply a more restrictive term from the fact that the employee has for some considerable period of time carried out only a restricted range of duties.[93] The critical issue is whether the requirements of the business "for employees" has ceased or diminished and it is immaterial that the volume of work has not altered[94] or that an expected business expansion for which employees were specially recruited did not take place;[95] nor is it relevant to find out the reason for the reduction in requirements for employees.[96] Determining whether there has been a reduction in requirements for employees to do work of a particular kind demands careful scrutiny of the functions required by the business and the skills and competence of employees and it is often a question of degree whether requirements for employees to do particular work have reduced. The following cases illustrate the approach that is necessary when considering whether requirements for employees to do work of a particular kind have ceased or diminished.

(a) *Vaux and Associated Breweries v. Ward.*[97] Mrs Ward was dismissed from her job as a waitress when her employers refurbished the pub in which she was employed changing its name from the Star and Garter Tavern to the Steamboat Inn. However it was held her dismissal was not attributable to redundancy because although after the refurbishment her employers chose to replace her with attractive, younger waitresses — in keeping with the new atmosphere the employers wished to create — there was no reduction in their requirements for employees to do work of a particular kind, namely the job of a waitress.

(b) *Murphy v. Epsom College.*[98] Mr Murphy was one of two plumbers employed to maintain the heating system and do general plumbing work but after alterations to the system he indicated he would restrict the type of work he would do to it. This resulted in Mr Murphy being dismissed following the employer's decision to appoint a heating technician to maintain the improved system as well as to do general plumbing work. Murphy was dismissed for redundancy because his employers, having appointed a heating technician with different skills and qualifications who, as well as doing general plumbing, had to perform functions which were more extensive and responsible than those Mr Murphy was competent to perform, no longer required two plumbers; their requirements now were a plumber and a heating technician/plumber.

---

[91] *Glitz v. Watford Electric Co* [1979] IRLR 89, EAT (job-title of "clerk/typist" held wide enough to require the employee to do photocopying).

[92] *Greater Glasgow Health Board v. Pate* [1983] SLT 90, IH.

[93] *Nelson v. BBC* [1977] ICR 649, CA. Consider also the validity of an *ad hoc* agreement to permit the transfer of an employee to a job he was not bound by contract to perform. Would such an agreement "purport to limit the operation of a provision of the Act" (EPCA, s. 140(1)) and therefore be void by EPCA, s. 140(1)? See *Tocher v. General Motors Scotland Ltd* [1981] IRLR 55, EAT.

[94] *North Yorkshire CC v. Fay* [1985] IRLR 247, CA; *Gorictree Ltd v. Jenkinson* [1985] IRLR 3, EAT; *Willcox and Lane v. Hastings* [1987] IRLR 298, CA. Cf. *Lesney Products & Co Ltd v. Nolan* [1977] IRLR 77, CA.

[95] Cf. *O'Hare v. Rotaprint Ltd* [1980] ICR 94, EAT.

[96] *Association of University Teachers v. University of Newcastle* [1988] IRLR 10, EAT.

[97] [1969] 7 KIR 309, DC. And see *Loudon v. Crimpy Crisps Ltd* [1966] ITR 307, IT and *European Chefs (Catering) Ltd v. Currell* [1971] ITR 37, DC.

[98] [1985] ICR 80, CA, affirming [1983] ICR 715, EAT. And see *Robinson v. British Island Airways Ltd* [1978] ICR 304, EAT.

(c) *Johnson v. Nottinghamshire Combined Police Authority.*[99] Johnson was one of several clerical workers working a standard 5 day, 38 hour week, employed by the police authority. To release more police officers from routine clerical work Johnson and her fellow workers were asked to change their work pattern so that they would work the same number of hours but at different times of the day and over a 6 day week. When they refused to comply with this pattern they were dismissed and claimed their dismissals were due to redundancy. However their claims were rejected because the changes in the time of work did not alter the essential nature of the work it being noted that while the statutory definition of redundancy[100] expressly refers to the place of employment the same cannot be said for the time at which work is done.[101]

6.7 Bumping.

"Bumping" describes what may frequently occur in a redundancy situation when, for example, a long serving employee capable of doing a variety of jobs in his employer's business is, on his redundancy, kept on in employment by being transferred into the job of another (usually more recently recruited) employee who, as a consequence is dismissed. An early example is seen in *Gimber & Sons Ltd v. Spurret*[102] in which Mr Spurret was held entitled to a redundancy payment on being dismissed when another employee, whose sales territory had disappeared in a reorganisation, took over his job as warehouse manager. Lord Parker, C.J. approved the following passage in the decision of the industrial tribunal — "if there is a reduction in the requirements for employees in one section of . . . a business and an employee who becomes surplus or redundant is transferred to another section of that business, an employee who is displaced by the transfer of the first employee and is dismissed by reason of that displacement is dismissed by reason of redundancy." While the generality of such a statement has been subsequently questioned[103] the effect is that an employee who is employed to do job "X" is entitled to a redundancy payment where the requirements for employees to do job "X" have not ceased or diminished provided they have ceased or diminished in relation to employees who do job "Y". The reason for this is that the definition of redundancy[104] does not expressly require that the redundant employee be one employed on the particular kind of work the requirements for which have ceased or diminished.[105] An important consequence of permitting an employer to argue that a "bumped" or displaced employee is dismissed by reason of redundancy is to enable him to overcome the first obstacle in defending an unfair dismissal complaint by proving the reason for dismissal was redundancy.[106]

---

[99] [1974] ICR 170, CA.

[100] EPCA, s. 81(a).

[101] However changing the time of work may also involve a change in the particular kind of work; see *Archibald v. Rossleigh Commercials Ltd* [1975] IRLR 231, IT; *Macfisheries Ltd v. Findlay* [1985] ICR 160, EAT.

[102] [1967] ITR 308, DC.

[103] *Gardner v. Adams (Dalkeith) Ltd* [1972] ITR 81, NIRC.

[104] EPCA, s. 81(2)(b).

[105] *Cf.* the comments in *Elliot Turbomachinery Ltd v. Bates* [1981] ICR 218, EAT. Also it would not seem difficult to imply a connection between the work for which there is a reduced requirement and the work performed by the dismissed employee; otherwise why does the statute create the idea of "work of a particular kind?"

[106] See Chapter Five para. 5.48.

ALTERNATIVE EMPLOYMENT

6.8 Offers of renewal and re-engagement

Even after an employee has been dismissed on grounds of redundancy his right to receive a redundancy payment may be defeated by his employer[107] offering to renew his contract or re-engage him. However whether the right to receive a redundancy payment is defeated depends on the suitability of the employment offered and the reasonableness of the employee's refusal of re-employment; thus, generally, where an employer offers to continue the employment of an employee he will lose his right to a redundancy payment if the new employment is suitable and he unreasonably rejects the offer or, having accepted the offer on a trial basis, he unreasonably terminates the new employment. However this is the result of a set of complicated statutory provisions which are strictly applied.[108] Although it is no longer[109] necessary for the employer's offer of renewal or extension[110] (of an existing contract) or re-engagement (under a new contract) to be in writing[111] it must be made (and communicated to the employee)[112] before[113] the ending of the original contract and must take place immediately on the ending of that contract or after an interval of not more than 4 weeks thereafter.[114] Where a change has occurred in the employee's terms of employment notice of such a change must be intimated *via* a revised or updated written statement issued in accordance with the relevant statutory provision.[115] However it has to be emphasised that as there is no duty to issue a revised written statement before the new employment beings[116] it cannot be regarded as an alternative to the offer of renewal or re-engagement which must be made before the ending of the original contract and although not required to be in formal, comprehensive terms must be more than a vague indication that the contract may be extended for a few days.[117]

6.9 Same terms, different terms and trial periods.

Where an employee accepts an offer of employment on the same terms he is not regarded as having been dismissed[118] and the law assumes that such an offer constitutes suitable employment so that an employee who declines such an offer is entitled to receive a redundancy payment only if his refusal is reasonable.[119] Where the offer is of employment on different terms[120] an employee's

---

[107] Employer in this context includes an associated employer or a new owner of a transferred business (EPCA, ss. 82(7), 94(2), (3)).

[108] See, for example, *E & J Davis Transport Ltd v. Chattaway* [1972] ICR 267, NIRC.

[109] *Cf.* Redundancy Payments Act 1965, s. 2 (4) (repealed).

[110] EPCA, s. 153(1).

[111] Accordingly an offer may be made collectively by the posting of a notice.

[112] Thus an employee who is off sick when the offer is made will not have received it unless it is sent directly to him (*Maxwell v. Walter Howard Designs Ltd* [1975] IRLR 77).

[113] See *E & J Davis Transport Ltd v. Chattaway* [1972] ICR 267, NIRC.

[114] EPCA, s. 82(3).

[115] EPCA, s. 82(3).

[115] EPCA, s. 1 as amended by EA, 1989 s. 13; see Chapter Two para. 2.10.

[116] See Chapter Two para. 2.10.

[117] Compare *Singer Co (UK) Ltd v. Ferrier* [1980] IRLR 300, EAT with *Kitching v. Ward, Watson and Taylor* [1967] ITR 464, DC.

[118] EPCA, s. 84(1).

[119] *Ibid.* s. 82(5).

[120] Generally a difference in only one term will mean the offer is or different terms but trivial differences are disregarded (*Rose v. Henry Trickett & Sons Ltd* [1971] ITR 211, DC).

entitlement to a redundancy payment depends on whether the employment offered is suitable and, if the employee refuses the offer of suitable employment, whether his refusal is reasonable. If the employment offered is unsuitable the reaction of the employee to the offer does not affect his right to receive a redundancy payment[121] but if the offer is of suitable employment an unreasonable refusal of the offer results in loss of redundancy payment.[122] Where before the original contract has ended the employee receives an offer of employment on different terms and renewal or re-engagement takes place immediately[123] on the ending of the original contract (or within 4 weeks thereof) the employee is not to be regarded as dismissed but a statutory trial period comes into play[124] and if either the employer or the employee terminates the new employment during the trial period then the employee is treated as having been dismissed at the date the original contract ended and for the reason(s) it ended.[125] However this is subject to the qualification that where it is the employer who terminates during the trial period the reason for the termination must relate to the change to the new employment whereas where termination is by the employee a dismissal for the reason the original employment was terminated is reinstated whatever the reason for the employee terminating the new employment.[126] Thus where termination takes place during the trial period the original dismissal is reinstated but an employee who unreasonably terminates the new employment is not entitled to a redundancy payment if the new employment was suitable.[127]

Because of these provisions it is important to be able to determine when the period begins and ends and statute provides that it shall begin with the ending trial of the employment under the prior (original) contract and end with the expiration of a period of 4 weeks beginning with the date on which the employee starts work under the new contract.[128] If the trial period exceeds the statutory limits the employee whose employment is terminated will not be able to claim the reinstatement of the dismissal under the original contract and the phrase "period of four weeks" means four consecutive weeks calculated according to the calendar.[129] Thus when an employee's employment terminated by reason of redundancy at midnight on 21st December 1986 and he was offered alternative employment commencing immediately it was held the statutory trial period could not be extended to take into account the period of 7 days the factory was closed for Christmas holidays; it was immaterial that the employee had not had a trial period of 4 weeks during which he was actually working.[130] While it is possible for a trial period to be extended by agreement between the employee and his employer[131] the purpose of the extension must be to retrain

---

[121] EPCA, s. 82(3)(5).

[122] *Ibid.*

[123] EPCA, s. 84(2).

[124] EPCA, s. 84(1), (3).

[125] EPCA, s. 84(b).

[126] *Ibid.*

[127] *Ibid.* Where an employer refuses to allow the employee to have a trial period that can affect the reasonableness of his (the employee's) decision to reject the new employment: *Elliot v. Richard Stump Ltd* [1987] IRLR 215, EAT.

[128] EPCA, s. 84(4).

[129] *Benton v. Sanderson Kayser Ltd* [1989] IRLR 19, CA.

[130] *Ibid.*

[131] The agreement need not be a formal probative document but in addition to specifying the length of the extension it must cover matters like status, pay and job description (*McKindley v. William Hill (Scotland) Ltd* [1985] IRLR 492, EAT.

the employee[132] and must be (1) in writing, (2) between the employer and the employee (or his representatives), (3) made before the employee starts work under the new contract and (4) specific about the date the trial period ends and the conditions which apply thereafter.[133] Thus extending a trial period to allow the employee an opportunity of deciding whether he could adapt to changed hours of work and night work is not permitted because it is not for retraining the employee.[134] It is necessary to appreciate the difference between a statutory trial period and the time an employee has to decide whether he will rescind his contract following a repudiation or conduct amounting to anticipatory breach by the employer. The relationship between the statutory trial period and, what might conveniently be termed, the common law trial period is illustrated by *Turvey v. C. W. Cheyney & Son Ltd*[135] in which Turvey, without being dismissed, agreed to try alternative work he was not contractually bound to do. However having worked at the new job for more than 4 weeks Turvey left because he did not find the job suitable and it was held that the statutory trial period was in addition to the common law trial period so that he had a reasonable time to decide whether to accept the new employment; only after the expiry of such a reasonable time would the statutory trial period begin to run.[136]

6.10 Is employment suitable; is refusal reasonable?

The answers given in response to these questions depend very much on the facts and circumstances of each case — they are questions of fact for determination by the industrial tribunal[137] and there is no rule that to be suitable the employment must be substantially equivalent to the employment which has come to an end.[138] Generally the onus of proof is on the employer to prove the employment offered is suitable and that the employee was unreasonable in refusing it.[139] To demonstrate how each case is dependent on its own facts and circumstances compare the following decisions. In *Cahuac and Others v. Allen Amery Ltd*[140] Mrs Cahuac was employed at the premises of her employers, Allen Amery Ltd, in Minerva Street, Hackney, London E2, when they moved to other premises in Goswell Road, London EC1 where she was offered employment but declined. The industrial tribunal held that the employment at Goswell Road was not suitable because it would involve a 40 minute bus journey, whereas Mrs Cahuac lived within a short walk of the Minerva Street premises; she looked after her widowed mother whom she could tend to during her lunch hour while employed at Minerva Street; the cost of travel to Goswell Road would reduce Mrs Cahuac's pay by 7% while the amount of travelling time would be greatly increased. In *Kerr v. National Coal Board*[141] on Mr Kerr's dismissal he was offered, but refused, employment at another colliery. His reasons for refusal were that the work was dangerous bearing in mind that he was deaf in one ear

---

[132] EPCA, s. 84(4).
[133] *Ibid.*, s. 84(5).
[134] *Meek v. I J Allen Rubber Co Ltd* [1980] IRLR 21, EAT.
[135] [1979] ICR 341, EAT.
[136] And see *Air Canada v. Lee* [1978] ICR 1202.
[137] *Kerr v. National Coal Board* [1970] ITR 48; *Hitchcock v. St Annes Hosiery Co Ltd* [1971] ITR 98, D.C.
[138] *Standard Telephone and Cables Ltd v. Gates* [1981] 21, EAT.
[139] *Jones v. Aston Cabinet Co Ltd* [1973] ICR 292, NIRC.
[140] [1966] ITR 313.
[141] [1970] ITR 48, CS. Also see *Bruce v. National Coal Board* [1967] ITR 167, IT; *Taylor v. Kent County Council* [1969] ITR 294, QBD.

and for health reasons (he suffered from chronic *otitis medio*) he could not travel the 20 miles by bus to the new colliery. However the Court of Session, emphasising the question of fact, upheld the decision of the industrial tribunal that he had been unreasonable in refusing the employment offered.[142]

BUSINESS TRANSFERS

6.11 Redundancy and the transfer of a business

Frequently a redundancy situation arises when the business[143] in which an employee is employed is transferred to a new owner.[144] Where such a transfer takes place and certain statutory conditions are satisfied[145] an offer of employment by the new owner is equated with an offer by the old owner so that an unreasonable refusal of suitable employment by the new owner will result in the employee losing any entitlement to a redundancy payment.[146] Where the employee accepts an offer by the new owner the statutory trial period operates but if the employment is terminated (either by the employee or the new owner) the employee is deemed to have been dismissed by the old owner against whom a claim for a redundancy payment may be made.[147] However these provisions must be placed in the context of the Transfer of Undertakings (Protection of Employment) Regulations 1981[148] which provide for the statutory transfer of contracts of employment which are in existence when an undertaking is transferred; the new owner (transferee) of the undertaking is statutorily substituted for the old owner (the transferor) in the contract of employment and, clearly where such a substitution takes place there is no scope for the application of the statutory provisions[149] which equate an offer by the new owners with an offer by the old, the new owner being regarded as party to the contract of employment.[150] The Regulations apply to a transfer from one person to another of an undertaking

---

[142] And see *Soutar v. Henry Balfour & Co Ltd* [1966] ITR 383, IT; *Ryan v. Liverpool Warehousing Co Ltd* [1966] ITR 69, IT. From the Outer House decision in *British Steel Corporation v. Dingwall* 1976 SLT 230 it may be inferred that a substantial drop in wages would itself render the employment unsuitable.

[143] "Business includes a trade or profession and any activity carried on by a body of persons, corporate or incorporate" (EPCA, s. 153(1)).

[144] The change in ownership may be by "sale or other disposition or by operation of law" (EPCA, s. 94(1)(a)) but does not include the transfer of shares in a limited company. In the latter situation there will be a transfer of shares but the business remains in the ownership of the limited company, no change of employer occurring.

[145] By the combined effect of EPCA, ss. 82(3) and 94(3) these are that the new owner must make the offer (of renewal or re-engagement) before the employee's contract with the old owner ends and employment by th enew owner must take effect within 4 weeks of it so ending. But a failure to satisfy these conditions does not break continuity (*Secretary of State for Employment v. de Rosa* 1974 SLT 214, HL).

[146] EPCA, s. 94. *Cf.* s. 150, Sch. 12, para. 13 (ownership passing to personal representatives).

[147] EPCA, ss. 84(6), 94(2). The substitution of a new owner does not itself affect the questions of whether the new employment is different or whether the employee has unreasonably refused the offer. (s. 94(4))

[148] SI 1981 No 1794. The regulations were enacted to give effect to Directive 77/187, and in line with *Litster v. Forth Dry Dock and Engineering Co Ltd* [1989] IRLR 161, HL it is necessary to construe the regulations to comply with the Directive which itself has been interpreted by the ECJ: *P Bork International A/S v. Foreningen of Arbejdsledere i Danmark* [1989] IRLR 41; *Berg und Busschers v. Besselen.* [1989] IRLR 447.

[149] EPCA, s. 94.

[150] Transfer of Undertakings etc. Regulations reg. 5.

(or part of one) which is in the nature of a commercial venture[151] — which has been held to exclude a school with charitable status[152] — so that the contracts of (1) employees who were employed immediately before the transfer and (2) employees who would have been so employed but for their having been unfairly dismissed before the transfer[153] have effect after the transfer as if made originally between the respective employees and the new owner (transferee)[154] to whom all the transferor's rights and liabilities are transferred and to whom are imputed the transferor's acts in relation to the employees.[155] Thus where a commercial undertaking is transferred an employee's entitlement to a redundancy payment depends on whether his contract of employment, with its connected rights and duties, is transferred to the transferor. If it is not, whether or not the transferor offers suitable employment on the statutory conditions[156] the employee's right to a redundancy payment and against whom that right should be enforced are regulated by the ordinary rules set out above although it should be noted that where an employee is dismissed by, and receives a redundancy payment from, the transferor but is re-engaged by the transferee the dismissal combined with the receipt of the payment will fracture any continuity of employment the employee had accumulated.[157] If, on the other hand, the employee's contract of employment is statutorily transferred to the transferee he has no right to resist employment by the transferee unless he can prove a repudiation of the contract for example by the transferor substantially changing its terms or that the change in the identity of the employer is significant and to his detriment.[158] Absent such matters, resignation by the employee will not be a dismissal and will result in the loss of a right to a redundancy payment. However where such matters do occur the employee will have the right to decide whether to "accept" the repudiation and rescind the contract claiming a redundancy payment on the basis of continuous employment with transferor and transferee[159] or

---

151 *Ibid.* regs. 2, 3. What is transferred must already be in the nature of a commercial venture: *Expro Services v. Smith* [1991] IRLR 156, EAT.

152 *Woodcock v. Committee of the Friends School, Wigton and Glenwise Ltd* [1986] IRLR 490, EAT. And see *Rastill v. Automatic Refreshment Services Ltd* [1978] ICR 289, EAT and *Hadden v. University of Dundee Students' Association* [1985] IRLR 449, EAT in which Lord MacDonald opined that a commercial venture could include one run deliberately at a loss.

153 This is the effect of *Litster v. Forth Dry Dock and Engineering Co Ltd* [1989] IRLR 161, HL. And see Chapter Five para. 5.69.

154 Reg. 5(1).

155 Reg. 5(2). And see *Macer v. Abafast Ltd* [1990] IRLR 137, EAT in which the need to attach the same meaning to EPCA , Sch. 13 para. 17(2) and reg. 6 was subordinated to need to ensure rights based on continuity of employment were preserved where the business in which the employee worked was transferred. According to *Macer* "provided there has been a valid transfer of a business from A to B the continuous period of service of an employee with A may be added to the continuous period of service with B so as to establish a qualifying period of employment".

156 See EPCA, ss. 82(3), 94(3).

157 EPCA, Sch. 13, para. 12.

158 Reg. 5(5).

159 See *Bullard v. Marchant* [1986] ICR 389, EAT; *Macer v. Abafast Ltd* [1990] IRLR 137, EAT.

whether to affirm the new contract.[160] Alternatively it may be argued there has been a termination of employment followed by an offer of alternative employment in which case the statutory trial period will operate and whether the employee will be entitled to a redundancy payment will depend on the suitability of the employment offered and the reasonableness of the employee's refusal.

6.12 What is a business?

This question is relevant to redundancy payments law[161] and the Transfer of Undertakings (Protection of Employment) Regulations 1981.[162] However although "business" includes a trade or profession and "any activity carried on by a body of persons, whether corporate or incorporate[163] and is to be given a wide meaning[164] British courts have emphasised the distinction between the acquisition of a business as a going concern and the mere acquisition of its assets.[165] Essentially the British courts require the adoption of a macroscopic view of the economic activity that is transferred; what the individual employee actually does is irrelevant.[166] A striking illustration of their approach occurs in *Melon v. Hector Powe Ltd*[167] in which one company transferred to another the lease of a clothing factory, the transferee company taking over stock and work in hand. The House of Lords held however that what occurred was not the transfer of a business but the mere transfer of assets because before the transfer the factory was employed exclusively in providing garments to be offered for sale either by the transferor company or one of its associated companies whereas after the transfer the transferee company made garments of differing quality for whatever customers it could attract. Of course whether there is a transfer of a business is a question of fact but such a transfer may occur where a franchise, licence or tenancy is transferred and where a tenancy is transferred from one tenant to another the landlord may become the owner of the business for the moment between the termination of the old tenancy and the start of the new one.[168] Although it has been held that where a business transfer takes place an employee who claims a redundancy payment must prove all the ingredients necessary to satisfy his claim, including that what was transferred was a "business" and continuity of employment[169] this decision may not attach enough significance to the Transfer of

---

[160] While an employee will be allowed a reasonable time to make his decision, working on the changed terms under protest will not be regarded as affirmation (*Marriott v. Oxford and District Cooperative Society Ltd (No 2)* [1970] 1 QB 186, CA). And see Chaper Four para. 4.5.

[161] EPCA, s. 94.

[162] Reg. 2(1); see too EPCA, Sch. 13 para. 17(2).

[163] EPCA, s. 153(1).

[164] *H A Rencoull (Joiner and Shopfitters) Ltd v. Hunt* [1967] ITR 475, *per* Lord President Clyde.

[165] Contrast the approach of the European Court of Justice in cases like *P. Bork International A/S v. Foreningen of Arbejdsledere i Danmark* [1989] IRLR 41.

[166] *Lloyd v. Brassey* [1969] ITR 100, CA; *Baileys Executors v. Co-operative Wholesale Society Ltd* 1976 SLT 92.

[167] 1981 SC (HL) 1.

[168] *Young v. Daniel Thwaites & Co Ltd* [1977] ICR 877, EAT; *Premier Motors (Medway) Ltd v. Total Oil Great Britain Ltd* [1983] IRLR 471, EAT; *Mannin Management Services v. Ward* (IDS Brief 393, 7 Feb 1989) CA. And see *Landsorganisationen i Danmark v. Ny Molle KRO* [1989] IRLR 37, ECJ.

[169] *Secretary of State for Employment v. Cohen and Beaupress Ltd* [1987] IRLR 169, EAT, on the view that the presumption of continuity in Sch. 13 para. 1(3) applies only to employment with a single employer.

Undertaking (Protection of Employment) Regulations 1981 which transfer not just the contract of employment but also rights and duties in connection therewith.[170]

STRIKES AND LOCK-OUTS

6.13 Special rules about misconduct, strikes and lock-outs

Although generally dismissal for misconduct does not entitle an employee to a redundancy payment[171] this is qualified where, after the employer has given notice of termination by reason of redundancy or after a period of lay-off or short-time workings[172] the employee has given notice of his intention to claim a redundancy payment the employer terminates the contract because of the employee's conduct in circumstances such that he is entitled to terminate without notice.[173] In such a case the employee's right to receive all or part of a payment depends on whether that would be just and equitable.[174] Whether an employer is entitled to terminate without notice depends on whether the employee has repudiated the contract using the same approach as that to be adopted when dealing with an allegedly unfair constructive dismissal.[175] However the special rule about dismissal for misconduct after notice of termination for redundancy or notice of intention to claim a payment is further modified where the conduct which entitles termination without notice is the employee's participation in a strike.[176] In such a case the employee does not lose all right to a redundancy payment; however if he fails to make up for the days lost by his being on strike, entitlement to part or all of the payment depends on an industrial tribunal's discretion.[177] The special rules regarding strikes were extensively examined in *Simmons v. Hoover Ltd*[178] whose conclusions may be summarised thus: an employee who is dismissed for striking after notice of redundancy will not automatically lose his right to a payment, whereas an employee who takes strike action first and is dismissed for redundancy during it is not entitled to a payment.

PAYMENTS AND EXCLUSIONS

6.14 Claiming and calculating a redundancy payment

(a) *The claim.* To perfect his entitlement to a redundancy payment in accordance with domestic provisions[179] an employee must within 6 months of

---

[170] Reg. 5(2). And see *Macer v. Abafast Ltd* [1990] IRLR 137, EAT.

[171] And see the express provision to this effect in EPCA, s. 82(2)(a) where the misconduct justifies summary dismissal/rescission.

[172] See para. 6.3(d).

[173] EPCA, s. 92(2), (3).

[174] *Ibid.* s. 92(3). And see *Lignacite Products Ltd v. Krollman* [1979] IRLR 22, EAT in which the EAT emphasised the discretion entrusted to the industrial tribunal and upheld a tribunal's award of 60% of a payment to an employee convicted of theft from his employer during his period of notice. *Cf. Jarmain v. E. Pollard & Co Ltd* [1967] ITR 406.

[175] *Bonner v. H. Gilbert Ltd* [1989] IRLR 475, EAT.

[176] EPCA, s. 92(1) "Strike" and "lock-out" are to receive the meanings given in EPCA, Sch. 13 para. 24 (s. 92(5)).

[177] *Ibid.* s. 110. Similarly an employee's termination without notice because of the employer's lock-out is not a (constructive) dismissal (s. 92(4)).

[178] [1977] ICR 61 at 79, EAT.

[179] Different consideration may apply where — as is now competent following *Barber v. Guardian Royal Exchange Assurance Group* [1990] IRLR 240, ECJ — entitlement is based

the relevant date[180] either agree and receive a redundancy payment or make a written claim for one,[181] although late claims may be admitted by an industrial tribunal.[182] In a redundancy payment claim the onus of proof may shift from one party to the other depending on the issue being contested. Thus it is for the employee to prove he has been dismissed[183] whereas where alternative employment is offered the employer must prove compliance with the statutory conditions.[184] However, significantly, it is generally[185] presumed that employment has been continuous[186] and that dismissal is due to redundancy[187] so that where, for example, several factors together result in a dismissal it is for the employer to prove that a reduction in the requirement of the business was not the main causative factor.[188] Ironically since the introduction in 1972 of protection against complaints of unfair dismissal[189] employers seek to prove that redundancy is the reason for dismissal — however in such complaints no recourse to the statutory presumption that dismissal is due to redundancy is permitted.

(b) The payment. The amount of a redundancy payment is to be determined by reference to a statutory formula which takes account of the dismissed employee's continuous employment, age and "week's pay"[190] at date of dismissal. Only the most recent 20 years of continuous employment may be taken into account[191] with employment before the 18th birthday being discounted.[192] Broadly the payment is calculated as follows:

> for each year (of continuous employment)
> between 18 and 22 years of age — half a week's pay
> between 22 and 41 years of age — a week's pay
> between 41 years of age and the normal non-discriminatory retiring age or the employee's 65th birthday whichever occurs first — one and a half week's pay.[193]

---

on Art. 119 of the EEC Treaty. Note although the discriminatory provisions of EPCA, s. 82(1) have been removed by EA, 1989 s. 16 questions of indirect discrimination based on the statutory rules of continuous employment still remain and could be challenged using Art. 119: see *Bilka-Kaufhaus GmbH v. Weber von Hartz* [1987] ICR 110, ECJ and *Rinner-Kuhn v. FWW Spezial Gebaudereinigung* [1989] IRLR, 493, ECJ. And see Chapter Seven.

[180] See para. 6.4.
[181] EPCA, s. 101(1)(a)-(d).
[182] *Ibid.* s. 191(1).
[183] The statutory concept of dismissal in s. 83 is exhaustive (*Dixon v. British Broadcasting Corporation* [1978] ICR 357, EAT).
[184] The employer cannot merely require the employee to prove his refusal was reasonable (*Cartin v. Botley Garages Ltd* [1973] ITR 150, NIRC).
[185] Cf. *Sec. of State for Employment v. Cohen and Beaupress Ltd* [1987] IRLR 169, EAT (transfer of a business).
[186] EPCA. Sch. 13, para. 1(3).
[187] EPCA, s. 91(2).
[188] *Hindle v. Percival Boats Ltd* [1969] ITR 86, CA, *per* Widgery LJ at p. 97. And see *Harrison v. Chamberlain Studios Ltd* [1966] ITR 162, IT (employer failed to rebut presumption that dismissal of Communist Party member who was alleged to be security risk was by reason of redundancy).
[189] See Chapter Five.
[190] EPCA, Sch. 14 para. 8 imposes a (reviewable) maximum amount. And see Chapter Three para. 3.12.
[191] EPCA, Sch. 4, para. 3.
[192] *Ibid.*, s. 151(4) as substituted by EA, 1982, Sch. 2, para. 7(1). Cf. Unfair dismissal.
[193] *Ibid.*, Sch. 4 para. 2 as amended by EA, 1982 ss. 29, 21(3); EA, 1989 s. 16.

Unless there operates a non-discriminatory earlier normal retiring age employees are excluded from entitlement to a redundancy payment on attaining 65 years of age[194] and for each month worked after the 64th birthday the redundancy payment is reduced by one twelfth.[195]

6.15 Exclusions, rebates and the Redundancy Fund

Employees who do not have two years' contituous employment and those who have reached 65 years of age or an earlier non-discriminatory normal retiring age are excluded from receiving a redundancy payment and[195a] various groups or classes of employee are excluded either expressly or because they do not have contracts of employment.[196] Thus an employee who ordinarily works outside Great Britain is not entitled to a redundancy payment unless on the relevant date[197] he is in Great Britain in accordance with his employer's instructions[198] and various employees are excluded from entitlement to a statutory redundancy payment because they are covered by a collective agreement which has been the subject of an exemption order by the Secretary of State.[199] Generally an agreement or contract to reduce an employee's entitlement to receive a redundancy payment is void[200] but this rule is subject to the important exception that an employee who enters into a contract for a fixed term[201] of two years[202] or more may lawfully (either by a written clause in the contract of employment or by entering a separate exclusion agreement in writing[203]) exclude his right to a redundancy payment which would be payable on the expiry of the fixed term contract without its renewal.[204] It must be emphasised however that such an exclusion clause only operates in the case of the expiry and non-renewal of the fixed term contract; it would have no effect if the employee were dismissed (for redundancy) during the term. Where the exclusion agreement is arrived at during the currency of a fixed term contract of sufficient length it will not necessarily be incorporated into any extension of the original contract[205] and where there has been a succession of fixed term contracts it is the length of the final one which determines whether any exclusion of redundancy rights is valid.[206] Entitlement to a rebate from the Redundancy Fund on paying a redundancy payment is now repealed[207] and the Redundancy Fund is merged with the National Insurance Fund.[208]

---

[194] EPCA, s. 82(1) as amended by EA, 1989 s. 16.

[195] EPCA, Sch. 4(1)(2) as amended by EA, 1989 s. 16(2).

[195a] EPCA, ss. 81(1)(4), 82 (1) as amended.

[196] *E.g.* police officers/cadets: *Robertson v. Bell* 1969 SLT 119; *Wiltshire Police Authority v. Wynn* [1980] ICR 649, CA. And see Chapter Two.

[197] See para. 6.4.

[198] EPCA, s. 141 (4). And see ibid. ss. 100(2) (certain relatives), 144 (mariners and sharefishermen). But note EPCA, s. 146 (dockworkers) was repealed by Dock Work Act, 1989. And see Chapter Five para. 5.7.

[199] EPCA, s. 96. See *e.g.* Redundancy Payments Exemption Order 1980 (SI 1980 No. 1052.)

[200] EPCA, s. 140. And see *Tocher v. General Motors Scotland Ltd* [1981] IRLR 55, EAT.

[201] See Chapter Five para. 5.16.

[202] *Cf.* Unfair dismissal; see Chapter Five para. 5.10.

[203] EPCA, s. 142 (3).

[204] *Ibid.* s. 142(2).

[205] *Ibid.* s. 142(4).

[206] *British Broadcasting Corporation v. Ioannou* [1975] ICR 267, CA.

[207] WA, 1986 s. 27; EA, 1989 s. 17.

[208] EA, 1990 s. 13.

Chapter Seven

DISCRIMINATION IN EMPLOYMENT

INTRODUCTION

7.1 That the contract of employment is based on consent, freely given, and that it involves the notion of *delectus personae*[1] emphasises that concluding a contract of employment will necessarily involve the consideration of many factors and criteria which are subjective in their conception and application. Consideration will be given to personal qualities ranging, on the employee's side, from education to appearance and, on the employer's side, from a good industrial relations record to the operation of a profit sharing scheme. In theory the terms of each contract of employment reflect a willingness of each party to accept those terms. Of course there are limits imposed by law on that otherwise essential freedom to decide with whom one will contract and on what terms one will contract. For example a contract of employment for an illegal purpose is not enforceable[2] and statute frequently attaches sanctions to the insertion of certain terms in contracts of employment either generally or in relation to particular classes of employee. Thus contracts of employment cannot be lawfully terminated if less notice than that prescribed by statute is given,[3] nor can they exclude or limit the operation of many statutory employment rights.[4] Also statute has forbidden certain types of work being done by women, young persons and children.[5] What these legal rules have in common is that they seek to prevent a contract of employment being concluded at all or on certain terms. Some could truly be described as "discrimination" laws because their direct result is that employees of one class are treated differently from employees of other classes. The different treatment is often, from the employee's point at any rate, less favourable.[6] Such well-meaning but unfavourable treatment has even been carried over into more recent legislation which itself was designed to ensure members of certain classes were no longer treated less favourably merely because of membership of a particular class.[7] Thus until the 1970s discrimination against

---

[1] Lord Fraser, *Master and Servant*, p. 66.

[2] Stair I, 10, 13(3); Bell, *Principles*, s. 35. And see *Tomlinson v. Dick Evans "U" Drive Ltd* [1978] ICR 639 and *Hyland v. J. H. Barker (North West) Ltd* [1985] IRLR 403 in which payment of an illegal tax-free allowance rendered the contract illegal for the period of payment. And see Chapter Three paras. 3.49 *et seq.*

[3] EPCA, s. 49(3).

[4] EPCA, s. 140; SDA 1975, s. 77 as amended by SDA 1986, s. 6.

[5] See, for example, the Factories Act 1961, Part VI.

[6] See, for example the Factories Act 1961, s. 86 (now repealed by the Sex Discrimination Act 1986) whereby the working hours and therefore the earning potential of female factory workers were restricted.

[7] See Sex Discrimination Act 1975, s. 51 prior to substitution by EA 1989, s. 3(3), and *Greater London Council v. Farrar* [1980] ICR 266 (decided before the enactment of SDA 1986, s. 5), *Page v. Freight Hire (Tank Haulage) Ltd* [1981] ICR 299 (decided before the enactment of EA 1989).

employees of certain classes, notably women and members of different races and ethnic groups, was endorsed through the freedom to contract with whom and on what terms one liked and, in some instances, was required by ostensibly protective legislation.[8]

In the 1970s and 1980s, with the passage of the Equal Pay Act 1970, the Sex Discrimination Acts 1975 and 1986 and the Race Relations Act 1976 statute began to make inroads on the freedom of contract by proscribing criteria like sex, marital status, race, nationality and ethnic origin. Deciding not to contract with, to terminate contractual relations with or to deal with a person to his detriment by reference to any of the above criteria was declared unlawful, giving the victim in employment recourse to an industrial tribunal.[9] Further, many discriminatory legislative provisions have been repealed or amended by the Sex Discrimination Act 1986 and with some exceptions legislative provisions which require an act of discrimination to be committed are overridden by the Employment Act 1989.

It is important to note however that discrimination is not unlawful unless and until the law declares it to be so. Thus although it is unlawful to discriminate against a married person on the grounds of his or her marital status[11] it is not unlawful to discriminate against a single person on the grounds of his or her marital status although it is unlawful to treat a single woman differently from a single man on the grounds of marital status.[12] However, unfavourable treatment because of pregnancy is sex discrimination.[12a] Similarly it is not unlawful to treat a person less favourably on the grounds of his religion[13] or his political opinions or beliefs[14] or apply a policy or not recruiting homosexuals or others of whose sexual proclivities or private morality he disapproves;[15] and until the passage of the Employment Act 1990[16] the employer could lawfully refuse to engage a trade unionist or employ only members of a particular trade union.[17] Therefore although certain types or groups of persons may derive some protec-

---

[8]   There were some minor exceptions whereby statute had removed certain forms of discriminatory treatment of particular groups. Thus the Sex Disqualification (Removal) Act 1919 provides a person should not be disqualified by sex or marriage from exercising any public function or holding any civil or judicial office or from carrying on any profession. And see the now repealed Race Relations Acts 1965, 1968. For a survey of the legislative approach to sex discrimination see W. B. Creighton, *Working Women and the Law* (1978).

[9]   See paras.7.20, 7.27. Victims of sexual or racial discrimination in fields other than employment have their disputes resolved by the courts (SDA 1975, s. 66; RRA, s. 57).

[10] EA 1989, ss. 1, 2.

[11] SDA 1975, s. 3.

[12] *Ibid.* s. 1(2).

[12a] See *Dekker v. Stichting Vormingscentrum etc* [1991] IRLR 27, ECJ., *cf. Webb v. EMO Air Cargo (UK) Ltd* [1990] IRLR 124, EAT.

[13] But see *Mandla v. Dowell Lee* [1983] ICR 385, HL discussed at para. 7.22. In Northern Ireland discrimination on religious grounds is unlawful by virtue of the Fair Employment (Northern Ireland) Act 1976.

[14] *Cf.* Fair Employment (Northern Ireland) Act 1976. However, in Scotland discrimination based on religious or political beliefs by a public body could probably be challenged by the flexible remedy of judicial review.

[15] And see *Saunders v. Scottish National Camps Association Ltd* [1981] IRLR 277, IH, *Boychuk v. Symons Holdings Ltd* [1977] IRLR 395, EAT.

[16] EA 1990, s. 1.

[17] Of course dismissal or action short of it because of union membership, non-membership or activities was unlawful (EPCA, ss. 58, 23 as amended by EA 88, s.11); see Chapter Five, para. 5.57, Chapter Nine, para. 9.47.

tion from general employment laws like unfair dismissal law or from statutes designed to give the type or group special legal entitlements[18] employment law only proscribes generally discrimination on the grounds of sex, marital status, race and union membership, non membership or activities.[19]

SEX DISCRIMINATION

7.2 The law against sex and marital status discrimination is found principally[20] in the Equal Pay Act 1970,[21] the Sex Discrimination Acts 1975, 1986 and Article 119 of the European Economic Community Treaty along with Council Directives 75/117 and 76/207.[22]

EQUAL PAY

7.3 Domestic provisions

The Equal Pay Act 1970 which became effective at the same time as the Sex Discrimination Act 1975,[23] was amended by that Act and by the Equal Pay (Amendment) Regulations 1983.[24] The Equal Pay Act is designed to prevent discrimination in contractual terms and conditions of employment between men and women;[25] clearly it cannot directly[25a] benefit women (men) whose terms of employment are worse than those of other women (men). The terms (whether they relate to pay or not) of every contract under which a woman is employed[26] are deemed to include an equality clause which has the effect of modifying any less favourable terms in, and inserting any terms which are absent from, the woman's contract when it is compared with the man's contract.[27] In *Hayward v. Cammell Laird Shipbuilders Ltd*[28] the House of Lords held that in the Act the word "term" should receive its natural meaning, namely, "a distinct provision or part of a contract which has sufficient content to permit a comparison from the point of view of the benefits it confers with a similar provision or part of

---

[18] See for example the Disabled Persons Employment Act 1958 (as amended by the National Health Service Act 1977) and the Rehabilitation of Offenders Act 1974.

[19] For coverage of discrimination based on trade union membership etc., see Chapter Nine, para. 9.47.

[20] The Sex Disqualification (Removal) Act 1919 removes sex disqualifications in public offices and professions.

[21] The scope of the Act was considerably increased by the Equal Pay (Amendment) Regulations 1983.

[22] See paras. 7.11, 7.12.

[23] The two Acts became effective on December 29, 1975.

[24] S.I. 1983 No. 1794 made under the European Communities Act 1972.

[25] The EqPA is worded so that it benefits women but it is expressly provided that it applies equally to men and their treatment relative to women: s. 1(3). And see *Duke v. GEC Reliance* [1988] IRLR 118 in which Lord Templeman emphasises that the Act deals with contractual discrimination.

[25a] Of course the indirect effect of one successful equal pay claim may be that pay differentials of other (female) workers are affected.

[26] "Employed" means employed under a contract of service or apprenticeship or a contract personally to execute any work or labour: s. 1(6).

[27] EqPA, s. 1(2).

[28] [1988] IRLR 257.

another contract".[29] Thus it is correct to compare the term about basic pay in the woman's contract with the term about basic pay in the man's, whereas it is wrong to compare the entire remuneration packages in the two contracts.[30]

There are three situations in which a woman is entitled to receive pay and other contractual benefits equal to those of a man — when she and the man are employed on (1) "like work"[31], (2) "work rated equivalent"[32] and (3) "work of equal value".[33] However the woman and the man with whom she claims equal pay and benefits must be employed "in the same employment"[34] which restricts the effect of the legislation to men and women employed by the same employer (or any associated employer)[35] at the same establishment or at establishments in Great Britain at which common terms and conditions of employment are observed generally or for employees of the relevant class.[36] To determine whether such common terms exist it is incorrect to compare the terms of the complainant with those of the selected comparators of the opposite sex because the concept of common terms and conditions necessarily contemplates a wide range of employees whose individual terms will vary greatly as between each other.[37]

7.4 Like work

For a woman to be employed on like work her work and that of the man with whom she compares herself must be of the same, or of a broadly similar, nature and any differences between their jobs must not be of practical importance in relation to terms and conditions of employment.[38] Until the introduction of the equal value entitlement[39] the concept of like work was of great significance because in the absence of an employer introducing a job evaluation study, which rates the work of employees no matter what kind of work they do, the only method of obtaining equal pay was to prove the woman was doing like work with a man. Since the introduction of the equal value entitlement, absent a job

---

[29] *Ibid. per* the Lord Chancellor Mackay p. 259; and see *Barber v. Guardian Royal Exchange Assurance Group* [1990] IRLR 240, ECJ to the effect that genuine transparency of pay structures was assured only if the principle of equal pay applied to each of the elements of remuneration. Cf. *Enderby v. Frenchay Health Authority* [1991] IRLR 44, EAT.

[30] The practical effect of their Lordships' decision may lead to "leap-frogging" *i.e.* mutual enhancement of benefits until equality is reached: but see *Leverton v. Clwyd C C* [1989] IRLR 28, HL discussed at para. 7.7.

[31] EqPA, s. 1(2)(a).

[32] *Ibid.* s. 1(2)(b).

[33] *Ibid.* s. 1(2)(c) inserted by Equal Pay (Amendment) Regulations 1983.

[34] *Ibid.* s. 1(2)(a), (b), (c).

[35] Employers are associated if one is a company of which the other (directly or indirectly) has control or if both are companies of which a third person (directly or indirectly) has control — *ibid.* s. 1(6)(c). This definition of associated employers is also found in EPCA, s. 153(4) and is limited to situations where at least one employer is a company — *Gardiner v. Merton London Borough Council* [1981] IRLR 472. And see *South West Launderettes Ltd v. Laidler* [1986] IRLR 305 and *Charnock v. Barrie Muirhead* [1984] ICR 641.

[36] EqPA s. 1(6). Note (1) this offers greater scope than Art. 119 of the EEC Treaty which is confined to men and women who work at the same establishment (*Macarthys v. Smith* [1980] ICR 672, CA); (2) the issue of common terms of employment is relevant only where the applicant and the comparator(s) are employed at different establishments.

[37] *Leverton v. Clwyd C C* [1989] IRLR 28, HL in which it was held that a nursery nurse at one establishment was entitled to claim equal pay with male clerical workers at another; and see *Thomas v. NCB* [1987] 757, EAT.

[38] EqPA, s. 1(4).

[39] See para. 7.6.

evaluation study, equal pay no longer depends on the existence of like work.[40] Whether the man and woman are employed on like work is essentially a matter for the tribunal of first instance[41] which should not adopt "too pedantic" an approach.[42] A correct comparison involves a consideration of the whole of the respective jobs[43] and the duties actually performed as distinguished from those set out in the contract[44] and although under the domestic law the like work entitlement applies only where the man and woman are employed contemporaneously this limitation is overridden by European Community law.[45] Although additional responsibility and working shifts can prevent jobs being like work[46] jobs do not cease to be like work merely because they are performed at different times.[47]

7.5 Work rated equivalent

A woman is employed on work rated equivalent to that of a man only where their respective jobs have been given an equal value on a study to evaluate the jobs to be done by all or any of the employees in an undertaking — a job evaluation study.[48] Until the introduction of the equal value entitlement only by being employed on work rated equivalent could a woman claim the same pay and other contractual benefits as a man who was not employed on like work. Although there is no duty on an employer to conduct a job evaluation study, where such a study has been conducted and results in different values for the woman's job and that of the man, a claim that the work of the woman is of equal value to that of the man is defeated.[49] However to meet the requirements of the legislation[50] the job evaluation study must be analytical in nature[51] al-

---

[40] However if a woman and the man with whom she claims equality are employed on like work, no recourse may be had to the equal value entitlement. (EqPA, s. 1(2)(c)). And see *Pickstone v. Freemans plc*, [1988] IRLR 357, HL to effect that s. 1(2)(c) does not prevent an equal value claim because some (token) man is employed on like work; it only prevents an equal value claim where the woman and the comparator(s) is employed on like work.

[41] The EAT has indicated in *Capper Pass Ltd v. J B Lawton* [1976] IRLR 366 and *Waddington v. Leicester Council for Voluntary Service* [1977] IRLR 32 that s. 1(4) involves a two-stage inquiry. (1) Are jobs of a broadly similar nature? If yes, (2) Are differences of practical importance?

[42] *Capper Pass Ltd v. J B Lawton, ibid.*

[43] *Maidment v. Cooper & Co* [1978] IRLR 462, EAT.

[44] *Shields v. Coomes Holdings Ltd* [1978] IRLR 263, CA; *Waddington v. Leicester Council for Voluntary Service* [1977] IRLR 32, EAT.

[45] See *Macarthys v. Smith* [1980] ICR 672, CA.

[46] *Eaton Ltd v. Nuttal* [1977] IRLR 71, EAT (additional responsibility); *Thomas v. NCB* [1987] IRLR 451, EAT (shift-working).

[47] *NCB v. Sherwin* [1977] ICR 700, EAT; *Dugdale v. Kraft Foods Ltd* [1977] ICR 48 in which the EAT approved of industrial tribunals awarding equal basic pay by discounting the extra premium the male night worker received as compensation for his inconvenient hours.

[48] EqPA, s. 1(5). It also provides for a woman to be regarded as employed on work rated equivalent but for the evaluation being made on a system setting different values for men and women.

[49] *Ibid.* s. 2A(2).

[50] S. 1(5) requires the study to evaluate the demands made on the worker under various headings, for instance, effort, skill and decision.

[51] *Bromley v. H & J Quick Ltd* [1988] IRLR 249, CA in which support for such an interpretation of s. 1(5) was derived from *Rummler v. Dato-Druck GmbH* [1987] IRLR 32, ECJ in which it was held that Directive 75/117 (Equal Pay) requires that job evaluation schemes consider the nature of the work objectively.

though it may be sufficient to analyse only certain bench-mark jobs.[52] Thus an employer will not be able to rely on a job evaluation study to defend an equal pay claim unless the jobs of the woman and the man with whom she makes a comparison have been analysed in terms of the demands made on the jobholders under various headings like effort, skill and decision-making; allocating a value to the jobs of the applicant or comparator by "slotting" their jobs into a grading structure arrived at by analysing benchmark jobs will not be regarded as a valid job evaluation study.[53] However, where a proper job evaluation study has been carried out the industrial tribunal is bound to act on the conclusions and content of the study[54] and although the House of Lords has held[55] a woman can rely on a job evaluation study to claim equal pay as soon as the study has resulted in the woman's job being given a value equal to that of a man even although the employers have not yet adopted the study or adjusted their pay structures, there is no completed job evaluation study unless and until the parties, normally the employer and the trade unions, have accepted its validity.[56]

7.6 Work of equal value

Until 1984 according to domestic law entitlement to equal pay depended on a woman being employed on "like work" or "work rated equivalent", the latter being dependent on the woman's employer conducting a job evaluation study. European Community law[57] however is less restrictive conferring equal pay rights where members of the opposite sex carry out the same work or work to which equal value is attributed[58] and in *EC Commission v. United Kingdom*[59] the European Court of Justice held that the United Kingdom, by making equal pay for different work (but to which equal value was attributed) depend on the employer agreeing to a job evaluation study, had failed to adopt such measures as European Community law required. To remedy the failure the Equal Pay Act 1970 was amended with effect from 1 January 1984, by the Equal Pay (Amendment) Regulations 1983,[60] so that along with equal pay claims based on "like work" and "work rated equivalent" a claim that the woman and a man are employed on "work of equal value" lies to an industrial tribunal.[61] However the procedure to be followed by a tribunal on an "equal value" claim is different[62]

---

[52] *Bromley v. H & J Quick Ltd* [1988] IRLR 249, CA *per* Woolf LJ p. 256. However where only bench-mark or representative jobs have been analysed under certain headings an employee will be able to contend that her job is materially different from the bench-mark job in which case the job evaluation study will not satisfy s. 1(5).

[53] *Bromley v. H & J Quick Ltd, ibid.*

[54] *Greene v. Broxtowe D C* [1977] IRLR 34, EAT.

[55] *O'Brien v. Sim-Chem Ltd* [1980] IRLR 373, HL.

[56] *Arnold v. Beecham Group Ltd* [1982] IRLR 307, EAT. However the EAT indicated that the parties could accept the validity of a study substantially before it is implemented.

[57] EEC Treaty, Art. 119; Dir. 75/117.

[58] Dir. 75/117, Art. 1.

[59] [1982] IRLR 333.

[60] S.I. 1983 No.1794.

[61] Even though the equal pay claim might raise questions regarding the validity of the statutory authority on which the rates of pay are based the correct procedure is still by way of a complaint to an industrial tribunal and not judicial review to challenge the statutory authority in the ordinary courts *R. v. Secretary of State for Social Services, ex parte Clark*, [1988] IRLR 22..

[62] For details of the procedure to be followed see the Industrial Tribunal (Rules of Procedure) (Scotland) Regulations 1985 (S.I. 1985 No. 17).

from that when the claim is based on "like work" or "work rated equivalent". Thus on an equal value claim where a dispute arises about the value of any work the tribunal is prohibited from determining whether any work is of equal value unless (1) it is satisfied there are no reasonable grounds for deciding the work is of equal value or (2) it has received from a member of the panel of independent experts[63] a report on whether the work in question[64] is of equal value.[65] Although there may be other reasons for a tribunal concluding there are no reasonable grounds for deciding the work is of equal value[66] it is statutorily declared that there shall be no such grounds where the jobs of the woman and her comparator(s) have been given different values on a job evaluation study[67] and that study was not itself discriminatory.[68] Nor may an equal value claim be brought if the woman and her chosen comparator(s) are employed on like work or work rated equivalent.[69] It has been held that an employer is entitled to pay higher salaries to predominantly male pharmacists and psychologists than to predominantly female speech therapists even where they were assumed to be engaged on work of equal value because in a case of unintentional pay discrimination it was necessary to identify a condition which the complainant could not comply with [69a] but the decision has been criticised.[69b]

7.7 Genuine material factor

Where a woman is employed on work of equal value, entitlement to equal pay does not arise if the employer can prove that the variation between the woman's contractual benefits and those of the man with whom she compares herself is "genuinely due to a material factor which is not the difference of sex",[70] but where the claim is based on the woman doing like work or work rated equivalent loss of entitlement to equal pay only occurs where the variation is genuinely due to a "material difference".[71] The reason for the apparently different criteria for losing entitlement to equal pay is largely due to the restrictive interpretation given to "material difference" by the Court of Appeal in *Clay Cross (Quarry Services) Ltd v. Fletcher*.[72] In order to ensure that such a restrictive

---

[63] The Advisory, Conciliation and Arbitration Service designates certain experts to be members of the panel (EqPA, s. 2A(4)).

[64] This will involve a comparison of the woman's work with that of her chosen comparator(s).

[65] EqPA, s. 2A.

[66] See, for example, *Kirby v. Cawoods (Fish Curers) Ltd* (I.T. Case No. 10673/84) in which the womens' work was regarded as "repetitive" with "little skill content" and performed in "more ambiant (sic) temperature" while the man's job involved "his knowledge", "a range of work" and "responsibilities"; his work was so different that there were no reasonable grounds for concluding the work was of equal value.

[67] The study must analyse the work of the woman and her comparator(s) under various headings like skill, effort, decision. See para. 7.5.

[68] EqPA, s. 2A(2).

[69] This is the effect of the wording of s. 1(2)(c) as interpreted in *Pickstone v. Freemans plc* [1988] IRLR 357, HL. This interpretation prevents an employer using a token man — doing either like work or work rated equivalent to the womens' — to defeat an equal value claim.

[69a] *Enderby v. Frenchay Health Authority* [1991] IRLR 44, EAT.

[69b] See [1991] IRLR 42-43.

[70] EqPA, s. 1(3).

[71] *Ibid.*

[72] [1979] ICR 1. The Court of Appeal took the view that s. 1(3) permitted consideration only of matters which were part of the "personal equation" (*e.g.* length of service, qualifications and preservation of special status "red-circling") and not extraneous factors (*e.g.* market forces or other economic or administrative reasons).

interpretation did not affect equal value claims when that entitlement was introduced the new and wider concept of "material factor" was introduced. However for all practical purposes the distinction between a material "factor" and a material "difference" has been removed by the decision of the House of Lords in the Scottish appeal of *Rainey v. Greater Glasgow Health Board*[73] which held that the meaning given to "material difference" by the Court of Appeal in *Clay Cross (Quarry Services) Ltd v. Fletcher*[74] was "unduly restricted"[75]; the proper meaning of those words — when account was taken of European Community law as contained in *Jenkins v. Kingsgate (Clothing Productions) Ltd*[76] and *Von Hartz v. Bilka-Kaufhaus*[77] — permitted taking account of personal and extraneous but objectively justified factors like economic or administrative matters. Thus the variation between the pay of Mrs Rainey a prostethist recruited directly into the National Health Service at Whitley Council pay rates and male prostethists who had previously been employed in the private sector and were recruited en bloc into the National Health Service at the rates of pay they had enjoyed in the private sector and subsequently increased by collective bargaining was genuinely due to a material difference other than the difference of sex because the employers could not have established the prostethist service within a reasonable time if the males who were previously employed in the private sector had not been offered the rate of pay they had been receiving there and from the administrative view it would have been highly anomalous if those prosthetists like Mrs Rainey were, for the future as well as the present, to have a salary scale and negotiating machinery different from the rest of those employed in the National Health Service.

Although it is for the industrial tribunal to decide whether the reason for the variation between the contracts could be objectively justified the following have been held sufficiently material to exclude the right to equal pay — regional variations in pay and other conditions,[78] "red-circling",[79] longer service resulting in incremental differences,[80] different qualifications,[81] different pay rates for part-time and full-time workers[82] where the difference in rates are reasonably necessary to achieve some objective other than an objective related to the sex

---

[73] [1987] IRLR 26. If *Rainey* had been decided before the Equal Pay (Amendment) Regulations 1983 were enacted it might not have been necessary for the doubtful distinction between a material factor and a material difference to have been enacted at all.

[74] [1979] ICR 1.

[75] In *Albion Shipping Agency v. Arnold* [1981] IRLR 525 the EAT restricted the rule in *Fletcher* to cases where employment was contemporaneous.

[76] [1981] IRLR 228, ECJ.

[77] [1987] IRLR 317, ECJ.

[78] *NAAFI v. Varley* [1976] IRLR 408, EAT. It may also be argued that the relevant employees are not in the same employment; see para. 7.3.

[79] This term is used to denote employees who are given exceptional terms of employment because, for example, they have agreed to transfer to a less well paid and lower status job on condition their terms of employment remain unchanged. See *Snoxell & Davies v. Vauxhall Motors Ltd* [1977] ICR 700 EAT and *Methven v. Cow Industrial Polymers* [1979] IRLR 277, EAT. *Cf. NCB v. Sherwin* [1978] IRLR 122, EAT.

[80] *Shields v. Coomes (Holdings) Ltd* [1978] IRLR 263. However mere longer service will not necessarily be material: *Goutcher v. Monteith Building Services*, (unreported, s/172/76), the first Scottish equal pay case.

[81] *Murray v. Lothian Regional Council*, (unreported s/1783/76). *Cf. Sampson v. Polikoff Universal Ltd* (unreported 9141/76).

[82] *Handley v. Mono Ltd* [1978] IRLR 534.

of the workers,[83] the fact that the jobs are done at different times[84] and the need to ensure the efficient carrying on of the employer's business.[85] As a result of the decision of the House of Lords in *Hayward v. Cammell Laird (Shipbuilders) Ltd*[86] a woman who can mount a successful case based on "like work", "work rated equivalent" or "equal value" is entitled to equality with regard to each "term" of her contract. Thus she is entitled to, for example, the same basic pay as her male comparator but the fact that she has some other contractual benefit (for example entitlement to holiday pay or paid sick leave) which the man does not enjoy may be regarded as a material factor distinguishing her case from his.[87]

7.8 Bringing an equal pay claim

Since entitlement to equal pay is achieved through the statutory implication of an equality clause into the woman's contract it follows that a failure to pay in accordance with an operative[88] equality clause is a breach of contract giving an action in the ordinary court. However the court is empowered to (1) strike out any claim or counter claim based on an equality clause where it could be "more conveniently disposed of separately by an industrial tribunal" or (2) sist its own proceedings while directing the claim be referred directly to an industrial tribunal.[89] The normal route for an equal pay claim therefore is by way of a claim presented to an industrial tribunal[90] which can award damages and arrears of remuneration in respect of the period of two years prior to the claim being made.[91] Although the claim will normally be brought by an employee or ex-employee there is provision for the Secretary of State for Employment to bring a claim on behalf of women[92] and for an employer to obtain an order declaratory of his and the employee's rights.[93] Where the claim is based on "like work" or "work rated equivalent" the procedure before the tribunal is regulated by the tribunal's ordinary rules of procedure.[94] However where the claim is based on the work being of "equal value" special rules of procedure operate[95] which re-

---

[83] *Jenkins v. Kingsgate (Clothing Productions) Ltd* [1981] IRLR 389.

[84] See *Thomas v. NCB* [1987] IRLR 451, EAT.

[85] *Rainey v. Greater Glasgow Health Board* [1987] IRLR 26, [1987] SLT 146, HL.

[86] [1988] IRLR 257; and see *Barber v. Guardian Royal Exchange Assurance Group* [1990] IRLR 240, ECJ.

[87] *Leverton v. Clwyd CC* [1989] IRLR 28, HL. And see the view expressed by Lord Goff in *Hayward v. Cammell Laird (Shipbuilders) Ltd* [1988] IRLR 257 referring to *Reed Packaging Ltd v. Boozer* [1988] ICR 391, EAT that he might be prepared to accept the submission that the total value of all the contractual terms could be a material factor so as to prevent equality being obtained in one particular term.

[88] Clearly it will not be operative if the inequality is due to a material factor.

[89] EqPA, s. 2(3).

[90] In *British Railways Board v. Paul* [1988] IRLR 20 the EAT has held that the need to have been employed by the employer/respondent within the six months preceding the date of claim in s. 2(4) does not apply when the claim is being made by an individual; s. 2(4) only applies to a reference to a tribunal by the court under s. 2(3) or the Secretary of State under s. 2(2). Thus, besides general law, there is no statutory time limit for bringing an equal pay claim, nor is a period of continuous employment required.

[91] EqPA, s. 2(1), (5).

[92] *Ibid.* s. 2(2).

[93] *Ibid.* s. 2(1A).

[94] Industrial Tribunals (Rules of Procedure) (Scotland) Regulations 1985 (SI 1985 No. 17) Sch. 1. Note that where the complaint involves the Equal Pay Act a tribunal must issue full reasons for its decision (*ibid.* Rule 9(5)(a)).

[95] *Ibid.* Sch. 2.

quire the tribunal to instruct an independent expert (from a panel of experts designated by ACAS)[96] to report on whether the work is of equal value unless (1) there are no reasonable grounds for determining the work is of equal value,[97] (2) the work of the woman and the man have been given different values on a valid[98] job evaluation study[99] or (3) at a preliminary stage the tribunal takes the view that the employer has proved the variation between the contracts is genuinely due to a material factor.[100]

The Independent expert. Where the tribunal refers the question of equal value to an independent expert the subsequent procedure can be fairly involved but can be summarised thus.[101] The expert receives written information about the parties to the case, where the applicant works and the name of the comparator the value of whose work is involved.[102] The expert is required to take account of representations, summarise to the parties the information and representations received and report to the tribunal his conclusion (or failure to reach one) on the question of the value of the respective jobs.[103] If the expert has not reported to the tribunal within 42 days he may be required to report on his progress and the tribunal may revoke the expert's instructions to prepare a report and require that another report be prepared.[104] A report, once submitted, results in the hearing being resumed — with at least 14 days' notice to the parties beginning with their receipt of the report — and the report being admitted as evidence unless the tribunal sees fit to reject it[105] in which case a new report has to be instructed.[106] Assuming the report is not rejected by the tribunal at the resumed hearing parties are entitled to give evidence, call and cross examine witnesses

---

[96] EqPA, s. 2A(4).

[97] Rules of Procedure, Rule 7A(1). Although the rules of procedure do not require that such a conclusion (that there are no reasonable grounds for determining the work is of equal value) be based on evidence the EAT has indicated that where evidence has been presented to the tribunal the correct approach is to take account of such evidence and look at the matter in the round; the tribunal should not limit itself to considering the originating application alone: *Dennehy v. Sealink UK Ltd* [1987] IRLR 120.

[98] To be valud the job evaluation study itself must not discriminate on grounds of sex: EqPA, ss. 1(5), 2A(3).

[99] Rule 7A(1); EqPA, ss. 2A(2).

[100] EqPA, s. 1(3). Although s. 2A(1) and Rule 7A(1) seem to suggest that a tribunal may decline reference to an expert only where there are no reasonable grounds for determining the work to be of equal value the EAT in *Forex Neptune (Overseas) Ltd v. Miller* [1987] ICR 170, *McGregor v. GMBATU*, [1987] ICR 505 and *Reed Packing Ltd v. Boozer* [1988] IRLR 333 has taken the view that Rule 8(2E) (which empowers a tribunal to hear evidence and submissions on whether the inequality is due to a material factor before it requires an expert to report) also permits the tribunal having heard the relevant evidence to uphold the employer's defence and dismiss the claim without reference to an expert. And see *R. v. Secretary of State for Social Services, ex parte Clark* [1988] IRLR 22 to the effect that a defence under s. 1(3) cannot be taken as a preliminary point; it must be supported by evidence.

[101] The details of the procedure are contained in Rules 7A and 8 in Sch. 2 to the Industrial Tribunals (Rules of Procedure) (Scotland) Regulations 1985.

[102] Rule 7A(2).

[103] Rule 7A(3).

[104] Rule 7A(5).

[105] Rule 7A(6), (7), (8), (9). The tribunal may also require an expert to explain a report or to give further consideration to certain matters. (Rule 7A(10)).

[106] *Ibid.*

and address the tribunal.[107] The tribunal or a party to the proceedings may require the expert who prepared the report to attend for cross-examination by any party; any party may call only one expert witness — who may be cross-examined — to give expert evidence on the question which formed the subject of the independent expert's report.[108] There is no restriction on the number of non-expert witnesses who may be called although no evidence may be introduced if it relates to any matter of fact on which the independent expert based his report.[109] On completion of the resumed hearing the tribunal then decides[110] whether the respective jobs are of equal value or that the employer has proved there is a material factor between the woman's case and the man's. To assist the expert in preparing his report the tribunal is empowered, on the application of the expert, to require any person to provide for the expert's consideration information or documents which are relevant to the question of equal value.[111] It is an offence to unreasonably fail to comply with such a requirement[112] although there is a right to apply to the tribunal to have the requirement varied or set aside.[113]

7.9 Collective matters

Although in some cases an employer may agree to extend the decision of an industrial tribunal to employees doing the same job as a successful complainant, strictly, the decision of an industrial tribunal requires to be observed only with regard to the parties in each case.[114] However a complaint which is similar to complaints which have already been the subject of a tribunal decision may be regarded as vexatious and therefore struck out.[115] Of course many terms of individual contracts of employment have their origins in a collective document which is, expressly or by implication, incorporated into the contracts of employment of individual employees. It follows therefore that if discriminatory terms and conditions can be eliminated at source the terms of employment in the many individual contracts incorporating such collective documents will not themselves reflect the discrimination. It was to facilitate the elimination of discrimination at source that the Equal pay Act in its original form provided[116] that

---

[107] Rule 8(2).

[108] Rule 8(2A), (2B).

[109] Rule 8(2C). But note the exception in Rule 8 (2D) which deals with facts relating to the defence of a genuine material factor and where the failure of an expert to reach a conclusion is due to the refusal/omission of any person to provide the expert with such information as a tribunal may require.

[110] Note it is the decision of the tribunal and not the independent expert. His report is merely part of all the evidence before the tribunal. The tribunal must append to its decision the expert's report (Rule 9(4A)).

[111] Rule 4(1A). Certain persons including conciliation officers are exempt from this requirement to produce information/documents (Rule 4(1B)).

[112] EPCA Sch. 9, para. 1(7).

[113] Rule 4(2A).

[114] Thus all females who do the same kind of work may require to apply; see, for example, the unreported cases 9142/76-9159/76 brought against Polikoff Universal Ltd and the background to *Thomas v. National Coal Board* [1987] IRLR 451, EAT in which claims by 1500 women were reduced to a sample of 14 on the instruction of the tribunal, but the decisions would not be binding on any other cases.

[115] *Ashmore v. British Coal Corporation* [1990] IRLR 283, CA.

[116] Ss. 3, 4, 5.

collective agreements,[117] which had different provisions for men and women could be referred to the Central Arbitration Committee[118] for amendment.[119] However the statutory procedure of referring discriminatory provision in collective agreements and wages regulation orders[120] has been repealed by the Sex Discrimination Act 1986[121] and the Wages Act 1986[122] respectively. Discrimination in collective agreements and employers' rules is now dealt with under the Sex Discrimination Act 1975[123] which renders void any collective term or employer's rule which would be modified by, or supplemented by, the operation of an equality clause. The effect of this provision is that a term in a collective agreement — itself not legally enforceable *inter partes* which provides for the inclusion of an unlawful[124] term in a contract of employment is void. However this presupposes that terms are inserted into contracts of employment by the collective agreement whereas the orthodox British view is that the contract of employment, being the legal nexus between employee and employer, accepts or adopts terms of collective agreements.[125] Without incorporation by acceptance or adoption the term of the collective agreement exists in a legal vacuum and the precise effect of this statutory effort to deal with discrimination in collective agreements and employers' rules must await judicial elucidiation.[126]

7.10 Exclusion from the Equal Pay Act

Although the Act applies to employment for the purposes of a government department and statutory bodies and offices it does not extend to military service or any women's service administered by the Defence Council.[127] The Act applies whether or not the proper law of the contract under which the person is employed is the law of any part of the United Kingdom.[128] An equality clause does not affect terms of employment which result from complying with laws regulating the employment of women[129] or which afford special treatment to

---

[117] Wages regulation orders and agricultural wages orders were also included.

[118] See Chapter Eight, para. 8.32.

[119] In *R. v. CAC ex parte Hy Mac Ltd* [1979] IRLR 461 it was held that a reference to the CAC could only occur in respect of provisions which were directly discriminatory, *i.e.* which applied to men only or women only.

[120] The procedure for referring to the CAC agricultural wages orders which contain provisions applying to women or men was retained. Unlike ss. 3 and 4, s. 5 (as amended by EPA 1975, s. 125(1)) is not repealed. Where the CAC has declared what amendments are necessary to remove the discrimination the Scottish Agricultural Wages Board must give effect to them — EqPA, s. 5(1).

[121] S. 9.

[122] S. 32(2).

[123] S. 77, as amended by SDA 1986, s. 6.

[124] Unlawful in the sense of being contrary to an equality clause where there is no material factor to justify it.

[125] See Chapter Two.

[126] The amendments to SDA 1975, s. 77 were enacted to comply with the requirements of European Community law: see *EC Commission v. UK* [1984] IRLR 29. Compliance with European Community Law could have been achieved by remodelling EqPA, ss. 4, 5 and 6 to give the CAC wider powers to deal with discriminatory collective agreements etc.

[127] EqPA, s. 1(8), (9). But see s. 7 which seeks to ensure that pay allowances and leave of men and women in the forces are the same without giving them the right to complain to a tribunal or court.

[128] *Ibid.* s. 1(11).

[129] Many such laws are now repealed; see part III of the schedule to SDA 1986.

women in connection with pregnancy or childbirth.[130] Although an equality clause will apply to any terms relating to membership of an occupational pension scheme which deal with the equal access provisions of the Social Security Pensions Act 1975[131] it will not apply to terms related to death or retirement[132] or any provision made in connection with retirement other than a term or provision which, in relation to retirement, gives access to promotion transfer or training or provides for a woman's dismissal[133] or demotion.[134]

7.11 The European Community provisions

The law on equal pay is complicated because Article 119 of EEC Treaty is of direct application, that is it creates binding legal rights and duties within the Scottish legal system which override contradictory domestic legislation and can be relied on by individuals in private and public employment.[135] It is now settled that Article 119 rights can be enforced through industrial tribunals.[135a] Article 119 requires each member state to maintain the application of the principle that "men and women should receive equal pay for equal work"[136] and is amplified by EC Council Directive 75/117[137] which provides that the "principle of equal pay" means, for the same work or for work to which equal value is attributed, the elimination of all discrimination on grounds of sex with regard to all aspects and conditions of remuneration and, where a job specification study is used, it must not discriminate on grounds of sex.

---

[130] EqPA, s. 6(1)(a), (b) as amended by SDA 1986, s. 9(1). And see *Coyne v. Exports Credits Guarantee Dept.* [1981] IRLR 51, in which the employers unsuccessfully tried to use s. 6(1)(b) to justify less favourable treatment of a pregnant employee.

[131] Ss. 53-59.

[132] "Retirement" includes voluntary retirement: EqPA, s. 6(2).

[133] "Dismissal" is to be construed in accordance with SDA 1975, s. 82(1A).

[134] EqPA, s. 6(1A) (a), (b) as amended by SDA 1986, s. 2(4). This amendment was introduced as a consequence of the decision of the ECJ in *Marshall v. Southampton and South-West Hampshire Area Health Authority* [1986] IRLR 140 which dealt with the equivalent section of the Sex Discrimination Act 1975 (s. 6(4)) and its compliance with European Community law. By making similar amendments to both the EqPA and the SDA 1975, discrimination in relation to retirement is unlawful whether it results from a term in the contract which is the province of the EqPA or from a policy/practice of an employer which is the province of the SDA.

[135] *Defrenne v. SABENA* [1976] 547, ECJ; *Jenkins v. Kingsgate (Clothing Production) Ltd* [1981] IRLR 228, ECJ. And see *Albion Shipping Agency v. Arnold* [1981] IRLR 525, EAT and *Garland v. British Rail Engineering* [1982] IRLR 257, HL. It may also be used as an aid to construing a domestic statute passed to bring domestic law into line with EC law — see *Pickstone v. Freemans plc* [1988] IRLR 357, HL and *Duke v. GEC Reliance Ltd* [1988] IRLR 118, HL. For further discussion of the direct applicability of EC provisions see D. J. Lasok & J. W. Bridge *Law and Institutions of the European Communities*, (1991).

[135a] *McKechnie v. UBM Building Supplies (Southern) Ltd, The Times*, May 9, 1991; *S. of S. for Scotland and Greater Glasgow Health Board v. Wright & Hannah* [1991] IRLR 187, EAT.

[136] "Pay" is defined by Art. 119 to mean "the ordinary basic or minimum wage or salary and any other consideration, whether in cash or in kind, which the worker receives, directly or indirectly, in respect of his employment from his employer and equal pay without discrimination based on sex means: (a) that pay for the same work at piece rates shall be calculated on the basis of the same unit of measurement; (b) that pay for work at time rates shall be the same for the same job.

[137] Dir. 75/117 is merely interpretative; it does not create any rights additional to those contained in Art. 119 itself (*Jenkins v. Kingsgate (Clothing Productions) Ltd* [1981] IRLR 228, ECJ).

Because of its direct applicability and that it is essentially a statement of the principle of equal pay for equal work rather than a series of detailed statutory rules there is scope for conflict between the detailed rules of the Equal Pay Act 1970 and the general principle of Article 119. In one important respect Article 119 is more restricted than the 1970 Act because the former, even when read with Directive 75/117, is limited to inequality in pay[138] (whether payable under the contract or not[139]) whereas the latter deals with inequality in pay and other contractual terms. Thus although the provision of a supplementary pension financed solely by the employer falls within the scope of Article 119[140] as does the repayment to a male employee of his compulsory contribution to a retirement benefit[141] a compulsory deduction from the salary of males but not females to finance a widows' pension scheme does not.[142] However Article 119 does apply to payments under a contracted-out pension scheme and it is therefore unlawful for a man made compulsorily redundant to be entitled to claim only a deferred pension when a woman in the same position is entitled to an immediate pension.[143] Article 119 is concerned with payments in cash or in kind, and does not extend to social security or pension schemes imposed by law,[144] and it is therefore unlawful to deduct from a woman's occupation pension her state retirement pension.[145] Whether the disparity is truly one of pay and therefore within Article 119 or one of social security benefits and therefore not within Article 119 requires an examination of each case individually having regard to the relevant national legislation.[146] Because Article 119 is concerned with ensuring equal pay for work of equal value it follows that it is not restricted to work which is performed contemporaneously[147] and it may be used to challenge indirect discrimination in the form of different rates of pay or other benefits for part-time and full-time workers. If the different rates of pay or pension for part-time workers affect a far greater number of women than men they will infringe Article 119 unless the employer can show that the difference is based on objectively justified factors, like productivity or efficiency, unrelated to any discrimination based on sex.[148] It is also arguable that the statu-

---

[138] *Bilka-Kaufhaus GmbH v. von Hartz* [1987] ICR 110, ECJ.

[139] *Barber v. Guardian Royal Exchange Assurance Group* [1990] IRLR 240, ECJ. "Pay" thereore includes redundancy/termination payments whether statutory, contractual or *ex gratia;* and see *Hammersmith & Queen Charlotte's Special Health Authority v. Cato* [1987] IRLR 483, EAT. and *McKechnie v. UBM Building Supplies (Southern) Ltd, The Times,* May 9, 1991, EAT.

[140] *Bilka-Kaufhaus GmbH v. von Hartz* [1987] ICR 110, ECJ.

[141] *Worringham v. Lloyds Bank* [1981] IRLR 178, ECJ.

[142] In *Newstead v. Dept. of Transport and H.M. Treasury* [1988] IRLR 66 the ECJ held the compulsory deduction was neither a benefit paid to a worker nor a contribution paid by an employer on behalf of the worker. There was no difference between the gross salaries of men and women.

[143] *Barber v. Guardian Royal Exchange Assurance Group* [1990] IRLR 240, ECJ.

[144] *Defrenne v. Belgium* [1974] 1 CMLR 494, ECJ.

[145] *Roberts v. Birds Eye Walls Ltd,* [1991] IRLR 19, EAT.

[146] *Bilka-Kaufhaus GmbH v. von Hartz* [1987] ICR 110, ECJ, *per* Advocate General Darmon.

[147] *Macarthy's v. Smith* [1980] ICR 672, ECJ.

[148] *Jenkins v. Kingsgate (Clothing Productions) Ltd* [1981] ICR 592, ECJ; *Bilka-Kaufhaus GmbH v. von Hartz* [1987] ICR 110, ECJ. Whether such objective justification exists is for the domestic tribunal to decide. And see *Rinner-Kuhn v. FWW Spezial Gebaudereinigung* [1989] IRLR 493, ECJ (exclusion of part-time workers from sick pay required by law); *Kowalska v. Freie und Hansestadt Hamburg* [1990] IRLR 447, ECJ (exclusion of part-time workers from severance pay); *Nimz v. Freie und Hansestadt Hamburg* [1991] IRLR 222, ECJ (full-time employees do not necessarily acquire skills more quickly).

tory rules regarding continuous employment themselves are indirectly discriminatory.[148a] However Article 119 does not require that employers organise their payment systems to take account of the particular difficulties faced by persons which family responsibilities.[149] Where a job evaluation system is used neither Article 119 nor Directive 75/117 prohibits the use in such a system of the criterion of muscle demand or muscular effort or the heaviness of the work if the work requires the use of a certain degree of physical strength provided the system as a whole, by taking account of other criteria, precludes any discrimination on grounds of sex and, because work which is objectively the same attracts the same rate of pay whether done by a man or a woman, the use of values reflecting the average performance of workers of one sex is contrary to Directive 75/117.[150]

OTHER FORMS OF SEXUAL DISCRIMINATION

7.12 The European Community provisions

To supplement Article 119 which deals only with equality of remuneration[151] Directive 76/207 extends equality of treatment irrespective of sex, marital or family status to access to employment and training and working conditions, including conditions governing dismissal.[152] The Directive also prevents discrimination on the grounds of pregnancy[152a] and this stiffens the protection afforded to pregnant workers by domestic law.[152b] Article 5(1) of Directive 76/207 is directly applicable in that it can be relied upon by an individual in a domestic court or tribunal against a member state or an agency which is an "emanation of the state".[153] The theory is that a member state cannot plead its own failure to implement a European Community directive in an issue between an individual and the member state or an agent or organ of the state. Thus where domestic legislation permitted employers to discriminate between men and women with regard to the ages at which they could be required to retire[154] an employee could rely on Directive 76/207 to base her case against her public authority employer which was treated as an "emanation of the state".[155] According to the European Court of Justice a body (whatever its legal form) which has

---

[148a] See *Rinner-Kuhn v. FWW Spezial Gebaudereinigung* [1989] IRLR 493, ECJ; *Secretary of State for Scotland and Greater Glasgow Health Board v. Wright and Hannah* [1991] IRLR 187, EAT.

[149] *Bilka-Kaufhaus GmbH v. von Hartz* [1987] ICR 110, ECJ.

[150] *Rummler v. Dato-Druck GmbH* [1987] IRLR 32, ECJ. However the job evaluation/grading system must take into account criteria for which workers of each sex may show particular aptitude.

[151] *Bilka-Kaufhaus GmbH v. von Hartz* [1987] ICR 110, ECJ.

[152] Dir. 76/207, Art. 5(1).

[152a] *Dekker v. Stichting Vormingscentrum* [1991] IRLR 27, ECJ; cf. *Hertz v. Aldi Marked K/S* [1991] IRLR 31, ECJ.

[152b] See the comparative approach adopted by the EAT in *Webb v. EMO Air Cargo* [1990] IRLR 124.

[153] *Marshall v. Southampton and South West Hampshire Area Health Authority* [1986] IRLR 140, ECJ; *Becker v. Finanzamt Munster-Innenstadt* [1982] ECR 53, ECJ.

[154] See the SDA 1975, s. 6(4) before its amendment by the SDA 1986, s.2.

[155] *Marshall v. Southampton and South West Hampshire Area Health Authority* [1986] IRLR 140, ECJ. *Cf. Duke v. GEC Reliance Ltd* [1988] IRLR 118, HL. But see now *Marleasing SA v. La Commercial International de Alimentacion SA* (unreported, Case 106/89, ECJ.)

been made responsible, pursuant to a measure adopted by the state, for providing a public service under the control of the state and has for that purpose special powers beyond those which resulted from the normal rules applicable between individuals is a body against which a directive, which is capable of having direct effect, may be relied on.[155a] "Working conditions" include the need to satisfy rules regarding eligibility for a benefit or payment;[156] and "dismissal" is to receive a wide meaning and includes a requirement to retire[157] and the automatic termination of employment on becoming entitled to a company pension.[158] However, although it has been held that where eligibility to participate in an early retirement scheme merely reflects the different national retirement/pensionable ages for men and women there is no violation of Directive 76/207,[159] it has been questioned[159a] whether this is reconciliable with the decision in *Barber v. Guardian Royal Exchange Assurance Group*.[159b] Nor is the Directive infringed if in a mass redundancy scheme men and women of the same age can participate even although their normal retirement ages are different.[160] Member states are required to provide individuals with opportunities to pursue their claims about equal treatment by judicial process[161] and while the Directive 76/207[162] could allow a member state to restrict general policing duties to armed male officers it[163] does not permit special treatment of women except against risks, like pregnancy or maternity, which affect women as such.[164]

7.13 Domestic provisions

To complement the Equal Pay Act 1970 which deals only with discriminatory contractual provisions the Sex Discrimination Act 1975 was enacted to deal with non-contractual discrimination on the grounds of sex and marital status. In relation to employment the Sex Discrimination Act[165] deals with sexual discrimination by, first, defining discrimination[166] then indicating when it is unlawful to discriminate in the employment context[167] and finally listing the circumstances in which discrimination by an employer is lawful either because sex is a "genuine occupational qualificaton"[168] or the type of employment is excluded

---

[155a] *Foster v. British Gas Corporation* [1990] IRLR 353, ECJ, applied *The Times* April 19, 1991, HL.

[156] *Burton v. British Railways Board* [1982] ICR 329, ECJ.

[157] *Marshall v. Southampton and South West Area Health Authority* [1986] IRLR 140, ECJ.

[158] *Beets-Proper v. F. Van Lanschot Bankiers* [1986] ICR 706, ECJ.

[159] *Burton (ibid.).* This is the result of reading Art. 1(2) of Dir. 76/207 in light of Art. 7 of Dir. 79/7 which deals with elimination of discrimination in social security matters.

[159a] *McKechnie v. UBM Building Supplies (Southern) Ltd, The Times* May 9, 1991, EAT.

[159b] [1990] IRLR 240, ECJ.

[160] *Roberts v. Tate & Lyle* [1986] ICR 371, ECJ.

[161] Dir. 76/207, Art. 6. And see *Johnston v. Chief Constable RUC* [1987] ICR 83, ECJ in which it was held Art. 53(2) of the Sex Discrimination (Northern Ireland) Order 1976 by which the Secretary of State could, by certifying national security was involved, prevent an industrial tribunal from hearing a case, contravened the right to judicial process conferred by Art. 6 which could be relied on by an individual against a public authority. The equivalent provision for other parts of the UK is Sex Discrimination Act 1975, s. 52.

[162] Art. 2(2).

[163] Art. 2(3).

[164] *Johnston v. Chief Constable R.U.C. (ibid.).*

[165] The SDA 1975 was amended by the SDA 1986 in various respects and references are to the SDA 1975 as amended.

[166] SDA 1975, ss. 1-3.

[167] *Ibid.* ss. 6, 9, 37-42.

[168] *Ibid.* s. 7.

in some respects from the provisions of the Act.[169] The Act also creates the Equal Opportunities Commission (EOC) and invests it with powers of investigation and enforcement.[170] Many of the issues involved in sex discrimination also arise in racial discrimination which is covered later in this chapter.

7.14 Definition of discrimination

The Act applies to both direct and indirect discrimination on the grounds of sex and marital status.[171] It also protects a person who has been the victim of discrimination which takes the form of less favourable treatment because, for example, he has brought proceedings under the Act (or the Equal Pay Act)[172] and where the word "discriminate" is used it embraces discrimination as defined by sections 1, 2, 3 and 4;[173] while it is couched in terms of benefiting women the Act applies equally to men.[174] Clearly direct discrimination occurs where an employer treats or would treat[175] a woman less favourably on the ground of her sex.[176] Thus it includes the straightforward refusal to appoint a woman[177] permitting women to leave their work stations earlier than men,[178] reserving unpleasant, dirty work for men,[179] dismissal and compulsory retirement[180] and sexual harassment.[181] However it also includes unfavourable treatment which derives from the application of a gender-based criterion like state pension age which is different for men and women.[182] While unfavourable treatment of a woman on the grounds of her pregnancy has been regarded as sex discrimination, decisions differ in their approach. Thus some decisions[182a] advocate the "comparative" approach while others[182b] follow the reasoning of the European Court of Justice[182c] and hold that such treatment is direct sexual discrimination irrespective of an employer's comparable treatment of a man who, say, for health reasons, requires a period off work. Direct discrimination against a married person occurs when a married person is treated less favourably than an unmarried per-

---

[169] *Ibid.* ss. 17-21, 47, 48, 51, 52.

[170] *Ibid.* ss. 53-61, 67-75.

[171] *Ibid.* ss. 1, 2. 3.

[172] *Ibid.* s. 4.

[173] *Cornelius v. University College of Swansea* [1987] IRLR 141.

[174] SDA 1975, s. 2.

[175] It is not necessary that less favourable treatment actually occurs.

[176] SDA 1975, s. 1(1)(a).

[177] *Roadburg v. Lothian Regional Council* [1975] IRLR 283, EAT; *Greig v. Community Industry* [1979] IRLR 158.

[178] *Automotive Products v. Peake* [1977] IRLR 365, CA.

[179] *Ministry of Defence v. Jeremiah* [1979] IRLR 436, CA.

[180] *Coleman v. Skyrail Oceanic Ltd* [1981] IRLR 398, CA (dismissal of woman after marriage to man who worked for rival on assumption that husband was the "breadwinner"); *Hayes v. Malleable Working Men's Club and Institute* [1985] IRLR 367, EAT (dismissal of woman because of pregnancy) disapproving *Turley v. Allders Department Stores Ltd* [1980] IRLR 4, EAT; *Marshall v. Southampton and South-West Hampshire Area Health Authority* [1986] IRLR 140, ECJ (requiring women to retire earlier than men).

[181] *Porcelli v. Strathclyde Regional Council* [1986] ICR 564, IH.

[182] *James v. Eastleigh Borough Council* [1990] IRLR 288, HL.

[182a] *Hayes v. Malleable Working Men's Club and Institute* [1985] IRLR 367, EAT; *Webb v. EMO Air Cargo Ltd* [1990] IRLR, 124, EAT.

[182b] *Cairney v. Chivas Bros Ltd* (unreported case no. SCOIT 8/3804/90).

[182c] *Dekker v. Stichting Vormingscentrum etc.* [1991] IRLR 27, ECJ; *Hertz v. Aldi Marked K/S* [1991] IRLR 31, ECJ. Contrast the approach in *Dekker* with *Berrisford v. Woodard Schools Ltd* (unreported case no. 323/90), EAT).

son of the same sex.[183] In all cases of direct discrimination the reason of the alleged discriminator is irrelevant.[184]

7.15 Indirect discrimination

Indirect discrimination occurs when a gender-neutral requirement or condition, which cannot be objectively justified, is applied to both sexes but the proportion of one sex which can comply with it is considerably smaller than the proportion[185] of the other sex which can comply and by not being able to comply the person suffers a detriment.[186] Indirect discrimination may be described as "covert" discrimination because on the surface, by applying the same criterion to both sexes, there would appear to be equal treatment. However when the impact or effect of the criterion is considered it clearly disadvantages one sex more than the other.[187] Insisting that employees work a certain pattern or number of hours per week is a requirement or condition. Thus not permitting part-time work or job-sharing can be expressed as imposing a requirement or condition[188] that employees have to work a minimum number of hours per week which, arguably, is a requirement that fewer women, because of family responsibilities, can comply with[189] as is selecting for redundancy part-timers before full-timers[190] and requiring applicants to be between certain ages.[191]

Disproportionate effect

To determine whether a smaller proportion of one sex "can comply" with the requirement or condition the test to be used is a practical and not a theoretical one. Thus in *Price v. Civil Service Commission*[192] the fact that there were approximately the same numbers of men and women between the stipulated ages of 17 $\frac{1}{2}$ and 28 years fewer women than men could in practice comply because women between those ages were, to a considerably greater extent than men,

---

[183] *Bick v. Royal West of England Residential School for the Deaf* [1976] IRLR 326 (dismissal as from date of marriage).

[184] *James v. Eastleigh Borough Council* [1990] IRLR 288, HL.

[185] See *Greater Manchester Police Authority v. Lea* [1990] IRLR 372, EAT.

[186] SDA 1975, s. 1(1)(b). And see *James v. Eastleigh Borough Council* [1990] IRLR 288, HL.

[187] For an early appreciation of the importance of controlling indirect discrimination see *Griggs v. Duke Power Co* 401 US 424 (1971).

[188] The decision in *Clymo v. Wandsworth London Borough Council* [1989] IRLR 241, EAT, — that a contractual term that a job is full-time does not involve applying a requirement or condition but is part of the nature of the job — has been disapproved in *Briggs v. North Eastern Education and Library Board* [1990] IRLR 181, NICA. But note the racial discrimination case of *Meer v. London Borough of Tower Hamlets* [1988] IRLR 399, CA that a "requirement" must be mandatory and not merely one of several criteria which are taken into account; and see para. 7.23.

[189] *Home Office v. Holmes* [1984] IRLR 299, EAT.

[190] *Clarke and Powell v. Eley (IMI) Kynoch* [1982] IRLR 482, EAT; *Kidd v. DRG (UK) Ltd* [1985] IRLR 190, EAT.

[191] *Price v. Civil Service Commission* [1977] IRLR 291, EAT. Other instances of a requirement or condition with disproportionate effect have included a seniority test for allocation of more attractive work (*Steel v. Post Office* [1977] IRLR 288), a height and strength test for admission to certain types of work (*Thorn v. Meggitt Engineering Ltd* [1976] IRLR 241), operating a promotion procedure which was subjective and unadvertised (*Watches of Switzerland v. Savell* [1983] IRLR 141) and requiring previous experience in particular job (*Conway v. Queens University of Belfast* [1981] IRLR 137).

[192] [1977] IRLR 291, EAT.

due to family responsibilities unable to take up employment.[193] But an inability to comply with a requirement or condition must be judged at the time of the alleged act of discrimination.[194] Although the applicant must show disproportionate effect by adducing appropriate evidence tribunals have considerable scope and may rely on their own knowledge and experience for determining which is the correct "pool" with regard to which disproportionate effect should be judged.[195] The importance of the "pool" with respect to which disproportionate effect is to be judged is illustrated by *Pearse v. City of Bradford Metropolitan Council*[196] in which the applicant's statistical evidence related only to the academic staff of a college and not to those with appropriate qualifications which was the pool selected by the tribunal.

Justification

However even if the employee can show she has suffered a detriment because of the inability to comply with a requirement or condition which is of disproportionate effect there is no discrimination if the employer can show that the requirement or condition is justifiable irrespective of the sex of the person to whom it is applied.[197] It has been stated that what is justification is a question of fact for the industrial tribunal[198] and means what is acceptable to right-thinking people[199] but the better view requires the employer to demonstrate some objective reason for the application of the requirement or condition.[200]

Marital status

Indirect discrimination against a married person[201] occurs where an employer[202]

---

[193] *Cf. Wright v. Civil Service Commission* (unreported) 9324/79B in which W failed to show that an age-bar of 32 years for internal promotion had a disproportionate effect on women because there were more men than women in the "pool" of employees to which the age-bar was applied.

[194] *Clarke & Powell v. Eley (IMI) Kynoch* [1982] IRLR 482; the fact that C could have worked full-time was immaterial because there were no full-time jobs available when she was selected for redundancy. And see *Turner v. Labour Party Superannuation Fund* [1987] IRLR 101, CA that a woman may be able to comply by change of status before the date by which compliance is judged.

[195] *Kidd v. DRG (UK) Ltd* [1985] IRLR 190, EAT; *Greater Glasgow Health Board v. Carey* [1987] IRLR 484, EAT. Elaborate statistical evidence is not always necessary (*Briggs v. North Eastern Education and Library Board* [1990] IRLR 181, NICA).

[196] [1988] IRLR 379, EAT. See also *R. v. Secretary of State for Education, ex parte Schaffter* [1987] IRLR 53.

[197] SDA 1975, s. 1(1)(b)(ii).

[198] *Greater Glasgow Health Board v. Carey* [1987] IRLR 484; and see speech of Lord Fraser of Tulleybelton in *Mandla v. Dowell Lee* [1983] IRLR 385, HL.

[199] *Ojutiku v. M.S.C.* [1982] IRLR 418, CA.

[200] See *Hampson v. Department of Education and Science* [1989] IRLR 69, CA and *Pearse v. City of Bradford Metropolitan Council* [1988] 379 in which the remarks of Lord Keith in *Rainey v. Greater Glasgow Health Board* [1987] IRLR 26 at para. 20 were suggested to require a more stringent test than that contained in *Ojutiku*. And note the application of the test in *Briggs v. North Eastern Education and Library Board* [1990] IRLR 181, NICA.

[201] Note E.C. Directive 76/207 (Equal Treatment) is wider than domestic law by prohibiting not just discrimination against a married person on the grounds of marital status but also discrimination against married *and* single persons on the grounds of "marital or family status". And see *R v. Secretary of State for Education, ex parte Schaffter* [1987] IRLR 53.

[202] The rules preventing discrimination against married persons only apply to acts of discrimination in the context of employment (SDA 1975, s. 3).

applies without justification[203] a requirement or condition to both married and unmarried people but which is such that a considerably smaller proportion of married people than unmarried people of the same sex can comply with it and a married person suffers a detriment thereby, for example, by not being appointed to a job or being dismissed.[204] Instances of requirements with which fewer married people can comply include not employing people who have children[205] and selecting for redundancy part-time workers before full-time workers on the basis that fewer married women can comply with the need to work full-time to avoid primary selection for redundancy because fewer married women than unmarried women were free of family and domestic responsibilities.[206]

7.16 Discrimination in employment

Discrimination by employers is dealt with by Part II of the Sex Discrimination Act 1975[207] (complemented by the EOC's Code of Practice[207a])which renders unlawful discrimination[208] at an establishment in Great Britain by an employer[209] (a) in the arrangements he makes for determining who should be offered employment,[210] (b) in the terms on which employment is offered[211] unless it is a contractual term for the payment of money,[212] (c) by refusing to offer employment,[213] (d) in the way he affords access to promotion, training, benefits, facilities or services[214] and (e) by dismissing or subjecting to any other detriment.[215] Although the *de minimis* rule may present some differences of treatment being regarded as a detriment[216] it can be the same detriment as that which founds a

---

[203] See notes 198-200.

[204] SDA 1975, s. 3(1)(b).

[205] *Hurley v. Mustoe* [1981] IRLR 208, EAT; *Thorndyke v. Bell Fruit (North Central)* [1979] IRLR 1, which proceed on the view that a smaller proportion of married women can comply with the "no children" requirement than unmarried women.

[206] *Kidd v. DRG (UK) Ltd* [1985] IRLR 190.

[207] Part II also deals with discrimination by other bodies in the employment field-partnerships (s. 11), trade unions (s. 12), qualifying bodies (s. 13), vocational and training bodies (ss. 14, 16) and employment agencies (s. 15).

[207a] Code of Practice for Elimination of Discrimination on grounds of Sex and Marriage and the Promotion of Equality of Opportunity in Employment (1985).

[208] Note that in Part II "discriminate" means (1) to discriminate (directly or indirectly) on grounds of sex (s. 1) and marital status (s. 3) and (2) to discriminate by victimisation (s. 4) (*Cornelius v. University College of Swansea* [1987] IRLR 141, CA).

[209] The employee who commits the unlawful act is liable as is the employer where the act is in the course of the employee's employment (SDA 1975, s. 41). And see *Bracebridge Engineering Ltd v. Darby* [1990] IRLR 3, EAT and *Yaseen v. Strathclyde Regional Council* 1991 GWD 20-1200. Discrimination against contract workers is dealt with by s. 9.

[210] SDA 1975, s. 6(1)(a). And see *Roadburg v. Lothian Regional Council* [1976] IRLR 283; "arrangements" would include how a vacancy is publicised, how interviews are conducted, how application forms are constructed and the use of selection tests.

[211] *Ibid.* s. 6 (1)(b).

[212] *Ibid.* ss. 6(5), 8(3), (4).

[213] *Ibid.* s. 6(1)(c).

[214] *Ibid.* s. 6(2)(a), (b). But contractual money benefits are covered by the Equal Pay Act and generally services which are also offered to the public are excluded (*ibid.* s. 6(6), (7)). And note s. 50 which brings in indirectly provided benefits etc.

[215] The definition of dismissal is extended to include expiry of a fixed term contract and constructive dismissal (SDA 1986, s. 2(3)).

[216] *Schmidt v. Austicks Ltd* [1977] IRLR 360; *Ministry of Defence v. Jeremiah* [1980] ICR 13, CA.

claim of indirect discrimination[217] and it need not sound in financial terms[218] but it must involve a disadvantage.[219]

7.17 Genuine occupational qualifications

Even where a person has been the subject of unlawful discrimination it is possible for the employer to obtain a complete defence by proving that being a man or a woman is a "genuine occupational qualification" (GOQ) for the job or part of it.[220] However such a defence is not available where the discrimination is in the terms on which employment is offered or by dismissal or subjection to a detriment[221] nor, generally,[222] where the employer already has sufficient men or women to perform the duties for which sex is a genuine occupational qualification.[223] An employer's contention that being a man or a woman is a genuine occupational qualification is likely to be carefully examined.[224] Being a man (or a woman) is a genuine occupational qualification for a job only where (a) the essential nature of the job calls for a man for reasons of physiology (excluding physical strength or stamina[225]) or in dramatic performances or entertainment, for reasons of authenticity, so that the essential nature of the job would be materially different if carried out by a woman,[226] (b) for decency or privacy the job needs to be held by a man because (i) it is likely to involve physical contact with men in circumstances where they might reasonably object to its being carried out by a woman[227] or (ii) the holder of the job is likely to do his work in circumstances where men might reasonably object to the presence of a woman because they are in a state of undress or using sanitary facilities,[228] (c) the job is likely to involve working or living in a private home and needs to be done by a man because objection might reasonably be taken to allowing a woman to have the degree of social or physical contact with, or knowledge of intimate details of, the person living in the private home,[229] (d) the nature or location of the establishment makes it impracticable for the job-holder to live other than on

---

[217] *Home Office v. Holmes* [1984] IRLR 299, EAT.

[218] *Ministry of Defence v. Jeremiah* [1980] ICR 13, CA. Subjection to a detriment would include being selected for redundancy, a reduction in working hours, unpleasant working conditions, having to pay a baby-sitter and being the victim of sexual harassment. But requiring women but not men to wear overalls might not be a detriment (*Schmidt v. Austicks Bookshop Ltd* [1977] IRLR 360).

[219] *Porcelli v. Strathclyde Regional Council* [1986] ICR 564, IH.

[220] SDA 1975, s. 7(1)(3).

[221] *Ibid.* s. 6(1)(b), (2)(b).

[222] The exceptions are those genuine occupational qualifications which relate to (a) the job being done in a private home and (b) jobs for a married couple.

[223] SDA 1975, s. 7(4).

[224] See for example *Roadburg v. Lothian Regional Council* [1976] IRLR 283, EAT and *Sisley v. Britannia Security Systems* [1983] IRLR 404, EAT.

[225] While physical strength and stamina are excluded here it must be remembered that requiring all employees for a particular job to possess a certain degree of strength or stamina may be a requirement which, although of disproportionate effect on women, may be justifiable, in which case there would be no discrimination at all. See *Thorn v. Meggitt Engineering Ltd* [1976] IRLR 241.

[226] SDA 1975, s. 7(2)(a).

[227] See *Wylie v. Dee & Co Ltd* [1978] IRLR 103, EAT, *Sisley v. Britannia Security Ltd* [1983] IRLR 404, EAT and *Etam plc v. Rowan* [1989] IRLR 150, EAT.

[228] SDA 1975, s. 7(2)(b). It is not necessary that the job *requires* that people be in a state of undress: *Sisley*, above.

[229] *Ibid.* s. 7(2)(ba), added by the SDA 1986, s. 1.

the premises and (i) the only available premises are not equipped with separate sleeping accommodation and sanitary facilities and (ii) it is not reasonable to expect the employer to provide separate accommodation or facilities for women,[230] (e) where the work requires the job-holder to be a man because (i) it is a hospital, prison or place for providing persons with special care, supervision and attention and (ii) those persons are all men, and (iii) it is reasonable that the job should not be held by a woman,[231] (f) the job-holder provides individuals with personal services promoting their welfare education or the like and they can be more effectively provided by a man,[232] (g) the job is likely to involve working in a country whose laws or customs are such that a woman could not operate effectively[233] and (h) that the job is one of two to be held by a married couple.[234]

7.18 Special cases, exceptions and exclusions

Limited discrimination is permitted with regard to: (a) *police* — discrimination is permitted only with regard to (i) height, uniform or equipment and allowances in lieu, (ii) special treatment of women with regard to pregnancy or childbirth and (iii) pensions, special constables and cadets;[235] (b) *prison officers* — discrimination with regard to height is permitted and the governor of a prison need not be the same sex as the prisoners;[236] (c) *ministers of religion* — discrimination is permitted in so far as doctrine requires it.[237]

Part V contains several general exceptions to the operation of the Act of which the following have relevance for employment.

(a) Training. Although there is a freedom to discriminate with regard to training for certain work (where very few people of one sex, during the 12 month period preceding the act complained of have been engaged in that kind of work) for the purpose of (i) affording women only or men only training to fit them for that work, (ii) encouraging women only or men only to do that work or (iii) affording training for work for persons who have been excluded from full-time employment by family or domestic responsibilities this freedom does not extend to protecting any discrimination by an employer which is unlawful by section 6 of the 1975 Act.[238] However a similar exception is made specifically for employers who seek to afford training for employees[239] of one sex only to encourage or facilitate workers of that sex to take up work which has generally not been performed by members of that sex.[240]

---

[230] *Ibid.* s. 7(2)(c).

[231] *Ibid.* s. 7(2)(d).

[232] *Ibid.* s. 7(2)(e). And see *London Borough of Lambeth v. CRE* [1990] IRLR 281, CA.

[233] *Ibid.* s. 7(2)(g)

[234] *Ibid.* s. 7(2)(h).

[235] *Ibid.* s. 17.

[236] *Ibid.* s. 18.

[237] *Ibid.* s. 19.

[238] *Ibid.* s. 47 as amended by SDA 1986, s. 4. The principal effect of the amendments is to extend the limited exceptions in s. 47 to any person who provides training as opposed to designated training bodies.

[239] Note SDA 1975, s. 48(1)(a) applies only in respect of "employees". It would not therefore permit recruiting people of one sex only. However s. 48(1)(b), which is an alternative to s. 48(1)(a), is cast in wider terms of encouraging "women" to do certain work.

[240] SDA 1975, s. 48(1). Similar provision is made for trade unions and other organisations by s. 48(2), (3) and s. 49 permits such bodies to discriminte to ensure that on elected bodies there is a minimum number of persons of one sex.

(b) Statutory authority. Previously a discriminatory act was not unlawful if it was done to comply with a requirement of legislation passed before the 1975 Act itself.[241] Thus an employer who refused to permit a woman of child-bearing age to be concerned with the transport of dimethylformamide because of his duties under the Health and Safety at Work etc. Act 1974 was not required to prove that removing a woman from the job (tanker driver) was the only method of complying with his duties under the prior Act.[242] The position is now different as a result of the Employment Act 1989[243] which only permits discrimination if it is necessary to comply with (1) an existing statutory provision[244] concerning the protection of women or (2) a relevant statutory provision (within Part I of the Health and Safety at Work etc. Act 1974) for the purpose of protecting a particular woman or a class including that woman. However a statutory provision may only operate to defend an act of discrimination if it is for the purpose of protecting women as regards (a) pregnancy or maternity or (b) other circumstances giving rise to risks specifically affecting women.[245] However these provisions of the Employment Act 1989 are properly appreciated only when it is noted that the same Act (1) declares that legislation passed before the Sex Discrimination Act 1975 is of no effect if it requires an act of unlawful discrimination,[246] (2) empowers the amendment or repeal of such legislation by order,[247] (3) lists statutory provisions which, because they concern the protection of women, continue to excuse acts of discrimination[248] and (4) amends and repeals many statutory provisions which have operated to discriminate.[249]

(c) National security. A discriminatory act is not unlawful if it is done for the purpose of safeguarding national security[250] and although a Crown certificate that an act was done for such a purpose is conclusive[251] an individual cannot be deprived of enforcing by judicial process the rights conferred by EC Directive 76/207.[252] The Directive itself allows for exceptions on the grounds of public safety[253] but whether the exception can be relied upon is to be determined by the domestic tribunal taking into account whether the discriminatory action is appropriate and necessary to achieve public safety. Thus where the policy of not permitting female officers to carry firearms led to the non-renewal of the contract of a female police officer, whether the discrimination fell within the public safety exception was a matter to be determined by the domestic tribunal whose jurisdiction could not be excluded by ministerial certificate.[254]

---

[241] *Ibid.* s. 51 which also applies to an Act re-enacted after the passage of the SDA 1975.

[242] *Page v. Freighthire Tank Haulage Ltd* [1981] IRLR 13, EAT. And see *Greater London Council v. Farrar* [1980] ICR 266 (lawful refusal to employ female wrestler in order to comply with licence issued for premises under London Government Act 1963).

[243] S. 3(3) substitutes the original provision of SDA 1975, s. 51.

[244] This includes Acts passed before 16 November 1989 and instruments made under them no matter when made (*ibid.*).

[245] SDA 1975, s. 51 as substituted by EA 1989, s. 3(3).

[246] EA 1989, s. 1.

[247] *Ibid.* s. 2 and see s. 6.

[248] *Ibid.* s. 4; Sch. 1; and see s. 5 (exemptions regarding certain educational appointments).

[249] *Ibid.* s. 29; Schs. 6, 7.

[250] SDA 1975, s. 52.

[251] *Ibid.* s. 52(2).

[252] *Johnston v. Chief Constable of the R.U.C.* [1986] IRLR 263, ECJ. The decision in *Johnston* deals with the equivalent (but wider) provision in the Sex Discrimination (Northern Ireland) Order 1976 (Art. 53) which includes acts to protect public safety.

[253] Art. 2(2).

[254] *Johnston (ibid.).*

(d) Other exclusions. Part II of the Act relates to discrimination in the field of employment which is defined to mean "employment under a contract of service or apprenticeship or a contract personally to execute any work or labour, and related expressions shall be construed accordingly".[255] While this includes any contracts which involve personal performance of work or labour,[256] it will not include a contract with an individual for the distribution of newspapers unless its dominant purpose is that the party contracting to provide the services under the contract performs personally the work or labour which forms the subject matter of the contract.[257] However it is also unlawful to discriminate against contract workers viz. those who are employed by a third party who has a contract with the discriminator.[258] Although service for the Crown is treated as if it were under a contract of employment[259] military service is excluded from the Act's operation[260] and although it is not unlawful for the Crown to discriminate in appointing to an office or post[261] the Crown is prohibited from doing any act which would be unlawful if the Crown were the employer.[262]

Discrimination in employment is only unlawful if it occurs at an establishment in Great Britain.[263] Employment is at an establishment in Great Britain unless the employee does his work "wholly or mainly outside Great Britain"[264] and employment on a British registered ship or an aircraft or hovercraft registered in the United Kingdom is at an establishment in Great Britain unless the employee works wholly outside Great Britain.[265] Until the passage of the Sex Discrimination Act 1986 discrimination in relation to death or retirement was excluded from the operation of the Sex Discrimination Act 1975.[266] However as a result of the decision of *Marshall v. Southampton and South West Hampshire Area Health Authority*[267] in which the policy of requiring women but not men

---

[255] SDA 1975, s. 82(1).

[256] *Hugh-Jones v. St Johns College* [1979] ICR 848, EAT; *Quinnen v. Hovell* [1984] ICR 525, EAT.

[257] *Mirror Newspaper Group v. Gunning* [1986] ICR 145, CA: although in practice there was an element of personal supervision the dominant purpose of the contract was for the efficient distribution of newspapers. Another approach might be to require the contract contains an element of *delectus personae.* And see *Tanna v. Post Office* [1981] ICR 374, EAT.

[258] SDA 1975, s. 9. In *Rice v. Fon-A-Car* [1980] ICR 133, s. 9 was limited to where the contract worker is employed by a person/company who contracts with the principal to supply workers.

[259] SDA 1975, s. 85(1).

[260] *Ibid.* s. 85(4), (5).

[261] *Ibid.* s. 85(2).

[262] *Ibid.* s. 86. But note in *Knight v. Attorney-General* [1979] ICR 194 the EAT ruled that s. 86(2) does not give an industrial tribunal jurisdiction.

[263] SDA 1975, s. 6. Note the same limitation is not contained in s. 9 (contract workers) or any other provisions in Part II of the Act.

[264] *Ibid.* s. 10 (1). The area of the Act's application may be extended by Order in Council (s. 10(5)). The SDA 1975 and the EqPA have been extended to the continental shelf by the Sex Discrimination and Equal Pay (Offshore Employment) Order 1987. In 1987 only 1% of the continental shelf workforce was female.

[265] SDA 1975, s. 10(2). In *Haughton v. Olau Line (UK) Ltd* [1986] ICR 357 the Court of Appeal stated that s. 10 excludes claims by those whose work was wholly or mainly outside Great Britain unless done on a British registered ship, aircraft etc. and was not done *wholly* outside Great Britain; it therefore excluded a claim by an employee who worked mainly outside Great Britain on a German registered ship.

[266] SDA 1975, s. 6(4).

[267] [1986] IRLR 140, ECJ.

to retire at age 60 was held to contravene the Equal Treatment Directive 76/207 the 1975 Act was amended[268] so that discriminatory retirement provisions are now unlawful if they involve promotion, transfer, training, dismissal, demotion or subjecting to a detriment. Thus if an employer operates an age-bar for access to promotion, transfer or training expressed in relation to proximity to retirement the age-bar must be the same for men and women and although the amended exclusion in relation to retirement does not include voluntary retirement[269] permitting women to opt for voluntary retirement earlier than men could be contrary to the Equal Treatment Directive 76/207.[270]

7.19 Sexual harassment, advertisements and other discrimination

"Sexual harassment" is shorthand for activity which is easily recognisable as subjecting a person to "any other detriment"[271] and although there has been some debate about whether sexual harassment is properly within the province of sexual discrimination[272] in *Porcelli v. Strathclyde Regional Council*[273] the First Division held that sexual harassment is a particularly degrading and unacceptable form of sex discrimination which it must have been the intention of Parliament to restrain.[274] However as in any complaint of sexual discrimination the burden of proof is on the complainant, the industrial tribunal has to be satisfied that the harassment was on the grounds of the victim's sex.[275] Where a complaint of discrimination in the form of harassment is successful evidence as to the victim's sexual attitudes will be admissible in calculating compensation for injured feelings.[276]

It is also unlawful for any person (a) to operate a "discriminatory practice,"[277] (b) to publish or cause to be published an advertisement which indicates an intention to discriminate unlawfully unless the intended act would not in fact be unlawful,[278] (c) to instruct a person over whom he has authority, or who usually carries out his wishes, to do an act of unlawful discrimination or to procure that

---

[268] SDA 1986, s. 2.

[269] *Cf.* SDA 1975, s. 82(1).

[270] *Burton v. British Rail Engineering* [1982] ICR 329, ECJ; *Roberts v. Tate & Lyle Industries Ltd* [1986] ICR 371, ECJ. And see para. 7.11.

[271] *Wileman v. Minilec Engineering Ltd* [1988] IRLR 144, EAT. It is also a breach of contract for an employer to fail to investigate allegations of sexual harassment: *Bracebridge Engineering Co v. Darby* [1990] IRLR 3, EAT.

[272] See, for example, Pannick "Sexual Harassment and the Sex Discrimination Act", 1982 *Public Law* 42.

[273] [1986] ICR 564.

[274] In response to the argument, accepted by the industrial tribunal, that a man would have been treated in the same way Lord Brand opined that the sexual harassment involved (comparing Mrs Porcelli to pictures of nude females, offering her a screw nail while asking if she would like a screw and whether she could use a piece of laboratory equipment shaped like a penis) was a "form of unfavourable treatment to which a man would not have been vulnerable" while Lord Grieve described it as "a sexual sword used against the victim because she was a woman."

[275] *Balgobin v. Tower Hamlets London Borough Council* [1987] ICR 829, EAT.

[276] Thus in *Snowball v. Gardner Merchant Ltd* [1987] ICR 719 evidence that the complainant had, allegedly, referred to her bed as a "play-pen" was admitted because of its bearing on the extent to which her feelings had been injured.

[277] SDA 1975, s. 37. A discriminatory practice is the application of a requirement or condition which results in an act of discrimination within Part II (Employment) or which would be likely to result in such an act if the persons to whom it is applied were not all of one sex (*ibid.*).

[278] *Ibid.* s. 38(1), (2).

person to do such an act[279] and (d) to pressure another person to do an act of unlawful discrimination.[280] Although legal action in respect of such forms of unlawful discrimination can be brought only by the Equal Opportunities Commission[281] publishing an unlawful advertisement may also be the subject of a complaint by an individual who can show that the discriminatory advertisement falls into the category of "arrangements for the purpose of determining who should be offered employment.[282] "Advertisement" is widely defined to include public and internal or in-house advertisements.[283] However the publisher (for example a newspaper) of an unlawful advertisement can escape liability if he can prove he reasonably relied on a statement that the actual act of discrimination itself would not be unlawful.[284]

7.20 Enforcement

A person who believes he has been the victim of unlawful discrimination may present a complaint to an industrial tribunal within three months of the date of the act which forms the subject of complaint.[285] While the Equal Opportunities Commission may present a preliminary[286] complaint to an industrial tribunal,[287] generally[288] no proceedings shall be brought for unlawful discrimination except those provided by the Act itself and although a minister of the Crown has the power to bar the hearing of a case on the grounds of national security[289] the exercise of such a power is inconsistent with EC Directive 76/207.[290] If the industrial tribunal finds the complaint well-founded[291] it must make such of the following as it considers just and equitable: (a) an order declaring the rights of

[279] *Ibid.* s. 39. This would include instructing a personnel manager not to select males/females for a particular post unless the discrimination itself was lawful because, for example, the post was covered by a GOQ. And see the unreported industrial tribunal decisions in *EOC v. Jack Adams* (refusal to interview males referred by Jobcentre), *EOC v. Foulds and Riding (Synthetics)* (request that Careers Office send only female applicants for vacancies as "sorters") and *EOC v. British Car Auctions* (request that Jobcentre refers only females for a vacancy).
[280] SDA 1975, s. 40. The pressure has to take the form of offering a benefit or subjecting to a detriment but neither needs to be made directly to the person pressured.
[281] *Ibid.* ss. 37(3), 72(1).
[282] *Ibid.* s. 6 (1)(a). And see *Brindley v. Tayside Health Board* [1976] IRLR 364.
[283] SDA 1975, s. 82(1). Newspapers, radio, television, notices, signs, catalogues, pictures, models and films are all included.
[284] *Ibid.* s. 38(4). A false or misleading statement to the publisher is an offence (*ibid.* s. 38(5)).
[285] *Ibid.* ss. 63, 76(1). A complaint may be admitted outside the period if it is just and equitable and there are provisions for deeming the date of an act or omission to be extended until the end of a period (s. 76(b)).
[286] It is preliminary in the sense that it will facilitate the EOC itself taking action under s. 71 or s. 72 (application to sheriff court for interdict).
[287] *Ibid.* s. 73.
[288] There is a limited exception in respect of the Court of Session to review, reduce or suspend any order or determination (*ibid.* s. 62(3) as substituted by the Race Relations Act 1976, Sch. 4, para. 2).
[289] SDA 1975, s. 52.
[290] *Johnston v. Chief Constable of the R.U.C.* [1986] IRLR 263, ECJ. And see *von Colson & Kamann v. Nordrhein-Westfahlen* [1986] CMLR 430, ECJ to effect that while Dir. 76/207 leaves the matter of penalty to the Member States it has to be of such a nature so as to have actual disuasive effect. And see note 292.
[291] A complaint may of course be settled by conciliation at any stage prior to the industrial tribunal determining the matter (SDA 1975, ss. 64, 77).

the complainant and respondent, (b) an order requiring the respondent to pay compensation[292] and (c) a recommendation that the respondent take, within a specified time, action to obviate or reduce the effect of the discrimination on the complainant.[293] Where the discrimination complained of takes the form of dismissal the aggregate of (1) the compensatory award for unfair dismissal and (2) compensation for discrimination cannot exceed the maximum award[294] and a tribunal has no power to require a respondent to pay a specific wage to the complainant in respect of a future time.[295]

7.21 The Equal Opportunities Commission

The Equal Opportunities Commission (EOC) was established by the Sex Discrimination Act 1975 and is charged with (a) working towards the elimination of discrimination, (b) promoting equality of opportunity between men and women generally and (c) reviewing and suggesting amendment of the Sex Discrimination Act itself and the Equal Pay Act 1970 and other statutory provisions in so far as they require men and women to be treated differently.[296]

Formal investigations

The EOC is empowered, on prescribed terms of reference, to conduct formal investigations for the purpose of carrying out any of its duties.[297] The investigation may be general or in respect of named persons. However an investigation in respect of named persons must be preceded by a belief, which has to be based on sufficient evidence, that these persons are committing acts which are unlawful by virtue of the Sex Discrimination Act 1975 or the Equal Pay Act 1970.[298] Subject to certain limits[299] for the purpose of a formal investigation the Commission may serve a notice requiring the production of written information and attendance of any person to give oral information and produce documents in his possession or control.[300] To enforce a notice the EOC may apply to the sheriff

---

[292] SDA 1975, s. 65. The statutory maximum which includes injury to feelings is the same as the unfair dismissal compensatory award; and see *Noone v. North West Thames Regional Health Authority* [1988] IRLR 195. Where the complaint is one of indirect discrimination and is unintentional no compensation may be awarded (s. 66(3), (4)). In England it is possible for exemplary damages to be awarded (*City of Bradford Metropolitan Council v. Arora* [1991] IRLR 164, CA) but EC law does not require the maximum to be ignored (*Marshall v. Southampton etc Area Authority (No. 2)* [1990] IRLR 481, CA).

[293] SDA 1975, s. 65(1)(a), (b), (c). But a tribunal does not have power to order that a victim be promoted/appointed at next suitable vacancy: *British Gas plc v. Sharma* [1991] IRLR 101, EAT.

[294] EPCA, s. 76.

[295] *Irvine v. Prestcold Ltd* [1981] IRLR 281, CA. The loss of wages is to be dealt with under s. 65((1)(b) while s. 65(1)(c) deals with, for example, ensuring the complainant has equal opportunity of participating in training, etc.

[296] SDA 1975, ss. 63(1), 55. Detailed provision for the financing, staffing and proceedings of the Commission is set out in Sched. 3.

[297] *Ibid.* s. 58. And see Sex Discrimination (Formal Investigations) Regulations 1975 (S.I. 1975 No. 1993).

[298] *In re Prestige Group Plc* [1984] ICR 473.

[299] These are that, unless the formal investigation follows the issue of a non-discrimination notice, (a) the notice was authorised by the Secretary of State, (b) the investigation is confined to the acts specified in s. 59(2)(b) and (c) no order regarding information or documents may be made if a similar order could not be made by the Court of Session in civil proceedings (SDA 1975, s. 59(2)).

[300] SDA 1975, s. 59(1)-(3).

court[301] and it is an offence to wilfully alter, suppress, conceal or destroy a document or knowingly or recklessly to make a false statement.[302] Either during or after a formal investigation the EOC may make recommendations for changes in the policies or procedures of an employer to promote equality of opportunity or for changes in the law.[303] Any information given to the EOC for a formal investigation shall not be divulged[304] unless disclosure is (a) compelled by a court, (b) with the informant's consent, (c) in a summary which does not identify the informant or other person, (d) in a report published or available for inspection or (e) to other members of the EOC or its staff or for certain litigation to which the EOC is a party.[305]

Non-discrimination notices.

Where the EOC in the course of a formal investigation, believes that certain unlawful acts[306] are being or have been committed it may, after giving the addressee at least twenty-eight days in which to make representations, issue to the person (the addressee) believed to be committing the unlawful act a "non discrimination notice" which requires the person not to commit any such acts, inform the EOC that any necessary changes in his practices or arrangements have been taken and take appropriate steps for informing others concerned (for example employees, employment agencies) of such changes.[307] If the notice relates to employment there is a right of appeal within six weeks to an industrial tribunal[308] (if the notice relates to matters which are outside the jurisdiction of the industrial tribunals the right of appeal is to the sheriff court).[309] The tribunal has a wide discretion[310] to quash a notice or direct that it be replaced by an amended notice.[311] A non discrimination notice becomes final when an appeal is dismissed, withdrawn or abandoned or when the time for appealing expires.[312]

Orders, codes and assistance.

Additional powers are conferred on the Commission to permit it to deal with persistent discrimination. Thus in the period of five years after the service of a non-discrimination notice or a finding by a tribunal or court that a person has done an unlawful discriminatory act or has breached an equality clause, the EOC may apply to the sheriff court for an order restraining such a person from doing such an unlawful act.[313] The EOC may issue codes of practice for elimi-

---

[301] *Ibid.* s. 59(4), (5).

[302] *Ibid.* s. 59(6), (7).

[303] *Ibid.* s. 60(1). Unless the Secretary of State requires otherwise the Commission's report on a formal investigation is required to be published or available for inspection (*ibid.* s. 60, (2)-(7)).

[304] It is a criminal offence for the Commission, any Commissioner or any employee of the Commission to divulge any such information (*ibid.* 2.61(2)).

[305] *Ibid.* s. 61(1).

[306] These are set out in s. 67(1) to be (1) an unlawful discriminatory act, (2) a contravention of ss. 37, 38, 39 or 40 and (3) breach a term included by virtue of an equality clause.

[307] *Ibid.* s. 67(1)-(5). Where the Secretary of State can exercise the powers conferred by s. 25(2), (3) the Commission must give notice of unlawful acts to the Secretary of State.

[308] *Ibid.* s. 68(1). And see the Industrial Tribunal (Non-Discrimination Notice Appeal) (Scotland) Regulations 1977 (SI 1977 No. 1095).

[309] SDA 1975, s. 68(1)(b).

[310] *Commission for Racial Equality v. Amari Plastics Ltd* [1982] ICR 304.

[311] SDA 1975, s. 68(2), (3).

[312] *Ibid.* s. 82(4); an appeal is treated as dismissed even if the tribunal directs it to be amended under s. 68(3).

[313] *Ibid.* s. 71.

nation of discrimination and promotion of equality of opportunity in the field of employment [313a] such codes are admissible in evidence in proceedings before any industrial tribunal.[313b] An individual may apply to the EOC for assistance for bringing proceedings under the Sex Discrimination Act 1975 and it has a wide discretion for granting assistance which can range from giving advice to arranging legal representation.[313c]

RACIAL DISCRIMINATION

7.22 Introduction and definitions

The Race Relations Act 1976 and its complementary Code of Practice[314] regulate racial discrimination in the employment field. The Act follows the same scheme as that adopted by the Sex Discrimination Act 1975 in that it embraces the concepts of direct and indirect discrimination[314a], and discrimination by way of victimisation before setting out in Part II the circumstances in which discrimination is unlawful in the context of employment (subject to the exceptions set out in Part VI) while Parts VII and VIII deal with the constitution and powers of the Commission for Racial Equality (CRE) and the provisions for enforcement respectively.

However before dealing with these matters it is necessary to note that segregation on racial grounds is itself deemed to be less favourable treatment[315] and to mention two pivotal definitions specific to the Race Relations Act —

(a) "Racial grounds" means any of the following grounds — colour, race, nationality and citizenship or ethnic or national origins.

(b) "Racial group" means a group of persons defined by reference to colour, race, nationality or citizenship[316] or ethnic or national origins[317] and references to a previous racial group refer to any racial group into which a person falls.[318] Whether a group of persons constitutes an ethnic group was considered in *Mandla v. Dowell Lee*[319] with the word "ethnic" being construed relatively widely in a "broad, cultural/historic sense". Before a group can be regarded as an ethnic

---

[313a] *Ibid.* s. 56A inserted by RRA, sch. 4. And see Code of Practice for Elimination of Discrimination etc. (1985) approved by Secretary of State

[313b] *Ibid.*

[313c] SDA 1975, s. 75.

[314] Code of Practice for the Elimination of Racial Discrimination and the Promotion of Equality of Opportunity in Employment, prepared by the Commission for Racial Equality and approved by the Secretary of State under the Race Relations Act 1976 (hereinafter RRA), s. 47.

[314a] Cross reference should be made to paras. 7.14, 7.15.

[315] RRA, s. 1(2). Thus equal but separate toilet facilities would be discriminatory. *Cf. Pel v. Modgill and Ors* [1980] IRLR 142, EAT where one racial group congregated in one section of the business of their own volition.

[316] On the question of nationality and citizenship see *Orphanos v. Queen Mary College* [1985] IRLR 349, HL.

[317] In *Tejani v. Superintendent Registrar for District of Peterborough* [1986] IRLR 502, CA, there was no discrimination of grounds of "national origins" where less favourable treatment was because the complainant was born abroad without any reference to any particular place or country of origin; but see the speech of Lord Fraser of Tullybelton in *Orphanos v. Queen Mary College* [1985] IRLR 349, HL.

[318] RRA, ss. 3(1), 78(1). A racial group can itself be comprised of two or more distinct racial groups (s. 3(2)) or more than one ethnic group (*London Borough of Lambeth v. CRE* [1990] IRLR 231, CA).

[319] [1983] ICR 385, HL.

group it must regard itself, and be regarded by others, as a distinct community by virtue of certain characteristics. The essential characteristics of an ethnic group are (1) a long shared history, of which the group is conscious as distinguishing it from other groups, and the memory of which it keeps alive; (2) a cultural tradition of its own, including family and social customs and manners often but not necessarily associated with religious observance.[320] Thus it has been accepted that Sikhs are one of a group defined by references to ethnic origins and applying to "no turban" or a "no hats" rule has been held to set up a case based on indirect discrimination.[321] Similarly Jews form an ethnic group[322] and while a notice stating "Sorry no travellers" indirectly discriminated against gypsies who were regarded as forming an ethnic group because they were a minority with a long shared history, a common geographical origin, distinctive customs or language derived from Romany and a common culture[323] an ability to speak a particular language (Welsh) did not of itself define membership of a particular ethnic group.[324]

7.23 Direct and indirect discrimination and victimisation

Direct discrimination occurs where one person is treated (or would be treated) less favourably than other persons on racial grounds.[325] It is probably not necessary that the complainant/victim is a member of a racial group before a complaint of direct discrimination will lie. Thus employees dismissed for refusing to carry out instructions not to admit or serve coloured customers were held to be treated less favourably on racial grounds.[326] However, although it may be an offence under the Public Order Act 1986[327] the use of racially insulting words to describe an employee does not amount to less favourable treatment unless the person who used the words intended the employee to overhear them or knew the insulting words would be passed on to the employee.[328] An employer's motive or intentions are irrelevant so that treating a black employee less favourably by changing his employment not because the employer is prejudiced against the employee but because he is being discriminated against by his fellow employees contrary to the employer's wishes is nevertheless unlawful.[329]

Cases of indirect racial discrimination are dealt with in broadly the same way as cases of indirect sexual and marital status discrimination although of course

---

[320] *Ibid., per* Lord Fraser of Tullybelton at p. 390. Other relevant but not essential characteristics are (a) a common geographical origin, or descent from a small number of common ancestors; (b) a common language, not necessarily peculiar to the group; (c) a common literature peculiar to the group; (d) a common religion different from that of neighbouring groups or from the general community surrounding it and (e) being a minority or being an oppressed or a dominant group within a larger community.

[321] *Mandla v. Dowell Lee* [1983] ICR 385, HL; *Gurmit Singh Kambo v. Vaulkhard, The Times* December 7, 1984, CA.

[322] *Seide v. Gillette Industries Ltd* [1980] IRLR 427, EAT.

[323] *CRE v. Dutton,* [1989] IRLR 8, CA.

[324] *Gwynedd County Council v. Jones, The Times* July 28, 1986, EAT.

[325] RRA, s. 1(1)(a).

[326] *Zarczynska v. Levy* [1978] IRLR 532, EAT; *Showboat Entertainment Centre Ltd v. Owens* [1984] IRLR 7, EAT. Similarly a white woman refused a job because her husband was West Indian has had her complaint heard (*Wilson v. T B Steelwork Co Ltd* 1978 COIT 706/441).

[327] S. 18 prohibits the use of insulting or abusive words likely to stir up racial hatred.

[328] *De Souza v. The Automobile Association* [1986] IRLR 103, CA.

[329] *R v. CRE, ex parte Westminster City Council* [1984] IRLR 230. And see *Din v. Carrington Viyella Ltd* [1982] IRLR 281, EAT.

the latter are not concerned with the notion of the "racial group". Thus indirect racial discrimination is concerned with overtly neutral employment rules or practices having an adverse effect on members of one or more particular racial groups, and occurs where one person applies to another a requirement or condition which he applies (or would apply) to persons not of the same racial group as that other person but (1) which is such that the proportion of persons of the same racial group as that other who can comply[330] with it is considerably smaller than the proportion of persons not of that racial group who can comply with it, (2) which he cannot show to be justifiable irrespective of the colour, race, nationality or ethnic or national origins of the person to whom it is applied and (3) which is to the detriment of that other person because he cannot comply with it.[331]

Justifiable. "Justifiable" means capable of being justified and is a question of fact.[332] Although it has been doubted whether the meaning of "justifiable" adopted by the Court of Appeal in *Ojutiku v. Manpower Services Commission*[333] is consistent with the meaning of justifiable in the context of sex discrimination the House of Lords has recently approved[334] the Court of Appeal's analysis[335] of the judgments in *Ojutiku* that although its previous decision in that case is binding with regard to the meaning of "justifiable" that word merely connotes a value judgment and in accordance with the judgment of Stephenson L.J. in *Ojutiku* it requires an objective balance between the discriminatory effect of the requirement and the reasonable needs of the person applying it; thus there is no significant difference between that test and the one adopted by the House of Lords in *Rainey v. Greater Glasgow Health Board*[336] that to justify a material difference (in the context of equal pay) the employer has to show a real need on the part of the undertaking, objectively justified. The following requirements or conditions have been held to be justifiable in particular circumstances, (a) forbidding beards on grounds of hygiene,[337] (b) requiring that a female nurse conform with the uniform prescribed by regulations by not wearing trousers,[338] (c) requiring employees to wear protective headgear,[339] (d) requiring previous managerial experience[340] and (e) requiring highly qualified and skilled employees to produce written reports in English promptly.[341] On the other hand the following have been held not to be justifiable: (a) a requirement that labour-

---

[330] As in the Sex Discrimination Act the words "can comply" are to mean "can in practice comply" (*Mandla v. Dowell Lee* [1983] ICR 385, HL; *Raval v. DHSS and Civil Service Commission* [1985] ICR 685, EAT.

[331] RRA, s. 1(1)(b).

[332] *Per* Lord Fraser of Tullybelton in *Orphanos v. Queen Mary College* [1985] IRLR 349 at 353.

[333] [1982] IRLR 418.

[334] *Hampson v. Department of Education and Science* [1990] IRLR 302 *per* Lord Lowry at p. 307.

[335] [1989] IRLR 69.

[336] [1987] IRLR 27.

[337] *Singh v. Rowntree Mackintosh Ltd* [1979] IRLR 199, EAT; *Panesar v. Nestle Co Ltd* [1980] IRLR 64, CA.

[338] *Kingston and Richmond Area Health Authority v. Kaur* [1981] IRLR 336, EAT.

[339] *Singh v. British Rail Engineering Ltd* [1986] ICR 22, EAT. But see now Employment Act 1989, s. 12 to the effect that a requirement that a Sikh on a construction site wear a safety helmet instead of a turban is a requirement which cannot be shown to be justifiable.

[340] *Ojutiku v. Manpower Services Commission* [1982] IRLR 418, CA.

[341] *Chin v. British Aerospace plc* [1982] IRLR 56, CA.

ers complete application forms in English in their own handwriting,[342] (b) a requirement that pupils attending a Christian school did not wear a turban[343] and (c) a requirement that students who had not been ordinarily resident in the European Community for three years pay higher fees.[344]

Requirement or condition. However a requirement or condition has to be justifiable without regard to the racial group to which the complainant belongs.[345] Although it must make it more difficult to establish a case of indirect discrimination it has been confirmed[346] that the decision in *Perrera v. Civil Service Commission (No. 2)*[347] to the effect that a requirement or condition means an absolute bar or a "must" has to be followed unless it can be distinguished. Accordingly a claim of indirect discrimination could not succeed where a selection criterion — the need to have previous experience of Tower Hamlets — was merely one factor taken into account in not considering a job application.[348]

Racial group. In view of the significance of the "racial group" when issues of proportionality are being considered it is important for industrial tribunals to identify clearly the racial group in respect of which the proportional inability to comply (with a requirement or condition) was to be assessed and a failure to do so is illustrated by the decision in *Tower Hamlets London Borough Council v. Quayyum*[349] in which the Employment Appeal Tribunal suggested that a complaint of indirect racial discrimination be tackled by (1) identifying the colour, race, nationality or ethnic origin of the complainant, (2) ascertaining whether there is a racial group of similar colour or nationality or ethnic origin as the complainant, (3) considering whether there has been imposed a requirement or condition irrespective of race, nationality or ethnic origin and finally (4) deciding whether the proportion of the racial group (to which the complainant belongs and to which the requirement or condition applies) is considerably smaller than the relevant comparable proportion of the indigenous population.[350]

Victimisation. Like the Sex Discrimination Act 1975[351] the Race Relations Act 1976 contains a provision[352] whose purpose is to ensure that victims of racial discrimination shall not be deterred from raising proceedings under the Race Relations Act. Thus it is provided[353] that a person (the discriminator)

---

[342] *Isa & Rashid v. B.L. Cars* (1981) COIT 1103/125. And see the Code of Practice on racial discrimination, para. 1.13.

[343] *Mandla v. Dowell Lee* [1983] ICR 385, HL. Lord Fraser observed, however, "it might be possible for the school to show that a rule insisting on a fixed diet, which included some dish (for example pork) which some racial groups could not conscientiously eat was justifiable if the school proved the cost of providing special meals for the particular group would be prohibitive.

[344] *Orphanos v. Queen Mary College* [1985] IRLR 349, HL; but note no reference was made to s. 41(2) to effect that nothing in Parts II to IV or RRA makes unlawful discrimination on basis of length of residence in UK if done to comply with a requirement of the Crown.

[345] *Orphanos (ibid.).*

[346] *Meer v. London Borough of Town Hamlets* [1988] IRLR 399, CA.

[347] [1983] IRLR 166, CA.

[348] *Meer v. London Borough of Tower Hamlets* [1988] IRLR 399, CA.

[349] [1987] ICR 729, EAT.

[350] In practice this may often be the comparison but the position is probably correctly stated by Lord Fraser of Tullybelton in *Orphanos v. Queen Mary College* [1985] IRLR 349 at 353 (in a case dealing with nationality), ". . . consider . . . the group consisting of Cypriot [the complainant's] nationality and compare it with the group consisting of persons not of Cypriot . . . nationality, *i.e.* consisting of all persons (except Cypriots) of every nationality from Chinese to Peruvian inclusive."

[351] S. 4.

[352] S. 2.

[353] *Ibid.*

discriminates — though not on racial grounds[354] — against another if he treats that other person (the victim) less favourably than he treats or would treat other persons and does so because the victim has or will do any of the following: (a) brought proceedings under the Race Relations Act,[355] (b) given evidence or information in connection with proceedings[356] under the Act, (c) otherwise done anything under or by reference to the Act[357] or (d) alleged in good faith that someone has contravened the Act.[358] The correct approach is to compare the treatment accorded to the victim with the treatment the discriminator has applied or would apply to persons who have not done an act in paragraphs (a) to (d) above.[359] However, more importantly, the less favourable treatment must be by reason of the fact that the victim had done an act set out in one of the paragraphs (a) to (d) and the complaint will fail if the less favourable treatment would have occurred irrespective of the victim doing such an act. Thus in *Aziz v. Trinity Taxis Ltd*[360] the complainant, an Asian taxi operator, failed to establish discrimination by victimisation when he was expelled from an association of taxi operators after making secret tape recordings of conversations held with other members even although the existence of the tape recordings was disclosed in industrial tribunal proceedings because "the evidence [did] not establish that the fact that the recordings were made by [Aziz] by reference to the race relations legislation in any way influenced [the alleged discriminator] in expelling [Aziz] from membership'.[361]

7.24 Racial discrimination and employment

Part II of the Race Relations Act 1976 deals with discrimination in the employment field. It is unlawful for a person in relation to employment[362] by him[363] at an establishment in Great Britain[364] to discriminate[365] against another, (a) in the

---

[354] Discrimination on racial grounds is covered by s. 1. In view of the decisions in *Zarczynska v. Levy* [1978] IRLR 532, EAT, and *Showboat Entertainment Centre Ltd v. Owens* [1984] IRLR 7, EAT could it be argued that certain discrimination by way of victimisation could also be covered by s. 1?

[355] The proceedings do not have to be brought against the discriminator.

[356] The proceedings need be neither against the discriminator nor brought by the victim.

[357] Although "under" relates to a specific statutory provision under which an act was done, "by reference to" has a much wider meaning; thus an act can be done by reference to the Race Relations Act if it is done by reference to it "in the broad sense, even though the doer does not focus his mind specifically on any provision of the Act", *per* Slade LJ, *Aziz v. Trinity Taxis Ltd* [1988] ICR 534 at 542, CA.

[358] RRA, s. 2.

[359] *Aziz v. Trinity Taxis Ltd* [1988] ICR 534, CA, overruling, on this point, *Kirby v. Manpower Services Commission* [1980] ICR 420, EAT.

[360] [1988] ICR 534, CA.

[361] *Ibid. per* Slade L.J. at 548.

[362] "Employment" which by s. 16 includes the police is defined by s. 78(1).

[363] Liability may attach to the employer and the individual employee who discriminates (RRA, ss. 32, 33).

[364] For the meaning of "employment at an establishment in Great Britain" see s. 8; and note s. 9 which disapplies ss. 4 and 7 in respect of persons employed on a ship who were engaged outside Great Britain. In *Deria v. General Council of British Shipping* [1986] IRLR 108, CA, it was held that whether there is employment in Great Britain depends on what the parties intended at the date of the act complained of. And note that nothing in s. 4 applies to persons not ordinarily resident in Great Britain in connection with employment to provide training in skills which are to be exercised wholly outside Great Britain (s. 6).

[365] "Discriminate" means on racial grounds or by way of victimisation (*Cornelius v. University College of Swansea* [1987] IRLR 141, CA).

arrangements made for offering employment,[366] (b) in the terms on which employment is offered or afforded,[367] (c) by refusing to employ a person,[368] (d) in access to promotion, transfer, training, benefits, facilities or services[369] and (e) by dismissing or subjecting a person to some other detriment[370] and in this context "detriment" is not limited to circumstances akin to dismissal or disciplinary action but includes any situation in which a reasonable worker would or might feel disadvantaged in the circumstances and conditions in which he had therefore to work.[371] It does not have to be a different detriment from that shown in making a case of indirect discrimination[372] and is wide enough to embrace racial harassment.[373] Discrimination in relation to partnerships,[374] trade unions,[375] qualifying and vocational training bodies,[376] employment agencies[377] and public training agencies[378] is also unlawful.

7.25 Genuine occupational qualifications

However none of the discrimination in paragraphs (a)-(e) above is unlawful if the employment is for the purposes of a private household.[379] Also akin to the Sex Discrimination Act 1975[380] the Race Relations Act provides that discrimination within (a), (c) and (d) above is not unlawful where being a member of a particular racial group is a genuine occupational qualification (GOQ) for the job.[381] A GOQ may be used to defend an act of discrimination (a) where the job involves participation in a dramatic performance or other entertainment in a capacity for which a person of a particular racial group is required for reasons of authenticity,[382] (b) the job involves participation as an artist's or photographic model in the production of a work of art, visual image, or sequence of visual images for which a person of a particular racial group is required for reasons of

---

[366] RRA, s. 4(1)(a). This includes advertisements, application forms and other literature, interviews, instructions to personnel officers etc. And see Code of Practice paras. 1.5-1.14.

[367] RRA, s. 4(1)(b), (2)(a).

[368] RRA, s. 4(1)(c). *Johnson v. Timber Tailors (Midlands) Ltd* [1978] IRLR 146.

[369] RRA, s. 4(2)(b). But note the partial exemption where the employer provides the services etc. to the public (s. 4(4)).

[370] RRA s. 4(2)(c).

[371] *De Souza v. The Automobile Association* [1986] IRLR 103, CA. Thus referring to an employee as "the wog" would constitute subjecting her to a detriment if it was intended that she should hear the remark and she could reasonably feel disadvantaged thereby.

[372] *The Home Office v. Holmes* [1984] IRLR 299, EAT.

[373] *Barclays Bank plc v. Kapur* [1989] IRLR 387, CA.

[374] RRA, s. 10.

[375] *Ibid*, s. 11.

[376] *Ibid*, s. 12, 13.

[377] *Ibid*, s. 14.

[378] *Ibid*, s. 15.

[379] *Ibid*, s. 4(3). Note this exemption does not apply to discrimination by victimisation (s. 2) nor to discrimination against contract workers (s. 7) and the circumstances may allow an ordinary claim of unfair dismissal under EPCA.

[380] S. 7. And see para 7.17.

[381] RRA, s. 5(1): but note, similar to s. 7(3), (4) of the Sex Discrimination Act 1975, s. 5(3), (4) permits the operation of a GOQ even where only part of the duties involve a GOQ but not where such duties could be done by existing employees of the relevant racial group. Thus provided a duty is not so trivial as to be disregarded it is not for the tribunal to evaluate the importance of the duty: *Tottenham Green Under Fives' Centre v. Marshall* (No. 2) [1991] IRLR 162, EAT.

[382] *Ibid*, s. 5(2)(a).

authenticity,[383] (c) the job involves working in a place where food or drink is provided to, and consumed by, members of the public in a particular setting for which a person of a particular racial group is required for reasons of authenticity[384] or (d) the holder of the job provides persons of a particular racial group with personal services promoting their welfare and those services can most effectively be provided by a person of that racial group.[385]

However although the "provision of welfare" and "effective provision of services" are issues of fact for the industrial tribunal,[386] as a matter of principle the provisions relating to GOQs generally should be narrowly or strictly construed and the particular GOQ relating to the provision of personal services envisages circumstances where there is direct contact — mainly face to face, or where there could be susceptibility in personal, physical contact — and where language or a knowledge and understanding of cultural and religious background are of material importance.[387] Also the particular racial group in respect of whom the personal services are to be provided by the job holder has to be clearly identified.[388]

7.26 Exceptions

In addition to the exceptions already mentioned certain general exceptions operate in relation to employment. Thus although generally conferring preferential treatment on a racially disadvantaged group — positive discrimination — is unlawful an employer may encourage, by affording them access to facilities for training or otherwise, employees[389] of a particular racial group to do work which during the previous year has generally not been done by employees of that racial group.[390] Additionally the exceptions in respect of (1) affording special treatment to meet the needs of a particular racial group[391] and (2) facilities for persons not ordinarily resident in Great Britain[392] may be relevant to employers. For example offering a training course only to employees who are members of a particular racial group which has a special need for such training would be covered by the exception (1) above.[393] Nothing in the Race Relations act 1976 may compromise national security[394] or acts done (1) in pursuance of an enactment (or instrument made thereunder by a Minister) or Order in Council or (2) to comply with any condition or requirement imposed by a Minister by virtue

---

[383] *Ibid.* s. 5(2)(b).

[384] *Ibid.* s. 5(2)(c).

[385] *Ibid.* s. 5(2)(d).

[386] *Tottenham Green Under Fives' Centre v. Marshall* [1989] IRLR 147, EAT.

[387] *London Borough of Lambeth v. CRE* [1989] IRLR 379, EAT, affirmed [1990] IRLR 231, CA; accordingly s. 5(2)(d) did not justify the Borough of Lambeth limiting two managerial jobs in their Housing Benefit department ot black Afro-Caribbean or black Asian candidates because over half the tenants dealt with fell into those groups.

[388] *Tottenham Green Under Fives' Centre v. Marshall* [1989] IRLR 147, EAT.

[389] Thus discriminatory recruitment is not permitted; see *Riyat v. London Borough of Brent* (COIT 1405/59).

[390] RRA, s. 38(1), (2). And see the complementary provisions of s. 38(3) which qualifies s. 11 (trade unions, professional organisations and employers' associations) and s. 37 (positive discrimination permitted by official training agencies).

[391] *Ibid.* s. 35.

[392] *Ibid.* s. 36; and see s. 6.

[393] Note that by s. 40 the benefit of these exceptions can be obtained not just where an employer provides the training course etc. but also where he arranges for another person to do so.

[394] RRA, s. 42.

of any enactment.[395] However the phrase "in pursuance of" is to be narrowly construed to avoid defeating the object of the Race Relations Act.[396] Thus refusing to employ a person who is required to, but does not, have a work permit may be defended by relying on the fact that the requirement that the person has a work permit is done in pursuance of an enactment.[397]

7.27 Enforcement

Individuals who believe they have been the victims of unlawful racial discrimination enforce their rights by presenting a complaint to an industrial tribunal within three months[398] of the alleged discriminatory act taking place. Where a copy of such a complaint is sent to a conciliation officer he must endeavour to promote a settlement and as an alternative, but without prejudice to an eventual complaint to an industrial tribunal, an individual may request the services of a conciliation officer.[399] In the event of an industrial tribunal upholding a complaint it may make such of the following as it considers just and equitable — (a) a declaratory order, (b) an order requiring the respondent to pay to the complainant a sum of compensation, and (c) a recommendation that the respondent take action to reduce the effect on the complainant of any act of discrimination to which the complaint relates.[400] With the exception of an application for judicial review no proceedings other than those provided by the Act may be brought in respect of an act of unlawful discrimination[401] and the amount of compensation that may be awarded by an industrial tribunal is subject to a statutory maximum[402] and while no compensation may be awarded in respect of unintentional indirect discrimination[403] compensation may include a sum in respect of injury to feelings whether or not compensation is payable for other heads of loss.[404]

---

[395] *Ibid.* s. 41(1); and see s. 41(2), discussed in *Saviani v. Inland Revenue Commissioners* [1981] QB 458, regarding discriminatory treatment on basis of nationality or residence in accordance with ministerial decisions. *Cf. Orphanos v. Queen Mary College* [1985] IRLR 349, HL.

[396] *Hampson v. Department of Education and Science* [1990] IRLR 302 HL, disapproving, in part, *General Medical Council v. Goba* [1988] IRLR 425, EAT. According to Lord Lowry at p. 307 the fallacy of a wide construction "can be recognised when one reflects that almost every discretionary decision such as that which is involved in the appointment, promotion and dismissal of individuals in, say, local government, the police, the National Health Service and the public sector of the teaching professions, is taken against a statutory background which imposes a duty on someone."

[397] As to work permits see the Statement of Immigration Rules for Control of Entry (H. C. Papers 1972-73, nos. 80, 81, as amended by Statement of Changes in Immigration Rules 1989 H.C. 388). Work permits are generally not required by nationals of EC member states; the exceptions are Spain and Portugal whose nationals will continue to require work permits until 1 January 1993.

[398] RRA, ss. 54, 68. But note the distinction between a "deliberate omission" (s. 68(7)(c)) and an "act extending over a period" (s. 68 (7)(b)) for calculating the time limit: *Barclays Bank plc v. Kapur* [1991] IRLR 136, HL.

[399] *Ibid.* s. 55.

[400] *Ibid.* s. 56(1). But see *British Gas plc v. Sharma* [1991] IRLR 101, EAT.

[401] *Ibid.* s. 53(1), (2).

[402] *Ibid.* s. 56(2), (3). The amount must not exceed the maximum that may be awarded under EPCA, s. 75 (compensatory award).

[403] RRA, ss. 56(1)(b), 57(3).

[404] *Ibid.* ss. 56(1)(b), 67(4). *Cf. Coleman v. Skyrail Oceanic Ltd* [1981] IRLR 398, CA. And see the indications on *quantum* in *Noone v. North West Thames Regional Health Authority* [1988] IRLR 195, CA.

7.28 The Commission for Racial Equality

The Commission for Racial Equality (CRE) was established by the Race Relations Act 1976[405] with powers and responsibilities similar to those of the EOC.[406] The duties of the CRE are (a) elimination of racial discrimination by way of victimisation, (b) promotion of equality of opportunity and good relations between persons of different racial groups[407] and (c) to review the working of the Race Relations Act and prepare proposals for amending it[408] and, to perform these, it has the following powers — (a) the preparation and issue of codes of practice in the field of employment;[409] (b) conducting formal investigations in connection with carrying out its statutory duties but before doing so the terms of reference of the investigation must be set in accordance with the appropriate statutory provisions;[410] where the CRE proposes to conduct a formal investigation into a named-person it should have formed the belief, and state so in the terms of reference, that the persons named in the terms of reference might have done or might be doing unlawful acts of a kind specified in the reference[411] and (c) issuing and enforcing non-discrimination notices, which are recorded in a public register,[412] in respect of certain discriminatory acts.[413] A person on whom a non-discrimination notice has been served may appeal against it within six weeks[414] and a notice may not be formally served without the addressee being given the opportunity of making representations of which the CRE must take account.[415] Where the CRE fears that discrimination may be persisted in it may apply to the sheriff court for an interdict to restrain further acts of unlawful discrimination[416] and proceedings in respect of certain types of unlawful discrimination are reserved to the CRE.[417] In cases where a complaint may be brought by an individual the CRE may grant assistance including (a) giving advice, (b) procuring a settlement, (c) arranging for legal advice and (d) providing other appropriate assistance.[418]

---

[405] S. 43; Sch. 1.

[406] See para. 7.21.

[407] And note the duty to make reports on recommendations in the context of a formal investigation (s. 51); as to the timing and publication of reports see *CRE v. Amari* [1982] IRLR 252, CA.

[408] RRA, s. 43(1).

[409] *Ibid.* s. 47. A draft is submitted to the Secretary of State for approval and laying before Parliament. A code is admissible evidence in industrial tribunal proceedings (S. 47(10)).

[410] *Ibid.* ss. 48, 49.

[411] *R. v. CRE, ex parte Hillingdon London Borough Council* [1982] 3 WLR 159, HL; In *In re Presige Group plc* [1984] 1 WLR 335, HL, it was stated the CRE must have some grounds for suspecting unlawful discrimination albeit they were no more than tenuous because at that stage they had not yet been tested.

[412] RRA, s. 61.

[413] *Ibid.* ss. 58, 60, 62.

[414] S. 59.

[415] S. 58(5); but the process of making and considering such representations is not in the nature of a judicial hearing (*R. v. Commission for Racial Equality, ex parte Cottrell & Rothon* [1980] 1 WLR 1580, QBD).

[416] S. 62. And note the ability of the Commission to make a preliminary complaint to an industrial tribunal under s. 64(1).

[417] S. 63. The reserved provisions relate to s. 30 (instructions to discriminate), s. 31 (pressure to discriminate) and s. 29 (discriminatory advertisements). Regarding advertisements see the equivalent provisions in the Sex Discrimination Act 1975 discussed at para. 7.19.

[418] S. 66.

ONUS OF PROOF

7.29 Onus of proof

In common with other legal disputes a person who claims that another person has discriminated against him has to prove that to be the case. However where the reason for treating a person in a particular way plays such an important part it is difficult to obtain direct evidence of discrimination; circumstantial evidence from which certain inferences may be drawn will frequently be all that is available. The onus of proof can be further complicated by the fact that at different stages of a complaint of discrimination the issue requiring proof will be put forward either by the complainant or the respondent. For example once a complainant has proved that she has been subjected to less favourable treatment on the grounds of her sex the employer may wish to argue that the discrimination can be defended by showing there is a genuine occupational qualification for the relevant job or that an appropriate exclusion or exception is applicable. In those instances it is for the employer/respondent to prove the existence of the defence he puts forward. Similarly where the complainant makes out a case of indirect discrimination it would be for the respondent to show the requirement or condition is justifiable. Acknowledging the difficulty of proving discrimination, courts and tribunals have frequently attempted to assist a complainant by holding that the onus of proof shifts from the complainant to the respondent and a failure by the latter to prove he did not discriminate results in a finding for the complainant.[419] However that approach has been criticised because although an industrial tribunal can infer discrimination in the absence of a satisfactory explanation[420] it is wrong to understand *Khanna v. Ministry of Defence*[421] and *Chattopadhyay v. The Headmaster of Holloway School*[422] as implying that the burden of proof is formally cast on the respondent; the burden of proof of discrimination is on the applicant, and to prove it on the balance of probabilities.[423]

A complainant's task of proving discrimination may be eased by an industrial tribunal ordering recovery or inspection of documents as might be granted by a sheriff.[424] Production of a document will be ordered if it is regarded by the tribunal chairman as relevant to the proceedings and in cases where confidential information may be involved whether disclosure will be ordered depends on whether the tribunal chairman considers it necessary to fairly dispose of the proceedings.[425] Thus an employer has been ordered to produce a schedule showing, over the 2 year period prior to the complainant's application, the number of white and non-white persons who had applied for particular posts catego-

---

[419] See *Moberley v. Commonwealth Hall* [1977] IRLR 176, EAT; *Wallace v. South Eastern Education and Library Board* [1980] IRLR 193, NICA; *Dornan v. Belfast City Council* [1990] IRLR 179, NICA; *Baker v. Cornwall CC* [1990] IRLR 194, CA.

[420] *Noone v. North West Thames Regional Health Authority* [1988] IRLR 195, CA.

[421] [1981] IRLR 182, EAT.

[422] [1981] IRLR 487, EAT.

[423] *London Borough of Barking v. Camara* [1988] IRLR 378, CA. This of course applies to proving whether discrimination has taken place but it would not affect issues in respect of which the onus is clearly placed on the employer/respondent, *e.g.* s. 1(1)(b)(ii) (whether a condition is justifiable). And see the analysis of the question of the burden of proof in *British Gas plc v. Sharma* [1991] IRLR 101, EAT.

[424] Industrial Tribunal (Rules of Procedure) (Scotland) Regulations 1985 (S.I. 1985 No. 17, Sch. 1, rule 4(1)(b)(ii)).

[425] *Science Research Council v. Nasse* [1979] ICR 921, HL.

rised as to whether or not they had been appointed because the statistical information contained therein was relevant to the complaint.[426] However it has been suggested that production of documents will not be ordered if such an order would be oppressive.[427]

Additionally a person who believes he has been the victim of discrimination may send to the alleged discriminator a statutory questionnaire.[428] The questions and any replies are admissible as evidence in tribunal or court proceedings and although the recipient is not under any legal duty to respond to the questions a tribunal or court may infer from a failure to reply or making an evasive reply the recipient committed an unlawful act.[429] Although legal aid is not available for applicants to industrial tribunals[430] the EOC and the CRE may grant assistance in respect of complaints based on the Sex Discrimination Act 1975, the Equal Pay Act 1970 and the Race Relations Act where (1) the case raises a question of principle, (2) it is unreasonable to expect an applicant to deal with a case unaided or (3) for any other special consideration;[431] a codes of practice giving practical guidance on the avoidance and elimination of sexual and racial discrimination and the promotion of equal opportunity have been issued by the EOC and the CRE and while a failure to observe a code does not render a person liable to proceedings the provisions of the codes are admissible in proceedings before an industrial tribunal.[432]

AIDS, DISABILITY AND SPENT CONVICTIONS

7.30 As indicated earlier [433], certain vulnerable classes of applicant and employees may derive protection from general legal principles, others from special rules.

AIDS. People who have Acquired Immune Deficiency Syndrome (AIDS) which is generally understood to be caused by the Human Immunodeficiency Virus (HIV) may be the subject of discrimination in relation to employment through

---

[426] *West Midlands Passenger Transport Executive v. Singh* [1988] IRLR 186, CA disapproving *Jalota v. I.M.I. (Kynoch) Ltd* [1979] IRLR 313, EAT. But an employer will not be ordered to prepare a document which in effect creates evidence (*Carrington v. Helix Lighting Ltd* [1990] IRLR 6, EAT).

[427] *West Midlands Passenger Transport Executive v. Singh* [1988] IRLR 186, *per* Balcombe L.J. at 189. Ordering the production of documents may be oppressive because the material might not be readily to hand and expensive to provide or because its effect will unreasonably extend the length and cost of the hearing.

[428] The form of the questionnaire and of the recipient's reply have been prescribed by the Secretary of State under SDA 1975, s. 74; see Sex Discrimination (Questions and Replies) Order 1975 (S.I. 1975 No. 2048). The Order also sets out the time limits and manner of service of the questions and replies. And see RRA s. 65.

[429] SDA 1975, s. 74(2); RRA, s. 65(2). And see *Carrington v. Helix Lighting Ltd* [1990] IRLR 6, EAT regarding use of second (supplementary) questionnaire.

[430] Industrial tribunals are not mentioned in the Legal Aid (Scotland) Act 1986 but the EAT is.

[431] SDA 1975, s. 75. And see RRA, s. 66 regarding equivalent powers of the CRE.

[432] SDA 1975, s. 56A; RRA, s. 47.

[433] See para. 7.1

fear — seldom real, often imagined — and prejudice.[434] Although no rule of law specifically protects against such discrimination[435] it is arguable that applying a policy of not employing people who suffer from AIDS or HIV could support a case of indirect sexual or racial discrimination. Thus it could be argued, at least in terms of present statistics, that such a policy disproportionately disadvantages men and would require to be justified for it to be lawful.[436] Alternatively to refuse to employ a person from an African country where the incidence of AIDS is very high could be unlawful direct racial discrimination ,[437] whereas to apply a policy of not recruiting applicants who had spent many years in such countries could be seen to be indirect discrimination against their nationals and require to be justified. Provided no sexual discrimination is committed it is not unlawful to refuse to employ a person because of his/her lifestyle or private morality although it has been held that a law which prohibits (male) homosexual activity constitutes an interference with a person's right to respect for his private life as guaranteed by Article 8 of the European Convention on Human Rights.[438]

Disability. Rather ironically although disabled people are the subject of special statutory protection[439] the lofty principles of the legislation are placed in proper perspective by statistics which demonstrate only token observance and by the fact that a disabled person who is refused employment in breach of these special provisions has no legal procedure or remedy which he himself can initiate. However the responsible government department considers that prosecution of recalcitrant employers is less productive than education, advice and encouragement.[440.]

Spent convictions. Although ex-offenders receive special treatment by the Rehabilitation of Offenders Act 1974 in that neither a "spent" conviction (including a failure to disclose) nor any of its ancillary circumstances is a "proper ground" for dismissal or exclusion from office or a profession or for prejudicing a person in employment[441] the legislation creates no special remedies for people whose rights are infringed. Thus although the dismissal of an employee because of a "spent" conviction cannot be used to found a fair dismissal[442] such protection comes from the ordinary law of unfair dismissal and would be of no avail to an employee who lacked the requisite period of continuous employment. Similarly it is not clear what remedy would be available to an applicant who was refused employment because he had a spent conviction no matter how "improper" such exclusion might be.

---

[434] For a detailed analysis of this area of the law see B.W. Napier "AIDS Sufferers at Work and the Law" in *Vulnerable Workers: Psychosocial and Legal Issues.* M Davidson, J Earnshaw (eds.)

[435] See "Guide to AIDS in the Workplace" published jointly by Department of Employment and Health and Safety Executive (1988).

[436] SDA 1975, s. 1(1)(b).

[437] RRA 1976 s. 1(1)(b).

[438] *Norris v Ireland. The Times* October 10, 1988, ECHR.

[439] Disabled Persons (Employment) Acts 1944, 1958; and see the Chronically Sick and Disabled Persons Act 1970 and the Disabled Persons Act 1981 (access to and accommodation at work) and the Companies Act 1985, s. 235 (company policy on disabled employees).

[440] See Code of Good Practice on the Employment of Disabled People (MSC, 1985); Employment and Training for People with Disabilities: Consultative Document (Department of Employment, 1990).

[441] Rehabilitation of Offenders Act 1974 s. 4; but see the Rehabilitation of Offenders Act 1974 (Exceptions) Order 1975, SI 1985 No. 1023.

[442] *Hendry v. Scottish Liberal Club* [1977] IRLR 5, IT and see *Torr v. British Railways Board* [1977] IRLR 84, EAT.

Chapter Eight

MACHINERY FOR EMPLOYMENT DISPUTES

INTRODUCTION

8.1 This chapter will concentrate upon those agencies and institutions charged with the resolution of disputes which arise in an employment law context. There are some agencies such as the Advisory, Conciliation and Arbitration Service (ACAS) and the industrial tribunals which have been created specifically to deal with certain forms of employment law disputes in ways directed by the statutory provisions which created them. Their actual functions will be discussed in more detail later in this chapter. Equally, the Central Arbitration Committee (CAC) is the only statutory agency in labour law which has been created in order to exercise arbitration functions. Despite the creation of the above agencies which are unique to employment law, one cannot under-estimate the importance of the civil courts which also exercise a wide jurisdiction in this field. The jurisdiction of the courts is important in two senses. First, they continue to exercise a significant first instance jurisdiction in such common law matters as breach of contract[1] and delictual liability (this latter area is particularly important as regards the law of industrial conflict). Further, the whole question of judicial review is becoming an increasingly important issue for employment law. The other sense in which the courts are important arises through the jurisdiction of the Inner House of the Court of Session in Scotland and the Court of Appeal in England and Wales to hear appeals from the Employment Appeal Tribunal which itself is charged with hearing appeals from the industrial tribunals and the certification officer.

INDUSTRIAL TRIBUNALS

8.2 Composition and jurisdiction

Industrial tribunals were first created by the Industrial Training Act 1964 to hear appeals from employers against their assessment for industrial training levy. The accompanying regulations[2] which established these tribunals recognised the need for a separate system of industrial tribunals for Scotland with their own personnel and administrative arrangements. This separate jurisdiction has been maintained ever since. However, the work of the industrial tribunals has changed

---

[1]   The Department of Employment made an announcement in March 1990 that it intended to give industrial tribunals jurisdiction to hear breach of contract cases by implementing EPCA, s. 131. It was made clear that a tribunal will only have jurisdiction if both the conditions set out in s. 131(3) are satisfied. This means that the complaint must arise to be outstanding on the termination of the employee's contract and arise in circumstances which already give rise to proceedings before a tribunal under some other statutory provision. At time of writing the necessary order has not yet been laid before Parliament.

[2]   See the Industrial Tribunals (Scotland) Regulations 1965, S.I. 1965 No. 1117 as amended by S.I. 1967 No. 302, S.I. 1972 No. 638 and S.I. 1977 No. 1474.

substantially since the 1964 Act and they have acquired a wide and extensive jurisdiction to adjudicate upon a large number of employment law questions. As was noted in Chapter Five, one reason why industrial tribunals were selected as the appropriate adjudicative bodies to hear labour law complaints was because they appeared to possess the virtues of relative accessibility, informality, speed and lack of expense. To this end legal aid is not available before industrial tribunals, although an applicant may be able to use the Legal Advice and Assistance Scheme for advice on the presentation of his case and have a case supported by the Equal Opportunities Commission or the Commission for Racial Equality. One issue that will be considered in this chapter is the extent to which these virtues have been eroded over the years through the growth of legalism which reduces the opportunities for unrepresented litigants to present effectively their own cases. Tribunals should also enjoy the confidence of both sides of industry since they are tripartite bodies consisting of a legally qualified chairman and two "wingpersons" or "lay members" — one selected from employer bodies and the other from organisations representing employees and are independent of the Department of Employment.

8.3 Membership

As has already been noted, an industrial tribunal consists of a chairman and two lay members.[3] Chairmen of industrial tribunals in Scotland are appointed by the Lord President of the Court of Session and must be advocates or solicitors of at least seven years' standing.[4] There is also a president of the Industrial Tribunals for Scotland who exercises overall supervision of the Scottish tribunals[5] and is responsible for selecting the chairman and the two members for each hearing.[6] The members are selected from two panels of persons appointed by the Secretary of State, one member being taken from each panel. The members of one panel are appointed after consultation with any organisation or association of organisations representative of employers and the other panel is appointed after consultation with any organisation or association of organisations representative of employed persons.[7] The lay members are appointed because of their knowledge and experience of industrial relations matters and can make use of their industrial experience in order to help the tribunal reach its decision. However, the lay members cannot rely on their industrial experience to such an extent that it leads to a decision which is contrary to the plain meaning of a statutory provision.[8] All three members have the same voting rights and partici-

---

[3] *Ibid.* reg. 5(1). In a sex discrimination case one of the tribunal members should be a woman and in a race discrimination case one of the members should possess special knowledge or experience of race relations in the employment field. However, a failure to select such a person does not affect the legality of the tribunal's composition. See *Habib v. Elkington & Co Ltd* [1981] ICR 435, EAT.

[4] *Ibid.* reg. 5(2).

[5] For the office of president generally see reg. 3.

[6] *Ibid.* regs. 6(2) and (3).

[7] *Ibid.* reg. 5(3). The most obvious bodies who are consulted are, on the employer's side, the CBI, and for employed persons the TUC and STUC. Other employer associations such as the Convention of Scottish Local Authorities are also consulted. Until 1981 only the TUC and STUC were consulted as bodies of employed persons. In April 1981 the Secretary of State announced that consultations would take place with non-TUC bodies such as the Management, Professional and Staff Liaison Group. See generally Linda Dickens *et al. Dismissed: A Study of Unfair Dismissal and the Industrial Tribunal System* (Oxford, 1985).

[8] *British Coal Board v. Cheesbrough* [1988] IRLR 351, CA.

pate equally in the activities of the tribunal, although it is the chairman who conducts the hearing and writes and signs the decision. Decisions may be by majority. At present in Scotland there is a president, 8 full-time chairmen, 21 part-time chairmen and 240 lay members.[9]

8.4 Administration

The industrial tribunals in Scotland are administered by the Secretary of Tribunals and an assistant secretary. It is the secretary who exercises many of the procedural duties associated with industrial tribunals and he is responsible for the day to day administration of the Scottish system. The secretary operates from the Central Office of the Industrial Tribunals (Scotland) in Glasgow which is the administrative headquarters of the Scottish tribunals and is the place where originating applications to the tribunal should be made. There are also area offices in Edinburgh, Aberdeen and Dundee where a tribunal will hear cases from those areas. When a tribunal is hearing a case there will be a clerk appointed by the Secretary of Tribunals to deal with the administrative details.

8.5 Jurisdiction

It is not intended to provide an exhaustive list of the types of complaint which are competent before industrial tribunals. For more detailed information on the rules for qualification and entitlement to each of the rights referred to below the reader is referred to the appropriate chapter which deals with the substantive law pertaining to the relevant statutory rights.[10] However, the following should provide some indication of the width and variety of case which a tribunal is entitled to hear. The jurisdiction of industrial tribunals includes:

(a) claims for equal terms and conditions of employment under the Equal Pay Act 1970;

(b) appeals against improvement notices and prohibition notices issued under the Health and Safety at Work etc. Act 1974 and complaints relating to time off work for safety representatives under the Safety Representatives and Safety Committees Regulations 1977;[11]

(c) complaints under Part II of the Sex Discrimination Act 1975 and appeals against non-discrimination notices;

(d) complaints that an employer has failed to consult with a trade union regarding redundancies under the Employment Protection Act 1975;

(e) complaints under Part II of the Race Relations Act 1976 and appeals against non-discrimination notices;

(f) complaints of unfair dismissal under the Employment Protection (Consolidation) Act 1978, Part V;

(g) complaints about entitlement to redundancy payments and the amount of such payments under the Employment Protection (Consolidation) Act 1978, Part VI;

(h) miscellaneous employment protection rights under the Employment Protection (Consolidation) Act 1978 (e.g. written particulars of terms and conditions of employment, guarantee payments, action short of dismissal on trade union membership grounds, time off for trade union duties and activities, time off for public duties, time off for ante-natal care, right to return to work after pregnancy and written statement of reasons for dismissal)

[9] *Industrial Tribunals in Scotland: Fact Sheet* May 1991.
[10] For a detailed discussion of the contract of employment see Chapter Three.
[11] S.I. 1977 No. 500.

(i) complaints of unreasonable exclusion or expulsion from a trade union under the Employment Act 1980;

(j) complaints that an employer has not informed and consulted with a trade union under the Transfer of Undertakings (Protection of Employment) Regulations 1981;[12]

(k) complaints alleging unauthorised deductions from pay under the Wages Act 1986;

(l) complaints alleging injustifiable union discipline under the Employment Act 1988;

(m) complaints that a person has been denied access to employment on union membership grounds under the Employment Act 1990.

However there can be no doubt that in terms of volume of cases the industrial tribunal's jurisdiction over unfair dismissal complaints constitutes its most important function.[13]

8.6 Procedure

The procedure applicable before the industrial tribunals in Scotland is regulated by the Industrial Tribunals (Rules of Procedure) (Scotland) Regulations 1985.[14] Proceedings are commenced before the tribunal by presenting to the Secretary of Tribunals an originating application in writing.[15] This application must set out the name and address of the applicant, the name and address of the person(s) against whom relief is sought and the grounds of complaint.[16] Once the application has been received it is the duty of the secretary to enter the particulars of it in the register and to forthwith send a copy to the respondent.[17] The respondent also receives a notice of appearance (Form IT3) which must be returned to the secretary within 14 days.[18] A respondent who fails to return a completed notice within this time will lose his entitlement to take any further part in the tribunal proceedings.[19] A completed notice of appearance will contain the full name and address of the respondent and, if he intends to resist the application, sufficient particulars to show the grounds of his defence.[20]

8.7 Conciliation

An important feature of most types of industrial tribunal application is the authority exercised by ACAS to conciliate a settlement of the dispute. These

---

[12] S.I. 1981 No. 1794.

[13] See "Industrial Tribunals - An Update" (1991) Department of Employment Gazette 303 and *Industrial Tribunals in Scotland Fact Sheet* where in 1989-90 67.1 per cent of applications registered by the Secretary concerned unfair dismissal and in 1990-91 this figure was 64.3%

[14] SI 1985 No. 17. There are also special rules in Sch. 2 which deal with the procedural aspects of a complaint of equal pay for work of equal value. These are discussed in Chapter Seven.

[15] *Ibid.* Sch. 1, rule 1. There is an appropraite form which an applicant can complete entitled Form IT1. However, so long as the applicant provides all the necessary information in writing, any form of application will suffice: *Coates v. C J Crispin Ltd* [1973] ICR 413, NIRC.

[16] *Ibid.* rules 1(a)-(c).

[17] *Ibid.* rule 2. The Secretary can refuse registration where the application does not disclose a proper ground of complaint. See rule 1(2).

[18] *Ibid.* rule 3(1).

[19] *Ibid.* rule 3(2).

[20] *Ibid.* rule 3(1).

conciliation powers are most important in unfair dismissal applications, in equal pay cases and in complaints alleging unlawful sex or race discrimination.[21] Usually ACAS can expect to conciliate a settlement in around 40 per cent of applications where it has the authority to conciliate.[22] In Scotland the Secretary of Tribunals will send copies of all the relevant documents to ACAS and will notify the parties that the services of a conciliation officer are available to them.[23] A conciliation officer must endeavour to promote a settlement of the complaint if either party requests him to do so, or if he believes that there is a reasonable prospect of conciliation succeeding.[24] In an unfair dismissal complaint, the officer is first required to promote reinstatement or re-engagement of the applicant on equitable terms, and only if this fails or is not requested, should he attempt to promote agreement as to the amount of compensation.[25] If the conciliation officer succeeds in achieving a settlement between the parties that settlement will be recorded on ACAS Form COT3 which is signed by the parties. A copy of the form will be sent to the Secretary of Tribunals, so that the complaint can then be dismissed by the chairman. An applicant who does sign Form COT3 cannot proceed with a complaint to an industrial tribunal based on the same facts[25] unless his agreement to settle the complaint can be vitiated in some way.[26]

8.8 Preliminary matters

There is a number of preliminary matters which can arise before a complaint actually gets to a tribunal hearing. There is a provision whereby either party can seek an order from the tribunal requiring the other party to furnish in writing further particulars of his case.[28] Clearly a person who will be appearing before a tribunal should ensure that he has all the necessary documents for the hearing and can rely on all his witnesses agreeing to give evidence on his behalf. However, there may be occasions when necessary documents are in the possession of the other party who should provide them when so requested. If he should fail to do so an application can be made to the tribunal for recovery and inspection of documents (including the right to take copies).[29] Equally, a party who is experiencing trouble ensuring that witnesses attend the hearing can apply to the tribunal for a witness order requiring the attendance of any person as a witness and, where necessary, requiring that person to produce any document relating to the case.[30] A person who fails to comply with an order for recovery

[21] For an exhaustive list of the types of case where ACAS has the power to conciliate see W. Leslie, *Industrial Tribunal Practice in Scotland* (Edinburgh, 1981) at pp. 128-129.

[22] See, for example, ACAS Annual Report for 1988, Table 13 and ACAS Annual Report for 1989, Table 11.

[23] Industrial Tribunals (Rules of Procedure) (Scotland) Regulations 1985, Sch. 1, rule 17(7) and rule 2.

[24] See, for example, EPCA, s. 134(1).

[25] EPCA, s. 134(2).

[26] *Moore v. Duport Furniture Products Ltd* [1982] ICR 84 HL.

[27] See *Hennessy v. Craigmyle & Co* [1986] ICR 461, EAT.

[28] Industrial Tribunals (Rules of Procedure) (Scotland) Regulations 1985, Sch. 1 rules 4(1)(a) and 4(1)(b)(i).

[29] *Ibid.* rule 4(b)(ii). For the procedure which operates in sex and race discrimination cases where documents are claimed to be confidential see the decision of the House of Lords in *Science Research Council v. Nasse* [1979] ICR 921.

[30] *Ibid.* rule 4(b)(iii). The party must state his reasons for the witness order: *Dada v. Metal Box Co Ltd* [1974] ICR 559, NIRC.

and inspection or a witness order can be prosecuted and on summary conviction can be fined up to level 3 on the standard scale.[31] Finally, there may be occasions where it is necessary for the tribunal to convene a preliminary hearing in order to consider a question of jurisdiction. For example, in an unfair dismissal case the respondent may argue that the complainant is not an employee or that he lacks the necessary period of continuous employment in order to make a competent complaint. This issue will have to be decided in the complainant's favour before the case can proceed to a full hearing.

8.9 Pre-hearing assessments

There is one further issue which can arise before a case goes to a full hearing. This concerns the possibility that there will be a preliminary hearing in order to ascertain the prospects of success for either party. At time of writing the procedure regulations provide for a system of pre-hearing assessment whereby a full tribunal can be required by either party or on its own motion at any time before the hearing to consider the contents of the complaint or the defences and any other written or oral representations.[32] If the tribunal decides that one of the parties has no reasonable prospect of success it can indicate to that party that if he continues with his case an order of expenses may be made against him at the full hearing.[33] If the case does proceed to a full hearing the result of the pre-hearing assessment is made available at the end of that hearing to the differently constituted tribunal which heard the case in full. Expenses can be awarded at the full hearing if, in the opinion of the tribunal, a party has in bringing or conducting the proceedings acted frivously, vexatiously or otherwise unreasonably.[34]

8.10 Pre-hearing reviews

There can be no doubt that the system of pre-hearing assessment has not been a success.[35] The procedure was first introduced in 1980 in order to weed out hopeless or ill-founded cases. Yet by the government's own admission the pre-hearing assessment system has not achieved this objective.[36] Accordingly, a consultation paper on tribunal procedure was published in May 1988 which recommended that at the pre-hearing stage either party could be required to pay a deposit of up to £150 as a condition of proceeding further. Section 20 of the Employment Act 1989 gives statutory effect to this recommendation and gives the Secretary of State increased powers to make regulations to provide for a

---

[31] EPCA, s. 128(3), Sch. 9, para. 1(7).

[32] Industrial Tribunals (Rules of Procedure) (Scotland) Regulations 1985, Sch. 1, rule 6(1).

[33] *Ibid.* rule 6(2).

[34] *Ibid.* rule 11(1).

[35] The statistics as regards pre-hearing assessment are discussed in "Industrial Tribunal - An Update" (1991) Department of Employment Gazette 303. This article shows that there were only 517 pre-hearing assessments in Great Britain with an expenses warning being made in 271 cases in 1988-89. The figures for 1989-90 are 545 pre-hearing assessments ordered and 274 expenses warnings. In Scotland the figures are even more stark. In the period from April 1, 1990 to March 31, 1991 there were only 8 pre-hearing assessments. See *Industrial Tribunals in Scotland: Fact Sheet* (May 1991).

[36] See the White Paper *Building Businesses . . . Note Barriers* (1986, Cmnd. 9794). This document recommended the introduction of a fee of £25 for all applicants to industrial tribunals. The fee would be refunded if the applicant was successful. This proposal was withdrawn after consultation with interested parties because many respondents considered that it constituted a tax on justice.

new pre-hearing stage (pre-hearing review) to be carried out by such person as may be determined by the regulations, or by the tribunal itself. In practice, it is likely that pre-hearing reviews will be conducted by the Chairman alone. The regulations will include a provision which will authorise the tribunal at pre-hearing review to make an order requiring a party to the proceedings, if he wishes to continue, to pay a deposit of up to £150.[37] The regulations will also prescribe the manner in which the amount of any such deposit is to be determined, the consequences of non-payment, and the circumstances in which the deposit, or any part of it, may be refunded to the party who paid it, or, alternatively, paid over to the other party.

8.11 The hearing

If a case is to go to full hearing a notice of hearing will be issued by the Secretary of Tribunals at least 14 days before the date fixed. It is the practice of the tribunals in Scotland to consider both the merits of the case and the question of remedies at the hearing, so that the parties should be in a position to lead evidence on both of these points.[38] A party to the hearing may appear in person or be represented by counsel or by a solicitor or by a representative of a trade union or an employers' association or by any other person whom he desires to represent him.[39] Tribunals are encouraged to avoid formality in their proceedings and are not bound by any enactment or rule of law relating to the admissibility of evidence in proceedings before the courts.[40] Despite the informal nature of tribunal hearings, recent studies have suggested that parties who present their own cases still encounter difficulties in case preparation and presentation.[41] In Scotland there are no opening statements at the hearing and witnesses are excluded until they give their evidence on oath or by affirmation.[42] If the applicant fails to appear or be represented at the hearing the tribunal may dismiss his application. Alternatively, and in any other case where a party fails to appear, the tribunal can dispose of the case in the absence of that party or adjourn the hearing to a later date.[43]

8.12 The decision, interest and expenses

As has already been noted, decisions of industrial tribunals can be unanimous or by majority with the chairman only having a second or casting vote in cases where for some reason the tribunal has been reduced to two members.[44] The decision may be given orally at the end of the hearing or reserved, but in either case must be recorded in writing and signed by the chairman.[45] In most cases a tribunal is only required to give its reasons in summary form. However, in

---

[37] EA 1989, s. 20(2) and note the Secretary of State has the power to increase the deposit from time to time.

[38] For the position in England see *Iggesund Converters Ltd v. Lewis* [1984] ICR 544, EAT.

[39] Industrial Tribunals (Rules of Procedure) (Scotland) Regulations 1985, Sch. 1, rule 7(6).

[40] *Ibid.*, rule 8(1).

[41] See generally Linda Dickens *et al Dismissed: A Study of Unfair Dismissal and the Industrial Tribunal System* (Oxford, 1985). This is an issue to which we shall return later in the chapter.

[42] Industrial Tribunals (Rules of Procedure) (Scotland) Regulations 1985, Sch. 1, rule 8(4).

[43] *Ibid.* rule 8(3).

[44] *Ibid.* rule 9(1).

[45] *Ibid.* rule 9(2).

equal pay, sex and race discrimination cases, in cases concerned with union membership reasons, dismissal for pregnancy or the sisting of a third party or where an applicant alleges unreasonable exclusion or expulsion from a trade union, the tribunal is required to record its decision in full.[46] Further, full reasons may be provided in other cases where it appears to the tribunal at any time that they should be given in full or there is a request by one of the parties to the case either at the hearing or within 21 days of the date when the summary reasons were sent to the parties.[47] It is now possible for interest at the rate of 15% to be levied on late payments of compensation awarded by industrial tribunals.[48] It is rare for expenses to be awarded to the successful party after an industrial tribunal hearing.[49] Expenses can only be awarded:

(a) where a party has acted frivolously, vexatiously or otherwise unreasonably;

(b) where the tribunal has postponed or adjourned the hearing on the application of a party and the other party has incurred any expenses; or

(c) where, in an unfair dismissal complaint, an adjournment or postponement has been caused by the respondent's failure to adduce evidence on job availability and the applicant has expressed a wish to be reinstated or re-engaged which has been communicated to the respondent at least seven days before the hearing, or the proceedings arose out of the respondent's failure to permit a return to work after pregnancy.

8.13 Review and appeal

Except in the case of a minor clerical error, the decision of an industrial tribunal can only be altered by review or by means of an appeal to the Employment Appeal Tribunal. A tribunal has the power to review its own decision on the following grounds:

(a) the decision was wrongly made because of an error by the tribunal staff;

(b) a party did not receive notice of the proceedings leading to the decision;

(c) the decision was made in the absence of one of the parties;

(d) new evidence has become available since the decision provided that its existence could not have been reasonably known of or foreseen;

(e) the interests of justice require such a review.[50]

An application for review may be made at the hearing or at any time until 14 days after the date when the decision is sent to the parties.[51] If, in the opinion of the president or the chairman of the tribunal, the application has a reasonable prospect of success, a full tribunal will be convened which may confirm, vary or revoke the earlier decision.[52] The purpose of review is to enable the tribunal to reconsider its decision in the light of some procedural error or the discovery

---

[46] *Ibid.* rule 9(5)(a).

[47] *Ibid.* rule 9(5)(b)-(d).

[48] See Industrial Tribunal (Interest) Order 1990 (SI 1990 No. 479) which provides for interest to be applied after 42 days from the date that the decision is sent to the parties.

[49] In 1988/89 expenses were awarded by the tribunals in Britain in only 207 cases and in 1989-90 this figure was 185. See "Industrial Tribunals - An Update" (1991) Department of Employment Gazette 303.

[50] Industrial Tribunals (Rules of Procedure) (Scotland) Regulations 1985, Sch. 1, rule 10(1)(a)-(e).

[51] *Ibid.* rule 10(2).

[52] *Ibid.* rules 10(3) and (4).

of new evidence, it is not intended as a means of providing a dissatisfied party with a second opportunity to succeed before the tribunal.[53]

EMPLOYMENT APPEAL TRIBUNAL

8.14 General

The Employment Appeal Tribunal was first established in 1975[54] and continues to operate under the powers conferred upon it by the Employment Protection (Consolidation) Act 1978.[55] It is a superior court of record[56] and is a tripartite body like the industrial tribunals. It consists of a number of judges of the High Court or Court of Appeal who are nominated by the Lord Chancellor, at least one judge of the Court of Session nominated by the Lord President, and a number of other members (the appointed members) who are appointed by the Queen on the joint recommendation of the Lord Chancellor and Secretary of State.[57] The appointed members are persons who appear to the Lord Chancellor and Secretary of State to have special knowledge or experience of industrial relations, either as representatives of employers or as representatives of workers.[58] A hearing of the Employment Appeal Tribunal will be made up of a judicial member who acts as chairman and usually two, although possibly four, appointed members taken in the same proportion from each side of industry.[59] Decisions can be by majority. The Employment Appeal Tribunal has a central office in London and a Scottish office in Edinburgh although it can sit anywhere in Great Britain.[60] The members of the Employment Appeal Tribunal can also sit anywhere in Great Britain and it is not unusual for the President of the Employment Appeal Tribunal, an English judge, to sit in Edinburgh. A party may appear before the Employment Appeal Tribunal in person or be represented by counsel or by a solicitor or by a representative of a trade union or employers' association or by any other person.[61] Expenses can only be awarded if, in the opinion of the Employment Appeal Tribunal, the proceedings were unnecessary, improper or vexatious, or there was unreasonable delay or other unreasonable conduct in bringing or conducting them.[62]

8.15 The principal task of the Employment Appeal Tribunal is to hear appeals on points of law from decisions of the industrial tribunals.[63] It also hears ap-

---

[53] *Flint v. Eastern Electricity Board* [1975] ICR 395.

[54] EPCA, S. 87.

[55] EPCA, ss. 135, 136.

[56] EPCA, s. 135 and Sch. 11, para. 12.

[57] EPCA, s. 135(2).

[58] EPCA, s. 135(3).

[59] EPCA, Sch. 11, para. 16. For examples of a tribunal of 5 see *Webb v. Emo Air Cargo (UK) Ltd* [1990] IRLR 124 and *Enderby v. Frenchay Health Authority,* [1991] IRLR 44.

[60] EPCA, Sch. 11, paras. 13 and 14.

[61] EPCA, Sch. 11, para. 20.

[62] EPCA, Sch. 11, para. 19.

[63] EPCA, s. 136(1). It might appear surprising that there should be two laypersons sitting on a tribunal which is hearing appeals on points of law. However, the President of the EAT, Sir John Wood, has argued that the appointed members are essential. He argued that it is the mix of experience in industrial problems, coupled with their knowledge of industrial practice and the ways in which the law is being seen to be worked that is all important. He also saw their role as vital in cases of considerable factual complexity. See "The Employment Appeal Tribunal as it Enters the 1990s" (1990) 19 ILJ 133.

peals on questions of law from decisions of the certification officer under the Trade Union Act 1913 and Trade Unions (Amalgamations, Etc.) Act 1964 and appeals on questions of law and fact from his decisions under the Trade Union and Labour Relations Act 1974, s. 8 (listing of trade unions) and the Employment Protection Act 1975, s. 8 (certificates of independence).[64] Appeals on questions of fact or law are also competent from industrial tribunals under the Employment Act 1980, ss. 4 & 5 (unreasonable exclusion or expulsion from a trade union). The Employment Appeal Tribunal also exercises a limited originating jurisdiction to determine applications for compensation under the Employment Acts 1980, s. 5 and 1988, s. 5 (right not to be unjustifiably disciplined). There is a further right of appeal on a point of law with leave of the Employment Appeal Tribunal or Court of Session, to the Inner House of the Court of Session.[65]

8.16 Errors of law

In *Watling v. William Bird & Son (Contractors) Ltd*[66] Phillips J. declared that proving an error of law on the part of the tribunal entailed the appellant establishing one or more of the following:

(a) that the tribunal misdirected itself in law, misunderstood the law or misapplied the law; or

(b) that it misunderstood the facts or misapplied the facts; or

(c) that the decision was either perverse or that there was no evidence to justify the conclusion which was reached.

In a similar vein, Lord President Emslie declared in *Melon v. Hector Powe Ltd*[67] as follows:

"The law is clear that where it cannot be shown that the tribunal of original jurisdiction has either misdirected itself in law, entertained the wrong issue, or proceeded upon a misapprehension or misconstruction of the evidence, or taken into account matters which were irrelevant to its decision, or has reached a decision so extravagant that no reasonable tribunal properly directing itself on the law could have arrived at, then its decision is not open to successful attack. It is of no consequence that the appellate tribunal or court would itself have reached a different conclusion on the evidence."

8.17 Misdirection

Clearly, the simplest error to detect is that disclosed by head (a). This head would cover such obvious errors as a wrong construction of a statutory provision or a misapplication of its terms. The other two types of error are more difficult to classify; particularly since there has been a tendency over the last ten years for the Employment Appeal Tribunal and the appeal courts to narrow the grounds of appeal. Indeed, since the decision of the Court of Appeal in *Sheridan v. British Telecommunications Plc*[68] it is doubtful whether head (b) can still be classified as a separate ground. Here it was argued that head (b)

---

[64] EPCA, s. 136(2) and (3).
[65] EPCA, s. 136(4). In England and Wales there is a right of appeal to the Court of Appeal.
[66] (1976) 11 ITR 70.
[67] *Melon v. Hector Powe Ltd* [1980] IRLR 80 at p. 82 approved by Lord Fraser of Tullybelton on appeal to the House of Lords at [1980] IRLR 477.
[68] [1990] IRLR 27.

was not a separate category and thus not a sufficient ground for appeal unless the misunderstanding or misapplication amounted to an error of law on the basis that there was no evidence to support it. This view appears to merge the second and third heads of appeal. Certainly, this was the position adopted by McCowan L.J. in *Sheridan* who, when discussing the three heads, declared —

"I have no difficulty in understanding and accepting the first and third, but I am bound to say for my part I have difficulty in accepting the second as a separate category. Either the second means nothing more than the third, or it means something less. If the latter, I would respectfully doubt if it can be right since this would suggest that the EAT is entitled to allow an appeal if it takes a different view of the facts from that of the Industrial Tribunal."[69]

8.18 Perversity

As far as head (c) is concerned, the traditional test for perversity is to show that no reasonable tribunal properly directing itself could, upon the facts before it, have come to the conclusion which it did.[70] It is vital that when the Employment Appeal Tribunal applies this test it ensures that it does not substitute its own views for those of the industrial tribunal. This significant factor has caused the appellate courts to take a narrow view of what amounts to a perverse decision. In *Retarded Children's Aid Society Ltd v. Day*[71] the Court of Appeal approved the statement of the Employment Appeal Tribunal that it would be a very rare case indeed for the Employment Appeal Tribunal to conclude that a tribunal had arrived at a result not tenable by any reasonable tribunal properly directed in law. Moreover, Russell L.J. in the same case counselled the Employment Appeal Tribunal to avoid "searching around with a fine tooth-comb" for a point of law so as it could take a different view from that of the industrial tribunal.

This reluctance to interfere with the decisions of industrial tribunals has been a major aspect of statutory employment law in the 1980s. In *Spook Erection Ltd v. Thackray*,[72] for example, the Second Division reminded the Employment Appeal Tribunal that the adequacy of an employer's procedures in an unfair dismissal case is essentially a question of fact for the tribunal to decide and re-emphasised that the Employment Appeal Tribunal could only overrule the tribunal when it had moved outside the range of reasonable decisions open to a reasonable tribunal. Finally, May L.J. in the Court of Appeal in *Hereford and Worcester County Council v. Neale*[73] argued that there was an instinctive element to the question of perversity when he stated that an appellate body should

---

[69] *Ibid.* at p. 29.

[70] See, for example, *Global Plant Hire Ltd v. Secretary of State for Social Services* [1972] 1 QB 139 and for its application in the context of industrial tribunals see *Palmer v. Vauxhall Motors Ltd* [1977] ICR 24 where the EAT also applied the dicta of Lord Radcliffe in *Edwards v. Bairstow* [1956] AC 14 at p. 36.

[71] [1978] ICR 437. For a recent Scottish case where the EAT was held to have substituted its views for those of the tribunal see *Scottish Midland Co-operative Society v. Cullion* [1991] IRLR 261 IH.

[72] [1984] IRLR 116 where the Second Division applied the statement of Lord President Emslie in *Melon v. Hector Powe Ltd* [1980] IRLR 80.

[73] [1986] IRLR 168. The Court of Appeal has warned of the dangers of this approach in *Piggott Bros & Co Ltd v. Jackson, The Times,* May 20, 1991 where it was stated that to find a decision perverse the appeal tribunal must be able to identify a finding of fact unsupported by any evidence or a clear misdirection in law.

only reverse a tribunal's decision if it could be said "My goodness, that was certainly wrong"!

THE COURTS AND THE TRIBUNALS

8.19 Legalism
It has already been suggested in this chapter that industrial tribunals have been criticised for operating in an unnecessarily legalistic manner. Although it is arguable that the Scottish industrial tribunals have avoided some of the worst aspects of legalism in comparison with their counterparts in England and Wales, it is still the case that the industrial tribunal system has been criticised for not delivering the levels of accessibility, informality, speed and lack of expense as had been hoped. The question of legalism has been raised at two levels. First, there is the question of the complex nature of the employment laws which tribunals are required to interpret and apply. Second, it has been argued that the physical arrangements for hearings, the tribunal procedure itself and the requirement that tribunals rely upon the adversarial system all contribute towards an atmosphere which inhibits parties (and applicants, in particular) from arguing their own cases.[74] ACAS has also been concerned about the growth of legal representation before industrial tribunals. The Annual Report for 1989, for example, declared "1989 saw mounting concern about the nature of proceedings in some industrial tribunal jurisdictions and the expenses often incurred by the parties in bringing and defending cases. In part this derived from the apparently irreversible increase in the use of legal representation in many jurisdictions, which was a feature of the decade as a whole; and which undoubtedly led to an increase in the time taken to clear applications".[75]

8.20 Issues of fact
Judges and policy-makers have been aware of these criticisms of the industrial tribunals. Attempts have been made to speed up the procedure before tribunals. For example, as has already been noted, the procedure regulations were amended in 1985 to permit tribunals to give their reasons in summary form in certain types of case and the introduction of a system of pre-hearing scrutiny must be viewed, in part, as an attempt to reduce the burden of cases on tribunals.[76] As far as the judges are concerned they have responded principally to the first charge that tribunals administer an area of law which is now too complex. Their response has taken a number of different forms. First, there has been a tendency to categorise most issues as questions of fact, thus limiting the opportunities for appeal to the Employment Appeal Tribunal. This is an issue which permeates

---

[74] These points are discussed in much more detail in Linda Dickens *et al Dismissed: A Study of Unfair Dismissal and the Industrial Tribunal System* (Oxford 1985); the Justice *Report on Industrial Tribunals* (1987) and Hazel Genn & Yvette Genn *The Effectiveness of Representation at Tribunals: A Report to the Lord Chancellor* (1989).

[75] ACAS Annual Report for 1989 at p. 17. In Scotland in 1990/91 35.0 per cent of applicants were legally represented at industrial tribunal hearings and 56.1 per cent of respondents had legal representation. See *Industrial Tribunals in Scotland: Fact Sheet* (May 1991).

[76] There is also a procedure in England and Wales whereby appeals to the EAT can be scheduled for a preliminary listing in order to assess whether or not the appeal discloses a genuine point of law. See EAT Listing Direction 1985. The procedure does not apply in Scotland.

most of the statutory employment protection laws but is most noticeable as regards such questions as to whether or not an applicant is an employee,[77] whether or not an employer has acted reasonably when dismissing an employee,[78] and the meaning of justifiable in cases of indirect discrimination.[79] This determination to leave most issues to be determined by the tribunal as a finding of fact is no better illustrated than by the case law as to whether employees were dismissed while taking part in industrial action.[80] Much of the uncertainty in this area has been fuelled by the reluctance of the EAT and the appellate courts to classify disputes over the meaning of many of the key statutory words and phrases as disclosing questions of law.

8.21 Errors of law

This tendency to classify issues as raising pure questions of fact has been taking place in tandem with another theme prevalent in appellate decisions of the last ten years *viz* the narrowing of the definition of an error of law. As we noted in the last section, doubts have been cast on the width of application of Phillips J.'s definition of an error of law in *Watling*. In many cases a potential appellant's only means of appeal is to argue that the decision is perverse. However, as was noted in *Regarded Children's Aid Society Ltd v. Day*[81] it will be rare for the Employment Appeal Tribunal to hold that an industrial tribunal has reached a decision which is so perverse that no reasonable tribunal, properly instructed as to the relevant law, could have come to.

8.22 Guidelines

Finally on this issue, the view that industrial tribunals should be left to reach their own decisions as industrial juries has also led in recent years to a discouragement of guideline authorities. There was a time, particularly in the early years of the Employment Appeal Tribunal, when it was prepared to give guidance to the tribunals as to how they should interpret some of the key provisions of statutory employment law. This was intended ". . . to introduce into the decisions of something over 60 industrial tribunals up and down the country, dealing day after day with questions of this kind something in the nature of a uniform approach".[82] This tactic ensured that the tribunals were briefed properly on the legal issues and also brought some certainty to the law. On the other hand, it had the effect of developing a large body of case law in an area where lay people were encouraged to participate and, so it was argued, of encouraging the likelihood of appeals. The guideline approach to employment issues was criticised by the Court of Appeal in *Bailey v. BP Oil (Kent Refinery) Ltd*[83] where Lawton L.J. reminded tribunals that

---

[77] *O'Kelly v. Trusthouse Forte plc* [1983] ICR 728 CA; *Nethermere (St Neots) Ltd v. Taverna* [1984] ICR 614 CA. See also *Lee v. Chung* [1990] IRLR 236 where the Judicial Committee of the Privy Council approved the statement of the law in *O'Kelly* and declared that where the relationship is to be determined by an investigation and evaluation of the factual circumstances in which the work is performed, the question should be regarded by an appellate court as one of fact to be determined by the trial court.

[78] *Spook Erection Ltd v. Thackray* [1984] IRLR 116 IH.

[79] See, for example, *Greater Glasgow Health Board v. Carey* [1987] IRLR 484, EAT.

[80] See, for example, *Coates and Venables v. Modern Methods & Materials Ltd* [1982] ICR 763 CA; *Naylor v. Orton & Smith Ltd* [1983] IRLR 233 EAT.

[81] [1978] ICR 437, CA.

[82] Phillips J. "Some Notes on the Employment Appeal Tribunal" (1978) 7 ILJ 137.

[83] [1980] ICR 642.

each case must depend upon its own facts and argued that it was wrong for either the Court of Appeal or Employment Appeal Tribunal to set out guidelines, to make rules or to establish presumptions. The attack on guideline authority was supported by Waite J. when he was President of the Employment Appeal Tribunal. He was concerned to prevent the growth of legalism before industrial tribunals and to create an environment where lay people could conduct their cases with the same confidence as professional representatives. In the view of Waite J. a preoccupation with guideline authority put this objective in jeopardy. He considered that "[i]t should seldom be necessary (and may sometimes even be unwise) for an industrial tribunal to frame its decisions by reference to any direction other than the express terms of the statute".[84]

8.23 Guidelines in Scotland

If anything, the Employment Appeal Tribunal in Scotland and the Court of Session have had even less respect for guideline authority. The traditions of the Scottish legal system with its reliance on principle rather than precedent have had an impact on the conduct of employment law cases before the industrial tribunals. Thus the question of guideline authority has been less of an issue in Scotland since there has not been the same tendency to cite a plethora of previous decisions to the tribunals. Equally, the Employment Appeal Tribunal in Scotland and the Court of Session have considered that tribunals need little guidance beyond the statutory language for the meaning of the key concepts such as fairness or reasonableness. Thus perhaps the most well-known of the remaining guideline cases, *Williams v. Compair Maxam Ltd*,[85] which deals with the reasonableness of the employer's procedures on redundancy, has not received wholehearted backing in Scotland.[86]

8.24 Re-emergence of guidelines?

Nonetheless, it may be that under the current president of the Employment Appeal Tribunal, Wood J., the value of guideline authority is being reappraised. In a recent article,[87] Wood J. argued that there was some virtue for the industrial tribunals to have access to what he referred to as "guidance cases". These were cases where the Employment Appeal Tribunal was not necessarily indicating how the law could properly be applied, but rather indicating industrial practice. In this regard, Wood J. placed particular importance on the role of the lay members as people with experience of industrial relations and argued that their views ". . . are given with one voice, it is the expression of opinion from *both* sides of industry and to seek to eliminate these cases is, to my mind, to waste the reservoir of experience which is contained within the Employment Appeal Tribunal".[88] There are already a number of cases where the Employment Appeal Tribunal, with Wood J. as the judicial member, has sought to provide guidance on good practice for employers as regards dismissal procedures. In

---

[84] *Anandarajah v. Lord Chancellor's Department* [1984] IRLR 131. See also "Lawyers and Laymen as Judges in Industry" (1986) 15 ILJ 32.

[85] [1982] ICR 156, EAT.

[86] See, for example, *Buchanan v. Tilcon Ltd* [1983] IRLR 417, IH; *A Simpson & Son (Motors) Ltd v. Reid* [1983] IRLR 401, EAT; *Meikle v. McPhail (Charleston Arms)* [1983] IRLR 351, EAT.

[87] "The Employment Appeal Tribunal as it Enters the 1990s" (1990) 19 ILJ 133.

[88] *Ibid.* at p. 139.

Linfood Cash & Carry Ltd v. Thomson,[89] for example, the Employment Appeal Tribunal provided a tenpoint guide on the steps that an employer might take when dealing with allegations about an employee's conduct!

ACAS

8.25 Although ACAS came into operation in 1974 its constitution and powers are regulated by statute.[90] ACAS has the general duty of promoting the improvement of industrial relations, and in particular of encouraging the extension of collective bargaining machinery.[91] It is directed by a council which consists of a full-time chairman and nine other members appointed by the Secretary of State (although there is power to increase this number to 15). The ACAS Council conforms to the traditional tripartite arrangements for British industrial relations bodies since of the nine other members three are selected from organisations representing employers, three from trade unions and three are independent people such as academics. ACAS cannot be subject to directions from any minister as to the way in which it exercises its functions and has the authority to appoint its own staff subject to the consent of the Secretary of State as to numbers.[92] It has a head office in London and a regional office for Scotland in Glasgow. There is also a Welsh regional office in Cardiff and seven regional areas in England. ACAS is required to make an annual report on its activities and those of the CAC to the Secretary of State, which will be laid before Parliament and published.

8.26 Conciliation — general

ACAS exercises conciliation functions in relation to collective labour disputes and also provides conciliation facilities for a wide range of industrial tribunal complaints. As regards collective conciliation, where a trade dispute exists or is apprehended ACAS may, at the request of one of the parties to the dispute or of its own volition, offer its assistance to the parties with a view to bringing about a settlement.[93] This assistance will be by conciliation or by other means, and may include the appointment of a person from outside the service to settle the dispute.[94] ACAS is also directed when exercising its collective conciliation functions to have regard to the desirability of encouraging the parties to use any appropriate agreed procedures for negotiation or settlement of disputes.[95] It is clear that use of these facilities is voluntary. This means that ACAS does not normally intervene in a collective dispute unless and until any agreed procedures for direct negotiations or for the resolution of difficulties by internal appeals machinery have been exhausted. ACAS has noted that it is becoming increasingly common for reference to its facilities to be written into agreed procedures as the final stage for the settlement of disputes.[96]

---

[89] [1989] IRLR 235. See also *Whitbread & Co plc v. Mills* [1988] IRLR 501, EAT.

[90] EPA, ss. 1-6, Sch. 1.

[91] *Ibid.* s. 1(2).

[92] *Ibid.* s. 1 and Sch. 1 paras. 6-8 and para. 11.

[93] ACAS still maintains a wide authority to offer conciliation facilities in trade disputes since the narrowing of the definition of a trade dispute in TULRA, s. 29(1) which was introduced by EA 1982, s. 18 does not apply to ACAS. The original definition of a trade dispute is maintained for ACAS duties by EPA, s. 126A(1).

[94] EPA, s. 2(2).

[95] *Ibid.* s. 2(3).

[96] ACAS Annual Report for 1989, ch. 2.

8.27 Conciliation and industrial tribunals

ACAS also has a duty to conciliate in complaints presented to industrial tribunals alleging unfair dismissal, breaches of statutory employment protection rights (but not redundancy payments),[97] failures to consult trade unions on proposed redundancies, breaches of the equal pay and sex and race discrimination legislation, breaches of the Wages Act 1986 and complaints of unreasonable exclusion and expulsion from a trade union, unjustifiable union disciplinary action and refusal of employment on grounds related to trade union membership. In Scotland the Secretary of Tribunals sends copies of all the relevant documents to the Scottish regional office of ACAS and informs the parties of the availability of ACAS's conciliation services. A conciliation officer can endeavour to promote a settlement of a complaint without it being determined by the tribunal if, either, he is requested to do by both the complainant and the respondent or, in the absence of such request, where the officer considers that he has a reasonable prospect of success.[98] ACAS also has the authority to conciliate in cases which have not been presented to industrial tribunals so long as the case entails a matter which could form the basis of a tribunal complaint and provided that either of the parties to the dispute has requested the services of the conciliation officer[99] and such cases have become an increasingly important element of ACAS's individual conciliation caseload.[100] The success of the conciliation process requires that the parties and ACAS recognise the confidential nature of their discussions. Accordingly, anything communicated to a conciliation officer in connection with his conciliation functions shall not be admissible in evidence before a tribunal, except with the consent of that person.[101]

8.28 Arbitration

ACAS does not actually conduct any arbitrations. Instead, it has the authority, where a trade dispute exists or is apprehended, at the request of one or more of the parties and with the consent of all of them, to refer all or any matters to which the dispute relates for settlement by arbitration either by persons appointed by ACAS but who are neither officers nor employees of the service or by the CAC.[102] In deciding whether to refer a matter to arbitration ACAS must consider the likelihood of the dispute being settled by conciliation, and where there are appropriate agreed procedures for negotiation must not refer a matter to arbitration until these procedures have been exhausted unless there is a special reason which justifies arbitration.[103] ACAS's ability to refer a matter to arbitration depends upon the agreement of all the parties and is therefore a voluntary process so that the arbitration award is not legally binding on the parties. Nonetheless, it is the policy of ACAS, when arbitration is being sought, to ask the parties to give an unqualified undertaking that the arbiter's award will be accepted as settling the disputed issue.[104] ACAS reported in its Annual Report for 1989 that after a number of years when arbitration had been in decline that there appeared to be a renewed awareness of the potential benefits of arbitration

---

[97] See generally EPCA, s. 133.
[98] EPCA, s. 133(2).
[99] *Ibid.* s. 133(3).
[100] ACAS Annual Report for 1989, ch. 4.
[101] EPCA, s. 133(6).
[102] EPA, s. 3(1).
[103] *Ibid.* s. 3(2).
[104] See generally ACAS Annual Report for 1989, ch. 3.

and mediation. One particular development in the field of arbitration has been the growth of "pendulum" or "straight choice" arbitration.[105] This system reduces the flexibility of the arbitration process by requiring the arbiter to choose one or other of the two competing propositions advanced by the parties. ACAS believes that pendulum arbitration is much better suited to non-pay issues. However, where the dispute is over pay its advantages are less clear because of its inhibiting effect upon employer/union negotiations.

8.29 Advice

ACAS has very broad powers to provide free advice to employers, employers' associations, workers and trade unions, on request or of its own volition, on any matter concerned with industrial relations or employment policies. Such advice may include the following:

(a) the organisation of workers or employers for collective bargaining purposes;

(b) trade union recognition;

(c) negotiation machinery and joint consultation;

(d) disputes machinery and grievance procedures;

(e) questions relating to communications between employers and workers;

(f) facilities for trade union officials;

(g) procedures relating to the termination of employment;

(h) disciplinary matters;

(i) manpower planning;

(j) recruitment, retention, promotion and vocational training;

(k) payment systems.[106]

ACAS can also publish general advice on any matter concerned with industrial relations. It has used this power extensively to produce advisory booklets, handbooks and occasional papers.[107] ACAS believes that its general duty to promote the improvement of industrial relations lies at the heart of its advisory work. It has also used this function as a means of encouraging the growth and assisting the development of employee involvement in business.[108]

8.30 Inquiry

ACAS may, if it thinks fit, inquire into any question relating to industrial relations generally or to industrial relations in any particular industry, undertaking or part of an undertaking.[109] The findings of any such inquiry may be published.

8.31 Codes of Practice

ACAS is authorised to issue Codes of Practice containing practical guidance for the purpose of promoting the improvement of industrial relations.[110] When ACAS proposes to issue a Code it must first prepare and publish a draft of that Code and must consider any representations about the draft and may modify it ac-

---

[105] For an analysis of the growth of pendulum arbitration in Britain see Roy Lewis "Strike-free Deals and Pendulum Arbitration" (1990) 28 BJIR 32.

[106] EPA, s. 4(1).

[107] Over half a million copies of two Handbooks *Employing People* and *Discipline at Work* have been printed to date. See Annual Report for 1989, ch. 5.

[108] *Ibid.* ch. 5.

[109] EPA, s. 5(1).

[110] *Ibid.* s. 6(1).

cordingly.[111] Thereafter the draft will be transmitted to the Secretary of State who may either approve of it, in which case it will be laid before both Houses of Parliament, or if he does not approve of the draft, publish details of his reason for withholding approval.[112] So long as no resolution is passed by either House negativing the draft, ACAS will issue the Code in the form of the draft and the Code will come into effect on such day as the Secretary of State by order appoints.[113] A failure on the part of any person to observe any provision of a Code of Practice does not of itself render that person liable to any proceedings; but in any proceedings before an industrial tribunal or the CAC any ACAS Code is admissible in evidence, and if any provision of the Code appears to the tribunal or the CAC to be relevant it will be taken into account.[114] Currently, ACAS has issued three Codes of Practice — on Disciplinary Practices and Procedures, Disclosure of Information to Trade Unions for Collective Bargaining Purposes and on Time Off for Trade Union Duties and Activities, (reissued in revised form in May 1991). In 1987 ACAS sought to revise and expand its Code of Practice on Disciplinary Procedures. However, the Secretary of State did not approve of it and so the original Code which came into force on 20 June 1977 continues to operate.[115]

CAC

8.32 The Central Arbitration Committee was formerly the Industrial Arbitration Board and before that the Industrial Court. It consists of a chairman appointed by the Secretary of State after consultation with ACAS and other members who are appointed by the Secretary of State from persons nominated by ACAS because of their experience of industrial relations.[116] The CAC's functions are performed on behalf of the Crown, but it is not subject to directions of any kind from any minister as to the manner in which it exercises those functions.[117] The CAC was intended to be an arbitration body which exercised a wide authority over a number of different statutory matters. However, the legislation of the 1980s has denuded the committee of many of its functions. Currently, it possesses the power to arbitrate in two circumstances. First, it can arbitrate on a matter which has been referred to it by ACAS at the request and with the consent of all the parties.[118] Second, it can adjudicate on complaints by independent trade unions alleging failures by employers to disclose information for collective bargaining purposes.[119]

---

[111] *Ibid.* s. 6(3).
[112] *Ibid.* s. 6(4).
[113] *Ibid.* s. 6(8).
[114] *Ibid.* s. 6(11).
[115] It should also be remembered that the Secretary of State has the power to issue Codes of Practice for certain matters. He has issued Codes on Picketing, Closed Shop Agreements and Arrangements and on Trade Union Ballots on Industrial Action.
[116] EPA, s. 10 and Sch. 1, para. 14. The CAC must include some members whose experience is as employers' representatives and others who have represented workers.
[117] *Ibid.* s. 10 and Sch. 1, para. 27.
[118] *Ibid.* s. 3(1)(b).
[119] See generally EPA, s. 19.

Chapter Nine

THE LAW OF COLLECTIVE BARGAINING

INTRODUCTION

9.1 The unique feature of the system of industrial relations operative in Britain is the limited extent to which the law directly regulates collective bargaining between employers and trade unions. In the past the attitude of the State has been to create an environment where the law provides as much support as it can towards the promotion and furtherance of collective bargaining but interferes as little as possible in the actual process. Thus, unlike the United States and Canada, for example, there has never been a legal duty upon trade unions and employers to bargain collectively in this country. The approach of the law has been to eschew any involvement in the collective bargaining process. This approach has been described by Kahn-Freund as a system of "collective laissez-faire".[1]

9.2 Voluntarism

In 1968 the Donovan Commission Report considered that the distinctive feature of British industrial relations was the extent to which the state remained aloof from the process of collective bargaining in private industry.[2] However, the report identified serious problems with British collective bargaining arising from the conflict between the formal system of industry wide bargaining and the informal system of plant level bargaining. Yet Donovan recognised that collective bargaining had to be supported and promoted by the state since it constituted the most fair and effective means of settling terms and conditions of employment. Consequently, the commission's recommendations for reform were not based on the belief that the traditional system should be abandoned but rather on a need to ensure its voluntary reform and extension. One important recommendation consistent when this objective was that there should be a statutory agency, the Industrial Relations Commission, charged with encouraging employers and trade unions to improve their bargaining arrangements themselves without reference to external interference. Equally, further statutory supports to collective bargaining were recommended such as the authority to be given to the Industrial Relations Commission to deal with recognition disputes, the relaxation of the rules permitting the abolition of Wages Councils where it could be established that voluntary collective bargaining could operate effectively, and the extension of the authority of the industrial court (now the Central Arbitration Committee) to hear complaints over the refusal by an employer to observe relevant terms and conditions.[3]

---

[1] Otto Kahn-Freund, "Labour Law" in M. Ginsberg (ed.), *Law and Opinion in England in the 20th Century* at p. 224.

[2] Report of the Royal Commission on Trade Unions and Employers Associations (the Donovan Report) Cmnd. 3623, at para. 39.

[3] See generally the Donovan Report, Chapter V.

9.3 Statutory intervention

The approach of the Donovan Commission, therefore, reflected the view that the voluntarist nature of British collective bargaining should not only continue but be encouraged. The Industrial Relations Act 1971, however, rejected this philosophy in favour of one which supported the improvement of collective bargaining by creating a legal framework to ensure that the parties acted in a reasonable and responsible way towards each other.[4] This legal framework was swiftly repealed by legislation passed by the incoming Labour government in 1974,[5] following which there was developed and enacted a series of statutory supports to collective bargaining along lines similar to those recommended by the Donovan Commission. Some of these were enacted as part of the government's stated preference for collective bargaining as the exclusive means for setting terms and conditions of employment at the workplace.[6] Others were enacted as part of the obligations placed upon the United Kingdom as a member of the European Economic Community.[7]

The most important statutory supports which were enacted during this period were as follows:

(a) the power of the Advisory Conciliation and Arbitration Service (ACAS) to have a request for recognition referred to it by an independent trade union and to investigate and report;[8]

(b) the right of recognised independent trade unions to seek disclosure of information for the purpose of collective bargaining;[9]

(c) the duty imposed upon employers to consult with representatives of recognised independent trade unions as regards redundancies.[10]

9.4 As well as this, new and increased powers were enacted which complemented and built upon a number of existing legislative provisions encouraging the extension of collective bargaining. Legislation was introduced, for example, to extend the work of Wages Councils.[11] This not only extended the scope of Wages Councils to make orders applying to other terms and conditions apart from wages and holidays but also made provision for the creation of Statutory Joint Industrial Councils which were supposed to act as halfway houses between the regulated forum of the Wages Council and free collective bargaining.[12] Legislation enhanced the jurisdiction of the Central Arbitration Committee (CAC) by not only continuing its existing power to hear complaints by unions that employers were observing terms and conditions of employment which were less favourable than recognised terms, but also by giving it the right to

---

[4] Although the Industrial Relations Act created a procedure for union recognition (IRA, ss. 45-55) it also presumed that collective agreements were legally binding (IRA, ss. 34-35). See Thomson and Engleman, *The Industrial Relations Act: A Review and Analysis* at pp. 126-7.

[5] TULRA, s. 1 and s. 25.

[6] Encapsulated in statutory form by the direction to ACAS in EPA, s. 1(2) to encourage the extension of collective bargaining.

[7] As we shall see, some of the present statutory supports to collective bargaining only exist because of the U.K.'s duty to implement EEC Directives.

[8] EPA, ss. 11-16.

[9] *Ibid.* ss. 17-21.

[10] *Ibid.* ss. 99-107 based on EEC Council Directive No. 75/129.

[11] See EPA, ss. 89-96 and later, Wages Councils Act 1979.

[12] Wages Councils Act 1979, s. 10.

hear a wider type of complaint.[13] This operated so that in the absence of recognised terms a union could also complain that the employer was observing terms less favourable than the general level of terms and conditions in the particular trade, industry or section.[14] The CAC also had jurisdiction under the Fair Wages Resolution 1946 to arbitrate on claims that a government contractor was failing to observe terms and conditions recognised in the industry or area. It is clear from the above that the government believed that this indirect approach was the best way of extending collective bargaining.

9.5 Moreover a number of statutory rights were also created or developed which although applying to individual employees only acquired true significance through the organisational strength of trade unions at the collective level.[15] Their purpose, therefore, was to protect and encourage union organisation at the workplace. The most important of the statutory rights which were created at this time and which applied to the individual employee but which really only have significance where a trade union was recognised by an employer for collective bargaining purposes were as follows:

(a) the right not to be dismissed or to have action short of dismissal taken on the grounds of trade union membership or activities;[16]

(b) the right given to an employee who is a union official to time off with pay in order to carry out trade union duties;[17] and

(c) the right given to an employee to unpaid time off to take part in trade union activities.[18]

The legislation of this time also sought to improve and strengthen union security arrangements. The most important example of this aspect of the law concerned the provisions in the Employment Protection (Consolidation) Act 1978 on the closed shop. These authorised the creation of union membership agreements and made dismissal for non-union membership unfair only in the special circumstance of the religious objector.[19]

PRESENT LEGAL FRAMEWORK

9.6 The decade of the 1980s has seen the disappearance or erosion of many of these statutory supports. The power that ACAS formerly enjoyed to recommend that a union be recognised by an employer for collective bargaining purposes has been repealed.[20] (There was no doubt that some of the early court decisions created difficulties for ACAS in the exercise of its functions over union recognition;[21] indeed, the chairman of ACAS was moved to argue in a letter to the

---

[13] EPA, Sch. 11, para. 1 repealing Terms and Conditions of Employment Act 1959, s. 8. See B. Bercusson, "The New Fair Wages Policy: Schedule 11 to the Employment Protection Act" (1976) 5 ILJ 129.

[14] EPA, Sch. 11, para. 2(b).

[15] Lord Wedderburn, *Worker and the Law*, 3rd edn., pp. 309-310.

[16] EPCA, ss. 58 and 23-26.

[17] *Ibid.* s. 27.

[18] *Ibid.* s. 28.

[19] TULRA, s. 30(1) and EPCA, s. 58.

[20] EA 1980, s. 19.

[21] *Powley v. ACAS* [1978] ICR 123; *Grunwick Processing Laboratories Ltd v. ACAS* [1978] ICR 231, HL; *UKAPE v. ACAS* [1979] ICR 303, CA. See generally R. Simpson, "Judicial Control of ACAS" (1979) 8 ILJ 69.

then Secretary of State for Employment in 1979 that the procedures could no longer operate satisfactorily.[22]) This repeal has meant that at the present moment there is no legal provision creating a regime for the compulsory recognition of trade unions in Great Britain.[23] As was noted in Chapter Eight, while ACAS still retains some authority over union recognition questions through its statutory power to provide conciliation or other assistance to parties involved in a trade dispute,[24] few of the measures enacted by previous governments and aimed at the encouragement of collective bargaining remain on the statute book.

9.7 The role of the law

ACAS still has the general duty of promoting the improvement of industrial relations, and in particular of encouraging the extension of collective bargaining.[25] However, other legislative changes of the 1980s could be considered as being inconsistent with the continued support for the merits of collective bargaining. It appears that the continuance of collective bargaining in its present form is no longer a primary objective. Instead, other priorities have underpinned much of the government's legislation of the 1980s.[26] Some of the changes such as those prohibiting union membership or union recognition requirements in contracts[27] can be viewed as examples of a policy of legal restriction of trade unions. Other changes such as the substantial limitations placed upon the operation of Wages Councils by the Wages Act 1986 and the government's recent suggestion[28] that they be abolished completely illustrate the government's preference for the operation of the market as the means of setting terms and conditions of employment for many employees. Even in those activities where collective bargaining continues, the government appears to have a preference for local bargaining over national collective agreements in order to avoid inflationary wage deals. Moreover, a major emphasis of the legislation since 1980 has been the need to protect the rights of the individual. Thus the Employment Acts 1980, 1982 and 1988 ensured the removal of all the previous statutory supports for the post-entry closed shop; whereas the Employment Act 1990 tackles the pre-entry closed shop by creating for the first time a right not to be denied access to employment on the ground of non-membership of a trade union. The effect of the changes introduced by the Employment Act 1988, in particular, ensure that now under British law the right to join and the right not to join a trade union must be considered as equal and correlative rights. These changes also have a de-stabilising effect upon existing collective bargaining arrangements.

9.8 The Transfer Regulations and individual rights

There has been one legislative measure this decade which goes against this trend. This concerns the provisions of the Transfer of Undertakings (Protection of Employment) Regulations 1981[29] which (a) continue a union's recognition rights after the relevant transfer of a business so long as that business retains its

---

[22] See ACAS Annual Report for 1979, Appendix C.
[23] For the position under some public sector statutes, see para. 9.16.
[24] See EPA, s. 2.
[25] EPA, s. 1(2).
[26] For a more detailed analysis of these priorities, see, for example, the Editor's Introduction to *Kahn-Freund's Labour and the Law* (3rd edn., Davies & Freedland).
[27] EA 1982, ss. 12-14.
[28] See the Consultation Paper issued by the Department of Employment in December 1988.
[29] S.I. 1981 No. 1794.

separate identity and (b) grant information and consultation rights in respect of the transfer to representatives of recognised independent trade unions.[30] However, these regulations were only introduced in compliance with the United Kingdom's obligations under EEC law when default proceedings were threatened against this country for a failure to implement the requisite directive.[31] It is fast becoming the case, therefore, that most of the statutory supports which remain are those which the British government must provide under its obligations as a member of the EEC. Yet even the Transfer Regulations are being subjected to close scrutiny by the government at present because of the supposed negative effect that the information and consultation provisions have had on some privatisation arrangements.[32] On the whole the individual rights of trade unionists have not been affected greatly by the Conservative government's labour legislation apart from the changes in relation to the dismissal of employees taking part in industrial action introduced by the Employment Acts 1982 and 1990. Indeed, in one sense members' rights have been increased as a result of the provisions introduced by the former, which creates larger awards of compensation not only to cover the dismissal of the non-unionist but the trade union member and activist as well, and the right provided by the latter not to be denied access to employment because of trade union membership. In both of these cases it must also be recognised, however, that these enhanced rights were only introduced as part of a package of measures aimed primarily at protecting the non-member. Finally, in keeping with the Government's encouragement for collective bargaining conducted at local level the Employment Act 1989 introduced restrictions on a union official's rights to paid time off work.[33]

It is now time to look at the present legislative provisions concerning collective bargaining in more detail.

COLLECTIVE BARGAINING

9.9 Meaning and status of a collective agreement

The purpose of collective bargaining is to provide a mechanism whereby terms and conditions of employment for a given group of employees are reached by means of negotiation and agreement between an employer or association of employers and a trade union or confederation of unions. As was noted in Chapter Two, there is no system in British law which permits these collectively agreed terms automatically to form part of an employee's terms and conditions of employment. This must be brought about by some arrangement which permits the incorporation of collectively agreed provisions into the individual contracts of employment of the employees concerned. This system makes no distinction between the terms of employment of the union member compared with those of the non-unionist. A collective agreement is also likely to have another function and that is to act as an "industrial peace treaty"[34] setting the method and procedure by which disputes between management and labour can be resolved. It is unlikely that this aspect of the collective agreement will be incorporated into the employees' contracts. The importance of the collective agreement as a means

---

[30] Discussed in more detail at para. 9.35.
[31] See Bob Hepple "The Transfer of Undertakings (Protection of Employment) Regulations" (1982) 11 ILJ 29.
[32] See statements made by ministers after the failure of the Yard Group to acquire the National Engineering Laboratory at East Kilbride in June 1988 because of trade union involvement.
[33] See para. 9.54.
[34] See generally *Kahn-Freund's Labour and the Law*, ch. 6.

of ensuring order has been judicially noted in Scotland although Lord McDonald may have overstated the position when he declared in one case[35] "[w]here employers negotiate a detailed agreement with a recognised union they are entitled to assume that all employees who are members of the union know of and are bound by its provisions. There could be no stability in industrial relations if this were not so".

9.10 National and plant level agreements

The two most significant features of British collective bargaining are the different levels at which negotiations are conducted and the lack of precision as regards the contents of collective agreements. Bargaining may be conducted at national level involving associations of employers. The purpose of these agreements is to set minimum terms and conditions which apply to all employees within a given description in the industry. It is likely that these agreements will be augmented by bargaining at local or plant level. The purpose of these local negotiations is to deal with the problems of applying the national agreement to the special circumstances of the area. Equally, bargaining may be conducted exclusively at the local plant or factory.[36] In the last few years there has definitely been a movement supported by the government towards a more localised system of bargaining: indeed, in the public sector there has been an attempt to target higher wage increases to employees in particular geographical areas or types of work. As far as the language of British collective agreements is concerned it is often vague and although there is evidence that agreements are becoming more formalised[37] there can be no doubt that they still lack the detail and sophistication of, for example, those in the United States.

9.11 Legal enforceability of the collective agreement

Statute declares that any collective agreement shall be conclusively presumed not to have been intended by the parties to be legally enforceable and this presumption can be overcome only by ensuring that the agreement is in writing and that it contains a provision, however expressed, which declares that the parties intend the agreement to have legal effect.[38] This is consistent with the decision of Geoffrey Lane J. in *Ford Motor Co Ltd v. AEF*[39] to the effect that under English common law a collective agreement was not a legally enforceable contract. Looking at the wording of such agreements, their nature and the climate of opinion at the time,[40] the judge concluded that the parties did not intend that collective agreements should be enforceable. Instead, they were intended to be binding in honour only.

9. 12 The position in Scots law

There is some limited support for this decision in *International Tailors' Machinists' and Pressers' Union v. Goldberg*[41] where it was held that an employer was not bound by a written undertaking that he had given to a trade union that

---

[35] *Gray Dunn & Co Ltd v. Edwards* [1980] IRLR 23 at p. 24, EAT.

[36] These issues are discussed in more detail in the Donovan Commission Report ch. III.

[37] See Brown (ed.), *The Changing Contours of British Industrial Relations: A Survey of Manufacturing Industry*.

[38] TULRA, s. 18(1)(a) and (b).

[39] [1969] 2 QB 303.

[40] Geoffrey Lane J. referred in particular to several articles by Otto Kahn-Freund and to the Report of the Donovan Commission.

[41] (1903) 19 Sh. Ct. Rep. 312.

he would not hire non-union labour on the basis that this undertaking was a mere voluntary and gratuitous act. However, one academic writer[42] has argued that under Scots law an intention to create legal relations is always presumed to exist in commercial or industrial cases.[43] Accordingly, a collective agreement as a form of industrial agreement should be assumed to create a legally binding relationship at the time when the agreement is made. Therefore, if the Scottish courts were to reach the same conclusion as the *Ford* case at common law, it would have to be on different grounds, for example, the need for certainty as to the terms of a valid contract.[44]

9.13 The statutory presumption

The existence of s. 18 of the Trade Union and Labour Relations Act 1974 renders these arguments otiose. Unless a contrary intention is expressed in writing s. 18 ensures that a collective agreement is conclusively presumed not to be a legally binding contract. There are no decisions of the Scottish courts on the language of s. 18. However, two English decisions shed light upon its effect. In the first,[45] it was held that the effect of the presumption in s. 18 was to ensure that a collective agreement was not a contract at all in the eyes of the law. Indeed, it was merely an arrangement between the parties the enforcement of which was to be achieved, if at all, by other means. Accordingly, it is wrong to view a collective agreement as a form of contract which statute has made unenforceable in the courts. It has no contractual status whatsoever.

9. 14 Rebutting the presumption

Moreover, if the parties wish the agreement to be legally enforceable the written term which is intended to rebut the presumption must clearly express this desire. This was held in the second case, *National Coal Board v. National Union of Mineworkers*,[46] where there was a clause in the agreement between the coal board and the union which declared that "the parties hereto be bound thereby accordingly". The union argued that the use of the word "bound" displayed an intention that the agreement should be legally binding. However, Scott J. concluded that the statutory presumption had not been displaced. It was his view that a statement in a collective agreement that the parties are to be bound by that agreement cannot be equated with a statement that the parties intend the agreement to be legally enforceable. At the very least for the presumption to be rebutted the collective agreement must contain a statement showing that the parties have directed their minds to the question of legal enforceability and have decided in favour of such enforceability.

UNION RECOGNITION

9.15 It has been noted that the original statutory provisions[47] permitted ACAS to inquire and report on a request for union recognition by an independent trade union. In exercising these powers ACAS had to have regard to the desirability

---

[42] James Casey "Collective Agreements: Some Scottish Footnotes" 1973 JR 22.
[43] See Stair 1.10.6: 1.10.13.
[44] And see Chapter Two, paras. 2.9, 2.14.
[45] *Monterosso Shipping Co Ltd v. International Transport Workers Federation* [1982] IRLR 468.
[46] [1986] IRLR 439.
[47] EPA, ss. 11–16.

of settling the issue by conciliation. ACAS was also obliged in the course of its inquiries to ascertain the opinions of the workers affected by the issue by any means it thought fit, and this would often involve the use of a questionnaire. At the end of its inquiries ACAS was required to make a report which set out its findings and where necessary make a recommendation for recognition by the employer. This recommendation was not legally binding. If the employer chose to ignore it all that ACAS could do was to attempt to settle the matter by conciliation. The ultimate sanction was for the union to complain to the CAC that the employer was not complying with ACAS's recommendation, and to have incorporated into the contracts of the relevant employees particular terms and conditions of employment except a term requiring the employer to recognise the applicant union.[48]

9.16 The repeal of the statutory procedure

There were some who argued that the provisions on union recognition did not go far enough.[49] However, the courts, at least initially, adopted the view that the procedure involved an interference with individual liberty.[50] In *Grunwick Processing Laboratories Ltd v. ACAS*[51] Lord Salmon, for example, considered that it was the court's duty to ensure that the rights of the individual were not lost except in strict accordance with the statutory procedure. As already pointed out, this statutory procedure was discontinued in 1980.[52] Thus apart from the provisions of certain statutes applying in the public sector which impose a duty of consultation with "appropriate"[53] organisations or organisations appearing to represent "substantial proportions"[54] of employees there is no legal obligation upon an employer to recognise a trade union. To a large extent, therefore, unions must rely on self-help in order to obtain recognition rights. However, the extent to which a union can apply self-help measures is limited since it is unlawful for a union to pressure an employer to impose a union-only or union-recognition requirement in contracts[55] or for the union to take industrial action to enforce union membership.[56]

9.17 Recognition for collective bargaining

Despite the lack of an enforceable union recognition procedure many of the remaining statutory supports to collective bargaining still only operate where a trade union is recognised for collective bargaining purposes. Thus the concept of union recognition is still a central aspect of the law. It is defined to mean the

---

[48] See, for example, *Phoenix Timber (Grangemouth) Ltd v. TGWU* (CAC Award No 272).
[49] During the 1977-78 Session of Parliament two Private Member's Bills were introduced which would have increased the powers of ACAS particularly as regards obtaining access to the names of employees whose opinions the Service had to ascertain. These Bills are discussed by B. James and R. C. Simpson in "Grunwick v. ACAS" (1978) 41 MLR 372.
[50] See Browne-Wilkinson J. in *Powley v. ACAS* [1978] ICR at p. 135; Lord Denning MR in *Grunwick Processing Laboratories Ltd v. ACAS* [1978] ICR 231 at p. 237 and in *UKAPE v. ACAS* [1979] ICR 303 at pp. 316-317. Later House of Lords' decisions took a less damaging tack. See *UKAPE v. ACAS* [1980] ICR 215.
[51] [1978] ICR 231 at p. 268, HL.
[52] EPA, ss. 11-16 repealed by EA 1980, s. 18.
[53] *R. v. Post Office ex parte ASTMS* [1981] ICR 77, CA.
[54] *R. v. British Coal Corporation ex parte Union of Democratic Mineworkers* [1988] ICR 38, DC. See also *Cannon v. Secretary of State for Scotland* 1964 SLT 91.
[55] EA 1982, s. 14. See Chapter Eleven, para. 11.47.
[56] EA 1988, s. 10. See Chapter Eleven, para 11.48.

recognition of the union by the employer, or two or more associated employers, to any extent for the purpose of collective bargaining.[57] Collective bargaining is defined by the same sub-section to mean negotiations relating to or connected with one or more of the following matters:

(a) terms and conditions of employment;

(b) engagement or non-engagement, or termination or suspension of employment or the duties of employment;

(c) allocation of work;

(d) matters of discipline;

(e) membership or non-membership of a union;

(f) facilities for union officials;

(g) machinery for negotiation or consultation.

9.18 The act of recognition

There is no doubt that before a union can be considered to be recognised by an employer in terms of the above definition there must be consent[58] or a meeting of the minds of the parties.[59] This requires the employer to acknowledge the role of the union and for the union to assent to such acknowledgement. This is best achieved through some form of express agreement to this effect. More difficult is the case where a decision about recognition has to be resolved by reference to the actings of the parties. In such a case, as Lord McDonald declared in *Transport and General Workers' Union v. Dyer*,[60] the actings ". . . must be clear and unequivocal, usually though not necessarily, involving a course of conduct over a period of time". This approach which sets a heavy burden of proof on the party claiming recognition[61] has been applied in subsequent cases. The thrust of these decisions is summed up in the statement of Lord Denning M.R. in *National Union of Gold, Silver & Allied Trades v. Albury Brothers Ltd*[62] that "a recognition issue is a most important matter for industry: and therefore an employer is not to be held to have recognised a trade union unless the evidence is clear". Usually the employer's conduct should establish no only a willingness on his part to discuss but also to negotiate about one or more matters listed above. It would not be sufficient proof of recognition for the union merely to show that the employer is a member of an association with whom it negotiates.[63] On the other hand, this factor could be an element in establishing recognition if there are other facts in the case which also point in this direction.[64]

9.19 Under the statutory definition it is competent for a union to be recognised "to any extent" for the purpose of collective bargaining. This phrase does not refer to the strength of conviction of the recognition but to the subject matters

---

57 EPA, s. 126(1).

58 *TGWU v. Dyer* [1977] IRLR 93.

59 *National Union of Tailors and Garment Workers v. Charles Ingram & Co Ltd* [1977] ICR 530.

60 [1977] ICR 93, EAT.

61 As Kilner Brown J. stated in *Joshua Wilson & Brothers Ltd v. Union of Shop, Distributive & Allied Workers* [1978] ICR 614, EAT the side of the scales labelled recognition must "go down with a bump".

62 [1979] ICR 84 at p. 89, CA.

63 *Albury Brothers, ibid.*

64 *Joshua Wilson & Brothers Ltd v. USDAW* [1978] ICR 614, EAT.

to which it relates.[65] Thus there is nothing to prevent a union acquiring partial recognition and exercise as a result rights which are conditional on being recognised for collective bargaining. However, the case law does make a distinction between negotiating rights which is the essence of recognition and mere rights to represent members. A union would not be considered recognised for collective bargaining purposes where its role is restricted simply to representing its members in individual grievances before the employer.[66] The distinction also applies as regards a collective agreement which grants full negotiating rights over some matters but as regards other matters only offers rights of representation. In such circumstances a union cannot complain about a failure on the part of the employer to disclose information about a method of evaluating work if this is an aspect of terms and conditions where only representation rights have been accorded.[67]

STATUTORY SUPPORTS FOR COLLECTIVE BARGAINING

9.20 Disclosure of information

An employer must disclose to the representatives of an independent trade union on request all the information relating to his undertaking as is in his possession for the purposes of all stages of collective bargaining.[68] This duty only arises where the union is recognised for collective bargaining purposes. Information need not be disclosed by an employer, therefore, where the union only possesses representation rights in relation to the type of information which the union is seeking.[69] Equally, there is no duty to disclose where, for example, the information is required to assist the union in its campaign against privatisation since this does not fall within the statutory concept of collective bargaining.[70] Two further conditions must be satisfied before the duty applies. The request must be for information without which the trade union representatives would be to a material extent impeded in carrying out collective bargaining and it must be in accordance with good industrial relations practice for the information to be disclosed.[71] Beyond this there is no further definition in the statute as to the types of information for which there is a duty to disclose. However, the ACAS Code of Practice on Disclosure of Information to Trade Unions for Collective Bargaining Purposes[72] does provide examples of the types of information which might be relevant to collective bargaining. These are under the headings of pay and benefits; conditions of service; manpower; performance and financial matters. This list is by no means exhaustive, and the Code stresses that it would be far better if the parties could reach agreement over the matters relevant for disclosure.

9.21 *Exempted information.* On the other hand the employer is exempt from disclosing certain types of information.[73] An employer need not disclose:

---

[65] *Per* Lord McDonald in *TGWU v. Dyer* [1977] IRLR 93 at p. 94, EAT.

[66] *USDAW v. Sketchley Ltd* [1981] ICR 644, EAT.

[67] *R. v. CAC ex parte BTP Tioxide Ltd* [1981] ICR 843.

[68] EPA, s. 17.

[69] *BTP Tioxide Ltd, op cit.*

[70] EPA, s. 126(1) and see *Civil Service Union v. CAC* [1980] IRLR 274.

[71] EPA, s. 17(1)(a) and (b).

[72] ACAS Code No. 2 effective August 22, 1977.

[73] EPA, s. 18(1).

(a) any information the disclosure of which would be against the interests of national security;

(b) any information the disclosure of which would involve contravening a prohibition imposed by or under an enactment;

(c) any information which has been disclosed to the employer in confidence,[74] or which the employer has otherwise obtained in consequence of the confidence reposed in him by another person;

(d) any information relating specifically to an individual, unless he has consented to its disclosure;

(e) any information the disclosure of which would cause substantial injury to the employer's undertaking for reasons other than its effect on collective bargaining;

(f) any information obtained by the employer for the purpose of bringing, prosecuting or defending any legal proceedings.

9.22 *Commercial information.* One specific head which leaves scope for widely divergent views is that which exempts disclosure where "substantial injury" is likely to be caused to the employer's undertaking. Although this phrase is not defined, the Code does give some guidance as to the types of information where disclosure might cause substantial injury. The examples provided include cost information on individual products; detailed analysis of proposed investment; marketing or pricing policies and price quotas or the make-up of tender prices. Moreover, the Code advises that substantial injury is likely to arise where disclosure would result in certain customers being lost to competitors, or suppliers refusing to supply necessary materials, or an impairment in the ability of the employer to raise funds.[75] Also an employer is not required to produce or allow for inspection any document other than the one prepared for the purpose of conveying the information[76] and there is no requirement on an employer to compile or assemble information which would entail an amount of work or expenditure out of reasonable proportion to the value of the information in the conduct of collective bargaining.[77]

9.23 *Enforcement.* Enforcement of these provisions is by means of an application by the union to the CAC.[78] However, where there is a reasonable likelihood that the complaint can be settled by conciliation the CAC has the authority to refer the matter to ACAS. In such a case it is the duty of ACAS to attempt to promote a settlement. Where conciliation fails or no reference has been made, the CAC will proceed to determine the complaint. The principal remedy where the whole or part of the complaint is well-founded is for the CAC to make a declaration. In such a case the CAC is required to specify the information which should have been disclosed and the period of time within which the employer ought to disclose that information. Where the employer refuses to comply with the terms of the declaration the union is entitled to make another complaint to the CAC[79] which entitles the union to submit a claim for improved terms and

[74] Discussed by Forbes J. in *CSU v. CAC* [1980] IRLR 274.
[75] Para. 15.
[76] EPA, s. 18(2)(a).
[77] EPA, s. 18(2)(b).
[78] EPA, s. 19. See H. Gospel & P. Willman, "Disclosure of Information: the CAC Approach" (1981) 10 ILJ 10.
[79] EPA, s. 20.

conditions for the class of employees specified in the complaint. If this further complaint is upheld the CAC is empowered to make an award requiring the employer to observe the terms and conditions which the union has specified in its claim or such other terms as it thinks appropriate.[80] The sanction under this procedure, therefore, is not to force disclosure, but to impose upon the employer an obligation to improve the employees' terms and conditions of employment. These terms become part of the contracts of employment of each of the employees concerned and can be enforced where necessary by an action for breach of contract in the civil courts.

9.24 The right to consultation

Statute places upon an employer a duty to consult with employee representatives in three specific circumstances. An employer must consult on health and safety matters so as to ensure that he and his employees can co-operate effectively in promoting and developing measures to ensure health and safety and to check the effectiveness of these measures.[81] There is also a duty to consult as regards proposals for redundancies and as regards the transfer of the employer's undertaking. These last two obligations have been introduced in compliance with the United Kingdom's membership of the EEC.

9.25 *Consultation on redundancy.* The statutory procedure[82] for handling redundancies (which is intended to comply with the United Kingdom's obligations under the EEC Directive on Collective Redundancies[83]) also imposes a duty to consult. This only arises where the employer proposes to dismiss as redundant an employee of a description in respect of which an independent trade union possesses recognition rights.[84] Redundancy has the same meaning here as it does in Part VI of the Employment Protection (Consolidation) Act 1978 as regards an employee's entitlement to a redundancy payment.[85] Thus there would be a duty to consult where the employer no longer requires the work which an employee has been performing and proposes to dispense with his services because of lack of funds or new technology even although there is still a demand for that type of work.[86] On the other hand, if the employer intends to deal with the problem by some other method which does not involve any dismissals (such as redeployment or the non-filling of vacancies) the statutory procedure does not operate.

9.26 *Consultation with representatives.* The duty is to consult with representatives of independent trade unions, *viz.* officials or other persons authorised to carry on collective bargaining with the employer.[87] The employer must ensure, therefore, that any consultations only take place with those union officials who have responsibility for conducting collective bargaining with him.[88] However,

---

[80] EPA, s. 21(3).
[81] Health and Safety at Work etc Act 1974, s. 2(6). Further discussion of this subject is outwith the scope of this work.
[82] EPA, ss. 99-107.
[83] Council Directive No 75/129.
[84] EPA, s. 99(1).
[85] Discussed in more detail in Chapter Six, paras. 6.5-6.7.
[86] *Association of University Teachers v. University of Newcastle-upon-Tyne* [1987] ICR 317, EAT.
[87] EPA, s. 99(2).
[88] *Amalgamated Union of Engineering Workers v. Sefton Engineering Co Ltd* [1976] IRLR 319, EAT.

once this provision has been satisfied the duty to consult will apply to all of those employees whom the employer is proposing to dismiss. The only condition for consultation is that the employees concerned be of a description for which an independent trade union has acquired recognition rights. Once this has been established the duty to consult will operate regardless of whether or not the employees concerned are union members.

9.27 *Commencing consultation.* The employer is required to begin consultation at the earliest opportunity regardless of the number of employees to be dismissed. Where, however, the employer is proposing to dismiss 100 or more employees at one establishment within a period of 90 days or less, consultation must begin at least 90 days before the first of these dismissals takes effect.[89] Equally, where the proposal is to dismiss 10 or more employees at one establishment within a period of 30 days or less, consultation must begin at least 30 days before the first of these dismissals takes effect.[90] It is clear that any consultation must begin as soon as the employer proposes to make redundancies. This means, for example, that an employer would be breaking the consultation requirements where he began to consult with the union at the same time as individual notices of dismissal had been sent out to the affected employees.[91] This would be the case even although the first dismissal would not take effect until after the periods for consultation mentioned in the statute had expired.[92] Equally, an employer would be in breach of his statutory obligations where the employees' dismissal notices and a memorandum to the union setting out details of the redundancies were sent out simultaneously.[93] On the other hand there must be something concrete to put before the union. As Lord McDonald stated in *Association of Patternmakers & Allied Craftsmen v. Kirvin Ltd*,[94] s. 99 of the Employment Protection Act ". . . connotes a state of mind directed to a planned or proposed course of events. The employer must have formed some view as to how many are to be dismissed, when this is to take place and how it is to be arranged".

9.28 *Multi-location businesses.* The reference to the dismissals being at one "establishment" has also created difficulties for there is no definition of this word for the purposes of consultation. This issue has obvious implications for the timing of any consultations for an employer running a multi-location business like retailing. In *Barratt Developments (Bradford) Ltd v. Union of Construction, Allied Trades and Technicians*[95] the company had employees engaged in house-building at 14 different sites each with a temporary shed housing the foreman and a telephone link to head office. Due to a reduction in demand it was decided that redundancies were necessary. As a result, 24 employees working at eight of the company's sites were given one week's notice of dismissal and

---

[89] EPA, s. 99(3)(a).

[90] EPA, s. 99(3)(b) as amended by the Employment Protection (Handling of Redundancies) Variation Order 1979, SI 1979 No 958.

[91] See, for example, *Sovereign Services Ltd v. TGWU* [1990] ICR 31, EAT.

[92] *National Union of Teachers v. Avon County Council* [1978] ICR 626; *E Green & Son (Castings) Ltd v. ASTMS* [1984] ICR 352.

[93] *General & Municipal Workers' Union v. British Uralite Ltd* [1979] IRLR 409.

[94] [1978] IRLR 318 at p. 310. See also *APEX v. Leyland Daf Ltd* [1991] IRLR 194 where the EAT held that an employer should be taken as "proposing" to discuss employees as redundant so as to be under an immediate duty to consult when a specific proposal has been formulated.

[95] [1978] ICR 319.

at the same time the union was notified about the impending dismissals. The union argued that these eight sites amounted to one establishment and that since more than ten employees were being dismissed at one time the amount of prior notification that had been given was inadequate. It was held that the question of what was an establishment was essentially one of fact and that the industrial tribunal in this case had been right to conclude that it would be contrary to common and business sense to regard each of these sites as a separate establishment. Accordingly, the company had provided insufficient time for consultation. It was significant that in this case all the important decision-making functions were exercised at head office. In another case where the facts disclose that far greater autonomy resides with the management at each location the decision might be different.

9.29 *The extent of the duty.* The extent of the consultation duty is to be found in the statutory requirement that an employer disclose in writing to union representatives the following:

(a) the reasons for the proposals;

(b) the numbers and descriptions of employees whom it is proposed to dismiss as redundant;

(c) the total number of employees of the appropriate description employed by the employer at the establishment in question;

(d) the proposed method of selection;

(e) the proposed method of carrying out the dismissals.[96]

In the course of any consultations the employer is under a duty to consider any representations made by the union representatives and to reply to these, and, if they are rejected, to state his reasons for doing so.[97]

9.30 *Qualification of the duty.* The duty to consult is qualified by the Employment Protection Act 1975 s. 99(8) which provides that where there are special circumstances which render it not reasonably practicable for the employer to comply with any of the above requirements, he must take all such steps towards compliance as are reasonably practicable in the circumstances. This is also a matter for the tribunal to decide. The Court of Appeal considered the meaning of "special circumstance" in *Clarks of Hove Ltd v. Bakers' Union*[98] where the employers had been in financial difficulties for some time. After their last hopes of financial aid had disappeared they dismissed 368 of their employees for redundancy and ceased trading on the same day. The Bakers' Union — the recognised trade union — complained to an industrial tribunal that the employers had failed to consult at least 90 days before the first dismissals were to take effect. The employers argued that there were special circumstances excusing their lack of consultation. The Court of Appeal held that insolvency was not necessarily a special circumstance. Everything would depend on the cause of that insolvency. A sudden disaster, either physical or financial, which suddenly struck a company making it necessary for the business to close could be capable of being a special circumstance. On the other hand, if the insolvency came about after a gradual run-down of the company such a circumstance would not be special.

---

[96] EPA, s. 99(5).

[97] *Ibid.* s. 99(7).

[98] [1978] ICR 1076.

9.31 *Special circumstances.* In general terms, therefore, to be a special event the occurrence must be something out of the ordinary or uncommon. A similar approach has been applied in Scotland in the *Kirvin* case[99] where Lord McDonald declared that insolvency would not be a special case where it was foreseeable. However, he did take the view that it would be a special circumstance for an employer to delay consultation until it became clear that the last potential purchaser of the business as a going concern had disappeared and that a receiver would have to be appointed. It has also been held to be a special circumstance where a prospective employer withdrew from negotiations and a receiver was appointed immediately by the bank.[100] On the other hand, this defence cannot operate where the employer's excuse for a failure to consult was his genuine belief that there was no recognised trade union.[101]

9.31 *Failure to consult.* The sanction for breach of these provisions is for an industrial tribunal to declare that a complaint by a recognised trade union is well-founded and to make a protective award.[102] The purpose of this award is to require the employer to continue to pay the wages of the employees who are the subject of the complaint for a protected period. Individual employees have no right to complain under this procedure, although any award will apply to union members and non-unionists alike. The duration of the protective award will be for such period as the tribunal considers just and equitable in all the circumstances, having regard to the seriousness of the employer's default.[103] However, the duration of any award is subject to certain maximum periods. In the case of 100 or more dismissals conducted within 90 days of less, the maximum award is for 90 days; in the case of 10 or more dismissals within 30 days or less it is 30 days; in all other cases the maximum length of the protective award is 28 days.[104] Any employee covered by the award is entitled to one week's wages for each week of the protective award subject to deduction of any contractual payment made by the employer to the employees. Employees who fail to receive their protective awards have the right to complain to an industrial tribunal. If the tribunal finds that the complaint is well-founded it will order the employer to pay the sum of money which is due.[105]

9.33 *The protective award.* There has been some judicial disagreement within the Employment Appeal Tribunal as regards the purpose of the protective award. In *Talke Fashions Ltd v. Amalgamated Society of Textile Workers and Kindred Trades*[106] Kilner Brown J. considered that the purpose of the award was not to punish employers for their failure to consult. Instead, it was intended merely to compensate the employees for any losses they had incurred as a result of the employer's default. This appears to be the dominant view in England, although in recent times protective awards have become more punitive.[107] In Scotland, on the other hand, Lord McDonald has declared in *Kirvin*[108] that since a tribunal

---

[99] [1978] IRLR 318, EAT.
[100] *USDAW v. Leancut Bacon Ltd* [1981] IRLR 295, EAT.
[101] *Joshua Wilson & Brothers Ltd v. USDAW* [1978] ICR 614, EAT.
[102] EPA, s. 101(3).
[103] *Ibid.* s. 101(5).
[104] *Ibid.* s. 101(5)(a)-(c).
[105] *Ibid.* s. 103(3).
[106] [1977] ICR 833, EAT.
[107] See Smith & Wood, *Industrial Law*, 4th edn., at pp. 60-61.
[108] [1978] IRLR 318.

was required to take account of the seriousness of the employer's default in assessing the period of the award, this introduced a punitive element into the jurisdiction of industrial tribunals in this area.

9.34 Notification to the Secretary of State

There is also an obligation placed upon an employer to notify the Secretary of State for Employment over mass redundancies. Where he proposes to dismiss as redundant 100 or more employees at one establishment within a period of 90 days or less at least 90 days prior written notice of these dismissals should be given. In the case where 10 or more employees are being dismissed from one establishment within 30 days or less at least 30 days notice is required.[109] Representatives of any recognised union are entitled to a copy of the notice. The only sanction now available for a failure to notify the Secretary of State is a fine on level 5 of the standard scale after summary conviction.[110]

9.35 Consultation on the transfer of an undertaking

The Transfer of Undertakings (Protection of Employment) Regulations 1981[111] constitute the United Kingdom's response to the Directive[112] of the EEC safeguarding employees' rights in the event of a transfer of an undertaking. Unlike the case of consultation on redundancies the Government chose to comply with its EEC obligations on this occasion by means of regulations made under the European Communities Act 1972. The regulations fulfil two purposes. First, they ensure that when the transfer of a business takes place the contracts of employment of the employees concerned will be transferred automatically from the one employer to the other.[113] Second, they require that when an employer proposes to transfer his business or part of it to another employer, both employers inform and in certain circumstances consult with representatives of the relevant trade unions about the proposed transfer. Moreover, as we have seen, union recognition rights can also be transferred and it is also declared that any collective agreement operating before the transfer will continue to apply after the transfer becomes effective.[114] However, as regards the continued operation of the collective agreement, the transferee is only required to honour its terms as regards those employees who were employed in the undertaking at the date of the transfer. The transferee is not obliged to honour its terms as regards those employees recruited after that date.[115]

9.36 *The nature of the duty.* The duty to inform and consult only arises where there is a relevant transfer[116] and where there is a recognised trade union. Further, the obligations only operate where there is an employee who will be affected by the transfer. This covers any employee of the transferor or the transferee (whether or not employed in the undertaking or the part of the undertaking to be transferred) who may be affected by the transfer or may be affected by

---

[109] EPA, s. 101(1).
[110] *Ibid.* s. 105(1).
[111] S.I. 1981 No. 1794.
[112] See the Council Directive No. 77/187.
[113] Reg. 5 discussed in more detail in Chapter Three.
[114] Reg. 6.
[115] See the decision of the European Court of Justice in *Landsorganisationen Ii Danmark v. Ny Molle KRO* [1989] IRLR 37.
[116] See Reg. 3.

measures taken in connection with it.[117] In the case of the duty to inform, the transferor employer must inform representatives of his own workforce about his intention to transfer them. The duty on the transferee employer is to inform the representatives of those of his own employees who will be affected by the transfer. The information must be provided long enough before a relevant transfer to enable consultations to take place. This is all that the regulations say about the timing of the information. However, in the only case to shed light on this question[118] Millet J. argued that the crucial issue was for the information to be provided as soon as measures are envisaged. This is the primary obligation under the regulations. The information should be provided therefore, as long a possible before the transfer is to take place. Moreover, in the case where no measures are envisaged before the transfer there is no requirement that information be provided before that transfer.

9.37 *The duty to inform.* The representatives should be informed about:
    (a) the fact that the relevant transfer is to take place, when it is to take place and the reasons for it;
    (b) the legal, economic and social implications of the transfer;
    (c) the measures, if any, which it is envisaged will be taken in relation to those employees in connection with the transfer; and
    (d) where the employer is the transferor, the measures which the transferee envisages he will take in connection with the transfer in relation to the employees being transferred.[119]

The necessary information for this last head must be given by the transferee to the transferor at such a time as will enable the latter to perform this duty. The information which union representatives are to receive should be delivered to them, or sent by post to an address notified by them to the employer, or sent by post to the union's head office.[120]

9.38 *When does it operate?* The nature of this duty to inform is vague. However, some light has been shed on its restrictive nature by the judgment of Millett J. in *Institution of Professional Civil Servants v. Secretary of Defence.*[121] There the judge confirmed that the obligation to provide information about measures which are envisaged under heads (c) and (d) only arises where some definite plan or proposal has been formulated which it is intended to implement. Where no measures are envisaged there is no need to inform. This may mean that these obligations will not assist unions to obtain information on such matters as manpower, redundancy and changes in working practices to which they might claim that they are entitled under head (d). For, although Millet J. accepted that the word measure has a wide import and involved any action, step or arrangement about these matters, he also argued that the use of the word "will" excluded mere hopes or possibilities. Consequently, an employer would have to formulate some definite plan or proposal which he is intending to implement before a duty to inform under head (d) would arise.

---

[117] Reg. 10(1).
[118] *Institution of Professional Civil Servants v. Secretary of State for Defence* [1987] IRLR 373.
[119] Reg. 10(2).
[120] Reg. 10(4).
[121] [1987] IRLR 373.

9.39 *The duty to consult.* The regulations also impose a duty of consultation. This duty arises where the employer envisages that he will be taking measures in relation to employees who are affected by the transfer.[122] The employer is required in the course of these consultations to consider any representations made by union representatives, to reply to them, and, if he rejects any of their representations, to state his reasons.[123] Consultation with union representatives is only compulsory where an employer envisages that he will be taking measure in connection with the transfer. This is the only topic for which consultation is mandatory. There is no obligation on an employer under the regulations to consult on any of the other topics for which information has been provided. This would be a voluntary matter for the employer alone to decide.[124] Where there are special circumstances rendering it not reasonably practicable for the employer to perform his information and consultation duties, he is required to take all such steps towards performing any duty as are reasonably practicable in the circumstances.[125] Since this is a similar defence to that applicable in redundancy consultation it can be presumed that that case law will also apply to a transfer of an undertaking.

9.40 *Failure to inform or consult.* A complaint that there has been a breach of these provisions must be presented to an industrial tribunal by the appropriate union within three months of the transfer. Where the complaint is well-founded the tribunal will make a declaration to that effect and will award appropriate compensation to the employees concerned.[126] An employee who has not been paid in pursuance of this order can complain to the tribunal, and if the complaint is well-founded the employer will be ordered to pay the sum due.[127] However, the maximum compensation which can be awarded under this procedure is limited to two weeks' wages.[128]

9.41 Wages councils

The early councils. Wages councils are the successors to the trade boards which were first created in 1909 as a response to popular concern about the conditions of employment which operated in the so-called "sweated trades". They are tri-partite bodies made up of representatives of employers and workers and independent members charged with setting minimum standards for a particular group of workers within their authority. They were first called wages councils by the Wages Councils Act 1945 and in 1975 their powers were enhanced by granting them the authority for the first time to make their own orders which had the force of law and by allowing them to determine the date when such orders would take effect. New bodies entitled statutory joint industrial councils were also created to act as bridges between the wages council and free collective bargaining. The previous legislation was consolidated by the Wages Council Act 1979. This Act was in turn repealed by Part II of the Wages Act 1986.

---

[122] Reg. 10(5).
[123] Reg. 10(6).
[124] See the decision of Millett J. in *IPCS* case [1987] IRLR 373 at p. 376.
[125] Reg. 10(7).
[126] Reg. 11(4).
[127] Reg. 11(5).
[128] Reg. 11(11).

9.42 *The Wages Council and government policy.* As has already been noted, the aim of the earlier legislation was to create machinery for the establishment of terms and conditions of employment wherever collective bargaining was weak or non-existent. The aim of the wages council was to ensure that any employee covered by its ambit would not be paid terms and conditions any less favourable than those specified in the relevant order. This system was criticised by the Conservative government of 1983-87 on at least two grounds. First, it was argued that wages councils interfered with the natural operation of the job market. They prevented employers offering and job-seekers accepting jobs at rates of pay which both parties would otherwise have been prepared to accept. The second government criticism concerned the length and complexity of many of the wages councils' order. This rigidity in the orders allegedly inhibited employers in developing sensible wage structures.[129]

9.43 *The Wages Council today.* The provisions of Part II of the Wages Act 1986 were enacted to remedy these difficulties. Thus to ensure that young workers will not be priced out of jobs through the setting of wage rates above those which the market can bear, wages councils have lost the right to exercise any functions in relation to workers under the age of 21.[130] Although the Wages Act 1986 permits the continued operation of wages councils for all other workers, it does introduce a number of reforms aimed at simplifying the procedure. The essential tri-partite nature of the wages council has been maintained but the Secretary of State now has the authority to increase the number of independent members on a wages council from three to five.[131] Moreover, the Act has created a specific requirement that the employer representatives on a wages council should be selected from an employers' association which the Secretary of State believes is representative of small businesses.[132] No member of a wages council can now hold office for more than three years, and the authority that existed formerly to transform a wages council into a statutory joint industrial council has disappeared entirely.[133]

9.44 *The powers of the Wages Council.* The Wages Act 1986 also abolished the power of a wages council to make orders covering all terms and conditions of employment. Instead, only two rates can be set by a wages council order. A single minimum hourly rate can be set which will apply to all the workers covered by the order and a single minimum hourly overtime rate can also be laid down for time worked in excess of basic hours.[134] In addition, an order can also fix a maximum limit for amounts deducted from a worker's pay to cover the cost of living accommodation provided by the employer.[135] In setting the minimum rate the wages council must pay specific regard to the effect that the rate will have on the level of employment of the workers to whom it will apply, and in particular in those areas where the remuneration received by such workers is generally less than the national average for such workers.[136] This is further

---

[129] See the Consultative Paper issued by the Department of Employment in March 1985.

[130] WA, s. 12(3).

[131] *Ibid.* s. 12(4), Sch. 2, para. 1(b).

[132] *Ibid.* Sch. 2, para. 2(2).

[133] *Ibid.* Sch. 2, para. 8(1).

[134] *Ibid.* s. 14(1). See also Chapter Three, paras. 3.13, 3.14.

[135] *Ibid.* s. 14(1)(c).

[136] *Ibid.* s. 14(6)(a).

reinforcement of the importance of the job market as a mechanism for setting wage rates. These rates apply to all workers, full-time and part-time alike. The rate cannot distinguish between workers in different parts of the country nor the different categories of work carried out by workers covered by the order. Special rules do apply to the piece worker who is a worker whose pay is calculated by reference to the number of items of work executed by him or by a group of which he is a member.[137] The aim of these rules is to ensure that piece rates are set at a level which reflects the minimum hourly rate. This is to be achieved by setting the piece rate at a rate equivalent to that which the ordinary worker executing the work in question could earn in any given time worked by him in any week, being not less than the amount of remuneration due under the order in respect of the time so worked.[138]

9.45 *Creation coverage and abolition of wages councils.* There is nothing in the Wages Act 1986 authorising the creation of any new wages councils. The setting of minimum wage rates has been restricted, therefore, to the 26 wages councils which existed immediately before the commencement of Part II of the Act. However, the procedure for the abolition or variation of a wages council has been simplified. Under the earlier legislation a wages council could be abolished by the Secretary of State on his own volition, or as a result of an application made by a joint industrial council, jointly by organisations of workers and employers representing a substantial proportion of the workers or by an organisation of workers representing a substantial proportion of the workers covered by the council.[139] Applications for abolition could be referred to ACAS for report and invariably such referrals were made. The Wages Act 1986 permits the Secretary of State to abolish, by order, a wages council at any time.[140] There are three matters to which the Secretary of State must have regard before abolition. He must take into account the current level of remuneration among the workers in relation to whom the wages council would cease to operate; he must consider such other matters as appear to him to be appropriate; and he must consult with such persons or organisations as appear to him to be appropriate.[141] There is no specific requirement that ACAS be consulted. Equally, there is now no formal procedure by which employer organisations or worker organisations can initiate abolition. The same basic rules also apply where the Secretary of State intends to vary an order so as to exclude specific employers or to transfer workers from one wages council to another.

9.46 At one time there was a strong possibility that wages councils would be abolished entirely. The government issued a consultation document in December 1988 which considered as one of the options the complete abolition of wages councils. The major reason provided in support of this view was that wages council awards continued to prevent employers from developing pay systems wholly in accordance with the best interests of their business. However, largely through the opposition of some employers towards any proposal to abolish the wages council system it would seem that the government has had a change of mind.

---

[137] *Ibid.* s. 15(4).
[138] *Ibid.* s. 15(2).
[139] Wages Councils Act 1979, s. 5.
[140] WA, s. 13(1).
[141] *Ibid.* s. 13(2).

UNION ORGANISATION — THE RIGHT TO ASSOCIATE

9.47 In Britain the right of workers to join and to take part in the affairs of trade unions is protected by means of three specific rights: (i) a right not to be refused employment because of trade union membership,[142] (ii) a right not to have action short of dismissal taken against them because of trade union membership or activities[143] and (iii) a right not to be dismissed on the grounds of union membership or activities.[144] Each of these three rights also applies to a person who is not a member of a trade union. The protection against refusal of employment on union membership grounds marks a new departure for British law because for the very first time applicants for employment enjoy protection against discrimination because of their membership or non-membership of a trade union.

9.48 Refusal of employment

The Employment Act 1990 renders it unlawful to refuse a person employment because he is, or is not, a member of a trade union; or because he is unwilling to accept a requirement:

(i) to take steps to become or cease to be, or to remain or not to become, a member of a trade union, or

(ii) to make payments or suffer deductions in the event of his not being a member of a trade union.[145]

Although this provision is aimed principally at the practices of the pre-entry closed shop it applies also to the applicant for employment who is denied a job because he is a union member. However, the protection given to union members seeking employment differs in two material respects from the right not to suffer action short of dismissal or the right not to be unfairly dismissed. First, it does not protect the applicant from discrimination as far as his trade union activities are concerned — arguably a major omission as regards active trade union members. Second, the right applies to membership of any trade union and is not restricted to those unions which hold a certificate of independence from the certification officer.[146]

9.49 *Deemed refusals of employment.* A person is taken to have been refused employment if he seeks a job with a person and that person does any of the following:

(a) refuses or deliberately omits to entertain and process his application or enquiry;

(b) causes him to withdraw or cease to pursue his application or enquiry;

(c) refuses or deliberately omits to offer him employment;

(d) makes him an offer of employment (which he does not accept) the terms of which are such as no reasonable employer who wished to fill the post would offer; or

(e) makes him an offer of such employment but withdraws it or causes him not to accept it.[147]

---

[142] EA, 1990, s. 1.
[143] EPCA, ss. 23-26.
[144] EPCA, s. 58.
[145] EA, 1990, s. 1.(1)
[146] For the meaning of "independence" see Chapter Ten, para. 10.15.
[147] EA, 1990, s. 1(5).

Further, it is conclusively presumed that a person has been refused employment for being a member or not being a member of a trade union when an advertisement is published which indicates or might reasonably be understood as indicating (a) that employment to which the advertisement relates is open only to a person who is, or is not a union member, or (b) that there will be requirements about taking steps to join or resign from a trade union or about making payments or suffering deductions in the event of not being a union member and a person who does not satisfy any of the above conditions seeks employment to which the advertisement relates and is refused that employment.[148] Finally, where there is an arrangement or practice under which employment is offered only to persons put forward or approved by a union — a "hiring hall" arrangement — and the union puts forward or approves only persons who are union members, a person who is not a union member and who is refused employment because of that arrangement or practice is to be taken as having been refused employment because he is not a union member.[149] All of the above provisions apply equally to an employment agency acting on behalf of the employer as it does to the employer himself, and it is unlawful for such an agency to refuse a person any of its services because he is or is not a union member, or because he is unwilling to accept a requirement to become or cease to be, or to remain or not to become, a union member.[150] While "employment agency" is defined in very broad terms[151] as meaning a person, who, for profit or not, provides services for the purpose of finding employment for workers or supplying employers with workers,[152] a trade union is not to be regarded as an employment agency by reason of services provided only to members.[153]

9.50 *Remedies.* Applicants for employment who believe that they have been discriminated against on any of the above grounds have the right to complain to an industrial tribunal.[154] If the tribunal finds the complaint to be well-founded it can award compensation and can recommend that the respondent take within a specified period such action as appears practicable in order to obviate or reduce the adverse effect of his conduct upon the complainant; the maximum amount of compensation that a complainant can receive is the maximum compensatory award in an unfair dismissal complaint.[155] The complainant or respondent may sist a third party to the proceedings where the respondent claims that he was induced to act as he did because of pressure which a trade union or other person exercised on him by calling, organising, procuring or financing a strike or other industrial action, or by threatening to do so; if the tribunal awards compensation it can order that the award be paid jointly or wholly by the third party.[156]

9.51 Action short of dismissal

The right against action short of dismissal on grounds of union membership or activities operates in two circumstances. First, where the employer takes action

---

[148] *Ibid.* s. 1(3).
[149] *Ibid.* s. 1(4).
[150] *Ibid.* s. 2.(1).
[151] *Ibid.* s. 3(1).
[152] For the width of operation of the similar definition in race and sex legislation see *CRE v. Imperial Society of Teachers of Dancing* [1983] IRLR 315.
[153] EA 1990, s. 3(3).
[154] *Ibid.* Sch. 1, para. 2.
[155] *Ibid.* Sch. 1, para. 5.
[156] *Ibid.* Sch. 1, para. 7.

short of dismissal for the purpose of preventing or deterring the employee from being or seeking to become a member of an independent trade union, or penalises him for doing so. This right is also breached where the employer's action prevents or deters the employee from taking part in the activities of an independent trade union at any appropriate time, or penalises him for doing so.[157] As far as the non-member is concerned, it is also unlawful for an employer to take action to compel an employee to be or become a member of any trade union or of a particular trade union or of one of a number of particular trade unions.[158] In all cases it must be shown that the employer's action was taken against the employee as an individual.[159] This means that in the context of union membership grounds it would not be action short of dismissal where the employer's action is aimed at the union but that action also has a consequential effect upon union officers and members who are employees.[160] An employee can only complain where the action affects him otherwise than merely as a member or officer of the union. Nevertheless, where the action took the form of withholding a pay rise from the members of a particular union, it was held that such action constituted action against each member of the union as an individual since a person is entitled to his pay as an individual employee.[161] Action in the form of disciplinary action[162] or the transfer of an employee to a less desirable job[163] is undoubtedly action short of dismissal for this purpose. However, it has been doubted whether a threat by an employer to dismiss in the future can amount to action short of dismissal.[164]

9.52 Dismissal

As was noted in Chapter Five, the right not to be unfairly dismissed applies where the reason (or, if more than one reason, the principal reason) was that the employee was, or proposed to become a member of an independent trade union or had taken part, or proposed to take part, in the activities of an independent trade union at an appropriate time.[165] Equally, it is an automatically unfair dismissal to dismiss an employee because he is not a member of any trade union, or of a particular trade union, or has refused or proposed to refuse to become or remain a member.[166] Although the protection against dismissal for union activities is undoubtedly the more significant right for the union member, it has been held in *Discount Tobacco & Confectionery Ltd v. Armitage*[167] that the union membership protection should be broadly defined so as to cover any incident of trade union membership such as making use of the essential services of a union officer to negotiate on the member's behalf. This decision hinges upon the view that the right not to be unfairly dismissed on the ground of union membership also applies so as to protect the consequences of that membership as well.

---

[157] EPCA, s. 23(1)(a) and (b).

[158] *Ibid.* s. 23(1)(c).

[159] *Ibid.* s. 23(1).

[160] *Ridgway v. National Coal Board* [1987] IRLR 80, CA.

[161] Decision of majority (Nicholls and Bingham L.JJ.) in *Ridgway*, May L.J. dissenting.

[162] *British Airways Engine Overhaul v. Francis* [1981] IRLR 9, EAT.

[163] *Robb v. Leon Motor Services Ltd* [1978] ICR 506, EAT.

[164] *Brassington v. Cauldon Wholesale Ltd* [1978] ICR 405, EAT.

[165] EPCA, s. 58(1)(a) and (b).

[166] *Ibid.* s. 58(1)(c). This protection is discussed in much more detail in Chapter Five, paras. 5.57-5.59.

[167] [1990] IRLR 15, EAT.

9.53 Job applicants and new members

The protections against dismissal and action short of dismissal only apply after employment has commenced. However even after a trade union activist has obtained employment he is only protected from discriminatory action in respect of trade union activities which took place after his employment had begun and the statutory protections do not cover trade union activities outside of and before the particular employment had begun.[168] It should also be noted that the statutory protections may well be of limited effect as regards employees who have recently joined a union during a campaign to obtain recognition rights. In *Carrington v. Therm-a-stor Ltd*[169] the Court of Appeal held that four employees who had been dismissed after their union had made a request to be recognised by their employer had not been dismissed for an automatically unfair reason because the reason for their dismissal was the union's request for recognition and not because they *personally* had joined or proposed to take part in the union's activities.

9.54 Activities of a trade union

An employee is protected from dismissal and action short of dismissal for taking part in the activities of an independent trade union. There is no definition of the word "activities" and it has been held that this lack of definition was deliberate since the word connotes a wide variety of possibilities varying with the circumstances of each case.[170] "Activities" should be reasonably, and not too restrictively, interpreted[171] but includes forming a union branch,[172] calling a meeting to consider the recognition of an employee as a shop steward[173] and complaining to the union about the provision of safety cover.[174] Moreover, it is not restricted to activities involving the status of an employee as a trade unionist. It might even apply where a meeting of women union members is called in order to pass a resolution complaining about the union's inability to obtain equal pay with the men.[175] On the other hand, the mere fact that an employee who makes representations to an employer is a trade unionist does not necessarily make those representations the activities of a trade union. In *Chant v. Aquaboats Ltd*[176] a union member who was not an accredited shop steward was held not to be taking part in union activities when he organised a petition complaining about safety standards which was signed by a majority of employees who were not union members. Equally, where the employee carries out wholly unreasonable, extraneous or malicious acts in support of union activities none of the statutory protections will apply.[177] This might also be the case where the employee indulges in union activities simply in order to ventilate a private grievance.[178] It is undoubtedly the case that going on strike or taking part in

---

[168] *City of Birmingham District Council v. Beyer* [1977] IRLR 211, EAT.
[169] [1983] ICR 208.
[170] *Chant v. Aquaboats Ltd* [1978] ICR 643, EAT.
[171] *Dixon v. West Ella Developments Ltd* [1978] ICR 856, EAT.
[172] *Lyon v. St James Press Ltd* [1976] ICR 413, EAT.
[173] *Marley Tile Co Ltd v. Shaw* [1980] ICR 72, CA.
[174] *Dixon v. West Ella Developments Ltd* [1978] ICR 856, EAT.
[175] *British Airways Engine Overhaul Ltd v. Francis* [1981] IRLR 9, EAT.
[176] [1978] ICR 643, EAT.
[177] *Lyon v. St James Press Ltd* [1976] 413, EAT.
[178] *Per* Goff L. J. in *Marley Tile Co Ltd v. Shaw* [1980] ICR 72 at p. 79.

industrial action short of a strike are not protected activities for the purposes of either dismissal or action short of dismissal.[179]

9.55 "Appropriate Time"

This right to take part in union activities is circumscribed by the requirement that the activities take place at an appropriate time. This is defined as a time either outside working hours, or, alternatively, within working hours where, in accordance with arrangements agreed with or consent given by his employer, the employee is permitted to take part in those activities.[180] The best course would be to ensure that there is some express agreement defining the terms of this right. However, the requirement that union activities should take place outside working hours unless the employer has consented has not been interpreted as involving a complete embargo on the use of the employer's premises. It would be legitimate for employees to use the employer's premises for union business at times when no work is being done such as during meal breaks or tea breaks so long as their contracts entitle them to be on those premises at that time.[181] The exercise of this right might even involve the employer tolerating minor infringements of his strict legal rights so long as no harm is caused and the employees who are taking part in those activities on his premises are doing so at a time when they are not actually working.[182]

9.56 Implied consent

As has been noted, the greater right to participate in union affairs during working hours can only be exercised with the employer's consent or agreement. Although such consent need not be stated expressly and can be implied, clear evidence of its existence must be established. Mere silence on the part of the employer is unlikely to suffice. In *Marley Tile Co Ltd v. Shaw*[183] the Court of Appeal held that the silence of the employer when an employee denied the status of shop steward announced his intention to hold a meeting during working hours did not imply consent. Equally, a statement in an employee's written particulars providing a right to take part in union activities at an appropriate time does not constitute the necessary agreement or consent nor does it provide any guidance as to what is meant by appropriate time.[184]

9.57 Remedies for action short of dismissal

An employee who alleges that action short of dismissal has been taken against him because of his union membership or trade union activities or because of non-union membership has the right to complain to an industrial tribunal. It is for the employer to establish that the action was not taken on trade union membership grounds.[185] If the complaint is upheld, the tribunal has the authority to make a declaration and to award compensation to the employee. The amount of

---

[179] *Drew v. St Edmondsbury Borough Council* [1980] ICR 513, EAT. The effect of EPCA, s. 62 upon a dismissed striker's right to complain of unfair dismissal is discussed in Chapter Five, paras. 5.62-5.67.

[180] EPCA, s. 23(2) and s. 58(2).

[181] *Post Office v. Crouch* [1974] ICR 374, HL. A decision reached under the equivalent provisions of IRA.

[182] *Per* Lord Reid in *Crouch, ibid.* at pp. 398-400.

[183] [1980] ICR 72.

[184] *Robb v. Leon Motor Services Ltd* [1978] ICR 506, EAT.

[185] EPCA, s. 25(1).

compensation awarded is such as the tribunal considers just and equitable in all the circumstances having regard to the infringement of the complainant's rights and to any loss sustained by him which is attributable to the employer's action.[186] It has been held[187] that the purpose of the award is to compensate an employee for the infringement of his rights, it is not intended to act as a fine against the employer. The amount should be calculated by reference to any monetary loss suffered by the employee plus an additional sum to compensate for non-pecuniary loss. It might be appropriate when assessing compensation to take account of the fact that an employee's sincere desire to enjoy the benefits of trade union membership have been frustrated as a result of the employer's actions.

9.58 Remedies for dismissal

An employee who has been dismissed because of his trade union membership and activities has the same rights of complaint to an industrial tribunal as an employee who has been dismissed for non-union membership. As was noted in Chapter Five these include the right to interim relief and the right to receive enhanced levels of compensation if dismissal for an automatically unfair reason is established.

TIME OFF

9.59 Trade union duties

The original statutory provisions[188] created a right to time off with pay during working hours for employees who were officials[189] of recognised independent trade unions in two circumstances. First, they were entitled to time off to enable them to carry out those duties as officials which were concerned with industrial relations between their employer and any associated employer and their employees.[190] They were also entitled to time off in order to undergo training in aspects of industrial relations which were relevant to their duties and which had been approved by the TUC or by their own union.[191] The case law on the right to time off adopted a liberal interpretation of this provision. In *Sood v. GEC Elliot Automation Ltd*[192] for example, although it was held that there was no statutory right to time off simply to attend meetings of union officials where information would be exchanged, it was accepted that the right to time off should not be restricted exclusively to those purposes falling within the statutory definition of recognition. Moreover, it need not even have been restricted to the industrial relations structure of the employer. The Court of Appeal confirmed this approach in *Beal v. Beecham Group Ltd*[193] where that court held that work preparatory to

---

[186] *Ibid.* s. 26(1).

[187] *Brassington v. Cauldon Wholesale Ltd* [1978] ICR 405, EAT.

[188] EPCA, s. 27 before amendment by EA 1989.

[189] An official is defined by TULRA, s. 30(1) as a person who is an officer of the union or a branch or section or who (not being such an officer) is elected or appointed in accordance with the union's rules to be a representative of its members or some of them.

[190] EPCA, s. 27(1)(a).

[191] *Ibid.* s. 27(1)(b). Cf. the provisions for time off for training for safety representatives in the Safety Representatives and Safety Committees Regulations 1977 SI 1977 No. 500 where there is no need for TUC or union approval. See *White v. Pressed Steel Fisher* [1980] IRLR 176, EAT.

[192] [1979] IRLR 416, EAT. See also *RHP Bearings Ltd v. Brookes* [1979] IRLR 452, EAT.

[193] [1982] ICR 460.

collective bargaining could give rise to a right to time off with pay. It was reiterated that the right of a union official to time off was not restricted by the extent of his union's recognition rights and the court accepted that it could encompass attendance at meetings with other officials of the union employed by the same or an associated employer called to plan union negotiating strategy prior to collective bargaining taking place.

9.60 *Development of the right to time off.* In another Court of Appeal decision, *Thomas Scott & Sons (Bakers) Ltd v. Allen,*[194] the right to paid time off was extended even further. In this case it was held that attending a meeting with union officials was within the industrial relations duties of a shop steward even although the meeting related to a matter over which the union had no authority to bargain collectively with that employer. This was on the basis that it was a shop steward's duty to give senor officials the benefit of his experience at meetings. The only limitation on the right to paid time off was that the official's duties had to have a connection with industrial relations between an employer and his employees. However, it is possible that an official might have a right to paid time off in order to attend a meeting called to plan a union's campaign against the repeal of an Act of Parliament so long as it can be established that the repeal of that Act will have some impact on the continued operation of the employer's arrangements for collective bargaining.[195]

9.61 *Time off for training.* The right to time for training was also liberally interpreted, particularly in England. In *Young v. Carr Fasteners Ltd*[196] for example, it was held that an employee had the right to time off to attend a training course on pensions even although the employer's own pension scheme did not call for any union involvement because advising about pensions was as much about industrial relations as negotiating and advising about wage levels. A different approach to this question has been adopted in Scotland[197] where it was held that an employee had to show that the subject of the course was directly related to his duties as a union official. Moreover, before paid time off could be granted it had to be the purpose of the course to teach material which would be of assistance in negotiation with the employer. This decision is more in keeping with the current statutory regime for time off.

9.62 *Restricting the right to time off.* The scope for time off under both of the above heads has been considerably narrowed[198] by restricting an official's right to time off for union duties to time off in relation to matters over which the union has obtained recognition rights with his particular employer. Now the right to time off is restricted to carrying out duties concerned with matters specified in a statutory list[199] and in relation to which the trade union is recog-

---

[194] [1983] IRLR 329.

[195] See the decision of the Court of Appeal in *Adlington v. British Bakeries (Northern) Ltd* [1989] IRLR 218 reversing the decision of the EAT reported at [1988] ICR 488. See also *Luce v. London Borough of Bexley* [1990] IRLR 422 where the EAT argued that whether a trade union organised lobby of Parliament is a trade union activity depends upon whether it is in some way linked to the employment relationship between the employee, the employer and the trade union.

[196] [1979] IRLR 420, EAT.

[197] *Menzies v. Smith & McLaurin Ltd* [1980] IRLR 180, EAT.

[198] EA, 1989, s. 14.

[199] TULRA, s. 29(1).

nised by the employer; or any other matters so listed where the union is not recognised but which are matters that the employer has agreed that the union may perform functions on behalf of his employees. The right to time off in order to undergo training is now also restricted to training which is relevant in relation to those duties for which recognition has been obtained.[200] These statutory changes ensure that there will be no repetition of decisions such as that in the *Allen* case where entitlement to time off for duties unconnected with collective bargaining was upheld. On the other hand, there are aspects of the decisions in both *Sood* and *Beal* which would be decided in the same way under the current definition since they related to time off in connection with negotiations with the employer over matters in the statutory list. However, it is clear that paid time off under either head can now only be granted where it relates to a matter which forms part of the recognition rights which the employee's union enjoys with his employer. This exclusion of industrial relations duties and the restriction of the right to matters involving the employee's own employer are consistent with the government's objective of weakening national collective bargaining and encouraging bargaining at local level so as to create greater flexibility in the setting of wage rages.

9.63 *The extent of the right to time-off.* An employee is only entitled to take such time off as is reasonable in all the circumstances.[201] Equally, the purposes, occasions and conditions attached to any time off must also be reasonable. Guidance on these questions is provided by the ACAS Code of Practice on Time Off for Trade Union Duties and Activities.[202] Para. 12 of the Revised Code contains a detailed list of the matters for which time off should be granted (assuming that the union has collective bargaining rights). These cover:

(a) terms and conditions of employment, or the physical conditions in which employees are required to work (*e.g.* pay, hours of work, holiday pay and entitlement, sick pay arrangements, pensions, vocational training, equal opportunities, notice periods, the working environment, utilisation of machinery and other equipment);

(b) engagement or non-engagement, or termination or suspension of employment or the duties of employment, of one or more workers (*e.g.* recruitment and selection policies, human resource planning, redundancy and dismissal arrangements);

(c) allocation of work, or the duties of employment as between workers and groups of workers (*e.g.* job grading, job evaluation, job descriptions, flexible working practices);

(d) matters of discipline (*e.g.* disciplinary procedures, representing members at internal interviews, appearing for members before agreed outside appeal bodies or industrial tribunals);

(e) trade union membership or non-membership (*e.g.* representational agreements, induction arrangements);

(f) facilities for officials of trade unions (*e.g.* accommodation, equipment, names of new workers to the union);

---

[200] EA, 1990, s. 14.
[201] EPCA, s. 27(2).
[202] ACAS Code No. 3. The original Code was brought into force on April 1, 1978. The present revised code took effect on May 13, 1991.

(g) machinery for negotiation and consultation and other procedures (*e.g.* collective bargaining, grievance procedures, joint consultation, communicating with members or officials).

The Code also recommends that union officials have the right to reasonable time off in order to prepare for negotiations and meetings, inform members of their progress and to explain the results to members.

9.64 *Reasonable time-off.* As has already been noted, the amount of time off is that which is reasonable in all the circumstances. This issue has also been judicially considered but without any definite guidelines being laid down because it is for the tribunal to decide the question of reasonableness on the facts. This point is illustrated in the *Allen* case[203] where the Court of Appeal refused to disturb the finding of the tribunal that it was not unreasonable in the circumstances for the employer to refuse paid off to all eleven shop stewards who had requested time off in order to attend their meeting. Although this approach is consistent with that applied in other areas of employment law it does have a number of questions unanswered.

For instance, it is not clear whether it would be legitimate for an employer who believes that a request for paid time off for union duties is unreasonable, to grant such time off on an unpaid basis. May L.J. was clearly of the view in *Allen* that an employer would be entitled to offer time off without pay in such circumstances. However in *Beecham Group Ltd v. Beal (No. 2)*[204] it was held that if it was established that the time off was for industrial relations duties, the employer could not impose a condition that it be unpaid. It would be legitimate, however, for an employer when assessing the reasonableness of a particular request to take account of the amount of paid and unpaid time off which that employee has already received.[205] The amount of pay that an employee receives for time off is that amount which he would have received had he worked his normal hours, although an employee paid by piece rates will receive an amount calculated by reference to his average hourly earnings for that work.[206]

9.65 Trade union activities

As far as trade union activities are concerned, an employee is entitled to take time off without pay to take part in the activities of a recognised independent trade union of which he is a member, together with any activities where the employee is acting as the representative of his union.[207] Like time off for trade union duties, the amount, purposes, occasions and conditions under which time off can be taken for those activities are those that are reasonable in all the circumstances. It would be lawful for an employer to refuse time off for union activities to an employee who has already taken a considerable amount of time off for other purposes.[208] The ACAS Code of Practice is once again useful for guidance on this issue. The Code (para. 21) advises, for example, that employees should be permitted reasonable time off in order to attend workplace meetings to discuss and vote on the outcome of negotiations, meeting full-time

---

[203] [1983] IRLR 329. See also Code of Practice, Section 4.
[204] [1983] IRLR 317, EAT.
[205] *Wignall v. British Gas Corporation* [1984] ICR 716, EAT.
[206] EPCA, s. 27 (3).
[207] *Ibid.* s. 28.
[208] *Wignall op. cit.*

officials, voting in properly conducted ballots on industrial action or in union elections. There is no right to time off, however, in order to participate in industrial action whether or not that action is in contemplation or furtherance of a trade dispute.[209]

9.66 Remedies

An employee who is denied the right to time off for trade union duties, relevant training or activities has the right to complain to an industrial tribunal.[210] There is also a right of complaint where the employer has granted time off for trade union duties but has failed to pay the wages that fell due. Where a complaint against a refusal to allow time off is made the tribunal has the authority to make a declaration to that effect and may also award such compensation as it considers just and equitable having regard to the employer's default and any loss sustained by the employee attributable to that refusal.[211] By analogy with the right to compensation for action short of dismissal for trade union membership or activities, the purpose of any award of compensation should not be to punish the employer for his default.[212] Where the complaint relates to a failure by the employer to pay the employee for the time off for trade union duties, the tribunal is entitled to order the payment of the amount which it considers that the employee is due.[213]

---

[209] EPCA, s. 28(2).
[210] *Ibid.* s. 30(1). ACAS can also exercise conciliation functions over such complaints: EPCA, s. 133(1).
[211] *Ibid.* s. 30(2).
[212] See *Brassington v. Cauldon Wholesale Ltd* [1978] ICR 405, EAT.
[213] EPCA, s. 30(3).

Chapter Ten

THE LEGAL REGULATION OF TRADE UNIONS

INTRODUCTION

10.1 The internal affairs of trade unions are regulated both by common law principles and by statute. As far as Scots common law is concerned a trade union is a voluntary unincorporated association with no separate legal identity from that of its members. The nearest analogous organisations are the non-established churches or social clubs. In the same way as the constitution of a club regulates the rights of the members so, in the case of a union, the rule book constitutes the contract of membership. It is the rule book which sets out a person's rights to join, to be disciplined and even to take part in the affairs of the union. As we shall see, the practice of the Scottish courts has been to examine these rules closely in order to establish the contractual rights of the member.[1] One important theme which will be explored in this chapter is the extent to which the courts no longer regard this voluntary association/social club model as suitable when reviewing the conduct of trade unions. There can be no doubt that in modern times trade unions exercise important functions in society far beyond those of the social club. The practice of the closed shop is the most obvious manifestation of the economic power of trade unions. However, the very process of collective bargaining also had important implications for the union member, the employer and for society as a whole, particularly when resort is made to industrial action. It will be important to discover to what extent the law has taken account of these factors in its present attitude towards trade union government.

10.2 Trade unions originally operated in a hostile legal environment where the law provided little or no legal protection for their activities or against abuse of their funds.[2] However, with the enactment of the Trade Union Act 1871, a new legal regime was created whereby trade unions were permitted to regulate their own internal affairs without the threat that their activities would be tainted with illegality.[3] This legislation set the tone for the approach of the State towards internal union affairs. Thus until the decade of the 1980s and with the exception of the period of the Industrial Relations Act 1971 the role of legislation

---

[1] See, for example, *Martin v. Scottish Transport and General Workers Union* 1951 SC 129, 1952 SC (HL) 1.

[2] *Procurator Fiscal v. Wool-Combers in Aberdeen* (1762) M 1961 and *Barr v. Carr* (1766) M 9564. See also *Hornby v. Close* (1867) LR 2 QB 153; *Farrer v. Close* (1869) LR 4 QB 602.

[3] See, in particular, TUA, s. 3 which declared that the purposes of a trade union were not to be considered unlawful simply because they were in restraint of trade and TUA, s. 4 which sought to exclude the courts from entertaining certain types of legal action against trade unions.

had been to provide a legal framework where trade unions could organise their own affairs without external interference. As Kahn-Freund has observed[4] "in this country, it has, on the whole, been common ground that in the dilemma between imposing standards of democracy and protecting union autonomy the law must come down on the side of union autonomy". This policy has now been rejected in favour of one which seeks to ensure that trade unions behave in a manner which conforms with certain democratic standards as laid down in statute. Thus the Trade Union Act 1984 and the Employment Act 1988, for example, ensure that union executive ballots and political fund ballots must be conducted by secret postal ballot. Moreover, the legislation of the 1980s has displayed a belief in the primacy of the rights of the individual union member above and beyond the collective interests of his trade union. As we shall see, for example, statute prevents a union from disciplining a union member who has refused to obey a lawfully executed strike call.[5]

DEFINITION OF A TRADE UNION

10.3 The original definition of a trade union as enacted by the Trade Union Act 1871 was undoubtedly wider than the one operative in modern times since it also applied to employers' associations and even to trade associations unconnected with industrial relations.[6] The present statutory definition of a trade union concentrates upon both the nature of the organisation and upon its objects by providing that a trade union is "an organisation (whether permanent or temporary) which . . . consists wholly or mainly of workers of one or more descriptions and is an organisation whose principal purposes include the regulation of relations between workers of that description or those descriptions and employers or employers' associations".[7] An organisation which is made up wholly or mainly of constituent associations or affiliates can also be a trade union in law so long as either the organisation itself or its constituents or affiliates consist wholly or mainly of workers and also regulate worker/employer relations.[8]

10.4 The members

The members of a trade union must be wholly or mainly workers. A worker is defined as a person who works or normally works or seeks to work under a contract of employment or any other contract (whether express or implied, and, if express, whether oral or in writing) so long as in the case of this latter type of contract the person is required to perform personally any work for another party to the contract who is not his professional client.[9] The term worker is clearly wider in scope than that of employee. However, certain groups of workers cannot be members of trade unions. Members of the police service and those in the armed forces are specifically excluded from the statutory definition.[10] On the other

---

[4] *Kahn-Freund's Labour and the Law* (3rd edn., Davies & Freedland) at p. 274.

[5] EA 1988, s. 3.

[6] See *G & J Rae v. Plate Glass Merchants' Association* 1919 SC 426; *Edinburgh Master Plumbers' Association v. Munro* 1928 SC 565; *Edinburgh & District Aerated Water Manufacturers' Defence Association v. Jenkinson & Co* (1903) 5 F 1159.

[7] TULRA, s. 28.

[8] TULRA, s. 28(1) (b). It is unclear whether the TUC or STUC satisfies the definition of a trade union. See Kidner *Trade Union Law* (2nd edn.) at p. 3.

[9] TULRA, s. 30(1); and see *Carter v. Law Society* [1973] ICR 113.

[10] TULRA, s. 30(1).

hand, both civil servants[11] and national health service staff[12] are expressly declared to be workers.

10.5 The organisation's objects

The fact that a trade union must be an organisation whether permanent or temporary has been described as being "pregnant with elasticity".[13] As a very minimum the union must posses some of the attributes of an organisation. In *Frost v. Clarke & Smith Manufacturing Co Ltd*[14] a claim that an employees' works committee could be a trade union was rejected because it possessed none of the organisational qualities expected of such a body. It had no name, no constitution and no rules, it held no meetings, kept no minutes, and did not have any officers, property or funds. A union must also have the regulation of worker/employer relations as one of its principal objects. This entails establishing that the organisation has some ambition to regulate the relations between an employer and workers by means of collective bargaining. It is not enough for the organisation simply to be involved in organising industrial action.[15] At the very least the organisation must have attempted to obtain recognition rights from an employer.[16] There is nothing to prevent an organisation which seeks to promote the professional interests of its members from satisfying the statutory definition. So long as it is also involved in some way in worker/employer relations it will be a trade union in law. In deciding this question the court is entitled to look beyond the organisation's rules and to consider how it operates in practice.[17]

10.6 Legal Status

There is no doubt that in the past the exact legal status of a trade union was uncertain. As we have seen, Scots common law considered that a trade union had no legal existence separate from the membership. Consequently, it could not sue in its own name — although it could take advantage of the procedures which permitted an unincorporated body to sue by the addition of certain of its members clothed with such responsibility.[18] However, with the enactment of the 1871 Act which *inter alia* granted a trade union the right voluntarily to register with the Chief Registrar of Friendly Societies the English courts construed this provision as bestowing upon it a near corporate status.[19] The exact position in Scotland was unclear. Lord President (Inglis) declared in *Aitken v. Associated Carpenters and Joiners of Scotland* [20] that the 1871 Act made "no change . . .

---

11 TULRA, s. 30(1).

12 TULRA, s. 30(2).

13 *Per* Megarry J. in *Midland Cold Storage v. Steer* [1972] 1 Ch 630.

14 [1973] IRLR 216.

15 *Midland Cold Storage v. Turner* [1972] ICR 230.

16 *Turner, ibid.*

17 *British Association of Advisers and Lecturers in Physical Education v. National Union of Teachers* [1986] IRLR 497 CA.

18 See the decision of Lord McLaren in *Renton Football Club v. McDowall* (1891) 18 R 670; *Wilson v. Scottish Typographical Society* 1912 SC 534.

19 *Taff Vale Railway Co v. Amalgamated Society of Railway Servants* [1901] AC 426 HL; *ASRS v. Osborne* [1910] AC 87 HL; *National Union of General and Municipal Workers v. Gillian* [1946] KB 81 CA; *Bonsor v. Musicians' Union* [1956] AC 104 HL. *Cf.* Lord Macdermott in *Bonsor, ibid.* at pp. 143-144.

20 (1885) 12 R 1206 at p. 1211.

into the constitution of these societies. They remain voluntary associations of which the law can take no special cognisance as collective bodies". This approach was followed in a later sheriff court decision.[21] On the other hand, in *Johnstone v. Associated Ironmoulders of Scotland* [22] Lord Skerrington, following the decision of the House of Lords in *Amalgamated Society of Railway Servants v. Osborne*[23] concluded that a trade union was an example of "a statutory quasi-corporation". Moreover, in later Scottish cases registered trade unions were sued in their descriptive names alone without the addition of any of their responsible members or trustees.

10.7 The present provisions on union status reassert the position at common law by declaring that a trade union "shall not be, or be treated as if it were a body corporate".[24] However, the Act does provide trade unions with certain corporate characteristics. Trade unions are capable of making contracts, suing or being sued in their own names and of being the subjects of criminal prosecution.[25] It is also the case that any judgment, order or award made against a union by a court can be enforced against it to the same extent and in the same manner as if the union were a body corporate.[26] The purpose of providing these corporate characteristics is not to create a near corporation but rather to overcome the specific difficulties which can arise particularly under English law when an unincorporated body is raising or defending a court action. This contention is supported by the decision of O'Connor J. in *Electrical, Electronic, Telecommunications and Plumbing Union v. Times Newspapers Ltd*[27] where it was held that the union could not sue in damages for defamation. Any such action had to be based upon the possession of a personality and reputation and the clear and unambiguous statutory direction that a trade union should not be treated as a body corporate denied it that necessary personality.

10.8 Restraint of trade

There can be no doubt that one major obstacle to the development and growth of trade unions was the common law doctrine of restraint of trade. The law considered that the objects of trade unions were unlawful because they restrained a person's freedom to earn a living in whatever occupation and upon whatever salary or wage that person could obtain. In particular, where a trade union sought to achieve its objectives by the threat or use of industrial action[28] or by the negotiation of closed shop agreements[29] it was held at common law to be an illegal organisation. The position under Scots common law was summarised by Lord President (Dunedin) in *Wilkie v. King*[30] who declared that "trades unions were judged by the decisions of the court to be illegal organisations in restraint of trade, and, as such illegal associations, were denied the assistance of the

[21] *International Tailors', Machinists' and Pressers' Union v. Goldberg* (1903) 19 Sh Ct Rep 312.
[22] (1911) 2 SLT 478.
[23] [1910] AC 87.
[24] TULRA, s. 2.
[25] TULRA, s. 2(1) (a), (c) and (d).
[26] TULRA, s. 2(1) (e).
[27] [1980] QB 585.
[28] *McKernan v. United Operative Masons' Association* (1874) 1 R 453.
[29] *Bernard's Executrix v. National Union of Mineworkers* 1971 SC 32.
[30] 1911 SC 1310 at p. 1314.

courts in recovering under any contracts made by them". Thus from a Scottish perspective it was not so much the fact that a trade union possessed an unincorporated status as common law which constituted an obstacle to the courts entertaining its legal actions, since, in any case, the Scottish courts had already devised ways of permitting an unincorporated body to sue and be sued at common law, but, rather, it was the restraint of trade doctrine which denied a union the necessary authority to pursue or defend a court action.

10.9 Statutory intervention

Statute remedied this situation by declaring that the purposes of a trade union should not be considered unlawful by reason merely that they were in restraint of trade.[31] The exact scope of this provision became the subject of doubt as a result of the opinion of Sachs L.J. in *Edwards v. Society of Graphical and Allied Trades*.[32] There he declared that it only protected the purposes of trade unions and did not therefore prevent the courts from holding that a specific union rule was void and in restraint of trade when it was not "proper" for the attainment of those purposes. Consequently, statute now declares that not only shall the purposes of a trade union not be unlawful so as to make any agreement or trust void or voidable by reason only that they are in restraint of trade, but also that no union rule shall be unlawful or unenforceable for the same reason.[33] However, it is possible that even this extended provision may not insulate the rules of a trade union from judicial scrutiny. In *Greig v. Insole*[34] Slade J. suggested that a distinction might be made between rules which are in restraint of trade and rules which restrain a person's right to work. He considered that as regards this latter category of rule the courts may not by prevented from interfering where an association exercises a virtual monopoly right to control entry to a particular trade or profession.

10.10 Ownership of property

The property of a trade union vests in its trustees.[35] Such vesting of property is in trust for the union itself. On this basis, the union must be the sole beneficiary. However, as a result of its unincorporated status the members are entitled to represent their union "collectively and severally".[36] The rights and obligations of the member, therefore, depend not on the notion of property but upon the contract of membership which all union members possess.[37] In the case of a union's branch funds, however, much will depend upon the terms of the union rule book when ascertaining who enjoys the beneficial rights to that property. In *News Group Ltd v. Society of Graphical and Allied Trades*[38] the Court of Appeal held that the branch property was being held in trust for the members of the branch and not the union, because the clear purport of the rules was to vest that property in trustees who held it on behalf of the branch members for the

---

[31] TUA 1871, s. 3.
[32] [1971] Ch 354 CA.
[33] TULRA, s. 2(5).
[34] [1978] 1 WLR 302.
[35] TULRA, s. 2(1) (b).
[36] *Per* Lord Lindley in *Yorkshire Miners' Association v. Howden* [1905] AC 256 at p. 280.
[37] *Cf.* the rights of members in other forms of unincorporated association under Scots law. See, in particular, *Murray v. Johnstone* (1896) 23 R 981.
[38] [1986] ICR 716.

time being. However it is unlawful for a union's property to be used in order to reimburse an individual who has been fined or is likely to be fined for the commission of a relevant offence or for contempt of court[39] and for a union to offer indemnity to an individual as regards a fine for any such offence or for contempt of court.[40] If a union should fail to take the necessary proceedings in order to recover unlawful payments made to individuals from union funds any union member can seek the authorisation of the court to pursue such an action at the union's expense.[41]

10.11 The trustee's responsibilities

Union trustees are bound by the normal law of trusts and owe fiduciary duties as regards their stewardship of the union property. Thus trustees can be removed from office by the court at common law if they act in such a way as to show that they are not fit and proper persons to administer the union's assets.[42] Under Scottish common law this could entail the appointment of a judicial factor by the court to take over the management of the union's assets.[43] In any case, statute now gives the courts important new powers to intervene at the suit of a member when trustees have carried out their functions, or are proposing to carry out their functions, in such a manner as to cause or permit any unlawful application of the union's property.[44] Alternatively, a member can also seek the assistance of the court where the trustees have complied, or are proposing to comply, with an unlawful direction given to them under the union's rules.[45] If the court is satisfied that the member's application is well-founded it can make such order as it considers appropriate. Without prejudice to these general powers, the power of the court on such an application includes:-

(a) power to require the trustees to take all such steps as the order may require for the protection or recovery of the union's property;

(b) power to appoint a judicial factor on the property of the union; and

(c) power to remove one or more trustees from office.[46]

EMPLOYERS' ASSOCIATIONS

10.12 Unlike the earlier legislation modern law recognises employers' associations as separate and distinct organisations.[47] It is clear that such an association can either be a body corporate or unincorporated. An unincorporated employers' association is provided with the same corporate benefits in respect of title to sue etc. as is granted to a trade union. However, it is clear that, unlike the trade union, an unincorporated employers' association is a quasi corporation.[48] An employers' association can remain unincorporated even although it has more

---

[39] EA 1988, s. 8(1) (a).

[40] EA 1988, s. 8(1) (b).

[41] EA 1988, s. 8(3).

[42] See the decision of Mervyn Davies J. in *Clarke v. Heathfield, The Times*, December 1, 1984. Approved on appeal at [1985] ICR 203 CA.

[43] *Munro v. Edinburgh & District Trades Council Social Club* [1989] GWD 6-240.

[44] EA 1988, s. 9(1) (a).

[45] EA 1988, s. 9(1) (b).

[46] EA 1988, s. 9(3)

[47] TULRA, s. 3.

[48] *EETPU v. Times Newspapers Ltd* [1980] QB 585.

than twenty members and would otherwise require to be incorporated under s 716 of the Companies Act 1985.[49] An unincorporated employers' association enjoys the same exemption from the restraint of trade doctrine as does a trade union. However, its corporate counterpart has its rules and purposes protected only insofar as they relate to the regulation of relations between employers and workers or trade unions.[50]

THE ROLE OF THE CERTIFICATION OFFICER

10.13 The Certification Officer exercises an extensive independent statutory jurisdiction over trade union affairs.[51] The Office was first created by the Employment Protection Act in 1975. However, as well as being given the authority to award certificates of independence to trade unions the Certification Officer also had transferred to him certain functions which were exercised formerly by the Chief Registrar of Friendly Societies. There is authority for an Assistant Certification Officer for Scotland to be appointed.[52] This officer has the responsibility for maintaining the lists of trade unions and employers' associations whose principal offices are in Scotland. The original duties of the Certification Officer have been extended considerably by the legislation of the 1980s. He is responsible for the administration of the scheme whereby independent trade unions are entitled to claim payment towards expenditure incurred in the conduct of secret postal ballots for certain prescribed purposes[53] and his jurisdiction has been extended to hear complaints over the conduct of union executive elections,[54] and the conduct of political fund ballots.[55]

10.14 List of trade unions and employers' associations

The Certification Officer, or his assistant in Scotland, is required to maintain a list of organisations which satisfy the statutory definition of a trade union[56] and also a list of employers' associations. Therefore, the only requirements for inclusion on the list of trade unions are that the organisation be made up wholly or mainly of workers and that it has the regulation of worker/employer relations as one of its principal purposes. There is a right of appeal against a refusal to list or against a withdrawal from the list.[57] The listing of a trade union is a simple process, and by itself is has very little significance. Indeed, there are certain obligations which are imposed upon a trade union even where it remains unlisted. Thus any organisation which meets the statutory definition of a trade union whether listed or not is required to maintain proper accounting records, to have those accounts audited and to submit annual returns to the Certification

---

[49] TULRA, s. 3(4).

[50] TULRA, s. 3(5).

[51] See EPA, s. 7 and Sch. 1. Although ACAS provides the Certification Officer with the necessary staff, accommodation and finance, he is independent of both ACAS and the Secretary of State in the exercise of his functions.

[52] EPA, s. 7(4).

[53] EA 1980, s. 2.

[54] TUA, s. 6.

[55] EA 1988, s. 16.

[56] TULRA, s. 8.

[57] TULRA, s. 8(7).

Officer. The main benefit of listing is that it is a prerequisite for any union which intends to seek a certificate of independence form the certification officer. The only other important benefit is that a listed trade union is guaranteed tax relief for expenditure on provident funds.[58]

10.15 Independence

In deciding whether to issue a certificate of independence the Certification Officer is guided by the statutory definition of an independent trade union.[59] This declares that a trade union is independent when it is not under the domination or control of an employer or a group of employers or of one or more employers' associations; and is not liable to interference by an employer or any such group or association (arising out of the provision of financial or material support or by any other means whatsoever) tending towards such control. Any union seeking a certificate must satisfy the Certification Officer that it meets both parts of the test. As regards the first requirement that the union should not be dominated or controlled by the employer, it has been suggested that this might require both a subjective and an objective approach.[60] However, it has been the second limb of the definition which has been the major barrier to the acquisition of a certificate of independence. Most unions who have been denied a certificate have failed because they could not prove that they were not liable to interference tending towards employer control.

10.16 Interference by an employer

The approach of the Certification Officer towards this second limb has been to ask how vulnerable the organisation is to employer interference. This test has been criticised as being more suited to discovering whether the union was subject to employer domination or control.[61] Nevertheless, the Court of Appeal has made it clear that the appropriate test under limb 2 is vulnerability to employer interference.[62] This requires the Certification Officer to look beyond the issue of the quality of relations between union and employer and to consider such factors as the extent to which the union has to rely on employer financed or employer provided facilities for its existence. The duty of the Certification Officer is to assess the independence of a trade union on the basis of these statutory criteria. The effectiveness of the union in collective bargaining is irrelevant except insofar as it impinges upon independence. Equally, the Certification Officer has no authority to consider the impact that certification will have on existing collective bargaining arrangements.[63]

[58] TULRA, s. 9(3).
[59] TULRA, s. 30(1).
[60] *Association of HSD (Hatfield) Employees v. Certification Officer* [1979] ICR 21, EAT.
[61] *Squibb UK Staff Association v. Certification Officer* [1977] IRLR 335, EAT.
[62] *Squibb UK Staff Association v. Certification Officer* [1979] ICR 235.
[63] This is a matter which has caused some TUC-affiliated trade unions to criticise the role of the Certification Officer. See his Annual Report for 1977 at p. 12. The Certification Officer has the power to withdraw a certificate from a union which is no longer independent. See EPA, s. 8(7).

10.17 The relevant criteria

The Certification Officer has drawn up a series of criteria which he takes account of when deciding whether or not to issue a certificate. These criteria have been approved.[64] They are

(1) *History* If there is evidence in the recent past that the union has received employer support and encouragement, this is a powerful argument against certification.

(2) *Membership Base* A union which recruits from the employees of a single employer is much more vulnerable to employer interference than a broadly based union.

(3) *Organisation and Structure* Looking at the union rules and its practices as well, the union should be organised in such a way as to enable the members to play a full part in the union's decision-making process free from employer interference or involvement.

(4) *Finance* A union with weak finances and inadequate reserves is more likely to be susceptible to employer interference that one with a strong financial base.

(5) *Employer-Provided Facilities* The greater a union's reliance on such facilities the more vulnerable it must be to employer interference.

(6) *Collective Bargaining Record* A weak record does not of itself indicate employer dependence. On the other hand, proof of a strong record and the display of a robust attitude in negotiation will be significant and, indeed, may even outweigh other factors unfavourable to the union's case.

There is no need for a union to satisfy each of these criteria separately. The final decision will be based on "the whole nature and circumstances" of the application.[65]

10.18 The importance of independence

In contrast to the issue of listing, there are considerable and numerous advantages which accrue to a trade union which has been awarded a certificate of independence. Privileges accrue to both the union and to its members. For example, union members have protection so far as their trade union membership and activities are concerned;[66] have the right to time off for trade union activities[67] and can be appointed as safety representatives.[68] Amongst the advantages which accrue to an independent trade union are the rights to information for collective bargaining;[69] to consult with a trade union over redundancies,[70] to obtain funds from the Certification Officer for the cost of postal ballots;[71] and to use the employer's facilities for secret ballots.[72]

---

[64] *Blue Circle Staff Association v. Certification Officer* [1977] ICR 224, EAT.

[65] Annual Report of the Certification Officer for 1979 at pp. 10-11.

[66] EPCA, ss. 23-26.

[67] EPCA, ss. 27-28.

[68] Health and Safety at Work etc. Act 1974, s. 2(4).

[69] EPA, ss. 17-21.

[70] EPA, Part IV.

[71] EA 1980, s. 1.

[72] EA 1980, s. 2.

10.19 Mergers

The Trade Union (Amalgamations) Act 1964 recognises two forms of merger; a transfer of engagements and an amalgamation. In the former case only members of the union seeking to transfer are balloted. If the ballot result is for transfer, the membership of the transferor organisation joins the transferee union with the result that the transferor union ceases to exist in law. In the case of an amalgamation two or more unions will come together in order to form one new union with new rules. All the unions involved must return a membership vote in favour of merger before such an amalgamation can take place. The Certification Officer's authority over union mergers has been delegated to the Assistant Certification Officer for Scotland in the case of transfers where the transferee union is based in Scotland and in the case of amalgamations where the new union will have its principal office north of the border.

10.20 Procedure

Before any transfer or amalgamations can take place a number of steps laid down in the Act and accompanying Regulations[73] must be carried out.

The completion of these steps is necessary before the Certification Officer can authorise the merger. As a first step, the Certification Officer must be given the opportunity to approve the instrument setting out the terms of the merger. There is also a requirement that a notice which explains the merger proposals be drawn up and distributed to the members who will be voting on it. This must also be approved by the Certification Officer. There will then be a ballot which takes the form of a resolution upon which the members vote.

10.21 The ballot

The fundamental aspect of the procedure is the ballot. There are three basic requirements for the conduct of this ballot. First, every member of the union must be entitled to vote on the resolution.[74] This means that the union cannot restrict the vote to certain classes of member even if the union rule book provides this authority.[75] Second, every member of the union must be allowed to vote without interference or constraint and must, so far as reasonably possible, be given a fair opportunity of voting.[76] The phrase "without interference of constraint" has been interpreted by the Certification Officer as being concerned with intimidation, physical interference and the like.[77] There is nothing to prevent a union campaigning in favour of a particular ballot result. The third requirement is that the method of voting must involve the marking of a voting paper by the person voting.[78] The Act does not demand that the ballot be secret

---

[73] See the Trade Unions and Employers' Associations (Amalgamations, etc) Regulations, 1975, S.I. 1975 No. 536 as amended by the Trade Unions and Employers' Associations (Amalgamations etc.) Regulations 1978, S.I. 1978 No. 1344.

[74] TU(A)A, s. 1(2) (a).

[75] *McLaren and Ognall and Association of Cinematograph, Television and Allied Technicians,* CO Annual Report, 1979, p. 18; *Young and National Union of Agricultural and Allied Workers,* CO Annual Report, 1982, p. 21.

[76] TU(A)A, s. 1(2) (b).

[77] *Clare and Eagle Star Staff Association,* Annual Report, 1981, p. 19; *Ammonds and Society of Lithographic Artists, Designers, Engineers and Process Workers,* Annual Report, 1982, p. 20.

[78] TU(A)A, s. 1(2) (c).

or that it be conducted by post. Beyond these three conditions a union has the discretion to arrange for the vote to be taken in any manner it thinks fit.[79] A simple majority of those voting is all that is required for the resolution to be carried. However, this is subject to the union's rules. Thus, for example, any provision in the union rule book which demands a larger majority or which requires that a certain proportion of members vote in the ballot for the resolution to be carried would be effective and binding in such circumstances.

10.22 Registration of the transfer

If the resolution is approved in the ballot is for the union or unions concerned to request the Certification Officer to register the instrument. There are two important points about registration. First, the Certification Officer would be entitled to refuse to register the instrument if its terms are inconsistent with the rules of a participating union.[80] Second, registration can only be effected after a period of six weeks has elapsed in order to enable complaints from members about the conduct of the merger process to be received.[81] Any complaint made to the Certification Officer during this time will prevent the instrument from being registered until that complaint is finally determined.[82] Once the instrument is recorded, however, the merger will become effective and there will be an automatic transfer of union property without any express conveyance.[83]

10.23 Union accounts

Both listed and unlisted trade unions[84] and employers' associations are required to keep proper accounting records and to establish and maintain a satisfactory system of control of those records.[85] The records must be such as to give a true and fair view of the state of affairs of the union.[86] Union branches are also required to comply with these provisions.[87] Formerly, a member did not have any statutory right to inspect the union's accounts although such a right may well have been provided under the rule book.[88] However, now a union is required to keep its accounting records available for inspection and to ensure that union members have the right to inspect those records on request.[89] A member who is exercising his right to inspect has the statutory right to be accompanied by an accountant.[90] A union must also ensure that a properly qualified auditor has been appointed to make a report on these accounts.[91] The auditor's report

---

[79] TU(A)A, s. 2(2). Although there is no requirement that a merger ballot be postal, the expenses of such ballots can be reimbursed by the Certification Officer. See EA 1980, s. 2(3) (e) and para. 10.57.

[80] *R v. Certification Officer, ex parte* AUEW (Engineering Section) [1983] ICR 125.

[81] TU(A)A, s. 1(5).

[82] TU(A)A, s. 4(2). There is a right of appeal on a point of law to the EAT. TU(A)A, s. 4(8).

[83] TU(A)A, s. 1(5).

[84] The only excluded organisations are those which consist wholly or mainly of representatives of constituent or affiliated organisations — TULRA, s. 10(1).

[85] TULRA, s. 10(1) and (2).

[86] TULRA, s. 10(3).

[87] TULRA, s. 10(4).

[88] For the extent of this right see *Dodd v. Amalgamated Marine Workers' Union* [1924] 1 Ch 116 CA; *Taylor v. National Union of Mineworkers (Derbyshire Area)* [1985] IRLR 65.

[89] EA 1988, s. 6.

[90] EA 1988, s. 6(3) (b).

[91] TULRA, s. 11(3). It is necessary for a union's rules to make provision for the appointment and removal of an auditor — TULRA, Sch. 2 para. 11.

which is included in the annual return made to the Certification Officer must state whether the accounts present a true and fair view of the union's financial position.[92]

10.24 Annual returns

All trade unions and employers' associations are required to submit annual returns to the Certification Officer for each calendar year.[93] Any such return must contain a revenue account, a balance sheet, and any other accounts required by the Certification Officer.[94] A copy of the union's current rules should also be included in the return together with a note of any changes in the union's officers or in the address of its head office.[95] It is the duty of the Certification Officer to keep these annual returns available for public inspection at all reasonable hours.[96] Both trade unions and employers' associations are under an obligation to provide any person who so requests with a copy of the rule book and the most recent annual return.[97]

SECESSION AND DISSOLUTION

10.25 There is an implied term in every union rule book permitting a member to resign from the union on giving reasonable notice and after complying with any reasonable conditions.[98] Thus a union has no legal remedy if a large number of members decide to resign from the union at the same time. However, the position is undoubtedly different when those disaffected members seek to leave the union as one distinct unit, for example, where a branch or section of the union decides to secede. In such a case, secession is only competent where there is a specific union rule providing for such an event. If a union does not possess such a rule it would be necessary for one to be created before the severance of any branch of the union would be legitimate.[99] Moreover, even where secession is permitted under the rules, those leaving the union have no right to any of its property, unless there is a specific union rule granting them rights over the union's property as well.[100] Usually, the union's property will remain vested in its original trustees. The need for express rule book authority also applies where it is the union which seeks to dissolve one of its branches. It has been held that such dissolution would only be legitimate where there is an express provision in the rule book clothing the union with such power.[101] Equally, it would not be competent for the union to rely on the general power given to the executive council by the rules to manage the affairs of the union as authority for dissolution of a branch.

---

[92] TULRA, Sch. 2, para. 19.
[93] TULRA, s. 11(2).
[94] TULRA, Sch. 2, para. 2.
[95] TULRA, Sch. 2, para. 2.
[96] TULRA, s. 11(5).
[97] TULRA, s. 11(4).
[98] TULRA, s. 7.
[99] *John v. Rees* [1970] Ch 345.
[100] *Burnley, Nelson, Rossendale and District Textile Workers Union v. Amalgamated Textile Workers Union* [1986] IRLR 298.
[101] *Maddock v. EETPU* 1972 SLT (Sh Ct) 54.

10.26 There is no statutory provision which requires a union to possess a rule authorising its dissolution where necessary.[102] However, such a rule would be advisable because under the common law an unincorporated association has no right to dissolve itself without the consent of every member.[103] If a union does not possess a dissolution rule it is always free to adopt one so long as it complies with all the democratic requirements necessary before any additional rules can by created. Where no such rule exists a simple resolution authorising winding-up passed at a delegate meeting of the union will not be sufficient.[104] There must be an express rule setting out the dissolution procedure and that procedure must be followed to the letter. A union should also possess a rule which explains in detail how its assets are to be distributed on dissolution. Otherwise the general law should be applied. This should ensure that the union's net assets are distributed amongst the members. However, the exact method of calculation for distribution of those assets is as yet unclear.[105]

MEMBER'S RIGHTS AT COMMON LAW

10.27 There is no doubt that in law the union rule book constitutes a contract of membership between the member and his union.[106] However, there is also both statutory[107] and judicial[108] authority for the view that the contract is between the members *inter se*. Any action raised by a member alleging unfair treatment by his union must be based upon breach of this contract. It will be the provisions of the rule book, as a contract, which will be relied upon by the courts to resolve any disputes about the extent of members' rights on the basis that those rules constitute "an exhaustive code".[109] The Scottish courts have always relied upon the notion of contract as the mechanism for reviewing the internal affairs of all unincorporated voluntary associations and not just trade unions.[110] This sets the position in Scotland apart from that under English law where at least initially a member's rights were thought to be based on property[111] and where in more modern times alternative bases for review of trade union affairs have been canvassed.[112]

---

[102] It is possible that a union could be wound up as an unregistered company under Part XXI of the Companies Act 1985.

[103] *Free Church of Scotland v. Overtoun* (1904) 7 F (HL) 1.

[104] *Gardner v. McLintock* (1904) 11 SLT 654.

[105] Compare *Re Printers and Transferors Amalgamated Trades Protection Society* [1899] 2 Ch 184 with *Re Sick and Funeral Society of St John's Sunday School* [1973] Ch 51.

[106] See, for example, the judgment of Lord Blades in *Martin v. Scottish TGWU* 1951 SC 129 particularly at 136.

[107] See EA 1982, s. 15(7) which defines a union's rules as meaning "the written rules of the union . . . forming part of the contract between a member and the other members".

[108] See, in particular, the speech of Lord MacDermott in *Bonsor v. Musicians' Union* [1956] AC 104.

[109] *Martin v. Scottish TGWU* 1951 SC 129.

[110] See *Robinson v. Scottish Amateur Athletic Association* (1900) 7 SLT 356; *Anderson v. Manson* 1906 SC 838.

[111] *Rigby v. Connol* (1880) 14 Ch D 482.

[112] Lord Denning, for example, sought to argue that union rules were akin to bye-laws. See his judgments in both *Bonsor v. Musicians' Union* [1954] Ch 479 and *Cheall v. Association of Professional, Executive, Clerical and Computer Staff* [1982] ICR 543. This theory has been rejected by the House of Lords in both *Faramus v. Film Artistes Association* [1964] AC 925 and in *Cheall* [1983] ICR 398. The idea that a member may have a cause of action based on status was firmly rejected by Lord President Cooper as being "completely false" in *Martin v. Scottish TGWU* 1951 SC 129 at 143.

10.28 If the union rule book is the source for the terms of the contract of membership, this must also mean that the law would expect that any disciplinary action would comply with rule book requirements. As has been stated, there is ample authority in Scotland that all voluntary associations must comply with their constitutions when disciplining members. However, another ground of action has also been recognised and this arises where the member complains that there has been a denial of natural justice.[113] Thus even where the association complies with its constitution its decision may still be impugned by reference to natural justice rules because the member had no notification of the charge against him or had not been given any opportunity to be heard in his defence.[114] As we shall see, these two grounds of review still constitute the bedrock upon which a member's rights to complain about a union's decision to discipline or expel him have been built.

10.29 Patrimonial loss

Before examining the application of this area of the law to trade unions in more detail, one final point has to be made. This concerns the additional requirement that not only does a member suing an unincorporated body have to show some breach of the rules but most also establish patrimonial loss. This entails establishing that the pursuer has been deprived of something more substantial than merely the enjoyment of membership,[115] although loss of status or reputation might be enough.[116] There is no doubt that in the early cases, and, particularly those decided during the time of the Trade Union Act 1871, the need to establish patrimonial loss was a major obstacle in the path of a member suing his union.[117] Nowadays it is no longer an issue. An averment of breach of the contract of membership by a trade union member seems to constitute sufficient patrimonial interest to permit the action to proceed.[118]

10.30 Admission

The fact that there is no contract in existence between the applicant and the union has made it far more difficult for the courts to discover a theoretical tool with which to review a union's decision to exclude a person from membership. There is no doubt that at least initially the courts adopted a fairly benign attitude to union exclusion cases. Indeed, in the only major case on the subject in Scotland — *Martin v. Scottish Transport and General Workers' Union*[119] — the House of Lords restricted themselves exclusively to an examination of the union's rules in order to discover whether the decision to exclude complied with them. In this case the pursuer had become a member of the union in 1940 and was placed in a category which restricted membership to the duration of the war. In

---

[113] See Lord Justice-Clerk Aitchison in *M'Donald v. Burns* 1940 SC 376.

[114] *Walker v. Amalgamated Union of Engineers and Foundry Workers* 1969 SLT 150.

[115] *Ellis v. Neilston Bowling Club* 1987 GWD 3-81.

[116] Per Lord Prosser in *Gunstone v. Scottish Women's Amateur Athletic Association* 1987 SLT 611.

[117] *Aitken v. Associated Carpenters and Joiners of Scotland* (1885) 12 R 1206; *Drennan v. Associated Ironmoulders of Scotland* 1921 SC 151.

[118] See, for example, *McGregor v. National and Local Government Officers' Association* 1979 SC 401.

[119] 1952 SC (HL) 1.

1948 the union resolved to terminate his membership. Martin sought a declarator that he was still a union member and reduction of that resolution. Lord Normand accepted that it was for the union to decide its own rules over admission. It was held, therefore, that since there was no authority in the rule book to admit a person into temporary membership the pursuer's purported membership was *ultra vires*. Thus although Martin had enjoyed *de facto* rights of membership he had never in law been a member. This broad approach was followed in the later House of Lords decision in *Faramus v. Film Artistes' Association*[120] where the judges were not prepared to question the application of a union rule which had the effect of barring the plaintiff from membership because of criminal convictions even although these related to offences committed almost twenty years before during the German occupation of Jersey. This conclusion was reached despite their Lordships' recognition that since Faramus' employment was the subject of a closed shop agreement, loss of union membership would also entail loss of employment.

10.31 Although the *Martin* case still remains the last word on the law of Scotland as regards union admission decisions, there have been cases decided by the English courts which have developed some legal basis with which to review union admission decisions. This has come about through the development of the concept of a right to work. The original architect of this theory was Lord Denning who believed that powerful organisations such as trade unions should be prevented from denying individuals the right to exercise their skills in their chosen area of employment. In the area of union admission policies the right to work theory has been used to declare invalid union refusals to admit[121] or re-admit[122] applicants where the union acted arbitrarily or capriciously in processing those applications. Its most effective application arose in cases where there was a closed shop.[123]

10.32 Hepple has argued that the concept of a right to work is merely "a reformulation in positive terms of the old doctrine or restraint of trade"[124] applied to protect the individual. Nevertheless, other judges have recognised its existence. Sachs L.J., for example, has referred to a right of equal opportunity to obtain work under English law.[125] Another judge[126] has acknowledged that the notion of a right to work is a category of public policy wider than restraint of trade. It entitles the courts to review the application of job controls by trade unions and other professional bodies in order to ensure fair treatment for applicants.[127] Megarry V.-C. in *McInnes v. Onslow Fane*[128] has argued that it should be more properly referred to as a liberty to work. This case is important because it provides a clear indication about the direction taken by English law on this subject.

---

[120] [1964] AC 925.
[121] *Nagle v. Feilden* [1966] 2 QB 633. See also *Lee v. Showmen's Guild* [1952] 2 QB 329.
[122] *Edwards v. SOGAT* [1971] Ch 354.
[123] *Edwards, ibid*; *Goring v. British Actors' Equity Association* [1987] IRLR 122.
[124] "A Right to Work?" (1981) 10 ILJ 65 at pp. 79-80.
[125] *Edwards v. SOGAT* [1971] 1 Ch 354 at p. 383.
[126] Slade J. in *Greig v. Insole* [1978] 1 WLR 302.
[127] See also Browne Wilkinson V.-C. in *Goring v. British Actors' Equity Association* [1987] IRLR 122.
[128] [1978] 3 All ER 211.

Here Megarry V.-C. argued that unions must act fairly in exercising their authority to exclude or expel. In most admission cases, this simply means that a union should ensure that its decision is reached honestly without bias or caprice. However, in other cases where a person has a legitimate expectation that he will be admitted into membership because the union is merely acting as a confirming body or the person has been a member previously, higher standards of fairness are required. The nature and extent of this higher duty was not explained by Megarry V.-C. However, Elias has argued that such a higher duty not only permits the courts to review the substantive unfairness of a union admission rule but also ensures that the courts' right of review is no longer confined exclusively to closed shop cases.[129] Although there is no express authority on this point in Scotland,[130] it is submitted that the courts in Scotland would apply a similar concept, at least in the sense of providing an applicant facing union job controls with a right to fair and equal treatment.

10.33 Discipline and expulsion

As has already been noted, Scots law has always recognised two bases for reviewing the activities of an unincorporated association. The first has involved discovering whether the organisation has acted in breach of its rules and the second has concerned the application of the rules of natural justice. It is also legitimate for a judge to intervene where there is evidence of malice or bad faith so that the decision can be challenged on the basis that it is not one which could have been reached *bona fide*.[131] As far as trade unions are concerned this latter ground for review has been refined so that it now involves a consideration of whether or not the decision was one which a reasonable trade union could have reached.[132]

10.34 As far as breach of the rules is concerned it is clear that if a union is intending to discipline or expel a member it must ensure that it has both the necessary authority in its rule book and that it complies with those rules. The court will always demand that a union comply with rule book requirements on the basis of the contract of membership. Thus if a union conducts its disciplinary procedures in breach of its rules or imposes a penalty which is not authorised by the rule book, the member will be entitled to sue the union for breach of contract. A union must ensure, for example, that the person or body conducting the disciplinary proceedings has the necessary authority under the rules;[133] and that any disciplinary penalty imposed against a member is implemented at a time specified in the rule book.[134] The Scottish courts have been just as deter-

---

[129] "Admission to Trade Unions" (1979) 8 ILJ 111.
[130] The *Lee* decision was applied in Scotland by Lord Allanbridge in *Partington v. NALGO* 1981 SC 299 but only as regards the question of expulsion.
[131] *Dawkins v. Antrobus* (1881) 17 Ch 615.
[132] *Lee v. Showmen's Guild* [1952] 2 QB 329 applied in Scotland by Lord Allanbridge in *Partington v. NALGO* 1981 SC 299.
[133] See, for example, *Bonsor v. Musicians' Union* [1956] AC 104 HL where it was held that an expulsion by a branch secretary was unlawful because he had no such authority under the rules.
[134] In *Blackall v. National Union of Foundryworkers* (1923) 39 TLR 431 it was held that B's expulsion was unlawful because he was expelled two days earlier than the rule about expulsion for arrears would allow.

mined as their English counterparts to ensure that the requirements of the rule book are enforced to the letter. In *McGregor v. National and Local Government Officers' Association*,[135] for example, Lord Dunpark held that a union which had rescinded a decision to expel a member could not reinstate that decision simply by means of a resolution of the annual conference. If disciplinary action was to be reactivated this entailed starting these proceedings afresh so that the member enjoyed all the procedural safeguards as provided by the rules and could exercise his full rights of appeal as prescribed by the rule book.

10.35 Expulsion and the Bridlington Rules

The same strict approach has also been applied by the courts as regards union expulsion decisions which comply with a disputes decision of the TUC under its Bridlington Rules. The thrust of these rules is to avoid inter-union disputes over organisation and negotiation rights. It is not lawful, for example, for a union to expel a member in conformity with an award of a disputes committee where it has no specific provision authorising such expulsion under its own rules.[136] Moreover the Bridlington Principles themselves have been subjected to very close scrutiny by the courts.[137] However, where it appears that neither the Bridlington Rules nor the expelling union's own rules have been misapplied the courts cannot intervene simply because the decision to expel is unreasonable.[138] It is clear, therefore, that in this area where a union makes rules which it considers to be in the best interests of its members and applies those rules to the letter it would normally be beyond judicial challenge.[139] The STUC also applies the Bridlington Rules. However, where a trade union has been suspended from membership of the TUC for breach of Bridlington the STUC has no right automatically to invoke the same penalty in Scotland simply because it has a reciprocal agreement with the TUC. Such suspension requires the express authority of a specific STUC rule.[140]

10.36 The content of union rules

Union rule books normally provide for two types of offence — a specific offence where an express rule of the union has been broken and a blanket offence for conduct which the union believes is detrimental or prejudicial to its interests. In both cases the courts have applied a strict construction of the rules. Where the allegation is that a member has broken a specific disciplinary rule, it must be established that the actual conduct satisfies the terms of that offence. For example, a union would not be justified in disciplining a member who left a mandatory meeting early when the rule book merely required attendance at such meetings.[141] Equally, where such a rule is ambiguous or unclear the court will

---

[135] 1979 SC 401.

[136] *Spring v. National Amalgamated Stevedores and Dockers Society* [1956] 2 All ER 221.

[137] See *Rothwell v. APEX* [1975] IRLR 375 where it was held that a transfer of engagements does not constitute organisation activities under Bridlington. See also the majority decision of the Court of Appeal in *Cheall v. APEX* [1982] ICR 543.

[138] *Cheall v. APEX* [1983] ICR 398, HL.

[139] See the speech of Lord Diplock in *Cheall, ibid*, at p. 405.

[140] See *EETPU v. STUC, Glasgow Herald*, 10 August 1988, where Lord Davidson accepted an undertaking from the STUC that it would lift its suspension of the EETPU because it was admitted that the STUC did not possess the power to suspend affiliated unions under its constitution.

[141] *McLelland v. NUJ* [1975] ICR 116.

apply the meaning which is more favourable to the member concerned.[142] Where a member is charged with a blanket offence, the function of the court is to discover whether the facts as proved are reasonably capable of establishing that offence. In *Silvester v. National Union of Printing, Bookbinding and Paper Workers*[143] for example, it was held that a member who had refused to work overtime contrary to the instructions of his union branch had not acted in a manner detrimental to the interests of his union because there was no union rule which made the working of overtime compulsory.

10.37 The blanket offence cases raise the question about how far the courts are prepared to go in examining the facts and the interpretation which the union has placed upon them. There is an obvious tension in the area of union discipline between the interest of the union to determine its own affairs and the right of the individual member not to be unreasonably treated. In the early days this tension was reflected in the court's insistence that it would only intervene where there was no evidence of rule book irregularities nor any denial of natural justice if it could be proved that the actual decision was reached in bad faith.[144] This test was very similar to that applied in the case of a social club. The modern test for trade unions, however, is to consider whether the facts are reasonably capable of supporting the decision reached. There is no doubt that an important factor in the development of this test has been the recognition that union disciplinary decisions can affect a person's livelihood.[145] The test grants to the court a discretion to consider factual questions as well as legal ones. Its scope is best illustrated by the decision of the Court of Appeal in *Lee v. Showmen's Guild*.[146] In that case Lee had been expelled from the Guild for "unlawful competition" by taking a site at a fair which had already been allocated to another member. In considering the extent to which the courts could review the disciplinary decision of a trade union, Lord Denning argued that union disciplinary committees performed two functions. First, they construed the rules and, second, they applied those rules to the facts. The second issue may appear to be solely a question of fact. However, Lord Denning argued that the two issues were so inextricably mixed together that they could not be separated. This decision undoubtedly enlarged the scope for judicial intervention. In the end, the Court of Appeal held unanimously that the facts in this case did not establish the offence and concluded that the union had come to a decision which no reasonable union could have reached.

10.38 Discipline and industrial action

It has been in the area of union disciplinary proceedings against the member who fails to take part in industrial action that this test has been most important. Its widest application was that of Templeman J. in *Esterman v. NALGO*[147] who suggested that a member being disciplined for not taking part in industrial ac-

---

[142] *Amalgamated Society of Carpenters v. Braithwaite* [1922] 2 AC 440 HL.

[143] (1966) 1 KIR 679. See also *Kelly v. NATSOPA* (1915) 31 TLR 632 CA.

[144] *Maclean v. Workers' Union* [1929] 1 Ch 602; *Wolstenholme v. AMU* [1920] 2 Ch 388.

[145] See Somervell L. J. in *Lee v. Showmens' Guild* [1952] 2 QB 329 and Lord Allanbridge in *Partington v. NALGO* 1981 SC 299.

[146] [1952] 2 QB 329.

[147] [1974] ICR 625.

tion had the right to doubt whether the union had the authority to issue such instructions in the first place. Templeman J. paid lip service to the now traditional test as to whether this was a decision which no reasonable union could have reached. However, as Davidson has argued, the *Esterman* case inverts the test because it concentrates upon whether it was reasonable for the member being subjected to the disciplinary process to refuse to engage in industrial action.[148]

10.39 The Scottish courts have also recognised that where a member is being disciplined for non-participation in industrial action the facts must be reasonably capable of supporting the disciplinary decision reached. However, the *Esterman* decision has been specifically distinguished in Scotland on the basis that it goes beyond the *ratio* of the *Lee* case.[149] In *Partington v. NALGO*[150] Lord Allanbridge declared invalid a decision to expel the pursuer for returning to work during a strike. He argued that the correct test was whether the facts were reasonably capable of establishing a breach of the union's rules. In deciding whether the facts did prove the offence Lord Allanbridge declared that the union had to look outside its own rules and also consider the terms of the pursuer's contract. The fact that Partington's contract had a term which had been reached after agreement between NALGO and the employer that he would be required to provide safety cover during industrial action rendered the expulsion unlawful. A reasonable union in this case would not only have taken account of its rules but also the terms of the agreement which recognised the employer's right to require members to return to work in order to provide safety cover.

10.40 Natural justice and discipline

It has been held in Scotland that a union disciplinary committee acts in a quasi-judicial manner.[151] It is upon this footing that a union must comply with the rules of natural justice, although such an issue is no longer significant since the modern law applies the rules to administrative proceedings as well.[152] Under Scots law the rules of natural justice constitute implied terms of the contract of membership and it would therefore be unlawful for any trade union to attempt to exclude their operation.[153] Natural justice demands that at the very least a member should have proper notice of the charge against him and a fair opportunity to be heard in his defence.[154] The union disciplinary committee should also act in an unbiased way. Each of these issues will be considered in turn.

10.41 Fair notice involves giving the member sufficient notice of the charge against him so as to enable him to prepare his defence and sufficient time within which to do so. This notice should specify the offence(s) the member is alleged to have committed, the rule(s) which have been violated and any rel-

---

[148] *The Judiciary and the Development of Employment Law* at p. 100.
[149] See Lord Allanbridge in *Partington v. NALGO* 1981 SC 299.
[150] 1981 SC 299.
[151] *Milton v. Nicholson* 1965 SLT 319.
[152] *Ridge v. Baldwin* [1964] AC 40 HL; *Breen v. Amalgamated Engineering Union* [1971] 2 QB 175 CA.
[153] *McDonald v. Burns* 1940 SC 376.
[154] *Walker v. Amalgamated Union of Engineers and Foundry Workers* 1969 SLT 150; *Lawlor v. Union of Postal Workers* [1965] Ch 712.

evant penalties.[155] A union cannot give the member notice of one charge and then find him guilty of an offence under another rule for which he has received no notice.[156] Equally, where a union is relying upon the report of an investigation conducted by a union official, it cannot take disciplinary action on the basis of that report until the member has been informed about the report's contents. This is to ensure that the member has a fair opportunity to correct or contradict any adverse comments made in it.[157] It would also be a breach of the rules for a disciplinary committee to consider a record of previous complaints outwith the presence of the member concerned.[158]

10.42 A member must be given the opportunity to be heard in his defence. This is to enable him to rebut the charge, or, if that is not possible, at least to explain the circumstances under which the breach of the rules was committed.[159] A failure to provide such a hearing even in an "open and shut" case will render the decision of the disciplinary committee *ultra vires* and invalid.[160] The member's right to a hearing is not an absolute one — it only operates to the extent of providing a fair opportunity to be heard. Thus if the member does not avail himself of this opportunity the union would be entitled to proceed with the case in his absence so long as it could established that he had proper notice of the charges.[161] The test applied in Scotland to assess the fairness of those proceedings is "whether the proceedings were truly and essentially consistent with fair justice between man and man or whether on the other hand they were such as to permit of any possibility of injustice".[162] It is not competent for some defect in the procedure before the disciplinary committee to be corrected by means of an appeal to a higher union tribunal.[163] It is undoubtedly the case in Scotland that a member has the right to request that he be represented by counsel and that the union must grant this request where the nature of the charge is likely to affect reputation or livelihood.[164]

10.43 It is a fundamental requirement of the rules of natural justice that nobody should be judge in their own cause. A strict application of this rule creates difficulties in trade union cases because there is a sense in which the association is both prosecutor and judge. Moreover, it is invariably lay people who are involved in a trade union's disciplinary procedures. Accordingly, the task of the

---

[155] *Walker, ibid.*

[156] *Annamunthodo v. Oilfield Workers' Trade Union* [1961] AC 945 PC.

[157] *Walker v. Amalgamated Union of Engineers and Foundry Workers* 1969 SLT 150.

[158] *Tait v. Central Radio Taxis (Tollcross) Ltd* 1989 SLT 217.

[159] *Burn v. National Amalgamated Labourers' Union* [1920] 2 Ch 364.

[160] *Burn, ibid.* See also Megarry J. in *John v. Rees* [1970] Ch 345 at 402 who declared that "the path of the law is strewn with examples of open and shut cases which, somehow, were not".

[161] *Annamunthodo v. Oilfield Workers' Trade Union* [1961] AC 945.

[162] *Per* Lord Stott in *Walker v. Amalgamated Union of Engineers and Foundry Workers* 1969 SLT 150 at 151-152 applying the dicta of Lord President Clyde in *Black v. John Williams & Co* 1923 SC 510.

[163] *Jamieson v. Central Federation of Homing Pigeon Societies* (11 January 1983, unreported) Lord Dunpark following *Leary v. National Union of Vehicle Builders* [1970] 2 All ER 713.

[164] *Walker v. Amalgamated Union of Engineers and Foundry Workers* 1969 SLT 150 distinguishing the decision of Maugham J. in *Maclean v. The Workers' Union* and applying the dictum of Lord Denning M.R. in *Pett v. Greyhound Racing Association* [1968] 1 QB 125.

members of a union's disciplinary committee is to have "a will to reach an honest conclusion after hearing what was urged on either side and a resolve not to make up their minds before hand".[165] This involves not only ensuring that there is no actual bias but that there can be no appearance of bias. If, for example, a member is expelled by a union committee which has as its non-voting chairman the person who pressed for charges in the first place, justice is not seen to be done since there must be a impression that the dice are loaded against the member.[166]

10.44 Exhaustion of internal remedies

Any union rule which seeks to prevent a member complaining to the courts against expulsion from that union is a nullity in law.[167] However, there was a time when the member had to exhaust all stages of his union's disciplinary procedure before he could approach the courts.[168] Nowadays, the courts will not demand that internal remedies are exhausted. This is on the basis of one of two propositions. In the first case, if the union rule book should declare expressly that a member must first exhaust all internal remedies, the courts will not be bound by this rule since their jurisdiction cannot be ousted. In this case, the member may have to show cause why the court should interfere with the contractual position. On the other hand, if the rule book merely provides for a right of appeal, the court can more readily grant relief without recourse to any domestic remedies.[169] This basic approach was followed by Lord Allanbridge in the *Partington* case [170] who entertained the member's action before he had appealed to the union's national council because it was considered that the interpretation of the rule book fell exclusively within the province of the courts and because the judge was concerned about the injustice which might result if court action were delayed.

10.45 The question of injustice is one which has also surfaced in other cases where a member is being disciplined for not taking part in industrial action. In *Porter v. NUJ*.[171] for example, the House of Lords was even prepared to grant the member interim relief before the disciplinary proceedings had commenced. Such relief may now be exceptional because it has been held by the Court of Appeal in *Longley v. NUJ*[172] that an injunction should only be granted to prevent a hearing from taking place where there was evidence that the disciplinary tribunal had acted improperly in the past or was likely to do so. Parliament has also been concerned to ensure that members should not be prevented from complaining to the courts by union rules which provide for inordinately long and drawn out internal procedures. Thus statute now ensures that where court proceedings relate to a grievance which a member began to pursue against his union under its rules more than six months before applying to the court, the court should not dismiss, sist or adjourn those proceedings on the ground that

---

[165] *Per* Viscount Simon in *White v. Kuzych* [1951] AC 585 at 596 PC.
[166] *Roebuck v. National Union of Mineworkers (Yorkshire Area) (No 2)* [1978] ICR 676.
[167] *Lee v. Showmen's Guild* [1952] 2 QB 329.
[168] *White v. Kuzych* [1951] AC 585.
[169] Goff J. in *Leigh v. NUR* [1970] Ch 326 at 334.
[170] 1981 SC 299.
[171] [1980] IRLR 404.
[172] [1987] IRLR 109.

further procedures for resolving the grievance are available under the union's rules.[173] There is provision for an extension of this period where the reason for the delay in resolving the grievance is attributable to the unreasonable conduct of the member who initiated the court case.[174]

STATUTORY CONTROL OF ADMISSION, DISCIPLINE AND EXPULSION

10.46 Both the Sex Discrimination Act 1975 and the Race Relations Act 1976 contain provisions which outlaw discrimination on grounds of sex or marital status or on racial grounds by trade unions and employers' associations. The Acts protect not only applicants for membership[175] but those in membership as well.[176] Until recently, the only other major statutory control on a union's treatment of its members was the statutory protection against unreasonable exclusion or expulsion from a trade union.[177] However this only applies where in accordance with a union membership agreement (UMA), a person is required to belong to a specified trade union or one of a number of specified trade unions. It is clear, therefore, that these provisions have to be viewed as an important element in the Conservative Governments' attempts to eradicate closed shop abuses.[178] A complaint lies initially to an industrial tribunal which may grant a declaration. Thereafter, there is a right to compensation either from the industrial tribunal where the union has complied with the terms of the declaration or from the Employment Appeal Tribunal where the union has ignored the industrial tribunal's order. An industrial tribunal is directed to award such a sum as it considers appropriate for the purpose of compensating the applicant for the loss sustained in consequence of his exclusion or expulsion.[179] This sum cannot exceed the maximum of 30 times the maximum week's pay for a basic award for unfair dismissal plus the maximum compensatory award.[180] The Employment Appeal Tribunal is authorised to award such a sum as is just and equitable in all the circumstances.[181] In this case the award will not only consist of the above two heads of compensation but also an additional sum of up to 52 times a maximum week's pay.[182] Any award of compensation can be reduced either because the applicant has failed to mitigate his loss,[183] or because some action of his has caused or contributed to that loss.[184]

---

[173] EA 1988, s. 2.
[174] EA 1988, s. 2(2).
[175] SDA, s. 12(2); RRA, s. 11(2).
[176] SDA, s. 12(3); RRA, s. 11(3).
[177] EA 1980, s. 4.
[178] See *NATSOPA v. Goodfellow* [1985] ICR 187 EAT where Bristow J. declared that "the mischief aimed at by s. 4 is that the closed shop would allow a union arbitrarily to debar from employment an outsider who wanted a job and was willing to be a member of the union" (at 191).
[179] EA 1980, s. 5(4) (a).
[180] EA 1980, s. 5(7).
[181] EA 1980, s. 5(4) (b).
[182] EA 1980, s. 5(8).
[183] EA 1980, s. 5(5).
[184] EA 1980, s. 5(6).

10.47 Reasonableness and union rules

The issue of reasonableness is central to these provisions[185] and it is expressly stated that the mere fact that the union has complied with the requirements of its rule book in exercising its admission or expulsion functions will not be conclusive in assessing the reasonableness or otherwise of a union's conduct.[186] This specific provision creates uncertainty for a trade union's recruitment or discipline policies.[187] However, some guidance is provided by the Department of Employment's Code of Practice on Closed Shop Agreements and Arrangements. This Code advises unions to apply fair and clear rules when handling applications for admission or disciplinary matters, and warns them that they should only exclude or expel a person where there is a closed shop when there has been a full compliance with all those rules and procedures. The Employment Appeal Tribunal has also made it clear that acting in conformity with the rule book should never be an irrelevant consideration in terms of the reasonableness of a union's behaviour.[188]

10.48 Scope of the statutory provision

The purpose of the provision is to provide protection to outsiders who are seeking employment in a particular industry.[189] Consequently, it does not apply to existing members who are seeking the agreement of their union to work additional shifts;[190] nor to any exclusion from a branch or section of the union unless that branch or section is specifically referred to in the UMA.[191] If there is no specific reference to a union branch in the UMA, the only way that any exclusion from it could be a breach of the statutory protection would be where it is the employer's practice only to accept as employees members of the union who have been referred by the particular branch.[192] It has now been declared that an applicant complaining of unreasonable exclusion need not point to a particular job which it is open to him to accept but which he cannot accept because of his lack of a union card.[193] On the other hand, it is legitimate for a union to take account of the levels of unemployment amongst existing members in a particular industry when exercising its admission functions[194] and a member who has resigned from the union is not protected because the statutory definition of expulsion is not broad enough to cover cases of "constructive" expulsion, i.e. where the union's conduct is such as to give the member no alternative but to resign.[195]

10.49 Unjustifiable discipline

The above provisions only operate as far as a union's disciplinary functions are concerned when a member has been expelled in circumstances where there is a relevant UMA. Equally, the Closed Shop Code, although it advises unions, for

---

[185] EA 1980, s. 4(5).
[186] EA 1980, s. 4(5).
[187] See Lewis and Simpson, *Striking A Balance? Employment Law After the 1980 Act* at p. 111.
[188] *National Graphical Association v. Howard* [1983] IRLR 445.
[189] *NATSOPA v. Goodfellow* [1985] ICR 187.
[190] *Goodfellow, ibid.*
[191] *NATSOPA v. Kirkham* [1983] ICR 241.
[192] *TGWU v. Tucker* (decision of the EAT on 29 October 1986, unreported, EAT 376/85).
[193] *Clark v. NATSOPA (SOGAT 82)* [1985] IRLR 494.
[194] *NGA v. Howard* [1983] IRLR 445.
[195] *McGhee v. TGWU* [1985] IRLR 198.

example, not to discipline members who refuse to take part in industrial action because that action was unlawful or in breach of their professional or other code of ethics is also restricted to UMA situations.[196] A new and much more extensive right applying to all forms of union disciplinary action without reference to any closed shop agreement has now been created by the Employment Act 1988.[197] This provision although aimed at union disciplinary action against the non-striking member applies in a large number of instances. The 1988 Act creates a protection against unjustifiable discipline where the member is disciplined for any of the following:-

(a) failing to participate in or support a strike or other industrial action by his own union's members or by others;

(b) indicating opposition to or a lack of support for any such strike or other industrial action;

(c) failing to contravene, for any purpose connected with the strike or other industrial action, any requirement imposed by his contract of employment or any other agreement between the member and any person for whom he works or normally works;

(d) making any assertion that the union, any official or representative or a trustee has contravened or is proposing to contravene any requirement imposed by the union's rules or by an agreement (such as a collective agreement) or by any enactment or rule of law;[198]

(e) encouraging or assisting any person to perform an obligation imposed upon him by his contract of employment or any other agreement between that person and a person for whom he works or normally works;

(f) encouraging or assisting any person in the making or attempted vindication of any assertion that the union, any official or representative or trustee has contravened or is proposing to contravene any requirement imposed by the union's rules or by an agreement or by any enactment or rule of law;

(g) consulting the Commissioner for the Rights of Trade Union Members or the Certification Officer;

(h) asking for advice or assistance from the Commissioner or Certification Officer with respect to any matter whatever;

(i) consulting or asking advice or assistance from any other person with respect to a matter which forms or might form the subject matter of an assertion that the union or one of its officials, representatives or trustees has contravened a requirement;

(j) contravening any requirement imposed by or in consequence of any determination constituting an infringement of the rights of an individual under this section;

(k) proposing to engage in conduct set out above;

(l) doing anything preparatory or incidental to engaging in any of the conduct set out above.

---

[196] Para. 61. It is likely that the Secretary of State will revoke this Code in the near future under the powers granted to him by EA 1990, s. 12.

[197] EA 1988, s. 3.

[198] This would cover, for example, an allegation that there has been a failure to ballot or to hold an election in conformity with statutory requirements.

10.50 The 1988 Act (s. 3(5)) also specifies the types of action which a union can take against a member which constitute disciplinary action.[198a] These are:-

(a) expulsion from the union or any of its branches or sections;[198b]

(b) requiring the member to pay any sum to the union, to any branch or section or to any person whatever (*e.g.* a donation to a charity);

(c) requiring that sums paid by the member by way of subscription should be treated as unpaid or paid for a different purpose;

(d) depriving the member of, or access to, any of the benefits, services or facilities which would normally be provided or made available to members (*e.g.* preferential insurance rates for members);[198c]

(e) advising or encouraging another trade union or branch or section of that other union not to accept the individual as a member;

(f) subjecting the individual to any other detriment.[199]

10.51 Complaint of unjustifiable discipline

A member has the right to complain to an industrial tribunal within three months of the date of the unjustifiable disciplinary action.[200] Any attempt by a union to preclude such a complaint is void.[201] If the complaint is well-founded the tribunal will make a declaration to that effect.[202] Thereafter the individual is entitled to compensation. Where the union has revoked the disciplinary action the application for compensation will also be to an industrial tribunal. Otherwise the individual's right is to complain to the Employment Appeal Tribunal. In both cases the amount awarded will be that which is just and equitable in all the circumstances.[203] The maximum compensation available under this provision is thirty times the maximum week's pay for a basic award for unfair dismissal plus the maximum compensatory award.[204] However, in the case of an application to the Employment Appeal Tribunal there is a minimum award of compensation which is an amount equal to the minimum basic award for trade union membership or non-union membership dismissals.[205] Any applicant under this provision has a duty to mitigate his loss and may also have his compensation reduced because he has caused or contributed to the disciplinary action.[206]

UNION DEMOCRACY AT COMMON LAW

10.52 The rights of union members to participate in the affairs of their unions depend just as much upon a strict construction of the rule book as do their

---

[198a] See generally *Medhurst v. NALGO* [1990] IRLR 459, EAT.

[198b] This provision will only be breached once the expulsion has taken place. See *TGWU v. Webber* [1990] IRLR 462, EAT.

[198c] The suspension of a member is a breach of s. 3(5) (d) since it involves depriving that person of access to benefits, services or facilities. See *NALGO v. Killorn & Simm* [1990] IRLR 464, EAT.

[199] This same word has been construed broadly in anti-discrimination legislation to mean being placed at a disadvantage. See the decision of the Court of Appeal in *Ministry of Defence v. Jeremiah* [1979] IRLR 436.

[200] EA 1988, s. 4(1) and (2).

[201] EA 1988, s. 4(7).

[202] EA 1988, s. 4(4).

[203] EA 1988, s. 5(5).

[204] EA 1988, s. 5(8). This award cannot be exceeded because of injury to feelings. See *Bradley v. NALGO* [1991] IRLR 159, EAT.

[205] EA 1988, s. 5(8).

[206] EA 1988, s. 5(6) and (7).

rights over discipline or expulsion. It is the rule book which sets out the constitution of the union in the eyes of the law. The extent to which the Scottish courts rely on the rule book as the means of establishing a member's democratic rights is best illustrated by the statement of Lord President Cooper in *Martin v. Scottish TGWU*[207] who argued that the rules of a trade union are as fundamental and exhaustive a statement as the memorandum and articles of association of a limited company. Any deviation from the requirements of the rule book would show that the union has acted beyond its constitution and make it amenable to the *ultra vires* doctrine. In order to pursue such an action in court the member need only show that he has been denied his constitutional right to participate fully in the democratic affairs of his union.[208] However, where a member applies for an interdict to prevent further *ultra vires* conduct by the union that person must remain in membership of the union throughout the whole course of the action.[209] The Scottish decisions in this field have been fixed firmly upon the *ultra vires* doctrine. This may be the reason why our courts have not found it necessary to consider the application of the rule in *Foss v. Harbottle*[210] to trade unions. This is a doctrine which restricts the circumstances in which an individual member can sue for alleged irregularities in procedure on the basis that the proper plaintiff should be the association itself. The English courts have applied it in the trade union field[211] and it was recently considered in one of the English decisions arising out of the miners' strike of 1984-85.[212] However, its application to trade unions has never been judicially considered in Scotland.

10.53 The member and the rule book

There is English authority to the effect that in this area union rule books should not be interpreted literally or like a statute. Some account should be taken of the authors of union rules and their likely readership.[213] No such statement has been made by any Scottish judge. The Scottish approach has been to subject union rules to a close and detailed analysis. This is best illustrated by the decision of the First Division in *Paterson v. NALGO*[214] where it was held that the respective powers of the union's conference as compared to the National Executive Council (NEC) were contained in the rule book as a constitutional document. Moreover, it was declared that the conference cannot rely on its power to direct the general policy of the union as authority for making decisions which clearly fall within the competence of the NEC under the rules. It is also wrong to view a union's conference as analogous to the general meeting of an unincorporated society since in this latter case every single member has the right to attend, whereas in the case of the union conference attendance is restricted to delegates.[215] One area where the need to follow rule book requirements closely is paramount concerns union authorisation for industrial action. If

---

[207] *Martin v. Scottish TGWU* 1951 SC 129 at 142.
[208] See the decision of Lord Cameron at first instance in *Paterson v. NALGO* 1977 SC 345.
[209] *Donaghy v. Rollo* 1964 SC 278.
[210] (1843) 2 Hare 461.
[211] *Cotter v. National Union of Seamen* [1929] 2 Ch 58; *Edwards v. Halliwell* [1950] 2 All ER 1064; *Hodgson v. NALGO* [1972] 1 WLR 130.
[212] *Taylor v. NUM (Derbyshire Area)* [1985] IRLR 99.
[213] The cases are analysed and discussed by Warner J. in *Jacques v. AUEW (Engineering Section)* [1986] ICR 683.
[214] 1977 SC 345.
[215] See Lord Johnston in *Paterson, ibid*, at 359.

the union's rules demand a ballot, for example, any failure to ballot or a defect in balloting procedures will render subsequent industrial action unlawful. Consequently, the votes in support of industrial action must at least reach the necessary majority specified in the rules,[216] and the ballot must not be held at a time which is too remote from the date of the proposed action.[217] Any authorisation of union expenditure in support of such action is also unlawful at common law, and any union officer who so authorised that expenditure could be held personally liable for breach of fiduciary duty.[218]

10.54 A full compliance with the requirements of the union's rules is particularly important where the union is seeking to change those rules. A change in the rules of a union cannot be implied from conduct alone.[219] Equally, where a particular rule change requires a successful ballot of the members, the union cannot avoid this procedure simply by calling a rules revision conference to repeal the balloting requirement and then change the rule at a later union conference. It has been held that a rule requiring a ballot of the members prior to any such change is an entrenched provision, so that no lawful change in the rule can be accomplished without the necessary ballot.[220]

10.55 The rule book and officials

A union must also ensure that it complies with the rule book in its treatment of union officers or officials. Thus if a union wishes to suspend a person from office it must make sure that it has that specific authority in its rules.[221] The courts apply a very strict construction of the rules affecting union officers. For example, it does not follow that a union would be acting lawfully at common law when it insists that candidates for the office of President be members of a particular political party, even although there is a union rule requiring the holder of that office to be a member of that party. In such a case, the question of a person's election to that office is too remote at the time of nomination to insist that a candidate hold a particular political allegiance.[222] The courts also adopt the same strict approach if a person is being dismissed from office. For example, the union can only implement those disciplinary sanctions which the rules authorise. A union officer appointed for a fixed term under a contract of employment who is also a member and who is challenging a union decision to dismiss him has two options under Scots common law. He can sue for damages for breach of his contract of employment, or he can seek reduction of the decision to dismiss on the basis that it is *ultra vires*.[223] If he chooses the former route he must be able to prove the existence of the contract.[224] As regards the authority to dismiss it has been held in *Milton v. Nicolson*[225] that a union's general powers under the rule book to conduct the business of the union are sufficient

---

[216] *Taylor v. NUM (Derbyshire Area)* [1984] IRLR 440.

[217] *Taylor v. NUM (Yorkshire Area)* [1984] IRLR 445.

[218] *Taylor v. NUM (Derbyshire Area)* [1985] IRLR 99. See also EA 1988, ss. 8-9.

[219] *Wilson v. Scottish Typographical Society* 1912 SC 535.

[220] *Jacques v. AUEW (Engineering Section)* [1986] ICR 683.

[221] *Burn v. National Amalgamated Labourers' Union* [1920] 2 Ch 364.

[222] *Leigh v. NUR* [1970] Ch 326.

[223] See Lord President Cooper in *Nisbet v. Percy* 1951 SC 350 particularly at 355. An employed official who has sufficient service could also seek a remedy for unfair dismissal under EPCA, Part V.

[224] *Nisbet, ibid.*

[225] 1965 SLT 319.

authority for the dismissal of a union official. There is no doubt that any dismissal of a union officer from that office must also comply with the rules of natural justice.[226] The rules may even apply where a union official has a legitimate expectation that his election to a particular post will be confirmed by the executive and this does not happen.[227] Certainly, they would operate where there are allegations of improper behaviour against that candidate.[228] However, natural justice rules would not necessarily apply to a union delegate attending a Labour Party Conference whose nomination is withdrawn by his union because it is doubtful whether the withdrawal of such a nomination is a disciplinary measure relating to an office in the union.[229]

UNION DEMOCRACY UNDER STATUTE

10.56 There can be no doubt that one major thrust of the Conservative Government's trade union legislation of the 1980s has been to attempt to make trade unions more responsible and more responsive to the wishes of their members. As the Green Paper which preceded the Trade Union Act 1984 declared ". . . union leaders are seen to be out of touch with their rank and file and often appear to be neither representative of the majority of their members nor directly responsible to them".[230] In particular, the Government has sought to ensure the primacy of the secret postal ballot over other forms of union democracy because of its belief that his form of balloting constitutes the most accurate means of ascertaining the views of the members.[231] At first postal balloting was encouraged indirectly through the scheme authorised by the Employment Act 1980 which enables the Certification Officer to refund certain costs incurred by independent trade unions in the conduct of postal ballots. The Trade Union Act 1984 took this a stage further by introducing a rebuttable statutory presumption that union executive election ballots and political fund ballots would be conducted by post. The Employment Act 1988 completes this process by stipulating that the secret postal ballot is the only lawful means of electing a union's executive or voting on a political fund. Moreover, the impact of the legislation of the 1980s has been to create one uniform system for the election of all members of a union's principal executive committee (PEC) and President and General Secretary.

10.57 Reimbursing ballot costs

The Employment Act 1980[232] empowered the Secretary of State to create a scheme allowing independent trade unions to claim reimbursement of expenses for certain ballots from the Certification Officer. The actual scheme which has been created by regulations[233] is more tightly drawn than the enabling legislation since it only applies to secret postal ballots and also restricts the ballot

---

[226] *Stevenson v. United Road Transport Union* [1977] ICR 893 CA.

[227] *Breen v. Amalgamated Engineering Union* [1971] 2 QB 175.

[228] See judgment of Megaw L. J. in *Breen, ibid*, at p. 200.

[229] *Hudson v. GMB* [1990] IRLR 67.

[230] *Democracy in Trade Unions* (1983) Cmnd 9571 at p. 3.

[231] See *Trade Unions and their Members* (1987) Cm. 95 at p. 25.

[232] EA 1980, s. 1.

[233] Funds for Trade Union Ballots Regulations 1984 S.I. 1984 No. 1654 as amended by the Funds for Trade Union Ballots (Amendment) Regulations 1988 S.I. 1988 No. 1123 and the Funds for Trade Union Ballots (Amendment No. 2) Regulations 1988 S.I. 1988 No. 2116.

purposes for which funds are available. The scheme provides funds for ballots for the following purposes:-

(a) calling or ending a strike or other industrial action;

(b) carrying out elections to a union's PEC as required by the Trade Union Act 1984 and Employment Act 1988;

(c) carrying out elections required by the union's rules for the posts of president, chairman, secretary, or treasurer of the union or any other elected post which a person holds as employee of the union;

(d) amending the union's rules;

(e) obtaining a decision about an amalgamation or transfer of engagements under the Trade Union (Amalgamations etc) Act 1964;

(f) deciding whether a union with a political fund wishes to retain that fund;

(g) accepting or rejecting a proposal by an employer relating to remuneration, hours of work, level of performance, holidays or pensions.[233a]

Funds cannot be obtained for ballots to elect worker representatives although this purpose is an appropriate ballot purpose as far as the enabling legislation is concerned.

10.58 Conditions for re-imbursement

There are also a number of conditions about the conduct of the ballot which have to be satisfied before the Certification Officer can authorise payment.[234] The first condition is that the method of voting must be by the marking of a voting paper. Every voter must be allowed to vote without interference or constraint on the part of the union or any of its members, officials or employees. It is a fundamental requirement of the scheme that so far as reasonably practicable a voter should be sent a ballot paper by post to his home address and be given a convenient opportunity to return the paper by post.[235] The member must be able to vote without incurring any direct cost.[236] The result of the ballot must be determined solely by counting the individual votes cast fairly and accurately.[237] It is now clear that in determining the outcome of the ballot the Certification Officer should take account of the rules of the applicant union.[238] The Certification Officer is empowered to repay two types of expense — stationery and printing expenditure and postal costs. Since the TUC's change of policy in 1986 concerning the use of the scheme by affiliated trade unions substantial sums of money have been paid out.

10.59 Electing the Principal Executive Committee

In the past trade unions were left to arrange their own methods of electing members to their PEC. So long as the union complied with its rules the law did not interfere with union election arrangements. The Conservative governments of the 1980s, however, expressed considerable disquiet that unions were not

---

[233a] Reg 5(a)-(b). See also *R v. Certification Officer, ex parte Royal College of Nursing* [1991] IRLR 258.

[234] See generally reg 11. Under the 1988 Amendment (No. 2) Regulations it is also necessary for the union to ensure that the ballot has been indepdently scrutinised where appropriate.

[235] Reg 11(c).

[236] Reg 11(b) (ii).

[237] Reg 11(e).

[238] See the decision of the House of Lords in *R v. Certification Officer ex parte Electrical Power Engineers' Association* [1990] IRLR 398 overruling the decision of the Court of Appeal reported at [1990] IRLR 98.

properly consulting their members in such elections. Eventually, when the government became convinced that the unions were not prepared to instigate voluntary reforms, legislation was enacted to ensure that all unions conducted certain elections in a particular way despite anything to the contrary in their rules.[239] Initially the statutory requirements about union executive elections applied only to those members of a union's PEC who had a deliberative or casting vote. And it was possible for a union to hold a workplace or semi-postal ballot where the union was satisfied that there were no reasonable grounds for believing that such ballots could not satisfy the requirements of, secrecy, freedom form interference or constraint and fairness and accuracy in the counting of votes required for postal ballots.[240]

10.60 Now the Employment Act 1988 ensures that a union must elect and re-elect at least every five years all members of its PEC and its President and General Secretary as well, by the sole method of a secret postal ballot. Accordingly, a union is now required to send the voting paper to a member's home address or any other address which he has requested in writing to be treated as his postal address and to give that member a convenient opportunity to vote by post.[241] Each voting paper must specify the address to which and the date by which it is to be returned, and be consecutively numbered.[242] The 1988 Act does exempt special register bodies from its requirements insofar as elections of non-voting PEC members, and the President and General Secretary are concerned.[243] Also exempted from these election requirements are persons who are entitled to attend a PEC merely to provide the committee with factual information or with technical or professional advice.[244] Equally, union presidents and general secretaries whose positions are purely ceremonial are exempted so long as they are neither voting members of the PEC nor union employees, hold office for less than thirteen months and have not held that position within the previous twelve months.[245] There are also special exemptions for union leaders and PEC members who are approaching retirement.[246]

10.61 Candidature

No member of a trade union can be unreasonably excluded from standing as a candidate at an election.[247] It is arguable that this right is infringed when a union prevents members of a particular political party from standing for office. The test for unreasonable exclusion is to consider the practical application of the union's arrangements. A procedure which does not specifically exclude a union member from standing would be unreasonable if it effectively precludes any real possibility that the ordinary member will put himself forward.[248] The Act clearly prohibits a union from requiring, whether directly or indirectly, that a

[239] TUA, s. 3.
[240] TUA, ss. 1-2(7).
[241] TUA, s. 2(7) and s. 9(1). S. 3 has been repealed by EA 1988, s. 14(2).
[242] EA 1988, s. 33 and Sch. 3, para 5.
[243] EA 1988, s. 12(1) which adds a new s. 1(6A)-(6C) to TUA.
[244] TUA, s. 1(6A) (b).
[245] TUA, s. 1(6C).
[246] EA 1988, s. 12(5).
[247] TUA s. 2(9).
[248] *Paul v. NALGO* [1987] IRLR 43.

candidate be a member of a political party.[249] This provision reinforces the decision in the *Leigh* case[250] already discussed, and candidates are entitled to draw up an election address in their own words and to have that address sent out with the voting papers without incurring any cost.[251]

10.62 The conduct of the ballot

All the members of the union who are voting should have an equal entitlement to vote, that they can exercise this right without interference from, or constraint imposed by, the union or any of its members officials or employees and that, so far as reasonably practicable, they vote without incurring any direct cost.[252] The ballot must be conducted in secret and the outcome must be determined by counting the number of votes cast directly for each candidate, and all those votes must be fairly and accurately counted.[253] These provisions are now reinforced by the system of independent scrutiny of PEC, president and general secretary and political fund ballots. It is for the union to appoint its own independent scrutineer for each ballot, although there are regulations which specify the categories of person or organisation who can act as scrutineers.[254] The scrutineer must supervise the production and distribution of all voting papers, be the person to whom these papers are returned and retain custody of them for at least one year after the announcement of the election result.[255] He is also required to make a report to the union stating the number of voting papers distributed, the number of papers returned to him, the number of valid votes cast for each candidate and the number of spoiled papers.[256] The report must also state whether the scrutineer is satisfied that there are no reasonable grounds for believing that the ballot contravened any statutory balloting requirement, that the security arrangements for the production, storage, distribution, return or other handling of the voting papers and for the counting of them were, so far as reasonably practicable, sufficient to minimise the risk of any unfairness or malpractice and that he was able to carry out his functions without interference.[257] The Employment Act 1990 (s. 5(5)) has placed additional obligations upon trade unions to announce the name of the scrutineer in advance of the election and to include his name on each voting paper.

10.63 In order to facilitate the requirement that PEC ballots be open to all members a statutory duty is imposed on trade unions to compile and thereafter to maintain, by means of a computer or otherwise, a register of the names and proper addresses of members.[258] This register must, so far as reasonably practicable, be

---

[249] TUA, s. 2(10).
[250] *Leigh v. NUR* [1970] Ch 326.
[251] EA 1988 s. 13.
[252] TUA, s. 2(6).
[253] TUA, s. 2(8). It may be legitimate to have regard to the rules of the union on this question. See the decision of the House of Lords in *R. v. Certification Officer ex parte EPEA* [1990] IRLR 398.
[254] Trade Union Ballots and Elections (Independent Scrutineer Qualifications) Order 1988 S.I. No. 2117. This authorises solicitors and accountants and organisations such as the Electoral Reform Society to act as independent scrutineers.
[255] EA 1988, s. 15(4).
[256] EA 1988, s. 15(5) (a)-(d).
[257] EA 1988, s. 15(5) (e) and (f) and s. 15(6).
[258] TUA, s. 4.

kept up to date and be accurate, and any member has the right free of charge at any reasonable time, to check whether or not he is included on that register and, if he so requests, to receive a copy of his entry either for no fee or on the payment of a reasonable fee.[259] There are occasions when a union can lawfully exclude certain classes of members under its rules from voting, so long as every member in that class is excluded.[260] Equally, so long as the union has the authority in its rules, a union can maintain separate constituencies for PEC elections. Thus the union can restrict the right to vote by reference to trade or occupation, geographical area, separate section or any combination of the above.[262]

10.64 These statutory obligations are enforced through rights provided to every member of the union. A member can complain either to the Court of Session (High Court of Justice for England and Wales) or to the Certification Officer.[262a] The power of the Certification Officer is restricted to the making of a declaration only. This specifies the breaches which the union has committed. The more potent remedy — the enforcement order — is only available before the courts. This can be made at the same time as the declaration or after it, since there is nothing to prevent a member applying to the courts for a remedy in respect of a matter which has already been dealt with by the Certification Officer.[262b] The order may require the union to ensure the holding of an election, to take the necessary steps to remedy its breach of the Act and to abstain from specified acts so that a repetition of the breach does not take place.[263] If the enforcement order is not observed any member (and not just the one who made the original application) can apply to the Court of Session to enforce obedience.[264] This enables contempt of court proceedings to be taken against the union.

THE COMMISSIONER FOR THE RIGHTS OF TRADE UNION MEMBERS

10.65 The Secretary of State has authority to appoint a Commissioner for the Rights of Trade Union Members.[265] The Commissioner has the power to provide assistance to a union member who is contemplating or is already taking certain proceedings against his union or one of its officers. The assumption underpinning this provision is that union members acting on their own behalf experience considerable disadvantages in pursuing cases against their unions in the courts and tribunals. Accordingly, the Commissioner is directed to assist a union member in a number of ways. She may

   (a) pay for any legal advice from a solicitor or advocate;

   (b) make arrangements for the giving of that advice;

   (c) make arrangements for the representation of the applicant or for the provision of such assistance as is usually provided by a solicitor or advocate in the preliminary or incidental stages of such proceedings; and

   (d) bear the costs of any such representation.

[259] TUA, s. 4(2A) added by EA 1988, s. 33 and Sch. 3, para. 5(3).
[260] TUA, s. 2(1).
[261] TUA, s. 2(2).
[262] TUA, s. 2(3).
[262a] TUA, s. 5(1).
[262b] TUA, s. 6(3) and see *Lenahan v. UCATT* [1991] IRLR 78.
[263] TUA, s. 5(7).
[264] TUA, s. 5(11).
[265] EA 1988, s. 19.

In exercising this discretion the Commissioner is not obliged to provide assistance in every case. The decision to do so may well depend upon whether the case raises a question of principle, whether given the complexity of the case it is reasonable to expect the member to pursue the case unaided and whether the case involves a matter of substantial public interest.[266] There are also special rules where a member seeks assistance from the Commissioner in a case where the Certification Officer has already made a declaration concerning a breach of the balloting requirements for PEC elections or for political funds and the member intends to enforce the declaration before the courts.[267] In such case the Commissioner must grant assistance if the applicant has a reasonable prospect of securing the making of the enforcement order.[268]

10.66 Where assistance may be given

The Commissioner can assist a union member to pursue an action[269] in the following circumstances

(a) where the union has breached the statutory balloting provisions[270] required for official industrial action;[271]

(b) where a member has been denied the right to inspect union accounts;[272]

(c) where union trustees have caused or permitted any unlawful use of union property;[273]

(d) where the union has breached the balloting provisions as regards political funds;[274]

(e) where the union has failed to bring or to continue any court proceedings against the use of union funds for indemnifying unlawful conduct;[275]

(f) where there has been a failure to ballot properly for PEC elections;[276]

(g) where the union has unlawfully applied its funds for political purposes.[277]

The Act also gives the Secretary of State the power exercisable by statutory instrument to extend the authority of the Commissioner to cover any other proceedings against a trade union, trade union official or the trustees of a union's property. The Government announced in 1989 that it was contemplating extending the powers of the Commissioner to cover proceedings against a trade union alleging a breach of its rule book requirements where the complaint was viewed as a matter of substantial public interest.[278] These proposals have now been given statutory effect by the Employment Act 1990 which authorises the Commissioner to provide assistance to a member who alleges that the union has

---

[266] EA 1988, s. 20(4).

[267] EA 1988, s. 20(5).

[268] EA 1988, s. 20(5) (c).

[269] EA 1988, s. 20(7).

[270] EA 1988, s. 1.

[271] For example, the Commissioner has supported legal action by union members alleging failures to receive ballot papers for industrial action during the NUR dispute with British Rail in 1989. See *Financial Times* 22 June 1989.

[272] EA 1988, s. 6.

[273] EA 1988, s. 9.

[274] EA 1988, s. 16.

[275] EA 1988, s. 8(3).

[276] TUA, s. 5.

[277] TUA 1913 s. 3(1).

[278] *Removing Barriers to Employment* (1989) Cm 655 ch 4.

breached or is threatening to breach its rules. The Commissioner can grant assistance in the following cases-

(a) appointment or election to, or the removal of a person from, any office;

(b) disciplinary proceedings by the union (including expulsion);

(c) the authorising or endorsing of industrial action;

(d) the balloting of members;

(e) the application of the union's funds or property;

(f) the imposition, collection or distribution of any levy for the purposes of industrial action;

(g) the constitution or proceedings of any committee, conference or other body.[278a]

The Commissioner cannot grant assistance for any of the above matters unless it appears to her that the breach of the rules affects or may affect, union members other than the applicant, or that similar breaches of the rules have been or may be committed in relation to other members of the union.[278b]

TRADE UNIONS AND POLITICS

10.67 The starting point for any discussion on this point must be the decision of the House of Lords in *Amalgamated Society of Railway Servants v. Osborne*[279] in 1910. There it was held that the Trade Union Act did not confer any power authorising a trade union to maintain a political fund. This decision was quickly followed in Scotland in *Johnstone v. Associated Ironmoulders of Scotland*[280] where Lord Skerrington held that a union rule which allowed the association to take such steps as necessary for labour representation was *ultra vires*. In *Wilson v. Scottish Typographical Society*[281] the effect of the *Osborne* judgement was extended by the Second Division to cover unions which had not registered under the Trade Union Act 1871. It was clear, therefore, that if trade unions were to be able to finance and to participate in political activities statutory intervention was required. This came in the form of the Trade Union Act 1913 which continues largely to provide the modern legal framework for expenditure by trade unions on political purposes.[282]

10.68 The Trade Union Acts 1913, 1984

The 1913 Act continues to fulfil three functions. First it provides a mechanism by which the members of a trade union can be balloted in order to approve the creation and maintenance of a political fund. Second, it creates a system whereby those union members who do not wish to contribute to the fund can be exempt from paying the political levy, and, third, it ensures that an exempt member who does not contribute cannot be put at any disadvantage as a union member save in relation to the fund's administration. The original framework of the 1913 Act operated unchanged (with the exception of the period between 1927 and 1946 when members had to contract in as regards the payment of the political levy) until the enactment of the Trade Union Act 1984. This Act was passed because of the Conservative Government's concern that ballots to create

[278a] EA 1990, s. 10(2).
[278b] EA 1990, s. 10(5).
[279] [1910] AC 87.
[280] (1911) 2 SLT 478. See also *McArdle v. United Society of Boilermakers* (1915) 1 SLT 437.
[281] 1912 SC 535.
[282] See generally K. D. Ewing *Trade Unions, the Labour Party and the Law.*

political funds were one-off affairs. Under the 1913 Act once a union had balloted to create a political fund it never had to ballot again to obtain authorisation for the continuance of that fund. Thus under the 1984 Act unions have to ballot at least every ten years in order to maintain their political funds. The 1984 Act also extended the definition of political objects because of government concern that unions were using their general funds to finance campaigns which were really political in nature. Union members may now complain to the Certification Officer about a breach of the balloting arrangements for political funds.[283]

10.69 Political objects

If a union wishes to spend money on a political object it must possess a political fund which has been approved in a ballot of the members. The following forms of expenditure are defined by the 1913 Act[284] as constituting political objects.

(a) contributions to the funds of, or on the payment of any expenses incurred directly or indirectly by, a political party;

(b) the provision of any service or property for use by or on behalf of any political party;

(c) payments in connection with the registration of electors, the candidature of any person, the selection of any candidate or the holding of any ballot by the union in connection with any election to a political office;

(d) payments to maintain any holder of a political office;

(e) payments towards the holding of any conference or meeting by or on behalf of a political party or of any other meeting the main purpose of which is the transaction of business in connection with a political party;

(f) payments on the production, publication or distribution of any literature, document, film, sound recording or advertisement the main purpose of which is to persuade people to vote for a political party or candidate or to persuade them not to vote for a political party or candidate.[285]

10.70 Political fund ballots

As we have seen, there must be a ballot to approve the creation of a political fund and a review ballot at least every ten years to maintain it. These ballots must be in accordance with union rules approved by the Certification Officer. Entitlement to vote in the ballot must be accorded equally to all members of the union. Any person voting must be entitled to do so without interference or constraint and so far as reasonably practicable must be able to do so without incurring any direct cost. The ballot must be conducted postally[286] in secret by means of the marking of a voting paper by the person voting and the votes cast must be fairly and accurately counted.[287] Moreover, the voting paper must clearly specify the address to which, and the date by which, it is to be returned and the union must ensure that the voting papers are consecutively numbered.[288] Both the Court of Session and the Certification Officer have jurisdiction to hear com-

---

[283] EA 1988, s. 16.

[284] TUA 1913, s. 3(3) as amended by TUA 1984, s. 17(1).

[285] The meaning of para (f) is discussed by Browne-Wilkinson V.-C. in *Paul and Fraser v. NALGO* [1987] IRLR 413.

[286] EA 1988 s. 14.

[287] TUA 1913, s. 4(1A)-(1E).

[288] EA 1988, s. 33 and Sch. 3, para. 1.

plaints about irregularities in the conduct of political fund ballots.[289] These must be subjected to independent scrutiny in the same way as PEC elections

10.71 TUA 1984 also introduced a series of requirements as regards the management of the political fund. It is made clear that no property can be added to the fund other than from contributions by members, donations from other persons (other than the union itself) and income which accrues to the fund in the course of administering its assets.[290] The Act also forbids the union using assets from its general fund in order to discharge liabilities incurred by the political fund.[291] Any union which fails to obtain a majority in a review ballot for continuation of its political fund must take all necessary steps to ensure that political contributions are discontinued as soon as reasonably practicable.[292] Any union member can request repayment of any political contributions he has made after the political fund resolution has ceased to have effect.[293] Further, all expenditure on political objects must cease within six months of the date of the adverse ballot result.[294] A union which loses a political fund review ballot may, if it wishes, transfer the assets in that fund into its general fund so that they can be spent on non-political objects, or, alternatively, it may simply retain its political fund and freeze the assets contained therein.[295] In this latter case the union would have to obtain a positive vote in a subsequent ballot in order to revive the union's right to spend money on political objects.

10.72 Despite criticisms of the system whereby union members who do not wish to contribute to the political fund are required to seek exemption from the payment of the political levy,[296] TUA 1984 retains the system of contracting-out.[297] If a union does vote to create or maintain a political fund that union must give notice to the members of their right to contract-out of the political levy and inform them that an exemption notice is available from the union or of its branches or from the Certification Officer.[298] So long as the exemption notice is returned to the union within one month, the member's exemption will operate from the date on which the notice was given. Otherwise, the exemption will become effective from the first of January following.[299] An exempted member cannot be excluded from any of the benefits of the union, nor can he be placed in any respect either directly or indirectly under any disability or at any disadvantage compared with other members of the union (except in relation to the control and management of the political fund) simply because he is exempt.[300]

---

[289] TUA 1984, s. 16 and EA 1988, s. 16.
[290] TUA 1984, s. 14(1).
[291] TUA 1984, s. 14(3).
[292] TUA 1984, s. 15(3).
[293] TUA 1984, s. 15(4).
[294] TUA 1984, s. 15(1).
[295] TUA 1984, s. 15(3) (b) and s. 15(7).
[296] An unsuccessful attempt was made by some Tory backbenchers to add a clause to the then Bill which would have provided for contracting-in. See HC, *Official Report*, Parl. Debs, Vol 57, No 133, Cols 721-761. The clause was defeated by 472 votes to 57.
[297] However, the TUC has issued a Statement of Guidance on Political Funds to affiliated unions. See Report of TUC General Council to 1984 Congress at pp. 84-85.
[298] TUA 1913, s. 5(1). This provision also permits a member to give notice at any time of his intention to contract-out.
[299] TUA 1913, s. 5(2).
[300] TUA 1913, s. 3(1) (b). For the meaning of disability or disadvantage see, for example, *Cleminson v. POEU* [1980] IRLR 1 CO.

The right to exclude an exempt member from control and management of the political fund does not permit a union denying that person the right to stand for union office.[301] The Certification Officer has the authority to hear complaints about irregularities in the management of a union's political fund or alleging discriminatory treatment against an exempt member.[302] There is a right of appeal on a question of law to the EAT.[303]

10.73 One area of controversy under this provision concerns a union's treatment of its exempt members. In particular, disquiet was expressed at the practice whereby unions charged exempt members the full subscription (including the political fund element) and then repaid them the political levy portion. Occasionally, this was done at the beginning of the year, but more often the political levy was paid in arrears. The lawfulness of these practices was considered by the EAT in *Reeves v. TGWU*[304] where the member was required to pay the full subscription and then was refunded the political levy as an exempt member. Some refunds were given in arrears of payment and some were paid in advance. It was argued that both types of refund were unlawful since they placed him at a disability or disadvantage. The Certification Officer held that those refunds paid in advance were lawful but that those paid in arrears were in breach of the 1913 Act. The EAT, on appeal, concluded that it was not only legitimate for a union to repay an exempted member's political levy in advance, it was also lawful for refunds to be paid in arrears so long as they were made as soon as reasonably possible after the collection of subscriptions by the employer. This point has now been dealt with in TUA 1984, s. 18 which declares that where an exempt member has certified in writing to the employer that he has contracted-out, that employer must ensure that no amount representing a contribution from the political fund can be deducted from his wages. It is therefore a breach of this provision for an employer to refuse to deduct this smaller subscription from the wages of an exempted member. This ensures that an employer will have to provide different levels of deduction for union subscriptions, depending on whether or not the member pays the political levy, when carrying out check-off arrangements. An exempt member who alleges that his employer has failed or has refused to deduct a rate of subscription which does not include the political fund element has a right of complaint to the sheriff court.[305] The court has the power to award a declarator and can make an order requiring the employer to take such steps as the order may specify in order to ensure that the employer's failure is not repeated.[306]

---

[301] *Birch v. NUM* [1950] Ch 602.
[302] TUA 1913, s. 3(2).
[303] TUA 1913, s. 5A.
[304] [1980] IRLR 307.
[305] TUA 1984, s. 18(4) (6).
[306] TUA 1984, s. 18(5).

Chapter Eleven

THE LAW OF INDUSTRIAL CONFLICT

INTRODUCTION

11.1 There can be no doubt that without the intervention of Parliament through the provision of immunities against legal action, the organisation of industrial action in Scotland would be fraught with legal difficulties. Except in the unusual case where union members have given proper notice of termination to their employer, the act of calling employees out on strike ensures that not only are the members in breach of their contracts of employment when they participate in the action but the union and its responsible officers, at the very least, are also liable in delict for inducing breaches of those contracts. Thus some statutory protection for industrial action is necessary if that action is to be organised without the fear of proceedings in the civil courts. As we saw in Chapter Ten, it might have been difficult for any legal action to be sustained against the trade union concerned because of its unincorporated status at common law. However, in 1901 the House of Lords held in *Taff Vale Railway Co. v. Amalgamated Society of Railway Servants*[1] that a trade union registered under the Trade Union Act 1871 possessed a quasi-corporate status and accordingly it became competent to bring a court action against a union which authorised industrial action.

11.2 Statutory immunities

It was as a direct result of this decision that Parliament enacted the Trade Disputes Act 1906. This statute is important not only because it gave trade unions complete immunity in law for actions in delict but also because it developed the concept of the "golden formula" which protected union officers and the like *inter alia* for inducing breaches of their members' contracts of employment when the industrial action was "in contemplation or furtherance of a trade dispute". Thus in deciding how to protect those who authorise industrial action in Britain the law has sought to provide protection through a system of immunities for those who organise that action rather than create a positive right to strike as in many Continental legal systems. This notion of a "golden formula" defence remains the bedrock for the operation of the immunities.[2] However, the particular delicts which can apply to industrial action have been developed considerably by the courts since 1906. Moreover, the present law no longer grants trade unions complete protection against legal actions in delict.[3] This means that their legal position is now the same as that of any other person who is responsible for calling industrial action. It is also worth pointing out that statutory developments have also redefined the meaning

[1]   [1901] AC 426.
[2]   TULRA, s. 13.
[3]   EA 1982, s. 15 repealing TULRA, s. 14.

of a trade dispute[4] in British Law and have outlawed virtually all secondary action.[5]

11.3 English decisions

There are three further introductory points that have to be made before examining the present state of the law in more detail. The first is that much of the development of the law in this field has been carried out by the English courts. In Scotland the common law delicts remain imprecise and underdeveloped in comparison with their English counterparts. This can make it difficult on occasions to state definitively the Scots law on the relevant delicts. Consequently, unless there is appropriate Scottish authority reference will be made to the important English decisions. Second, given the fact that the immunities are intended to give protection against the operation of certain common law delicts, any redefinition or extension of these delicts is likely to have an effect upon the scope of the immunities. It is certainly the case that Parliament has had to extend the immunities on a number of occasions in order to take account of common law developments.[6] As we shall see, it is even arguable that certain forms of primary action might be unlawful because they entail delictual liability in circumstances where there is no corresponding statutory immunity. Lastly, it must be noted that the statutory immunities protect only those who organise or authorise the action. The law provides no protection for those employees who participate in the industrial action — even where that action is in contemplation or furtherance of a trade dispute. If their participation in the action involves a breach of their contracts of employment, the employer is entitled to sue for damages,[7] or, more likely, to treat those breaches as material and summarily dismiss the employees concerned. As far as unfair dismissal law is concerned, in the case of official action, so long as all the strikers are dismissed and none taken back within three months of dismissal an industrial tribunal would have no jurisdiction to hear complaints of unfair dismissal from those who were dismissed unless the industrial action is unofficial; in the case of unofficial action participants may be dismissed selectively.[8]

11.4 In *Merkur Island Shipping Corporation v. Laughton*[9] Lord Diplock declared that this area of the law should be approached in three stages. First, does the common law provide the pursuer with a cause of action against the defender? Second, if the pursuer satisfies this requirement, has the pursuer's cause of action been removed as a result of immunities in the Trade Union and Labour Relations Act 1974, s. 13? Third, if one of these immunities does apply, has the pursuer's cause of action been restored by any of the statutory developments

---

[4] EA 1982, s. 18 amending TULRA, s. 29.

[5] EA 1990, s. 4.

[6] See, for example, the enactment of the Trade Disputes Act 1965 to provide statutory relief for the delict of intimidation which had been applied to trade unions by the House of Lords in *Rookes v. Barnard* [1964] AC 1129 and the extension of immunity to cover inducement of breach of all contracts by the Trade Union and Labour Relations (Amendment) Act 1976 in accordance with the recommendations of the Royal Commission on Trade Unions and Employers' Associations 1965-68 (Donovan Commission) Cmnd. 3623 who had argued that the earlier legal decisions had created a "legal maze". See paras, 892-893 of the Report.

[7] *NCB v. Galley* [1958] 1 All ER 91 CA.

[8] EPCA, s. 62 and s. 62A. For the equivalent provisions on redundancy see EPCA, s. 92.

[9] [1983] ICR 490 HL.

which have restricted the scope of protected industrial action? This is the approach to this subject which will be adopted in this chapter.

THE COMMON LAW

11.5 (a) Conspiracy

The essence of conspiracy is a combination of two or more persons to commit an unlawful act or to commit a lawful act by unlawful means. A conspiracy cannot be committed by one person alone. It is clear that there are two forms of conspiracy which can give rise to liability in delict. The first arises where two or more persons combine in order to injure the pursuer through the use of means which are unlawful in themselves and which do not depend on the combination for their illegality. The second exists when two or more persons combine in order to injure the pursuer using lawful means, but where their predominant purpose is not to advance their own legitimate interests. In both cases it is now clear that there must be an intention to injure the pursuer[10] who must also establish that he has suffered some patrimonial loss.[11] The critical question as regards the first form of the delict concerns the meaning of unlawful means. There can be no doubt that any conspiracy to commit a delict[12] or to commit a crime[13] would be unlawful. There has been some doubt expressed as to whether combining in order to break a contract can constitute an unlawful conspiracy[14] although the preponderance of opinion is now in favour of liability.[15] At one time it was thought that this form of delictual liability was established as soon as the unlawful means were proved. However, it now seems as a result of the decision of the House of Lords in *Lonrho Ltd v. Shell Petroleum Ltd*[16] that it is also necessary to show some intention to injure the pursuer.

11.6 *Simple conspiracy.* The second form of conspiracy — simple conspiracy to injure — became important as far as industrial conflict law is concerned through the trilogy of cases decided by the House of Lords in the late Victorian era.[17] The effect of one of these decisions, *Quinn v. Leathem*,[18] ensured that an otherwise lawful act could become unlawful if it was done by two or more persons and with the intent to injure a third party.[19] Clearly, such a principle

---

[10] *Lonrho Ltd v. Shell Petroleum Co Ltd (No. 2)* [1982] AC 173.

[11] See the decision of the House of Lords in *Crofter Hand Woven Harris Tweed Co Ltd v. Veitch* 1942 SC (HL) 1.

[12] *Crofter, ibid; Sorrell v. Smith* [1925] AC 700 HL.

[13] However, a conspiracy to breach a penal statute may not constitute unlawful means. See the decision of the House of Lords in *Lonrho Ltd v. Shell Petroleum Co Ltd (No 2)* [1982] AC 173.

[14] See the speech of Lord Devlin in *Rookes v. Barnard* [1964] AC 1129 at p. 1210.

[15] See "Trade Unions and Trade Disputes", *Stair Memorial Encyclopoedia of the Laws of Scotland,* Vol. 23, (1991) para. 850.

[16] [1982] AC 173. This decision has been construed by the Court of Appeal as requiring proof of a predominant purpose to injure for both types of conspiracy. See the decision of the Court of Appeal in *Metall und Rohstoff AG v. Donaldson Lufkin & Jenvette Inc* [1989] 3 WLR 563. The House of Lords has now overruled *Metall und Rohstoff* in part by declaring that there is no need to establish a predominent purpose in the case of a conspiracy using unlawful means. An intention to injure will suffice. See *Lonrho plc v. Fayed* [1991] 3 All ER 303.

[17] *Mogul SS Co v. Mcgregor Gow & Co* [1892] AC 25; *Allen v. Flood* [1898] AC 1; *Quinn v. Leathem* [1901] AC 495.

[18] [1901] AC 495.

[19] *Sorrell v. Smith* [1925] AC 700, HL.

would have a significant impact on the legality of industrial action since the very basis of such action involves employees combining together to cause economic harm to their employer's business. However, later cases have reduced the impact of this delict by taking a broad interpretation of the predominant object behind the action and by accepting a defence of justification. Thus if the union can show that its predominant purpose is to pursue genuine trade union objectives the pursuer will have no cause of action even although his business is being injured as a result. In *Crofter Hand Woven Harris Tweed Co v. Veitch*,[20] for example, island mill-owners combined with the union to keep out the pursuer because his yarn was produced on the mainland. As part of this campaign, the union instructed its members, without breaking their contracts, to boycott the pursuer's yarn so as not only to protect the local industry but also to ensure that the local mill-owners improved the wages of their employees and permitted the extension of union membership. The House of Lords held that since the interests of the union and the employer were similar because both wanted to protect the local tweed industry which relied upon home produced wool there was no unlawful conspiracy by the union and its members.[21] On the other hand, where the predominant object is to pursue a grudge against a former union member by seeking to have him dismissed a conspiracy to injure will be established since this is not a legitimate union objective.[22]

11.7 (b) Inducement of breach of contract

This form of illegality was established as far as English law is concerned in *Lumley v. Gye*[23] where an opera singer was induced to break her contract of employment by singing at another theatre. This decision has been followed in Scotland in *Rose Street Foundry and Engineering Co v. Lewis & Sons*.[24] It is clear that the delict does not just apply to an inducement to break a contract of employment but extends to inducing a breach of any type of contract.[25] The delict is committed where one person intentionally and without lawful justification procures or induces a breach of a contract between two other persons causing damage to one of them.[26] This delict takes three forms.

(a) *Direct inducement* where the defender (U) directly approaches one of the contracting parties (B) and persuades him to break his contract with a third party (A). See Figure 1.

In this case A will have a cause of action against U for inducement for breach of contract.

(b) *Direct procurement* where one of the contracting parties is forced to break the contract as a result of an unlawful act committed against him by the defender such as false imprisonment, trespass or theft.

---

[20] 1942 SC (HL) 1. See also *Scala Ballroom (Wolverhampton) Ltd v. Ratcliffe* [1958] 3 All ER 220 where it was held that a boycott of a dance hall by members of the Musician's Union in protest at a colour bar did not constitute an unlawful conspiracy because the union was pursuing its legitimate interests.

[21] See also *Reynolds v. Shipping Federation* [1942] 1 Ch 28 where a union's action to enforce a closed shop was held not to be an unlawful conspiracy because it was intended to advance the business interests of employers and employed alike.

[22] *Huntley v. Thornton* [1957] 1 All ER 234.

[23] [1853] 2 E&B 216.

[24] 1917 SC 341.

[25] See the judgment of Lord President Cooper in *British Motor Trade Association v. Gray* 1951 SC 586 at p. 599.

[26] *Per* Lord Russell in *Gray, ibid*, at p. 603.

FIGURE 1.

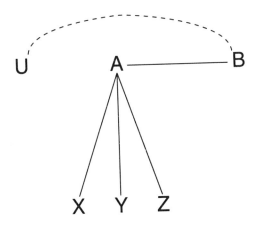

(c)   *Indirect procurement or inducement* this arises where the defender (U) is able to induce a breach of the pursuer's (A) contract with B (the other contracting party) by inducing the employees (K, L & M) of B to break their contracts of employment bringing about a consequent breach of the contract between A and B.[27] See Figure 2.

FIGURE 2.

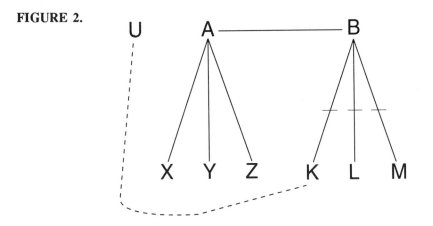

Once again A will be able to sue U for inducement of breach of contract.

It is the first and third versions of the delict which are most important as far as industrial action is concerned.

---

[27] See the judgment of Evershed M. R. in *DC Thomson & Co Ltd v. Deakin* [1952] 1 Ch 646 at p. 678. This is the most likely form of the delict for trade dispute purposes. However, it can be committed by the commission of any unlawful act by a third party which causes one of the contracting parties to break the contract. This point is developed further later in this chapter.

11.8 The elements of the delict

There are a number of elements to this delict. These were best outlined by Jenkins L.J. in *D C Thomson & Co Ltd v. Deakin*[28] which is still relied upon today as the basis for the delict albeit that some of the strict requirements mentioned by Jenkins L.J. have been diluted. First, the inducer must have knowledge of the contract and intend to bring about its breach. As far as knowledge is concerned at one time it was thought that this required the defender to possess a knowledge of the precise terms of the contract.[29] Now, however, general knowledge about the existence of the contract is enough.[30] Indeed, it is possible for the courts to deem that the inducer had knowledge of the existence of contracts from the circumstances of the case.[31] Moreover, it would not be a defence for the inducer to argue that he genuinely believed that there was no such contractual term between the parties which could be broken.[32]

11.9 *Intention.* In one of the few authoritative statements on this branch of the law in Scotland Lord Russell declared in *BMTA v. Gray*[33] that the defender's actings must be intentional. However, the present English position is that the tort is no longer one of intention since liability can be established where the inducer acts recklessly or turns a blind eye to the likelihood of breach.[34] The present state of the law in Scotland is unclear although there is a recent Outer House decision in a landlord and tenant case to the effect that the delict is still one of intention and that "turning a blind eye" is not sufficient unless such action is tantamount to enable the court to conclude that the actings were in effect intentional.[35] If one can induce a breach without intending to damage the actual pursuer this has obvious implications for the range of people who have title to sue for inducement of breach of contract in a trade dispute. This issue was discussed in the County Court in England in *Falconer v. ASLEF & NUR*[36] where a passenger on British Rail sued the two unions for damages for inducement of breach of contract. He had bought his ticket in advance but was unable to travel on the appointed day because of industrial action. The unions' defence that F was not the object of the action and that any damage to passengers was merely consequential was rejected by the judge as being both naive and divorced from reality. In his view the action could succeed because the intention of the unions was to direct the strike against passengers in order to put pressure on the employers. In any case the unions also acted recklessly because they knew and appreciated the effects of their action upon F and his contract but nevertheless pursued it.

11.10 On the other hand in *Barretts & Baird (Wholesale) Ltd v. IPCS*[37] Henry J. introduced an element of predominant purpose in order to establish liability. He argued that where the industrial action was called in order to improve the

---

[28] *Ibid*, at pp. 696-697.

[29] See *DC Thomson, ibid.*

[30] *Stratford & Son Ltd v. Lindley* [1965] AC 269 HL applied in Scotland by Lord Milligan in *Square Grip Reinforcement Ltd v. MacDonald* 1968 SLT 65.

[31] *Merkur Island Shipping Corporation v. Laughton* [1983] ICR 490.

[32] *Metropolitan Borough of Solihull v. NUT* [1985] IRLR 211.

[33] 1951 SC 586 at p. 603.

[34] *Emerald Construction Co v. Lowthian* [1966] 1 WLR 691.

[35] *Rossleigh Ltd v. Leader Cars Ltd* 1987 SLT 355. See particularly the decision of Lord Mayfield at p. 360.

[36] [1986] IRLR 331.

[37] [1987] IRLR 3.

members' terms and conditions of employment the union would not be held liable for inducing consequent breaches of commercial contracts if these were merely "unavoidable by-products". There is no direct authority on this point in Scotland, although statements by Lord Milligan in *Square Grip Reinforcement Ltd v. Macdonald*[38] could be construed as supporting the *Falconer* decision because he argued that although actual knowledge of the terms of the contract on the part of the defender could not be proved, liability could be established when the defender should have realised that his action would injure the pursuer and cause a breach of contract. However, despite the fact that Henry J.'s view does have the advantage in a labour law context of limiting the legal consequences of industrial action, it has to be acknowledged that in other areas of the law there is no need to prove a predominant intention to injure the plaintiff for the purposes of the tort.[39] In Scotland, of course, the issue may yet be resolved purely on the basis that the defender did not intend to damage the pursuer.[40]

11.11 *Inducement or advice?* Second, it must be shown that the defender definitely and unequivocally persuaded, induced or procured the breach of an existing contract.[41] This requirement is particularly important as far as direct inducement is concerned. The issue here is to discover the forms of direct approach to one of the contracting parties which can constitute the necessary persuasion for the purposes of the delict, for example, would it be unlawful persuasion for a union officer merely to inform a supplier that a customer was in dispute with his employees? In *D. C. Thomson & Co Ltd v. Deakin*[42] this question appeared to be answered in the negative because the court suggested that merely to advise one of the contracting parties about the current state of facts would not constitute the necessary persuasion for the delict. However in the only major case on this topic in Scotland a contrary view was expressed. In *Square Grip Reinforcement Ltd v. Macdonald*[43] Lord Milligan adopting a similar approach to that of Lord Pearce in *J T Stratford & Son Ltd v. Lindley*[44] took the view that informing customers that the union had a recognition dispute with the other contracting party amounted to inducement of breach of contract because the union was "desperately anxious" to achieve a successful conclusion to the dispute. It would be important in deciding whether the approach amounted to inducement to consider the relative positions of the parties involved in order to assess the impact of the information upon the contract-breaker.[45]

11.12 *Indirect inducement.* As far as indirect inducement is concerned it is also necessary to show in a trade dispute context that the employees concerned did actually break their contracts of employment and that the breach of the contract between A and B came about as a necessary consequence of the employees' breaches of their contracts of employment. The necessary consequence point

---

[38] 1968 SLT 65 at p. 72.
[39] See the decision of the Court of Appeal in *Lonrho plc v. Fayed* [1988] 3 WLR 631.
[40] *Rossleigh Ltd v. Leader Cars Ltd* 1987 SLT 355.
[41] *BMTA v. Gray* 1951 SC 586 at p. 603. In England the Court of Appeal has held in *Union Traffic Ltd v. TGWU* [1989] IRLR 127 that interlocutory relief could be provided in order to prevent a party inducing a breach of a future contract.
[42] [1952] 1 Ch 646.
[43] 1968 SLT 65 at pp. 72-73.
[44] [1965] AC 269 at p. 333.
[45] *Square Grip Reinforcement Ltd v. MacDonald* 1968 SLT 65.

has not proved a major obstacle in the cases.[46] It simply entails the pursuer showing as a matter of practical possibility that the other contracting party did not perform his contract.[47] Much more important is the requirement that the breach of the contract between A and B be procured by unlawful means. If there is no unlawful means there can be no delictual liability for indirect inducement of breach of contract.[48] In the context of industrial action, unlawful means will usually be established by the employees of B being called upon by their union to take strike action or boycott goods destined for delivery to or collection from A: although, as we shall see, the unlawful means can exist in other ways such as inducement of breach of statutory duty. Whatever action the employees of B actually take, must entail a breach of their contracts of employment. This means that the necessary illegality would be lacking where B, having been informed of the union's dispute with A, withdraws his instructions to his employees to deliver goods to A so that the employees are never put in a position to break their contracts.[49]

11.13 *Justification*. In the *BMTA* case[50] Lord Russell declared that it was also necessary to show that the defender had acted without lawful justification. Although this is a widely recognised defence, it has been applied very restrictively in trade dispute cases. It would not be a defence in a case involving industrial action to show that that action was called without any malice or ill-will towards the pursuer.[51] The only occasion where a defence of justification has been accepted in an employment case is *Brimelow v. Casson*[52] where it was acknowledged that the defendants were justified in inducing theatre proprietors to refuse the use of their theatres to the plaintiff when it was clear that the wages he was offering his chorus girls were so low that there was a danger that some of them would seek to supplement their income through immoral behaviour. As we shall see shortly, this specific delict has been extended considerably, certainly as far as English law is concerned, so that there is now a broad innominate tort of interference with contractual relations.

11.14 (c) Intimidation

The basis of intimidation involves the pursuer suffering damage as a result of action by a third party which that party is forced to take because of unlawful threats made to the third party by the defender. This form of liability was developed by the House of Lords in the context of industrial action in *Rookes v. Barnard*.[53] Previously it was thought that intimidation only applied to threats

---

[46] See, for example, the decision of the House of Lords in *Stratford & Son Ltd v. Lindley* [1965] AC 269 reversing the decision of the Court of Appeal on this point (reported at [1965] AC 276). See also *Merkur Island Shipping Corporation v. Laughton* [1983] ICR 490, HL.

[47] *Per* Jenkins L. J. in *DC Thomson & Co Ltd v. Deakin* [1952] 1 Ch 646 at p. 697.

[48] See the judgment of Lord Denning M. R. in *Torquay Hotel Co Ltd v. Cousins* [1969] 2 Ch 106 at pp. 138-139 reversing his earlier statement in *Daily Mirror Newspapers Ltd v. Gardner* [1969] 2 QB 768.

[49] *DC Thomson & Co Ltd v. Deakin* [1952] 1 Ch 646.

[50] *BMTA v. Gray* 1951 SC 586 at p. 603.

[51] *South Wales Miners' Federation v. Glamorgan Coal Co* [1905] AC 239. *Cf Findlay v. Blaylock* 1937 SC 21.

[52] [1924] 1 Ch 302.

[53] [1964] AC 1129.

which were in themselves unlawful, usually threats of physical violence, although it might have extended to cover any crime or delict.[54] The *Rookes* case makes it clear that the concept of intimidation is wide enough to cover threats to break a contract. In that case the plaintiff was held to have a cause of action against a number of his fellow employees for intimidation when their employer terminated his contract of employment by proper notice. The basis for this was that his dismissal came about as a direct result of threats to take industrial action by the other employees in breach of their contracts of employment. Clearly, this form of liability has significant implications for those organising industrial action[55] since the critical element is that the defender must make an unlawful threat — something that may arise frequently in the preliminary stages before any industrial action is actually taken. If this is the case, then, it is of no moment whether the damage caused to the pursuer by the person who has been threatened is committed lawfully through, for example, the termination of a contract by proper notice. There is no express authority on this form of liability in Scotland although there are some older Scottish cases where a threat to break a contract has been held to constitute an actionable wrong.[55a] However, it must be accepted that a wrong of the type envisaged by the judges in the *Rookes* case would fall within the general principle of *culpa* in the Scots law of reparation. Thus we can assume that a wrong of the same kind as intimidation would be recognised by the Scottish courts.[56]

11.15 (d) Interference with contractual relations or with trade or business

As we saw earlier in this chapter there is no doubt that it is an actionable wrong to induce a breach of contract. However, in the last twenty years or so liability has been extended to encompass another form of wrong *viz* interference with the performance of a contract. This arises where the defender interferes with the performance of a contract without actually causing either of the contracting parties to break it. Although there are statements in the *Thomson* case[57] which could be construed as being wide enough to encompass this type of liability its origins can be traced to the decision of the Court of Appeal in *Torquay Hotel Co Ltd v. Cousins.*[58] In that case the contract which was the target of the union's action had a *force majeure* clause. This allowed the contract to be terminated without breach in the event of industrial action. When industrial action was called at the hotel the company which supplied the hotel with heating oil activated the *force majeure* clause. Thus we had the situation where it was obvious that the *force majeure* clause was implemented because of the industrial action. However, technically, there was no breach of contract. The majority of the court considered that the clause only provided an immunity as between the contracting parties and therefore concluded that Cousins was still responsible for inducement of breach of contract. However, Lord Denning

---

[54] See K. W. Wedderburn "Intimidation and the Right to Strike' (1964) 27 MLR 257.

[55] One other feature of the *Rookes* case was the fact that the House of Lords also held that the union officer who had informed the employer about the likelihood of strike action could be held responsible for a conspiracy to intimidate for which there was then no trade disputes protection. See Wedderburn, *ibid*, at pp. 272-275.

[55a] See, for example, *Hewit v. Edinburgh & District Operative Lathsplitters and Lathdriver's Association* [1906] 14 5LT 489, OH.

[56] See J. T. Cameron "Intimidation and the Right to Strike" 1964 SLT (News) 81.

[57] [1952] 1 Ch 646. See, in particular, the judgment of Jenkins L. J. at pp. 696-694.

[58] [1969] 2 Ch 106.

M.R. considered that there was also a tort of interference with contractual relations which arose where a third person prevents or hinders one of the contracting parties from performing his contract so long as that interference is deliberate.

11.16 *Interference without breach.* This view has been supported by Lord Diplock in *Merkur Island Shipping Corporation v. Laughton*[59] He argued that the analysis of the law in the *Thomson* case was restricted to inducement of breach of contract simply because this was the legal issue which the facts in that case disclosed. In Lord Diplock's opinion, although he used the expression "breach" in that case, Jenkins L.J. did not intend to restrict the tort of actionable interference with contractual rights to situations where a breach of contract was actually induced. Thus as far as English law is concerned, an interference with the performance of a contract will give rise to liability in tort even although no breach of contract has been induced. It most likely arises where the action of the defender prevents or hinders the performance of the pursuer's contract without a breach.[60] It is important to discover whether this wrong applies in both the direct and indirect forms of the tort. In *Cousins*, Lord Denning certainly envisaged that both forms of interference would give rise to liability. As far as indirect interference is concerned there can be no doubt that there must be unlawful means — usually through the employees of one of the contracting parties being induced to break their contracts of employment. However, in the case of direct interference, it would seem that mere interference alone without the commission of some other unlawful act by the inducer would not be tortious.[61] There is no clear authority on the existence of this form of liability in Scots law. However, Lord Cameron in *St Stephen Shipping Co Ltd v. Guinane*[62] did accept without argument that it would be unlawful in Scotland to interfere with the performance of an existing contract. The exact limits of this form of liability still await clearer articulation and analysis.

11.17 In the *Thomson* case[63] Evershed M.R. argued that at the time of the enactment of the Trade Disputes Act in 1906 it was unlikely that the law recognised that a person would be liable for merely interfering in some way with the trade or business of some other person. However, English law now undoubtedly recognises this type of liability so long as, and this is crucial, the defender uses unlawful means.[64] Interference with trade or business was certainly relied upon by Lord Denning in *Daily Mirror Newspapers Ltd v. Gardiner*[65] and in the *Cousins* case[66] and it was referred to by Lord Reid in both *Stratford v. Lindley*[67] and *Rookes*.[68] There is, therefore, ample authority in English law to support its existence. Indeed, in English law, it is likely that the concept of wrongful in-

---

[59] [1983] ICR 490.
[60] *Merkur, ibid, per* Lord Diplock at p. 506.
[61] See the judgment of Lord Denning M. R. in *Acrow (Automation) Ltd v. Rex Chainbelt Inc* [1971] 3 All ER 1175 CA.
[62] 1984 SLT 25.
[63] [1952] 1 Ch 646 at p. 688.
[64] *Torquay Hotel Co Ltd v. Cousins* [1969] 2 Ch 106.
[65] [1968] 2 QB 768 at p. 783.
[66] [1969] 2 Ch 106 at p. 139.
[67] [1965] AC 269.
[68] [1964] AC 1129.

terference with trade or business constitutes a broad category of tortious liability encompassing the other specific delicts to which we have already referred.[69] In the *Merkur* case[70] Lord Diplock certainly recognised the existence of a common law tort of interfering with the trade or business of another person by doing unlawful acts. There is no express authority on this point in Scotland. However, if the Scottish courts were to follow the English position the delict would be committed where damage is caused intentionally to the pursuer's business by the use of unlawful means. It is undoubtedly the case that the wrong is only actionable when there is proof of unlawful means — there would be no wrong where the interference is brought about by means which are themselves lawful. The exact scope of the unlawful means is not yet clear although it is not restricted to procuring another person to break a subsisting contract nor to interfering with the performance of that contract. As a final point there is authority in a trade disputes case that it is a strong requirement of the delict that the defender's predominant purpose must be injury to the pursuer and not his own self-interest.[71] However, in *Lonrho plc v. Fayed*[72] the Court of Appeal held that it was not necessary to establish a predominant intention to injure for the purposes of the tort, it is enough if the unlawful act is in some sense directed against the plaintiff or is intended to harm him.

11.18 *What constitutes unlawful means?* It has already been noted that although the existence of unlawful means is critical to the delict of interference with business the exact limits of those means for the purposes of liability have not been fully defined. Commission of another delict or of a crime would constitute the necessary unlawful act. Equally, as we shall see, inducement of breach of a statutory duty can constitute unlawful means — although not the breach of a penal statute.[73] The area of doubt is whether a breach of contract would be enough.[74] This is a point which is discussed by Henry J. in *Barretts & Baird (Wholesale) Ltd v. IPCS*.[75] In this case, it was held that the plaintiffs had an arguable case against a number of fatstock officers employed by the Meat and Livestock Commission for interference with their business by unlawful means when the officers took part in a one day strike causing disruption to their business through the non-availability of EEC subsidies. The critical aspect of this case was Henry J.'s holding that the unlawful means existed in the form of the officers' breaches of their own employment contracts when they took part in

---

[69] See Patrick Elias and Keith Ewing "Economic Torts and Labour Law: Old Principles and New Liabilities" (1982) 41 Cam LJ 321.

[70] [1983] ICR 490. See also *Barretts & Baird (Wholesale) Ltd v. IPCS* [1987] IRLR 3; *Associated British Ports v. TGWU* [1989] IRLR 305 CA, [1989] IRLR 399 HL; *Lonrho plc v. Fayed* [1989] 3 WLR 631 CA.

[71] *Per* Henry J. in *Barretts & Baird (Wholesale) Ltd v. IPCS* [1987] IRLR 3 at 10 misapplying the speech of Lord Diplock in *Lonrho Ltd v. Shell Petroleum Co Ltd (No 2)* [1982] AC 173.

[72] [1989] 3 WLR 631. See, in particular, the judgment of Dillon L. J. at p. 637.

[73] *Lonrho Ltd v. Shell Petroleum Co Ltd (No 2)* [1982] AC 173.

[74] In *Rookes v. Barnard* [1964] AC 1129 the House of Lords had held that a breach of contract was unlawful means for the purposes of intimidation, but left open the question of whether it would be so for the purpose of other delicts. See, for example, Lord Devlin at p. 1210.

[75] [1987] IRLR 3.

the action. He came to this conclusion because of the repeal of the Trade Union and Labour Relations Act 1974 s. 13(3)(b) by the Employment Act 1980, s. 17(8). This provision had declared that "a breach of contract in contemplation or furtherance of a trade dispute shall not be regarded as the doing of an unlawful act for the purpose of establishing liability in [delict]". Its repeal forced Henry J. to accept that a simple breach of contract would be enough to constitute the necessary unlawful means for liability for wrongful interference with another's business.[76]

11.19 (e) Other actionable wrongs

In this developing area of the law there have been a number of other potential forms of liability which have been discussed in the cases. The importance of most of these is that given their novelty, no immunity is provided in the Trade Union and Labour Relations Act 1974 against their application to trade unions in a trades disputes case. One possible wrong which has been discussed is inducement of breach of statutory duty. In *Meade v. Haringey LBC*[77] industrial action was called involving school janitors and cleaners. When the council closed the schools a number of parents sought an injunction against the council for failing to comply with its statutory duties under the Education Acts. In the Court of Appeal both Lord Denning M.R. and Eveleigh L.J. considered that it was not only competent to sue the council for breach of statutory duty but also that a cause of action lay against the union for inducing such a breach.

11.20 *Breach of statutory duty.* An important element in this delict is to discover whether the statute does actually impose a mandatory duty upon the person induced which the pursuer alleges has been broken as a result of the defender's inducements. This will entail a careful examination of the terms of the relevant statute.[78] The dangers of this type of liability for primary industrial action and the extent to which the appropriate statute will have to be scrutinised are illustrated in *Associated British Ports v. TGWU*.[79] There the union sought to call a strike of dockers as part of its campaign for similar terms and conditions to be applied to the dockers which they had previously enjoyed under the National Dock Labour Scheme. The Court of Appeal held that the scheme imposed a statutory duty upon registered dockers to work for such periods as were reasonable so that the union was inducing a breach of this statutory duty by calling the dockers out on strike. While this decision was reversed by the House of Lords,[80] it was simply on the ground that the Court of Appeal was wrong in its interpretation of the scheme. In the view of the House of Lords it did not place a clear statutory duty on the dockers to perform work. Their Lordships did not question the existence of such a wrong and so the dicta of the Court of Appeal are still relevant. The other important aspect of this form of liability is that

---

[76] As has already been noted, the action against the employees for interference failed because the plaintiffs could not show that the action was taken with the predominant purpose of injuring them. This holding must now be open to doubt as a result of the Court of Appeal's decision in *Lonrho plc v. Fayed* [1989] 3 WLR 631.

[77] [1979] ICR 494. See also the judgment of Lord Denning M. R. in *Associated Newspaper Group v. Wade* [1979] ICR 664 where he also argued that an interference with press freedom would also involve liability.

[78] *Per* Henry J. in *Barretts & Baird (Wholesale) Ltd v. IPCS* [1987] IRLR 3.

[79] [1989] IRLR 305.

[80] [1989] IRLR 399.

there is no doubt that in certain circumstances inducing a breach of statutory duty can constitute the necessary unlawful means for the purpose of wrongful interference with the pursuer's trade or business.[81] However, the critical point is to show that the statutory contravention is independently actionable so that the pursuer has a right to sue *per se*.[82] Once again liability will turn upon the exact terms of the statute concerned.[83]

11.21 *Economic duress*. A final potential form of liability which could apply to trade unions is economic duress. This arises where one party to a contract is forced to enter into that contract or to agree to one of its terms because of unlawful coercion by the other party. In such a case the innocent party can argue that the contract is voidable and seek restitution of any money paid under it. The House of Lords has held in *Universe Tankships Inc of Moinrovia v. ITWF*[84] that this form of liability is applicable in trade dispute cases. In this case it was held that the plaintiffs could seek restitution of $6,480 which they had been forced to pay into the union's welfare fund as a result of industrial pressure caused when the union authorised the blacking of one of their ships. There is no authority on this proposition in Scotland. However, it is doubtful whether such a cause of action would apply given the underdeveloped state of the law relating to force and fear and duress.[85]

THE IMMUNITIES

11.22 Introduction

Once a pursuer has established that he has a cause of action at common law it is then necessary to discover whether that right to sue had been removed by any of the statutory immunities. Before any immunity operates, it must be shown that the industrial action was called "in contemplation or furtherance of a trade dispute" and is therefore protected by the golden formula. However, immunity is not provided against all the forms of delictual liability that are likely to arise in the course of a trade dispute.

11.23 The scope of s. 13

The Trade Union and Labour Relations Act 1974 s. 13(4) declares that an agreement or combination to do any act done in contemplation or furtherance of a trade dispute shall not be actionable in delict if the act is one which, if done without that agreement or combination, would not be actionable in delict. This immunity applies in the case of simple conspiracy to injure — that is the case where two or more persons combine in order to injure the pursuer by lawful means, but have an unlawful predominant purpose. However, there is no protection in the case where the combination seeks to achieve its objective by

---

[81] *Barretts & Baird (Wholesale) Ltd v. IPCS* [1987] IRLR 3.

[82] *Lonrho Ltd v. Shell Petroleum Ltd (No 2)* [1982] AC 173.

[83] See generally the litigation arising out of the dockers' strike of 1989. See *Associated British Ports v. TGWU* [1989] IRLR 291 HC; [1989] IRLR 305 CA; [1989] IRLR 399 HL.

[84] [1982] ICR 262. See also the decision of the Court of Appeal in *Dimskal Shipping Co SA v. ITWF* [1990] IRLR 102.

[85] The present state of Scots law in this area is discussed by Andrew Thompson "Economic Duress" 1985 SLT (News) 85 and Ewan McKendrick "Economic Duress — A Reply" 1985 SLT (News) 277.

means which would be unlawful if perpetrated by one person alone. The Trade Union and Labour Relations Act 1974 s. 13(1)(a) protects both the direct and indirect forms of the delict of inducement of breach of contract if done in contemplation or furtherance of a trade dispute. The provision also extends its protection to cover cases of interference with the performance of a contract or inducing interference with the performance of a contract. When initially passed this provision only applied to inducement or interference with a contract of employment. Immunity was extended to cover all types of contract in 1976.[86] This immunity has remained unchanged since that date and in the case of primary action it is unaffected by any of the statutory changes enacted in the 1980s and in 1990. Immunity is also provided against the delict of intimidation.[87] An act done in contemplation or furtherance of a trade dispute will not be actionable in delict on the ground only that it consists in the defender threatening that a contract (whether one to which he is a party or not) will be broken or its performance interfered with, or that he will induce another person to break another contract or to interfere with its performance. This protection was first introduced by the Trade Disputes Act 1965 in order to negate the decision of the House of Lords in *Rookes v. Barnard*[88] and in 1976 it was extended to cover intimidation of any type of contract.[89]

11.24 There are a number of other wrongs which can be committed in the course of industrial action for which statute provides no protection. For example, there is no protection for assault or trespass although arguably until 1982 there existed immunity for the consequences of a trespass since statute[90] protected any interference with trade, business or employment of some other person, or with the right of some other person to dispose of his capital or his labour as he wills.[91] More importantly, as has already been noted, there is no immunity against the new actionable wrongs. Thus there is no protection against economic duress or inducement of breach of statutory duty.

11.25 The position is rather more complicated in the case of an interference with business by unlawful means. The repealed Trade Union and Labour Relations Act 1974 s. 13(2) might have been relevant since, as we have seen, it sought to protect an interference with a person's trade, business or employment. However, it was made clear by Lord Reid in *Rookes v. Barnard*[92] that this provision only provided protection if it was ever decided that a person could be liable for simple interference with business and nothing more. As we know, such interference is only actionable where unlawful means are used. It seemed

---

[86] TULR(A)A 1976, based on the proposals of the Donovan Commission (1968, Cmnd. 3623) which had recommended that in order to bring clarity to this area of the law the immunities should be extended to cover inducement of breach of contract. See paras 891-894.

[87] TULRA, s. 13(1) (b).

[88] [1964] AC 1129.

[89] TULR(A)A 1976, s. 3(2).

[90] TULRA, s. 13(2) was repealed by EA 1982, s. 21(3).

[91] See the interpretation placed upon this provision by the First Division as regards the legality of factory occupations in *Plessey PLC v. Wilson* 1983 SLT 139.

[92] [1964] AC 1129 at p. 1177.

therefore, that s. 13(2) protected nothing.[93] However, in *Hadmor Productions Ltd v. Hamilton*[94] Lord Diplock suggested that s. 13(2) was intended to cover interference by unlawful means. No authority was cited in support of this proposition and certainly one writer has argued that it was *per incuriam*. [95] The better view is that Lord Reid's assessment in *Rookes* is correct. Since the repeal of s. 13(2) by the Employment Act 1982,[96] there is now no specific statutory protection against interfering with business by unlawful means. However, there may be some indirect protection against liability. This would arise where the means adopted to bring about the interference are themselves declared not actionable by s. 13. Thus if the interference involved employees being induced to break their contracts of employment the necessary unlawful means would not exist since this form of inducement cannot from the basis of an action under the Trade Union and Labour Relations Act 1974, s. 13(1)(a).[97]

11.26 Golden Formula

The parties to a dispute. Once it has been established that the delict which the defender is alleged to have committed is one covered by s. 13 the next task is to consider whether it was done in contemplation or furtherance of a trade dispute. This entails discovering whether or not there is a trade dispute and then considering whether or not the industrial action is in contemplation or furtherance of that dispute. The first question raises two issues. First we must consider who can be the parties to a trade dispute and then examine the definition of a trade dispute provided by statute. A trade dispute means a dispute between workers and their own employer.[98] To qualify as a worker the person must be employed by the employer in dispute, or, in the case of a person who has ceased to be employed by that employer, either have had his employment terminated in connection with the dispute, or, prove that the termination of his employment was one of the circumstances giving rise to the dispute. It would seem that the present definition would exclude inter-union disputes or demarcation disputes since these are unlikely to involve the workers' employer.[99] It also ensures that workers cannot use this provision as a means of taking solidarity action in support of other trade unionists, since they are not employed by the employer in dispute. The only way by which these other workers would be

---

[93] As Lord Wedderburn put it, TULRA, s. 13(2) was of "limited value since it has been made clear that such interference is not a tort anyway, so there is nothing to protect". See K. W. Wedderburn "The Trade Union and Labour Relations Act" (1974) 37 MLR 525 at 539.

[94] [1982] IRLR 102 at p. 109. Lord Diplock's interpretation of s. 13(2) was followed by the First Division in *Plessey PLC v. Wilson* 1983 SLT 139.

[95] See K. D. Ewing "Industrial Action: Another Step in the 'Right' Direction" (1982) 11 ILJ 209 at 214.

[96] EA 1982, s. 21.

[97] See the speech of Lord Diplock in *Hadmor Productions Ltd v. Hamilton* [1982] IRLR 102 at p. 109.

[98] TULRA, s. 29(1). Formerly under the original provisions of s. 29(1) a trade dispute could be between workers and workers or workers and employers. The present restrictive definition was introduced by EA 1982, s. 18. It should be noted that a dispute between a trade union and an employer does satisfy the present statutory definition of a dispute between workers and their employer, since a union has the authority to negotiate terms and conditions on behalf of its members. See the decision of Millett J. in *Associated British Ports v. TGWU* [1989] IRLR 291.

[99] TULRA, s. 29(6).

protected would be by establishing that they had a separate dispute with their own employer. The present definition would also exclude a dispute with another employer in the same group of companies as the workers' employer. In such a case the workers would have no trade dispute with their own employer because of the judges' reluctance to lift the "corporate veil".[100]

11.27 *The subject matter of a trade dispute.* A trade dispute must relate wholly or mainly to one or more of the following —

(a) terms and conditions of employment, or the physical conditions in which any workers are required to work;

(b) engagement or non-engagement, or termination or suspension of employment or the duties of employment, of one or more workers;

(c) allocation of work or the duties of employment as between workers or groups of workers;

(d) matters of discipline;

(e) the membership or non-membership of a trade union on the part of a worker;

(f) facilities for officials of trade unions; and

(g) machinery for negotiation or consultation, and other procedures, relating to any of the foregoing matters, including the recognition by employers or employers' associations of the right of a trade union to represent workers in any such negotiation or consultation or in the carrying out of such procedures.[101]

11.28 The above definition covers a large number of issues. As far as terms and conditions of employment are concerned, it is clear that this phrase has a wide meaning and covers not only the express and implied terms of the contract but also customary arrangements applied in practice by the parties.[102] The only limitation appears to be that it is restricted to those terms which regulate the relationship between the employee and his employer.[103] As regards head (c) concerning allocation of work, given that a trade dispute is now restricted to disputes between workers and their employer, disputes over the allocation of work are only covered where the work is being reallocated between workers employed by the same employer. It does not apply where the employer chooses to reallocate the work to an outside agency.[104]

11.29 Some matters lie outside the definition. Strikes which are primarily political are not covered;[105] nor is industrial action aimed at showing employee disapproval of the employer's policy of selling his products to a particular coun-

---

[100] *Dimbleby & Sons Ltd v. NUJ* [1984] ICR 386 HL.

[101] TULRA, s. 29(1).

[102] *BBC v. Hearn* [1977] ICR 685 approved by the House of Lords in *Hadmor Productions Ltd v. Hamilton* [1982] IRLR 102.

[103] *Per* Lord Diplock in *Universe Tankships Inc of Monrovia v. ITWF* [1982] ICR 262. Both Lord Scarman and Lord Brandon dissented from this view and placed a wider interpretation on this phrase.

[104] *Dimbleby & Sons Ltd v. NUJ* [1984] ICR 386 HL.

[105] See, for example, *Express Newspapers Ltd v. Keys* [1980] IRLR 247. The general strike of 1926 was held to be illegal by Astbury J. in *National Sailors' and Firemen's Union v. Reed* [1926] Ch 536.

try.[106] The most important point about this definition is that the dispute must "relate wholly or mainly" to one or more of the matters listed above. This phrase was inserted by the Employment Act 1982, s. 18 to replace the original requirement that the dispute be "connected with" one or more of the above-noted matters. This previous phrase undoubtedly covered a wider category of dispute and had been interpreted broadly by the courts. The only requirement was that the dispute had to have some genuine connection with one of the matters listed in (a)-(g). It was therefore irrelevant that the dispute was primarily concerned with some extraneous subject-matter like a political issue provided that the dispute was also concerned with one of the matters listed.[107]

11.30 The current definition is much more restrictive. The meaning of the present phrase has been considered by the Court of Appeal in *Mercury Communications Ltd v. Scott-Garner*[108] where it was concluded that although the union had called industrial action because of the fear of redundancies amongst its members given the liberalisation and ultimate privatisation of British Telecom, the main reason for the action was the union's opposition to the government's privatisation programme. This case makes it clear that judges may be required to make a critical choice as to what is the predominant purpose or main matter behind the action. In doing so they must consider the reason for the dispute very carefully[109] and this may entail considering the contents of statements made by union officers both before and during the action. As the *Mercury* case illustrates under the present definition there can be no such thing as a mixed industrial/political strike. One or other of these two possibilities must be selected as the main reason for the action. This state of affairs means that public sector unions, in particular, have to be very careful about how they manage their disputes with employers. This point is illustrated by the case arising out of the proposed repeal of the National Dock Labour Scheme.[110] Millett J. had to decide whether the union's strike call was in protest at the government's proposal to abolish the scheme or against the port employers for replacement terms and conditions of employment after the scheme was abolished. The judge considered that initially these two issues were intermingled. However, the union had clearly been

---

[106] *BBC v. Hearn* [1977] ICR 685. In this case the Court of Appeal held that the H had no immunity when he authorised industrial action to protest against the BBC's decision to televise the FA Cup Final to South Africa. However, Lord Denning M. R. conceded that had the union sought to include as a term and condition of employment of its members, a right not to be involved in broadcasts to South Africa, this might make the dispute a trade dispute.

[107] *NWL Ltd v. Woods and Nelson* [1979] ICR 755 HL. See also the decision of the House of Lords in *Hadmor Productions Ltd v. Hamilton* [1982] IRLR 102 where it was held that a trade dispute did exist when ACTT sought to prevent "facility companies" being permitted to broadcast on the ITV network. The House of Lords accepted that although the dispute was mainly about the union's objection to such companies being granted network time the dispute also concerned fears about redundancies amongst ACTT members and on this basis was a trade dispute. See also *General Aviation Services (UK) Ltd v. TGWU* [1975] ICR 276.

[108] [1984] ICR 74. *Cf Hadmor, ibid.*

[109] *Per* Dillon L. J. in *Mercury, ibid*, at p. 123.

[110] See, for example, the tactics of the TGWU prior to the calling of a dockers' strike after the abolition of the National Dock Labour Scheme. See *Associated British Ports v. TGWU* [1989] IRLR 399.

able to separate them. Thereafter, the union only threatened strike action in relation to its dispute with the employers over the terms and conditions of employment applying to the dockers after the scheme was repealed. Accordingly Millett J. concluded that the dispute was a trade dispute because it wholly related to the matters specified in the statutory definition.

11.31 There are two further points about the statutory definition of a trade dispute. First it is possible to have a trade dispute in relation to matters occurring outside the United Kingdom. For this to happen, however, it must be shown that the person(s) whose actions in the United Kingdom are said to be in contemplation or furtherance of a trade dispute are likely to be affected in respect of one of the matters listed.[111] Second, a trade dispute can still exist in law even where the employer accedes to the union's demands because an act, threat or demand done or made by one person or organisation against another which, if resisted, would have led to a trade dispute, shall, notwithstanding that the other submits to the act or threat or accedes to the demand, be treated as being done or made in contemplation or furtherance of a trade dispute.[112]

11.32 *"Contemplation"*. Once it has been established that there is a trade dispute the next step is to show that the action taken was called in contemplation or furtherance of that dispute. As far as "in contemplation" is concerned it is clear that this phrase refers to something which is impending or likely to occur. There must be some objective event or situation which is before the defender's mind. A person would not be acting in contemplation of a trade dispute where he has a resolve in regard to something which is as yet wholly within his mind and is of an entirely subjective character.[113] The dispute must be real and imminent. Accordingly, preparing for something which is merely a possibility and not certain to arise cannot be considered to be in contemplation.[114]

11.33 *"Furtherance"*. The essence of "in furtherance" is that the dispute should be in existence and that the act is done in the course of it and for the purpose of promoting the interests of one of the parties to it.[115] The meaning of this phrase has been the subject of considerable judicial disagreement in the past. In the 1970s the Court of Appeal sought to define this phrase narrowly as a means of restricting the categories of lawful industrial action. Three strands of approach could be identified in the cases. First, the motive test which required unions to organise industrial action for a legitimate trade object and not for some extraneous motive;[116] second, the remoteness test which restricted lawful industrial action to action which directly furthered the dispute;[117] and the objective test which

---

[111] TULRA, s. 29(3).

[112] *Ibid*, s. 29(5).

[113] See generally Lord Shaw of Dunfermline in *Conway v. Wade* [1909] AC 506 at p. 522.

[114] *Bent's Brewery Co Ltd v. Hogan* [1945] 2 All ER 570.

[115] *Per* Lord Loreburn in *Conway v. Wade* [1909] AC 506 at p. 512, and Lord Shaw of Dunfermline, *ibid*, at p. 522.

[116] *Star Sea Transport Corporation v. Slater* [1979] 1 Lloyd's Rep 26 CA.

[117] *Beaverbrook Newspapers v. Keys* [1978] ICR 582; *Associated Newspapers Group v. Wade* [1979] ICR 664.

required that the action be "reasonably capable" of furthering the dispute.[118] These qualifications on the statutory language were swept away by the House of Lords. In *NWL Ltd v. Woods and Nelson*[119] the House of Lords declared that the motive test was wrong and inconsistent with the intention of Parliament. Then in *Express Newspapers Ltd v. McShane*[120] the objective test was rejected by the House of Lords in favour of a subjective approach which concentrated upon the state of mind of the defender and simply required him to show that he had an honest belief that the action would further the dispute.[121] This approach was later confirmed by the House of Lords in *Duport Steels Ltd v. Sirs*[122] where it was reiterated that the important task for the judges was to give effect to the statutory language. The net effect of these three decisions was to re-establish that "furtherance" requires nothing more than an honest purpose to assist one party to the dispute.[123] Before it can be shown that a union is not furthering a dispute it must be established that the union called the action without any intention of pursuing trade dispute objectives.[124] The test is not restricted by any limitations based upon causation or the non-wisdom of the action taken.

PRESENT STATUTORY DEVELOPMENTS

11.34 Even where a union has established that the action is in contemplation or furtherance of a trade dispute and that it involves the commission of one or more of the protected delicts that action could still give rise to a civil claim because of a failure to comply with certain requirements laid down in the legislation of the 1980s and in 1990. Three limitations on the immunities will be discussed *viz* secondary action; action not authorised by a secret ballot and action to enforce union membership or recognition requirements.

11.35 (a) Secondary industrial action

Prior to its repeal by the Employment Act 1990 s. 4, s. 17 of the Employment Act 1980 limited the legality of industrial action taken against a person other than the employer in dispute. It outlawed all forms of industrial action taken beyond a first customer or supplier of the employer in dispute and severely restricted legitimate secondary action. The framework provided by s. 17 gave statutory effect to some of the concepts developed by the Court of Appeal in their decisions of the 1970s when it became clear that the House of Lords was not prepared to endorse the Court of Appeal's approach, although statutory in-

---

[118] *Express Newspapers Ltd v. McShane* [1979] ICR 210 CA. Lord Denning M. R. would have applied an even narrower objective test than that of the majority of the court. In his view before action could be held to further a dispute it had to provide "practical" assistance. See his judgment at p. 218.

[119] [1979] ICR 744.

[120] [1980] ICR 42.

[121] This was the majority view. Lord Wilberforce, although concurring in the result, applied an objective test that the action should be reasonably capable of achieving its objective. See his speech at 54-56. Lord Salmon also added the rider that the honest belief should be on reasonable grounds. See *ibid* p. 60.

[122] [1980] ICR 161.

[123] See R. C. Simpson "Gilt Back on the Formula" (1980) 43 MLR 319.

[124] *Associated British Posts v. TGWU* [1989] IRLR 291, HC.

tervention was recommended by their Lordships.[125] Section 17 has been criticised for lacking clarity[126] but its aim was to ensure that certain forms of secondary action were unlawful unless a number of gateways were passed. In particular, s. 17(1) declared that statutory immunity would not apply where there has been an interference of or an inducement to breach a contract which is not an employment contract and where the secondary action does not satisfy any of the requirements listed later in the section. Thus the principal aim of s. 17 was to regulate industrial action involving a secondary employer's commercial contracts.

11.36 *The Employment Act 1990.* Section 17 created three situations or gateways in which secondary action could be protected. The first was secondary industrial action taken at a first customer or supplier of the employer in dispute; the second was secondary action involving an associated employer and the third concerned the delictual secondary effects of lawful primary picketing. Now only the third gateway, remains. This gateway, as reconstituted by the Employment Act 1990, is now the sole type of legitimate secondary action. The Employment Act 1990 fulfils the recommendations contained in the Green Paper, *Removing Barriers to Employment*[127] and ensures that in future lawful secondary action will be restricted to acts which affect an employer who is not a party to the dispute only where they are induced in the course of lawful primary picketing. Thus the gateways to legality which were contained in the Employment Act 1980, s. 17(3) and (4) are swept away and immunity will only be available to secondary action which fulfils the following requirements. There is secondary in relation to a trade dispute, when, and only when, a person:

(a) induces another to break a contract of employment or interferes or induces another to interfere with its performance, or

(b) threatens that a contract of employment under which he or another is employed will be broken or its performance interfered with, or that he will induce another to break a contract of employment or to interfere with its performance,

and the employer under the contract of employment is not the employer party to the dispute.[127a]

These requirements for protected secondary action are only satisfied if the action is done in the course of such attendance as a picket as is declared lawful by the Trade Union and Labour Relations Act 1974, s. 15. This will require the picket to be peaceful and for the action to be conducted either by a worker employed (or, in the case of a worker not in employment, last employed) by the

---

[125] See in particular the speeches of Lord Diplock and Lord Scarman in *Duport Steels Ltd v. Sirs* [1980] ICR 161.

[126] See the judgment of Donaldson M. R. in *Merkur Island Shipping Corp v. Laughton* [1983] ICR 178 at p. 207 and the speech of Lord Diplock in the same case at [1983] ICR 490 at p. 510. British employment legislation has also been criticised by the International Labour Organisation as being too complex. See the Observations of the Committee of Experts on a complaint by the TUC and NUM in 1989. The complicated nature of the secondary action provisions was one of the reasons given by the Department of Employment for the introduction of EA 1990. See *Removing Barriers to Employment* (Cm 655, March 1989) at para. 3. 10.

[127] March 1989, Cm. 655.

[127a] EA 1990, s. 4(2).

employer party to the dispute or by a trade union official who is attending in order to accompany a member of that union whom he represents.

11.37 The effect of these measures is to compartmentalise industrial action by restricting it exclusively to the employer in dispute. Henceforth only the consequential secondary effects of such primary action may attract immunity from the Trade Union and Labour Relations Act 1974. This state of affairs is enhanced by the Employment Act 1990, s. 4(4) which prevents unions extending a primary dispute to involve another employer in order to circumvent these extended restrictions on secondary action. This provision declares that an employer must not be treated as party to a dispute between another employer and workers of that employer; and where more than one employer is in dispute with his workers, the dispute between each employer and his workers must be treated as a separate dispute. On the other hand, the same provision prevents an employer who is one of a number who are involved in a trade dispute from arguing that protected primary action should lose its immunity because it could also involve secondary action of a type which no longer enjoys the Trade Union and Labour Relations Act 1974 immunity. Thus it is declared that an act in contemplation or furtherance of a trade dispute which is primary action in relation to that dispute may not be relied on as secondary action in relation to another dispute.[128]

11.38 (b) Strike ballots

As we saw in Chapter Ten, the Trade Union Act 1984 was passed in order to give statutory effect to the government's policy of ensuring that trade unions became more responsive to the views of their members. As well as requiring ballots for union executive elections and for the periodic review of political funds that Act also obliges trade unions to conduct secret ballots before authorising official industrial action. The original provisions of the Act have been amended by the Employment Acts 1988 and 1990. If a union fails to ballot or ballots in a manner which does not comply with these statutory provisions it will lose any immunity which it might otherwise enjoy for that action. Thus, even although the industrial action falls within the golden formula or is legitimate secondary action, immunity will be lost if the action has been called by the union and it has failed to comply with the statutory balloting provisions. Equally, it is no defence for a union to argue that it is impossible for it to organise a ballot which complies with the legislation because such ballots are not authorised by its rules;[129] union members also have a right of complaint.

11.39 *When a ballot is required.* The balloting provisions only apply where a union has authorised or endorsed[130] industrial action which entails the commission of certain prescribed delicts. A ballot must be held where the action entails employees being induced to break or to interfere with the performance of their contracts of employment.[131] Equally, a union must ballot if the action is intended to induce a person to break or to interfere with the performance of a

---

[128] EA 1990, s. 4(5).

[129] *Shipping Co Uniform Inc v. ITWF* [1985] IRLR 71.

[130] For the meaning of "authorised or endorsed" see EA 1982, s. 15 as amended by EA 1990, s. 6, and para. 11.50.

[131] TUA 1984, s. 10(1).

commercial contract through the union inducing a breach or an interference with another person's contract of employment.[132] These are the only occasions where a ballot is required. Thus there is no need to ballot where the union seeks directly to break or interfere with a commercial contract without actually inducing any breach or interference with a contract of employment. Nor would a union be required to ballot where the action takes the form of a threat to induce any of the above.

11.40 *The result of not balloting or a defective ballot.* Under the original provisions the remedy for a failure to ballot properly was for immunity to be withdrawn; accordingly, the employer or any person affected by that action could apply to the courts for relief. This is still the case. However, in 1988 union members who are likely to be, or have been, induced to take part in the action were given a right to complain to the courts for an order where there has been a failure to ballot in accordance with the statutory requirements.[133] The effect of this order is to require the union to take such steps as will ensure that union members are no longer induced to take part or to continue to take part in the action.[134] The right given to members is wider than that provided to employers and others since it operates in any case where the member has been asked to take part in any industrial action which has not been sanctioned by a properly constituted ballot. The only requirement here is that the industrial action either involve a strike, meaning any concerted stoppage of work, or other action by persons employed under contracts of employment.[135] Thus in the case of a complaint raised by a member the sole issue is whether industrial action as broadly defined is likely to be or has been called. There is no need to establish that the action also entails employees being induced to break or to interfere with their contracts of employment. This means that the Employment Act 1988 has had the indirect effect of widening the categories of industrial action for which a ballot is necessary. Thus this additional right of complaint would apply to any disruptive action[136] such as a refusal to work voluntary overtime even although technically it does not involve breaches of employment contracts. In the end of the day, however, the difference between these two forms of complaint may be slight since the courts, certainly in England, have taken a broad view of the categories of industrial action which entail interference with the performance of a contract of employment.[137]

11.41 *The effect of a ballot.* The continuance of immunity depends upon whether or not the action has been endorsed with the support of a ballot. The necessary ballot support will only exist if there is a majority yes vote.[138] Moreover, the

---

[132] TUA 1984, s. 10(2).

[133] EA 1988, s. 1.

[134] EA 1988, s. 1(2).

[135] EA 1988, s. 1(7).

[136] Case law under EPCA, s. 62 concerning dismissal in connection with a lock-out, strike or other industrial action might be relevant here. See, for example, *Power Packing Case Makers Ltd v. Faust* [1983] ICR 292 where the Court of Appeal formed the view that s. 62 was intended to apply to all forms of disruptive industrial action.

[137] See, for example, *Metropolitan Borough of Solihull v. NUT* [1985] IRLR 211 where it was held that the union had a duty to ballot for action involving, *inter alia*, the withdrawal of lunchtime supervision of pupils which the teachers had thought was voluntary.

[138] TUA 1984, s. 10(3) (b).

mandate it provides only lasts for a period of four weeks from the date of the ballot.[139] The union must authorise or endorse the industrial action by the expiry of this period. Such a tight schedule may cause problems for a union particularly in the case where the yes vote is being used as a bargaining lever in negotiations with the employer. If the union does not decide to call any action during the four week period it will have to ballot again. The only occasion where the union can avoid this is where industrial action has already been called under the authority of a ballot and that action is suspended temporarily in order to allow for the re-start of negotiations with the employer.[140] Unions might also find themselves conducting another ballot when the employer seeks to challenge the legitimacy of the industrial action approved by the first ballot and this process together with any appeals lasts for more than the four week period.[141] However, a trade union may apply to the court for an order excluding the period of any court proceedings from the calculation of the four weeks.[142] This remedy will arise where for the whole or part of the four week period the calling or organising of industrial action is prohibited by virtue of a court order which subsequently lapses or is discharged, recalled or set aside, or by virtue of an undertaking given to the court from which the union is subsequently released or by which it ceases to be bound. In such a case the union may apply to the court for an order that this period should be ignored. Such an application must be made forthwith upon the prohibition ceasing to have effect and no application can be made after the end of the period of eight weeks beginning with the date of the ballot.[142a] The court need not make an order if it appears to it that the result of the ballot no longer represents the views of the members concerned, or an event is likely to occur as a result of which those members would note against industrial action if another ballot were to be held.[142b]

11.42 *Who may vote?* A union must also be careful in selecting the members who are entitled to vote. It must ensure that all those members get a vote whom it is reasonable at the time of the ballot for the union to believe will be induced to take part in the action and no others.[143] Immunity will be lost if a union asks members to take part in the action who have been denied entitlement to vote.[144]

---

[139] TUA 1984, s. 10(3) (c) and EA 1990, s. 8(1). The date of the ballot is defined by TUA, s. 10(5).

[140] *Monsanto PLC v. TGWU* [1986] IRLR 406.

[141] See, for example, the experience of the TGWU during the docks dispute of 1989. The union had to ballot afresh because of the length of time it took for the litigation associated with this dispute to be completed. Lord Campbell of Alloway introduced a Bill in the House of Lords in October 1989 which would have suspended the operation of the four weeks for the period of the litigation. Although the Bill successfully completed all its stages in the House of Lords it fell through lack of time. See HL Debs, 31 October 1989, cols 185-202.

[142] EA 1990, s. 8.

[142a] EA 1990, s. 8(3)

[142b] EA 1990, s. 8(4) There is no appeal from the court's decision on this matter: EA 1990, s. 8(5).

[143] TUA 1984, s. 11(1).

[144] TUA 1984, s. 11(2). However, in *British Railways Board v. NUR* [1989] IRLR 349 the Court of Appeal held that s. 11(2) does not invalidate a ballot where a union inadvertently fails to give some members who will be asked to take part in the action an opportunity to vote. The question of a member's opportunity to vote is a matter which is dealt with by TUA, s. 11(6) which introduces a requirement of reasonable practicability. Vinelott J. argued at first instance in the same case that s. 11(2) would only invalidate a ballot where the failure to distribute ballot papers was of such a magnitude that it might affect the result. See [1989] IRLR 345.

However, the ballot will not be invalidated simply because a union has inadvertantly failed to give a member an opportunity to vote. There must be something more than trifling errors in the conduct of the ballot for TULRA immunity to be withdrawn.[145]

11.43 *Separate constituencies.* The question of constituency has been compounded further by a presumption in favour of separate ballots if a union should ballot members employed at different places of work.[146] However, this presumption can be displaced if the union can establish that it was reasonable for it to believe and it did believe that each of the members employed at the different places of work had a factor relating to his terms and conditions of employment or to his occupational description in common with one or more of the other members entitled to vote which he does not have in common with any other employees employed by the same employer who have been denied a vote.[147] Where a union is relying on a common factor which is shared by employees at different workplaces who have the same employer it must ensure that all of the employees who could be selected in this way are entitled to vote. A place of work in relation to any person who is employed means the premises occupied by his employer at or from which that person works.[148] So workplaces are defined by reference to the particular premises of the employer where the employee works. Although the definition of place of work is far from exhaustive and problems can arise as to whether a union should have conducted separate ballots it is a defence for the union to argue that it was reasonable to believe and the union did believe that all the employees had the same place of work.[149]

11.44 *The ballot rules.* There are also detailed statutory rules as regards the conduct of the ballot. First and foremost, the method of voting must be by the marking of a voting paper by the person voting.[150] Thus a show of hands vote would entail loss of immunity. However, unlike other types of ballot, industrial action ballots can still be conducted at a member's place of work, although they may also be conducted at a place which is more convenient to him. Members can be given a convenient opportunity to vote by post or to vote immediately before, immediately after, or during working hours at their place of work.[151] They must be entitled to vote without interference or constraint and the voting must be so far as reasonably practicable secret and without any direct cost to them.[152] Votes must be fairly and accurately counted and those voting should be informed as soon as reasonably practicable about the result.[153] The most controversial aspect of these arrangements concerns the form of the ballot paper.

---

[145] *British Railways Board, ibid.*

[146] EA 1988, s. 17.

[147] TUA 1984, s. 11(1B) added by EA 1988, s. 17(1).

[148] TUA 1984, s. 10(3) as substituted by EA 1988, s. 17(3).

[149] TUA 1984, s. 10(1B) added by EA 1988, s. 17(1).

[150] TUA 1984, s. 11(3).

[151] Thus s. 11(6) is sufficiently flexible to permit workplace ballots, postal ballots or semi-postal ballots or even a combination of the above. If a postal ballot is held, the expenses incurred in such a ballot can be reclaimed from the Certification Officer. See EA 1980, s. 1(3) (a).

[152] TUA 1984, ss. 11(5) and (7).

[153] TUA 1984, ss 11(7) and (8).

11.45 *The ballot question.* Under the original provisions unions were expressly required when seeking authorisation for industrial action to ask a question (however framed) which required the members to indicate on the basis of YES or NO whether or not they were prepared to break their contracts of employment.[154] Since the amendments introduced in 1988[155] the members need only be asked whether or not they would be prepared to take part in a strike or in action short of a strike. A union which is contemplating strike action and action short of a strike must ensure that the ballot paper gives the members the opportunity to vote separately on each of these questions. A single "rolled-up" question would not satisfy these balloting requirements.[156] That action must be in support of an issue which constitutes a trade dispute. Immunity would be lost if the union poses a question, either wholly or in part, which asks whether the member would be prepared to take part in action involving issues which are not trade dispute matters.[157] Moreover, the ballot paper must also contain a statement in these exact words *viz* "If you take part in a strike or other industrial action, you may be in breach of your contract of employment".[158] This statement cannot be qualified or commented upon by anything else on the ballot paper. It is now also necessary for trade union to specify on the ballot paper who, in the event of a favourable vote, will be authorised to call the action.[158a] Industrial action will lose the support of that ballot unless it is called by the specified person.[158b] It has been argued that the form of the ballot paper constitutes an attempt by the State unduly to influence the decision of those voting as to whether they would be prepared to withdraw their labour.[159] Yet it does seem that strike ballots have become a permanent feature of negotiating processes and that in the bulk of cases a large majority in favour of industrial action is returned in a high turnout of members.[160]

11.46 *Ballots and the Code of Practice.* One final point about strike ballots concerns the increased powers given to the Secretary of State to issue Codes of Practice. The Employment Act 1988, s. 18 extends the existing powers of the Secretary of State to issue Codes of Practice so that he now has the authority to issue codes for the purpose of promoting what appear to him to be desirable practices in relation to the conduct by trade unions of ballots and elections.[161] A Code of Practice on Trade Union Ballots on Industrial Action came into effect on 11 April 1990 and a revised code came into force on May 20, 1991. The

---

[154] TUA 1984, s. 10(4).

[155] EA 1988, Sch. 3.

[156] *Post Office v. UCW* [1990] IRLR 143.

[157] *London Underground Ltd v. NUR* [1989] IRLR 341.

[158] TUA 1984, ss. 11(3) and (4) as substituted by EA 1988, s. 33 and Sch. 3 para. 5(8) (c) and (d). In *London Underground Ltd, ante,* it was held that where the ballot asks a number of questions on which the member's approval for industrial action is sought each one of these issues must be capable of constituting a trade dispute.

[158a] EA 1990, s. 7(1) adding s. 11(4A) to TUA 1984. See *Tanks and Drums Ltd v. TGWU, The Times,* July 10, 1991.

[158b] EA 1990, s. 7(2).

[159] Ewan McKendrick "The Rights of Trade Union Members: Part I of the Employment Act 1988" (1988) 17 ILJ 141.

[160] This is certainly the view expressed by ACAS in a number of its Annual Reports. See, in particular, ACAS Annual Report for 1987.

[161] These Codes are admissible in evidence and can be relied upon by a court or tribunal when determining a case. See EA 1980, s. 3(8).

original was a watered-down version of the earlier draft code which was criticised by a variety of organisations including the TUC, ACAS and the CBI. The Code not only advises on the current statutory arrangements but also gives additional advice not founded upon any statutory enactment as regards the conduct of strike ballots. For example, the Code advises that when considering whether to call industrial action after a successful yes vote a union should take into account such matters as the serious consequences for the members (such as dismissal), the possibilities of using the facilities of ACAS and the size of the majority and the number of those voting in the ballot relative to those with entitlement to vote. Equally, the code also advises unions to ensure that adequate arrangements are made for the independent scrutiny of strike ballots although there is no statutory requirement for independent scrutiny of industrial action ballots as there is for PEC and political fund ballots. The courts may experience difficulty in deciding to what extent this latter category of advice can be taken into account when determining the validity of a ballot on industrial action.

11.47 (c) Pressure to impose union membership or recognition requirements

Any term in a contract for the supply of goods or services is void if that term seeks to impose union membership requirements.[162] Moreover, it is a breach of statutory duty if on the ground of union membership a person fails to include the name of a particular person on a list of approved contractors; or, terminates a contract for the supply of goods or services; or, excludes a person from the right to tender for the supply of goods or services.[163] Further any term which purports to require a party to a contract for the supply of goods or services to grant recognition rights to a trade union or to negotiate or consult with any union official is void.[164] It is also a breach of statutory duty to discriminate against a person on grounds of union recognition in any of the circumstances already outlined.[165] These provisions are reinforced by the withdrawal of immunity where a person induces or attempts to induce another to incorporate a term in a contract of the types described above or seeks to induce a person to discriminate against another in any of the circumstances already outlined.[166] Thus a person who has been denied the right to tender for a contract because he refuses to provide union-only labour may not only have a cause of action against the person who prevented him from tendering but also against the trade union which induced that person to exclude him. Further, a union has no immunity where it seeks to interfere with the supply (whether under a contract or not) of goods or services by inducing or threatening to induce employees to break or interfere with their contracts of employment if the supplier is not the employer under the contracts of employment and the reason, or one of the reasons, for the interference is the fact or belief that the supplier does not or might not recognise, negotiate or consult with a trade union.[167]

---

[162] EA 1982, s. 12(1).

[163] *Ibid*, s. 12(2).

[164] *Ibid*, s. 13.

[165] *Ibid*, s. 13(2).

[166] *Ibid*, s. 14.

[167] *Ibid*, s. 14(3) as substituted by EA 1988, s. 33 and Sch. 3, para. 4. The original provisions applied to industrial action to enforce union-only requirements. See *Messenger Group Newspapers Ltd v. NGA (1982)* [1984] IRLR 397.

11.48 The Employment Act 1982, ss. 12 and 13 are intended to prevent employers, particularly local authorities, from enforcing the closed shop by indirect means, while s. 14 seeks to deter trade unions from pressurising employers to insist that contractors provide union-only or recognition-only labour or by forcing union recognition upon a supplier by means of real or threatened industrial action against some other employer. These proscriptions have now been reinforced and extended by the Employment Act 1988, s. 10 which removes immunity from actions in delict where the reason, or one of the reasons, for which the act is done is the fact or belief that a particular employer is employing, has employed or might employ a person who is not a member of any trade union, a member of a particular trade union, or is not a member of one of a number of particular trade unions. Alternatively, immunity can be lost where the act is done because the employer is failing, has failed or might fail to discriminate against any such person. The discrimination takes the form of conduct which treats employees or applicants for employment differently, according to whether or not those persons are union members and is more favourable to those who are.[168] This loss of immunity will apply regardless of whether or not the action is taken against a third party employer or is targeted at the actual employer who refuses to employ union-only labour. In sum, these provisions concentrate upon the subject matter of a dispute and withdraw immunity even where there is a primary dispute and where the action has been supported by a majority of voters in a properly organised ballot.

UNION LIABILITY

11.49 The 1982 Act

As we saw at the start of this chapter the Trade Disputes Act 1906 granted trade unions complete immunity from actions in delict. This arrangement was continued by the Trade Union and Labour Relations Act 1974.[169] However, this provision was repealed in 1982[170] so that trade unions are now in the same position as their officials and only have protection from legal action if they can establish immunity under the Trade Union and Labour Relations Act 1974, s. 13. The result is that unions are liable for unlawful industrial action if, but only if, that action was authorised or endorsed by a responsible person.[171] Initially this requirement was satisfied where the action was authorised or endorsed by any of the following:

(a) by the principal executive committee (PEC);

(b) by any other person empowered by the union's rules to authorise or endorse acts of the kind in question;

(c) by the president or general secretary;

(d) by any other official who is an employed official;

(e) by any committee of the union to whom an employed official regularly reports.[172]

---

[168] EA 1988, s. 10(2).
[169] S. 14.
[170] EA 1982, s. 15.
[171] EA 1982, s. 15(2).
[172] EA 1982, s. 15(3).

11.50 The 1990 Act

However these rules on the liability of trade unions for industrial action have been amended by the Employment Act 1990[173] which widens the categories of people who can authorise or endorse industrial action on behalf of a trade union and stiffens the rules on repudiation[174] with the result that an act will be taken to have been authorised or endorsed by a trade union if it was done, or was authorised or endorsed —

(a) by any person empowered by the rules to do, authorise or endorse acts of the kind in question; or

(b) by the PEC or the president or general secretary; or

(c) by any other committee of the union or any other official of the union (whether employed by it or not).[174a]

The principal effect of this change has been to make unions responsible for the acts of shop stewards or committees of shop stewards who call or take part in industrial action even although the union rule book does not authorise or may even specifically deny shop stewards the right to call industrial action on behalf of their union. This also means that unions are required to ballot members to obtain their support for industrial action called by a shop steward unless the repudiation rules discussed in the next paragraph are activated. The idea of union responsibility is developed further by providing that as far as para. (c) is concerned any group of persons constituted in accordance with the rules of the union is a committee of the union; and that an act shall be taken to have been done, authorised or endorsed by, or by any member of, any group of persons of which he is a member, the purposes of which include organising or co-ordinating industrial action.[175] These vicarious liability rules apply notwithstanding anything in the rules of the union, or in any contract or rule of law.[176]

11.51 *Repudiation.* An act shall not be taken to have been authorised or endorsed by the union by virtue of para. (c) if it was repudiated by the PEC or the president or general secretary as soon as reasonably practicable after coming to the knowledge of any of them.[177] For such repudiation to be effective a number of detailed requirements have to be fulfilled.[178] Written notice of the repudiation must be given to the committee or official in question without delay. Further, the union must do its best to give individual written notice of the fact and date of repudiation without delay to every member of the union who the union has reason to believe is taking part, or might otherwise take part, in the repudiated action and to the employer of every such member. The notice which the members receive must contain the following statement —

"Your union has repudiated any call for industrial action to which the notice relates and will give no support to such action. If you are dismissed while

---

[173] EA 1990, s. 6.
[174] It fulfils the proposals contained in the Green Paper, *Unofficial Action and the Law* (Cm 821, October 1989).
[174a] EA 1990, s. 6(3) substitutes a new s. 15(3) in EA 1982.
[175] EA 1982, s. 15(3A) as substituted by EA 1990, s. 6(2).
[176] *Ibid*, s. 15(3B) as substituted.
[177] *Ibid*, s. 15(4) as substituted.
[178] *Ibid*, s. 15(6) as substituted or amended.

taking unofficial industrial action, you will have no right to complain of unfair dismissal."[179]

If the union should fail to comply with any of these notice requirements, the repudiation must be treated as ineffective. A party to a commercial contract which has or may be interfered with and who has not received written notice of the repudiation may request the PEC president or general secretary to confirm the repudiation within three months and a failure to confirm forthwith in writing will render that repudiation ineffective.[179a] Finally enhanced powers are given to a court which is granting an interdict against a trade union to require the union to take such steps as the court considers appropriate for ensuring —

(a) that there is no, or no further, inducement of persons to take part or to continue to take part in industrial action; and

(b) that no person engages in any conduct after the granting of the interdict by virtue of having been induced before it was granted to take part or to continue to take part in industrial action.[180]

11.52 Delicts outwith s. 13

These statutory rules setting out the liability of a trade union only apply where the acts in question entail the commission of a delict listed in the Trade Union and Labour Relations Act 1974, s. 13. If another type of wrong is committed such as trespass or nuisance[181] or the proceedings against the union are for contempt of court[182] a union's liability will depend upon the common law. The exact nature of a union's vicarious liability at common law was discussed in *Heaton's Transport (St Helens) Ltd v. TGWU*[183] where the House of Lords had to consider the scope of the authority of a shop steward where the union's rules were unclear. In this case it was held that union officers not only bind their union when they act in conformity with their express authority but that they also possess some sort of implied authority which also makes the union responsible for their acts. The exact extent of this implied authority is unclear although when considering its scope reference can be made to the union rule book, its customs and practices and even to a shop steward's handbook.[184]

11.53 Damages

The effect of these provisions is to make trade unions the subjects of court proceedings. In the past when trade unions enjoyed blanket immunity, actions raised by employers against union officials tended to be for interdicts only. Interdicts can now be awarded against the union as well. However, given the fact that unions do have assets there is an increased likelihood that employers will sue trade unions in damages where unlawful industrial action has caused them loss. However the Employment Act 1982 places limits on the amount of

---

[179] See Chapter Five para. 5.67 for the unfair dismissal rules for unofficial industrial action introduced by EA 1990, s. 9.

[179a] EA 1982, s. 15(6A) as substituted by EA 1990, s. 6(6).

[180] EA 1982, s. 15(9) as added by EA 1990, s. 6(8).

[181] *Thomas v. NUM (South Wales Area)* [1985] ICR 886; *News Group Newspapers Ltd v. SOGAT 82* [1987] ICR 181.

[182] *Express & Star Ltd v. NGA (1982)* [1986] IRLR 222 CA.

[183] [1973] AC 15.

[184] *Heaton's, ante. Cf General Aviation Services (UK) Ltd v. TGWU* [1976] IRLR 224.

damages which can be awarded against trade unions in actions in delict. The present limits are as follows:

(a) £10,000, if the union has less than 5,000 members;

(b) £50,000, if it has 5,000 or more members but less than 25,000 members;

(c) £125,000, if it has 25,000 or more members but less than 100,000 members;

(d) £250,000, if it has 100,000 or more members.[185]

Clearly, these limits only apply where the pursuer can establish that his losses are at least as much as the appropriate maximum statutory award. On the other hand, if the employer was awarded damages against the union and the industrial action continued, he would be at liberty to sue the union anew for further damages. It is also worth pointing out that the limits are only applicable to an action by an individual pursuer. If there are a number of pursuers each can sue and be awarded the appropriate maximum sum assuming that the necessary level of loss can be established. Finally, it must be stressed these limits only apply in relation to damages actions in delict.[186] They have no relevance in the case of a fine against a union for contempt of court.[187]

11.54 *Protected property.* Certain categories of union property are protected in terms of damages awards. Where a pursuer is seeking to recover damages or expenses against a trade union, its trustees acting in their official capacity, or, its members or officials on behalf of themselves and all the other members, no part of that amount can be recovered against the union's protected property.[188] This encompasses any property

(a) belonging to trustees otherwise in their capacity as such;

(b) belonging to any member of the union otherwise than jointly or in common with the other members;

(c) belonging to any official of the union who is neither a member nor a trustee;

(d) comprised in a political fund; or

(e) comprised in a provident benefits fund.[189]

---

[185] EA 1982, s. 16(3). The Secretary of State may by order vary these limited — EA 1982, s. 16(4).

[186] Moreover, certain actions in delict and quasi-delict are also exempted from the above limits. Thus actions for personal injury for negligence, nuisance or breach of duty; or actions for breach of duty in connection with the ownership, occupation, possession, control or use of property (whether heritable or moveable) are not subject to the appropriate limits. See EA 1982, s. 16(2).

[187] See, for example, the fines imposed against the NGA in connection with the Stockport Messenger dispute discussed in John Gennard "The Implications of the Stockport Messenger Group Dispute' (1984) 15(3) IRJ 7.

[188] EA 1982, s. 17(1).

[189] EA 1982, s. 17(2). "Provident benefits" includes any payment, expressly authorised by the rules of the union, which is made to a member during sickness or incapacity from personal injury or while out of work, or to an aged member by way of superannuation, or to a member who has met with an accident or has lost his tools by fire or theft, and includes funeral expenses paid on the death of a member or his wife, or a payment as provision for the children of a deceased member — EA 1982, s. 17(3).

11.55 Award of interdicts

It was mentioned in the previous section that although it was always possible to sue a union official in damages for authorising unlawful industrial action, the usual remedy was that of interdict to stop the action taking place or to prevent it continuing. Although, as we have seen, damages actions are now competent against trade unions, it is still the case that even where the union is the defender the initial proceedings will be for interdict. The normal remedy is that of interim interdict.[190] This is on the premise that at some later date there will be a full trial of the action where a permanent interdict will be awarded and possibly damages as well. In most cases, however, the pursuer is happy to obtain a remedy which effectively ends the action and will not insist that the case proceed to proof.[191] This means that interim interdict can be considered as the primary remedy in industrial conflict cses.[192]

11.56 *Interim interdicts.* In order to prevent interdicts being awarded without the union being given the opportunity to state a defence where there is an application for an interdict in the absence of the union and the union has claimed, or in the opinion of the court would be likely to claim, that it acted in contemplation or furtherance of a trade dispute, the court shall not grant the interdict unless satisfied that all steps which in the circumstances were reasonable have been taken with a view to securing that notice of the application and an opportunity of being heard with respect to the application have been given to the union.[193] There is evidence from both sides of the border that judges have sometimes ignored these directions.[194] This is the extent of the statutory directions for the award of interdicts in Scotland.

11.57 *Statutory immunity in England and Wales.* There is, however, an additional provision applicable only south of the border. This declares that for the avoidance of doubt where an interlocutory injunction is sought against a union and the union claims that it acted in contemplation or furtherance of a trade dispute, the court shall, when exercising its discretion, have regard to the likelihood of the union establishing a statutory defence.[195] This provision was enacted in the wake of the decision of the House of Lords in *American Cyanamid Co v. Ethicon Ltd*[196] which had held that in interlocutory proceedings the im-

---

[190] See, for example, *Scottish & Universal Newspapers Ltd v. Smith* 1982 SLT 160.

[191] See the speech of Lord Diplock in *NWL Ltd v. Woods and Nelson* [1979] ICR 867 at 880 who declared that because of the "practical realities" trade disputes actions rarely came to full trial. In *Dimbleby & Sons Ltd v. NUJ* [1984] ICR 397 at 405-406. Lord Diplock argued that because of the Employment Acts 1980 and 1982 these practical realities were no longer apposite so that employees were much more likely to sue trade unions in damages.

[192] Although an employer may also seek interim suspension of a union's instruction to cease work. See the decision of Lord Cullen in *Maersk Co Ltd v. NUS* 1988 SLT 828.

[193] TULRA, s. 17(1).

[194] See, for example, K. D. Ewing's letter to the Editor of the Scots Law Times published at 1981 SLT (News) 99 who complains about the decision of the vacation judge in *Scottish & Universal Newspapers Ltd v. Smith* 1982 SLT 160 to grant interim interdict without appearance by the respondent. See also Sandra Fredman "The Right to Strike: Policy and Principle" (1987) 103 LQR 176 who points out that in *Barretts & Baird (Wholesale) Ltd v. IPCS* [1987] IRLR 3 an *ex parte* injunction was initially granted over the telephone.

[195] TULRA, s. 17(2).

[196] [1975] AC 396. Formerly under English it was necessary for the plaintiff to establish that he had a prima facie case i.e. one to which there was prima facie no defence.

portant issue was whether there was a serious issue to be tried and, if so, then to consider where the balance of convenience lay. This latter point entails discovering whether the plaintiff would suffer more damage by the non-award of the injunction than the defendant would if it was awarded. Although this was not a labour law case the decision did have important consequences for interlocutory relief in trades disputes. For if a plaintiff can be awarded an injunction simply by establishing that there is a serious issue to be tried there is an obvious danger that an injunction will be awarded to an employer in an industrial dispute case without any consideration as to whether or not the union can establish a statutory defence. The award of the injunction is all the more likely when one considers that given the nature of industrial action the employer will invariably be able to show that the balance of convenience lies with him because of the economic losses which he is or is likely to suffer. Since the award of the injunction is almost certain to end the dispute, the *American Cyanamid* approach would have meant that the case would have gone against the union without any real consideration of the substantive legal questions.[197]

11.58 *The position in Scotland.* It has been claimed that the reason why such a provision was not applied to Scotland was because Parliament thought that such a provision was unnecessary because it would merely have given effect to the existing Scots law.[198] This claim is borne out by the decision of Lord Avonside in *Square Grip Reinforcement Co Ltd v. MacDonald*[199] where a clear distinction was made between the merits of the case and the balance of convenience question. This case represents the traditional approach of the Scottish judges and entails a consideration of two questions. First, whether a *prima facie* or substantial case has been established; and, second, an analysis of where the balance of convenience lies. It has been argued that this approach gives substantial weight to the legal rights of the parties.[200] In the last few years, however, an alternative "palm tree"[201] approach has been applied in the Scottish cases. In this approach the question of the defender's legal rights is not considered as a separate issue but is subsumed within the question of the balance of convenience. Its application has been supported by Lord Fraser of Tullybelton in *NWL Ltd v. Woods and Nelson*[202] who declared that "[w]hether the likelihood of success should be regarded as one of the elements of the balance of convenience, or as a separate matter, seems to me to be an academic question of no real importance, but my inclination is in favour of the former alternative".

11.59 Nevertheless, there is a problem with this alternative approach in that the likelihood of establishing a trade dispute defence simply becomes one issue

---

[197] These points are discussed in the speeches of Lords Diplock and Scarman in *NWL Ltd v. Woods and Nelson* [1979] ICR 867.

[198] *Per* Lord Fraser of Tullybelton in *NWL Ltd, ibid,* at p. 884.

[199] 1966 SLT 232. The *Square Grip* case does illustrate one of the major problems for trade unions even with the traditional balance of convenience test, *i.e.* establishing that they would suffer financial loss if the interdict were awarded. As Lord Avonside put it in this case "[d]amage to the petitioners might be disastrous and irreparable. Damage to the respondents would be minimal". See his judgment at p. 234.

[200] K. D. Ewing "Interim Interdicts in Labour Law: A Case for Reform" (1981) JLSS 422.

[201] A soubriquet applied to this approach by Ewing, *ante.*

[202] [1979] ICR 867 at p. 884.

amongst others in establishing where the balance of convenience lies. A great deal is left to the discretion of the judge in establishing what weight to give to the likelihood factor. This is illustrated in *Scottish and Universal Newspapers Ltd v. Smith*[203] where Lord Cowie accepted that the defenders had a fair chance of establishing that there was a trade dispute and that they were acting in furtherance of it. However, he was of the opinion that this was only one of the elements which had to be taken into account when deciding where the balance of convenience lay. Other matters such as the economic consequences of the action for the pursuers had to be considered. In the end, Lord Cowie concluded that interim interdict should be issued because the balance of convenience lay heavily in favour of the pursuers since the industrial action was having "disastrous effects" on the viability of their business.[204]

11.60 This case illustrates the dangers of the alternative approach in a trade dispute case. It concentrates upon the economic losses sustained by the employer to the detriment of the statutory provisions providing immunity from legal action which Parliament has created. The most extreme example of this inversion of priorities is *Phestos Shipping Co Ltd v. Kurmiawan*[205] where the Second Division introduced an additional element to the balance of convenience question by arguing that the workers' grievances could be resolved better by legal action for breach of contract rather than by a strike when deciding whether or not the industrial action could continue. In this case Lord Justice-Clerk Wheatley considered that it was unnecessary for him to form a view as to whether or not the Lord Ordinary was correct on the substantive law. In his opinion, the balance of convenience was so overwhelmingly in favour of the pursuers given the amount of losses that they were sustaining that consideration of the legal issues was irrelevant. As one commentator has argued this decision turns the traditional test on its head because it permits legal questions to be ignored if the balance of convenience question is heavily in favour of one side.[206] This modern "palm tree" approach pays insufficient regard to the statutory immunity issue and is, on this basis, contrary to the intention of Parliament.

11.61 *Breach of interdict.* It is worth noting that Scots law demands that the pursuer must specify the reasons for his request for interdict in his written pleadings.[207] It is at the discretion of the court whether or not to grant the interdict and whether or not to award it in the exact terms sought. If the defenders should fail to comply with the terms of the interdict after it has been served on them the pursuer can commence proceedings for breach.[208] Such proceedings require the concurrence of the Lord Advocate.[209] The usual remedies are fines

---

[203] 1982 SLT 160.

[204] This decision was upheld by an Extra Division reported at 1982 SLT 162. See also *Star Offshore Services plc v. NUS* 1988 SLT 836 (Lord Allanbridge).

[205] 1983 SLT 388.

[206] Douglas Brodie (1984) 13 ILJ 170.

[207] See Lord M'Laren in *Fleming v. Liddesdale District Committee* (1897) 24 R 281.

[208] The difficulties that this procedure can present in cases such as factory occupations where there are a large number of defenders are illustrated in *Plessey Co plc v. Wilson* 1983 SLT 139 discussed by K. Miller at (1982) 11 ILJ 115.

[209] For the appropriate procedure for this type of case see W. W. McBryde and N. J. Downie *Petition Procedure in the Court of Session* (1980) at pp. 69-70.

or even imprisonment. Although there is no express authority on the point in Scotland sequestration of the assets of a trade union which has failed to obey an interdict does appear to be a competent remedy since it was used in the nineteenth century for breach of interdict in family law cases.[210] In England sequestration proceedings have become a regular feature of modern trade dispute cases. It would seem that in deciding whether the union can be held vicariously liable for the contempts of its officers or members it is the common law rules which must be applied.[211] Before a union will be entitled to return of its assets after they have been sequestrated it must be shown to have purged its contempt. Usually, this will entail some apology to the court although it may be enough for the union by its actions to recognise the authority of the court.[212]

THE LAW OF PICKETING

11.62 It is an obvious tactic for employees who are in dispute with their employer not only to withdraw their labour but also to picket outside his premises in order to turn back other employees and to prevent or disrupt the flow of goods or supplies entering or leaving those premises. It would seem that this activity is not *per se* unlawful.[213] However, it is very easy for pickets to commit civil wrongs such as nuisance or trespass. Moreover, pickets may also be in danger of breaking the criminal law through the common law offence of breach of the peace and the statutory offence of obstruction of a police officer in the execution of his duty, or, in extreme cases, the serious crime of mobbing and rioting.[214] There is also a specific statutory offence relevant to pickets contained in s. 7 of the Conspiracy and Protection of Property Act 1875. It is important to consider each of these in turn.

11.63 The immunities

It is lawful for a person in contemplation or furtherance of a trade dispute to attend at or near his own place of work for the purpose only of peacefully obtaining or communicating information, or peacefully persuading any person to work or abstain from working.[215] This provision restricts lawful picketing to an employee's own place of work. Under the original provisions[216] the only restriction on the location of a picket-line was that it could not take place outside a person's home. Changes introduced in 1980 sought to eradicate the practice of secondary picketing, and, in particular, render unlawful the activities of "flying pickets" *i.e.*, union members who were prepared to picket any factory or

---

[210] *Ross v. Ross* (1885) 12 R 1351; *Edgar v. Fisher"s Trs* (1893) 21 R 59.

[211] *Express & Star Ltd v. NGA (1982)* [1986] IRLR 222.

[212] *Read Transport Ltd v. NUM (South Wales Area), The Times* March 19, 1985. For a discussion of contempt under English law see Lord Wedderburn *The Worker and the Law* (3rd edn., 1986) at pp. 705-716.

[213] *Hubbard v. Pitt* [1975] ICR 308 CA.

[214] *Sloan v. Macmillan* 1922 JC 1.

[215] TULRA, s. 15(1) as substituted by EA 1980, s. 16.

[216] TULRA, s. 15.

business premises in the country in order to further a dispute.[217] Any attempt to argue under the present law that these people are not pickets but merely demonstrators appears to have been scotched by two recent decisions of the English courts.[218] Although the statutory language seems to create a right to picket since it declares that it shall be lawful etc. the House of Lords has held that such a view is inaccurate. In *Broome v. DPP*[219] it was made clear that statute merely protected the attendance of pickets at the places specified and then only if their attendance was for one of the protected purposes; nothing grants any authority to pickets to require other people to stop or even to listen to them. A picket who attempts to stop vehicles by standing in front of them is guilty of obstruction under English law[220] and could be arrested for a breach of the peace in Scotland.

11.64 *Conditions for immunity.* Before there can be any immunity for picketing under the civil law three requirements must be satisfied. The first is that the picketing must be undertaken in contemplation or furtherance of a trade dispute.[221] The second requirement is that the picketing must only be carried out by persons attending at or near their own place of work. There is some uncertainty about the exact meaning of "place of work" since it is not defined. The Secretary of State's Code of Practice on Picketing considers that the purport of this phrase is to permit attendance at an entrance to or exit from the factory, site or office at which the picket works. However, problems still remain where the factory or site is made up of a number of self-contained units. As far as the requirement that the picketing should be "at or near" that place of work, it is clear that the word "near" is to be interpreted in a realistic and purposive way which takes account of the particular circumstances of the case and the geographical location of the employer's premises. Thus pickets were still near their workplace when they had to picket at the entrance to an industrial estate which was some 1,232 yards from their employer's premises.[222]

11.65 Special rules are created for those employees who have more than one place of work (*e.g.* mobile workers) or where the location of their workplace makes picketing impracticable there (*e.g.* oilrig workers). In such cases a person's place of work is any premises of his employer from which he works or from which his work is administered.[223] The effectiveness of this provision for mobile workers is circumscribed by the requirement that the place which is picketed must be premises of the employer. Consequently, even where the workers, when working normally, perform many of their activities during the course

---

[217] This provision was used on a number of occasions during the miners' strike of 1984-85 by small employers concerned that such activity might put them out of business. See, for example, *Read (Transport) Ltd v. NUM (South Wales Area)* [1985] IRLR 67 and the unsuccessful actions raised by three Stirling road haulage firms to obtain interdicts against the Scottish Area of the NUM for secondary picketing — *Glasgow Herald* March 31, 1984. See also Roger Benedictus "The Use of the Law of Tort in the Miners' Dispute" (1985) 14 ILJ 176.

[218] *Thomas v. NUM (South Wales Area)* [1985] ICR 886, HC; *News Group Newspapers Ltd v. SOGAT 82* [1987] ICR 181.

[219] [1974] ICR 84.

[220] *Broome v. DPP* [1974] ICR 84.

[221] An issue discussed earlier in this chapter. See paras. 11.32-11.33.

[222] *Rayware Ltd v. TGWU* [1989] IRLR 134.

[223] TULRA, s. 15(2) as substituted by EA 1980, s. 16.

of their employment at the premises of one major customer, there will be no right to picket at that place since that location does not form part of their own employer's premises.[224] However, a dismissed worker can picket his former place of work so long as his last employment was terminated in connection with a trade dispute or the termination of his employment was one of the circumstances giving rise to a trade dispute.[225] This provision only applies for as long as the picket remains unemployed. It can provide an empty right particularly where the employer dismisses his employees employed at one factory (plant A) and then transfers all of the business which was formerly conducted there to another of his factories (plant B). In such a case the dismissed workers would be entitled to picket plant A but not plant B where their work is now being performed. Thus they would be restricted to picketing premises which the employer no longer uses![226] The third special case applies to union officials. They can picket at any place of work of a member of the union whom they are accompanying and whom they represent. An official who has been elected or appointed to represent a particular category of member or members in a particular area can only accompany those members on the picket line. However, a national official can represent all of the members.[227]

11.66 The third requirement for lawful picketing is that the only purpose of the picketing must be peacefully to obtain or communicate information or peacefully to persuade a person to work or abstain from working. If the picketing is not peaceful there can be no immunity in law.[228] Equally, if the picketing involves some other purpose, such as where pickets walk around in a circle in front of factory gates in order to seal them off from traffic,[229] there can be no immunity since this entails a purpose other than the specific statutory purposes. Picketing which is in breach of any of these requirements loses the statutory protection and also takes the activities of the pickets outwith the immunities provided by the Trade Union and Labour Relations Act 1974, s. 13. In such circumstances an employer would have a cause of action against the individual pickets,[230] the union officer who organised the picketing and against the union itself for such delicts as inducement of breach of contract, interference with contractual relations and intimidation.[231] Picketing involving large numbers of people is not *per se* illegal: although in such a case it would not be difficult to

---

[224] *Mersey Dock and Harbour Co v. Verrinder* [1982] IRLR 152.

[225] TULRA, s. 15(3) as added by EA 1980, s. 16.

[226] In *News Group Newspapers Ltd v. SOGAT 82* [1987] ICR 181 it was held that dismissed printers had no right to picket outside the company's new plant at Wapping since this had never been their place of work. They could only picket outside the company's premises in Bouverie St. which were no longer in use.

[227] TULRA, s. 15(4) added by EA 1980, s. 16(4). This provision ensures that the members on a picket line cannot be swamped by union officials brought in from other branches or districts of the union.

[228] *Messenger Newspapers Group Ltd v. NGA (1982)* [1984] IRLR 397.

[229] *Tynan v. Balmer* [1967] 1 QB 91. See also *Mersey Dock and Harbour Co v. Verrinder* [1982] IRLR 152 where the judge considered that the purpose of the picket line was not merely to obtain or communicate information; it was also intended to regulate the flow of container traffic between the pickets' employer and his major customer.

[230] *United Biscuits (UK) Ltd v. Fall* [1979] IRLR 110.

[231] See generally *News Group Newspapers Ltd v. SOGAT 82* [1987] ICR 181.

establish some ulterior purpose.[232] Further, picketing is not necessarily unlawful simply because it may involve the commission of offences under s. 7 of the Conspiracy and Protection of Property Act 1875 Act.[233] Nevertheless, the activities can go beyond s. 15 and therefore outwith the immunities conferred by s. 15 of the Trade Union and Labour Relations Act 1974 if they involve the commission of unprotected wrongs such as nuisance or trespass; or the picketing is secondary in nature.[234]

11.67 *Nuisance and trespass.* As far as nuisance is concerned there has been a conflict of authority in England as to whether picketing *per se* amounts to a nuisance, or whether it is necessary for there also to be some violence, obstruction, annoyance or molestation for the picketing to constitute a nuisance.[235] It is submitted that the correct view and the one supported by the most recent authorities[236] is that picketing alone does not constitute a nuisance. There must at the very least be some unreasonable obstruction of the highway[237] or possibly some unreasonable harassment of those wishing to work.[238] Although, there is no express authority on the point it is submitted that picketing would constitute a nuisance under Scots law so long as the picketing caused some annoyance to or interfered with the property rights of neighbouring proprietors.[239] A trespass can also be committed by pickets when they stray onto the lands of another without his permission. This is all the more likely where the picket develops into an occupation of the employer's premises. Formerly, there might have been some protection against the consequences of such an occupation since the First division had held in *Plessey Co Plc v. Wilson*[240] that where the occupation primarily involved interferences with the trade or business of the employer there could be a defence by the provision that an interference with the trade, business or employment of some other person would not be actionable in delict if it was done in contemplation or furtherance of a trade dispute.[241] However, as a result of the *Plessey* case, the provision was repealed.[242] This means that an employer is now free to obtain interdicts in order to prevent the continued unlawful occupation of his premises.[243]

---

[232] See the speech of Lord Reid in *Broome v. DPP* [1974] ICR 84.

[233] *Thomas v. NUM (South Wales Area)* [1985] ICR 886.

[234] Both grounds are discussed in *Thomas, ante,* and in *News Group Newspapers Ltd v. SOGAT 82* [1987] ICR 181.

[235] Compare *J Lyons & Sons v. Wilkins* [1899] 1 Ch 255 and *Ward Lock & Co v. Operative Printers' Assistants' Society* (1906) 22 TLR 327. See also *Hubbard v. Pitt* [1975] ICR 308 and *Mersey Dock and Harbour Co v. Verrinder* [1982] IRLR 152 and in Scotland *Galt v. Philp* 1983 SCCR 295.

[236] See *Thomas v. NUM (South Wales Area)* [1985] ICR 886 and *News Group Newspapers Ltd v. SOGAT 82* [1987] ICR 181.

[237] *News Group, ante.*

[238] *Per* Scott J. in *Thomas v. NUM (South Wales Area)* [1985] ICR 886 at p. 915. Doubted by Stuart Smith J. in *News Group, ante,* at p. 206. Under English law special damage has to be proved in order to establish a public nuisance.

[239] See Niall R. Whitty "Nuisance" in *Stair Memorial Encyclopaedia of the Laws of Scotland* (1988) Vol. 14 at para. 2046.

[240] [1983] IRLR 139. But see also the judgment of Lord Dunpark in *Phestos Shipping Co Ltd v. Kurmiawan* 388 at p. 391.

[241] TULRA, s. 13(2).

[242] EA 1982, s. 19(1).

[243] See the decision of Lord Clyde in *Caterpillar Tractors PLC v. Brannan, Glasgow Herald* March 26, 1987.

11.68 *Secondary action by primary pickets.* The activities of pickets even at their own place of work could involve unlawful secondary industrial action since their attempts to persuade lorry drivers etc. to turn back might result in them inducing breaches or interfering with contracts between employees and an employer who is not a party to the trade dispute. In order to ensure that immunity is retained in such circumstances picketing at a worker's own place of work is now the only form of protected secondary action so long as that worker's employer is a party to the dispute; the same rules also apply to union officials if they are accompanying union members whom they represent.[244]

11.69 The Code of Practice

Those responsible for organising pickets should also be aware of the Secretary of State's Code of Practice on Picketing. This Code advises the organiser *inter alia* to seek directions from the police on the number of people who should be present on the picket line. This advice is reinforced by para. 31 which declares that large numbers on a picket line are likely to give rise to fear and resentment amongst those wishing to cross it and recommends that pickets and their organisers should ensure that in general the number of pickets does not exceed six at any entrance to a workplace; frequently a smaller number will be appropriate. The Code of Practice is admissible in evidence and can be taken into account by a court[245] and para. 31 has had a significant impact on the conduct of picketing and has been relied upon by the courts in phrasing the terms of the injunction or interdict applicable where there has been mass picketing.[246] The Code has been criticised for being a misuse of the idea of Codes of Practice, particularly in relation to its advice on the role of the picket organiser and its section on essential supplies and services.[247] The present law and the code of Practice have also been criticised for the strains they place upon the police who have to control the behaviour of pickets and who may be required to decide where people should picket and in what numbers.[248] As a final point the Closed Shop Code advises unions not to discipline members who have crossed a picket line which it has not authorised or which was not at a member's place of work.[249] This advice has now been superseded by the statutory provision which protects a member against unjustifiable disciplinary action *inter alia* where he has failed to take part in a strike or other industrial action.[250]

11.70 Picketing and the criminal law

Pickets receive no protection as far as the criminal law is concerned. There are a number of crimes which can be committed by pickets. The most obvious are

---

[244] EA 1990, s. 4.

[245] EA 1980, s. 3(8).

[246] See the terms of the injunctions awarded by Scott J. in *Thomas v. NUM (South Wales Area)* [1985] ICR 886 and Stuart Smith J. in *News Group Newspapers Ltd v. SOGAT 82* [1987] ICR 181 which specifically restricted the number of pickets at any workplace to six. Attempts in both of these cases to avoid the Code by arguing that the people present were demonstrators and not pickets proved unsuccessful since they often broke ranks and dispersed to join the official picket line.

[247] I. T. Smith and J. C. Wood *Industrial Law* (4th edn., 1989) at p. 506.

[248] Lord Wedderburn *The Worker and the Law* (3rd edn., 1986) at p. 546.

[249] See the Code of Practice: Closed Shop Agreements and Arrangements (1983) at paras. 61-62.

[250] EA 1988, s. 3.

breach of the peace, obstruction of a police officer in the execution of his duty contrary to the Police (Scotland) Act 1967, s. 41, malicious mischief or vandalism and assault.[251] Even peaceful picketing may involve a breach of the peace since the offence can be committed where there is no actual disturbance, if it can be shown that the accused's conduct is likely to lead to a disturbance.[252] In English law there is a specific offence of obstruction of the highway contrary to the Highways Act 1980, s. 137. The width of this offence is illustrated by the decision of the House of Lords in *Broome v. DPP*[253] where it was held that a picket had been rightly convicted of obstruction when he stood in front of a lorry holding a placard and shouting at the driver to stop. There is no equivalent statutory offence in Scotland. However, there can be no doubt that a complaint of breach of the peace would be relevant in such circumstances so long as it can be shown that the picket's conduct might reasonably be expected to cause any person to be alarmed, upset or annoyed.[254]

11.71 Moreover, the criminal law also recognises that the police must be given some discretion as regards their control of picket-line behaviour. Under English law the most appropriate offence which enables the police to regulate the behaviour of pickets is that of resisting or wilfully obstructing a constable in the execution of his duty contrary to s. 51(3) of the Police Act 1964. It is clear that the courts have construed this offence as granting a police officer a reasonable discretion in deciding whether he is being obstructed. For example, in *Piddington v. Bates*[255] a police constable asked a picket to move away because he believed that two pickets were enough outside a factory and not three. One picket pushed gently past the policeman. He was arrested and subsequently convicted of obstruction of a police officer in the execution of his duty. In *Tynan v. Balmer*[256] the divisional court upheld the conviction of a picket organiser for obstruction of a police officer when he refused to obey instructions from the police that the pickets should stop walking around in a circle in front of a factory. In Scotland a complaint of obstruction of a police officer under the Police (Scotland) Act 1967, s. 41 would also be applicable in these circumstances.[257] A charge of breach of the peace would also be relevant since it is clear that under Scots law a refusal to move on when requested to do so by the police could competently be charged as a breach of the peace.[258] The wide nature of this common law crime undoubtedly gives the police

---

[251] This point is borne out by the statistics concerning arrests during the miners' strike of 1984-85. In Scotland of the 1015 people prosecuted here 678 were charged with breach of the peace, 249 with obstructing the police and 30 with vandalism. See generally Peter Wallington "Policing the Miners' Strike" (1985) 14 ILJ 145.

[252] See, for example, *Raffaelli v. Heatly* 1949 JC 101 (peeping Tom); *Young v. Heatly* 1959 JC 66 (improper remarks by teacher to pupils in private).

[253] [1974] ICR 84.

[254] See the statement on breach of peace by Lord Justice General Emslie in *Stewart v. Jessop* 1988 SCCR 492.

[255] [1960] 2 All ER 660.

[256] [1967] 1 QB 91.

[257] This provision is discussed by G. H. Gordon in *The Criminal Law of Scotland* (2nd edn., 1978) at para. 29-12.

[258] *Montgomery v. McLeod* 1977 SLT (Notes) 77.

considerable discretion in controlling the behaviour of pickets in Scotland.[259] In very serious cases where the behaviour of the pickets through sheer force of numbers is intimidatory or disturbs the public peace a charge of mobbing and rioting might be libelled.[260]

11.72 There is also a specific statutory offence contained in s. 7 of the Conspiracy and Protection of Property Act 1875 which is relevant to pickets. There was a time when prosecutions under this section appeared to have fallen into disuse.[261] However, there have been two recent reported prosecutions in Scotland and it was used widely in England as a means of regulating the behaviour of pickets during the miners' strike of 1984-85. Interestingly, only four such prosecutions were recorded in Scotland during this period.[262] Section 7 declares that every person who, with a view to compel any other person to abstain from doing or to do any act which such other person has a legal right to do or abstain from doing, wrongfully and without legal authority —

(1) uses violence to or intimidates such other person or his wife or children, or injures his property; or,

(2) persistently follows such other person about from place to place;[263] or,

(3) hides any tools, clothes or other property owned or used by such other person, or deprives him or hinders him in the use thereof; or,

(4) watches or besets the house or other place where such other person resides, or works, or carries on business, or happens to be, or the approach to such house or place, or,

(5) follows such other person with two or more other persons in a disorderly manner in or through any street or road,[264]
commits an offence.

11.73 It has always been accepted in Scotland that s. 7 creates only one offence. The five heads listed in the section which appear to set out particular categories of crime are regarded as merely different ways of committing the same offence. In all prosecutions it must be shown that the act complained of was done with a view to compel etc. and that it was done wrongfully and without legal authority. As far as this last point is concerned it appears that s. 7 does not make anything wrongful that was not wrongful before.[265] This means

---

[259] Indeed, it may even be used in order to prevent people joining a picket line so long as the police have a reasonable apprehension that a breach of the peace will be committed. The turning back of people intending to join picket lines by means of road blocks was certainly a tactic that the police adopted in both Scotland and England during the miners' strike. See Peter Wallington "Policing the Miners' Strike" (1985) 14 ILJ 145.

[260] *Sloan v. Macmillan* 1922 JC 1. The crime was libelled unsuccessfully against a number of pickets who picketed outside the Longannet Power Station during the miners' strike of 1972. See Peter Wallington "The Case of the Longannet Miners and the Criminal Liability of Pickets' (1972) 1 ILJ 219. No charges of mobbing and rioting were brought during the 1984-85 miners' strike. This was unlike the position in England where unlawful assembly and riot charges were brought. See Wallington (1985), *ante.*

[261] See Richard Kidner "Picketing and the Criminal Law" (1975) Crim LR 256.

[262] These points are discussed by Peter Wallington in "Policing the Miners' Strike" (1985) 14 ILJ 145.

[263] *Elsey v. Smith* 1982 SCCR 218 where it was held that this particular head of offence can be committed by a car following another car on the motorway.

[264] This head of offence can also be committed by persons in a car see *Elsey, ante.*

[265] *Ward Lock & Co v. Operative Printers' Assistants' Society* (1906) 22 TLR 327.

that the act complained of must attract either criminal or civil liability itself without reference to s. 7. It is not a defence to argue that the act has immunity from actions in delict under the Trade Union and Labour Relations Act 1974 s. 13. Acts which do attract such immunity still remain wrongful for the purpose of s. 7.[266] Looking to the five heads of offence listed in s. 7 several points can be made. First, as regards head 1, intimidation need not produce actual fear in the other person. It is enough if threats are used which would arouse in a person of common sense a natural alarm of personal violence or of violence to his family.[267] As far as watching or besetting is concerned, it is clear that a besetting can be committed both outside and inside the relevant place so that an occupation of an employer's premises by his employees can be a breach of s. 7.[268]

[266] *Galt v. Philp* 1983 SCCR 295.
[267] *Agnew v. Munro* (1891) 2 Wh 611.
[268] *Galt v. Philp* 1983 SCCR 295.

SUBJECT INDEX